Advanced Neuro MR Techniques and Applications

Advances in Magnetic Resonance Technology and Applications Series

Series Editors

In-Young Choi, PhD
Department of Neurology, Department of Radiology, Department of Molecular & Integrative Physiology, Hoglund Biomedical Imaging Center, University of Kansas Medical Center, Kansas City, KS, United States

Peter Jezzard, PhD
Wellcome Centre for Integrative Neuroimaging, Nuffield Department of Clinical Neurosciences University of Oxford, United Kingdom

Brian Hargreaves, PhD
Department of Radiology, Department of Electrical Engineering, Department of Bioengineering Stanford University, United States

Greg Zaharchuk, MD, PhD
Department of Radiology, Stanford University, United States

Titles published:

Volume 1 – Quantitative Magnetic Resonance Imaging – Edited by Nicole Seiberlich and Vikas Gulani

Volume 2 – Handbook of Pediatric Brain Imaging – Edited by Hao Huang and Timothy Roberts

Volume 3 – Hyperpolarized Carbon-13 Magnetic Resonance Imaging and Spectroscopy – Edited by Peder Larson

Volume 4 – Advanced Neuro MR Techniques and Applications – Edited by In-Young Choi and Peter Jezzard

Visit the Series webpage at https://www.elsevier.com/books/book-series/advances-in-magnetic-resonance-technology-and-applications

Advanced Neuro MR Techniques and Applications

Edited by

In-Young Choi
Department of Neurology
University of Kansas Medical Center
Kansas City, KS, United States

Peter Jezzard
Wellcome Centre for Integrative Neiroimaging
University of Oxford
Oxford, United Kingdom

Academic Press is an imprint of Elsevier
125 London Wall, London EC2Y 5AS, United Kingdom
525 B Street, Suite 1650, San Diego, CA 92101, United States
50 Hampshire Street, 5th Floor, Cambridge, MA 02139, United States
The Boulevard, Langford Lane, Kidlington, Oxford OX5 1GB, United Kingdom

Copyright © 2021 Elsevier Inc. All rights reserved.

No part of this publication may be reproduced or transmitted in any form or by any means, electronic or mechanical, including photocopying, recording, or any information storage and retrieval system, without permission in writing from the publisher. Details on how to seek permission, further information about the Publisher's permissions policies and our arrangements with organizations such as the Copyright Clearance Center and the Copyright Licensing Agency, can be found at our website: www.elsevier.com/permissions.

This book and the individual contributions contained in it are protected under copyright by the Publisher (other than as may be noted herein).

Notices

Knowledge and best practice in this field are constantly changing. As new research and experience broaden our understanding, changes in research methods, professional practices, or medical treatment may become necessary.

Practitioners and researchers must always rely on their own experience and knowledge in evaluating and using any information, methods, compounds, or experiments described herein. In using such information or methods they should be mindful of their own safety and the safety of others, including parties for whom they have a professional responsibility.

To the fullest extent of the law, neither the Publisher nor the authors, contributors, or editors, assume any liability for any injury and/or damage to persons or property as a matter of products liability, negligence or otherwise, or from any use or operation of any methods, products, instructions, or ideas contained in the material herein.

Library of Congress Cataloging-in-Publication Data
A catalog record for this book is available from the Library of Congress

British Library Cataloguing-in-Publication Data
A catalogue record for this book is available from the British Library

ISBN: 978-0-12-822479-3

For information on all Academic Press publications
visit our website at https://www.elsevier.com/books-and-journals

Publisher: Mara Conner
Acquisitions Editor: Tim Pitts
Editorial Project Manager: Emily Thomson
Production Project Manager: Prem Kumar Kaliamoorthi
Designer: Greg Harris

Typeset by VTeX

Contents

List of contributors ix
Preface xvii

PART 1 FAST AND ROBUST IMAGING

CHAPTER 1 **Recommendations for neuro MRI acquisition strategies** 3
Tony Stöcker

CHAPTER 2 **Advanced reconstruction methods for fast MRI** 21
Florian Knoll

CHAPTER 3 **Simultaneous multi-slice MRI** 37
Andreia S. Gaspar, Ana R. Fouto, and Rita G. Nunes

CHAPTER 4 **Motion artifacts and correction in neuro MRI** 53
André van der Kouwe

PART 2 CLASSICAL AND DEEP LEARNING APPROACHES TO NEURO IMAGE ANALYSIS

CHAPTER 5 **Statistical approaches to neuroimaging analysis** 71
Jeanette A. Mumford

CHAPTER 6 **Image registration** 83
Hui Zhang

CHAPTER 7 **Image segmentation** 95
Carole Helene Sudre

PART 3 DIFFUSION MRI

CHAPTER 8 **Diffusion MRI acquisition and reconstruction** 109
Hua Guo

CHAPTER 9 **Diffusion MRI artifact correction** 123
Jesper L.R. Andersson

CHAPTER 10 **Diffusion MRI analysis methods** 147
Szabolcs David, Joost Verhoeff, and Alexander Leemans

CHAPTER 11 **Diffusion as a probe of tissue microstructure** 157
Yaniv Assaf and Daniel Barazany

PART 4 PERFUSION MRI

CHAPTER 12 **Non-contrast agent perfusion MRI methods** 177
Matthias Günther

v

vi   Contents

CHAPTER 13   **Contrast agent-based perfusion MRI methods** **195**
Laura C. Bell, Sudarshan Ragunathan, and Anahita Fathi Kazerooni

CHAPTER 14   **Perfusion MRI: clinical perspectives** **211**
Kevin Yuqi Wang, Eric K. van Staalduinen, and Greg Zaharchuk

PART 5 FUNCTIONAL MRI

CHAPTER 15   **Functional MRI principles and acquisition strategies** **231**
Martina F. Callaghan and Nadège Corbin

CHAPTER 16   **Functional MRI analysis** **247**
Wei Zhang and Janine Bijsterbosch

CHAPTER 17   **Neuroscience applications of functional MRI** **261**
Essa Yacoub and Luca Vizioli

CHAPTER 18   **Clinical applications of functional MRI** **277**
Natalie L. Voets

PART 6 THE BRAIN CONNECTOME

CHAPTER 19   **The diffusion MRI connectome** **295**
Michiel Cottaar and Matteo Bastiani

CHAPTER 20   **Functional MRI connectivity** **309**
Eugene Duff

CHAPTER 21   **Applications of MRI connectomics** **323**
Jessica S. Damoiseaux, Andre Altmann, Jonas Richiardi, and
Sepideh Sadaghiani

PART 7 SUSCEPTIBILITY MRI

CHAPTER 22   **Principles of susceptibility-weighted MRI** **341**
Sagar Buch, Yongsheng Chen, and E. Mark Haacke

CHAPTER 23   **Applications of susceptibility-weighted imaging and mapping** **359**
Stefan Ropele

PART 8 MAGNETIZATION TRANSFER APPROACHES

CHAPTER 24   **Magnetization transfer contrast MRI** **373**
Seth A. Smith and Kristin P. O'Grady

CHAPTER 25   **Chemical exchange saturation transfer (CEST) MRI as a tunable relaxation
phenomenon** **387**
Moritz Zaiss, Felix Glang, and Kai Herz

CHAPTER 26   **Clinical application of magnetization transfer imaging** **403**
Francesca Bagnato

Contents **vii**

PART 9 QUANTITATIVE RELAXOMETRY AND PARAMETER MAPPING

CHAPTER 27   **Quantitative relaxometry mapping** 421
Mark D. Does

CHAPTER 28   **MR fingerprinting: concepts, implementation and applications** 435
Dan Ma

CHAPTER 29   **Quantitative multi-parametric MRI measurements** 451
Gunther Helms

PART 10 NEUROVASCULAR IMAGING

CHAPTER 30   **Neurovascular magnetic resonance angiography** 469
Kevin M. Johnson

CHAPTER 31   **Neurovascular vessel wall imaging: new techniques and clinical applications** 485
Chun Yuan, Mahmud Mossa-Basha, Zachary Miller, and Zechen Zhou

PART 11 ADVANCED MAGNETIC RESONANCE SPECTROSCOPY

CHAPTER 32   **Single voxel magnetic resonance spectroscopy: principles and applications** 503
Ivan Tkáč and Gülin Öz

CHAPTER 33   **Magnetic resonance spectroscopic imaging: principles and applications** ... 519
Wolfgang Bogner, Bernhard Strasser, Petr Bednarik, Eva Heckova,
Lukas Hingerl, and Gilbert Hangel

CHAPTER 34   **Non-Fourier-based magnetic resonance spectroscopy** 537
Peter Adany, In-Young Choi, and Phil Lee

PART 12 ULTRA-HIGH FIELD NEURO MR TECHNIQUES

CHAPTER 35   **Benefits, challenges, and applications of ultra-high field magnetic resonance** 553
Karin Markenroth Bloch and Benedikt A. Poser

CHAPTER 36   **Neuroscience applications of ultra-high-field magnetic resonance imaging:
mesoscale functional imaging of the human brain** 573
Jonathan R. Polimeni

CHAPTER 37   **Clinical applications of high field magnetic resonance** 589
Louise Ebersberger, Mark E. Ladd, and Daniel Paech

Index 609

List of contributors

Peter Adany
Hoglund Biomedical Imaging Center, University of Kansas Medical Center, Kansas City, KS, United States

Andre Altmann
Centre for Medical Image Computing (CMIC), Department of Medical Physics and Biomedical Engineering, University College London (UCL), London, United Kingdom

Jesper L.R. Andersson
FMRIB Centre, University of Oxford, Oxford, United Kingdom

Yaniv Assaf
School of Neurobiology, Biochemistry and Biophysics, Faculty of Life Science, Tel Aviv University, Tel Aviv, Israel
Sagol School of Neuroscience, Tel Aviv University, Tel Aviv, Israel
The Strauss Center for Computational Neuroimaging, Tel Aviv University, Tel Aviv, Israel

Francesca Bagnato
Neuroimaging Unit, Neuroimmunology Division, Neurology Department, Vanderbilt University Medical Center, Nashville, TN, United States
Department of Neurology, Nashville VA Medical Center, TN Valley Healthcare System, Nashville, TN, United States

Daniel Barazany
The Strauss Center for Computational Neuroimaging, Tel Aviv University, Tel Aviv, Israel

Matteo Bastiani
Wellcome Centre for Integrative Neuroimaging (WIN), Oxford Centre for Functional MRI of the Brain (FMRIB), University of Oxford, Oxford, United Kingdom
Sir Peter Mansfield Imaging Centre (SPMIC), University of Nottingham, Nottingham, United Kingdom

Petr Bednarik
High-field MR Center, Department of Biomedical Imaging and Image-guided Therapy, Medical University of Vienna, Vienna, Austria

Laura C. Bell
Division of Neuroimaging Research, Barrow Neurological Institute, Phoenix, AZ, United States

Janine Bijsterbosch
Department of Radiology, Washington University School of Medicine, Washington University in St. Louis, St. Louis, MO, United States

x   List of contributors

Wolfgang Bogner
High-field MR Center, Department of Biomedical Imaging and Image-guided Therapy, Medical University of Vienna, Vienna, Austria

Sagar Buch
Department of Radiology, Wayne State University School of Medicine, Detroit, MI, United States

Martina F. Callaghan
Wellcome Centre for Human Neuroimaging, UCL Queen Square Institute of Neurology, UCL, London, United Kingdom

Yongsheng Chen
Department of Neurology, Wayne State University School of Medicine, Detroit, MI, United States

In-Young Choi
Hoglund Biomedical Imaging Center, University of Kansas Medical Center, Kansas City, KS, United States
Department of Neurology, University of Kansas Medical Center, Kansas City, KS, United States

Nadège Corbin
Wellcome Centre for Human Neuroimaging, UCL Queen Square Institute of Neurology, UCL, London, United Kingdom
Centre de Résonance Magnétique des Systèmes Biologiques, UMR5536, CNRS/University Bordeaux, Bordeaux, France

Michiel Cottaar
Wellcome Centre for Integrative Neuroimaging (WIN), Oxford Centre for Functional MRI of the Brain (FMRIB), University of Oxford, Oxford, United Kingdom

Jessica S. Damoiseaux
Institute of Gerontology, Department of Psychology, Wayne State University, Detroit, MI, United States

Szabolcs David
PROVIDI Lab, Image Sciences Institute, University Medical Centre Utrecht, Utrecht, The Netherlands
Department of Radiation Oncology, University Medical Centre Utrecht, Utrecht, The Netherlands

Mark D. Does
Department of Biomedical Engineering, Vanderbilt University, Nashville, TN, United States
Institute of Imaging Science, Vanderbilt University Medical Center, Nashville, TN, United States

Eugene Duff
Department of Paediatrics, and Wellcome Centre for Integrative Neuroimaging, University of Oxford, Oxford, United Kingdom

List of contributors

Louise Ebersberger
German Cancer Research Center (DKFZ), Division of Radiology, Heidelberg,
Baden-Württemberg, Germany

Anahita Fathi Kazerooni
Department of Radiology, Perelman School of Medicine, University of Pennsylvania, Philadelphia,
PA, United States

Ana R. Fouto
Institute for Systems and Robotics and Department of Bioengineering, Instituto Superior Técnico,
Universidade de Lisboa, Lisbon, Portugal

Andreia S. Gaspar
Institute for Systems and Robotics and Department of Bioengineering, Instituto Superior Técnico,
Universidade de Lisboa, Lisbon, Portugal

Felix Glang
Magnetic Resonance Center, Max Planck Institute for Biological Cybernetics, Tübingen, Germany

Matthias Günther
Fraunhofer MEVIS, Bremen, Germany
University Bremen, Bremen, Germany
mediri GmbH, Heidelberg, Germany

Hua Guo
Center for Biomedical Imaging Research, Department of Biomedical Engineering, School of
Medicine, Tsinghua University, Beijing, China

E. Mark Haacke
Department of Radiology, Wayne State University School of Medicine, Detroit, MI, United States
Department of Neurology, Wayne State University School of Medicine, Detroit, MI, United States

Gilbert Hangel
High-field MR Center, Department of Biomedical Imaging and Image-guided Therapy, Medical
University of Vienna, Vienna, Austria

Eva Heckova
High-field MR Center, Department of Biomedical Imaging and Image-guided Therapy, Medical
University of Vienna, Vienna, Austria

Gunther Helms
Department of Clinical Sciences Lund (IKVL), Lund University, Lund, Sweden

Kai Herz
Magnetic Resonance Center, Max Planck Institute for Biological Cybernetics, Tübingen, Germany
Department of Biomedical Magnetic Resonance, University of Tübingen, Tübingen, Germany

xii   List of contributors

Lukas Hingerl
High-field MR Center, Department of Biomedical Imaging and Image-guided Therapy, Medical University of Vienna, Vienna, Austria

Kevin M. Johnson
Departments of Medical Physics and Radiology, University of Wisconsin – Madison, Madison, WI, United States

Florian Knoll
NYU School of Medicine, Department of Radiology, New York, NY, United States
FAU Department of Artificial Intelligence in Biomedical Engineering, Erlangen, Germany

Mark E. Ladd
German Cancer Research Center (DKFZ), Division of Medical Physics in Radiology, Heidelberg, Baden-Württemberg, Germany

Phil Lee
Hoglund Biomedical Imaging Center, University of Kansas Medical Center, Kansas City, KS, United States
Department of Radiology, University of Kansas Medical Center, Kansas City, KS, United States

Alexander Leemans
PROVIDI Lab, Image Sciences Institute, University Medical Centre Utrecht, Utrecht, The Netherlands

Dan Ma
Case Western Reserve University, Cleveland, OH, United States

Karin Markenroth Bloch
Lund University, Lund, Sweden

Zachary Miller
Department of Radiology, University of Washington, Seattle, WA, United States

Mahmud Mossa-Basha
Department of Radiology, University of Washington, Seattle, WA, United States

Jeanette A. Mumford
Stanford University, Stanford, CA, United States

Rita G. Nunes
Institute for Systems and Robotics and Department of Bioengineering, Instituto Superior Técnico, Universidade de Lisboa, Lisbon, Portugal

List of contributors   **xiii**

Kristin P. O'Grady

Vanderbilt University Institute of Imaging Science, Vanderbilt University Medical Center, Nashville, TN, United States

Department of Radiology and Radiological Sciences, Vanderbilt University Medical Center, Nashville, TN, United States

Gülin Öz

Center for Magnetic Resonance Research, Department of Radiology, University of Minnesota, Minneapolis, MN, United States

Daniel Paech

German Cancer Research Center (DKFZ), Division of Radiology, Heidelberg, Baden-Württemberg, Germany

Jonathan R. Polimeni

Athinoula A. Martinos Center for Biomedical Imaging, Massachusetts General Hospital, Charlestown, MA, United States

Department of Radiology, Harvard Medical School, Boston, MA, United States

Division of Health Sciences and Technology, Massachusetts Institute of Technology, Cambridge, MA, United States

Benedikt A. Poser

Maastricht University, Maastricht, The Netherlands

Sudarshan Ragunathan

Division of Neuroimaging Research, Barrow Neurological Institute, Phoenix, AZ, United States

Jonas Richiardi

Department of Radiology, Lausanne University Hospital and University of Lausanne, Lausanne, Switzerland

Stefan Ropele

Department of Neurology, Medical University of Graz, Graz, Austria

Sepideh Sadaghiani

Psychology Department, Beckman Institute for Advanced Science and Technology, University of Illinois at Urbana-Champaign, Urbana, IL, United States

Seth A. Smith

Vanderbilt University Institute of Imaging Science, Vanderbilt University Medical Center, Nashville, TN, United States

Department of Radiology and Radiological Sciences, Vanderbilt University Medical Center, Nashville, TN, United States

Department of Biomedical Engineering, Vanderbilt University, Nashville, TN, United States

Department of Ophthalmology, Vanderbilt University Medical Center, Nashville, TN, United States

xiv List of contributors

Tony Stöcker
German Center for Neurodegenerative Diseases (DZNE), Bonn, Germany

Bernhard Strasser
High-field MR Center, Department of Biomedical Imaging and Image-guided Therapy, Medical University of Vienna, Vienna, Austria

Carole Helene Sudre
MRC Unit for Lifelong Health and Ageing at UCL, University College London, London, United Kingdom
Centre for Medical Image Computing, University College London, London, United Kingdom
School of Biomedical Engineering and Imaging Sciences, King's College London, London, United Kingdom

Ivan Tkáč
Center for Magnetic Resonance Research, Department of Radiology, University of Minnesota, Minneapolis, MN, United States

André van der Kouwe
Athinoula A. Martinos Center for Biomedical Imaging, Massachusetts General Hospital, Charlestown, MA, United States

Eric K. van Staalduinen
Department of Radiology, Stanford University, Stanford, CA, United States

Joost Verhoeff
Department of Radiation Oncology, University Medical Centre Utrecht, Utrecht, The Netherlands

Luca Vizioli
Center for Magnetic Resonance Research (CMRR), Department of Radiology, University of Minnesota, Minneapolis, MN, United States
Department of Neurosurgery, University of Minnesota, Minneapolis, MN, United States

Natalie L. Voets
Wellcome Centre for Integrative Neuroimaging (FMRIB-WIN), John Radcliffe Hospital, University of Oxford, Oxford, United Kingdom

Kevin Yuqi Wang
Department of Radiology, Stanford University, Stanford, CA, United States

Essa Yacoub
Center for Magnetic Resonance Research (CMRR), Department of Radiology, University of Minnesota, Minneapolis, MN, United States

Chun Yuan
Department of Radiology, University of Washington, Seattle, WA, United States

List of contributors

Greg Zaharchuk
Department of Radiology, Stanford University, Stanford, CA, United States

Moritz Zaiss
Department Neuroradiology, University Clinic Erlangen, Friedrich Alexander University Erlangen-Nürnberg, Erlangen, Germany
Magnetic Resonance Center, Max Planck Institute for Biological Cybernetics, Tübingen, Germany

Hui Zhang
Centre for Medical Image Computing and Department of Computer Science, UCL, London, United Kingdom

Wei Zhang
Department of Radiology, Washington University School of Medicine, Washington University in St. Louis, St. Louis, MO, United States

Zechen Zhou
Philips Research North America, Cambridge, MA, United States

Preface

This book arose principally from a highly successful workshop titled "*Advanced Neuro MR: Best Practices for Technical Implementation*" that was organized by the International Society for Magnetic Resonance in Medicine, which took place in Seoul, South Korea, in 2018. It was clear from the workshop that there was a desire to summarize state-of-the-art neuroimaging in the form of an edited book. Many of the speakers at that workshop agreed to contribute to the book, and more experts were recruited to the effort. The result is a comprehensive summary of the field, provided by its leading researchers. We are deeply honored and grateful that such distinguished scientists and clinicians have contributed to the project.

The book is divided into twelve parts, covering a wide range of topics intended to be accessible to both experts and newcomers. Basic scientists involved in the methodology of neuro MR should find the book as equally valuable as should technically-oriented clinicians and neuroscientists who seek a deeper understanding of its principles. After beginning with introductory chapters on fast and robust imaging, and approaches to image analysis, the book focuses on advanced structural, functional, and physiological imaging, before covering other specialist MRI contrasts, such as magnetic susceptibility imaging, magnetization transfer, and relaxometry mapping. The book also covers neurovascular imaging and advanced magnetic resonance spectroscopy, and then summarizes the opportunities, challenges, and applications of ultra-high-field magnetic resonance. Please note that there is accompanying electronic content available for some chapters at: https://www.elsevier.com/books-and-journals/book-companion/9780128224793.

We would like to express our deepest gratitude to our authors for keeping to a rigorous submission schedule, despite the huge disruptions to their laboratories and personal lives caused by the global COVID-19 pandemic. We would also like to thank the Commissioning Editor at Elsevier, Tim Pitts, the Editorial Project Manager, Emily Thomson, and the Production Project Manager, Prem Kumar Kaliamoorthi, for their support and guidance from the book's conception to the final product. We hope that readers will find this a useful addition to the literature, and a valuable reference tool in their work.

In-Young Choi, Kansas City, KS, United States
Peter Jezzard, Oxford, United Kingdom

PART 1

Fast and robust imaging

CHAPTER

Recommendations for neuro MRI acquisition strategies

1

Tony Stöcker
German Center for Neurodegenerative Diseases (DZNE), Bonn, Germany

1.1 MRI hardware

Since the advent of MRI, the underlying system hardware has been substantially improved. MR image acquisitions have become faster, and at the same time the image quality has become better. Four factors were mainly responsible for these improvements: i) an increase of magnetic field strength (3 tesla or even 7 tesla) provides higher signal-to-noise ratio (SNR), ii) faster switching and more powerful gradient systems increase the speed of spatial encoding, iii) multi-channel receiver arrays increase SNR and also enable faster spatial encoding ("Parallel Imaging" – PI), and finally iv) faster and more powerful computers improve the image reconstruction quality. Based on these hardware improvements, novel imaging methods were developed which gave access to fast acquisitions of soft-tissue contrasts with high potential for neuroimaging application. The recommendations given here will focus on MR neuroimaging techniques at 3 tesla (3T). This is the current de-facto standard for many recent large-scale neuroimaging studies. 3T MRI scanners are widely available in the research landscape and, additionally, provide a good compromise between sensitivity and imaging artifacts. The latter typically also scale up with magnetic field due to susceptibility-induced inhomogeneity of the main field and inhomogeneity of the transmit radio frequency (RF) field, which scales with field-dependent wavelength. The latter effect becomes especially problematic at 7T and will be discussed in Chapter 35 of this book. The wavelength in the human body is about 30 cm at 3T, and therefore wave-effects in neuro MRI exist, but do not significantly compromise the image quality. Nevertheless, they need to be taken into account, especially when deriving quantitative tissue properties. Translating an optimized image acquisition from one field strength to another is a difficult task. Even if imaging artifacts are neglected, a theoretical or experimental SNR and CNR (contrast-to-noise ratio) analysis is cumbersome: many variables need to be considered, such as the sequence timing, tissue relaxation times, and the receiver coil properties. An excellent example of a detailed SNR & CNR analysis for 3T, 7T, and 9.4T MRI was given by Pohmann et al. (2016). Nevertheless, a crude estimate can be quickly performed by assuming that the SNR is proportional to the field strength, the voxel-volume, and the square-root of the acquisition time (due to incoherent noise cancellation). Adjusting a 3T MRI protocol with isotropic resolution to a 1.5T scanner with the goal of maintaining the SNR requires either an increase in voxel size (the edge length) by a factor of $\sqrt[3]{2} \approx 1.26$—while keeping the scan time constant —or an increase in acquisition time by a factor of 4, while keeping the resolution constant. In that way the recommendations of this chapter can be roughly extrapolated to other field strengths than 3T.

The other hardware components—the gradient system, the receiver arrays, and the image reconstruction computer—all have application-specific impact in neuro MR. A powerful gradient system is especially important for diffusion MRI. Typical MRI scanners have a maximum gradient strength of 40 mT/m ("milli-tesla-per-meter"), whereas some advanced products double that performance. If diffusion MRI is key to answering a research question, then an MRI scanner with high-performance gradients is recommended. If such a system provides a two-fold SNR gain for a dedicated diffusion MRI protocol, it saves a factor of 4 in scan time. Therefore higher investments for such a system may dramatically reduce scan time costs in subsequent studies. Today, phased array head coils with 32 (or more) individual elements are common. They can provide a substantial acquisition speed-up. The common technology provides PI acceleration factors between 2–8. PI reduces the acquisition time, and therefore the SNR. Thus PI acceleration capabilities strongly depend on the image resolution. PI reconstructions with large acceleration factors on low SNR data are computationally expensive. The performance of the image reconstruction computer is essential for high-throughput data acquisition. If the computer is busy reconstructing previously acquired data, execution of the next sequence(s) of the MR protocol is delayed. High-performance-computing extensions of the hardware may help, but are not considered for the recommendations in this chapter. Here, the description is based on the assumption that image acquisition and image reconstruction are performed on the MRI system to guarantee robust and high-throughput examinations. Subsequently, imaging data is exported to an external database for analysis. It should be noted that this is not easily possible with MRI raw data, i.e., the complex signals per receiver channel. Commercially available MRI scanners may have no functionality for realtime raw data export. Even if this would be the case, the huge size of MRI raw data can generate substantial problems. For example, a one hour MRI protocol can easily generate 1 Petabyte of raw data. Conversely, the smaller sized imaging data can be more easily stored and subsequently analyzed.

1.2 From signals to biomarkers

The richness and variety of neuro MR methods is impressive: information on biophysical tissue properties can be encoded in many ways into the MR signal. The MRI sequence first generates these signals by weighting the spin magnetization with the property of interest, then encodes spatial information into the signal, and finally acquires the raw data, which is transferred to the image reconstruction computer. The reconstructed images have an arbitrary intensity scaling. It is the task of image analysis to derive quantitative information from the images, which may serve as a potential biomarker of a specific normal biological or pathogenic process in the brain. Overall, many steps are involved from the generation of the MR signal to an image-derived biomarker of brain structure and function. These steps are highly interdependent: image acquisition, reconstruction, and analysis capabilities determine each other. Novel approaches try to combine image reconstruction and analysis into a single process, directly delivering the biomarker from the MRI raw data. This has consequences for the acquisition.

MRI-derived quantitative tissue properties have limited precision and accuracy. The precision describes the statistical error in the data, and the accuracy quantifies the acquisition bias. To a large extent the precision is determined by SNR and CNR, but image artifacts, e.g., induced by involuntary head motion, also degrade the precision. If the precision is low, image-derived quantities cannot serve as a robust biomarker. The precision can be estimated in test-retest experiments. If unknown, it is recommended to design a pilot study to estimate the precision. However, even if the precision is known, the effect size of the biological mechanism of interest is often unknown. A good estimate of the effect size requires studies with large sample size, including hundreds to thousands of subjects, which is not the case for many studies in human neuroscience, as noted by Button et al. (2013). Therefore a sound power analysis in advance of a new study is difficult. Often, the required sample size is estimated from previous knowledge. This is difficult due to the limited accuracy of MRI-derived quantities. In general, MRI introduces a measurement bias: often it is intended to weight the MR signal to a *single* tissue property, but other weightings are unavoidably present. For instance, the spatial encoding process always encodes—to a small extent—a diffusion weighting. If such effects are not built into the physical model of the quantity of interest, the fitting is biased. It is computationally too expensive to simultaneously account for all physical effects in the acquisition process. However, by changing experimental conditions, e.g., by adjusting the sequence timing parameters or by examining various MR phantoms with well-defined properties, it is possible to make predictions about the accuracy of a specific method. Fortunately, exact knowledge of the accuracy is not always required. If only the percentage change of a quantity in two experimental conditions is relevant for the interpretation, then meaningful conclusions may be drawn without knowledge of the accuracy. Still, the change will be biased by the acquisition process. Reproducibility is therefore only possible if the experimental conditions are maintained. For this reason, there is a strong need for harmonization of neuro MR protocols. The closer the experimental conditions between different studies, the better the results can be compared. On the other hand, harmonization of protocols often means "freezing" of protocols potentially over a long time, and therefore new methodological advances of image acquisition cannot be taken into account. Typically, a trade-off between efficiency (fast acquisition with high precision) and matureness (well-known accuracy and good reproducibility) has to be made. This consideration is a general important recommendation for neuro MRI acquisition strategies, which was taken into account for the protocol proposals presented in this chapter.

1.3 Spatial encoding strategies

The human brain is a highly structured and complex organ. The highly folded gyri and sulci form the gray matter of the human cortex. Its regions are connected by short- and long-ranging fiber bundles of axons, which form the white matter. Imaging the brain with MRI provides spatially resolved information on the scale of approximately a millimeter (the voxel size). Acquisition protocols can be adapted to investigate a specific region of interest (ROI) with higher resolution, but generally whole-brain imaging is desired: it enables the study of systemic brain structure and function, and it provides the possibility to compare tissue markers between different brain regions. For example, utilizing the hemispheric symmetry, tissue composition in a lesion can be compared to the counterpart region in the brain.

Since there is no preferred slice orientation for whole-brain MRI, isotropic spatial image resolution is generally advisable. For resolutions of one millimeter and below, this is preferably obtained with 3D spatial encoding. Here, the MRI sequence does not perform slice selection, but uses RF pulses that excite the whole human head (or a large slab through the head). The resulting MR signal is spatially encoded utilizing gradient waveforms, which define an appropriate trajectory in 3D k-space. The sampling points along the trajectory define the grid of the 3D Fourier transform for image reconstruction. There are infinite ways to traverse k-space, e.g., curved non-Cartesian trajectories are time-efficient. However, then the reconstruction problem is complicated. Thus most MRI sequences provided on commercial MRI systems employ Cartesian k-space encoding. This has several advantages: the image reconstruction problem is computationally less demanding and, additionally, minor gradient hardware

Chapter 1 Recommendations for neuro MRI acquisition strategies

imperfections typically have little or no effect on the final image. Moreover, a single generic image reconstruction algorithm can handle the raw data of arbitrary sequences. State-of-the-art Cartesian image reconstruction, including parallel imaging capabilities, are available on all modern MRI scanners. Therefore the recommendations of this chapter are confined to Cartesian acquisitions. However, the field of advanced image reconstruction capable by non-Cartesian MRI is rapidly evolving. Recent developments strongly benefited from deep learning, which improves reconstruction quality and reduces computation times dramatically. However, those methods are not standard and are more difficult to apply. An overview of recent developments is given in Chapter 2.

The gradient axes of 3D Cartesian MRI are given by the frequency-encoding axis and two phase encoding axes. The data are acquired simultaneously with the frequency-encoding gradient (or readout gradient), providing a fast sampling of k-space in this direction. The sampling along the two "spin-warp" phase encoding (PE) dimensions is repeated in a two-fold loop structure of the MRI sequence, which results in long acquisition times. The process can be substantially accelerated with parallel imaging, which under-samples k-space along the PE dimensions. Under-sampling is a violation of the Nyquist–Shannon sampling theorem and results in aliasing artifacts, the well-known fold-over artifacts in MRI. Parallel imaging (PI) removes (or avoids) these artifacts by utilizing the spatial sensitivity information of a multi-channel receiver array coil. Modern head coils with 32 or more channels have sensitivity variation along all three spatial dimensions. Therefore PI acceleration can be performed for both PE dimensions. 2D-PI is an important feature of 3D spatial encoding, and it can be well exploited in human head imaging. As mentioned, PI reduces the SNR due to the reduced sampling duration. Additionally, the noise is amplified by the g-factor ($g \geq 1$), which depends on the coil geometry and the encoding scheme (Pruessmann et al., 1999). Regions with large fold-over have a large g-factor. It can be substantially reduced using CAIPIRINHA sampling (Breuer et al., 2005), or for short "CAIPI" sampling. Shifting the under-sampling artifacts relative to one another for the two PE dimensions reduces fold-over, and therefore the g-factor. With CAIPI sampling, higher acceleration factors can be employed without sacrificing image quality.

There exist three more techniques to reduce the spatial encoding time of Cartesian acquisitions: partial Fourier (PF), elliptical sampling (ES), and echo planar imaging (EPI). All methods can be combined with each other and with PI. Partial Fourier takes advantage of the Hermitian symmetry in k-space, enabling a reduced sampling in one PE dimension, which can save 10–40% of scan time. Elliptical sampling (Bernstein et al., 2001) omits sampling of 2D-PE k-space outside an ellipsoid (a circle, in the case of isotropic spatial encoding), which defines the imaging resolution. Elliptical sampling saves approximately 25% of scan time and can be applied to many 3D neuro MRI acquisitions. EPI encodes multiple readouts after a single excitation with alternating frequency-encoding gradients and small PE gradient blips in between. EPI was introduced as a 2D single-shot method, acquiring a whole-slice after one RF excitation. The method can be extended to 3D-EPI with two PE dimensions, where for instance one PE dimension is encoded in the EPI train and the other PE dimension is segmented in an outer loop. However, segmenting both PE dimensions with respect to the excitation provides more flexibility for 2D-PI acceleration. Combining a double-segmented 3D-EPI acquisition with CAIPI sampling was recently introduced as skipped-CAIPI sampling (Stirnberg and Stöcker, 2021). Using the method with moderate EPI-factors (< 10) is, for instance, well-suited for high-resolution anatomical MRI.

Examples of efficient 2D phase encoding patterns are depicted in Fig. 1.1, where A and B form the basis for most of the neuro MR applications presented in the remaining sections of this chapter.

1.3 Spatial encoding strategies

Fig. 1.1A shows two-fold under-sampling with CAIPI shift (green squares are not acquired) and elliptical sampling. The encoding scheme is well-suited for 3D anatomical T_1-weighted and T_2-weighted sequences with a two-fold loop structure, where the outer loop encodes contrast and the inner loop samples a constant number of PE steps. The three red lines in Fig. 1.1A, show inner loop encodings for the first, middle, and last step of the outer loop. Fig. 1.1B shows the extension to double-segmented EPI acquisition with skipped-CAIPI sampling. The example depicts a 6-fold PI acceleration of 3D-EPI with 2D-PE segmentation. The yellow squares connected by yellow arrows are acquired in the first EPI train, the white squares connected by white arrows are acquired in the second echo train, and the process is repeated until all data are acquired. An example beyond Cartesian acquisitions is finally given in Fig. 1.1C, which shows the wave-CAIPI acquisition (Bilgic et al., 2015). Here, a corkscrew-trajectory along the readout dimension is utilized in addition to the 2D phase-encoding under-sampling. As opposed to Figs. 1.1A and B, this approach takes additional advantage of receiver sensitivity variation in the readout dimension, which reduces the g-factor and enables higher acceleration factors. However, 3D k-space sampling is no longer on a Cartesian grid, and therefore a dedicated image reconstruction algorithm is required.

In conclusion, 3D Cartesian acquisitions utilizing 2D parallel imaging with CAIPI sampling are well suited for rapid whole-brain neuroimaging. The encoding can be combined with other acceleration techniques, such as partial Fourier imaging, elliptical sampling, and EPI. Such methods are available on modern MRI systems and enable fast and robust neuro MRI applications.

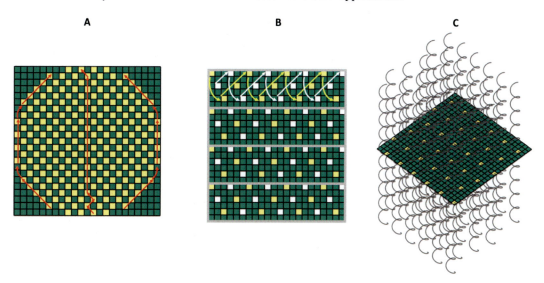

FIGURE 1.1

Parallel imaging (PI) acceleration schemes to optimally exploit the spatial sensitivity variation of modern MRI receiver head coils. (A) 2D phase encoding (PE) pattern with two-fold CAIPI under-sampling (green squares are not acquired) and elliptical sampling. (B) Extension to segmented 3D-EPI acquisitions, which acquire multiple PE steps per excitation. (C) Further extension to wave-CAIPI acquisitions, which additionally exploit receiver sensitivity variation in the readout dimension, however, at the expense of departing from the Cartesian grid.

8   **Chapter 1** Recommendations for neuro MRI acquisition strategies

1.4 Large-scale population imaging

A dedicated MR protocol for a single neuro MR method could last from a few minutes up to several hours, depending on the desired resolution and image contrast. Scanning human subjects limits the total scan time to approximately one hour; longer examinations may result in subject discomfort and strong motion artifacts. If a research question is linked to a special technique, the protocol can be designed accordingly. However, often the combination of complementary information from multiple contrasts increases the overall sensitivity. Therefore, a versatile MR protocol tries to combine several methods, each with a short scan time of several minutes, but still providing sufficient resolution and sensitivity. It is a good choice to use a well-tested MR-protocol from someone else, if it meets your own requirements. There exist several large-scale population imaging studies that developed multi-purpose MRI protocols. Using such a protocol has two advantages. Firstly, these protocols were thoroughly designed and tested. Secondly, newly acquired imaging data is compatible with the population study and results can be more easily correlated.

Different approaches exist to gather large-scale neuro MRI data. Retrospective imaging studies perform meta-analyses on large amounts of neuroimaging data across many different studies and sites; a prominent example is the ENIGMA study (http://enigma.ini.usc.edu/). Conversely, a prospective study collects data with identical set-up and methods tailored to the study questions. Usually, the MRI protocols of these studies have been extensively piloted. Table 1.1 gives an overview of four prospective population imaging studies. The original human connectome project (HCP) was the first large-scale imaging study to apply advanced MRI technology in more than 1000 healthy young adults. High performance gradient systems, as presently available in commercial MRI scanners, were developed in the context of the HCP. Meanwhile, several HCP sub-studies were launched, each addressing specific neuroscientific research questions, and each with a dedicated MRI protocol. Another approach is given by multi-center prospective studies, where imaging protocols are harmonized across many different sites and scanner types, aiming at increased sample size. A successful example of this approach is the Alzheimer's disease neuroimaging initiative (ADNI). The initial five-year study (ADNI-1) was twice extended (ADNI-2, and ADNI-3), where each time the MR protocols were adjusted to the newest technology, given by the common denominator available at the participating sites. There have been increasing efforts to utilize advanced MRI technology in large-scale population studies by means of dedicated centers, equipped with MRI systems exclusively for the study. The UK-Biobank study utilizes a 30 minutes neuro MRI protocol, with a target population of 100,000 subjects. A similar concept, with the additional goal of longitudinal examination, is implemented by the Rhineland study. The study utilizes a 60 minutes neuro MRI protocol obtained on two MRI systems equipped with high-performance gradients (80 mT/m). The study aims to include 20,000 subjects with re-examination every 3–4 years. All studies of Table 1.1 utilize 3T MRI systems. Detailed information on the MRI protocols is available on the respective web-sites. The next section outlines the one-hour MR protocol of the Rhineland study in more detail.

1.5 Example multi-purpose protocols

This section presents two example MR protocol proposals for multi-purpose neuroimaging applications. Imaging examples will be given in the next section, including more details on the individual

1.5 Example multi-purpose protocols 9

Table 1.1 Large-scale prospective population imaging studies with dedicated neuro MRI protocols. Detailed study information, including the MRI protocols can be obtained from the study web-sites.

Study Name	General Information
Human Connectome Project (HCP)	- original HCP (2009–2014): MRI with custom gradient hardware - 4 substudies (since 2015) on aging and developing brain - sample size / substudy: N ≈ 500–1,500 - https://humanconnectome.org
Alzheimers Disease Neuroimaging Initiative (ADNI)	- multi-center study in patient population (MCI & AD) - active since 2009, three study extensions (current: ADNI-3) - sample size: N ≈ 2,000 - http://adni.loni.ucla.edu
UK Biobank Imaging Study	- 4 dedicated study centers / MR-protocol inspired by HCP - brain, cardiac, & abdominal MRI / 30 min brain protocol - current/target N ≈ 25,000/100,000 (re-invite ≈ 10,000) - subjects recruited from the UK Biobank cohort (≈ 500,000) - https://www.ukbiobank.ac.uk
Rhineland Study	- 2 dedicated study centers / MRI with high-performance gradients - 8 h phenotyping per subject, including 60 min brain MRI protocol - current/target N ≈ 5,000/20,000 - longitudinal study (rescan every 3–4 years) - https://www.rheinland-studie.de (in German)

sequences and methods. Table 1.2A shows an advanced research protocol, which is (except for a missing body-fat exam) exactly the MRI-protocol of the Rhineland study. The total scan time is below one hour per subject. All sequences, except #1 and #8, employ 3D-acquisition with 2D acceleration and, if possible, elliptical sampling. Sequence #8, DWI, requires a different acceleration strategy, as will be explained in the next section. The first sequence is a short 3D scout, enabling automatic slice positioning of all subsequent acquisitions. The second sequence, 3DREAM (Ehses et al., 2019), acquires fast whole-brain B_0 and B_1 field maps, providing off-resonance and actual flip angle distribution. These maps are required for various calibration purposes in the analysis, e.g., for quantitative tissue parameter mapping. With the current available technology, it is not feasible to acquire all possible neuro MR contrasts of interest in one hour and, at the same time, high image quality and resolution. Therefore, the protocol is designed in two parts: the first 8 sequences form the core protocol with 45 minutes net scan time. Contrasts for the core protocol are assumed to be of higher relevance and will be acquired for every subject of the study. The second part is the free protocol. It consists of promising applications, however only one of them is acquired per subject. This keeps the total examination time below 1 h, and results in a smaller sub-population for each contrast of the free protocol. The specific choices for the core and free protocol were based on the general objectives of the Rhineland study. Since it is a long-term study, it might be possible that objectives will adapt, and therefore also the protocol will adapt. A sequence may move from the core protocol to the free protocol, or vice versa, or could be completely removed. Likewise, new emerging techniques may enter the free protocol. (The free protocol of the Rhineland study already uses more specific sequences, e.g., for hippocampal subfield imaging or $T_{1\rho}$ mapping.)

10   **Chapter 1** Recommendations for neuro MRI acquisition strategies

This acquisition strategy was considered to be both forward-looking and at the same time mature. It may serve as a recommendation for upcoming long-term studies. Finally, Table 1.2B presents a fast research protocol proposal, providing high-quality neuroimaging data in less than 10 minutes, which is well-suited for a clinical setting. The proposal includes fast perfusion imaging, which might be of interest in a patient population. Note that the anatomical images are acquired with 1.0 mm isotropic resolution, which is still the common standard in many advanced neuroimaging studies. The short scan times result from higher acceleration factors, which can be achieved with 2D acceleration.

Table 1.2 Example recommendations for neuroimaging protocols. All sequences provide whole-brain coverage with isotropic resolution. A) The research protocol of the Rhineland study, providing many promising MRI contrasts in a short scan time. The bottom rows printed in gray font form the optional free protocol (FP). B) Fast research protocol to acquire high-quality neuroimaging data in less than 10 minutes for several clinically relevant contrasts.

#	Contrast	Sequence Name	Resolution [mm³] & Matrix Size	PI Accel.	TA [min]	Main Features
			A			
1	Scout	GRE	$1.6 \times 1.6 \times 1.6$ $160 \times 160 \times 128$	3×1	00:14	auto align
2	field mapping	3DREAM	$5.0 \times 5.0 \times 5.0$ $54 \times 54 \times 48$	2×2^1	00:10	B_1 & B_0 maps
3	rs-fMRI	3D-EPI	$2.4 \times 2.4 \times 2.4$ $90 \times 90 \times 60$	1×6^2	10:25	TE/TR=30/570 ms 1070 volumes
4	T_1-weighted	ME-MPRAGE	$0.8 \times 0.8 \times 0.8$ $320 \times 320 \times 224$	1×2^1	06:35	$4 \times$TE: 1.6–6.5 ms elliptical sampling
5	T_2-weighted	3D-TSE	$0.8 \times 0.8 \times 0.8$ $320 \times 320 \times 224$	1×2^1	04:47	external ACS, PF=6/8 elliptical sampling
6	FLAIR	IR-3D-TSE	$1.0 \times 1.0 \times 1.0$ $256 \times 256 \times 176$	1×2^1	04:37	ext. ACS, ellipt. sampl.
7	QSM	ME-SC-3D-EPI	$0.8 \times 0.8 \times 0.8$ $270 \times 270 \times 176$	3×2^1	06:12	maps: $\Delta\omega, \chi, T_2^*$ $6 \times$TE: 7–32 ms EF=7, avg=4, PF=6/8
8	DWI (CS-DSI)	SMS-DW-SE-EPI	$.5 \times 1.5 \times 1.5$ $140 \times 140 \times 93$	MB 3	12:04	117 q-space samples b_{max}=6800 s/mm² TE=107 ms, PF=6/8
					45:04	
FP1	MPM	SC-3D-EPI	$0.8 \times 0.8 \times 0.8$ $270 \times 270 \times 176$	3×2^1	7:15	maps: PD, T_1, MT$_{sat}$ EF=7, PF=6/8, avg=5
FP2	Perfusion	te-PCASL 3D-GRASE	$3.3 \times 3.3 \times 3.3$ $64 \times 64 \times 36$	1×2^1	7:13	8×8 Hadamard time-enc. CBF+ATT maps EF=32, avg=7
FP3	CEST	ss-CEST-3D-EPI	$2.0 \times 2.0 \times 2.0$ $108 \times 108 \times 70$	1×6^2	6:56	45 freq. offsets, 2 B_1 amp. EF=21, PF=6/8
...	...					

continued on next page

Table 1.2 (*continued*)						
			B			
#	**Contrast**	**Sequence Name**	**Resolution [mm^3] & Matrix Size**	**PI Accel.**	**TA [min]**	**Main Features**
1	Scout	GRE	1.6 × 1.6 × 1.6	3×1	00:14	auto align
4	T_1-weighted	ME-MPRAGE	1.0 × 1.0 × 1.0 256 × 256 × 176	1×3^1	02:40	4×TE: 1.6-6.5 ms elliptical sampling
5	T_2-weighted	3D-TSE	1.0 × 1.0 × 1.0 256 × 256 × 176	2×2^1	01:47	external ACS, PF=6/8 elliptical sampling
8	DWI (DTI)	SMS-DW-SE-EPI	2.0 × 2.0 × 2.0 108 × 108 × 69	MB 3	2:14	33 directions TE=76 ms, b=1000 s/mm^2
7	Perfusion	te-PCASL 3D-GRASE	3.3 × 3.3 × 3.3 64 × 64 × 36	1×2^1	02:12	CBF map (single PLD) EF=32, avg=6
					09:05	

1.6 Acquisition of neuro MRI contrasts

Multi-purpose neuro MRI exams acquire several contrasts, providing complementary information on brain structure and function. Some MR techniques even provide quantitative information on the biophysical tissue composition inside the voxel. This section briefly highlights examples of the most important techniques. All methods will be discussed in greater depth in other chapters of this book. The images shown in this section were obtained with the MR protocol presented in Table 1.2A.

1.6.1 Brain anatomy

Imaging brain anatomy with high resolution is a key component for many neuro MRI exams. It serves as the basis for segmenting brain structures and performing morphometric analysis, e.g., to quantify brain atrophy in neurodegeneration. T_1-weighted 3D sequences, such as the MP-RAGE sequence, provide excellent image quality and contrast for brain segmentation. The sequence utilizes a global inversion in an outer loop, followed by an inner loop with a gradient-echo readout. Originally, the MP-RAGE loop structure was fixed to the phase encoding dimensions. However, the approach can be easily combined with 2D-CAIPI acceleration and elliptical sampling, which provides significant speed-up without sacrificing image quality (Brenner et al., 2014). High-resolution whole-brain imaging of brain anatomy with T_2-weighting can be efficiently obtained with a 3D turbo-spin echo sequence (3D-TSE). Again, 2D acceleration with elliptical sampling can be efficiently applied to the 2-fold loop structure of 3D-TSE (Busse et al., 2008). However, the strong signal from the eyes in T_2-weighted scans may lead to PI artifacts if the PI auto-calibration signal (ACS) is acquired during phases of eye motion. Therefore it is advisable to acquire the ACS in a fast prescan. The T_2-weighted images are less suited for brain segmentation, but they provide contrast for tissue boundaries which are difficult to detect with T_1-weighting, e.g., the border from gray matter to the dura. A combined segmentation requires both scans at the same resolution. With the aforementioned acquisition methods, both scans can be acquired with 0.8 mm resolution and good image quality in about 10 minutes. Fig. 1.2 depicts anatomical images acquired with the MR protocol of the Rhineland study. Here, one important detail is the bandwidth-matching between MP-RAGE and 3D-TSE. Typically, MP-RAGE has a lower readout encoding bandwidth than

3D-TSE, which results in subtle image artifacts and geometric distortions close to areas of tissue-air interfaces. Acquiring multiple gradient-echoes at higher bandwidth (ME-MP-RAGE) with subsequent signal-averaging maintains acquisition time and CNR and, additionally, provides a perfect registration to 3D-TSE (van der Kouwe et al., 2008).

FLAIR images are often acquired in clinical neuro MRI. FLAIR provides T_2-weighting with CSF signal nulling, obtained by applying a global inversion pulse before each excitation pulse of the 3D-TSE sequence. The contrast is well-suited for detecting white matter lesions (WM hyper-intensities). Although presumably possible, so far it has not been shown that the FLAIR contrast can be artificially generated from T_1- and T_2-weighted acquisitions. Therefore, FLAIR is part of the Rhineland study core protocol. It might be removed in the future if, for instance, artificial intelligence (AI) applications enable robust and fail-safe FLAIR predictions from the other anatomical scans. A FLAIR example is depicted in Fig. 1.2C. The image has 1.0 mm isotropic resolution with a total scan time of 4:37 min. Due to its reduced SNR, FLAIR cannot be acquired with comparable image quality, resolution, and scan time as the T_1- and T_2-weighted scans. All three acquisitions of Fig. 1.2 utilize the acceleration pattern depicted in Fig. 1.1A.

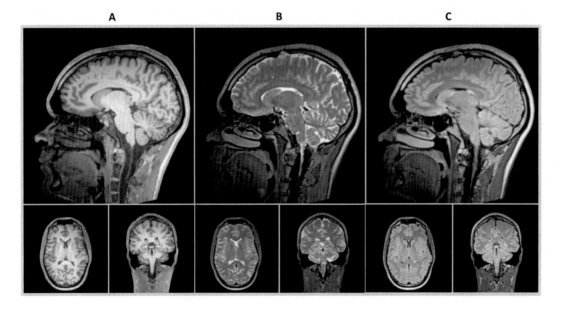

FIGURE 1.2

Examples of 3D whole-brain anatomical scans acquired at 3 tesla, which are well-suited for brain segmentation, morphometry, and lesion detection. A) T_1-weighting, B) T_2-weighting. C) FLAIR. The corresponding acquisition protocols are given in Table 1.2A (# 4,5,6).

1.6.2 Tissue microstructure

Modeling tissue microstructure with diffusion-weighted imaging (DWI) requires the acquisition of many images. Tens to hundreds of repetitions are common, varying the directions and the strength (b-value) of the diffusion weighting gradients. Chapters 8–11 of this book are dedicated to the acquisition and reconstruction of DWI data. For most applications the state-of-the-art sequence is SMS-DW-SE-EPI: a diffusion-weighted spin-echo EPI sequence with simultaneous-multi-slice acquisition. SMS utilizes multi-band (MB) pulses, which select multiple slices at the same time. As in conventional PI, the overlapping SMS signals can be separated with knowledge of the coil array receive sensitivities. Chapter 3 of this book provides a comprehensive introduction to the technique. SMS-EPI provides a "snapshot" acquisition of the DW-encoding per slice(s), avoiding motion-induced phase errors resulting from the DW-gradients, as they would occur with segmented 3D-EPI. Therefore SMS is the recommended acceleration technique for DWI. As mentioned in Section 1.1, DWI acquisitions benefit from high-performance gradients. This reduces the duration of the DW-gradients, and therefore the echo time, TE. Shorter TE leads to a higher SNR, which can be invested in higher resolution. For standard gradient systems with a maximum amplitude of 40 mT/m, an isotropic resolution of ≈ 2 mm is recommended. A gradient amplitude of 80 mT/m enables acquisitions with 1.5 mm isotropic resolution, as shown in the following examples. The repeated DWI acquisitions sample points in "diffusion space", also known as q-space. Each DW direction and b-value defines a point in q-space. The acquisition scheme is often linked to the analysis methods. Robust diffusion tensor imaging (DTI) requires a single $b \approx 1000$ s/mm^2 and approximately 30 directions, i.e., sampling a sphere (shell) in q-space, plus a $b = 0$ acquisition. Many biophysical microstructure models require acquisitions with varying b-value. A very successful approach is HARDI acquisition, which samples multiple shells (high angular diffusion imaging). An equidistant q-space sampling is called diffusion spectrum imaging (DSI). Many diffusion models can be derived from DSI data, however, the acquisition time is long. Fortunately, DSI acquisitions can be substantially accelerated by applying compressed sensing (CS) in q-space: the smooth variation of the q-space signal distribution enables a sparse signal representation. Using CS, the total distribution can be reconstructed from under-sampled q-space data. Fig. 1.3A shows the CS-DSI acquisition as utilized in the Rhineland study. 117 randomly distributed q-space samples are acquired, and CS reconstruction provides the full distribution sampled with 257 points. The corresponding acquisition parameters are given in Table 1.2A (#8), and a detailed discussion of the protocol was given by Tobisch et al. (2018). Fig. 1.3B depicts some derived measures of tissue microstructure. The concepts will be discussed in detail in Chapters 8–11 of this book. The top row shows maps from mathematically inspired diffusion models: fractional anisotropy (FA) and mean diffusivity (MD), from the tensor model, and the radial kurtosis (RK). The bottom row shows maps from biologically inspired diffusion models: neurite density (ND) and orientation dispersion (OD) from NODDI, and intra-axonal restricted volume fraction (FR) from CHARMED. Reliable FR estimates require sampling of high b-values up to $b \approx 6\text{--}7 \times 10^3$ s/mm^2. Fig. 1.3C shows results from deterministic fiber tracking, visualizing macroscopic structural connectivity of the brain. The tracking is based on voxel-wise estimates of the orientation distribution function (ODF), which is able to model multiple crossing fibers inside the voxel (c.f. lower left of Fig. 1.3C).

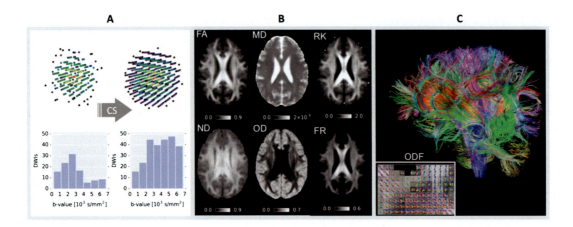

FIGURE 1.3

Diffusion spectrum imaging (DSI) with a compressed-sensing approach in q-space (A) enables fast acquisition of DWI data, which is suitable to reconstruct multiple tissue microstructure maps (B), as well as macroscopic brain structural connectivity or fiber tracking (C). The sequence details are given in Table 1.2A (#8). Figure adapted from (Tobisch et al., 2018).

1.6.3 The brain at work and rest

Similar to diffusion imaging, functional MRI (fMRI) also acquires a large number of images. The readout method of choice is gradient-echo EPI. Repeated imaging with T_2^*-weighting samples brain activity (the BOLD response) at high frame rate. The same sequence can be used to study brain activity resulting from certain stimuli (task-fMRI) or to investigate the functional connections between different brain regions in absence of external input (resting-state fMRI). Chapters 15 and 16 of this book provide a detailed introduction to fMRI data acquisition and analysis. Here, we name four important factors which determine the BOLD-sensitivity of the EPI acquisition: the echo time (TE), the repetition time per volume (TR), the total acquisition time (TA), and the temporal SNR (tSNR) of the EPI time series. At 3 tesla, TE $\approx$ 30 ms provides maximum BOLD-sensitivity. The tSNR is given by the mean voxel signal divided by its standard deviation. The tSNR depends on the image SNR, and therefore on the resolution. An isotropic resolution of 2–3 mm is a common and good choice for fMRI at 3 tesla. More samples of the time series yield a higher statistical power in the analysis. For instance, using a fixed TA of 10 min and TR of 600 ms yield 1000 whole-brain images. Such a high sampling rate is also beneficial for identification and removal of physiological noise (nuisance regression), i.e., cleaning signal variations due to heart beat and breathing, which contaminate the BOLD signal. Therefore, accelerated EPI acquisitions offer the best advantage. SMS-EPI acquisitions with multi-band acceleration factors MB $\approx$ 6–8 are common. This approach is utilized by large population studies, such as HCP and UK-Biobank. An alternative approach is 3D-EPI with 2D-CAIPI acceleration. Compared to slice-selective approaches, 3D acquisitions can achieve fat suppression in a faster and more elegant way. Since water-selective SMS pulses are not efficient, SMS-EPI utilizes standard fat suppression pre-pulses, which are time-consuming and also slightly influence the water signal. Instead, 3D-EPI can take advantage of short water-selective pulses, which excite the whole brain or a large slab. Moreover, since 3D-EPI at short TR operates in a steady state, the flip-angles are reduced (Ernst angle). This reduces the SAR (specific absorption rate) and makes the sequence particularly well suited for high field applications. Fig. 1.4 summarizes the results of a comparative study for fMRI acquisitions with SMS and 3D-EPI at 3 tesla (Stirnberg et al., 2017), which was performed in the piloting phase of the Rhineland study. The sequence diagrams in Fig. 1.4A schematically show the increased TR of SMS-EPI due to the fat suppression (FS) and multi-band (MB) excitation at the beginning, which can be achieved in shorter time with a water-selective excitation (WE) pulse for 3D-EPI (a binomial 1-1 hard pulse in the example). Thus, a TR-matched 3D-EPI sequence can utilize lower acceleration factors than SMS. This results in higher temporal SNR (tSNR) as depicted in Fig. 1.4B, where TR=530 ms and the acceleration factors were 8 and 6 for SMS and 3D-EPI, respectively. The tSNR analysis in gray matter (Fig. 1.4B, bottom) shows that the advantage further increases if additional nuisance regression and bandpass filtering is performed. Consequently, functional networks are more pronounced with 3D-EPI than with SMS-EPI, as shown in the resting-state analysis depicted in Fig. 1.4C. However, SMS-EPI also provides highly significant functional networks. In conclusion, both options are well-suited state-of-the-art options for fMRI at 3 tesla.

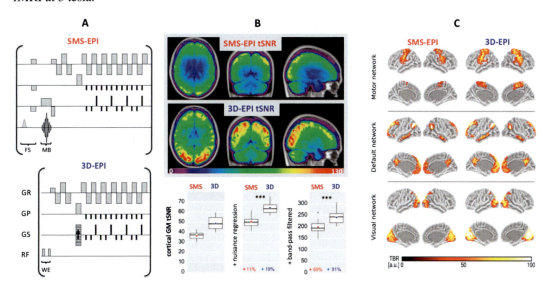

FIGURE 1.4

Comparison of functional MRI acquisitions with SMS-EPI and 3D-EPI: A) Sequence diagrams, B) temporal SNR analysis, C) resting-state network analysis. Details of the 3D-EPI acquisition protocol are given in Table 1.2A (#3). Figure adapted from (Stirnberg et al., 2017).

1.6.4 Brain perfusion

Constant blood supply provides the oxygen for healthy brain function. The process of blood penetrating brain tissue, first through larger arteries, and then to a dense network of small capillaries, is called perfusion. MRI can quantify the process by means of arterial spin labeling (ASL), which labels (typically inverts) the magnetization of inflowing blood. The T_1-recovery of the MR signal can be measured and, utilizing kinetic models of brain perfusion, the cerebral blood flow (CBF) can be estimated. ASL uses blood flow as an endogenous perfusion contrast. An overview of available techniques is given in Chapter 12 of this book. As always in MRI, a method-specific acquisition bias is present. Since CBF is a clinically relevant marker, protocol harmonization is especially important to quantitatively compare results. According to a consensus paper (Alsop et al., 2015), the proposed acquisition method is PCASL (pseudo-continuous ASL) with a 3D-GRASE readout. PCASL performs blood labeling in a single slice positioned below the brain and covering the major arteries. Labeling durations of a few seconds provide a stable perfusion weighting. After a post-labeling delay (PLD), whole-brain images are acquired with a 3D-GRASE readout, i.e., a multiple-spin-echo sequence employing an EPI train for each echo. The experiment is performed at least twice, with and without labeling, and the difference image provides the perfusion-weighted signal. Due to the low CNR of perfusion-weighted images, isotropic voxel-sizes of 3–4 mm are common and signal averaging of multiple repetitions is needed. If the data are acquired for a single PLD, robust CBF estimates can be drawn from short acquisitions of 2–3 minutes. In this case, the kinetic model is based on several assumptions about the physiology and MR tissue parameters, which might not hold over wide age-ranges and different patient groups. Acquisitions of multiple PLD information provide a more robust and less biased fit of CBF. In addition, applying a kinetic model to multi-PLD data enables an estimate of arterial transit times (ATT), i.e., the blood travel time required to reach a certain brain region. The recommended method of choice is so-called time-encoded PCASL (Teeuwisse et al., 2014), where the PLD is kept constant, but the labeling duration is varied with different block lengths for the label and control condition. The encoding scheme follows a Hadamard matrix, which can be inverted to reconstruct high-quality perfusion-weighted data for multiple PLDs. Moderate PI acceleration is additionally advisable as it reduces motion-induced artifacts and allows for the acquisition of more encoding steps for a fixed acquisition time. State-of-the-art perfusion imaging with a PI-accelerated time-encoded PCASL-3D-GRASE sequence provides stable estimates of CBF and ATT at approximately 3 mm isotropic resolution in a scan time below 10 minutes. An important extension of the approach enables probing of the permeability of the blood-brain-barrier (BBB). Here, the experiment has to be repeated several times with varying T_2-weighting, which can be conveniently applied during the PLD dead-time (Schmid et al., 2015). Fitting the exponential decay provides T_2 maps of the perfusion-weighted signal. Blood has considerably longer T_2 than gray matter. Therefore the observed decrease of T_2 at longer PLDs may be interpreted as water proton transition from the arterial compartment into the gray matter. A malfunction of the BBB due to disease would influence the result. The application has huge clinical potential; however, examinations times are still long. Fig. 1.5 shows examples of perfusion MRI results with a time-encoded PCASL-3D-GRASE sequence, as applied in the free protocol of the Rhineland study. Figs. 1.5A and B depict maps of cerebral blood flow (CBF) and the arterial transit time (ATT), respectively. Fig. 1.5C shows T_2-mapping results from an acquisition repeating the entire sequence seven times, each with a different T_2-weighting. The decrease of T_2 at late PLDs reflects transition of the labeled water molecules through the BBB. The total acquisition time for Fig. 1.5C was 45 minutes; however, robust T_2 maps may be already obtained with fewer T_2-weightings ($\approx$4–5).

1.6.5 Biophysical tissue properties

In quantitative MRI (qMRI) a series of weighted images is acquired. Fitting the data to a physical model enables mapping of biophysical tissue properties. Chapters 22–29 of this book are dedicated

1.6 Acquisition of neuro MRI contrasts

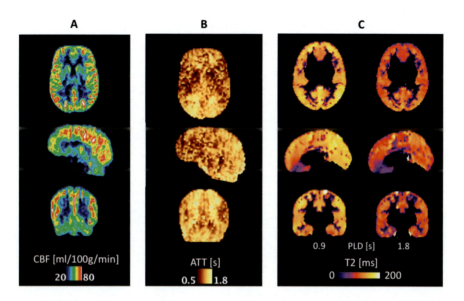

FIGURE 1.5

Whole-brain imaging of brain perfusion with a time-encoded PCASL-3D-GRASE sequence, which provides maps of cerebral blood flow (CBF) (A), and arterial transit time (ATT) (B). Fig. C depicts blood-brain permeability via T_2-mapping, obtained from an additional acquisition of multiple T_2-weightings. The acquisition protocol (without T_2-weighting) is given in Table 1.2A (# FP2).

to the most relevant methods currently applied in neuroimaging. This section presents examples to rapidly acquire quantitative tissue parameter maps. Quantitative-susceptibility-mapping (QSM) uses phase images of gradient-echo (GRE) acquisitions to reconstruct the magnetic susceptibility in tissue. This is, for example, an important marker of increased brain iron load as observed in many neurodegenerative diseases. If the GRE sequence acquires multiple echoes with appropriate timing, it is possible to additionally reconstruct maps of the effective transverse relaxation time, T_2^*, from the magnitude images. Applying the GRE sequence with appropriate flip angles for T_1- and PD-weighting (proton density), enables the reconstruction of T_1 and PD maps. An additional acquisition with an off-resonant preparation pulse for MT weighting enables the reconstruction of magnetization transfer saturation, MT_{sat}, which is a measure of proton magnetization exchange between larger molecules and water. The acquisition of all contrasts with subsequent reconstruction of the quantitative maps was termed multi-parameter mapping (MPM) by Weiskopf et al. (2013). The MT acquisition principle can be further extended to acquire more information about the molecular environment. The technique is known as CEST-imaging (chemical exchange saturation transfer). Snapshot-CEST repeats the off-resonant preparation with a train of preparation pulses, followed by a fast whole-brain GRE readout (Zaiss et al., 2018). If the acquisition is repeated with varying off-resonances, the data samples the so-called z-spectrum, a frequency-resolved quantification of proton exchange. The technique is less specific, but more sensitive than MR spectroscopy, enabling fast imaging of molecular information with isotropic resolution of ≈ 2 mm.

18 Chapter 1 Recommendations for neuro MRI acquisition strategies

All acquisitions can be efficiently obtained with the segmented skipped-CAIPI 3D-EPI (SC-3D-EPI) readout outlined in Section 1.3. Using substantial double segmentation as well as PI acceleration along both PE axes reduces the EPI factor, and therefore EPI-specific geometric distortions and other artifacts induced by field inhomogeneity. In this way, high quality images can be obtained in a short scan time. Fig. 1.6 shows examples of QSM, MPM, and CEST imaging, acquired with the MR protocol of the Rhineland study. The snapshot-CEST (ss-CEST) acquisition was repeated twice with varying B_1 amplitude to quantify the effect of B_1 variation on the z-spectrum. In this context, it has to be noted that all qMRI reconstructions require information on field inhomogeneities (B_0 and B_1 maps), which were obtained with the 3DREAM sequence (Table 1.2A, #2).

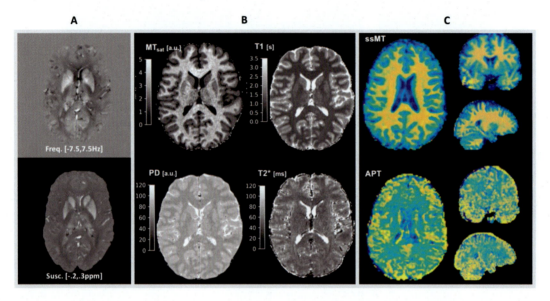

FIGURE 1.6

Quantitative MRI reconstructed from whole-brain skipped-CAIPI 3D-EPI acquisitions. A) off-resonance map (top) and derived quantitative susceptibility map (QSM, bottom). B) Multi-parametric-mapping (MPM) providing quantitative maps for T_1, T_2^*, PD, and MT_{sat}. C) Contrasts derived from whole z-spectrum CEST imaging: semisolid magnetization transfer (ssMT, top), and amide proton transfer (APT, bottom). Sequence details are given in Table 1.2A (#7, FP1, FP3, respectively).

1.7 Conclusions and future prospects

This chapter provided recommendations and examples for neuro MRI acquisition strategies. The discussion was confined to 3 tesla MRI, which is today the most commonly used system for neuroimaging research and advanced clinical applications. Many neuro MR applications require whole-brain imaging. Therefore the MRI acquisition should take advantage of 3D spatial encoding with 2D parallel imaging acceleration, if possible. Cartesian acquisitions are currently still the method of choice, as they can be robustly applied in high-throughput studies on commercial MRI systems. Using state-of-the-art receiver array coils, acceleration factors of 2–8 are possible, depending on the contrast and resolution of interest. For example structural T_1- and T_2-weighted anatomical imaging with high quality and 0.8 mm isotropic resolution can be obtained in approximately 5–6 minutes, respectively. The recommendations are based on MRI acquisition technologies which are both state-of the-art and widely available on modern MRI systems. The specific sequences are either available as products by the vendor or can be obtained via research agreements. The protocol design also has to consider the available image analysis tools. Ideally, the imaging data should be compatible with existing tools and well-suited for future analysis concepts.

Given the speed of MRI method development, the advanced MR protocols of today will be outdated in the (near) future. Recent advances in acquisition technology and image reconstruction will enable routine use of non-Cartesian acquisitions in the future. Writing the same chapter again in a few years would potentially name 7T as the current method of choice for neuro MR, enabling even faster acquisitions and better image contrast. Already today, the technology provides many promising contrasts which can be acquired in a single one-hour multi-purpose exam. As an example, this chapter presented the MR protocol of the Rhineland study. The methods provide biophysical information of the tissue composition within a single voxel. Quantitative tissue parameters, microstructure, and molecular information can be encoded with neuro MRI, all enriching our understanding of the structure and the function of the human brain. However, the clinical and diagnostic value still needs to be proven for many of these techniques. This will require more large-scale imaging studies in the general population and on patients in the future.

References

Alsop, D.C., Detre, J.a., Golay, X., Günther, M., Hendrikse, J., Hernandez-Garcia, L., Lu, H., Macintosh, B.J., Parkes, L.M., Smits, M., van Osch, M.J.P., Wang, D.J.J., Wong, E.C., Zaharchuk, G., 2015. Recommended implementation of arterial spin-labeled perfusion MRI for clinical applications: a consensus of the ISMRM perfusion study group and the European consortium for ASL in dementia. Magnetic Resonance in Medicine (ISSN 1522-2594) 73, 102–116. https://doi.org/10.1002/mrm.25197. http://www.ncbi.nlm.nih.gov/pubmed/24715426.

Bernstein, M.A., Fain, S.B., Riederer, S.J., 2001. Effect of windowing and zero-filled reconstruction of MRI data on spatial resolution and acquisition strategy. Journal of Magnetic Resonance Imaging (ISSN 1053-1807) 14 (3), 270–280. https://doi.org/10.1002/jmri.1183.

Bilgic, B., Gagoski, B.a., Cauley, S.F., Fan, A.P., Polimeni, J.R., Grant, P.E., Wald, L.L., Setsompop, K., 2015. Wave-CAIPI for highly accelerated 3D imaging. Magnetic Resonance in Medicine (ISSN 1522-2594) 73 (6), 2152–2162. https://doi.org/10.1002/mrm.25347. http://www.ncbi.nlm.nih.gov/pubmed/24986223.

Brenner, D., Stirnberg, R., Pracht, E.D., Stöcker, T., 2014. Two-dimensional accelerated MP-RAGE imaging with flexible linear reordering. Magma (New York, N. Y.) (ISSN 1352-8661) 27 (5), 455–462. https://doi.org/10.1007/s10334-014-0430-y. http://www.ncbi.nlm.nih.gov/pubmed/24510154.

Breuer, F., Blaimer, M., Heidemann, R.M., Mueller, M.F., Griswold, M., Jakob, P.M., 2005. Controlled aliasing in parallel imaging results in higher acceleration (CAIPIRINHA) for multi-slice imaging. Magnetic Resonance in Medicine (ISSN 0740-3194) 53 (3), 684–691. https://doi.org/10.1002/mrm.20401. http://www.ncbi.nlm.nih.gov/pubmed/15723404.

Busse, R.F., Brau, A.C., Vu, A., Michelich, C.R., Bayram, E., Kijowski, R., Reeder, S.B., Rowley, H.A., 2008. Effects of refocusing flip angle modulation and view ordering in 3D fast spin echo. Magnetic Resonance in Medicine (ISSN 1522-2594) 60 (3), 640–649. https://doi.org/10.1002/mrm.21680.

Button, K.S., Ioannidis, J.P.a., Mokrysz, C., Nosek, B.a., Flint, J., Robinson, E.S.J., Munafò, M.R., 2013. Power failure: why small sample size undermines the reliability of neuroscience. Nature Reviews. Neuroscience (ISSN 1471-0048) 14 (5), 365–476. https://doi.org/10.1038/nrn3475. http://www.ncbi.nlm.nih.gov/pubmed/23571845.

Ehses, P., Brenner, D., Stirnberg, R., Pracht, E.D., Stöcker, T., 2019. Whole-brain B1-mapping using three-dimensional DREAM. Magnetic Resonance in Medicine (ISSN 1522-2594) 82 (3), 924–934. https://doi.org/10.1002/mrm.27773.

Pohmann, R., Speck, O., Scheffler, K., 2016. Signal-to-noise ratio and MR tissue parameters in human brain imaging at 3, 7, and 9.4 tesla using current receive coil arrays. Magnetic Resonance in Medicine (ISSN 1522-2594) 75 (2), 801–809. https://doi.org/10.1002/mrm.25677.

Pruessmann, K.P., Weiger, M., Scheidegger, M.B., Boesiger, P., 1999. SENSE: sensitivity encoding for fast MRI. Magnetic Resonance in Medicine (ISSN 0740-3194) 42 (5), 952–962. http://www.ncbi.nlm.nih.gov/pubmed/10542355.

Schmid, S., Teeuwisse, W.M., Lu, H., van Osch, M.J.P., 2015. Time-efficient determination of spin compartments by time-encoded pCASL T2-relaxation-under-spin-tagging and its application in hemodynamic characterization of the cerebral border zones. NeuroImage (ISSN 1095-9572) 123, 72–79. https://doi.org/10.1016/j.neuroimage.2015.08.025.

Stirnberg, R., Stöcker, T., 2021. Segmented K-space blipped-controlled aliasing in parallel imaging for high spatiotemporal resolution EPI. Magnetic Resonance in Medicine 85 (3), 1540–1551. https://doi.org/10.1002/mrm.28486. https://onlinelibrary.wiley.com/doi/abs/10.1002/mrm.28486.

Stirnberg, R., Huijbers, W., Brenner, D., Poser, B.A., Breteler, M., Stöcker, T., 2017. Rapid whole-brain resting-state fMRI at 3 Tesla: efficiency-optimized three-dimensional EPI versus repetition time-matched simultaneous-multi-slice EPI. NeuroImage (ISSN 1053-8119) 163, 81–92. https://doi.org/10.1016/j.neuroimage.2017.08.031. http://linkinghub.elsevier.com/retrieve/pii/S105381191730678X.

Teeuwisse, W.M., Schmid, S., Ghariq, E., Veer, I.M., Van Osch, M.J., 2014. Time-encoded pseudocontinuous arterial spin labeling: basic properties and timing strategies for human applications. Magnetic Resonance in Medicine (ISSN 1522-2594) 72 (6), 1712–1722. https://doi.org/10.1002/mrm.25083.

Tobisch, A., Stirnberg, R., Harms, R.L., Schultz, T., Roebroeck, A., Breteler, M.M., Stöcker, T., 2018. Compressed sensing diffusion spectrum imaging for accelerated diffusion microstructure MRI in long-term population imaging. Frontiers in Neuroscience (ISSN 1662-453X) 12, 1–19. https://doi.org/10.3389/fnins.2018.00650.

van der Kouwe, A.J.W., Benner, T., Salat, D.H., Fischl, B., 2008. Brain morphometry with multiecho MPRAGE. NeuroImage (ISSN 1053-8119) 40 (2), 559–569. https://doi.org/10.1016/j.neuroimage.2007.12.025.

Weiskopf, N., Suckling, J., Williams, G., Correia, M.M., Inkster, B., Tait, R., Ooi, C., Bullmore, E.T., Lutti, A., 2013. Quantitative multi-parameter mapping of R1, PD(*), MT, and R2(*) at 3T: a multi-center validation. Frontiers in Neuroscience (ISSN 1662-4548) 7 (June), 95. https://doi.org/10.3389/fnins.2013.00095. http://www.pubmedcentral.nih.gov/articlerender.fcgi?artid=3677134&tool=pmcentrez&rendertype=abstract.

Zaiss, M., Ehses, P., Scheffler, K., 2018. Snapshot-CEST: optimizing spiral-centric-reordered gradient echo acquisition for fast and robust 3D CEST MRI at 9.4 T. NMR in Biomedicine (ISSN 1099-1492) 31 (4), 1–14. https://doi.org/10.1002/nbm.3879.

CHAPTER

Advanced reconstruction methods for fast MRI

2

Florian Knoll[a,b]

[a]*NYU School of Medicine, Department of Radiology, New York, NY, United States*
[b]*FAU Department of Artificial Intelligence in Biomedical Engineering, Erlangen, Germany*

2.1 Introduction to image reconstruction for fast MR imaging

Due to the nature of the acquisition physics and the use of magnetic gradient fields to perform spatial signal encoding, MR data points are acquired in frequency space (Fourier-, or k-space). This Fourier nature defines the essential properties of the image acquisition and reconstruction process. The number of required measurement points to obtain an image without aliasing artifacts is set by the well-known Nyquist–Shannon sampling theorem. The relationships between image domain and Fourier domain explain both the types of image artifacts that are specific to MRI due to certain corruptions during data acquisition, as well as particular features that can be facilitated to make the measurement process more efficient.

As the name suggests, image reconstruction is the task of obtaining corresponding images from measurement data that are acquired by the MR scanner. Image reconstruction is a field that has evolved constantly since the first conception of MRI, where it was performed with what would now be called a back-projection approach, similar to what is used in computed tomography. Developments in image reconstruction are closely related and often driven by corresponding developments in pulse sequences, which require new data processing strategies or correction mechanisms. Equally, new ideas for data acquisition are often inspired by progress in image reconstruction. The goal of this chapter is to provide an overview of a selection of developments in image reconstruction for fast MR imaging. It will cover both well-established methods that go back to the late 1980s, as well as currently ongoing research efforts. Pulse sequence developments are not included in this chapter, because they are the topic of the previous chapter. The specific topic of simultaneous multi-slice (SMS) acquisitions and their applications to neuroimaging are also not included here, because they are covered later in Chapter 3 (Simultaneous Multi-Slice MRI). Since this chapter does not cover details about pulse sequences and spin physics, a good starting point is the abstraction level of the well-known MRI signal equation:

$$f_j(k_x, k_y) = \int\limits_{-\infty}^{+\infty} \int\limits_{-\infty}^{+\infty} c_j(x, y) u(x, y) e^{-i(k_x x + k_y y)} dx dy. \tag{2.1}$$

Advances in Magnetic Resonance Technology and Applications, Volume 4, ISSN 2666-9099. https://doi.org/10.1016/B978-0-12-822479-3.00010-5
Copyright © 2021 Elsevier Inc. All rights reserved.

22   **Chapter 2** Advanced reconstruction methods for fast MRI

In Eq. (2.1), f_j is the MR signal of RF receive coil $j = 1, \ldots, n_c$, u is the underlying image, and c_j is the sensitivity profile of the receive coil j (Pruessmann et al., 1999). k_x and k_y are Fourier domain (k-space) spatial frequencies, whereas x and y are spatial coordinates in image space. In this chapter, all examples will be given in 2D. k_x will be used for the readout (frequency encoding gradient) direction and k_y for the phase encoding direction. Though they will not be shown in the didactic examples for this chapter, generalizations to 3D imaging and non-Cartesian acquisitions will be discussed in the context of each individual section. After discretization, the signal equation can be written in matrix-vector notation:

$$f_j = \mathcal{F}_\Omega C_j u. \tag{2.2}$$

In Eq. (2.2), C_j is a diagonal matrix that contains the sensitivity profile of the receive coil j, and $\mathcal{F}_\Omega$ is a Fourier operator that samples locations Ω in k-space. Together, the matrices C_j and $\mathcal{F}_\Omega$ define the mapping from image space to k-space, and are often referred to as the encoding or forward operator. At this abstraction level, the task of image reconstruction is to solve the corresponding matrix inversion problem for the unknown image u. Building on this foundation, this chapter will progressively add complexity to the solution of the image reconstruction problem. Developments are introduced chronologically, starting with constrained reconstruction based on partial Fourier acquisitions (Margosian et al., 1986; Cuppen and van Est, 1987), to parallel imaging (Sodickson and Manning, 1997; Pruessmann et al., 1999; Griswold et al., 2002), compressed sensing (Lustig et al., 2007), and finally novel developments that use concepts from deep learning (Wang et al., 2016; Hammernik et al., 2018; Zhu et al., 2018). The theoretical foundations of all these approaches have been described in detail in the respective publications as well as earlier review papers and textbooks; the didactic approach in this chapter is to provide practical hands-on insight into their properties. In some cases, rigorous notation is sacrificed for intuitive understanding. Discussions of MR hardware are also outside the scope of this chapter. Numerical experiments are conducted with a data set that is representative of a clinical neuroimaging exam. It should be noted that though these experiments were designed to be realistic, their main goal is to illustrate didactic concepts. The individual methods were not optimized to give the best possible performance for those particular data, and in some cases simplifications were made. The data and the source code that was used to obtain the results for the individual sections are available as additional online material.[1] Therefore this chapter can been seen as an instruction manual, and readers are encouraged to perform their own numerical experiments to deepen their understanding of the material.

2.2 Data acquisition for didactic example

For didactic consistency, the concepts in this chapter will be illustrated with data from a brain scan obtained at the Department of Radiology at NYU School of Medicine. Acquisition of the exam was part of a study approved by our local institutional review board (IRB). Data were acquired on a clinical 3T system (Siemens Magnetom Prisma), using 52 channels of a 64-channel head and neck coil. A T_2-weighted Turbo-Spin-Echo (TSE) sequence was acquired in the axial plane with the following sequence parameters: TR = 6000 ms, TE = 113 ms, in-plane resolution of 0.57×0.57 mm^2 covering

---

[1] https://www.elsevier.com/books-and-journals/book-companion/9780128224793.

a field of view of 220×220 mm^2 (matrix size 384×384), slice thickness 5 mm, echo train length = 18. No acceleration was performed at the data acquisition stage. A total of 30 slices was acquired, and a single slice at the center of the brain is used for all examples in this chapter. SVD-based channel compression from 52 to 16 receive channels was used to reduce the memory requirements and computation time of the experiments. The fully sampled ground truth reconstruction u was obtained via inverse Fourier transform and coil sensitivity-weighted combination of the individual receive channels. Coil sensitivities were obtained with ESPIRiT (Uecker et al., 2014).

2.3 Constrained reconstruction: partial Fourier acquisitions
2.3.1 Overview of partial Fourier imaging and the POCS algorithm

After the introduction of the k-space concept, it was soon discovered that there is an inherent redundancy in MRI data due to a basic property of the Fourier transform: The Fourier transform representation f of $u \in \mathbb{R}$ will have Hermitian symmetry $f^*(k_x, k_y) = f(-k_x, -k_y)$, where * denotes complex conjugation. The consequence for MR imaging is that under the assumption that the reconstructed image u is real valued, it should in principle be possible to acquire only half of k-space, and synthesize the missing coefficients by via Hermitian symmetry prior to performing an inverse Fourier transform. The practical consequence is that if such a half-Fourier acquisition is performed in the phase encoding dimension, the scan time will be reduced substantially, because the number of phase encoding steps is halved. Half-Fourier in the readout direction is commonly called an asymmetric echo, and is used to reduce the echo time TE. The problem is that, in practice, the underlying assumption that u is real valued is often violated due to motion or field inhomogeneities. The resulting image phase leads to image artifacts if Hermitian symmetry is enforced during the reconstruction. This issue leads to the development of reconstruction methods that enforce two constraints simultaneously: Hermitian symmetry and consistency with an estimated image phase (Margosian et al., 1986; Cuppen and van Est, 1987). The assumption behind these methods is that the image phase φ is smooth and can be estimated from a fully sampled center of k-space f_c:

$$\varphi = \angle(\mathcal{F}^{-1} f_c). \tag{2.3}$$

Partial Fourier reconstructions are covered in detail in existing textbooks and literature. For example, a comprehensive overview can be found in Liang et al. (1992). Therefore, in this chapter only a brief overview of one popular algorithm is presented, the iterative projection on convex sets (POCS) method. After initialization with the trivial zero-filled solution, the update step of one iteration is defined by alternating between two constraints:

$$u_1^{n+1} = |u_2^n| e^{i\varphi},$$
$$u_2^{n+1} = \mathcal{F}_{\Omega}^{-1}(\mathcal{R}(\mathcal{F}_{\Omega}(u_1^{n+1}))). \tag{2.4}$$

In Eq. (2.4), the first step enforces consistency of the reconstructed image with the estimated phase φ; the second step enforces data consistency with the acquired k-space data. This is enforced by replacing the k-space coefficients of the intermediate image u_1^n with the originally acquired data. This step is denoted by $\mathcal{R}$:

$$\mathcal{R} : \begin{cases} \mathcal{F}_{\Omega}(u_1^n)) = f, & \text{if } f \in \Omega \\ \mathcal{F}_{\Omega}(u_1^n) = \mathcal{F}_{\Omega}(u_1^n)), & \text{otherwise.} \end{cases}$$

24 **Chapter 2** Advanced reconstruction methods for fast MRI

u_2^n denotes the intermediate reconstruction result of POCS iteration step n, and the iteration is repeated until convergence.

2.3.2 Didactic experiments for partial Fourier imaging

Fig. 2.1 shows an example of a retrospectively simulated partial Fourier reconstruction for the brain data described in Section 2.2. A partial Fourier factor of 5/8 is simulated. Since this data set is from a TSE acquisition and does not show severe residual phase, the data were additionally modulated with a synthetic sinusoidal phase to enhance the effects of phase errors for didactic reasons. The results from this figure can be reproduced with the corresponding code package that is provided online. Readers are also encouraged to change the simulation settings (e.g., the amount of partial Fourier undersampling) and observe the effects on the results. Fig. 2.1 shows the inverse Fourier transform reconstruction from the full k-space as a ground truth reference, the partial Fourier k-space, the estimate of the image phase φ, and three reconstructions: (i) a trivial zero-filling reconstruction, (ii) a reconstruction that enforced strict conjugate symmetry of k-space, thus violating the residual image phase, and (iii) the iterative POCS reconstruction described in Eq. (2.4). 10 POCS iterations were performed. Error images to the ground truth reference are also shown for each reconstruction. The structural similarity index (SSIM) (Wang et al., 2004), a commonly used image quality metric ([0,1], 1 indicating identical images) in comparison to the reference, is shown for each reconstruction. These examples illustrate the basic properties of the individual reconstructions. As expected, the trivial zero-filling reconstruction leads to a substantial loss of high resolution, because the outer part of k-space is missing, but it results in no model mismatch, given that it enforces no *a-priori* information. The conjugate symmetry reconstruction recovers part of that resolution, but the model mismatch from ignoring the image phase leads to severe ringing artifacts. The POCS reconstruction shows the highest recovery of resolution and no obvious artifacts. However, it should be mentioned that this is contingent upon an accurate estimation of the image phase. If the phase estimate is poor, POCS will result in comparable artifacts to the conjugate symmetry reconstruction.

2.4 Parallel imaging
2.4.1 Overview of parallel imaging

Parallel imaging is currently the most widespread technique for fast MRI acquisitions. Multi-channel receive coils, which were originally developed to increase the signal-to-noise ratio of MR acquisitions, are now standard in clinical MRI scanners and every major vendor has parallel imaging in their product portfolio. A feature that parallel imaging shares with partial Fourier is that accelerated acquisitions are achieved by undersampling k-space. However, undersampling is performed differently. Instead of performing half-Fourier acquisitions, the sampling rate (the distance between two adjacent points in k-space) in the phase encoding direction is increased. According to basic Fourier relationships, this leads to a reduction of the field-of-view in the image domain. Therefore, in contrast to the loss of resolution in partial Fourier, a conventional zero-filling reconstruction leads to images with aliasing artifacts. The goal of the parallel imaging reconstruction process is to fill these missing parts of k-space by utilizing information from multiple receive coils.

Historically, parallel imaging is categorized in two groups: methods that perform data processing steps in image space after the Fourier transform, and methods where the major data processing steps are

2.4 Parallel imaging

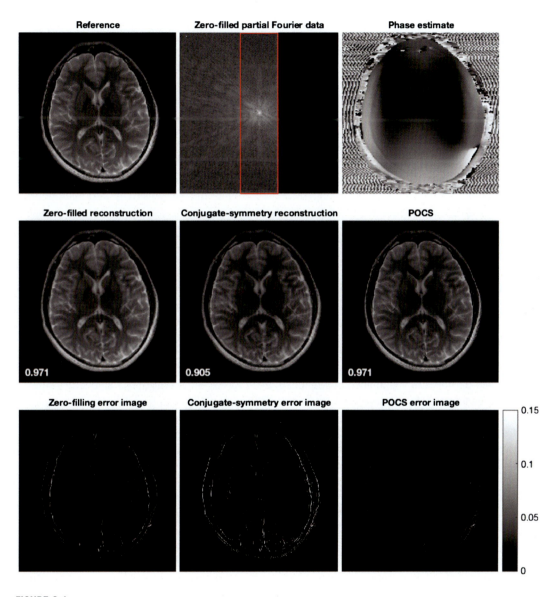

FIGURE 2.1

Partial Fourier reconstruction. First row: Reference inverse Fourier transform reconstruction from the full k-space, partial Fourier k-space, and estimate of the image phase φ. The central part of k-space that is used for the phase estimation is indicated with the red rectangle. Second row: A trivial zero-filling reconstruction, a reconstruction that enforced strict conjugate symmetry of k-space, thus violating the residual image phase and the iterative POCS reconstruction from the algorithm described in Eq. (2.4). SSIM in comparison to the reference is shown for each reconstruction. Third row: Error images to the ground truth reference.

26 **Chapter 2** Advanced reconstruction methods for fast MRI

performed in k-space, followed by a Fourier transform. The most well-known examples of these two groups are SENSE (sensitivity encoding) (Pruessmann et al., 1999) and GRAPPA (generalized auto-calibrating partial parallel acquisition) (Griswold et al., 2002). These two methods can be found under different acronyms on every recent MRI scanner of all major vendors. These two methods are discussed in the following subsections; high-level illustration of their respective data processing pipelines is presented in Fig. 2.2. In this figure, f_j^{Ω} denotes undersampled measurement data, u_j^{Ω} the corresponding undersampled images, f_j the recovered k-space, and u_j the corresponding images. C_j are estimations of the coil sensitivity profiles, and u is a combined, unaliased reconstruction. $\mathcal{F}^{-1}$ denotes the inverse Fourier transform; SENSE and GRAPPA stand for the respective unaliasing algorithms. Note that this notation is not rigorous, because when using parallel imaging, f_j and u_j are of course only approximations of the true underlying fully sampled data. They are subject to noise amplification (Pruessmann et al., 1999) and systematic errors due to imperfect calibration of the coil sensitivity information.

2.4.2 Image space parallel imaging: SENSE

As illustrated conceptually in Fig. 2.2, in image space-based parallel imaging methods, such as SENSE (Pruessmann et al., 1999), the elimination of aliasing artifacts is performed after the application of an inverse Fourier transform. In image space, the violation of the sampling theorem due to the increased distance of k-space samples in the phase encoding direction leads to a superposition of periodic repetitions of the original image u. Each pixel in the accelerated images u_j^{Ω} consists of a superposition of R (the acceleration factor) pixels from u, which are weighted according to the values of the coil sensitivities C_j at the corresponding pixel positions. If the number of receive coil elements is higher than the undersampling factor, an assumption that is generally true in real-world imaging settings, then the forward signal encoding model defined by Eq. (2.2) constitutes an overdetermined system of equations. Estimations of receive coil sensitivity maps C_j can be achieved via a separate reference scan with the body coil, or from a fully sampled area at the center of k-space. With this knowledge, the signal values of the original, unaliased image u can be recovered (unfolded) by solving this system of equations. Iterative inversion algorithms are commonly used for this task, and the didactic SENSE experiments that are discussed in Subsection 2.4.4 were performed with iterative conjugate gradient (CG)-SENSE (Pruessmann et al., 2001).

Though it is possible to use parallel imaging with arbitrary coil configurations, it is important that the individual receive coil elements deliver independent information in the undersampled phase encoding dimension. In practice, since the elements always overlap to a certain degree, the rank of the encoding matrix is reduced, and the matrix inversion can become ill-conditioned. This leads to noise amplification in the reconstructed image. Using the SENSE formalism, the reduced signal-to-noise ratio of an accelerated parallel imaging acquisition $\text{SNR}_{\Omega}(x, y)$ can be quantified as follows (Pruessmann et al., 1999):

$$\text{SNR}_{\Omega}(x, y) = \frac{\text{SNR}}{g(x, y)\sqrt{R}}. \tag{2.5}$$

In Eq. (2.5), $g(x, y) > 1$ is the so-called geometry factor that characterizes the lack of independent information in individual receive coil elements. Since the overlap of the elements depends on their respective spatial position, the g-factor changes over the field-of-view, and the image has a spatially varying SNR. This is one of the key properties of images that are reconstructed with parallel imaging.

2.4 Parallel imaging

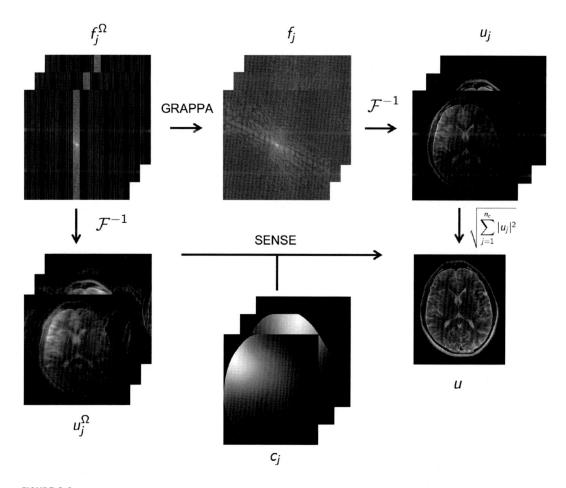

FIGURE 2.2

Graphical illustration of the pipelines behind the two most commonly used parallel imaging reconstruction principles, image space- and k-space-based parallel imaging. SENSE and GRAPPA, the two most widely used methods, are used as examples for the respective principles. A description of the notation is given in the main body of this chapter.

Noise amplification can be reduced by regularization of the matrix inversion, which can be achieved with the use of a-priori information in the form of additional constraints. This is discussed in Section 2.5.

2.4.3 k-space parallel imaging: GRAPPA

Rather than trying to unfold the aliased multi-coil images, the goal of k-space-based methods is to directly recover the k-space coefficients that were not sampled during data acquisition. Although they were historically developed separately from image space-based parallel-imaging methods, and the two

28   Chapter 2 Advanced reconstruction methods for fast MRI

approaches may appear to be fundamentally different, they are essentially just two points of view on the exact same underlying physics: multi-channel receive coils provide an additional way of spatial encoding that is complementary to the phase encoding gradient. In the k-space parallel-imaging formalism, this spatial distribution of the different coil elements is used to directly synthesize omitted phase encoding steps (Sodickson and Manning, 1997). An intuitive way to understand k-space-based parallel imaging is that an individual coil image u_j is a multiplication of the underlying image u, and the coil sensitivity C_j. The acquired k-space data f_j are therefore a convolution of the Fourier transform of the data $\mathcal{F}f_j$, with the Fourier transform of the respective coil sensitivity $\mathcal{F}C_j$. Due to their electrodynamic properties, coil sensitivities are smooth functions, and $\mathcal{F}C_j$ acts as a convolution kernel of limited size that distributes the information that is stored in a single k-space data point to its neighbors. Consequently, it is possible to recover missing points by a weighted linear combination of adjacent samples. In GRAPPA (Griswold et al., 2002), this is done by constructing a reconstruction kernel in k-space. The weights of this kernel are defined by the coil sensitivities, and they have to be estimated in a calibration step prior to the reconstruction. This calibration step can be compared to the estimation of coil sensitivity maps in image-space-based parallel imaging. This is done with the additional acquisition of so-called autocalibration or reference lines at the center of k-space. The result of a GRAPPA processing step is a complete set of k-space data f_j for all coils. To reconstruct an image u, individual coil images are first generated by applying a standard inverse Fourier transform $\mathcal{F}^{-1}$, and the resulting images u_j are combined to a single final image, for example via a square root sum of squares combination $u = \sqrt{\sum_{j=1}^{n_c} |u_j|^2}$. This pipeline is illustrated conceptually in Fig. 2.2.

The spatially varying reduction of SNR is an inherent feature of parallel imaging that depends on the properties of the used receive coil. Images that are reconstructed with a k-space parallel imaging method therefore show the same reduction in SNR as reconstructions from image space parallel imaging. However, the limited size of the GRAPPA convolution kernel serves as an implicit regularization of the reconstruction problem. Therefore the trade-off between image resolution, residual aliasing artifacts, and noise amplification is usually different between SENSE and GRAPPA, as well as between different implementations of the two methods.

2.4.4 Didactic experiments for parallel imaging

Didactic experiments were performed that replicate accelerated parallel-imaging protocols on clinical MRI scanners. Acceleration was simulated by performing equidistant reduction of k-space lines in the phase encoding direction, thus increasing the k-space sampling rate. The center of k-space was not undersampled. Two sets of experiments are shown in this section. The first experiment uses a k-space reduction factor of R=4 and 26 fully sampled reference lines at the center of k-space. The second experiment uses a reduction factor of R=6 and 16 reference lines. For didactic simplicity in the provided code package, only one set of coil sensitivity maps C_j from 26 reference lines was estimated for SENSE, and used to reconstruct data at both levels of acceleration. Since it is the more general and widely used version of the algorithm, the iterative conjugate gradient-based SENSE version (CG-SENSE) (Pruessmann et al., 2001) was used in the experiments. The numeric tolerance for the CG-algorithm was set to 10^{-4}. For the R=4 experiment, this resulted in 17 iterations, for the R=6 experiment, it resulted in 68 iterations. A 5×5 convolution kernel was used for GRAPPA.

The results of these experiments are shown in Fig. 2.3. Trivial zero-filling reconstructions are again shown for reference, and they illustrate the different corruption with this type of k-space undersam-

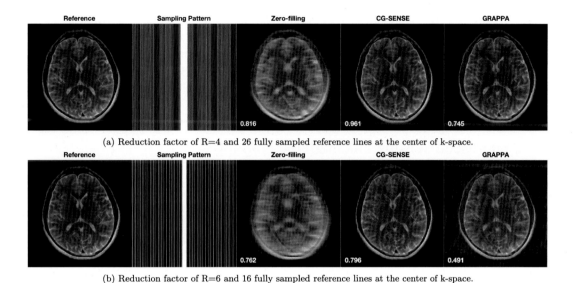

(a) Reduction factor of R=4 and 26 fully sampled reference lines at the center of k-space.

(b) Reduction factor of R=6 and 16 fully sampled reference lines at the center of k-space.

FIGURE 2.3

Parallel imaging reconstruction results from the widely used algorithms CG-SENSE and GRAPPA. The fully sampled reference, the sampling patterns, as well as a trivial zero-filling reconstruction are shown. SSIM in comparison to the reference is shown for each reconstruction. The substantially lower SSIM of the GRAPPA reconstructions is not representative of the actual image quality, but is the result of a systematic mismatch to the ground truth reference that was computed with the use of coil sensitivity maps.

pling in comparison to the partial Fourier acquisition in Section 2.3. The undersampled images now show visible aliasing artifacts in the phase encoding direction (left-right). Since the center of k-space was fully sampled, they also show a relative over-weighting of low-frequency information that manifests itself as image blurring. The SSIM to the fully sampled ground truth has again been calculated as a quantitative measure of image quality. With this particular receive coil, the acceleration in the first experiment does not lead to substantial degradation in image quality, as can be observed both quantitatively (SENSE SSIM of 0.961) and by qualitative visual assessment of the images. In contrast, the R=6 results are already corrupted by residual artifacts and noise amplification. The SSIM of the GRAPPA reconstruction is substantially lower for both acceleration factors. This illustrates an issue in the use of quantitative image quality metrics. As described above, GRAPPA first reconstructs unaliased individual coil images u_j, which are then combined in a second step via root sum of squares. This creates a different signal intensity weighting than the SENSE procedure, which weights the individual images with the conjugate of the receive coil sensitivities C_j. Since the fully sampled ground truth was computed with SENSE-type sensitivity weighting, and not root sum of squares, a systematic bias is introduced that leads to lower SSIM values for GRAPPA that are not representative of the true image quality. Therefore the GRAPPA SSIM values should not be compared directly to those of SENSE and the zero-filling reconstructions, but rather between the R=4 and R=6 GRAPPA reconstructions.

30   Chapter 2 Advanced reconstruction methods for fast MRI

As mentioned in the introduction, generalizations to 3D Cartesian imaging are straightforward in parallel imaging. Instead of one phase encoding direction, two phase encoding directions can be undersampled in this case, which leads to two-dimensional undersampling patterns. Extensions to non-Cartesian acquisitions are straightforward in the case of SENSE-type methods (Pruessmann et al., 2001). For GRAPPA-type methods, the extension to non-Cartesian imaging is more challenging.

2.5 Compressed sensing and machine learning

2.5.1 Compressed sensing

Section 2.3 introduced the concept of constrained reconstruction, in particular the constraint of k-space conjugate symmetry in partial Fourier imaging. Compressed sensing (CS) is another form of a constrained reconstruction that gained substantial popularity in accelerated MR imaging in the late 2000s, after the publication of the seminal paper by Lustig et al. (2007). The basis of CS is that images, including MR images, are inherently compressible. A well-known example of this phenomenon is JPEG image compression, which is widely used to reduce the file size of photographs without obvious visual degradation. The reason for this compressibility is that images can be represented with a substantially smaller number of non-zero coefficients than the number of image pixels in a certain domain (often called a sparse representation). Examples for such sparse representations are the discrete cosine transform (DCT) that is used in JPEG, or the wavelet transform that is used in JPEG 2000. In accelerated MRI, the goal is of course not to reduce the file size of the acquired images, but to decrease scan acquisition times. Similar to partial Fourier and parallel imaging, CS reduces the scan time by acquiring fewer samples in k-space. In contrast to the overdetermined image reconstruction problem in parallel imaging, if CS is not combined with parallel imaging the reconstruction problem is now underdetermined. The sparsity constraint then allows identifying one particular solution of this inversion problem, the solution with the sparsest representation. The form of this constraint defines the way k-space undersampling is performed in CS. Since noise does not allow a sparse representation, the goal in the design of the sampling trajectory is to make the aliasing artifacts as noise-like (incoherent) as possible. This can be achieved with pseudo-random k-space sampling in the phase encoding direction, as opposed to regular equidistant sampling in parallel imaging or half-Fourier imaging. Typical pseudo-random sampling patterns are shown in Fig. 2.4, together with zero-filling image reconstruction results that illustrate the incoherent structure of the aliasing artifacts. Due to the widespread use of parallel imaging for accelerated MRI, CS is now almost exclusively used in combination with parallel imaging. This extension was first introduced in (Block et al., 2007), which presented the underlying idea for the special case of non-Cartesian radial imaging. In this chapter, we go straight to the combined approach (PI-CS), but the original single-coil CS formulation can be seen as a special case of this formulation with only a single, constant-1, coil sensitivity map C_j. It should be pointed out that PI-CS creates an additional layer of complexity for the design of the sampling pattern. CS requires pseudo-random sampling to create incoherent artifacts, whereas the synthesis of missing k-space points in parallel imaging gets progressively harder the further away they are from a measured point. A successful undersampling pattern for PI-CS needs to balance these two requirements. Sampling pattern design is outside the scope of this chapter, but Poisson-disk sampling has been demonstrated to be a robust and flexible choice for combined PI-CS.

2.5 Compressed sensing and machine learning 31

Constrained image reconstruction for PI-CS is performed by solving the following optimization problem:

$$\min \|\mathcal{F}_{\Omega} C_j u - f\|_2^2 + \lambda \|\Psi(u)\|_1. \tag{2.6}$$

Eq. (2.6) consists of two terms that are balanced by a user-defined hyper-parameter λ, commonly called the regularization parameter. The first term is commonly called the data fidelity term, since it ensures that the reconstructed image u is consistent with the measured raw k-space data f. It serves the same role as the data fidelity step in POCS (Eq. (2.4)). C_j is again a diagonal matrix that contains the sensitivity profiles of the receiver coil j, and $\mathcal{F}_{\Omega}$ is a Fourier operator that samples locations Ω in k-space. The second term enforces the constraint that the reconstructed image is sparse in the transform domain Ψ. The choice of the transform domain depends on the target application. Popular choices for neuroimaging are wavelets (Lustig et al., 2007) and total variation-based methods (Block et al., 2007; Knoll et al., 2011).

The didactic experiments for this chapter were again designed to replicate accelerated protocols for a combined parallel imaging and CS-constrained reconstruction. This time, variable density pseudo-random undersampling of k-space was performed in the phase encoding direction, according to the sampling pattern design originally presented for CS in (Lustig et al., 2007). However, since we are using a combined parallel imaging and CS approach, the center of k-space was again not undersampled to obtain receive coil sensitivity maps. Two sets of experiments are shown. The undersampling factors are matched to the parallel imaging experiments in Section 2.4, R=4 and 26 fully sampled reference lines and R=6 and 16 reference lines. Total generalized variation (TGV) was used for the sparsity promoting term, and data processing exactly followed the presentation in (Knoll et al., 2011). The regularization parameter λ was set to $5 \cdot 10^{-6}$ and 1000 iterations were performed. The results of these experiments are shown in Fig. 2.4. The SSIM to the fully-sampled ground truth was again calculated as a quantitative measure of image quality. For the less aggressively accelerated case of R=4, a subtle SSIM improvement is achieved in comparison to regular parallel imaging (SSIM of 0.963 for PI-CS (TGV) vs 0.961 for SENSE). For R=6, a substantial improvement can be observed (SSIM of 0.926 for PI-CS (TGV) vs 0.796 for SENSE), because the nonlinear CS constraint stabilizes the reconstruction against the severe parallel imaging noise amplification and also helps to suppress residual aliasing artifacts.

In line with parallel imaging, generalizations to 3D Cartesian imaging are straightforward in CS. Instead of one phase encoding direction, two phase encoding directions can be undersampled, which is particularly beneficial, because it increases incoherence of the aliasing artifacts. The sparsifying transform can also be extended to 3D as well as to the time dimension for dynamic acquisitions. Extensions to non-Cartesian acquisitions are also possible. However, the combination of the increased computational demand of the nonlinear optimization in Eq. (2.6) with a 3D non-uniform Fourier transform (Fessler and Sutton, 2003) and a 3D sparsifying transform is still a limiting factor for clinical translation.

2.5.2 Machine learning

Recent years have seen a substantial increase in research activities around machine learning, in particular deep learning variants, for accelerated MR image reconstruction. The first corresponding pub-

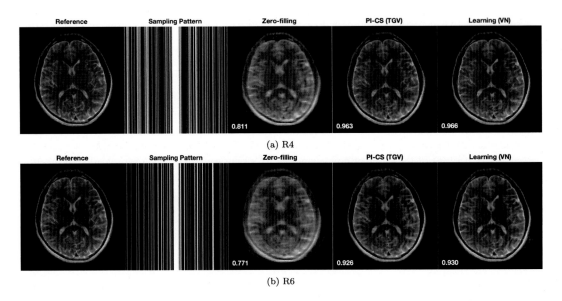

FIGURE 2.4

Combined parallel imaging and compressed sensing reconstruction results with a total generalized variation constraint (PI-CS (TGV)) and reconstructions obtained with a learned regularizer, following the framework of the variational network (VN). The fully sampled reference, the pseudo-random sampling patterns, as well a trivial zero-filling reconstruction are shown. SSIM in comparison to the reference is shown for each reconstruction.

lications appeared in 2016 and 2018 (Wang et al., 2016; Hammernik et al., 2018), and new work on this topic has been published continuously since then. A substantial number of these developments are based on supervised learning and build on the general idea of CS. This chapter will focus on these types of algorithm.

The role of the regularization term in CS is to promote the sparsest solution. Therefore, a successful sparsifying transform Ψ needs to provide a separation between the true image content and the artifacts that arise due to undersampling. The goal of machine learning is to improve the regularization in comparison to hand-crafted sparsifying transforms. Dictionary learning (Ravishankar and Bresler, 2011) can already be seen as an earlier predecessor of these more recent machine learning developments. The general idea of a supervised training process of a neural network for image reconstruction is illustrated in Fig. 2.5. The network takes undersampled k-space f as its input. Optionally, for models that also incorporate parallel imaging, such as (Hammernik et al., 2018), the estimates of the coil sensitivity maps C_j are provided as well. The network then performs a numerical operation that is similar to the optimization in CS (Eq. (2.6)) and the output is a reconstructed image u. The parameters of the neural network Θ define the regularization term and are learned from the training data. During training, the outputs of the network are intermediate reconstructions that are compared to the fully sampled ground truth reference via an error metric. A common choice for this error metric, due to its simplicity, is the mean squared error (MSE). The parameters of the network are then updated such that this error metric is minimized for all examples in the training data set. Mathematically, the training therefore corresponds

2.5 Compressed sensing and machine learning

to solving the following optimization problem:

$$\min L(\Theta) = \frac{1}{E}\sum_{e=1}^{E} ||u_e(\Theta) - u_e^{\text{ref}}||_2^2. \qquad (2.7)$$

In Eq. (2.7), $L(\Theta)$ is the training cost function that is minimized (MSE is shown in this example), E is the number of training examples, u_e is the output of the reconstruction network for example e with the current set of parameters Θ, and u_e^{ref} is the corresponding fully sampled reference. When all training examples are processed, one epoch in the training procedure is completed and the process is repeated until convergence. To avoid overfitting of the neural network to the training set, it is important to monitor the performance of the error metric on a separate validation set that is not used to update network parameters. A detailed description of training neural networks is outside the scope of this chapter and can be found in classic textbooks on machine learning and pattern recognition, for example, Duda et al. (1998).

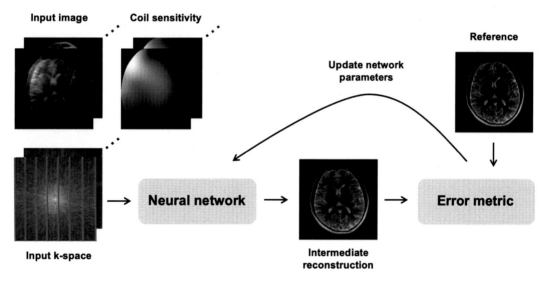

FIGURE 2.5

Conceptual illustration of the supervised training of a machine learning neural network model for the reconstruction of accelerated MR images.

Results from a machine learning reconstruction with a variational network (VN) (Hammernik et al., 2018) are shown in Fig. 2.4 for the same undersampling rates and sampling masks as the CS experiments in Section 2.5.1. The network architecture consisted of 10 layers with a learned regularizer of 24 11×11 filter kernels for the real and imaginary parts of the reconstructed image. The training was done exactly as described in (Hammernik et al., 2018). Please note that the training code for this experiment is not part of the code package that is available together with this chapter. Instead, the corresponding code is available in the code repository that was published together with the referenced manuscript.[2] Training data from 9 brain 2D TSE exams with similar protocols as described in Section 2.2 and with 30 slices each was used to train the network. The exam that is shown in Fig. 2.4 is a test case that was not used during training. The SSIM to the fully sampled ground truth was calculated as a quantitative measure of image quality. Subtle SSIM improvements over CS can be observed.

Generalizations to 3D and non-Cartesian imaging are also possible for machine learning reconstruction. However, in contrast to partial Fourier, parallel imaging, and CS, at the time of writing these are still actively ongoing research topics. Though the extension is straightforward from a conceptional point of view, the increased memory and computational demands make the implementation of the training challenging on currently existing GPU hardware.

2.6 Summary

Image reconstruction for fast MR acquisitions is an active field of research, and consistent progress has been made over a period of many years. Constrained partial Fourier reconstruction and parallel imaging have already been well-established in clinical protocols for many years, and they are used for numerous applications and body areas. Compressed sensing is a newer development and its clinical use is less mature at this stage, but all major vendors have implementations available as products for selected applications. The development of machine learning methods is still at a much earlier stage. Their reliability, stability, and robustness is a topic of increasing research interest (Antun et al., 2020), and their clinical value still needs to be demonstrated. Thorough comparisons of recently developed methods are also still lacking, as are large-scale and multi-center clinical studies. First initiatives in this direction are starting, for example in the form of publicly open image reconstruction challenges (Knoll et al., 2020).

Acknowledgments

The author acknowledges grant support from the National Institutes of Health under grants NIH R01EB024532, NIH P41EB017183 and R21EB027241.

References

Antun, V., Renna, F., Poon, C., Adcock, B., Hansen, A.C., 2020. On instabilities of deep learning in image reconstruction and the potential costs of AI. Proceedings of the National Academy of Sciences, 201907377. https://doi.org/10.1073/pnas.1907377117.

Block, K.T., Uecker, M., Frahm, J., 2007. Undersampled radial MRI with multiple coils. Iterative image reconstruction using a total variation constraint. Magnetic Resonance in Medicine 57, 1086–1098.

Cuppen, J., van Est, A., 1987. Reducing MR imaging time by one-sided reconstruction. Magnetic Resonance Imaging 5, 526–527. https://doi.org/10.1016/0730-725x(87)90402-4.

---

[2] https://github.com/VLOGroup/mri-variationalnetwork.

Duda, R.O., Hart, P.E., Stork, D.G., 1998. Pattern Classification, 2nd ed. Computational Complexity.

Fessler, J.A., Sutton, B.P., 2003. Nonuniform fast Fourier transforms using min-max interpolation. IEEE Transactions on Signal Processing 51, 560–574.

Griswold, M.A., Jakob, P.M., Heidemann, R.M., Nittka, M., Jellus, V., Wang, J., Kiefer, B., Haase, A., 2002. Generalized autocalibrating partially parallel acquisitions (GRAPPA). Magnetic Resonance in Medicine 47, 1202–1210.

Hammernik, K., Klatzer, T., Kobler, E., Recht, M.P., Sodickson, D.K., Pock, T., Knoll, F., 2018. Learning a variational network for reconstruction of accelerated MRI data. Magnetic Resonance in Medicine 79, 3055–3071. https://doi.org/10.1002/mrm.26977. arXiv:1704.00447.

Knoll, F., Bredies, K., Pock, T., Stollberger, R., 2011. Second order total generalized variation (TGV) for MRI. Magnetic Resonance in Medicine 65, 480–491. https://doi.org/10.1002/mrm.22595.

Knoll, F., Murrell, T., Sriram, A., Yakubova, N., Zbontar, J., Rabbat, M., Defazio, A., Muckley, M.J., Sodickson, D.K., Zitnick, C.L., Recht, M.P., 2020. Advancing machine learning for MR image reconstruction with an open competition: overview of the 2019 fastMRI challenge. Magnetic Resonance in Medicine, mrm.28338. https://doi.org/10.1002/mrm.28338.

Liang, Z.P., Boada, F.E., Constable, R.T., Haacke, E.M., Lauterbur, P.C., Smith, M.R., 1992. Constrained reconstruction methods in MR imaging. Reviews of Magnetic Resonance in Medicine 4, 67–185.

Lustig, M., Donoho, D., Pauly, J.M., 2007. Sparse MRI: the application of compressed sensing for rapid MR imaging. Magnetic Resonance in Medicine 58, 1182–1195.

Margosian, P., Schmitt, F., Purdy, D.E., 1986. Faster MR imaging: imaging with half the data. Health Care Instrumentation 1, 195–197.

Pruessmann, K.P., Weiger, M., Boernert, P., Boesiger, P., 2001. Advances in sensitivity encoding with arbitrary k-space trajectories. Magnetic Resonance in Medicine 46, 638–651.

Pruessmann, K.P., Weiger, M., Scheidegger, M.B., Boesiger, P., 1999. SENSE: sensitivity encoding for fast MRI. Magnetic Resonance in Medicine 42, 952–962.

Ravishankar, S., Bresler, Y., 2011. MR image reconstruction from highly undersampled k-space data by dictionary learning. IEEE Transactions on Medical Imaging 30, 1028–1041. https://doi.org/10.1109/TMI.2010.2090538.

Sodickson, D.K., Manning, W.J., 1997. Simultaneous acquisition of spatial harmonics (SMASH): fast imaging with radiofrequency coil arrays. Magnetic Resonance in Medicine 38, 591–603.

Uecker, M., Lai, P., Murphy, M.J., Virtue, P., Elad, M., Pauly, J.M., Vasanawala, S.S., Lustig, M., 2014. ESPIRiT - an eigenvalue approach to autocalibrating parallel MRI: where SENSE meets GRAPPA. Magnetic Resonance in Medicine 71, 990–1001. https://doi.org/10.1002/mrm.24751.

Wang, S., Su, Z., Ying, L., Peng, X., Zhu, S., Liang, F., Feng, D., Liang, D., 2016. Accelerating magnetic resonance imaging via deep learning. In: IEEE International Symposium on Biomedical Imaging (ISBI), pp. 514–517.

Wang, Z., Bovik, A.C., Sheikh, H.R., Simoncelli, E.P., 2004. Image quality assessment: from error visibility to structural similarity. IEEE Transactions on Image Processing 13, 600–612. https://doi.org/10.1109/TIP.2003.819861.

Zhu, B., Liu, J.Z., Cauley, S.F., Rosen, B.R., Rosen, M.S., 2018. Image reconstruction by domain-transform manifold learning. Nature 555, 487–492. https://doi.org/10.1038/nature25988. http://www.nature.com/doifinder/10.1038/nature25988. arXiv:1704.08841.

CHAPTER

Simultaneous multi-slice MRI

3

Andreia S. Gaspar, Ana R. Fouto, and Rita G. Nunes

Institute for Systems and Robotics and Department of Bioengineering, Instituto Superior Técnico, Universidade de Lisboa, Lisbon, Portugal

3.1 Historical overview

Simultaneous multi-slice (SMS) acquisitions were introduced in the 1980s before multi-channel coils were available. Initially, the motivation for applying multi-band (MB) pulses was to increase the obtained signal-to-noise ratio (SNR), with no reduction in the total acquisition time compared to standard multi-slice acquisitions. By sampling each k-space data point as many times as the number of simultaneously excited N slices, an averaging effect would occur, resulting in an SNR gain of $\sqrt{N}$. To achieve slice separation, radio-frequency (RF) phase modulation could be applied by varying the relative phase applied to each slice location, enabling Hadamard encoding, or by introducing a relative spatial shift within an enlarged virtual field-of-view (FOV).

It was only after the introduction of parallel imaging (PI) that Larkman et al. realized that SMS could enable a reduction in exam times, which is currently the main drive for its use. The N overlapping slices can be separated by taking advantage of spatial variations in the sensitivities of multi-channel coils, enabling an acquisition speed-up by the same factor of N (Larkman et al., 2001). Crucially, contrary to standard PI acceleration, which results in reduced k-space sampling, when an SMS acceleration factor of N is applied the reconstructed images suffer from a $\sqrt{N}$ SNR loss relative to a fully sampled volumetric (i.e., 3D-sampled) acquisition, but do not suffer from a $\sqrt{N}$ SNR loss relative to a conventional multi-slice 2D acquisition. Furthermore, provided that a favorable geometric arrangement of the coils is available, as in this initial demonstration, the so-called PI "g-factor" noise amplification can also become negligible, enabling an effective N-fold acceleration without a significant SNR loss compared to non-accelerated 2D acquisitions (Larkman et al., 2001).

Despite the promising results of this first implementation, it took over a decade for SMS to attract wider attention due to the challenges of applying SMS to brain imaging at that time. This first SMS demonstration made use of a spine array coil, using a transverse slice orientation to enable efficient slice separation. However, considering that brain imaging also frequently uses axial slices, the geometry of the head coils then available was not favorable to SMS, as coil sensitivity patterns would barely vary between planes.

As further described below, a key development was the realization that RF modulation could once again be used to introduce relative spatial shifts between overlapping slices, allowing advantage to be taken of in-plane coil-sensitivity variations to enable more efficient slice separation (CAIPIRINHA: controlled aliasing in parallel imaging results in higher acceleration) (Breuer et al., 2006).

Unfortunately, the introduction of relative spatial shifts through RF phase cycling is not applicable to single-shot sequences. The first application of SMS to functional MRI (fMRI) thus relied on using a more favorable slice prescription considering the available enveloping coils, by selecting a coronal slice orientation (Moeller et al., 2010). Although the introduction of gradient-based CAIPIRINHA shifts had already been demonstrated (Nunes et al., 2006), it was only with the introduction of blipped-CAIPI by Setsompop et al. (2012b) that interest in the application of SMS to other echo planar imaging-based (EPI-based) sequences became more widespread. This slice shifting method was first applied in diffusion MRI (dMRI) (Setsompop et al., 2012a), and the availability of head coils with multiple rings (with 16 or higher number of channels) further facilitated the separation of simultaneously excited axial slices (Feinberg et al., 2010).

Interest in SMS escalated after it was included in the imaging protocol of the human connectome project, having been shown to enable significant reductions in the acquisition times of dMRI acquisitions and to improve sensitivity for detecting brain activations with fMRI (Uğurbil et al., 2013).

3.2 Implementation of SMS

3.2.1 Simultaneous slice excitation

SMS requires the simultaneous excitation of multiple slices in different locations. This is possible by generating an MB RF pulse, which is characterized by an amplitude $A(t)$ (to specify the slice profile) and a phase modulation function (which combined with the slice-selective gradient enables specifying the phase ϕ_i and position x_i of each i slice). Intuitively, the simple addition of N single-band (SB) RF excitation pulses to excite different locations would create an MB RF pulse to simultaneously excite N slices (also known as the MB factor) whilst applying the same gradient G:

$$B_1(t) = A(t) \sum_{i=1}^{N} e^{i(\gamma G x_i t + \phi_i)}. \tag{3.1}$$

By setting the phase ϕ_i to be uniform across slices, the RF peak amplitude ($\max(|B_1|)$) would be proportional to the number of slices (N), and the peak power to its square (N^2). This implies that, with increasing MB factors, the peak power would quickly rise above the hardware limits (set by the RF amplifier), and that the patient safety limits would also be exceeded, namely the specific absorption rate (SAR), which quantifies RF power deposition. To reduce the peak amplitude of the combined RF pulse, time shifts can be applied to the individual pulses to avoid peak superposition; in this case the amplitude envelope of the combined RF pulse is modulated since the slices will be excited at slightly different times, as shown in Fig. 3.1. However, as well as resulting in a longer RF pulse duration, the excitation of the different slices is offset in time, and so the corresponding echoes will also occur at different times, which can be problematic in spin-echo sequences.

The alternative to avoid this RF duration increase is to optimize the phase of each slice independently instead, as represented in Fig. 3.2, resulting in a more moderate increase in the peak RF amplitude by a factor of $\sqrt{N}$ relative to the original SB pulse (Wong, 2012). Sharma et al. took a slightly different approach to solve this problem by optimizing asymmetric RF pulses with the Shinnar-Le Roux (SLR) method, and allowing for the peaks to occur at different times (i.e. root-flipping) (Sharma et al., 2016). The goal is to avoid coherent superposition of individual SB pulse peaks to enable a shorter MB RF pulse duration.

3.2 Implementation of SMS

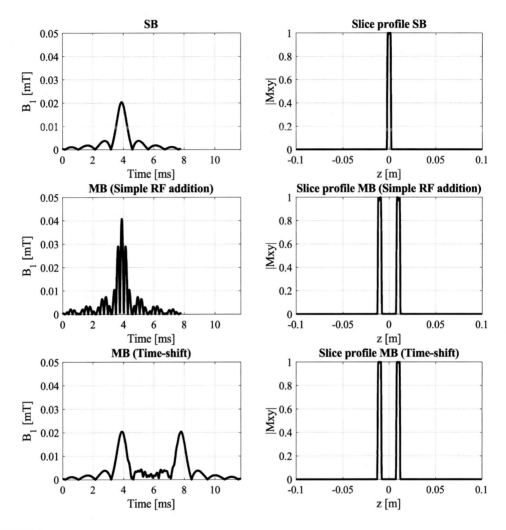

FIGURE 3.1

Example RF pulses showing, from top to bottom, the amplitude envelopes for single-band (SB), multi-band (MB) with simple addition, and MB with time-shifting, together with the respective profiles for N=2 slices on the right. When using simple RF addition to create the MB RF pulse, the peak amplitude goes up to $2*\max(|B_1^{SB}|)$, but the application of a time-shift, with a factor of 0.5 of the SB pulse duration, allows maintaining its amplitude almost at the same value as $\max(|B_1^{SB}|)$. However, this comes at the cost of an increment in RF pulse duration. This example considered a slice thickness of 2 mm and a slice separation of 20 mm.

Although the methods mentioned above allow avoidance of high peak amplitudes, the produced MB RF pulses must be further optimized to avoid high power deposition, particularly relevant for high MB factors. In this context, modulating the slice-selective gradient provides an additional degree of free-

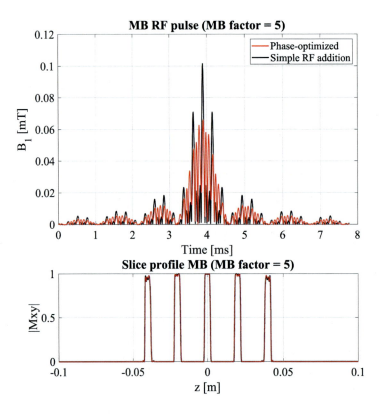

FIGURE 3.2

MB RF pulse envelopes (top) and respective excitation slice profiles (bottom) when simple RF addition (black), or phase optimization (red) is performed for an MB factor of 5. The amplitude peak reduction is of the order of 30% when the phase of each individual pulse is optimized. This example considered a slice thickness of 2 mm and slice separation of 20 mm. Note that since the simulated MB factor is odd, one of the slices is excited at position zero.

dom. One approach is Power Independent of the Number of Slices (PINS) (Norris et al., 2011), in which rectangular RF excitations are interleaved with gradient blips to excite each transmit k-space position in a sequential scheme, as represented in Fig. 3.3. In fact, the area of the gradient blips determines the periodic distance between slices, allowing for a total power deposition which does not depend on the number of excited slices, making PINS particularly appealing at high magnetic fields. The downside is that the RF pulse bandwidth is inversely proportional to the slice period, in a way that the minimum achievable slice thickness may be limited if the distance between slices is also small. In addition, the rate at which k-space is traversed is limited by the gradient slew rate.

Instead of relying on gradient blips, an alternative is to use VariablE Rate Selective Excitation (VERSE). This method consists of varying the slice selection gradient amplitude to traverse the transmit k-space at a slower rate at the peak of the RF pulse, enabling a lower RF pulse amplitude and a reduced power deposition. Time-optimal VERSE avoids long RF durations, while reducing the effect of gradient distortion. In addition, the optimization of VERSE for an SB pulse, before the MB modulation, has

3.2 Implementation of SMS

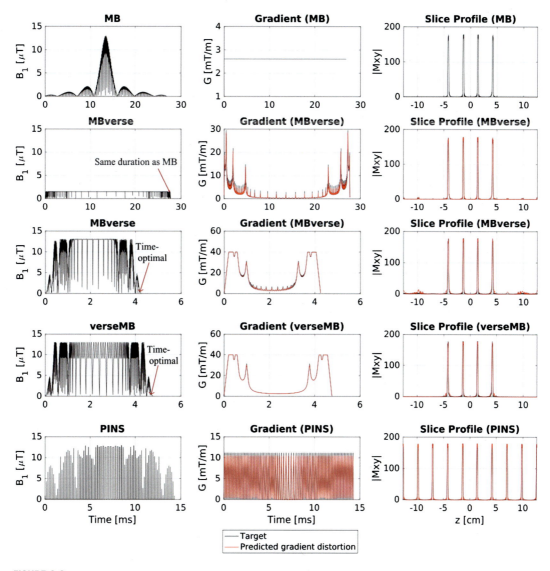

FIGURE 3.3

MB RF pulse implementations and respective gradients to reduce power deposition for an MB factor of 4, slice thickness of 2 mm, and slice gap of 28 mm. An MB RF pulse with constant gradient is presented along with three implementations of VERSE: MBverse keeping the same duration as the original MB RF pulse to illustrate the reduction in peak B_1; MBverse using time-optimized VERSE to shorten the RF pulse duration; and verseMB, in which VERSE is applied to the SB RF pulse followed by MB modulation, also time-optimized. In MBverse, sharp temporal gradient variations are required, which typical MRI systems are not capable of replicating, leading to spurious excitations outside the intended slices, as visible in the predicted slice profile; in contrast, verseMB presents less stringent gradient requirements and as a result enables a final slice excitation without distortions. A PINS RF pulse, the respective gradient blips, and the produced slice profile are also presented showing the expected periodic (and theoretically infinite) series of excited slices.

42 **Chapter 3** Simultaneous multi-slice MRI

been shown to avoid the undesirable excitation of satellite slices (Abo Seada et al., 2019), as shown in Fig. 3.3.

3.2.2 Introducing relative spatial shifts

As already mentioned, the possibility to introduce relative offsets between overlapping slices (CAIPIR-INHA) enabled better use to be made of the spatial variation in coil sensitivities when separating the individual slices (Breuer et al., 2006). This approach is based on the Fourier shift theorem, whereby introducing a phase ramp in k-space results in a spatial shift along the corresponding direction in image-space. To derive this result, we can start by considering, for simplicity, the 1D discrete Fourier transform, relating the k-space signal S composed of M samples separated by the distance Δk with the corresponding image ρ at the spatial coordinate y:

$$\rho(y) = \sum_{m=-\frac{M}{2}}^{\frac{M}{2}-1} S(m\Delta k)\, e^{jm\Delta k.y}, \tag{3.2}$$

it is then possible to demonstrate that we can introduce a shift of Δy in image-space by imposing a ramp phase pattern in k-space:

$$\rho(y + \Delta y) = \sum_{m=-\frac{M}{2}}^{\frac{M}{2}-1} S(m\Delta k)\, e^{jm\Delta k.(y+\Delta y)} = \sum_{m=-\frac{M}{2}}^{\frac{M}{2}-1} \left[S(m\Delta k)\, e^{jm\Delta k.y} \right] e^{jm\Delta k.\Delta y}. \tag{3.3}$$

The original implementation of CAIPIRINHA by Breuer et al. was developed for multi-shot spoiled gradient-echo readouts. It relied on the use of different SMS excitation pulses to impart the required phase ramps to shift different slices by a distinct distance in image-space (Breuer et al., 2006). An example is shown in Fig. 3.4a for an MB factor of 3, where phase cycling can be applied to shift two of the slices by -FOV/3 and FOV/3, respectively.

To implement the same spatial shifts in the case of a single-shot EPI sequence, gradient blips can be applied along the slice-select (SS) direction, as shown in Fig. 3.4b. CAIPI-blip patterns were introduced by (Setsompop et al., 2012b) and their key feature was the introduction of rewinding G_{ss} blips, instead of maintaining the same polarity throughout the whole EPI readout, as in an earlier implementation of SMS-EPI (Nunes et al., 2006). This enabled achieving larger relative spatial shifts, whilst avoiding a large phase dispersion along the through-slice direction, which would otherwise result in signal loss and image-blurring.

Though either an RF or a gradient-based approach could in principle be used for introducing relative slice shifts in multi-shot sequences, in practice CAIPI-blips can be more straightforward to implement when specific RF phase cycling is required, or if the RF phase is being used for magnetization spoiling purposes. This is the case when balanced Steady-State Free Precession (bSSFP), Turbo Spin-Echo (TSE), or RF-spoiled gradient-echo readouts are employed. Nevertheless, when using this type of readout, it may be desirable to avoid shift patterns which require very large rewinding blips, as these can potentially produce large eddy current fields resulting in image artifacts. Also, in the case of simultaneous multi-slab excitations, the dephasing effect of the CAIPI-blips may no longer be negligible and

3.2 Implementation of SMS

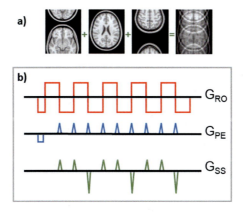

FIGURE 3.4

Application of relative slice spatial shifts. a) Example showing three simultaneously excited slices (MB=3), where the first is shifted by -FOV/3 and the third by FOV/3. b) Diagram of an EPI readout showing the readout gradients (G_{RO}), phase encode gradients (G_{PE}), and CAIPI-blips applied along the slice select direction (G_{SS}) to apply the shifts shown in panel a. To achieve these spatial shifts, two blips are applied, each corresponding to an area of Δk, after which the accumulated phase is rewound to avoid dephasing along the through-plane direction.

potentially produce detectable signal loss and blurring, depending on the amplitude of the CAIPI-blips, considering the slab thickness.

3.2.3 SMS image reconstruction

The application of SMS is connected to the principles of PI (see Chapter 2). PI is based on the fact that the geometry of coil sensitivity patterns can be used as prior information in the reconstruction to recover a complete image from incomplete data sampling. This approach can be performed in either the image (e.g., SENSitivity Encoding: SENSE), spatial frequency (e.g., GeneRalized Autocalibrating Partial Parallel Acquisitions: GRAPPA), or hybrid domains (Larkman and Nunes, 2007).

When a Cartesian acquisition is undersampled, the image reconstructed with a simple FFT presents a folding artifact since the FOV is decreased proportionally to the spatial frequency domain step (Δk) increase. SENSE uses the coil sensitivity information to unfold the overlapping pixels. As each pixel in the folded image corresponds to the sum of pixels arising from different locations, weighted by the corresponding coil sensitivities, it is possible to recover each pixel by inverting a coil sensitivity matrix. For example, if undersampling by a factor of 2, we can retrieve the pixels separated by 1/2 of FOV (P), by accounting for the sensitivities, at the correct locations, of at least two independent coils (C_1 and C_2) and the corresponding aliased pixels P_1 and P_2 by solving the following equation:

$$\begin{bmatrix} P_1(x,y) \\ P_2(x,y) \end{bmatrix} = \begin{bmatrix} C_1(x,y) & C_1(x, y+1/2\,FOV) \\ C_2(x,y) & C_2(x, y+1/2\,FOV) \end{bmatrix} \begin{bmatrix} P(x,y) \\ P(x, y+1/2\,FOV) \end{bmatrix}. \quad (3.4)$$

The capability for solving this problem depends on the coil geometry with respect to the undersampled direction. For example, if C_1 is very different from C_2 along the direction y, then it is easy to disentangle the superimposed pixels (i.e., the inversion of the coil sensitivity matrix is well-behaved). This can be quantified at each spatial location by the geometric g-factor, which relates to the covariance of the coil sensitivities: if their spatial pattern along the undersampled direction is very correlated (high g-factor), then they are not independent and the problem is ill-conditioned in a way that the noise in the final reconstructed image is amplified.

Adapting SENSE to SMS (slice-SENSE) similarly allows unfolding superimposed slices, where each pixel is a linear combination of pixels from different slices weighted by the respective coil sensitivities, as explained in Fig. 3.5. If the overlapping pixels are near each other and the respective coil sensitivities are too similar for robust separation, a relative spatial shift can be added (see the previous section), allowing noise amplification (g-factor) reduction.

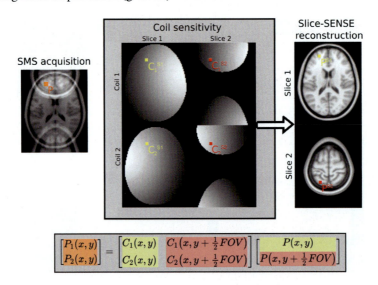

FIGURE 3.5

Slice-SENSE reconstruction framework. The SMS acquisition results in a superimposed image of both slices, where each pixel P_i is the linear combination of pixel P^{Sj} from slice j, weighted by the respective coil sensitivities C_i^{Sj}. This linear problem can be solved on a pixel-by-pixel basis by inverting each corresponding coil matrix C and multiplying it by the SMS acquired data.

Alternatively, signals from overlapping slices can be separated in the k-space domain using a GRAPPA-like reconstruction. This method involves the estimation of non-acquired k-space samples by linearly combining acquired k-space data from adjacent locations based on pre-calculated weights (GRAPPA kernel); see coil calibration section below. Similarly to slice-SENSE, the SENSE-GRAPPA method considers the superimposed SMS image as an undersampled version of an expanded FOV comprising the concatenation of the fully sampled individual slices (Blaimer et al., 2006), as explained in Fig. 3.6a. In this case, GRAPPA weights are also estimated from the k-space data obtained from a concatenated low-resolution reference image obtained from SB acquisitions.

Since coil sensitivity is assumed to be spatially smooth, small GRAPPA kernels that contain mainly low spatial-frequency components are applied. However, when this smoothness assumption is not valid, the reconstruction results can embody artefacts that are difficult to identify as such. This can be the situation when using spatial shifts, as the extended-FOV SMS image will have phase variations and discontinuities that may not always be possible to capture using kernels containing low-frequency information, and trained for both slices simultaneously.

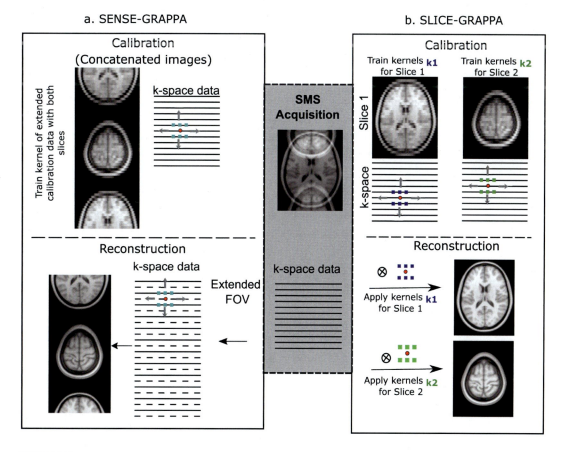

FIGURE 3.6

SENSE-GRAPPA and slice-GRAPPA methods for SMS reconstruction. a) In SENSE-GRAPPA, the kernel calibration is performed in an extended k-space built from the concatenation of low-resolution single-slice acquisitions and is then applied to the k-space SMS acquisition to simultaneously derive both slices in this extended FOV. b) In slice-GRAPPA, the calibration is performed separately in low-resolution data of each slice to derive two sets of kernels, one for each slice. The convolution of each kernel with the SMS k-space allows retrieving the respective slice.

To overcome this issue, Setsompop et al. proposed slice-GRAPPA, where separate GRAPPA weights are trained from the reference data to calculate N sets of kernels, one set for each slice. Each slice is then isolated from the aliased SMS data by convolution with its slice-specific GRAPPA kernel (Setsompop et al., 2012b), as illustrated in Fig. 3.6b. However, when the slice separation is not

46   Chapter 3 Simultaneous multi-slice MRI

perfect, and the kernel that should capture information arising only from a given slice also retrieves information from others, the reconstructed image is contaminated, presenting slice-leakage artifacts. The quantification of these artifacts can be crucial for data analysis and interpretation, especially in fMRI and dMRI, in which these spurious signal contributions can result in neuronal activation or structural connectivity being assigned to an incorrect location. In fact, knowing that the reconstruction is linear, this metric can be obtained by applying each slice-specific GRAPPA kernel to an individual SB image, enabling quantifying its contribution to other reconstructed slice locations. This approach can also be used to minimize leakage by constraining the kernel calculation to suppress contributions to other reconstructed slices.

Both SENSE-GRAPPA and slice-GRAPPA can be combined with in-plane PI undersampling acceleration; however, the way this is done differs between the two methods. In slice-GRAPPA, the slice-specific weights are first used to separate the simultaneously excited slices, followed by a standard PI 1D GRAPPA reconstruction to correct for phase-encoding in-plane aliasing. In SENSE-GRAPPA, the FOV can be additionally expanded along the phase-encoding direction, in a way that makes it possible to formulate a 1D problem for simultaneously solving both slice superposition and in-plane undersampling. An alternative is to elongate the FOV along the readout direction instead, when considering the SMS contribution, and applying a 2D GRAPPA reconstruction.

Although for simplicity this section focused on Cartesian k-space trajectories, SMS is also applicable to non-Cartesian data sampling schemes, following similar modifications as in standard PI (Larkman and Nunes, 2007).

3.2.4 Coil sensitivity calibration

As was clear from the previous section (Reconstruction), and similarly to standard PI, coil sensitivity maps are required to perform SMS image reconstruction. In the case of SMS-EPI applications, coil calibration is often performed using a separate low-resolution SB acquisition. Depending on the algorithm used to perform SMS reconstruction, these data can be used to estimate coil sensitivity maps in the image domain or to calculate the required GRAPPA kernels in k-space.

Regardless of the used reconstruction approach, to achieve accurate slice separation, care must be taken to ensure that the coil information is consistent with the main k-space data. This requires matching the geometric distortions caused by static B_0 field inhomogeneities, which can be done by keeping the same effective inter-echo-spacing; to achieve this when in-plane PI acceleration is used, a multi-shot calibration scan can be performed. Motion between shots could then become problematic if maintaining the same repetition time (TR), as in the main acquisition. However, given that the coil sensitivities are independent of the used image contrast, small excitation flip angles can instead be selected for the SB calibration scan. This enables faster magnetization recovery and enables all EPI segments required for a given slice to be sequentially acquired, instead of imaging other slices while waiting for a full (longer) TR, thus minimizing inter-shot motion (Polimeni et al., 2016). Even when using this approach, it is still essential to minimize motion occurring between the coil sensitivity calibration and the main measurements to avoid reconstruction artifacts. As we will discuss later when presenting the main SMS applications, this is particularly relevant for long scans, comprising many fMRI or dMRI volumes.

Another issue to consider in the case of EPI readouts is that the production of eddy current fields can result in ghosting artifacts due to inconsistencies between odd and even k-space lines. Since these fields are often slice-dependent, ghosting artifacts should be corrected for only after slice separation, instead of applying the standard correction methods to the multi-band k-space data, as this would only enable correcting for the average ghosting artifact (Setsompop et al., 2012a). This is particularly relevant when using CAIPI shifts of FOV/2, as the signal from a shifted slice could otherwise be confused with an artifactual ghost originating from another slice.

3.3 Current applications of SMS

The growing availability of SMS-compatible sequences for brain imaging has encouraged the development of a wide variety of applications. Typically, SMS is now used to enable faster fMRI (Moeller et al., 2010; Uğurbil et al., 2013) and dMRI (Setsompop et al., 2012a). Efforts have been made to extend this technique also to perfusion imaging with arterial spin labeling (ASL) (Kim et al., 2013; Li et al., 2015). All these applications share the same type of readout (single-shot EPI) and have benefited from the introduction of blipped-CAIPI combined with the progressive increase in the number of channels contained in receiver head coils. This has enabled MB acceleration factors of 2 to 3 to be commonly achieved with a negligible SNR penalty.

fMRI is a noninvasive technique widely used to infer the spatial localization of neuronal activity over time, relying on dynamic changes in the blood oxygenation resulting from a task or during resting state (see Chapters 15–18). A fast fMRI acquisition allows increased temporal resolution without increasing the exam duration. Inherently, signal fluctuations can be better characterized (higher sensitivity) as more data points are obtained, increasing statistical power. Alternatively, or at the cost of a more moderate reduction in the TR, SMS allows for the acquisition of a higher number of slices, enabling increased brain coverage without penalizing scanning time. Although optimal imaging outcomes rely on a variety of sequence parameters (e.g., the strength of the static field B_0, slice orientation relative to the coil geometry, etc), acceleration factors of up to 12 can be obtained, enabling a high temporal resolution (2 mm isotropic resolution, TR=400 ms (Uğurbil et al., 2013)). Nonetheless, there are some trade-offs linked to the use of rapid sampling that need to be considered. In general, lower SNR is found due to the reduced recovery of the longitudinal magnetization associated with the use of a much shorter TR value, despite the use of an optimal excitation flip angle (Ernst angle). However, the SNR also depends on the relative contribution of physiological noise components arising from cardiac and respiratory effects (i.e., ≈ 1 Hz and ≈ 0.3 Hz, respectively). In particular, by using fast sampling rates (TR less than 1 s), these noisy frequencies are more easily filtered out, since not only is their sampling more efficient, but also more sophisticated analysis techniques are made available (e.g., independent component analysis) to detect and minimize these contributions. Ultimately, fast fMRI analysis achieves greater statistical power and improved physiological noise correction, as exemplified in Fig. 3.7 (i.e., larger activation areas for TR of 0.8 s and 0.4 s than the more conventional TR=2.5 s). Despite increased SMS noise amplification, activation detection results are often satisfactory.

It should also be noted that head motion in these acquisition schemes should be considered as a significant confounding factor. In other words, the presence of substantial motion (of a few millimeters) can cause signal variations which result in false-positive and/or false-negative activations. It is important to bear in mind that both SMS and PI techniques rely on the spatial consistency between the acquired data and the coil sensitivity information required for slice-separation/image reconstruction. This means that both techniques are vulnerable to motion artifacts due to the variation of the head position in relation to the set of receiver coils. It is also common to combine SMS acceleration with in-plane

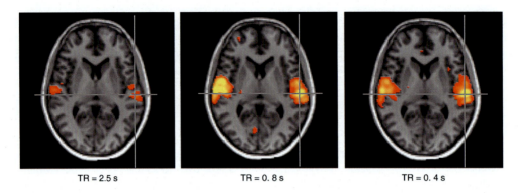

TR = 2.5 s   TR = 0.8 s   TR = 0.4 s

FIGURE 3.7

Illustrative example of improved statistical significance of resting-state networks detection (larger brain activation area) while using different slice acceleration factors. Although acceleration was achieved by combining multi-band excitation (without blipped-CAIPI) with the simultaneous echo refocused (SIR) sequence, this example serves to illustrate the gains achieved in statistical power by increasing temporal resolution. A single resting state is depicted by colored z-statistics map thresholded at Z=4. This fMRI data was obtained at 3T with 3 mm isotropic resolution for three different TR values: TR=2.5 s (no acceleration); TR=0.8 s (4-fold slice acceleration: MB=2, SIR=2); and TR=0.4 s (9-fold slice acceleration: MB=3, SIR=3). Reproduced with permission from (Uğurbil et al., 2013).

PI techniques, such as GRAPPA for reducing EPI-related geometric distortions. Fig. 3.8 presents an illustrative example of the effect of motion on a brain activation map obtained from a healthy volunteer, who was visually instructed to either remain still or to execute intentional movement repeatedly at 10 s after the onset of a visual stimulation block (visual paradigm: 3 blocks of alternating 20 s flickering checkerboard with 20 s fixation). Though retrospective processing techniques (e.g., alignment of the fMRI time series to a reference volume) can be applied to minimize the impact of motion, and is done for all the current large brain imaging projects, this may not be sufficient since inconsistencies between the main data and coil calibration information are not accounted for in this way. More recent studies have tested a combination of prospective and retrospective motion correction techniques to mitigate this effect. In practice, SMS-accelerated fMRI should be considered with care while studying uncooperative patients (presenting large head movements in the range of 5 mm and 5°) (Faraji-Dana et al., 2016).

Diffusion MRI is mostly used to probe microstructure in the brain. dMRI also benefits from fast sampling techniques to shorten the acquisition and increase q-space resolution (associated with diffusion-sampling) by enabling more diffusion directions and a higher number of diffusion-weightings (b-values). The most common sampling scheme acquired in the clinic typically includes one shell (b=1000 mm/s^2) and 6 to 32 diffusion directions, which are sufficient to fully characterize the tensor in diffusion-tensor imaging (DTI). In practice, this acquisition is used due to time limitations, as it can require several minutes without SMS. Nevertheless, more complex models have been developed to relate the dMRI signal to the white matter microstructure to better explain the actual biological environment. These models entail the acquisition of a growing number of diffusion volumes and multiple b-values, thus increasing the length of the exam, which may undermine its clinical feasibility. For example, with-

3.3 Current applications of SMS   49

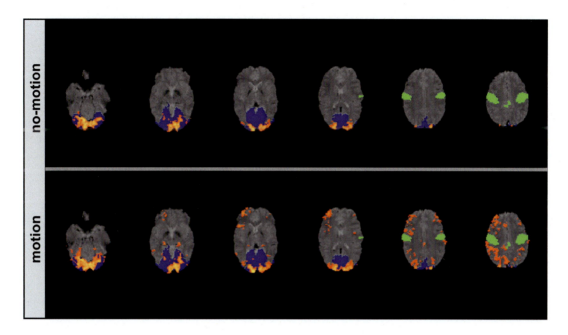

FIGURE 3.8

Illustrative example of brain activation maps (red-yellow) of a healthy volunteer overlaid on visual cortex (blue) and motor cortex masks (green) for no-motion (top) and motion conditions (bottom). Almost all activations were superimposed with the visual cortex (blue) when the subject was instructed to remain still, but when instructed to intentionally move, more activation clusters, many of which likely to represent false positives, were found outside of this region. These fMRI data were obtained by combining SMS-acceleration (MB=3) with GRAPPA (R=2), TR=1.69 s, using blipped-CAIPI to impose a relative spatial shift of FOV/3.

out SMS a diffusion-kurtosis imaging (DKI) protocol with 64 diffusion directions (two shells of b=1000 mm/s^2 and b=2000 mm/s^2) would take about 18 minutes, whereas a diffusion-spectrum imaging (DSI) protocol with 515 diffusion directions (and maximum b-value of 17000 mm/s^2) would take more than 1 hour. dMRI acquisition times have been reduced 3-fold using SMS with comparable results to unaccelerated acquisitions (Setsompop et al., 2012a). In practice, however, these acquisition schemes still require highly cooperative subjects, since they are very sensitive to motion (large head movements >10° should be avoided) (Herbst et al., 2017).

Lastly, another important application of SMS-EPI is perfusion imaging based on the ASL sequence (see Chapter 12). Perfusion is the process by which blood is delivered through the network of capillaries to the tissue. ASL is a brain imaging technique in which an inversion of the blood magnetization is done at a specific location (e.g., in the arteries present in the neck region) before entering the brain circulation, so that the labeled blood spins will function as an endogenous contrast agent. Then, two images are typically acquired: a baseline image (without labeling) and a tagged image. The difference between these two images can be interpreted as a measure of the perfusion of brain tissues. As the labeled magnetization is susceptible to relaxation decay, the imaging acquisition is limited to a specific time window. Thus SMS allows a greater brain coverage to be achieved during this period (Kim et al., 2013), while also altering the relaxation decay, which necessitates more complex modeling (Li et al., 2015).

SMS-compatible sequences are now included as product sequences by the main vendors, making them more commonly accessible. Both SMS and traditional PI techniques have benefited from the development of modern hardware, such as receiver coils with an increasing number of channels and improved geometry configurations. Though many more MB applications are emerging, especially in the field of body imaging, ensuring the quality of coil calibration data and in particular its consistency with the main acquisition, both spatially and in regards to off-resonance effects, is still a practical problem that needs to be tackled to accurately separate the overlapping slices.

3.4 Emerging applications and future outlook

Although SMS is still most often used in fMRI and dMRI, continuous developments on MB RF pulse design have been progressively enabling its application to other more RF-intensive pulse sequences. In fact, the ability to increase MB acceleration factors without prolonging RF pulse durations is critical for sequences such as TSE and bSSFP, for which these pulses take up a considerable fraction of the total sequence time.

An added challenge in the case of TSE is keeping within the SAR limits due to the high flip angles used for refocusing the magnetization; this is further aggravated when long echo trains are required (e.g., high spatial resolution or fast single-shot acquisitions). A possible solution is to use PINS RF pulses (Norris et al., 2011), but unless the undesirable slice replicas fall outside the coil sensitivity region, this may limit the acquisition to sagittal or coronal slice orientations. To avoid this issue, a standard MB RF pulse can be used for excitation, with the added advantage of enabling improved effective slice profiles. Still, PINS RF pulses tend to be long, limiting the achievable inter-echo spacing.

An alternative to standard gradient encoding, WAVE-CAIPI, has also been explored for SMS TSE imaging (Gagoski et al., 2015). It relies on the same principle underlying CAIPIRINHA, using gradient waveforms to maximize the distance between aliased voxels. In WAVE-CAIPI, sinusoidal gradients offset by 1/4 of a period are applied along the y and z directions overlapping with the standard frequency encode gradient x, resulting in a corkscrew k-space trajectory. Although image reconstruction becomes more computationally demanding, this approach allows the burden placed on coil sensitivity encoding to be reduced, enabling higher acceleration factors. Despite being compatible with both SMS and 3D acquisitions, WAVE-CAIPI has been more extensively applied to the latter.

The benefit of applying SMS to gradient-echo sequences is also affected by the MB RF pulse duration, particularly in the case of bSSFP, where it is the main constraint to the minimum achievable TR. Both TSE and bSSFP sequences would therefore benefit from shorter MB RF pulses. Abo Seada et al. have shown that it is possible to reduce the duration of MB RF pulses, while keeping the SAR under control, by applying VERSE to SB pulses prior to converting them to MB. This approach has the advantage of avoiding the need for fast temporal variations of the slice select gradient, which are hard to achieve in practice due to limitations in gradient hardware performance, thus avoiding spurious ghost contributions (Abo Seada et al., 2019); see Fig. 3.3.

MB RF pulses can be further shortened through the use of parallel RF transmission (pTX) (Deniz, 2019). We expect this technique to be key for enabling the application of SMS at ultra-high field MRI. In fact, promising results have recently been reported within the scope of the human connectome project, showing that pTX applied to MB pulses enables improved flip angle uniformity and reduced power deposition in dMRI at 7T. Ongoing efforts have been making transmit B_1 field calibration and RF pulse design procedures simpler and easier to apply. Given the growing availability of pTX in clinical MRI systems, it is only a question of time before this technology becomes standard in SMS applications.

To summarize, SMS is now a well-established technique, commonly used in neuroimaging studies. Although in this context fMRI and dMRI are still its main applications, recent developments in MB RF pulse design and the increased availability of pTX are expected to widen the impact of SMS in the future.

Acknowledgments

We acknowledge the Portuguese Foundation for Science and Technology (FCT) for financial support through grants SFRH/BD/120006/2016, PTDC/EMD-EMD/29686/2017, SFRH/BD/139561/2018 and POR Lisboa 2020 LISBOA-01-0145-FEDER-029675.

References

Abo Seada, S., Price, A.N., Schneider, T., Hajnal, J.V., Malik, S.J., 2019. Multiband RF pulse design for realistic gradient performance. Magn. Reson. Med. 81, 362–376.

Blaimer, M., Breuer, F.A., Seiberlich, N., Mueller, M.F., Heidemann, R.M., Jellus, V., Wiggins, G., Wald, L.L., Griswold, M.A., Jakob, P.M., 2006. Accelerated volumetric MRI with a SENSE/GRAPPA combination. J. Magn. Reson. Imaging 24, 444–450.

Breuer, F.A., Blaimer, M., Mueller, M.F., Seiberlich, N., Heidemann, R.M., Griswold, M.A., Jakob, P.M., 2006. Controlled aliasing in volumetric parallel imaging (2D CAIPIRINHA). Magn. Reson. Med. 55, 549–556.

Deniz, C.M., 2019. Parallel transmission for ultrahigh field MRI. Top. Magn. Reson. Imaging 28, 159–171.

Faraji-Dana, Z., Tam, F., Chen, J.J., Graham, S.J., 2016. A robust method for suppressing motion-induced coil sensitivity variations during prospective correction of head motion in fMRI. Magn. Reson. Imaging 34, 1206–1219.

Feinberg, D.A., Moeller, S., Smith, S.M., Auerbach, E., Ramanna, S., Gunther, M., Glasser, M.F., Miller, K.L., Ugurbil, K., Yacoub, E., 2010. Multiplexed echo planar imaging for sub-second whole brain FMRI and fast diffusion imaging. PLoS ONE 5, e15710.

Gagoski, B.A., Bilgic, B., Eichner, C., Bhat, H., Grant, P.E., Wald, L.L., Setsompop, K., 2015. RARE/turbo spin echo imaging with simultaneous multislice wave-CAIPI. Magn. Reson. Med. 73, 929–938.

Herbst, M., Poser, B.A., Singh, A., Deng, W., Knowles, B., Zaitsev, M., Stenger, V.A., Ernst, T., 2017. Motion correction for diffusion weighted SMS imaging. Magn. Reson. Med. 38, 33–38.

Kim, T., Shin, W., Zhao, T., Beall, E.B., Lowe, M.J., Bae, K.T., 2013. Whole brain perfusion measurements using arterial spin labeling with multiband acquisition. Magn. Reson. Med. 70, 1653–1661.

Larkman, D.J., Hajnal, J.V., Herlihy, A.H., Coutts, G.A., Young, I.R., Ehnholm, G., 2001. Use of multicoil arrays for separation of signal from multiple slices simultaneously excited. J. Magn. Reson. Imaging 13, 313–317.

Larkman, D.J., Nunes, R.G., 2007. Parallel magnetic resonance imaging. Phys. Med. Biol. 52, R15–R55.

Li, X., Wang, D., Auerbach, E.J., Moeller, S., Ugurbil, K., Metzger, G.J., 2015. Theoretical and experimental evaluation of multi-band EPI for high-resolution whole brain pCASL imaging. NeuroImage 106, 170–181.

Moeller, S., Yacoub, E., Olman, C.A., Auerbach, E., Strupp, J., Harel, N., Uğurbil, K., 2010. Multiband multislice GE-EPI at 7 tesla, with 16-fold acceleration using partial parallel imaging with application to high spatial and temporal whole-brain fMRI. Magn. Reson. Med. 63, 1144–1153.

Norris, D.G., Koopmans, P.J., Boyacioğlu, R., Barth, M., 2011. Power Independent of Number of Slices (PINS) radiofrequency pulses for low-power simultaneous multislice excitation. Magn. Reson. Med. 66, 1234–1240.

Nunes, R.G., Hajnal, J.V., Golay, X., Larkman, D.J., 2006. Simultaneous slice excitation and reconstruction for single shot EPI. In: 14th Annual Meeting of the International Society for Magnetic Resonance in Medicine, p. 293.

Polimeni, J.R., Bhat, H., Witzel, T., Benner, T., Feiweier, T., Inati, S.J., Renvall, V., Heberlein, K., Wald, L.L., 2016. Reducing sensitivity losses due to respiration and motion in accelerated echo planar imaging by reordering the autocalibration data acquisition. Magn. Reson. Med. 75, 665–679.

Setsompop, K., Cohen-Adad, J., Gagoski, B.A., Raij, T., Yendiki, A., Keil, B., Wedeen, V.J., Wald, L.L., 2012a. Improving diffusion MRI using simultaneous multi-slice echo planar imaging. NeuroImage 63, 569–580.

Setsompop, K., Gagoski, B.A., Polimeni, J.R., Witzel, T., Wedeen, V.J., Wald, L.L., 2012b. Blipped-controlled aliasing in parallel imaging for simultaneous multislice echo planar imaging with reduced g-factor penalty. Magn. Reson. Med. 67, 1210–1224.

Sharma, A., Lustig, M., Grissom, W.A., 2016. Root-flipped multiband refocusing pulses. Magn. Reson. Med. 75, 227–237.

Uğurbil, K., Xu, J., Auerbach, E.J., Moeller, S., Vu, A.T., Duarte-Carvajalino, J.M., Lenglet, C., Wu, X., Schmitter, S., de Moortele, P.F., Strupp, J., Sapiro, G., De Martino, F., Wang, D., Harel, N., Garwood, M., Chen, L., Feinberg, D.A., Smith, S.M., Miller, K.L., Sotiropoulos, S.N., Jbabdi, S., Andersson, J.L.R., Behrens, T.E.J., Glasser, M.F., Van Essen, D.C., Yacoub, E., Consortium, W.-M.H., 2013. Pushing spatial and temporal resolution for functional and diffusion MRI in the Human Connectome Project. NeuroImage 80, 80–104.

Wong, E., 2012. Optimized phase schedules for minimizing peak RF power in simultaneous multi-slice RF excitation pulses. In: 20th Annual Meeting of the International Society for Magnetic Resonance in Medicine, p. 2209.

Further reading

Barth, M., Breuer, F., Koopmans, P.J., Norris, D.G., Poser, B.A., 2016. Simultaneous multislice (SMS) imaging techniques. Magn. Reson. Med. 75, 63–81.

Moeller, S., Pisharady Kumar, P., Andersson, J., Akcakaya, M., Harel, N., Ma, R., Wu, X., Yacoub, E., Lenglet, C., Ugurbil, K., 2021. Diffusion imaging in the post HCP era. J. Magn. Reson. Imaging 54, 36–57.

Poser, B.A., Setsompop, K., 2018. Pulse sequences and parallel imaging for high spatiotemporal resolution MRI at ultra-high field. NeuroImage 168, 101–118.

CHAPTER

Motion artifacts and correction in neuro MRI

4

André van der Kouwe

Athinoula A. Martinos Center for Biomedical Imaging, Massachusetts General Hospital, Charlestown, MA,
United States

4.1 Introduction

MRI provides exquisite soft tissue contrast that is invaluable in diagnosing a wide variety of brain disorders in clinical practice and is widely used in brain research due to the range of attainable anatomical, physiological, and metabolic contrasts. There is a constant push towards more sensitive, higher resolution imaging. The introduction of coil arrays along with efficient encoding methods, as well as higher field strengths, have contributed to higher SNR and shorter scans. However, these acceleration techniques may be especially sensitive to instabilities in the acquired signal. In research, the gains in SNR are often traded for resolution, resulting in unprecedented detail, but requiring tens of minutes per scan with a narrow tolerance on signal stability. The primary contributor to signal instability in human neuroimaging is head motion during scans. Head position changes are accompanied by secondary changes that indirectly increase signal instability, such as changes in the B_0 magnetic field. Physiological processes, especially respiration and the cardiac cycle (manifesting as pulsatile flow and small tissue displacements), add to signal instability in acquisitions where the physiology is not the process of interest. In this chapter, we explore methods to reduce or compensate for nuisance signal dynamics caused by head motion during scans. Accurate and reproducible initial positioning of the field of view, together with accurate head tracking and a stable signal throughout a session with multiple scan types, are indispensable if the full information potential of each scan session is to be reflected in the results.

4.2 Establishing and maintaining a consistent brain anatomical coordinate system throughout a scan session

Though not a dynamic aspect of motion tracking, accurate initial positioning of the field of view is sometimes an important consideration, and can be compromised by subsequent motion. This occurs in single voxel spectroscopy (SVS), for example, where an estimate of metabolite concentrations in a volume of only a few milliliters may be desired. The acquisition requires a stable signal over several minutes. Position changes during the scan result in altered tissue composition of the voxel, accompanied by magnetic field changes (including the mean B_0 offset or average resonance frequency and higher-order spatial components). In spectroscopy, the magnetic field changes may be more obviously detrimental to the signal than tissue position changes, as they result in spectral line broadening and catastrophic failure of editing in the spectral editing sequences. We observed that children, having been told to keep still during scans, tended to move more between scans than within scans, with the result that the prescription of the SVS voxel on the initial scan did not always reflect the desired positioning (Hess et al., 2014). In these types of studies, an accurate match between the localizer used for field of view placement and the true head position is essential. Conversely, in imaging sequences, the influence of an unstable field is easier to neglect. BOLD EPI used in functional imaging is especially sensitive to field inhomogeneities. Since this technique generates a series of temporally closely spaced volumes, pose changes are intrinsically encoded in the data. Pose changes can easily be corrected by registration and resampling in post-processing (see Chapter 6), or prospectively using the acquired data or an external tracker. However, by using temporal SNR (tSNR) as a proxy for signal stability in any given voxel, we observe that registration and resampling do not restore tSNR in BOLD EPI. Simply examining the signal time course in a voxel, or the estimated T_2^*, shows discontinuities even after correction. The substantial residual error in the signal is due to B_0 and B_1 magnetic field changes secondary to motion. Since T_2^* reflects the homogeneity of the field within each voxel, rather than simply the average resonance frequency in each voxel, it is difficult to restore the signal when the field changes. Proper correction requires a spatially and temporally constant field across each voxel, or precise dynamic knowledge of the field if the correction is to be applied offline. The ideal motion correction strategy should track the anatomical region of interest selected on the initial localizer in a true anatomical coordinate system, keeping it constant throughout the scan session, while also stabilizing the B_0 and B_1 fields throughout the session.

4.3 Impact of motion on MRI scans

4.3.1 Clinical impact

Motion tracking methods are often developed with healthy volunteers performing deliberate motions while clinical patients are frequently in pain or discomfort and unable to keep still. Patients with Parkinson's disease or Huntington's disease may perform involuntary movements. Young children and patients with dementia or altered states of consciousness may not be able to follow instructions. Claustrophobic and anxious patients may not tolerate scanning at all. Technologists handle each case based on experience, and the most effective approaches may not require advanced technologies. Some of these approaches are mentioned in Section 4.3.3. In the U.S., imaging departments are remunerated for completed examinations. Therefore, while there is not necessarily an incentive to perform fewer examinations, current healthcare economics incentivize abbreviated examinations that suffice for diagnostic purposes, such as the "5-minute brain" protocol. In principle, these examinations may be less sensitive to motion insofar as the patient does not have to remain still as long, and scans can be repeated if the images are motion corrupted. In practice, accelerated encoding techniques may be more sensitive to motion, and some patients cannot remain still even for a short examination. It has been estimated that motion during clinical MRIs results in lost revenue of over $110,000 per scanner per year, as estimated in 2015 (Andre et al., 2015), while disproportionately affecting the sickest patients. Practical motion compensation techniques should provide images of diagnostic quality immediately on the scanner, while maintaining a streamlined clinical workflow.

4.3.2 Research impact

It has become evident that motion introduces not just variance, but bias in research studies. In people with autism, for example, it may be hypothesized that long-range connectivity and fractional anisotropy (FA) in white matter are reduced relative to neurotypical controls. However, studies with volunteers performing deliberate movements during scans show that motion during resting-state functional and diffusion scans results in reduced estimates of long-range connectivity and FA compared with scans in the same volunteers without motion. Since people with autism tend to move more than neurotypicals, the underlying reason for the observed differences is confounded (Deen and Pelphrey, 2012). Brain morphometry studies exhibit the same confound—motion during structural imaging has been shown to reduce brain volume and cortical thickness estimates, but these are frequently also the expected differences in the patient population that moves more during imaging. In a few cases where the study group exhibits increased cortical thickness or connectivity, it is an intervention, such as meditation that results in the changes, but in this case motion is expected to decrease in the study group relative to controls, so the confound remains.

4.3.3 Mitigating motion

The most common and simplest motion mitigation technique is the use of pillows to constrain head motion inside the head coil. Provided this does not interfere with surgical sites or hardware, such as ICP monitors, it is a simple way to restrict motion and dampen acoustic noise. We have observed slow drifts with some pillows, even with phantom scans, suggesting that some materials subside over time. Neck muscle relaxation may also manifest as drift. We also frequently observe small oscillatory head motions correlated with breathing. This may include small physical head rotations and translations and/or B_0-modulations induced by the changing chest volume. Immobilizing pillows that harden under vacuum and inflatable pads (Pearl Technology, Schlieren, Switzerland) are effective at limiting head motion. CaseForge (Berkeley, CA) provides a custom-machined polystyrene head case that fits an individual's head on the inside and the selected head coil on the outside. While restricting motion, the head case also positions the head consistently over multiple sessions. Consistent positioning and landmarking can reduce variance in the B_1 field and keep gradient nonlinearities the same in longitudinal studies.

Sedation and anesthesia are effective in reducing motion. However, anesthetics may be dangerous to the developing brain and the FDA recommends avoiding their use in young children when possible. Anesthetic use is seldom ethically justified in research scans. Child life specialists are therefore invaluable especially in research. Generally, psychological preparation of the participant may greatly improve compliance during scanning. Familiarizing patients with the procedure using literature, introductory videos, and a mock scanner have been effective. Participants have been trained to keep their heads still in the mock scanner by watching a movie, which freezes when head motion is detected by a

56   **Chapter 4** Motion artifacts and correction in neuro MRI

camera or an accelerometer affixed to the head. Feedback in the form of a graph or as a controller for a game has been used to motivate the patient to minimize head motion and to inform technologists when patients move (Nous Imaging, St. Louis, MO).

4.4 Data quality and motion metrics

Though many image quality metrics exist, as provided for example in the MRIQC package, the relationship between these metrics and motion is less well characterized. This is in part due to the complicated relationship between the time course of the motion and the encoding scheme of the acquisition. Ignoring the neck, lower jaw and spine, and perhaps the brainstem, the brain moves as a single rigid body. Simply expressing the six parameters describing a rigid body motion (three translations and three rotations) as a single value can be done in multiple ways. One approach is to add the translation distance (length of the translation vector) to the distance traversed by a point on a sphere with approximately the radius of the head that experiences the rotation. This represents the "worst case" displacement of a voxel in the head. Another metric is the average displacement of all the voxels in the head. Summarizing the motion over time adds uncertainty. Most signal energy is encoded near the center of k-space, whereas edges that may be important in resolving structures, such as vessels, are encoded at higher spatial frequencies. Therefore the relationship between the timing of the motion and the timing of the sequence is important, and sequences may be designed to minimize the impact of motion by virtue of their timing. For example, HASTE encodes slices independently and rapidly to freeze motion. Even though the positioning of the slices in the stack may be inconsistent, the expectation is that most individual slices are sharp. In acquisitions with 3D encoding, the entire volume is excited at every repetition throughout the scan, so all three dimensions are encoded in spatial frequency and transformed at the end of the scan. Position changes at any time during the scan therefore affect the entire volume and manifest as blurring and ghosts. This approach confers spin history immunity, whereas movement between slices of a 2D acquisition may result in spin history shadows between slices. Simulation of motion and "reverse correction" of prospectively corrected images can be helpful in evaluating motion correction strategies (see Fig. 4.1). The "reverse correction" technique approximates the images without correction by using the measured motion information to resample the k-space volume to how it would have been encoded without prospective motion correction, potentially recreating the under- or unsampled regions of k-space characteristic of uncorrected k-space encoding (Zahneisen et al., 2016; Slipsager et al., 2021). Current methods apply generally only to 3D-encoded acquisition schemes and also do not simulate secondary effects of motion such as B_0 and B_1 inconsistencies.

Image quality in clinical studies is often summarized by a radiologist's rating of diagnostic value on a Likert scale (0 = undiagnostic to 5 = no artifacts). Though some artifacts, such as background ghosting, may substantially reduce QA metrics, a radiologist may easily read through the artifact and rate the image as being suitable for diagnosis. For clinical purposes, the relevant metric is the radiologist's assessment of diagnostic quality.

4.5 Retrospective correction methods

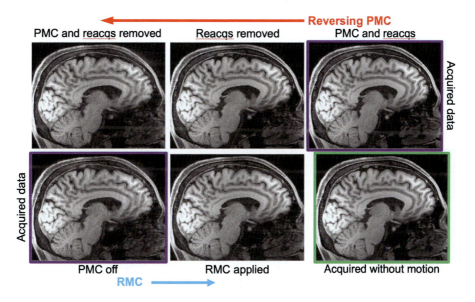

FIGURE 4.1
(Top row) "Reverse correction" is a useful tool for evaluating the performance of prospective motion correction (PMC) approaches. Here the method is used to demonstrate qualitatively the benefits of PMC with reacquisition using volumetric navigators in MPRAGE. "Reacqs" refers to prospectively reacquired slices of k-space. (Bottom row) Retrospective motion correction (RMC) of MPRAGE without PMC. All corrections were performed with a modified version of Retro-MoCo-Box (Gallichan et al., 2016).

4.5 Retrospective correction methods
4.5.1 Classical approaches

Data rejection, rather than correction, may be the most practical approach to retrospective correction. For example, BOLD and diffusion EPI acquisitions may include redundant data, of which only a subset is needed for parameter fitting. In non-redundant acquisitions, damaged k-space lines may be identified by comparison to a reference or with an external motion sensor. If lines are rejected, a non-uniform transformation is required to reconstruct the image. If the motion is known, the lines can be correctly incorporated into the reconstruction using a tool such as Retro-MoCo-Box (Gallichan et al., 2016). When motion information is unavailable, reconstruction may be performed iteratively in the image domain, optimizing for a cost function, such as image entropy or gradient image entropy, which minimizes motion-related ghosts (Atkinson et al., 1997). This is called "autofocus" optimization and is computationally expensive. "Super-resolution" assumes that high-frequency information beyond the Nyquist limit is aliased into the acquired data and can be accessed through multiple acquisitions with different sub-voxel shifts. This is not the case with phase encoding, but can be imposed deliberately by repeated random sampling and shifting in the slice direction. Such an approach is one of the few successful methods for imaging the moving fetal brain, a challenging problem best handled in the image domain,

58   **Chapter 4** Motion artifacts and correction in neuro MRI

because the fetal brain and surrounding tissue move independently and their signals become entangled in k-space (Studholme, 2011).

4.5.2 Machine learning approaches

Generative adversarial networks (GANs) have become popular in machine learning due to their ability to create very realistic images, such as human faces, text, and even music. Pairs of motion-corrupted and motion-free images were provided to train a GAN to "translate" between them. This approach produced "near-realistic motion-free images" from novel motion-corrupted images (Kustner et al., 2019). However, the process may alter or hide clinically important anatomical features according to the authors.

A more constrained approach is to estimate the motion explicitly from the k-space data, and then apply this correction in a traditional reconstruction, thus eliminating any possibility of biasing the reconstruction with prior knowledge of a brain. "Network accelerated motion estimation and reduction" (NAMER) uses a convolutional neural network as a framework to jointly search for motion parameters and the uncorrupted 2D image (Haskell et al., 2019). Machine learning is an active field, in which optimization algorithms that are evolving mutually with powerful GPUs are being adapted to the motion problem.

4.6 Methods of detecting motion and associated field changes in real time

4.6.1 Camera-based external motion trackers

Technology for tracking and modeling head and body motion with cameras and fiducials is well established in the movie industry. NDI Medical (Waterloo, Ontario, Canada) provides such a system designed for rigid tracking of surgical instruments using spherical markers and two cameras. A variant was adopted in MEG for head registration to anatomical MRI. The system can be used in the scanner fringe field and requires a direct line of sight into the scanner bore, which precludes some patients, constrained head coils, and some mirror assemblies. MRI-compatible in-bore camera-based systems requiring visible markers are commercially available (Kineticor, Honolulu, HI, HobbitView, San Jose, CA). A research variant uses a rotation-sensitive moiré interference pattern to measure marker orientation. In principle, these systems can measure the position of the marker with micron accuracy.

Markers attached to the face may be irritating to patients and young children and may be obfuscated behind parts of the head coil. Most importantly, the brain and marker must maintain a precise rigid relationship throughout the scan session as the marker is a proxy for brain pose. Markers attached to the upper jaw with a dental device reliably maintain this relationship, whereas markers on the forehead may be affected by facial expressions. One solution is to use multiple markers and verify the rigid relationship between them throughout the scan. This also helps with markers disappearing behind the head coil. A generalization is to use the entire face as the marker. A 3D face image can be acquired with stereoscopic cameras. However, structured light approaches are more reliable for depth estimation, and require only one camera. TracInnovations (Ballerup, Denmark) offers a markerless tracking system for MRI use (Fig. 4.2). The camera and light source are installed in a Faraday cage outside the scanner bore, and light is transmitted to and from the patient through optic fiber. By eliminating metal-containing

4.6 Methods of detecting motion and associated field changes in real time 59

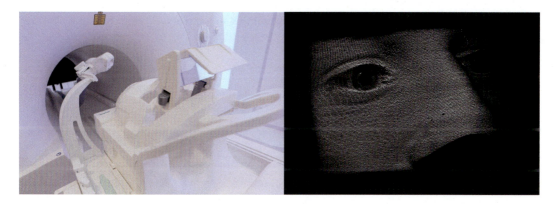

FIGURE 4.2

Markerless motion tracking. (Left) MRI scanner with head coil, optic fiber, and vision probe with view of patient's face (right). The entire visible surface of the face is used as the "marker", thus obviating the need for discrete attached markers.

hardware and electronics from inside the scanner bore, vibrations, RF energy absorption, and RF noise transmission are avoided.

4.6.2 Marker-based systems without cameras

A substantial challenge with camera-based systems is accurately establishing the relationship between the coordinate systems of the camera(s) and the scanner. The relevant scanner coordinate system is the coordinate system of the gradients, as these are responsible for spatial encoding of the MR image. Several marker- or sensor-based systems that directly sense their own orientation and position in the gradient fields have been designed. Robin Medical Inc. (Baltimore, MD) offers a system that uses one or more cube or flat sensors containing three or six miniature coils that measure position and orientation in the gradient fields through the voltage induced by magnetic induction. This requires a changing magnetic field, and therefore the sequence must either natively exhibit activity at frequent intervals on all three gradients, or very short deliberate excitation gradients must be added to the sequence. A map of the gradients may improve pose estimates, especially further from the gradient isocenter, where the fields are further from linear. Sensors have been added to stabilize the measurements further in experimental systems, such as a magnetometer to sense the main magnetic field and an accelerometer to measure the gravity vector. Inertial measurement units (IMUs) have become small and inexpensive due to cell phone applications. These small sensors use microelectromechanical systems (MEMS). IMUs measure angular velocity and linear acceleration about all three axes. Absolute pose estimates require integration, and therefore accumulate error. Inertial navigation system design is a mature engineering discipline with substantial associated control theory. A combined IMU with magnetometer and inductive coils, and an RF pickup for synchronization to the sequence, and control system to combine measurements, has been demonstrated. MEMS are slightly susceptible to gradient activity, and in a later generation version of the system the MEMS IMU was omitted, as it did not add sufficient information beyond the magnetometer and inductive coils (Fig. 4.3). The device has no physical connection to the scanner and uses RF communications within the scanner room to communicate positions to the scan controller (van Niekerk et al., 2019).

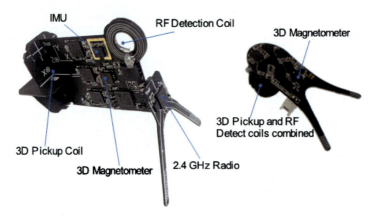

FIGURE 4.3

Wireless radio frequency triggered acquisition devices (WRADs) that mount to a patient's nose. An RF detect circuit synchronizes motion estimates with the pulse sequence so that gradient activity is sampled by the 3D pickup coil assembly at the correct time. A Hall effect magnetometer measures the main B_0 field vector. The 2.4 GHz radio communicates information from the WRAD to a computer outside the scanner that controls the sequence in real time. The second-generation device (left) included an inertial measurement unit (IMU) that was determined not to be necessary in the third-generation device (right).

A rigid pose is defined by three or more fiducials. Fiducials may be realized with small spheres of material providing strong localized signals (passive markers), or small coils tuned to couple inductively with the scanner receive coils (semi-passive markers) (Ooi et al., 2013). The resonance frequency or relaxation parameters of the material may be chosen to separate the marker signal from the signal of interest. Three orthogonal readouts (a marker-based "navigator") may be used to capture projections of the strong marker signals on three axes. With identical markers, the indexing of the markers after a pose change may not be unique. The indices may be resolved with non-identical markers or additional readouts that are not mutually parallel. Fully active markers are receive-coils with dedicated receivers. These require additional RF infrastructure, but each marker is indexed by a unique channel so there is no ambiguity.

4.6.3 Field cameras and probes

None of the aforementioned systems estimates properties of the B_0 or B_1 fields, except for the inductive coil and magnetometer systems that measure field properties at a single point in space. To fully characterize the field requires an array of sensors spaced consistently with the expected smoothness of the field. Extremely precise and rapid measurements at multiple points around the head are possible with commercial NMR field probes (Skope, Zürich, Switzerland). These systems can precisely measure and correct the gradients. An array of probes attached to the head can be used to estimate head position (Eschelbach et al., 2019), and to approximate the B_0 field within the head. However, it has been shown that measurements outside the head do not resolve the contours of the magnetic field in regions with sharp susceptibility gradients inside the head. In theory, sources within a closed surface cannot be predicted from measurements on the surface.

4.6.4 Navigators

Since the brain anatomical, functional, physiological, or metabolic characteristics we wish to measure are dependent directly on the MR signal, and the MR signal is modulated by position changes and their secondary effects, there is some elegance in using the MR signal itself to estimate motion's effects. Moreover, these measurements are encoded using the same gradient coordinate system, albeit potentially with sequence-dependent distortions and artifacts. The intimate coupling between motion and the MR signal is also the challenge with using the signal to characterize itself, the problem being how to disentangle the signal of interest, such as the image of the brain, from the nuisance signal, such as the change in head pose and associated field changes. Measuring the dynamic properties associated with an organ, such as cardiac or respiratory phase, head pose, or the B_0 field inside the head, is called "navigation". External tracking systems neatly separate motion navigation and imaging. Navigation can be achieved from the MR signal without any external equipment using a short experiment called a "navigator", an elemental sequence that is embedded at intervals within another sequence to characterize the dynamic changes during the main scan. The challenge is to separate navigation from imaging.

4.6.4.1 Self-navigation

Some sequences are naturally structured to generate navigators, and these are called "self-navigating". An example is 2D BOLD EPI, the technique used for fMRI. The sequence generates repeated snapshots of the head that are registered and resampled in post-processing before fitting the functional signal. In one instantiation, registration is done on the scanner immediately after each volume is collected, and the head pose is used to prospectively track the motion at every volume. The resulting volumes are thus registered without resampling, within a residual error due to the feedback delay. Slices within a volume may be inconsistent. Recently, slice- and multi-slice-to-volume registration have been explored, the latter being better constrained and practical, given the popularity of simultaneous multi-slice/multiband imaging (see Chapter 3). Multiple corrections per volume are possible. The experiment can be easily modified also to acquire phase, preferably at two echo times, to estimate the B_0 field map. Diffusion scans are approximately self-navigating, but the diffusion weighting biases the registration at each volume, especially at higher b-values. Distributing the low-b volumes throughout the acquisition helps to estimate head pose at regular intervals. A scheme was recently suggested in which the diffusion directions are ordered such that windows of three volumes are orthogonal or almost orthogonal, and trace-weighted images, that are immune from direction-dependence, can be calculated at each interval (Hoinkiss and Porter, 2017).

Fast- or turbo-spin-echo imaging is the most used clinical sequence. A widely adopted innovation is to repeat each 2D slice in an interleaved fashion, rotating between interleaved slices or "blades". This technique is called "PROPELLER" (Pipe, 1999). By reducing the width of the blades, the elliptical plane in k-space is still fully sampled at the end of the scan, but the center of k-space is sampled redundantly with a modest time-penalty (Fig. 4.4). A similar idea has been applied in radial imaging, in which the center of k-space is naturally more densely sampled. Windows of radial spokes can be combined to form low-resolution navigators throughout the scan. This approach is popular in cardiac imaging, where cardiac and respiratory gating are important, and has been demonstrated in brain imaging.

FIGURE 4.4

"PROPELLER" (Periodically rotated overlapping parallel lines with enhanced reconstruction) divides the 2D k-space plane into narrow "blades" that overlap at the center of k-space. The central region provides a lower-resolution image of the slice at each interval, and these navigators are registered to one another to correct for pose changes between blades, ensuring a reconstructed slice that is free of artifacts if there is within-plane motion.

4.6.4.2 K-space navigators

Since the head moves rigidly in three-dimensional "object space", spatial information is required for tracking. However, by choice of frequency/phase encoding with linear gradients, the acquired data is encoded in the spatial frequency domain ("k-space") with sinusoidal basis functions. Through the Fourier shifting property, we know that translations in the spatial domain are manifest as linear phase rolls in k-space. Rotations in object-space are manifest as rotations in k-space. Exploiting these properties, we can design efficient navigators that measure rigid body motion and field properties directly with efficient k-space trajectories.

For example, we can measure the translation vector with three mutually non-parallel (ideally orthogonal) readouts (straight lines in k-space). Translations are estimated by fitting the phase ramp along the readout (relative to a reference), or more easily by transforming the discrete data along the readout to the spatial domain with the FFT and cross-correlating with the reference. The FFT of a line through the center of k-space represents the projection of all material in the excited volume onto that axis. In perhaps the earliest instantiation of such a navigator, a rectanguloid region of the chest, including the diaphragm, oriented head-to-foot, was excited by the intersection of two thin slabs with 90° and 180° pulses. These "pencil-beam navigators" are still used for respiratory gating.

Rotations can be measured by cross-correlating the k-space magnitude signal along a circle around the center of k-space with a reference. This is called an "orbital navigator" (Fu et al., 1995). The radius of the circle determines the spatial resolution of the features that drive the registration. Three circles in mutually non-parallel planes suffice to fully characterize 3D rotation. Cross-correlation may

4.6 Methods of detecting motion and associated field changes in real time

be less accurate if the rotation is out-of-plane with all three circle navigators. A map of k-space at the radius of the navigators stabilizes the solution. Although very large rotations need not be mapped, a full sampling of the sphere can be achieved with a spiral trajectory along the surface of a sphere. This map itself can be the navigator, and this is called a "spherical navigator" (Welch et al., 2002). Registering the complete sphere is computationally burdensome. An efficient Lissajous sampling was recently proposed (Buschbeck et al., 2019).

An efficient combination of the line and circle navigators is realized in the "cloverleaf navigator" (van der Kouwe et al., 2006). This k-space navigator consists of a single trajectory of about 3 ms that includes three quarter-circles on the spherical surface and three straight lines through the center of k-space and delivers a rigid body estimate of head position. The method requires an initial map of k-space capturing possible out-of-plane rotations about the initial navigator. The map is acquired by rotating the gradient coordinate system through plausible rotations by gradient encoding. Since corrections are made in real time, the map captures only the expected range of rotations between navigators. Each pose estimate is noisy, and regularization improves tracking accuracy. The echo positions in the linear segments give the linear field offsets or shims.

4.6.4.3 Object-space navigators

Object-space navigators are navigators that capture data that can be transformed into an image of the object. Such navigators are simply registered to one another to estimate motion, such as the EPI time series. Though the resolution of the navigator may be low, the data acquired are highly redundant, and registration is possible with much better resolution than the size of the voxels. Exploiting this idea, EPI time series have been embedded in longer sequences. Typically, 3D EPI navigators are embedded in a 3D-encoded sequence so that excitation is consistent between the navigator and the main sequence. The navigators can be used for offline reconstruction or registered in real time to prospectively correct the main sequence. Such navigators are called "volumetric navigators (vNav)" (Tisdall et al., 2012). These have been demonstrated in various anatomical and spectroscopy sequences (see Fig. 4.5). The vNav is acquired in a few hundred milliseconds. Another approach is to collect three single planes with spiral readouts in an approach called PROMO, implemented in MPRAGE and a few other sequences (White et al., 2010). The 3-plane navigator may be repeated to resolve mutually out-of-plane motions, and a mask may be used to separate rigid from non-rigid parts of the head.

Navigators require careful coordination between the excitation that elicits the navigator signal, and the excitation of the main sequence, to prevent interference. The signals can be separated by frequency multiplexing. In one approach, fat-selective excitation is used for the navigator and water-only excitation for the main sequence (Gallichan et al., 2016). Scalp and marrow fat provide strong features for navigator registration. It was observed that such navigators can be highly accelerated due to sparsity, and the accelerated reconstructions are robust to small inconsistencies in position with respect to the coil sensitivity maps. Alternatively, if only the center slice of k-space is collected, this is called a "collapsed fat navigator". The fat projection on three planes suffices to track motion. Multiplexing is also possible using coils that tune to multiple nuclei.

Volumetric navigators can be realized with other acquisition schemes, such as segmented EPI, or spoiled gradient-echo readouts, which provide flexibility in timing and may reduce distortion. Such navigators have been inserted in SWI sequences. Since the susceptibility-weighted readout has a long TE, the navigator may be inserted with no time penalty before this readout. This implementation in-

64 Chapter 4 Motion artifacts and correction in neuro MRI

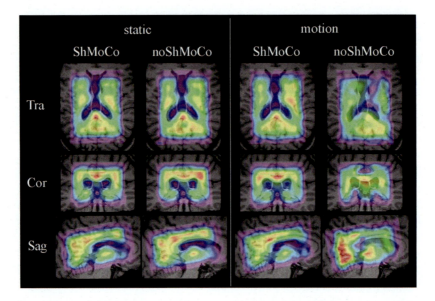

FIGURE 4.5

Three dimensional maps of NAA obtained in a volunteer with standard-resolution 3D-MRSI in the presence of moderate motion. Metabolic maps from four scans are displayed in three orthogonal planes. Odd columns display maps with ShMoCo (prospective shim and motion correction), and even columns display maps without ShMoCo. The two columns on the left show all three orthogonal slices for each of the two static scans as a reference. The two columns on the right display the slice orientations that illustrate the largest localization errors caused for specific head motions: (top) transversal for rotation about the head-foot axis, (center) coronal for translation in the head-foot (HF) direction, and (bottom) sagittal for rotation about the left-right (LR) axis. Reproduced with permission (Bogner et al., 2014).

cludes multiple navigator echo times to acquire the dynamic field map at 7T. Image correction is done in post-processing (Liu et al., 2020).

4.6.4.4 Coil-space navigators

Substantial spatial information is encoded by the geometry of the coil elements in an array, as exploited by methods such as GRAPPA and SENSE. Indeed, a very low-resolution image can be reconstructed from a single free induction decay ("FID", a measurement at the center of k-space) if there are sufficient and appropriately spaced receive coils. Detecting changes in position directly without the image is possible with a signal model that includes the coil sensitivities. The optimization is numerically challenging and simulating possible motions stabilizes the solution. Initially, this was done by having the person perform deliberate head movements at the start of the scan session and measuring the head positions using an independent method, such as localizer scans or an external tracker (Kober et al., 2011). More recently, it has been shown that the signal can be predicted numerically from an anatomical volume, and this provides robust motion estimates using FID navigators without the manual calibration step, including B_0 correction (Wallace et al., 2020).

4.7 Prospective correction   **65**

Methods have been developed that exploit the redundancy in the k-space data, provided by the signals from the multiple receive coils to jointly estimate motion and a corrected image without requiring independent pose estimates from navigators or a tracker. "Distributed and incoherent sample orders for reconstruction deblurring using encoding redundancy" (DISORDER) is a framework for optimally selecting the order of k-space sampling to improve convergence when joint motion and image estimation is formulated as a separable nonlinear least squares problem (Cordero-Grande et al., 2020).

4.7 **Prospective correction**

With the motion time-course, images can be corrected in post-processing, as described in Section 4.5 and in Chapter 6. The effects of the changing B_0 and B_1 fields can also be included. However, there are advantages to applying the corrections in real time. Perhaps the biggest practical advantage is that the images are available immediately on the scanner, an important consideration in the clinical workflow. Another important advantage is that missing information can be recovered in real time. For example, if a person's head shifts in the inferior direction during the acquisition of an ascending stack of 2D axial slices, a part of space will irretrievably be lost. The same is true of rotations in 3D acquisitions, though the effect on the image is less intuitive. Detecting and correcting for the lost data in real time ensures that minimal data are lost.

Rotation corrections are implemented by altering the mapping of the image coordinates to the gradient axes. That is, the allocation of the slice select, readout, and phase encode gradient waveforms to the scanner's logical X, Y, and Z axes (the physical gradients) is calculated from the initially prescribed field of view using a rotation matrix that may be adapted in real time so that the effective field of view follows the rotations of the head throughout the scan. The rotation matrix may become non-orthogonal through repeated corrections, no longer representing a pure rotation. Quaternions are preferred, as they cannot encode non-rotational distortions. The quaternion representation also avoids the order of rotations that must be defined when Euler angles are used, as well as the associated "gimbal lock" problem, though this problem is unlikely to arise in the context of small head rotations. Translations in an RF-selected slice direction are realized by changing the frequency of the slice-selective pulse. All these corrections must be performed in real time to avoid missing data. Translations in the readout and phase encode directions, on the other hand, are manifest only as phase changes in the k-space signal. The object correspondingly moves within the field of view, possibly wrapping over the edge, and back into the image on the opposite side if it moves too far, with no loss of information. Therefore, this part of the correction can be done at any time before the FFT, even after the scan is complete, by simply correcting k-space phase.

Every prospective tracking technique involves a lag, and part of the delay may be imposed by the physics of the experiment. For example, if the position estimate is determined after a slice-selective pulse, but before the readout, it cannot be used to correct the slice, as the selection is already memorialized by the spins, and this memory is not erased until the signal is spoiled or decays away. In this case, even a rapid external tracking system with millisecond delay cannot overcome causality. However, it is possible to rewrite history by repeating the experiment and replacing the corrupted signal. This is called "reacquisition". EPI time series and single voxel spectroscopy experiments are "self-reacquiring" in the sense that the same experiment is intrinsically repeated multiple times. One embodiment of the vNav system reacquires slices of k-space in the 3D MPRAGE or SPACE sequences, based on an assessment of the amount of motion that occurred during the acquisition of each slice. The worst slices are reacquired at the end of the scan. A variant of this idea is to detect when additional information is needed. For example, an FID navigator that is sensitive enough to detect motion but not accurate enough to quantify it may be used to trigger acquisition of a vNav if a motion threshold is exceeded.

Given a dynamic B_0 field map, most scanners only provide for real-time updates of the zeroth and first-order spatial components of the field. The zeroth-order component, or constant offset, is compensated by the system RF frequency (transmit and receive). The first-order shim component is realized by a constant offset on the system gradients, which are typically eddy current compensated and respond precisely on schedule as part of the sequence timing. Higher-order shim terms can be adjusted, but change asynchronously and are not eddy current compensated. Correcting higher-order components may require special additional hardware, such as real-time addressable shim coils (Resonance Research, Billerica, MA) or arrays.

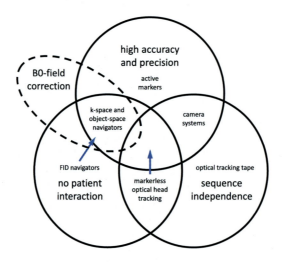

FIGURE 4.6

Desirable criteria for MRI motion correction techniques for brain imaging with current approaches. Arrows indicate recent progress. Adapted from (Maclaren et al., 2013).

4.8 Conclusion

In a review of prospective motion correction in brain imaging (Maclaren et al., 2013) highlighted three desirable properties of motion correction systems in an overlapping Venn diagram viz. "high accuracy and precision", "sequence independence", and "no patient interaction". Fig. 4.6 shows Maclaren's scheme with B_0-field correction added and blue arrows showing recent progress in the technology. Though some of the methods, such as markerless tracking, come close, we may never perfectly satisfy all four criteria. Complete sequence independence may not be possible given the constraints of physics, especially the unavoidable lag in prospective correction, and the implication that information may be lost if it is not reacquired. Therefore we are left with multiple approaches and multiple applications, with no single best approach for every application. Nevertheless, we have many excellent options, and the field is progressing rapidly.

References

Andre, J.B., Bresnahan, B.W., Mossa-Basha, M., Hoff, M.N., Smith, C.P., Anzai, Y., Cohen, W.A., 2015. Toward quantifying the prevalence, severity, and cost associated with patient motion during clinical MR examinations. J. Am. Coll. Radiol. 12 (7), 689–695.

Atkinson, D., Hill, D.L., Stoyle, P.N., Summers, P.E., Keevil, S.F., 1997. Automatic correction of motion artifacts in magnetic resonance images using an entropy focus criterion. IEEE Trans. Med. Imaging 16 (6), 903–910.

Bogner, W., Hess, A.T., Gagoski, B., Tisdall, M.D., van der Kouwe, A.J., Trattnig, S., Rosen, B., Andronesi, O.C., 2014. Real-time motion- and B0-correction for LASER-localized spiral-accelerated 3D-MRSI of the brain at 3T. NeuroImage 88, 22–31.

Buschbeck, R.P., Yun, S.D., Shah, N. Jon, 2019. 3D rigid-body motion information from spherical Lissajous navigators at small k-space radii: a proof of concept. Magn. Reson. Med. 82 (4), 1462–1470.

Cordero-Grande, L., Ferrazzi, G., Teixeira, R., O'Muircheartaigh, J., Price, A.N., Hajnal, J.V., 2020. Motion-corrected MRI with DISORDER: distributed and incoherent sample orders for reconstruction deblurring using encoding redundancy. Magn. Reson. Med. 84 (2).

Deen, B., Pelphrey, K., 2012. Perspective: brain scans need a rethink. Nature 491 (7422), S20.

Eschelbach, M., Aghaeifar, A., Bause, J., Handwerker, J., Anders, J., Engel, E.M., Thielscher, A., Scheffler, K., 2019. Comparison of prospective head motion correction with NMR field probes and an optical tracking system. Magn. Reson. Med. 81 (1), 719–729.

Fu, Z.W., Wang, Y., Grimm, R.C., Rossman, P.J., Felmlee, J.P., Riederer, S.J., Ehman, R.L., 1995. Orbital navigator echoes for motion measurements in magnetic resonance imaging. Magn. Reson. Med. 34 (5), 746–753.

Gallichan, D., Marques, J.P., Gruetter, R., 2016. Retrospective correction of involuntary microscopic head movement using highly accelerated fat image navigators (3D FatNavs) at 7T. Magn. Reson. Med. 75 (3), 1030–1039.

Haskell, M.W., Cauley, S.F., Bilgic, B., Hossbach, J., Splitthoff, D.N., Pfeuffer, J., Setsompop, K., Wald, L.L., 2019. Network Accelerated Motion Estimation and Reduction (NAMER): convolutional neural network guided retrospective motion correction using a separable motion model. Magn. Reson. Med. 82 (4), 1452–1461.

Hess, A.T., Jacobson, S.W., Jacobson, J.L., Molteno, C.D., van der Kouwe, A.J., Meintjes, E.M., 2014. A comparison of spectral quality in magnetic resonance spectroscopy data acquired with and without a novel EPI-navigated PRESS sequence in school-aged children with fetal alcohol spectrum disorders. Metab. Brain Dis. 29 (2), 323–332.

Hoinkiss, D.C., Porter, D.A., 2017. Prospective motion correction in diffusion-weighted imaging using intermediate pseudo-trace-weighted images. NeuroImage 149, 1–14.

Kober, T., Marques, J.P., Gruetter, R., Krueger, G., 2011. Head motion detection using FID navigators. Magn. Reson. Med. 66 (1), 135–143.

Kustner, T., Armanious, K., Yang, J., Yang, B., Schick, F., Gatidis, S., 2019. Retrospective correction of motion-affected MR images using deep learning frameworks. Magn. Reson. Med. 82 (4), 1527–1540.

Liu, J., van Gelderen, P., de Zwart, J.A., Duyn, J.H., 2020. Reducing motion sensitivity in 3D high-resolution T_2^*-weighted MRI by navigator-based motion and nonlinear magnetic field correction. NeuroImage 206, 116332.

Maclaren, J., Herbst, M., Speck, O., Zaitsev, M., 2013. Prospective motion correction in brain imaging: a review. Magn. Reson. Med. 69 (3), 621–636.

Ooi, M.B., Aksoy, M., Maclaren, J., Watkins, R.D., Bammer, R., 2013. Prospective motion correction using inductively coupled wireless RF coils. Magn. Reson. Med. 70 (3), 639–647.

Pipe, J.G., 1999. Motion correction with PROPELLER MRI: application to head motion and free-breathing cardiac imaging. Magn. Reson. Med. 42 (5), 963–969.

Slipsager, J.M., Glimberg, S.L., Højgaard, L., Paulsen, R.R., Wighton, P., Tisdall, M.D., Jaimes, C., Gagoski, B.A., Grant, P., van der Kouwe, A., Olesen, O.V., Frost, R., 2021. Comparison of prospective and retrospective motion correction in 3D-encoded neuroanatomical MRI. Magn. Reson. Med. https://doi.org/10.1002/mrm.28991.

Studholme, C., 2011. Mapping fetal brain development in utero using magnetic resonance imaging: the Big Bang of brain mapping. Annu. Rev. Biomed. Eng. 13, 345–368.

Tisdall, M.D., Hess, A.T., Reuter, M., Meintjes, E.M., Fischl, B., van der Kouwe, A.J., 2012. Volumetric navigators for prospective motion correction and selective reacquisition in neuroanatomical MRI. Magn. Reson. Med. 68 (2), 389–399.

van der Kouwe, A.J., Benner, T., Dale, A.M., 2006. Real-time rigid body motion correction and shimming using cloverleaf navigators. Magn. Reson. Med. 56 (5), 1019–1032.

van Niekerk, A., Meintjes, E., van der Kouwe, A., 2019. A wireless radio frequency triggered acquisition device (WRAD) for self-synchronised measurements of the rate of change of the MRI gradient vector field for motion tracking. IEEE Trans. Med. Imaging 38 (7), 1610–1621.

Wallace, T.E., Afacan, O., Kober, T., Warfield, S.K., 2020. Rapid measurement and correction of spatiotemporal B0 field changes using FID navigators and a multi-channel reference image. Magn. Reson. Med. 83 (2), 575–589.

Welch, E.B., Manduca, A., Grimm, R.C., Ward, H.A., Jack Jr., C.R., 2002. Spherical navigator echoes for full 3D rigid body motion measurement in MRI. Magn. Reson. Med. 47 (1), 32–41.

White, N., Roddey, C., Shankaranarayanan, A., Han, E., Rettmann, D., Santos, J., Kuperman, J., Dale, A., 2010. PROMO: real-time prospective motion correction in MRI using image-based tracking. Magn. Reson. Med. 63 (1), 91–105.

Zahneisen, B., Keating, B., Singh, A., Herbst, M., Ernst, T., 2016. Reverse retrospective motion correction. Magn. Reson. Med. 75 (6), 2341–2349.

PART 2

Classical and deep learning approaches to neuro image analysis

CHAPTER

Statistical approaches to neuroimaging analysis

5

Jeanette A. Mumford
Stanford University, Stanford, CA, United States

5.1 Linear model overview

A model is a mathematical approximation of reality, where some function of a given set of input variables aims to recreate an output variable. Consider an fMRI paradigm, where a subject is shown images of faces and houses. The goal of the model is to use the expected time courses for when a voxel reacts to a face and house, and produce an output closely matching the signal of a measured voxel's response to faces/houses (see Fig. 5.1). Let Y be a vector of length N that contains the time series data for a voxel, and let X_1 and X_2 be the expected time courses for face and house activation, respectively. In the case of the *linear* model, we assume Y is a linear combination of the X_i. Since measurement and models are not perfect, there is an additional error term vector, ϵ, describing this leftover variability giving,

$$Y = \beta_0 + \beta_1 X_1 + \beta_2 X_2 + \epsilon. \tag{5.1}$$

The parameter, β_0, describes the baseline value of the fMRI signal when the subject is not viewing a face or house (when X_1 and X_2 are zero), whereas β_1 and β_2 describe the amounts of face and house activation, respectively. Lastly, ϵ contains variability from the noise of the data as well as any unknown structured variability not captured by the model. The bottom panel of Fig. 5.1 shows how well the fitted model matches the original data and the parameter estimates.

The model can be expressed in matrix form, where all regressors are in a single matrix and all β_i are in a column vector, expressed as $Y = X\beta + \epsilon$, where Y is a vector of length N, X is a matrix of dimension $N \times p$, where p is the number of regressors, β is a column vector of length p and ϵ is a vector of length N. Fig. 5.2 shows these matrices for the fMRI task shown in Fig. 5.1 as well as a second model studying group differences in fractional anisotropy (FA). The linear model is used widely in neuroimaging analyses to relate various brain measures to different variables and compare them between groups. It is also used in a preprocessing step of resting state fMRI data to remove artifact. It can be used directly for prediction analyses or extended to build more advanced machine learning algorithms, such as neural networks. The broad differences in how this model is used for prediction and explanation are discussed next.

5.1.1 Linear model: prediction compared to explanation

The columns of X are typically referred to as *features* in prediction models, and *regressors* in models focused on explanation. The values within β are often called *feature weights* in the case of predic-

Advances in Magnetic Resonance Technology and Applications, Volume 4, ISSN 2666-9099. https://doi.org/10.1016/B978-0-12-822479-3.00014-2
Copyright © 2021 Elsevier Inc. All rights reserved.

71

72 Chapter 5 Statistical approaches to neuroimaging analysis

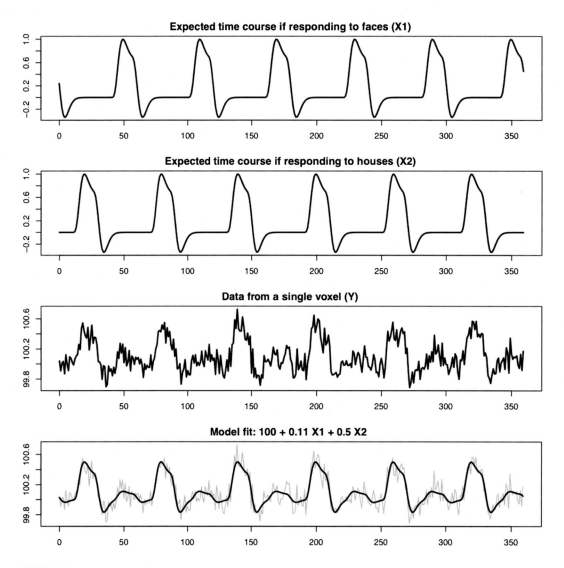

FIGURE 5.1

BOLD modeling example. The top two panels are the regressors, which are the expected time course one would see in response to a face and house. The third panel is the dependent variable, Y, a measured time course from a single voxel. The final panel shows the model fit in black and time course in gray. This particular voxel appears to have some activation for each of faces and houses, but to different degrees.

tion and *parameter estimates* in the case of explanation. Aside from these differences in nomenclature, the model $Y = X\beta + \epsilon$ has slightly different generalization goals for prediction and explanation.

5.1 Linear model overview 73

Face/House fMRI Analysis

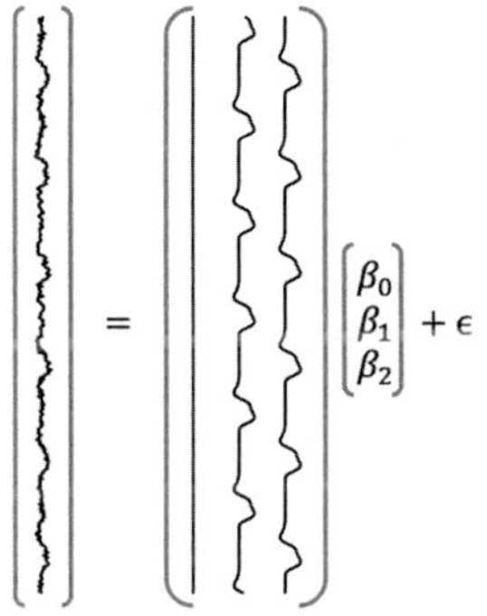

$$\vdots = \vdots \begin{bmatrix} \beta_0 \\ \beta_1 \\ \beta_2 \end{bmatrix} + \epsilon$$

HO: Face Activation = House Activation
HA: Face Activation > House Activation

HO: $\beta_1 - \beta_2 = 0$
HA: $\beta_1 - \beta_2 > 0$

HO: $c\beta = 0$
HA: $c\beta > 0$
$c = [0\ 1\ \text{-}1]$

Fractional Anisotropy difference between groups

$$\begin{pmatrix} 0.71 \\ 0.45 \\ 0.27 \\ 0.63 \\ 0.58 \\ -0.37 \\ -0.59 \\ -0.34 \\ -0.28 \\ -0.60 \end{pmatrix} = \begin{pmatrix} 1 & 0 \\ 1 & 0 \\ 1 & 0 \\ 1 & 0 \\ 1 & 0 \\ 0 & 1 \\ 0 & 1 \\ 0 & 1 \\ 0 & 1 \\ 0 & 1 \end{pmatrix} \begin{bmatrix} \beta_1 \\ \beta_2 \end{bmatrix} + \epsilon$$

HO: Control FA = Patient FA
HA: Control FA > Patient FA

HO: $\beta_1 - \beta_2 = 0$
HA: $\beta_1 - \beta_2 > 0$

HO: $c\beta = 0$
HA: $c\beta > 0$
$c = [1\ \text{-}1]$

FIGURE 5.2

Two model examples in matrix format with hypotheses and contrasts. The left shows the model from Fig. 5.1 in matrix form. Although the actual matrices would contain numbers, the time course images are used for interpretability. The parameters represent the intercept, face activation, and house activation, respectively (β_0, β_1, β_2). To test whether the faces activation was larger than houses activation, the hypotheses and contrast are shown. The right panel illustrates an analysis where fractional anisotropy (FA) measures for a region are compared between control subjects (first 5 subjects) and patients (last 5 subjects), where β_1 and β_2 are the means of the controls and patients, respectively. The hypothesis to test whether FA is larger for controls than patients is also shown.

When predicting, the focus is on how well the estimate of the vector, β (denoted $\hat{\beta}$), generalizes to other data sets. Specifically, if one data set is used to estimate $\hat{\beta}$, how well does $X\hat{\beta}$ match the actual values of Y when X and Y are from a new, independent data set. Importantly, in many cases, the feature's weights cannot be used to understand an underlying mechanism. For example, two features could be nearly identical and have feature weights with opposite signs or one may have a weight of 0, whereas the other is nonzero, which doesn't imply one feature is "better" than the other.

In the case of explanation, a more detailed story about the underlying mechanism is often of interest, and the goal is that the *model* generalizes well to other data sets. In other words, is this a reliable framework for explaining a story? The β estimates may change, but the hope is that the model still fits well. A different thought process is required when selecting regressors for the model and the method used to estimate β will typically yield inferential statistics that can be used to assess each parameter within β as well as linear combinations of the parameters. Regressor choice comes into play when avoiding what is called collinearity, which is discussed below. Collinearity makes interpretation difficult, but may not impede prediction.

5.2 Estimating the parameters of the linear model

Whether the goal is prediction or explanation, an estimate of the vector, β, is required. To begin, it will be assumed that the length of β, p, is much smaller than the number of observations, N. Generally this is required for explanation, although prediction often uses regularized estimation approaches that can handle $p > N$. The estimate for β, denoted by $\hat{\beta}$, aims to find an estimate of Y, $\hat{Y} = X\hat{\beta}$, that is close to the actual values of Y. How is "close" defined? The most typical approach, least squares estimation, measures closeness by the sum of the squared differences between the actual values and their estimates, $(Y - \hat{Y})^T (Y - \hat{Y})$, where T is the matrix transpose. This can also be expressed without using matrices. Assuming β has length 2, this would be

$$(Y - \hat{Y})^T (Y - \hat{Y}) = \sum_{i=1}^{N} (Y_i - (\hat{\beta}_0 + \hat{\beta}_1 X_{1,i}))^2. \tag{5.2}$$

Assuming $N < p$ and that no single column of X can be recreated by linear combinations of other columns of X, it can be shown that this estimate is given by,

$$\hat{\beta} = (X^T X)^{-1} X^T Y. \tag{5.3}$$

The estimated covariance of the vector, $\hat{\beta}$, is given by

$$\widehat{\mathrm{Cov}}\left(\hat{\beta}\right) = (X^T X)^{-1} \hat{\sigma}^2, \tag{5.4}$$

where $\hat{\sigma}^2$ is the estimated variance of the residual vector, ϵ, given by

$$\hat{\sigma}^2 = (Y - \hat{Y})^T (Y - \hat{Y})/(N - p). \tag{5.5}$$

This is the mean squared error scaled by the degrees of freedom or the number of observations, N, minus the number of parameters that have been estimated, p.

5.2.1 Bias and variance

The least squares estimate is unbiased, meaning if you were to repeat many studies and estimate β in each study, the average would equal the truth. Additionally, this estimate has the minimum variance among all unbiased estimates, which refers to the variability in the estimates across repeats of the study. It could be the case that a different estimator produces a biased estimate with a lower variance, but why would we want to bias our estimate? This is another difference between explanation and prediction. Variance can interfere with obtaining a good prediction and biasing some of the feature weights, typically shrinking them toward or setting them to zero can help improve prediction. On the other hand, biased parameter estimates may interfere with explanation. Generally, explanatory models stick within the category of unbiased estimators and avoid potential issues in interpretation by avoiding collinearity and require many more samples than parameters, $N > p$. Prediction models often have $N < p$ and balance bias and variance to improve out-of-sample prediction using regularized estimators instead of least squares.

5.2.2 Collinearity

When regressors are highly correlated, the variance of our estimated parameters is quite large, and this is especially problematic in explanatory modeling and is something to avoid, whereas is it less problematic in prediction. This will be illustrated with a simple example.

Assume we have 10 subjects for which we have the gray matter density measures from two highly correlated voxels and age. In the explanatory setting, the goal would be to understand how each of these voxels relates to age, whereas for prediction, we want to test whether we can accurately predict age with the gray matter density of these voxels. In both cases, the model of interest is the following: $Age = \beta_0 + \beta_1 GM_1 + \beta_2 GM_2 + \epsilon$ (Fig. 5.3). Using least squares estimation, the parameter estimates are found to be $\hat{\beta}_0 = -36.59$, $\hat{\beta}_1 = -5.82$ and $\hat{\beta}_2 = 7.59$, and all are statistically different from 0. These voxels are almost identical (correlation = 0.98), so how could their true relationships with age be so different with opposite signs? High collinearity is driving high variability in the estimated parameters, and these are of little use for explanation. Due to the lack in interpretability in the presence of collinearity, it is avoided in explanatory modeling settings. In this case, the researcher should either pick one voxel or create a summary measure of the two to use in the model.

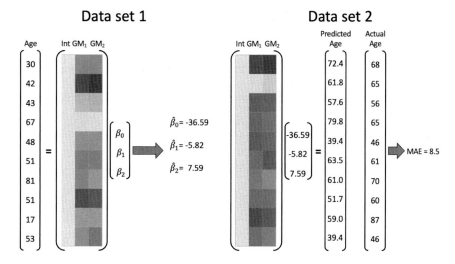

FIGURE 5.3

Collinearity's impact on explanation and prediction. Age is modeled as a function of gray matter density for two voxels, GM_1 and GM_2, where the GM density values are indicated in gray scale, and the intercept is a column of 1 s. The GM densities are highly correlated (> 0.95), and the high collinearity causes the estimates of β_1 and β_2, based on data set 1 (left), to be wildly different. This conflicts with the regressors being nearly identical. Although the parameters are not useful for explanation, prediction in a second data set (right) is decent, where the mean absolute error is 8.5 years.

Interestingly, this model does fine with prediction. One cannot assess predictive accuracy using the same data from which the parameter estimates were derived, so assume we have a second data set of the same measures in 10 new subjects. Fig. 5.3 shows that the predicted ages are decent, even though the parameter estimates weren't all that interpretable when viewing the model as explanatory. The mean

76 **Chapter 5** Statistical approaches to neuroimaging analysis

absolute error (MAE) between age and predicted ages is only 8.5 years, which isn't bad considering how small the sample used to fit the model is. This illustrates that feature weights may result in great predictions, when the weights themselves may not be interpretable.

5.3 Topics related to explanation

Explanatory analyses are typically built to test statistical hypotheses involving parameters in the model. Hypothesis tests have two parts: the thing you hope isn't true (the null hypothesis or H0) and the thing you hope is true (the alternative hypothesis or HA). Fig. 5.2 lays out 2 models and a hypothesis for each. Focusing on the second model, the goal is to find whether controls have larger FA than patients, making HA:$\beta_1 > \beta_2$ and H0:$\beta_1 = \beta_2$. We can test this hypothesis using the inferential steps below and properly controlling for false positives and designing studies with high power, or we can test for the ability to detect effects when present, which is also of great importance.

5.3.1 Contrast estimates

Often, hypotheses require combining multiple parameters in the model, for example, the FA analysis aims to test whether $\beta_1 > \beta_2$. This can be equivalently expressed as $\beta_1 - \beta_2 > 0$, so our statistic of interest should correspond to this difference. These linear combinations of parameter estimates are created by finding a row vector, c, such that the product, $c\beta$ yields the quantity of interest. In this case, $c = [1, -1]$ would be the appropriate contrast. Fig. 5.2 also displays the contrast for testing whether face activation is larger than house activation in the earlier discussed fMRI example. For a contrast, c, the estimated contrast of parameter estimates and corresponding variance are given by $c\hat{\beta}$ and $c\left[\widehat{\text{Cov}}\left(\hat{\beta}\right)\right]c^T$.

5.3.2 Inference

The first step in hypothesis testing, or inference, is defining your null and alternative hypotheses. Next you need a test statistic based on your data, and then you can calculate a p-value, which is used to assess your statistic. Continuing with the FA/group difference example, our model and contrast are shown in the right panel of Fig. 5.2. The t statistic used to evaluate this contrast estimate is given by the ratio of the contrast estimate and the standard error,

$$t = \frac{c\hat{\beta}}{\sqrt{\widehat{\text{Var}}\left(c\hat{\beta}\right)}} = \frac{c(X^T X)^{-1} X^T Y}{\sqrt{c(X^T X)^{-1} c^T \hat{\sigma}^2}}, \tag{5.6}$$

where Eqs. (5.3) and (5.5) define $\hat{\beta}$ and $\hat{\sigma}^2$. Under the assumption that the null is true, this statistic follows a t-distribution, which has a single parameter: the degrees of freedom (DoF). The DoF of the t-distribution reflect the variability, and as the DoF increase, the t-distribution will be very similar to the Gaussian distribution. The DoF are $N - p$ and reflect the quality of the estimate, $\hat{\sigma}^2$, which we are using in place of the true variance. For the FA example, we have $N = 10$ subjects and 2 parameters in our model, so the degrees of freedom are 8. The estimates are $\hat{\beta}_1 = 0.528$ and $\hat{\beta}_2 = -0.436$, yielding a contrast estimate of $c\hat{\beta} = 0.528 - (-0.436) = 0.964$ ($c = [1, -1]$). Lastly, $\widehat{Var}\left(c\hat{\beta}\right) = 0.0103$, yielding a t statistic of $t = 0.964/\sqrt{0.0103} = 9.50$. The next question is whether this would be expected if there was no signal in our data.

The p-value is commonly misinterpreted. We assume the null hypothesis is true, and then calculate the probability of observing our statistic or something more extreme than it under this null distribution. Note, "more extreme" refers to the direction of the alternative hypothesis. In this case, we would estimate the probability of 9.50 or larger under the null, a t distribution with 8 degrees of freedom, which is $p = 0.000006$. Seems pretty small, but how small is small enough? The most commonly used threshold is $p = 0.05$. The meaning of this threshold is that if we do not have any true signal in our data we will only make a mistake (false positive) 5% of the time. In this case, one would conclude there's a statistically significant group difference.

This and most hypothesis tests in neuroimaging are 1-sided, meaning the alternative focuses on a parameter of a particular sign. In all standard statistics software, the default p-values reflect 2-sided tests, testing whether the effect is simply different than 0. The two-sided p-values are typically twice as large, and therefore one-sided tests should be reserved for situations where we have strong evidence that the effect will be in a certain direction. Running two 1-sided tests in place of a single 2-sided test is bad practice, because it inflates the false positive rate, which will be discussed shortly. Although it is common to ignore in neuroimaging, it is worth working toward changing this practice and either running 2-sided tests by default or by adjusting properly when two 1-sided tests are run.

If the p-value is above 0.05, one cannot conclude that H0 is true since the p-value is conditional on the null hypothesis being true. The implication is that this type of test will not be useful if you are trying to prove if two things are the same, for example whether the mean is the same for patients and controls. A different analysis strategy or new hypotheses would be needed in this case.

5.3.3 Multiple comparisons

Assume you're analyzing 101,000 voxels, where 100,000 of these voxels contain no signal, whereas 1000 voxels do (Table 5.1). Assuming voxels are independent, a p-value cutoff of 0.05 implies there will be 5000 false positives or Type I errors. In reality, our voxels are not independent, so false positives will typically appear as small blobs on the brain that are tempting to interpret as real effects. To deal with this issue, we use methods for controlling the error rate. Although the Bonferroni correction is a well-known method for controlling Type I error; it assumes all tests are independent and is too conservative for imaging data. Instead, we typically focus on cluster-based statistics and correcting the error rates for these statistics. Although it is beyond the scope of this chapter, interested readers can refer to Lindquist and Mejia (2015), Eklund et al. (2016), and Chapter 7 of Poldrack et al. (2011) for more details.

5.3.4 Power

To understand power, let's focus on the second column of Table 5.1, where HA is true. If we have 80% power, that indicates we will detect 800 of the 1000 voxels that truly have signal. If one is interested in maximizing the power for a study, this must be considered prior to data collection. Generally, power will be increased if our t statistics are large, which will happen if the denominator of our statistic, or

78 **Chapter 5** Statistical approaches to neuroimaging analysis

Table 5.1 Illustration of Type I error and Power. Type 1 error conditions on H0 being true, whereas power conditions on HA being true.

	H0 true	HA true	
$p < 0.05$	5000 (Type I error)	800 (Power)	5800
$p \geq 0.05$	95,000	200 (Type II error)	95,200
	100,000	1000	101,000

the variance, is small: $c(X^T X)^{-1} c^T \hat{\sigma}^2$ (Eq. (5.6)). Assuming we cannot make the signal stronger or the residual variance smaller, power is modestly controlled through the sample size.

For a 1-sample t-test, the design matrix, X, consists of a single column of 1s such that $(X^T X)^{-1} = 1/N$, so doubling the sample size reduces the variance by a factor of $1/\sqrt{2}$. For most models, the power can be calculated as a function of N. If a good estimate of the value of β and σ can be made based on pre-existing studies, it is possible to calculate the power over a range of sample sizes. Typically the sample size associated with power larger than 80% or 90% is preferred. Further information about power analyses can be found in Mumford (2011) and Bausell and Li (2002).

5.3.5 Efficiency

As mentioned earlier, collinearity can interfere with interpretation in explanatory models due to high variability in the parameter estimates. In the case of fMRI analyses, most of the regressors that will go into the model for the time course data are known prior to data collection, because they mostly rely on parameters of the task design, such as the timing and order of stimuli. The BOLD signal we measure in fMRI studies is blurred and delayed from the actual neuronal signal, because we are measuring changes in blood oxygenation. This can often lead to collinearity in models if stimuli are not separated over time. Take, for example, an item recognition task where a subject is first shown a set of letters, say {A, T, E, M} (target), and after a brief pause they are shown a single letter, say T, and must respond "Yes" or "No" to indicate whether this single letter was contained in the preceding set (probe). For this illustration the yes/no response and correctness will be ignored. To study the brain processes for target and probe separately, we would need a separate regressor for each of the target and probe portions of the task. As shown in Fig. 5.4, the regressors will be more highly correlated if the time between the target and probe is short. The inverse of the quantity, $c(X^T X)^{-1} c^T$ from the denominator of our t statistic (Eq. (5.6)), is called efficiency and can be used to rank designs. In the case of the two designs in Fig. 5.4, the contrast estimate for either the target or probe for the second design is 1.97 times more efficient than the first, indicating the variance estimate for the contrast using the top design will be 1.97 times larger! There isn't a specific threshold for efficiency as it is only a relative measure that can be used to rank a set of study designs. It is important to consider during a behavioral pilot run prior to an fMRI study, to ensure any behavioral effects found there are not impeded by having to space out stimuli to meet the requirements of efficiency for a future fMRI study. Good resources for efficiency are Liu et al. (2001) and Kao et al. (2009).

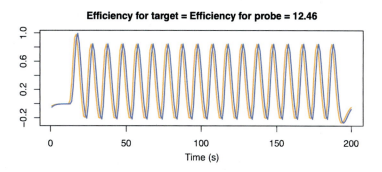
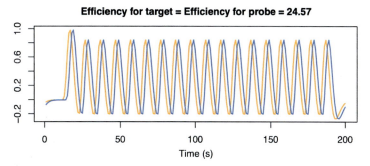

FIGURE 5.4

Regressors for an item recognition fMRI task that consists of a target (orange) and probe (blue). In the top panel, only 0.25 s elapse between the end of the target and beginning of the probe, whereas the bottom panel has a 1 s separation. Efficiency is equal for both the target and probe regressors in each design and is 1.97 times higher for the bottom design compared to the top, which means the variance of the parameter estimates is 1.97 times higher for the top design.

Typically one generates many task designs, calculates the efficiency of each, and then ranks them, but they may all have very high collinearity. One way to avoid this is to use the metric variance inflation factor (VIF), a collinearity assessment tool. It provides a VIF for each parameter in your model, and the goal is that all VIFs are below 5. Both designs in Fig. 5.4 have VIFs below 5 for the parameters (2.28 for each parameter in the top model and 1.56 for the bottom). The details of the VIF calculation will not be explored here, but see Chapter 11 of Rawlings et al. (1998) for more detail. VIF should be used to ensure collinearity has been avoided and efficiency can further refine the model choice to further reduce the variance.

5.4 Topics related to prediction

Although it is rare to use the linear regression model directly for prediction analyses, most prediction models can be thought of as extensions of this model. The main addition is to regularize parameter esti-

80 Chapter 5 Statistical approaches to neuroimaging analysis

mates by adding a little bias. Additionally, cross validation must be incorporated to estimate predictive performance. These topics are discussed below, and a great resource for machine learning is Hastie et al. (2001).

5.4.1 Cross validation

The goal in prediction is to test how well an estimate of $\hat{\beta}$ generalizes to new data. Specifically if one estimates $\hat{\beta}_{train}$ using a data set Y_{train}, X_{train}, then how close is Y_{test} to $X_{test}\hat{\beta}_{train}$ for a second data set Y_{test}, X_{test}? This was illustrated in Fig. 5.3. If, instead, one compares Y_{train} to $X_{train}\hat{\beta}_{train}$, the predictive ability will be overestimated. This occurs because a model will always fit the noise in the data to some extent, so the comparison of Y_{train} to $X_{train}\hat{\beta}_{train}$ will reflect both the ability to recreate signal and noise, whereas an independent data set will reflect the ability to recreate signal. For example, if data set 1 (Fig. 5.3) is used to both estimate β and test the predictive ability, the MAE is 3.95, which is much smaller than the out-of-sample prediction's MAE (8.5).

You can still obtain predictions for all observations in a single sample using cross validation. It begins by dividing the data into, say, 10 equally sized chunks. This would be for a 10-fold cross validation. If your data set had 200 subjects, you would randomly split the data into 10 sets of 20, and you would carry out the following steps:

1. Assign the first set of 20 subjects as test data and other 180 as train data.
2. Fit the model to the 180 training samples to obtain $\hat{\beta}_{train}$.
3. Predict values for the test data using $X_{test}\hat{\beta}_{train}$ and store these values for later.
4. Repeat steps 1–3 nine more times using each of the other sets of 20 subjects as test data.
5. Compare all 200 predicted values to their true values to assess accuracy.

The data in your test and train data must be independent or your accuracies will be inflated. The first time I ran a cross validation, I was excited to have a very high classification accuracy, but realized it wasn't realistic. I had multiple measures for each of 30 subjects and hadn't been careful that all data from a single subject were contained completely within the test or training data. By having some data for each subject in both data sets, the accuracy was inflated. This is referred to as a peeking bias.

How many folds should one have? Common choices are 5- or 10-fold cross validation, but the best choice is dependent upon how many samples you have in your data since larger training sets should yield better parameter estimates. For more details, see Chapter 7 of Hastie et al. (2001).

5.4.2 Regularization

Typically, one would not use a standard linear regression for prediction since there are often more features than observations. This is often referred to as "wide data" since the design matrix, X, is wider than it is tall. The idea of regularization goes back to the bias-variance tradeoff that was mentioned earlier. Although unbiased parameter estimates sound attractive, they can lead to highly variable predictions. Regularization focuses on the bias and variance separately, allowing one to arrive at a balance of the two that ends up reducing the overall prediction error compared to a least squares estimate. The biasing typically involves shrinking the feature weights to 0, where the degree of shrinkage is controlled by regularization parameters, and how this is done differs greatly between methods. A class of regularization methods referred to as "L1" will gradually shrink feature weights, and then suddenly set some weights to 0 as the shrinkage parameter increases. In this case, one cannot assign the same interpretation to feature weight estimates as we tend to do with standard linear regression parameter estimates. If two features are highly correlated, the L1-regularization is likely to simply set the feature weight of one of these to 0. It isn't choosing the "best" feature to have the nonzero weight. Lasso regression is a commonly used L1 regularized regression model.

Another commonly used regularization strategy is called "L2" and, instead, gently shrinks all feature weights, without shrinking some strictly to 0. Ridge regression is the most well-known version of this strategy. The parameter estimates are a bit more interpretable, but it is still a dangerous game to assign importance to different features. Even with least squares regression, the regressors work together to do a job. A regressor with a smaller parameter may be lending a hand to another regressor with a much larger parameter.

5.4.3 More advanced prediction models

The simplest machine learning approaches rely on human intervention to input meaningful features that can predict well. For example, if trying to classify images of a retina as being healthy or showing disease, processing steps may need to be applied to the image first to develop meaningful features, say lesion counts. Deep learning methods differ in that the algorithm takes over this job of creating more meaningful features to improve prediction. Although these methods may seem far removed from linear regression, there is a link between linear regression and simple neural networks, which can then be related to the more modern deep learning approaches. The goal here is to make that first connection in understanding.

Say a drywall expert, plumber, and electrician are working together to renovate homes, and the general idea is to relate the amount of time each worker spends on a home to the renovation quality (RQ). In this case, the model would be $RQ = \beta_1 t_{dw} + \beta_2 t_{elec} + \beta_3 t_{plumb} + \epsilon$. A graph depicting this model is shown in the left panel of Fig. 5.5 and reflects a standard linear regression model. In reality, the time each of these workers spends on the house and the resulting renovation quality depend on how much time they spent working together on different types of room, and then the overall renovation quality may be better explained by a function of the collective efforts in each room type. The assumption I'm making here is that for each house the electrician's time, for example, will be split across room types for all homes in the same way, and let's also assume the houses are all similar in terms of how many of each room type they have. The true relationship between time spent and renovation quality might be closer to what is shown in the right panel of Fig. 5.5. This is a simple linear feed forward neural network with one hidden layer. This single hidden layer contains two nodes or neurons which are, effectively, new and improved features. Although one does specify the number of nodes and layers, what the nodes represent isn't specified. They will be determined during the estimation and may not have an intuitive meaning, such as room type. Either way, each of the nodes within this layer consists of a weighted sum of a portion of each worker's time. For example, $l1 = \beta_{11} t_{dw} + \beta_{12} t_{elec} + \beta_{13} t_{plumb}$, which looks a lot like a linear model within a larger linear model. One level of complexity beyond this linear relationship is to instead allow for nonlinearities at each node. For example, $l1 = f1(\beta_{11} t_{dw} + \beta_{12} t_{elec} + \beta_{13} t_{plumb})$, where $f1$ is some nonlinear function that, for example, constrains the values in $l1$ to be between 0 and 1. Bias terms are typically also included to further control the contribution of each node's contribution by adding a constant, $l1 = f1(\beta_{11} t_{dw} + \beta_{12} t_{elec} + \beta_{13} t_{plumb} + \beta_{10})$. The number of parameters involved in this model is very high and the estimation is more involved than least squares regression. For more on deep learning methods see Nielsen (2015), which is freely available online.

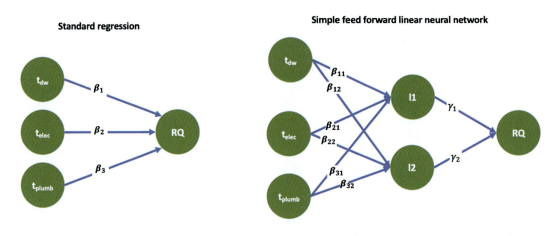

FIGURE 5.5

The left panel illustrates a simple linear regression model in graphic form. The right panel is a simple feed forward linear neural network with one layer consisting of two nodes.

References

Bausell, R., Li, Y.F., 2002. Power Analysis for Experimental Research: A Practical Guide for the Biological, Medical and Social Sciences. Cambridge University Press.

Eklund, A., Nichols, T., Knutsson, H., 2016. Cluster failure: why fmri inferences for spatial extent have inflated false-positive rates. Proceedings of the National Academy of Sciences 114, E4929. https://doi.org/10.1073/pnas.1602413113.

Hastie, T., Tibshirani, R., Friedman, J., 2001. The Elements of Statistical Learning: Data Mining, Inference and Prediction. Springer Series in Statistics.

Kao, M.H., Mandal, A., Lazar, N., Stufken, J., 2009. Multi-objective optimal experimental designs for event-related fmri studies. NeuroImage 44, 849–856. https://doi.org/10.1016/j.neuroimage.2008.09.025.

Lindquist, M., Mejia, A., 2015. Zen and the art of multiple comparisons. Psychosomatic Medicine 77, 114–125. https://doi.org/10.1097/PSY.0000000000000148.

Liu, T., Frank, L., Buxton, R., 2001. Detection power, estimation efficiency, and predictability in event-related fmri. NeuroImage 13, 759–773. https://doi.org/10.1006/nimg.2000.0728.

Mumford, J., 2011. A power calculation guide for fmri studies. Social Cognitive and Affective Neuroscience 7, 738–742. https://doi.org/10.1093/scan/nss059.

Nielsen, M., 2015. Neural Networks and Deep Learning. Determination Press.

Poldrack, R., Mumford, J., Nichols, T., 2011. Handbook of Functional MRI Data Analysis. Cambridge University Press.

Rawlings, J., Pantula, S.G., Dickey, D.A., 1998. Applied Regression Analysis: A Research Tool. Springer Texts in Statistics.

CHAPTER

Image registration

6

Hui Zhang

Centre for Medical Image Computing and Department of Computer Science, UCL, London,
United Kingdom

6.1 Introduction

Image registration emerged as a process of significant practical importance long before the dawn of the digital revolution in the 1940s. The process found its first application in color printing, where multi-color patterns are formed by layering together several mono-chromatic designs (Yoshida and Yuki, 1966). To produce the desired final multi-color prints, the alignment of the individual layers with respect to one another must be exact. During the course of printing, due to imperfections in machine components, individual layers can become misaligned, known as out of register. So processes were developed to detect and correct any misalignment to ensure accurate registration. These processes, known variably as printing registration or color registration, were the forebears of the topic of this chapter.

As the digital revolution ushered in the era of modern medical imaging that we know today, image registration has become an indispensable tool for many applications of imaging in healthcare (Hajnal et al., 2001; Hill et al., 2001). Though MRI was not among the first medical imaging technologies that had made use of image registration, it is arguably the one technique that has benefited the most. Among the MRI techniques reviewed in this book, a large majority require image registration as an essential preprocessing step. The reason for this is exactly what had motivated the invention of image registration for color printing. For many MRI techniques, as in color printing, the final image or images must be synthesized from a set of input images in exact correspondence. As the set of input images is acquired sequentially, imperfections over the course of acquisition, such as subject motion, can render some or all of the input to become out of register, necessitating the use of image registration.

However, today this is only one of the many important roles image registration plays in MRI, and in medical imaging more generally. The drive to meet this diverse set of needs has prompted a great variety of image registration techniques being developed over the past decades (Maintz and Viergever, 1998; Sotiras et al., 2013). Also, in the past few years, just as in many other fields, the remarkable success of deep learning in tackling general image analysis problems has led to an explosion of interest in using this emerging technology to reinvent image registration (Fu et al., 2020; Haskins et al., 2020). In this context, the aim of this chapter is to give an overview of the key applications of image registration in MRI, the classes of image registration techniques developed to address these challenges, and the future deep learning brings.

84   **Chapter 6** Image registration

6.2 **Applications**

The applications of image registration can be categorized, based on the subject or subjects of whom the images are acquired, into two broad types: within-subject (also known as intra-subject), when the images to be registered are all from the same subject, and between-subject (also known as inter-subject), when the images are from different subjects.

Within-subject applications were the original driver of image registration in medical imaging. In the 1980s, with the rapid advance in multiple medical imaging technologies that offer complementary information of the imaged subject, there was great interest in the fusion of data from different modalities. In particular, a major research focus was to enable the fusion of MRI and PET data from the same individual, as this would allow detailed physiological information, provided by PET, to be attributed to specific anatomical locations that can be more accurately ascertained with MRI than with PET. Within-subject image registration was required to correct differences in the positioning of the subject, in image resolution and in image distortion. Today, data fusion remains an important application of within-subject image registration, even in MRI-only exams, which typically include a battery of MRI modalities, many of which are covered in this book. As typical imaging sessions can last half an hour or more, it is impossible for even the most compliant participants to stay still over such a long period. In addition, different MRI modalities typically exhibit distinct image distortion and can also differ in image resolution, making within-subject image registration essential for multi-modal fusion.

The second class of within-subject applications, as first mentioned in the introduction, is to serve as a requisite pre-processing step for a number of MRI modalities that synthesize their output from a set of images acquired serially, often under varying experimental settings. Though in many instances, such as functional MRI, subject motion is the main cause for images becoming out of register, a prominent exception is diffusion MRI. The so-called multi-shell acquisition, commonly used for neuroimaging, can consist of hundreds of individual images acquired serially with two or more diffusion-sensitizing factors (b-values) and hundreds of different diffusion-sensitizing gradient directions. Different diffusion-sensitizing factors, coupled with different diffusion-sensitizing gradient directions, induce image distortion of varying magnitudes and forms (see Chapter 9). Thus, even in the absence of subject motion these images will be out of register. Within-subject image registration must be carried out before these images can be combined to estimate target quantities, such as diffusion tensors and fiber orientation distribution functions.

The final class of within-subject applications is to enable the use of serially-acquired MRI scans for assessing changes over time. The baseline MRI scan of an individual can be compared against one or more follow-up scans to quantify temporal changes to anatomical structures in terms of either morphology or contrast. Such comparison has been used to establish the growth trajectory of brain structures during normal development, as well as to quantify the pattern of accelerated brain atrophy in patients with dementia. Within-subject image registration is required here both to correct for, and to quantify, differences in morphology of the corresponding anatomies. Another important application is in image-guided neurosurgical navigation to compensate for the deformation of brain structures during neurosurgery, known as brain shift. Image-guided neurosurgery is planned with preoperative scans, but brain shift can lead to significant navigational errors that must be compensated for. This can be achieved by the acquisition of additional scans during operations. Registering pre- and intra-operative scans allows the extent of brain shift to be ascertained and be corrected for. This idea of estimating deformation from serial scans is also important for MR-guided radiotherapy, which typically involves a

6.2 Applications

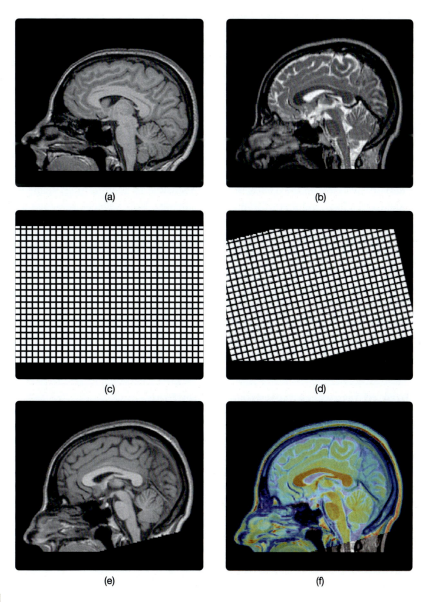

FIGURE 6.1

An illustration of image fusion with within-subject registration. Panels (a) and (b) show the T_1-weighted (T_1w) and T_2-weighted (T_2w) MRI brain scans of a healthy subject. A within-subject registration is applied to align the T_1w scan with its T_2w counterpart. This involves first finding a geometric transformation that places the T_1w scan into register with the T_2w scan. This transformation is visualized with a regular grid, shown in Panel (c), and the same grid after the transformation has been applied, shown in Panel (d). Panel (e) shows the T_1w scan after this transformation has been applied, which is now aligned with the T_2w scan. This realizes the fusion of the two different contrasts from the same subject, as shown in Panel (f). The code and the data used to generate this illustration are available as a GitHub public repository (Zhang, 2021) and also at https://www.elsevier.com/books-and-journals/book-companion/9780128224793.

86   **Chapter 6** Image registration

series of fractional treatments over multiple visits. With the development of hybrid MR-linac systems, MRI data can be readily acquired at each visit to provide an up-to-date picture of the treatment target (e.g., a brain tumor) and its surrounding structures. Registering scans from consecutive visits enables any positional and morphological changes in between the visits to be precisely quantified, allowing treatment plans to be adapted appropriately. With the fastest available MRI techniques, target motion can even be monitored and thus compensated for real time, promising a future of radiotherapy with unprecedented accuracy.

While within-subject applications prompted the earliest use of image registration, between-subject applications have been providing the impetus for the majority of research into image registration in the past two decades (Sotiras et al., 2013; Viergever et al., 2016). In particular, since MRI scanners became commercially available in the 1980s, it became feasible to acquire brain scans with exquisite anatomical details from a large number of living human beings. This advance heralded an exciting era of brain imaging research that has continued to this day, enabling neuroscientists to investigate the commonalities and variabilities of brain anatomy across a large cohort of individuals, as well as to study differences between cohorts, such as between healthy controls and individuals with dementia (Toga, 1998). The key challenge to overcome was the spatial alignment of scans from different individuals, as between-subject variations in brain size and shape turned out to be far greater than what could be accounted for with the early image registration methods developed for within-subject applications (Friston et al., 1995). Addressing this challenge of spatial normalization has spurred on the development of increasingly sophisticated image registration techniques that we will review later.

6.3 Structure of image registration algorithms

Though a large number of image registration algorithms have been developed over the years, they share a common structure and a standard set of building blocks, and differ from one another only in the implementation details of one or more of these building blocks. This section introduces this common structure and the standard components of an image registration algorithm. It will provide the conceptual framework for understanding the difference between the classes of algorithms reviewed in the next section and how deep learning can be used to develop the next-generation approaches.

The common structure and building blocks for image registration can be understood from a study of the workings of its forebear. In printing registration, to align two color layers, operators keep one layer fixed in place while adjusting the placement of the other. To judge how well the layers are aligned, they make use of the registration marks, two small marks etched onto each layer to indicate the positions that should correspond when layers are in register. Operators can conclude that the two layers are aligned when the distances between the corresponding registration marks are minimized. This example illustrates several important points about an image registration algorithm. The first is that the task of registering two images can be formulated as finding an adjustment to the placement of one image, the *moving image*, relative to the other, the *fixed image*, i.e., a *geometric transformation*, that places the moving image into alignment with the fixed image. The example also reveals the first essential building block of an image registration algorithm: a measure of alignment quality between two images, known as the *similarity measure*. A similarity measure shall be determined from some features of the image pair; the set of features chosen is often referred to as the *feature space*. In this example, the

6.3 Structure of image registration algorithms

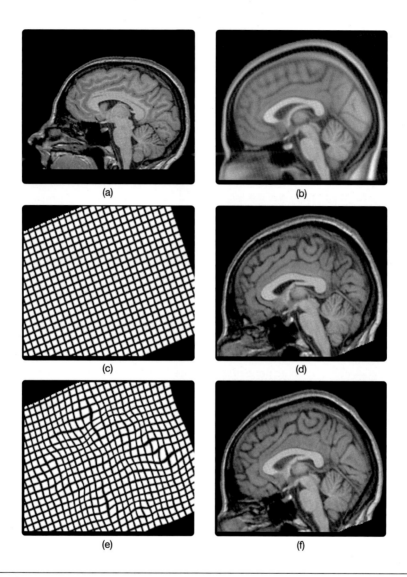

FIGURE 6.2

An illustration of spatial normalization with between-subject registration. Panel (a) shows the T_1-weighted (T_1w) MRI brain scans of a healthy subject. Panel (b) shows the MNI152 T_1w template developed by the Montreal Neurological Institute (MNI) from averaging brain MRI scans of 152 healthy subjects (Fonov et al., 2011). A between-subject registration is applied to align the T_1w scan with the MNI152 template. This involves first applying a linear registration to find a linear transformation that makes the T_1w scan broadly resemble the template in size and shape. The resulting linear transformation is visualized with its action on a regular grid as shown in Panel (c). The effect of this transformation on the T_1w scan is shown in Panel (d). Following the linear registration, a non-linear registration is applied to find a non-linear transformation to match the T_1w scan to the template in detail. Panel (e) visualizes the resulting non-linear transformation. Panel (f) shows the T_1w scan after this transformation has been applied, which is now spatially normalized with respect to the standard space defined by the template. The code and the data used to generate this illustration are available as a GitHub public repository (Zhang, 2021) also also at https://www.elsevier.com/books-and-journals/book-companion/9780128224793.

88 **Chapter 6** Image registration

registration marks on the color layers are used as the features; the similarity measure is some function of the distances between the corresponding registration marks.

Considering the printing registration example further, observe that the number of possible placement adjustments is infinite, but a trained operator can find the right adjustment in just a few moves by following a defined strategy. The strategy starts with picking, arbitrarily, one of the two registration marks. They then move one color layer relative to the other until the corresponding versions of this mark align. Next, they rotate one color layer relative to the other, about the aligned registration mark, until the corresponding versions of the second registration mark align. In practice, the rotation step may render the first registration mark to become slightly out of register, so the two steps need to be repeated a few times to achieve the final alignment. This further analysis illustrates the other two essential building blocks of an image registration algorithm. One is some *search strategy* to find the right geometric transformation from the infinite possibilities efficiently. In this example, the search strategy is an instance of alternating optimization. The other is the family of geometric transformations to be considered as potential candidates, known as the *transformation space*. This defines the space in which the search algorithm needs to search for the desired solution. Transformation space shall be chosen based on what is appropriate for the registration task at hand. In this example, geometric transformations must not deform color layers, thus the transformation space contains only translations (shifting left/right or up/down) and rotations.

In summary, an algorithm for registering two images is a procedure that follows some prescribed search strategy to seek a geometric transformation, within some pre-specified transformation space. The desired geometric transformation, when applied to the moving image, should maximize its alignment to the target image, as assessed by some pre-defined similarity measure defined over some feature space. The three essential ingredients of an image registration algorithm are thus: 1) a transformation space; 2) a search strategy through the transformation space; and 3) a similarity measure defined over some feature space (Brown, 1992).

6.4 **Taxonomy of image registration algorithms**

This section reviews the different classes of image registration algorithms available today, classified based on the essential building blocks introduced in the previous section.

6.4.1 **Classification based on transformation space**

One of the most common classification schemes based on transformation space is to categorize image registration algorithms as either *linear* or *non-linear*. An algorithm is considered linear if candidate transformations drawn from its transformation space always transform a set of parallel straight lines into another set of parallel straight lines; such transformations are known as linear, or *affine*, transformations. In contrast, an algorithm is considered non-linear if its transformation space includes candidates that can transform a straight line into a curve; such transformations are known as non-linear, or *deformable*, transformations.

Based on transformation space, image registration algorithms can also be classified as either *rigid* or *non-rigid*. An algorithm is considered rigid if its candidate transformations are linear, and additionally, preserve the length of straight line segments; such length-preserving linear transformations are

6.4 Taxonomy of image registration algorithms

known as rigid transformations. Printing registration is an example of a rigid algorithm, as translations and rotations are length-preserving. Rigid image registration is commonly used for within-subject applications, to correct for any differences in position and orientation between images of the same subject when no differences in size and shape are expected, such as motion correction. Fig. 6.1D illustrates the effect of a rigid transformation through its action on a regular grid shown in Fig. 6.1C. An algorithm is considered non-rigid if its transformation space includes candidates that are not length-preserving; such transformations are known as non-rigid transformations. Non-rigid transformations include all deformable transformations and non-rigid linear transformations. Between-subject applications typically require the use of non-rigid image registration to correct for significant differences in size and shape between subjects. In particular, non-rigid linear image registration is used to match *global* shape and size, as well as the position and orientation; an example is shown in Fig. 6.2C. Deformable image registration is then applied to match *local* shape and size; an example is shown in Fig. 6.2E. Some within-subject applications also require non-rigid image registration. One important example is the correction for eddy-current induced geometric distortions in diffusion MRI (see also Chapter 9). As mentioned in Section 6.2, the eddy current produced by a diffusion-sensitizing gradient induces a geometric distortion of the acquired image. It turns out that this geometric distortion can be well approximated as a non-rigid linear transformation. As a result, it is corrected for with non-rigid linear image registration. Moreover, the form of the non-rigid linear transformation is significantly dictated by the properties of the diffusion-sensitizing gradient. Some techniques exploit this relationship to produce a high-quality initial guess of the linear transformation required. Another example is the correction for susceptibility-induced geometric distortion in echo-planar imaging (EPI). Susceptibility differences across soft tissue interfaces with bone or air induce highly localized, and non-linear, geometric distortion. In the absence of any additional information, such as an otherwise identical acquisition but with the EPI phase-encoding direction reversed, the geometric distortion can be corrected for by aligning the EPI image to the T_1-weighted scan of the same individual with non-linear image registration.

Another useful way to categorize image registration algorithms is to use the dimensionality of transformation space. As the name suggests, the dimensionality of a transformation space is a measure of the size of the space to search for the optimal transformation; the larger the dimensionality is, the more challenging it is to find the optimal transformation efficiently. For a transformation space, its dimensionality is defined as the degrees of freedom (DoF) of the transformations belonging to the space. For example, rigid transformations have six DoF (three for translations and three for rotations); it is the smallest transformation space we have considered, thus the simplest to search for a solution transformation. General linear transformations, which have rigid transformations as a special case, have six additional DoF (three for scaling and three for shearing), making linear image registration more complex than its rigid counterpart. In contrast, non-linear transformations can have many orders of magnitude larger DoF. For example, consider one of the most popular families of non-linear transformations: free-form deformations, with cubic B-splines as the basis function set (Rueckert et al., 1999). The dimensionality of the corresponding transformation space is equal to $3n_x n_y n_z$ where n_x, n_y, and n_z are the number of so-called B-spline control points along x, y, and z axes. For registering a pair of standard high-resolution T_1-weighted scans, the typical choice for these numbers are $n_x = n_y = n_z = 40$; the resulting dimensionality is 192,000, which is 16,000 times that of linear transformations. However, the more recent development in non-linear image registration involves transformation spaces with dimensionalities that are an order of magnitude larger still (Sotiras et al., 2013).

90   **Chapter 6** Image registration

Transformation spaces of such large dimensionalities have been adopted to provide the flexibility to describe the complex morphological differences between subjects, but they also present two significant challenges. One is how to efficiently search for the right solution in such a large space; this challenge will be addressed later as part of the discussion on search strategy. The other is the potential for finding transformations that are inappropriate, e.g., those that leave folds or tears in a transformed image. Transformations that do not cause folding or tearing are known as *topology preserving*. In addition to topology preservation, we commonly require transformations to be *smooth*. Smoothness ensures that a transformation is differentiable. This property guarantees the existence of the *Jacobian matrix*, which can be thought of as the first-order derivative of a transformation. The determinant of this matrix, commonly known as the *Jacobian determinant* or just the *Jacobian*, provides a useful summary measure of local deformation: a value greater than 1 indicating expansion; a value below 1 but above 0 indicating compression. Importantly, it provides a practical means to check whether a transformation is topology preserving. A topology-preserving transformation must only have positive Jacobian determinants. In summary, desirable transformations should be both topology preserving and differentiable; such mappings are known as *diffeomorphic transformations* or *diffeomorphisms*.

Integral to each high-dimensional non-linear image registration is a strategy to prevent the algorithm from producing transformations that are not diffeomorphic; such strategies are known as transformation *regularization*. Regularization strategies provide an important way to classify deformable image registration algorithms. Broadly, they can be categorized as either *explicit* or *implicit* approaches. In explicit approaches, a regularization term is introduced to measure the suitability of a candidate transformation; the objective of the algorithm becomes finding the optimal transformation that maximizes a weighted sum of the similarity measure and the regularization term. Regularization terms are commonly formed from Jacobian determinants to penalize any values that are close to 0. In contrast, implicit approaches encode the desired properties of transformations by construction, i.e., in terms of the mathematical representation of a transformation. For example, free-form deformations, by the use of cubic B-spline basis functions, guarantee that the resulting transformations are smooth. Often, implicit approaches need to be combined with some explicit regularization. Free-form deformations again provide an example, as the construction does not ensure topology preservation. So it becomes necessary to additionally include a regularization term to discourage the use of any topology-breaking mapping.

6.4.2 Classification based on similarity measure

A great variety of similarity measures have been proposed for image registration (Brown, 1992; Maintz and Viergever, 1998; Hill et al., 2001). They can differ either in the choice of the feature space or in the way the features are used to assess image similarity. In the early days of medical image registration, the feature space is often a set of corresponding point landmarks which needs to be identified in advance, e.g., via manual inspection of an expert or some automated method. The similarity measure for such landmark-based image registration is usually the sum of squared distances between the corresponding landmarks. Evidently, printing registration is the earliest example of a landmark-based registration, with the registration marks serving as the landmarks. The landmark-based approach is intuitive, and when computers were not as powerful as today, had the advantage of being very memory and computationally efficient. But identifying corresponding landmarks is not straightforward, especially when a large number is required, e.g., for between-subject applications that need high-dimensional non-linear transformations. A natural generalization to the landmark-based approach is to use corresponding surfaces as the feature space. This takes advantage of the fact that it is considerably easier to identify corresponding surfaces in two images, as this does not require the onerous task of establishing point-wise correspondences as in landmark-based matching. This type of approach is particularly useful for aligning a specific anatomical structure, such as the hippocampus. The similarity measure for such surface-based matching is typically the sum of the closest distances between the vertices of one surface to the other. Today, landmark- and surface-based approaches are not commonly used outside some specific within-subject applications, where rigid or linear transformations are adequate. The feature space of choice now is the entire set of image voxels; similarity measures using this feature space are known as *voxel-based* or *intensity-based*.

Voxel-based similarity measures can be classified as being either intra-modal or inter-modal. Intra-modal similarity measures are designed for applications where two images are of the same modality. The sum of squared intensity difference (SSD), the simplest voxel similarity measure, is of this kind. It assumes that anatomically corresponding structures should have similar voxel values, and any difference can be attributed to noise. However, due to factors such as B_0 or B_1 field non-uniformity, intensity inhomogeneity within anatomically homogeneous tissue is often observed both within and between subjects, which can be substantial enough to lead to SSD performing poorly. Whereas this issue can be mitigated by applying intensity inhomogeneity correction as a pre-processing step, alternative similarity measures that make weaker assumptions about image intensity have also been developed. One popular example is the normalized cross-correlation (NCC), which is the correlation coefficient between the corresponding intensity values of an image pair. Compared to SSD, NCC only assumes that there is a linear relationship between intensities of anatomically corresponding voxels. However, this assumption is still too strong for relating intensities between images of different modalities. To support inter-modal registration with intra-modal similarity measures, one approach is to convert one of the images into the modality of the other. For example, this is used for correcting eddy-current induced distortion to account for contrast variations between volumes acquired with different diffusion-weighting factors and gradients. Alternatively, inter-modal similarity measures can be used, with the best known being the *mutual information* (Wells et al., 1996; Maes et al., 1997). Mutual information (MI) is an example of an information-theoretic similarity measure. It views image registration from the perspective of information theory, and recasts it as a prediction problem, for which the aim is to seek a transformation that maximizes the probability of predicting the moving image from the fixed image. The underlying assumption is that intensity values of anatomically corresponding voxels are good predictors of one another.

6.4.3 Classification based on search strategy

A considerable number of search strategies have been adopted for image registration (Brown, 1992; Maintz and Viergever, 1998; Hill et al., 2001). Despite the variety, they share a common feature, namely that they are *iterative* in nature. They work by first picking, from the transformation space of choice, an initial guess to serve as the *starting point* of the search. This initial estimate is then iteratively refined. At each iteration, the current estimate of the transformation is applied to the moving image. Then the similarity measure of choice is computed to assess the quality of alignment between the transformed moving image and the fixed image and, crucially, to propose a refinement to the current transformation estimate that can improve the alignment. The iterations continue until the improvement from the proposed refinement is deemed negligible, as measured by some pre-specified convergence criterion.

92 **Chapter 6** Image registration

Within the common framework of iterative search, different strategies vary in how they propose the refinement to the current transformation estimate. To illustrate the nature of the problem, consider the printing registration example again. Here, the transformation space consists of 2-D rigid transformations that allow translations (up/down and left/right) (2 DoF) and rotations (1 DoF). So any refinement has 3 DoF and can be viewed as a vector with a direction and a magnitude. In other words, the algorithm must decide not only the direction along which to make an adjustment but also how big the adjustment should be. There are broadly two approaches to choose the refinement direction. The alternating strategy used in the printing registration example is one approach, where refinements are always made for one DoF at a time, while keeping the rest fixed. This approach is straightforward to implement and is often used for linear registration. But it does not work well when the dimensionality of the transformation space is large, making it ill-suited for non-linear image registration. For deformable image registration, gradient-based strategies are standard, among which the simplest example is the gradient-ascent method. Here, the gradient vector of the similarity measure with respect to the transformation is computed. As an adjustment along the gradient vector locally produces the maximal increase in the similarity measure, the gradient direction is taken as the search direction. Once a search direction is chosen, deciding the magnitude of the adjustment turns out to be tricky, as it must ensure that the choice does not reduce the similarity measure. In practice, this is done either cautiously, by taking some pre-defined small adjustment and reducing it if required, or through trial and error.

One common challenge facing iterative searches is the presence of many *local maxima*. Depending on the initial guess, iterative searches can converge to any one of the local maxima, but only one of these corresponds to the correct alignment. To tackle this, two approaches have been developed. The most commonly used is the so-called *multi-resolution* strategy. Here, a pyramid of images are constructed by progressively blurring and downsampling, such that the images in the resulting pyramid capture spatial details across a range of scales. Registration begins with the images containing only the largest scale information, which tends to have much fewer local maxima. The transformation estimated at this scale is then used to initialize the subsequent registration with the images capturing the next scale details. This is repeated until the registration with the original images is run. The second approach is known as the *multi-start* strategy. As the name suggests, the idea is to repeat the registration from multiple starting points, with the hope that the correct matching will be reached from at least one of these initial guesses.

6.5 Image registration with deep learning

2012 has generally been marked as the year when deep learning first achieved its landmark breakthrough for image recognition. So it is remarkable that only just a year later, the first medical image registration method applying deep learning was published. Since then, research articles on this topic have grown exponentially and a number of review articles (Fu et al., 2020; Haskins et al., 2020) have already appeared, demonstrating considerable interest in exploiting deep learning to reinvent image registration. This final section of the chapter will give an overview of the broad strategies reported in the literature.

The strategy that appeared first is to use deep learning for crafting better similarity measures. The first example of this approach leverages deep learning's unique capacity to learn salient features in images for classification tasks. The idea is that features important for object recognition are usually also important for object matching. So a deep learning model, known as a convolutional-stacked autoencoder, was used to learn a novel representation of the class of images to be registered. Similarity between two images is assessed in terms of the similarity between their new representations. One limitation of this approach is that the images must be of the same modality. The more recent developments focused on similarity measures useful in inter-modal applications. One example is to train a deep learning model to classify aligned image patches from misaligned; the resulting model, when being presented a new pair of image patches, will produce a score between -1 and 1, with -1 to indicate the model's belief that the image pairs are misaligned, and 1 for otherwise. When applied to registration, at each iteration, the transformed moving image and the fixed image are divided into corresponding patches, and each pair of patches is scored by the model. The similarity measure can then be evaluated as the sum of the scores from all the patch pairs. One limitation of this approach is the need for existing aligned multi-modal images. More recent works have developed strategies that forgo this requirement.

Another strategy is to use deep learning to improve search strategy. As discussed in Section 6.4.3, avoiding local maxima is a distinct challenge for the standard iterative search. One approach to address this is using deep reinforcement learning, which is behind Alpha Go's famous success of beating the world's best human Go players. Here, a highly robust search strategy is learned from numerous previous attempts. The ability to learn from prior experience is the key advantage over conventional search strategies. A limitation of this approach is that it retains the iterative nature of image registration. A number of approaches have been developed to make image registration *one-shot*. These efforts can be categorized as either *supervised* or *unsupervised*. Supervised approaches work by training deep learning models that take a pair of images as input and predicts a transformation that puts the two images in register. They are known as supervised, because the models must be trained with pairs of images, for which correct transformations are known. The challenge to create such training data has motivated the development of unsupervised approaches, for which such data is not required. The breakthrough came from the invention of so-called spatial transformer network (STN), which allows geometric transformations to be encoded within deep learning models. During model training, for each pair of input images, the model parameters are tuned such that the predicted transformation maximizes some pre-specified similarity measure. In other words, it is essentially like running a conventional iterative image registration algorithm. The key difference is that the model learns from its past experience. As more pairs of training images are fed into the model, the model becomes progressively better at predicting the right transformation. Crucially, after the model is trained and when presented with a new pair of image to register, the model can predict the suitable transformation in one shot, without the need for multiple iterations. As a result, these methods can now perform image registration in just a fraction of the time required by conventional algorithms. For instance, for registering a pair of T_1-weighted scans, computational time can be reduced from approximately an hour to about a minute (Balakrishnan et al., 2019). More remarkably still, they can achieve such gain in computational efficiency while matching the registration performance of state-of-the-art conventional techniques. Advances like these make the future of deep-learning-powered image registration truly exciting to look forward to.

References

Balakrishnan, Guha, et al., 2019. VoxelMorph: a learning framework for deformable medical image registration. IEEE Transactions on Medical Imaging 38 (8), 1788–1800. https://doi.org/10.1109/TMI.2019.2897538.

Brown, Lisa G., 1992. A survey of image registration techniques. ACM Computing Surveys 24 (4), 325–376. https://doi.org/10.1145/146370.146374.

Fonov, Vladimir, et al., 2011. Unbiased average age-appropriate atlases for pediatric studies. NeuroImage 54 (1), 313–327. https://doi.org/10.1016/j.neuroimage.2010.07.033.

Friston, Karl J., et al., 1995. Spatial registration and normalization of images. Human Brain Mapping 3 (3), 165–189. https://doi.org/10.1002/hbm.460030303.

Fu, Fabo, et al., 2020. Deep learning in medical image registration: a review. Physics in Medicine and Biology 65 (20), 20TR01. https://doi.org/10.1088/1361-6560/ab843e.

Hajnal, Joseph V., Hill, Derek L.G., Hawkes, David J. (Eds.), 2001. Medical Image Registration, 1st ed. CRC Press. ISBN 9780429114991.

Haskins, Grant, Kruger, Uwe, Yan, Pingkun, 2020. Deep learning in medical image registration: a survey. Machine Vision and Applications 31 (8). https://doi.org/10.1007/s00138-020-01060-x.

Hill, Derek L.G., et al., 2001. Medical image registration. Physics in Medicine and Biology 46 (3), R1–R45. https://doi.org/10.1088/0031-9155/46/3Z201.

Maes, Frederik, et al., 1997. Multimodality image registration by maximization of mutual information. IEEE Transactions on Medical Imaging 16 (2), 187–198. https://doi.org/10.1109/42.563664.

Maintz, J.B. Antoine, Viergever, Max A., 1998. A survey of medical image registration. Medical Image Analysis 2 (1), 1–36. https://doi.org/10.1016/S1361-8415(01)80026-8.

Rueckert, Daniel, et al., 1999. Nonrigid registration using free-form deformations: application to breast MR images. IEEE Transactions on Medical Imaging 18 (8), 712–721. https://doi.org/10.1109/42.796284.

Sotiras, Aristeidis, Davatzikos, Christos, Paragios, Nikos, 2013. Deformable medical image registration: a survey. IEEE Transactions on Medical Imaging 32 (7), 1153–1190. https://doi.org/10.1109/TMI.2013.2265603.

Toga, Arthur (Ed.), 1998. Brain Warping, 1st ed. Academic Press. ISBN 9780126925357.

Viergever, Max A., et al., 2016. A survey of medical image registration - under review. Medical Image Analysis 33, 140–144. https://doi.org/10.1016/j.media.2016.06.030.

Wells, William M., et al., 1996. Multi-modal volume registration by maximization of mutual information. Medical Image Analysis 1 (1), 35–51. https://doi.org/10.1016/S1361-8415(01)80004-9.

Yoshida, Toshi, Yuki, Rei, 1966. Japanese Print-Making: A Handbook of Traditional & Modern Techniques, 1st ed. Charles E. Tuttle Company.

Zhang, Hui, 2021. Medical Image Registration Demo. https://github.com/garyhuizhang/MedicalImageRegistrationDemo.

CHAPTER

Image segmentation

7

Carole Helene Sudre[a,b,c]

[a]*MRC Unit for Lifelong Health and Ageing at UCL, University College London, London, United Kingdom*
[b]*Centre for Medical Image Computing, University College London, London, United Kingdom*
[c]*School of Biomedical Engineering and Imaging Sciences, King's College London, London, United Kingdom*

7.1 Introduction

Image segmentation consists in the delineation of objects of interest and results in attribution of a class to each voxel of the image and/or the definition of contours of objects of interest. In the context of neuroimaging, segmentation is generally an intermediate step, allowing for the extraction of measures of volume, location, and/or shape that have a clinical interest at the individual or population level. For instance, in the context of Alzheimer's disease, atrophy of the hippocampus has been shown to be a strong marker of the disease (Henneman et al., 2009). Comparison of extracted volumes to a normative population can then be used for diagnostic purposes. In the context of neuro-oncology, delineating the amount of pathological tissue and its location may inform the chosen strategy of care (Rees, 2011).

Beyond contours, the output of a voxel-based segmentation process may take multiple forms. In its most simple form, also known as hard or crisp segmentation, each voxel of the image will be allocated to a unique class. If only two classes are concerned (foreground and background), the result is known as binary segmentation. However, due to the finite resolution of the images, some voxels may contain more than one tissue that contribute to a certain proportion to the observed intensity. This is called partial volume effect and is particularly relevant in the context of neuroimaging due to the complexity of the observed tissues (cortical ribbon for instance). In this case, considering a whole voxel as belonging to a single class may lead to large measurement approximations (Tohka, 2014). A probabilistic segmentation output may then be used instead and interpreted as the proportion of each tissue responsible for the intensity in a given voxel.

A segmentation procedure can be described according to the degree of human input required for its completion, from the wholly manual delineation to the fully automated version, where no input is necessary. Manual segmentations are particularly dependent on the choice of protocol. Taking again the example of the hippocampus, definitions of some of the 70 protocols (Konrad et al., 2009; Geuze et al., 2005) were carefully analyzed by Boccardi and colleagues when attempting to reach a harmonized protocol (Boccardi et al., 2011).

Manual segmentations are usually highly time-consuming and prone to inter- and intra-rater variability. Despite these shortcomings, manual segmentation is generally used as a gold standard reference when evaluating new methodological solutions. For semi-automated segmentation methods, the input can take multiple forms with, for example, the edition of automated output, choice of seed points or

96 **Chapter 7** Image segmentation

sample voxels, delineation based on automatically determined thresholds, and many others. In contrast, automated methods do not require any operator information for input or for post-processing.

Approaches described for segmentation often rely on additional processing steps, either as a prerequisite for the framework (preprocessing steps) or to refine the output (post-processing step). In the context of neuroimaging, preprocessing steps may include skull-stripping, correction for acquisition artefacts, denoising, intensity normalization, or coregistration of multiple sequences acquired over the same scanning session. Post-processing may involve morphological operations, application of masks, smoothing or thresholding of the output.

Automated methods can themselves be characterized according to the degree of supervision (or prior knowledge) which they require, i.e., if they rely on existing examples of segmentation (obtained typically through manual annotation) or not. Some may prefer to classify them as discriminative or generative solutions. Typically, generative models propose a model that would allow recreation of the data, whereas discriminative models act as classifiers. In the remainder of the chapter, after presenting a few situations of segmentation tasks and their associated challenges, we will briefly present a range of automated segmentation approaches, such as atlas-based segmentation, thresholding or clustering methods, and feature-based classification methods from among those more recent deep learning frameworks. After a presentation of the challenges of longitudinal segmentation, the chapter will lastly touch on the topic of the evaluation of segmentation methods.

7.2 Segmentation contexts: need, challenges and further application

A few typical examples of segmentation tasks, their challenges, and how they are further used in practice are described in this section.

7.2.1 Total intracranial volume and brain segmentation

Though rarely used as standalone, the total intracranial volume (TIV) is an important factor to explain the variability of tissue volumes across individuals as directly related to head size. Having an adequate estimation of the TIV is therefore important to allow for appropriate comparison of individuals. It is one of the key confounders to be considered when assessing brain structure, and tissue volumes (Malone et al., 2015). Brain segmentation, on the other hand, is often considered as a key preprocessing step that can, in addition to providing brain volume measurement, help other downstream processing by removing all non-brain information.

7.2.2 Tissue segmentation

In the context of neuroimaging, tissue segmentation refers mainly to the separation between different tissue types, such as gray matter (GM), cerebrospinal fluid (CSF), and white matter (WM). Further distinction may separate cortical from deep gray matter. Segmentation of the cortical gray matter has notably seen considerable applications when assessing its volume or the thickness of the cortical ribbon, as they are key markers of the degree of brain atrophy in neurodegenerative diseases. Tissues are defined based on their biological constitution, whose physical properties result in different signal at the image level. For instance, on a classical T_1-weighted image of an adult brain, highly myelinated white matter appears lighter compared to the gray matter. Within tissue intensity, similarities are therefore one of the key aspects leveraged to perform automated segmentation. However, the segmentation outputs may be influenced by acquisition-related artifact that affect the signal intensity homogeneity (e.g., bias field), motion artifact, and the presence of pathology (e.g., legions) (Dora et al., 2017).

7.2.3 Structure segmentation

Structure segmentation consists of the separation of specific tissues into known structures classically defined, based on histopathology or known functions. Such structures may not display homogeneous intensity levels, and the boundary with neighboring structures may be difficult to determine. Separation of subcortical structures belong to this subtype and may be relevant to the assessment of specific pathological conditions. Atlas-based and other supervised techniques have been particularly well suited to address these segmentation problems. Additionally, multi-spectral solutions, using, for instance, tractography via diffusion imaging, have been proposed for some of these problems, when a given structure may be defined through its structural connectivity (e.g., thalamic nuclei). Structure segmentation is generally used to further assess structure volumetry or perform shape analysis or to create models of mechanical function (e.g., vessel segmentation).

7.2.4 Pathology segmentation

Damage to the brain tissue may lead to a change in the physical properties of the tissue that in turn can result in a different signal. Compared to other tissue and structure segmentation, for which location and shape are relatively stable, brain lesions may be found with greater variability in shape, size, and appearance throughout the brain. Quantification of the amount of damaged tissue and its location can then be used for diagnosis, prognosis, or disease modeling. The presence of tissue damage may, however, affect tissue and/or structure segmentation. For instance, if not accounted for, the presence of white matter lesions, common in ageing populations can affect gray matter segmentation (Levy-Cooperman et al., 2008). Segmentation of the damage may then be a first step to correct the images (e.g., lesion filling) and ultimately provide more accurate segmentation of healthy tissues (Chard et al., 2010).

Fig. 7.1 presents examples of TIV segmentation, tissue segmentation, structure segmentation (hippocampus), and pathology segmentation.

7.3 Approaches to automated segmentation

In the following, a few of the typical approaches to segmentation are briefly mentioned. These separate approaches have often been combined, to benefit from specific advantages and balance out possible shortcomings. Though some of these methods naturally account for the presence of noise and artefacts, others may require preliminary preprocessing (e.g., denoising and bias field correction) to perform best.

7.3.1 Thresholding methods

Thresholding methods are among the most straightforward segmentation methods. They can be particularly powerful in the case of homogeneous intensities or when intensity distributions across tissues

98 Chapter 7 Image segmentation

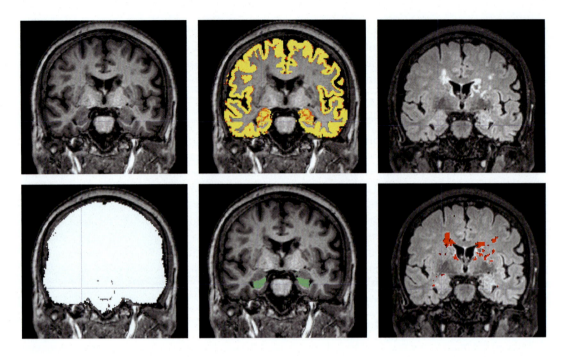

FIGURE 7.1

Illustration of different segmentation subtypes: Top row/left: example of coronal slice of a T_1-weighted scan; middle: gray matter segmentation overlaid on T_1; right: T_2-FLAIR coronal slice. Bottom row/left: TIV segmentation overlaid on T_1; middle: hippocampus segmentation overlaid on T_1; right: white matter hyperintensities lesion segmentation overlaid on FLAIR.

are well separated. Thresholding has, for instance, been proposed for white matter lesions due to the very abnormal signal intensity observed in this case. Thresholding is particularly sensitive to noise and intensity inhomogeneity as the target tissue may share similar intensity distributions with possible artifacts; for instance, CSF flow artifact may be as bright as the targeted lesions, and it is then additional information related to location that can help provide an accurate segmentation. The Otsu method is another well-known technique that assumes a bimodal distribution of the intensities, notably used for skull-stripping, that aims at finding the threshold that minimizes the variance in each of the separated classes. Thresholding techniques may be further combined with morphological operations to improve performance (Benson and Lajish, 2014).

7.3.2 Atlas-based segmentation and label fusion

Among the different existing approaches to automated segmentation, atlas-based solutions use directly another of the key aspects of image analysis, namely image registration (see Chapter 6). In this context, an atlas is defined as an image and its associated label map. In its simplest form, single atlas segmentation consists of finding the best transformation that maps the atlas image to the target image to segment, and applies it to the label to associate the transformed label to the segmentation. Many variants of this idea have been derived considering, for instance, multiple such labels that, once transformed to the target image need to be aggregated, a step also known as label fusion. In the presence of multiple atlases, the registration step is followed by a decision step designed to combine the possibly different answers coming from the different templates. Beyond majority voting, weights may be attributed to each of the template solutions either globally or locally, according to the quality of the transformation and the similarity between the atlas image and the target (Cabezas et al., 2011; Cardoso et al., 2015). Such an approach is naturally limited by the quality of the registration and by the representative nature of the set of atlases that have been manually segmented. Individual atlases may be combined after registration into a common space and averaged to create probabilistic atlases that can then be used as prior information when applying other methods, such as clustering-based methods

7.3.3 Edge-based methods

Edge-based methods, such as level set, edge-based active contours, or graph cut, attempt to define the boundary of specific regions or tissues. They often rely on the intensity gradient of the images, which may be affected by the presence of noise, artifact, or intensity inhomogeneities. Edge detection algorithms have often been combined with other segmentation methods to achieve necessary regularization (Huang et al., 2009). Edge-based deformable models, such as level set or active contours, aim at deforming an existing contour to minimize an energy function (Akram et al., 2017).

7.3.4 Clustering segmentation methods: mixture models, k-means and fuzzy clustering

Clustering methods consist of the classification of individual pixels into the groups that their intensity features are closest to. Whereas the k-means algorithm leads to hard classification, where a pixel is attributed to a cluster based on a measure of similarity to the features of the centroid of a given cluster, mixture models and FCM provide a soft / probabilistic classification. Initial centroids may be either picked manually (semi-automated) or guessed, based on the use of statistical priors. In the case of mixture models, the intensity histogram of the image is modeled as a weighted sum of known distributions, whose parameters are derived over the optimization procedure. Classically, the observed noise is modeled as Gaussian, thus resulting in Gaussian mixture models. Expectation-maximization algorithms are often adopted for the iterative optimization of the distribution parameters best suited to describe the data (Dempster et al., 1977). Those methods, prone to convergence to local minima, are strongly dependent on their initialization and may benefit from the use of statistical atlases. Fig. 7.2 illustrates the output from an expectation-maximization algorithm along with the corresponding intensity histogram.

One of their key assumptions is to consider each voxel as an independent sample. This may result in local inconsistency and speckly segmentations. To enforce neighborhood consistency, application of Markov random field approaches has been adopted as a possible solution. In addition, this framework allows for the modeling of intensity inhomogeneities, and this correction may further improve the segmentation output (Van Leemput et al., 1999). For instance, the bias field can be modeled as a weighted sum of spatially varying polynomial basis function, with weight parameters being optimized along with the distribution parameters. With fuzzy clustering, fuzzy weights are attributed to each voxel based on similarity measures to the centroid of each cluster. Because clustering methods do not naturally convey any spatial information and are not robust under intensity inhomogeneities, variants have been developed to account for these limitations (Dubey and Mushrif, 2016).

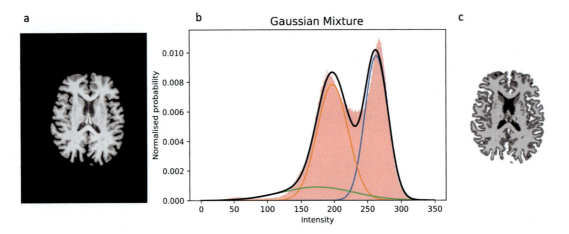

FIGURE 7.2

Example of application of Gaussian mixture model on a T_1-weighted image. a) Slice of the image to segment; b) Image intensity histogram and associated 3 tissue probability distribution from the Gaussian mixture model; c) Associated tissue segmentation on the selected slice. Note that the image was masked prior processing.

7.3.5 Region-based methods

In turn, region-based methods are mostly designed around regional consistency. Region-growing solutions start from seed voxels and progressively adopt neighboring voxels as elements of the target object according to their intensity and the gradient observed until a cut-off criterion is met. Combined with thresholding, this can be, for instance, used for lesion segmentation when seeds are chosen conservatively in the specific ranges of the histogram and further grown to encompass the overall lesions (Schmidt et al., 2012). Watershed and region-growing methods often require a post-processing step to allow for the merging of over-segmented regions.

7.3.6 Feature-based methods

In addition to intensities and locations, other features and information about the surrounding of each voxel can help in the classification of each voxel to a tissue or structure. Dictionary-based methods extract features over a patch around the voxel of interest and classify it. Such methods have been used for pathology segmentation, brain segmentation, and tissue segmentation. K-nearest neighbor methods can also be based on multiple engineered features to classify appropriately different voxels. Similarly, support vector machines and random forest classifiers may use features extracted from the intensity of a given voxel, texture, and location features from the surrounding to inform the classifier.

These have been used successfully for tissue, pathology, but also for structure segmentation. In the most recent years, deep learning has taken the forefront of state-of-the art segmentation solutions. Compared to methods where features are hand crafted, the optimization procedure also performs the design of the features of interest that are encoded through a series of convolutional kernels that allow for extraction of elements relevant for the ultimate classification at different image scales. Though routinely employed in bidimensional computer vision tasks, the computational cost and memory associated with these frameworks has long been a bottleneck to their adoption for application to 3D medical images. Currently, one of the most versatile networks used for segmentation is the so-called U-Net that performs feature extraction at different image scales (Ronneberger et al., 2015). Supervised networks, in which the target segmentation is learnt from fully annotated images, is most commonly used in deep learning. However, such approaches may require a large amount of high-quality annotation. Alternatively, models have been developed that combine both full label with weakly labeled data (Bontempi et al., 2020). Fully unsupervised networks have also been proposed for the purpose of anomaly detection (Baur et al., 2019). For deep-learning frameworks, robustness to artifacts and generalizability can either be achieved by proposing for training a large and varied set of labeled images and/or by artificially modifying the appearance of existing labeled images by applying image or intensity distortion using a process called augmentation.

7.3.7 Hybrid methods / multi-sequence or multi-modal approaches

Typically, to achieve best performance, two or more of the previously mentioned approaches are combined so as to gain from their combined strength and reduce the effects of their individual drawbacks. Combining edge-based and region-based method with further atlas-based correction appeared relevant for skull-stripping (Ségonne et al., 2004). Classically, atlas-based methods can be easily combined with clustering-based methods either at a single stage or in an iterative manner (Ashburner and Friston, 2005). In addition to the combination of approaches, combination of MRI pulse sequences can prove relevant due to differences in depicted tissue physical properties. Such approaches attempt to combine information coming from multiple sources of information. In the context of white matter lesion segmentation, T_2-weighted or FLAIR intensities are particularly relevant for the identification of out-of-distribution (lesion) voxels, whereas the information coming from the T_1-weighted scan helps in the localization with a clearer contrast between gray and white matter. Multi-sequence imaging has also proved useful for skull-stripping; thanks, for instance, to the sharp contrast generally observed between CSF and brain tissue in T_2-weighted sequences. Beyond multi-sequence structural approaches, combining information from functional and structural imaging (for instance, using PET and MR structural imaging) has been used to improve on the segmentation of tumors.

7.4 Longitudinal segmentation: challenge and approaches

Beyond a single time-point assessment of volume or shape of brain structures or pathology, assessment of evolution is an essential component in the clinical workflow, and being able to assess changes over time is essential. Therefore, being able to adequately segment over multiple time points is necessary. Although segmenting each time point independently appears as the most natural solution, this does not account for the topological consistency observed over time in an individual; processing two imaging time points as essentially different subjects suffers from the measurement noise at both time points and may mask any subtle real measurement change. In addition to all the possible acquisition-induced sources of error, outcomes of longitudinal segmentation are particularly sensitive to protocol and scanner changes over time. Using the multiple acquired time points to create a subject-specific template and use it to propagate information to the original time points is a possible solution that has been shown to yield more reliable results (Fox et al., 2011). Creation of this intermediary template requires ap-

102 **Chapter 7** Image segmentation

propriate registration. Choosing to aggregate the time points in an intermediate space is the generally preferred solution as choosing one of the time points may lead to biases due, for instance, to differences in interpolation (one image not being interpolated, whereas the others are). Such approaches have been used both for tissue and pathology segmentation (Reuter et al., 2012; Sudre et al., 2017).

7.5 **Segmentation evaluation**

Segmentation solutions can be assessed according to their **robustness** (i.e., how well does the solution perform in degraded conditions, such as motion artifact, noise, or decreased contrast and resolution?), **reproducibility** (i.e., are the results similar when providing two different scans from the same individual taken at very limited time interval?), **generalizability** (i.e., how good is the performance when changing either the scanning material or scanning individuals with other demographic characteristics such as older, younger, or at different disease stages?), and their general **accuracy**.

7.5.1 **Evaluation strategies**

Segmentation frameworks can be validated on simulated or real-world data. Simulated data have the advantage of not requiring any expert annotation, but must be realistic for the task at hand, and are often used as a preliminary step to address questions of robustness, in particular on large amounts of data. Such simulators have been designed for brain tissue (Brainweb) or pathology segmentation (Prastawa et al., 2009). Such simulators may allow for the observation of the direct impact of increased noise, or artifacts on the segmentation quality.

Reproducibility can be assessed by comparing volumetric results obtained when applying the segmentation framework in a test-retest setting, that is, applying the algorithm on images of the same individuals acquired with the same protocol within a limited time interval (typically the same day).

Assessment of generalizability may require observing the performance of the system on cohorts different in terms of acquisition protocols or individual demographics / pathology presentation. This aspect is crucial for supervised discriminative frameworks that learn and classify from existing examples. One of the common causes for poor generalization is overfitting that typically occurs when the learning capacities of the framework are too strong compared to the variability of the presented examples. This is a typical issue for deep learning frameworks. In all discriminative models, when tuning of parameters is required, nested cross-validation with training, validation and test sets is a possible way to avoid biasing the performance results and obtaining a distribution of performance that allows for further comparisons. The validation set is used to decide when to stop training (deep learning setting) or to choose the hyperparameter, and the test set is a completely held out set on which to assess the segmentation performance

Alternative ways of evaluating a segmentation output may be driven by the clinical output; therefore association of resulting biomarkers with clinical assessments may become surrogate markers of the quality of the processing. When specific shape or intensity characteristics are required, the validity of the segmentation can further be assessed according to the accuracy of these properties.

7.5.2 Ground truth and comparison to reference

Quality of a segmentation solution with respect to another solution or a reference can be measured in multiple ways, and using a single metric is rarely enough to properly assess all the desired characteristics relevant for clinical application. The choice of appropriate metrics depends greatly on the clinical relevance of the associated property. For instance, in the context of neuro-oncology and assessment for treatment planning, knowledge of the border of the tumor can be of particular interest to then adequately target the tissue to treat. Alternatively, when the number of objects is a key clinical marker, such as in multiple sclerosis, measures of connectivity will be important in the assessment of the proposed solution. Among the most used metrics, the quality of overlap between the proposed segmentation and the reference mask for a binary segmentation is often measured with the Sorensen–Dice coefficient. This measure is defined as the ratio between twice the volume of overlapping voxels and the sum of the volumes of the segmentation and the reference. While broadly used, this measure is known to be strongly dependent on the volume to segment, and tends to favor over-segmentation over under-segmentation. Multiple metrics have been proposed that reflect other or similar properties, and it is the choice of the researcher to select adequate nonredundant metrics; it is therefore essential for the proper comparison and evaluation of segmentation solutions (Cárdenes et al., 2009).

7.6 Conclusion

Image segmentation in the context of neuroimaging is a field of active investigation and encompasses a large diversity of tasks. Among the different automated approaches that have been proposed over the years, deep learning has recently shown excellent results. With new possibilities of imaging, faster acquisition and increased resolution, classical tasks are required to be performed faster and more accurately. Thus, new segmentation tasks are emerging, along with the knowledge that their output can be used for understanding and modeling diseases, as well as for diagnosis, prognosis, treatment and care planning.

References

Akram, Farhan, Garcia, Miguel Angel, Puig, Domenec, 2017. Active contours driven by local and global fitted image models for image segmentation robust to intensity inhomogeneity. PLoS ONE 12. https://doi.org/10.1371/journal.pone.0174813.

Ashburner, John, Friston, Karl J., 2005. Unified segmentation. NeuroImage 26 (3), 839–851. https://doi.org/10.1016/j.neuroimage.2005.02.018.

Baur, Christoph, Wiestler, Benedikt, Albarqouni, Shadi, Navab, Nassir, 2019. Deep autoencoding models for unsupervised anomaly segmentation in brain MR images. In: Brainlesion: Glioma, Multiple Sclerosis, Stroke and Traumatic Brain Injuries. In: Lecture Notes in Computer Science (Including Subseries Lecture Notes in Artificial Intelligence and Lecture Notes in Bioinformatics), vol. 11383. Springer Verlag, pp. 161–169.

Benson, C.C., Lajish, V.L., 2014. Morphology based enhancement and skull stripping of MRI brain images. In: Proceedings - 2014 International Conference on Intelligent Computing Applications, ICICA 2014. Institute of Electrical and Electronics Engineers Inc., pp. 254–257.

Boccardi, Marina, Ganzola, Rossana, Bocchetta, Martina, Pievani, Michela, Redolfi, Alberto, Bartzokis, George, Camicioli, Richard, et al., 2011. Survey of protocols for the manual segmentation of the hippocampus: preparatory steps towards a joint EADC-ADNI harmonized protocol NIH public access. Journal of Alzheimer's Disease 26 (3). https://doi.org/10.3233/JAD-2011-0004.

Bontempi, Dennis, Benini, Sergio, Signoroni, Alberto, Svanera, Michele, Muckli, Lars, 2020. CEREBRUM: a fast and fully-volumetric Convolutional Encoder-decodeR for weakly-supervised sEgmentation of BRain strUctures from out-of-the-scanner MRI. Medical Image Analysis 62 (May), 101688. https://doi.org/10.1016/j.media.2020.101688.

Cabezas, Mariano, Oliver, Arnau, Lladó, Xavier, Freixenet, Jordi, 2011. A review of atlas-based segmentation for magnetic resonance brain images. Computer Methods and Programs in Biomedicine 104 (December), 158–177.

Cárdenes, Rubén, de Luis-García, Rodrigo, Bach-Cuadra, Meritxell, 2009. A multidimensional segmentation evaluation of medical image data. Computer Methods and Programs in Biomedicine 96, 108–124.

Cardoso, M. Jorge, Modat, Marc, Wolz, Robin, Melbourne, Andrew, Cash, David, Rueckert, Daniel, Ourselin, Sébastien, 2015. Geodesic information flows: spatially-variant graphs and their application to segmentation and fusion. IEEE Transactions on Medical Imaging 34 (9), 1976–1988. https://doi.org/10.1109/TMI.2015.2418298.

Chard, Declan T., Jackson, Jonathan S., Miller, David H., Wheeler-Kingshott, Claudia A.M., 2010. Reducing the impact of white matter lesions on automated measures of brain gray and white matter volumes. Journal of Magnetic Resonance Imaging 32, 223–228.

Dempster, Arthur P., Laird, Nan M., Rubin, Donald B., 1977. Maximum likelihood from incomplete data via the EM algorithm. Journal of the Royal Statistical Society, Series B, Methodological 39 (1), 1–38.

Dora, Lingraj, Agrawal, Sanjay, Panda, Rutuparna, Abraham, Ajith, 2017. State-of-the-art methods for brain tissue segmentation: a review. IEEE Reviews in Biomedical Engineering 10, 235–249. https://doi.org/10.1109/RBME.2017.2715350.

Dubey, Yogita K., Mushrif, Milind M., 2016. FCM clustering algorithms for segmentation of brain MR images. Advances in Fuzzy Systems 2016. https://doi.org/10.1155/2016/3406406.

Fox, Nick C., Ridgway, Gerard R., Schott, Jonathan M., 2011. Algorithms, atrophy and Alzheimer's disease: cautionary tales for clinical trials. NeuroImage 57 (1), 15–18. https://doi.org/10.1016/j.neuroimage.2011.01.077.

Geuze, E., Vermetten, E., Bremner, J.D., 2005. MR-based in vivo hippocampal volumetrics: 1. Review of methodologies currently employed. Molecular Psychiatry 10 (2), 147–159. https://doi.org/10.1038/sj.mp.4001580.

Henneman, W.J.P., Sluimer, J.D., Barnes, J., van der Flier, W.M., Sluimer, I.C., Fox, N.C., Scheltens, P., Vrenken, H., Barkhof, F., 2009. Hippocampal atrophy rates in Alzheimer disease: added value over whole brain volume measures. Neurology 72 (11), 999–1007. https://doi.org/10.1212/01.wnl.0000344568.09360.31.

Huang, Albert, Abugharbieh, Rafeef, Tam, Roger, 2009. A hybrid geometric–statistical deformable model for automated 3-d segmentation in brain MRI. IEEE Transactions on Biomedical Engineering 56 (7), 1838–1848. https://doi.org/10.1109/TBME.2009.2017509.

Konrad, C., Ukas, T., Nebel, C., Arolt, V., Toga, A.W., Narr, K.L., 2009. Defining the human hippocampus in cerebral magnetic resonance images—an overview of current segmentation protocols. NeuroImage 47 (4), 1185–1195. https://doi.org/10.1016/J.NEUROIMAGE.2009.05.019.

Van Leemput, Koen, Maes, Frederik, Vandermeulen, Dirk, Suetens, Paul, 1999. Automated model-based bias field correction of MR images of the brain. IEEE Transactions on Medical Imaging 18 (10), 885–896.

Levy-Cooperman, Naama, Ramirez, Joel, Lobaugh, Nancy J., Black, Sandra E., 2008. Misclassified tissue volumes in Alzheimer disease patients with white matter hyperintensities: importance of lesion segmentation procedures for volumetric analysis. Stroke 39, 1134–1141. https://doi.org/10.1161/STROKEAHA.107.498196.

Malone, Ian B., Leung, Kelvin K., Clegg, Shona, Barnes, Josephine, Whitwell, Jennifer L., Ashburner, John, Fox, Nick C., Ridgway, Gerard R., 2015. Accurate automatic estimation of total intracranial volume: a nuisance variable with less nuisance. NeuroImage 104, 366–372. https://doi.org/10.1016/j.neuroimage.2014.09.034.

Prastawa, Marcel, Bullitt, Elizabeth, Gerig, Guido, 2009. Simulation of brain tumors in MR images for evaluation of segmentation efficacy. Medical Image Analysis 13 (2), 297–311. https://doi.org/10.1016/j.media.2008.11.002.

Rees, J.H., 2011. Diagnosis and treatment in neuro-oncology: an oncological perspective. British Journal of Radiology 84 (special issue 2), S82–S89. https://doi.org/10.1259/bjr/18061999.

Reuter, Martin, Schmansky, Nicholas J., Rosas, H. Diana, Fischl, Bruce, 2012. Within-subject template estimation for unbiased longitudinal image analysis. NeuroImage 61 (4), 1402–1418. https://doi.org/10.1016/j.neuroimage.2012.02.084.

Ronneberger, Olaf, Fischer, Philipp, Brox, Thomas, 2015. U-Net: convolutional networks for biomedical image segmentation. In: Medical Image Computing and Computer-Assisted Intervention – MICCAI 2015, pp. 234–241.

Schmidt, Paul, Gaser, Christian, Arsic, Milan, Buck, Dorothea, Förschler, Annette, Berthele, Achim, Hoshi, Muna, et al., 2012. An automated tool for detection of FLAIR-hyperintense white matter lesions in multiple sclerosis. NeuroImage 59, 3774–3783.

Ségonne, F., Dale, A.M., Busa, E., Glessner, M., Salat, D., Hahn, H.K., Fischl, B., 2004. A hybrid approach to the skull stripping problem in MRI. NeuroImage 22 (3), 1060–1075. https://doi.org/10.1016/j.neuroimage.2004.03.032.

Sudre, C.H., Cardoso, M.J., Ourselin, S., 2017. Longitudinal segmentation of age-related white matter hyperintensities. Medical Image Analysis 38. https://doi.org/10.1016/j.media.2017.02.007.

Tohka, Jussi, 2014. Partial volume effect modeling for segmentation and tissue classification of brain magnetic resonance images: a review. World Journal of Radiology 6 (11), 855. https://doi.org/10.4329/wjr.v6.i11.855.

PART 3

Diffusion MRI

CHAPTER

Diffusion MRI acquisition and reconstruction

8

Hua Guo

Center for Biomedical Imaging Research, Department of Biomedical Engineering, School of Medicine, Tsinghua University, Beijing, China

8.1 Introduction

Diffusion-weighted imaging (DWI) is one of the most important imaging techniques in MRI. It has been used widely in clinics for diagnosis and in neuroimaging studies for fiber tracking and microstructure mapping. Since DWI detects micro-scale random motion of water molecules, it needs to be sensitive to micro-scale motion, which also renders DWI very sensitive to physiological motion and bulk motion. Because of this, DWI has different acquisition requirements compared to traditional anatomical MR imaging. The most widely used acquisition technique is single-shot EPI (SS-EPI), which is immune to the motion-induced phase variations between excitations. However, its image quality is limited, and thus advanced acquisition and reconstruction techniques have been developed. To understand the primary techniques and recent developments, this chapter will focus on the introduction of EPI-based DWI acquisitions and reconstruction, including SS-EPI, multi-shot EPI (MS-EPI), point spread function (PSF) EPI, and 3D acquisitions, as well as the corresponding image reconstruction approaches. Also, some non-EPI diffusion methods, including spiral and PROPELLER, will be introduced. Due to the vast literature in this area, it will be impossible to cover every published DWI method. For the interested reader, please refer to the excellent reviews from other resources.

8.2 SS-EPI DWI

The most commonly used DWI acquisition sequence is based on single-shot spin-echo EPI (Fig. 8.1). After signal excitation and diffusion encoding, frequency and phase encoding (PE) gradients are played out for k-space traversal from one end to the other along k_y. A series of spatially encoded gradient echoes are formed through the signal encoding gradients under the envelope of the spin-echo and generate an image after inverse Fourier transformation. Due to its snap-shot imaging feature, SS-EPI has subject motion insensitivity, and thus has been the primary workhorse method for diffusion imaging.

However, SS-EPI's sampling scheme also introduces particular artifacts to diffusion images. One of the most common artifacts is known as a Nyquist ghost, which comes from the misalignment of k_y lines induced by hardware imperfections. In addition, SS-EPI images usually have relatively low spatial resolution, which is limited by T_2^* signal decay and the allowed readout window length. Furthermore, SS-EPI usually has low bandwidth along the PE direction. Therefore the extra phase accrual caused by

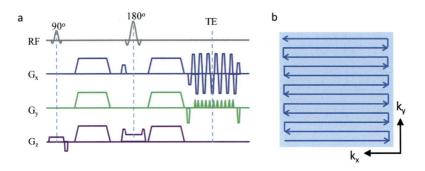

FIGURE 8.1

Sequence diagram for single-shot EPI DWI (a) and its k-space sampling trajectory (b).

magnetic field inhomogeneities can lead to geometric distortions, especially close to tissue boundaries with different susceptibilities (see also Chapter 9). To improve image resolution and to reduce distortions, tremendous efforts have been devoted and some of the improved strategies have been adopted by the major vendors.

8.3 Parallel imaging for DWI

In-plane parallel imaging, such as SENSitivity Encoding (SENSE) and GeneraLized Autocalibrating Partially Parallel Acquisition (GRAPPA), can increase the effective bandwidth along the PE direction by accelerating k-space traversal. Basically, parallel imaging with an acceleration factor of R can theoretically offer an R-fold distortion reduction over a fully sampled SS-EPI scan. Thus it is a straightforward method to reduce distortions in EPI. However, usually the value of R is limited as it leads to a signal-to-noise ratio (SNR) penalty, g-factor-induced noise amplification, and image artifacts (see Chapter 2). In practice, R is typically set as 2 or 3 for diffusion imaging. Thus EPI DWI still suffers from distinct distortions, especially at high magnetic field strengths or with high spatial resolution.

8.4 Multi-shot EPI DWI

Instead of acquiring signals in a single-shot for DWI, k-space filling can be achieved with multiple-shots, which provide higher sampling bandwidth in the PE direction to reduce distortions, and increase image resolution. Interestingly, during the application of diffusion encoding gradients, bulk subject motion or physiological motion, such as cerebrospinal fluid (CSF) pulsations, can cause phase variations between shots for multi-shot acquisitions (Anderson and Gore, 1994). Such phase variations must be corrected before shot combination; otherwise severe aliasing artifacts occur in the DWI images. To address this problem, there are two primary acquisition schemes for MS-EPI sampling: readout segmented EPI (RS-EPI) (Porter and Heidemann, 2009) and interleaved EPI (iEPI). Fig. 8.2 shows their sampling trajectories and the navigator acquisitions.

8.4 Multi-shot EPI DWI

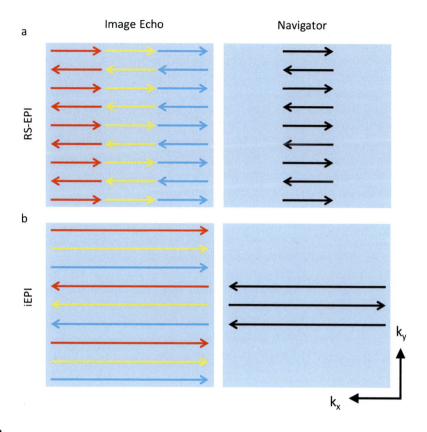

FIGURE 8.2

k-space sampling trajectories for RS-EPI and iEPI DWI. (a) RS-EPI splits k-space into a number of segments along the frequency encoding direction (in this case 3 segments) with different colors representing different excitations. Along with each segment, a low-resolution navigator with the same segment width as the image echo is acquired for motion recording. (b) iEPI interleaves k-space using a number of consecutive excitations (with different colors, with 3 interleaves used here as a demonstration). Also, a navigator is acquired after each image echo. For navigator-free iEPI, the navigator is removed from the sequence.

RS-EPI splits k-space into segments along the frequency encoding (FE) direction (Fig. 8.2a). For each segment, it is fully sampled or accelerated using parallel imaging along the PE direction. In this way, the reduced echo-spacing increases the bandwidth in the PE direction, which suppresses the distortion and T_2^* decay effect significantly. To record any motion-induced phase for correction in image reconstruction, a low-resolution navigator with the same segment length as the image echo is acquired after a second RF refocusing pulse. The navigator has the same distortion level as the image echoes. Thus the navigator can be used directly for nonlinear phase error correction, which will be introduced later.

The net distortion suppression is governed by the segment width and the maximum gradient slew rate. To further reduce geometric distortion and T_2^* decay artifacts, parallel imaging methods, such as

112 **Chapter 8** Diffusion MRI acquisition and reconstruction

GRAPPA, are often used for the image echo and navigator acquisitions in RS-EPI. Additionally, a recent study showed that variable segment length can be used to reduce image distortions more effectively.

Unlike RS-EPI, iEPI accelerates k-space traversal by interleaving the k_x lines along the PE direction (Fig. 8.2b). Because of the reduced readout length per interleave, phase accumulation along the PE direction decreases, and thus image distortion is suppressed. Any motion-induced phase errors between shots can be calibrated from a navigator scan (Fig. 8.2b) or a navigator-free acquisition can be adopted via parallel imaging reconstruction.

If a navigator is acquired in iEPI DWI, its low-resolution image usually has different distortion levels than the desired image. To address this, echo spacing should be reduced or undersampling can be used to minimize the distortion mismatch. An early study showed that the mismatch effect can be minimized when $R=2$ and/or k-space-based reconstruction is used to improve the reconstruction.

The iEPI acquisition method can also be used in a navigator-free mode to improve sampling efficiency, especially when a few shots are acquired with a highly dense RF receive coil (Skare et al., 2007). Then, phase correction is computed through parallel imaging, which will be introduced in the reconstruction section. In some scenarios, high-shot-number acquisitions are needed to suppress severe distortions, for example, in sagittal spine diffusion imaging. Due to the high undersampling factor (equal to the number of shots), navigator-free iEPI DWI approaches fail in this setting, and thus navigators have to be acquired.

Similar performance in terms of distortion suppression has been found between RS-EPI and iEPI DWI. For high-resolution DWI, iEPI has more potential in distortion reduction than RS-EPI when increasing the number of shots. However, RS-EPI can achieve a reasonable SNR with a shorter scan time than iEPI.

8.5 Image reconstruction for MS-EPI DWI

For image reconstruction of MS-EPI DWI data, the primary challenge concerns the motion-induced phase correction needed between shots. Depending on the sampling scheme, very different reconstruction methods have been developed and can be separated into two categories: navigated phase correction and navigator-free phase correction. We will introduce some commonly used methods here.

For navigated RS-EPI, given that the 2D navigator always has the same distortion level as the image echo, its low-resolution image can be used directly in the image domain without additional image registration (Porter and Heidemann, 2009). Specifically, once the navigator image is obtained, any 2D nonlinear phase variation can be removed from the main image data by performing a pixel-wise complex multiplication. Subsequently, well-trimmed segments are combined to form the full k-space for each coil. After inverse Fourier transformation, images from all coils are combined using a "square root of the sum of squares" (SOS) method. As such, the reconstruction of RS-EPI data is relatively straightforward.

For navigated iEPI DWI, the image reconstruction can be conducted in either the image domain or in the k-space domain. When a phased-array coil is used, the k-space signal can be expressed as (Miller and Pauly, 2003)

$$\mathbf{d}_{i,j} = \mathbf{F}_i \mathbf{S}_j \mathbf{P}_i \mathbf{f}, \quad \text{with } \mathbf{P}_i = \exp(i\mathbf{\Phi}_i) \tag{8.1}$$

Here i and j denote the index of each shot and each channel, respectively; $\mathbf{d}_{i,j}$ is the acquired signal; $\mathbf{F}_i$ is the Fourier encoding operator of the i-th shot; $\mathbf{S}_j$ is the coil sensitivity of the j-th channel; $\mathbf{P}_i$ is the exponential of the motion-induced phase variation of the i-th shot; $\mathbf{f}$ is the diffusion-weighted image to be reconstructed. Using SENSE reconstruction, if we treat $\mathbf{S}_j$ and $\mathbf{P}_i$ similarly, the image $\mathbf{f}$ can be solved via a least squares method:

$$\mathbf{f} = (\mathbf{E}_{i,j}^H \mathbf{\Psi}^{-1} \mathbf{E}_{i,j})^{-1} \mathbf{E}_{i,j}^H \mathbf{\Psi}^{-1} \mathbf{d}_{i,j}, \quad \text{with } \mathbf{E}_{i,j} = \mathbf{F}_i \mathbf{S}_j \mathbf{P}_i, \tag{8.2}$$

where $\mathbf{E}_{i,j}$ is the encoding matrix, $\mathbf{\Psi}$ is the noise correlation matrix. Eq. (8.2) shows that the phase correction is conducted pixel-wise in the image domain, which requires the navigator to have the same distortion characteristics as the image $\mathbf{f}$. Thus for navigated iEPI DWI, registration or tuning of the navigator sampling (undersampling) is needed for accurate phase correction, when the distortion does not match between the image and navigator due to their different sampling bandwidth.

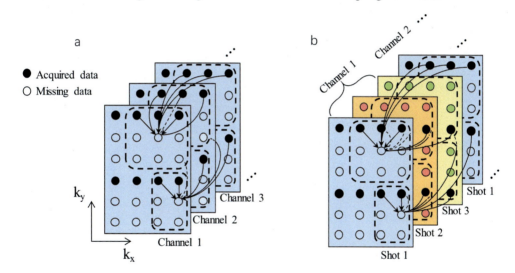

FIGURE 8.3

Image reconstruction with GRAPPA using the shot and coil information. (a) traditional GRAPPA using the coil channels. (b) GRAPPA interpolation for multi-shot DWI using different shots and coil channels. The missing data from each shot are interpolated by the acquired data from all shots and all RF channels (marked with arrows), with the weighting vectors calibrated using fully-sampled navigator data.

Instead of using the image-domain-based phase correction method, k-space-based reconstruction can also be used for multi-shot diffusion imaging, which can alleviate the image matching requirement (Ma et al., 2016). The basic principle is that the phase variation $\mathbf{P}_i$ in the image domain, similar to coil sensitivity, can be regarded as one kind of sensitivity encoding (Eq. (8.1)), thus the missing data can be synthesized using k-space correlations among different shots (and RF channels as well as averages; see Fig. 8.3), just like GRAPPA. Based on this theory, a compact kernel is used for data recovery, using only the acquired signals with significant contribution to the sample to be synthesized (Ma et al., 2016). The weighting coefficients for the interpolation are calibrated from the fully-sampled navigator data. Since navigators are used in k-space rather than via pixel-wise operations in the image domain, this method is less sensitive to mismatch between the image echo and navigator data. Additionally, the distortion level of the navigator can be suppressed via undersampling, making this method robust for navigated iEPI DWI. Results show that a joint reconstruction using the phase and coil information can perform much better than conventional GRAPPA that uses coil information alone (Fig. 8.4).

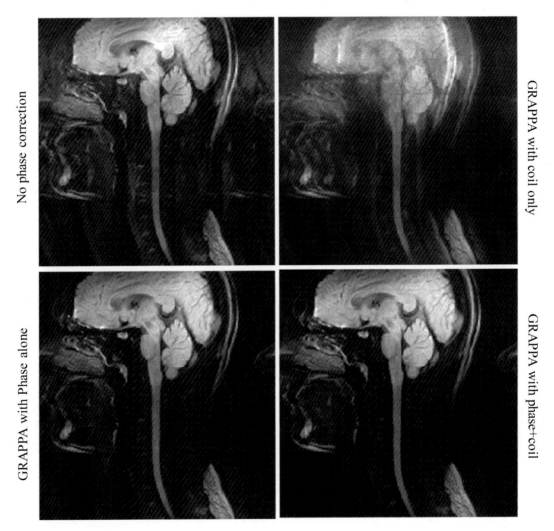

FIGURE 8.4

Image reconstruction using GRAPPA for 10-shot navigated iEPI DWI data acquired with a 16-channel neurovascular coil. The acquisition parameters were: resolution=$1.3 \times 1.3 \times 5$ mm^3, no in-plane or SMS acceleration, Signal averages=2, b=500 s/mm^2, FOV=250×250 mm^2, TE is 70 ms, TR is 3 cardiac cycles. The data were acquired on a 3T MRI scanner. Top left: inverse Fourier transformation of k-space data without phase correction; top right: GRAPPA reconstruction for each shot using coil information alone; bottom left: GRAPPA reconstruction for each shot using phase information alone; bottom right: GRAPPA reconstruction for each shot using both phase and coil information to recover full k-space. GRAPPA using phase information has superior performance.

For navigator-free iEPI DWI, multiplexed sensitivity-encoding (MUSE) (Chen et al., 2013) is an innovative and robust reconstruction method. The key principle is that it first uses SENSE to obtain the phase information of each shot, then the phase and multi-shot data are put into the reconstruction framework to jointly calculate the diffusion images. When the shot number is relatively small compared to the RF channel number (e.g., $R \leq 4$ with an 8-channel receive coil), the shot-to-shot phase variation aliasing artifacts in DWI can be successfully removed by MUSE without acquiring specific navigators. However, when using a high shot number, equivalent to a high SENSE reduction factor, extensions to the MUSE approach are needed to improve reconstruction reliability. They include self-feeding MUSE and POCSMUSE, which enable better phase estimation, even with a higher shot number. It has been shown that these MUSE-based techniques can improve the image SNR, and thus perform better than the conventional SENSE reconstruction of each shot separately (Chen et al., 2013).

Multi-shot sensitivity-encoded diffusion data recovery using structured low-rank matrix completion (MUSSELS) (Mani et al., 2017) is another alternative method to recover the images for navigator-free iEPI DWI. Different from MUSE, MUSSELS does not estimate the shot-to-shot phase information explicitly. The basic principle is that by introducing completion of a low-rank Hankel matrix using the annihilation relation between shots, MUSSELS can recover DWI data of each constituent shot. Specifically, assuming that the motion-induced phase maps are smooth, shift-invariant filters of finite support can be used to model them in k-space. Then an annihilation relation is derived between shots using these filters and a low-rank block-Hankel matrix is formed by extracting the multi-shot data with a sliding window. A reconstruction framework is derived based on structured low-rank recovery, which learns the filter implicitly to restore the missing data from each shot. Finally, images from all shots are combined using the SOS method.

For multi-shot EPI DWI, although the phase-variation-induced aliasing artifacts can be corrected most of the time, severe pulsatile brain motions, such as from cardiac-driven CSF pulsations occurring during the diffusion sensitizing period, can lead to excessive phase variations and signal loss. This can be seen in scans without cardiac gating. To avoid this, various corrupt data detection and compensation methods have been proposed, including reacquisition and data rejection techniques.

8.6 DWI with multi-band acquisitions

Diffusion imaging can be time-consuming, especially when multiple diffusion encoding directions are used. Thus, it may not be practical to use multi-shot methods for high angular diffusion imaging. Simultaneous multi-slice (SMS), or multi-band imaging, which excites multiple slices simultaneously and unfolds the aliased images using parallel imaging, is a great solution to reduce scan time (Larkman et al., 2001 and see Chapter 3). Although the slice unfolding for SMS also depends on the receiver coil design, it does not have $\sqrt{R_{SMS}}$ SNR penalty like its in-plane parallel imaging variant. Meanwhile, for a certain number, R_{SMS}, of simultaneously excited slices, the spatial extent along the slice direction increases by R_{SMS}-fold, making the SNR $\sqrt{R_{SMS}}$ times higher. Moreover, blipped-CAIPI (controlled aliasing in parallel imaging) can generate an in-plane image shift among simultaneously excited slices, and thus helps to improve the slice un-folding. As such, SMS has been successfully used in SS-EPI, RS-EPI, and iEPI DWI to improve their SNR efficiency.

For SMS-accelerated SS-EPI or MS-EPI DWI, SENSE, SENSE/GRAPPA (Blaimer et al., 2006), and slice-GRAPPA (Setsompop et al., 2012) can be used for the image reconstruction. In particular, for MS-EPI DWI, inter-shot phase variation should be corrected along with slice unfolding for SMS.

Both MUSE and MUSSELS have been extended to navigator-free iEPI DWI with SMS. On the other hand, the k-space data formed by SMS can be treated as an undersampled 3D k-space, which not only describes SMS encoding from a different viewpoint, but also provides great flexibility to the reconstruction. Then the traditional reconstruction methods for 3D k-space parallel imaging, such as 2D SENSE and 2D GRAPPA, can be used directly for SMS unfolding. If the aforementioned k-space method is used, the phase variation can also be treated as signal encoding (Dai et al., 2017). For navigated iEPI DWI with SMS, a 3D navigator is needed and can have a geometric mismatch with the image echo along both the PE and slice-selection directions. As such, k-space-based reconstruction has the capability to alleviate this problem.

8.7 Point spread function EPI

MS-EPI can suppress image distortion, but cannot remove it completely, even when a very large shot number is used. Point-spread-function (PSF)-encoded EPI has been proposed to achieve high-resolution, distortion- and T_2^* blurring-free imaging. Basically, in PSF-EPI, a set of PSF encoding gradients are inserted into the PE direction of the 2D EPI acquisition before the image-echo readout (Fig. 8.5a). This encoding scheme generates a 3D k-space data set consisting of k_x, k_y, and k_{psf} dimensions for each slice. At a given k_y position in the k_x-k_{psf} plane, all PSF-encoding signals at different k_{psf} are acquired at the same echo time. Accordingly, the phase accumulations induced by susceptibility and T_2^* decay are identical for the same k_y. Therefore there is no distortion and T_2^* blurring in the image from k_x-k_{psf}.

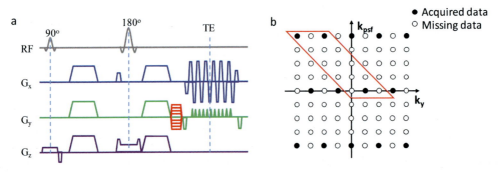

FIGURE 8.5

(a) The basic sequence diagram of PSF-EPI DWI. The gradient (in red) along G_y is applied before the EPI readout and changes shot-to-shot to achieve the additional PSF-encoding. (b) The tilted-CAIPI undersampling pattern in the k_{psf}-k_y dimension. The readout direction k_x is omitted.

However, due to the PSF encoding, its acquisition efficiency is very low, making it impractical for clinical applications. Traditional parallel imaging can be used for sampling acceleration; however, the efficiency improvement is limited, especially for multiple direction diffusion encoding. For further acceleration, a new acquisition and reconstruction framework, tilted-CAIPI, has been proposed for PSF-EPI with >20-fold acceleration (Dong et al., 2019). It exploits the inherent signal correlation in PSF-EPI and treats susceptibility-induced phase accumulation as an additional signal encoding to achieve high undersampling. Based on this principle, an optimized tilted 2D-CAIPI undersampling pattern

(Fig. 8.5b), with an acceleration factor of $R_{PE} \times R_{PSF}$, is used in k_y-k_{psf}. Subsequently, GRAPPA-like interpolation using a titled kernel along the k_y-k_{psf} diagonal line is employed to restore the undersampled data in k-space. Tilted-CAIPI can be combined with SMS and partial Fourier sampling along both the PE and PSF directions to further improve the acquisition efficiency. To correct for inter-shot phase variations, navigated or navigator-free acquisitions can be employed for diffusion imaging. Fig. 8.6 shows the superior performance of PSF-EPI DWI compared to iEPI with the same excitation numbers.

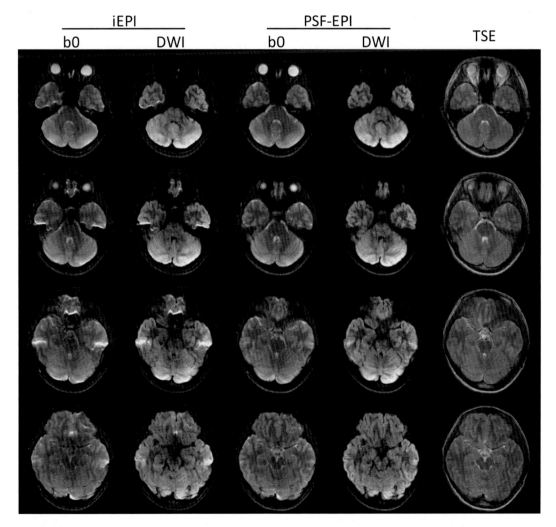

FIGURE 8.6

Comparison between 8-shot iEPI and 8-shot PSF-EPI for diffusion imaging at 3T. T_2^*w TSE images are also provided as a reference. The acquisition parameters for PSF-EPI were: resolution=$1.2 \times 1.2 \times 4$ mm^3, R_{PE}=4, R_{PSF}=18, TR/TE=2562/66 ms, partial Fourier along PE=0.75. iEPI used different TR/TE=3208/61 ms. The distortions seen in iEPI are well suppressed in the PSF images.

8.8 3D diffusion imaging

2D EPI can achieve high in-plane resolution for DWI; however, its slice resolution is relatively low. For 2D imaging, the slice resolution is determined by the slice profile of the RF excitation. To achieve an ideal slice profile, the duration of the RF pulse needs to be long, which is impractical. Additionally, the intrinsically low SNR in DWI makes high-resolution imaging even more challenging.

Although ultra-high magnetic fields (such as 7T) can be used to improve the image SNR, it may not work well for DWI. The limitation factors include increased B_0 and B_1 field inhomogeneities and increased specific absorption rate. More importantly, tissues have faster T_2/T_2^* signal decay at higher fields, which can affect the effective SNR significantly. One way to remedy this is to use powerful gradients, such as gradient inserts. However, they are not widely available yet.

Therefore, one commonly adopted strategy for high-resolution 3D DWI is to excite a thick slab, and then use specific sampling schemes with specific reconstruction methods to resolve the high slice resolution. 3D acquisition by gradient encoding in the slice direction provides higher SNR than a 2D acquisition by exciting a larger volume, and also more accurately defines the slice profiles, thus aiding isotropic DWI. Similar to multi-shot 2D DWI, physiological motion-induced phase variation during diffusion encoding needs to be corrected for each k_z encoding. Efforts have been expended to simplify this complex process by using methods such as driven equilibrium or cardiac triggering. The latest developments in 3D diffusion imaging include the following two methods: generalized slice dithered enhanced resolution (gSlider) and 3D multi-slab imaging.

The basic principle of gSlider is based on super-resolution reconstruction, in which a high-resolution along the slice dimension is calculated from a thick slab being excited multiple times. The desired thin slices in the slab are modulated by different RF pulses in different excitations. Then, by solving a linear equation $\mathbf{Af} = \mathbf{b}$, where $\mathbf{A}$ represents the slice profiles generated by different RF pulses, and $\mathbf{b}$ is the low-resolution image from the thick slab of each excitation, the high-resolution image $\mathbf{f}$ can be obtained. As for the implementation, the sub-slices in the thick slab are modulated sequentially by combinations of phase π through the slab-encoding RF pulse in different excitations, and their consequent slice profiles vary differently. Therefore the conditioning of the linear equation is improved significantly, and the reconstruction results are better than the alternative of shifting the slab partially. For each slab acquisition, SS-EPI is used, and thus phase variation correction is not needed. When combined with SMS, increased SNR efficiency can be obtained.

Multi-slab DWI is an alternative method for 3D imaging and has a great potential for SNR-efficient sampling (Frost et al., 2014; Engstrom and Skare, 2013). In multi-slab imaging, a large 3D imaging volume is split into thick slabs, and the acquisition is conducted slab by slab in an interleaved manner. Since the TR time is determined by the number of slabs, by combining with SMS the TR for 3D multi-slab can be reduced to around 2 seconds, which can achieve optimal SNR-efficiency for whole-brain diffusion imaging (Fig. 8.7). Both RS-EPI and iEPI have been used with SMS for high-resolution isotropic multi-slab DWI.

Since multi-slab signals are acquired in a multi-shot manner, inter-shot phase variations can occur spatially in all directions. Therefore, phase correction is more complicated than in 2D multi-shot DWI. In practice, either a 2D navigator or a 3D navigator can be used to correct for the phase variation. When the slab thickness is less than 30 mm, a 2D navigator works well.

For SMS-accelerated multi-slab DWI, only a 2D navigator for each slab can be acquired, due to the inter-slab gap-induced phase interference in the presence of k_z-encoding gradients. A synthesized

8.8 3D diffusion imaging   119

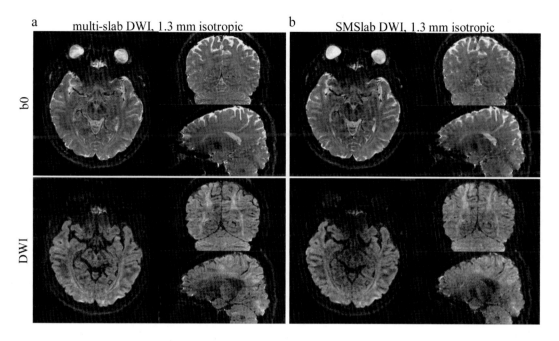

FIGURE 8.7

Comparison between multi-slab (a) and SMS-accelerated multi-slab (SMSlab) DWI (b) with 2-shot iEPI for in-plane sampling. Common acquisition parameters were: resolution=1.3 mm isotropic, $R_{in\text{-}plane}$=2, NSA=1, b=800 s/mm^2. Multi-slab used: slices/slab × kz oversampling=10×1.8, slab thickness = 14 mm, R_{SMS}=1; SM-Slab used: slices/slab × kz oversampling=6×1.33, slab thickness = 7 mm, R_{SMS}=2, TR=1.7 s. Multi-slab used a large oversampling factor to reduce the boundary artifacts while SMSlab used a boundary artifacts correction algorithm. The data were acquired on a 3T MRI scanner.

3D navigator that incorporates coil sensitivity information can be used to improve the phase correction accuracy.

The phase correction can be conducted in the image domain, such as using 3D-MB-MUSE for image reconstruction (Bruce et al., 2017). Also, the phase variations can be treated as a kind of image encoding as mentioned before, allowing the missing data to be recovered by k-space-based methods. In Dai's work (Dai et al., 2019), by jointly using RF and gradient encoding for image echo formation, a 3D k-space framework is proposed to solve the image reconstruction problem. Navigator-free acquisitions have also been investigated for SMS-accelerated multi-slab DWI.

Another challenge for multi-slab DWI is boundary artifacts, which are mainly induced by imperfect slice/slab profiles from the RF pulses and manifest as decreased signal intensity at the slab boundaries, aliasing artifacts and crosstalk between neighboring slabs. For SMS-accelerated multi-slab imaging, the artifacts can be even more complicated. To suppress the artifacts, researchers have proposed various innovative methods, which include oversampling along the slice direction, separating odd and even slabs, weighted averaging along the slab boundary, slab profile encoding and nonlinear inversion for slab profile encoding (Wu et al., 2016).

8.9 Non-EPI diffusion imaging

For non-EPI diffusion imaging methods, researchers have developed methods based on fast spin-echo (FSE), radial FSE, steady-state free precession, spiral, and PROPELLER acquisitions. The latter two methods will be introduced below.

As a fast acquisition method, spiral can be used for single-shot DWI acquisitions. One distinct disadvantage of spiral imaging is blurring artifacts due to off-resonance effects, which is different to EPI. Therefore, long readout windows have to be used with care. The use of a "field camera" is an effective way to control image blurring by accurately characterizing the gradient system, allowing long readout windows to be used. Another way to control the readout window length is to use parallel imaging or multi-shot acquisitions. An earlier study showed that single-shot spiral DWI can achieve significant SNR gains compared to SS-EPI DWI at 3T using traditional gradient coils. Additionally, when combined with a powerful gradient system (e.g., gradient strength: 200 mT/m, slew rate: 600 T/m/s), spiral DWI can achieve much shorter TEs (TE=19 ms with b=1000 s/mm^2), and thus higher SNR compared to SS-EPI. This provides a great means to maximize the signal yield and likely facilitate diffusion quantification.

If spiral is used in a multi-shot mode for high-resolution DWI, phase variation correction can be conducted using self-navigated interleaved spirals (SNAILS, Liu et al., 2004) or navigator-free acquisitions. SNAILS uses the densely oversampled region in the k-space center to correct for motion-induced phase variations. One merit for variable-density spiral is that the undersampling-induced aliasing artifacts are less coherent than standard Cartesian sampling, thus facilitating compressed sensing reconstruction. The problem for this sequence, however, is that the lengthened readout window aggravates image blurring if a field camera is not used. Although the readout duration can be shortened using more interleaves, the scan time increases correspondingly.

Compared to SNAILS, navigator-free methods have higher acquisition efficiency and fewer blurring artifacts, due to the shortened readout window. Similar to MUSE for iEPI DWI, interleaved spiral DWI without explicit navigators can also be reconstructed reliably using a parallel imaging calculation strategy. Multiple methods have been proposed, including SENSE+CG, POCS-ICE (POCS-enhanced inherent correction of motion-induced phase errors) (Guo et al., 2016) and PR-SENSE. Among them, POCS-based algorithms show a superior performance and have a stable convergence behavior, even when the number of shots is relatively large. Unlike iEPI sampling for DWI, the spiral trajectory always samples the k-space center for each shot, which helps better correct navigator-free spiral phase errors.

As an efficient acquisition method, fast spin echo (FSE) has been used for distortion-free diffusion imaging. Due to the use of multiple 180° pulses in FSE, the phase accumulation from either magnetic field inhomogeneities or eddy currents is reversed during the echo time such that the distortion that occurs in EPI can be avoided in FSE. Due to this trait, single-shot or multi-shot FSE-based DWI has been successfully developed.

One additional challenge for FSE DWI is that the Carr–Purcell–Meiboom–Gill (CPMG) condition needs to be met such that the initial phase of the transverse magnetization and the phase of the refocusing pulse should be identical. However, motion-induced phase during the application of diffusion gradients may disturb the transverse magnetization phase, and thus the CPMG condition for FSE signal formation no longer holds. Various methods have been introduced to circumvent this issue.

Among the variants of FSE-based diffusion imaging, PROPELLER DWI (Pipe et al., 2002) is a widely adopted technique due to its superior geometrical fidelity compared with the EPI-based methods (except PSF-EPI). PROPELLER collects data using a series of rotating blades containing multiple phase encoding lines (see also Chapter 4). The central circle of k-space sampled by all blades can serve as a self-navigator for motion information recording, and identifies blades with corrupted data. Therefore PROPELLER DWI has the capability to correct translation and rotation motion and motion-induced phase variations in diffusion imaging. To meet the CPMG condition, the refocusing pulses can vary their phases, for which PROPELLER shows better signal stability than Cartesian FSE DWI. To increase the sampling efficiency of PROPELLER DWI and reduce its energy deposition, some attractive techniques have been derived, including Turboprop, 3D variant radially oriented tri-dimensionally organized readouts (ROTOR), Steer-PROP, X-PROP, and so on. Recent works have explored using SMS to accelerate PROPELLER acquisitions.

8.10 Summary

With MRI hardware and computation method advancement, various diffusion acquisition and reconstruction methods have been developed to provide high-fidelity diffusion images with high spatial resolution and suppressed distortion or no distortion. Thus, image quality is close to or equivalent to anatomical images. Some among these methods have been adopted by the major MRI vendors. However, SS-EPI DWI is still the most commonly used method for clinical scanning due to its robustness, simplicity, and high scan efficiency. The advanced DWI methods, especially using multi-shot acquisition schemes, usually have lower sampling efficiency, and thus may not be suitable for high angular diffusion imaging. Limited by the trade-off between SNR, image resolution and sampling efficiency, diffusion imaging is still a key research area in MRI, and further efforts are needed to continue to push it forward.

Acknowledgments

The author would like to thank Dr Peter Jezzard for his time and effort in proofreading this chapter and for providing valuable comments. The author would also like to thank Xiaodong Ma, Yishi Wang, Erpeng Dai, Simin Liu, Jieying Zhang, and Xinyu Ye for contributing images and for helpful discussions.

References

Anderson, A.W., Gore, J.C., 1994. Analysis and correction of motion artifacts in diffusion weighted imaging. Magn. Reson. Med. 32, 379–387.

Blaimer, M., Breuer, F.A., Seiberlich, N., Mueller, M.F., Heidemann, R.M., Jellus, V., Wiggins, G., Wald, L.L., Griswold, M.A., Jakob, P.M., 2006. Accelerated volumetric MRI with a SENSE/GRAPPA combination. J. Magn. Reson. Imaging 24, 444–450.

Bruce, I.P., Chang, H.C., Petty, C., Chen, N.K., Song, A.W., 2017. 3D-MB-MUSE: a robust 3D multi-slab, multi-band and multi-shot reconstruction approach for ultrahigh resolution diffusion MRI. NeuroImage 159, 46–56.

Chen, N.K., Guidon, A., Chang, H.C., Song, A.W., 2013. A robust multi-shot scan strategy for high-resolution diffusion weighted MRI enabled by multiplexed sensitivity-encoding (MUSE). NeuroImage 72, 41–47.

Dai, E., Ma, X., Zhang, Z., Yuan, C., Guo, H., 2017. Simultaneous multislice accelerated interleaved EPI DWI using generalized blipped-CAIPI acquisition and 3D K-space reconstruction. Magn. Reson. Med. 77, 1593–1605.

Dai, E., Wu, Y., Wu, W., Guo, R., Liu, S., Miller, K.L., Zhang, Z., Guo, H., 2019. A 3D k-space Fourier encoding and reconstruction framework for simultaneous multi-slab acquisition. Magn. Reson. Med. 82, 1012–1024.

Dong, Z., Wang, F., Reese, T.G., Manhard, M.K., Bilgic, B., Wald, L.L., Guo, H., Setsompop, K., 2019. Tilted-CAIPI for highly accelerated distortion-free EPI with point spread function (PSF) encoding. Magn. Reson. Med. 81, 377–392.

Engstrom, M., Skare, S., 2013. Diffusion-weighted 3D multislab echo planar imaging for high signal-to-noise ratio efficiency and isotropic image resolution. Magn. Reson. Med. 70, 1507–1514.

Frost, R., Miller, K.L., Tijssen, R.H., Porter, D.A., Jezzard, P., 2014. 3D multi-slab diffusion-weighted readout-segmented EPI with real-time cardiac-reordered K-space acquisition. Magn. Reson. Med. 72, 1565–1579.

Guo, H., Ma, X., Zhang, Z., Zhang, B., Yuan, C., Huang, F., 2016. POCS-enhanced inherent correction of motion-induced phase errors (POCS-ICE) for high-resolution multishot diffusion MRI. Magn. Reson. Med. 75, 169–180.

Larkman, D.J., Hajnal, J.V., Herlihy, A.H., Coutts, G.A., Young, I.R., Ehnholm, G., 2001. Use of multicoil arrays for separation of signal from multiple slices simultaneously excited. J. Magn. Reson. Imaging 13, 313–317.

Liu, C., Bammer, R., Kim, D.H., Moseley, M.E., 2004. Self-navigated interleaved spiral (SNAILS): application to high-resolution diffusion tensor imaging. Magn. Reson. Med. 52, 1388–1396.

Ma, X., Zhang, Z., Dai, E., Guo, H., 2016. Improved multi-shot diffusion imaging using GRAPPA with a compact kernel. NeuroImage 138, 88–99.

Mani, M., Jacob, M., Kelley, D., Magnotta, V., 2017. Multi-shot sensitivity-encoded diffusion data recovery using structured low-rank matrix completion (MUSSELS). Magn. Reson. Med. 78, 494–507.

Miller, K.L., Pauly, J.M., 2003. Nonlinear phase correction for navigated diffusion imaging. Magn. Reson. Med. 50, 343–353.

Pipe, J.G., Farthing, V.G., Forbes, K.P., 2002. Multishot diffusion-weighted FSE using PROPELLER MRI. Magn. Reson. Med. 47, 42–52.

Porter, D.A., Heidemann, R.M., 2009. High resolution diffusion-weighted imaging using readout-segmented echo-planar imaging, parallel imaging and a two-dimensional navigator-based reacquisition. Magn. Reson. Med. 62, 468–475.

Setsompop, K., Gagoski, B.A., Polimeni, J.R., Witzel, T., Wedeen, V.J., Wald, L.L., 2012. Blipped-controlled aliasing in parallel imaging for simultaneous multislice echo planar imaging with reduced g-factor penalty. Magn. Reson. Med. 67, 1210–1224.

Skare, S., Newbould, R.D., Clayton, D.B., Albers, G.W., Nagle, S., Bammer, R., 2007. Clinical multishot DW-EPI through parallel imaging with considerations of susceptibility, motion, and noise. Magn. Reson. Med. 57, 881–890.

Wu, W., Koopmans, P.J., Frost, R., Miller, K.L., 2016. Reducing slab boundary artifacts in three-dimensional multislab diffusion MRI using nonlinear inversion for slab profile encoding (NPEN). Magn. Reson. Med. 76, 1183–1195.

CHAPTER

Diffusion MRI artifact correction

9

Jesper L.R. Andersson
FMRIB Centre, University of Oxford, Oxford, United Kingdom

9.1 Introduction

Diffusion MRI is a fantastic tool for assessing *in vivo* connectivity in the human brain, but it also has its fair share of challenges. These may pertain to acquiring data with high resolution, SNR, and diffusion contrast, or to following fiber bundles through complex configurations of crossing fibers. Or they may pertain to the problem of ensuring that data are free of distortions and the effects of subject movement; the latter is what this chapter is about.

Broadly speaking, methods for this can be divided into those that aim at alleviating or measuring the off-resonance field and/or movement through changes to acquisition and sequences, and those that attempt to estimate and correct for them after the fact. These are very much complementary and should not be seen as mutually exclusive. However, the focus of this chapter is on post-processing methods. I have chosen to focus largely on methods that I have worked on myself, rather than reviewing the field. This is not to diminish the large number of papers that have been published and the very important contributions that have been made by other groups and individuals.

The chapter is organized into two halves. The first half outlines what the problems are with distortions and subject movement for diffusion data. It explains the concept of an off-resonance field, and why that causes distortions in echo-planar images (Jezzard and Balaban, 1995). The distinction between the "susceptibility-induced off-resonance field", and the "eddy current-induced off-resonance field" is explained, and the etiology of each is outlined. After that, it discusses the effects of subject movement. These are both the gross effects common to any serial acquisition of echo-planar images, and effects that are specific to diffusion imaging, such as movement-induced signal dropout.

The second half explains how the different sources of distortions and the consequences of subject movement can be corrected.

9.2 Distortions

9.2.1 Why are echo-planar images distorted?

All MR imaging hinges on the idea of using gradients to manipulate the frequency/phase of the signal such that there is a known relationship between frequency and location. However, that relationship can be disrupted by something called an "off-resonance field". A useful intuition of an off-resonance field is to think of it as the difference between what you *think* the field is, and what it *really* is. Typical

124 **Chapter 9** Diffusion MRI artifact correction

off-resonance fields are very small compared to the gradients that are used for spatial encoding, small enough to be negligible in many situations. Because of their low strength, it is convenient to express the off-resonance field in Hz, i.e., translate the field to what it corresponds to in precession frequency of water. Typical off-resonance fields are of the order a few tens to a couple of hundred Hz.

However, echo-planar images are particularly sensitive to off-resonance fields, and fields of the magnitude alluded to above can cause significant distortions. This is because a whole 2D k-space is acquired after a single excitation, using "blips" to advance one step at a time along the phase-encode direction between consecutive traversals of the frequency-encode direction in alternating directions. Taken together, these blips are equivalent to a very weak gradient being on for a long time. It is so weak that it is of the same order of magnitude as a typical off-resonance, resulting in a bandwidth in the phase-encode direction of 10–30 Hz/pixel. The bandwidth per pixel determines how many Hz the off-resonance field has to be for the signal to be displaced by one pixel.

Hence, the distortions encountered in echo-planar images consist of displacement of signal along the phase-encode direction. If neighboring voxels are displaced by different amounts, caused by rapid change of the off-resonance field in the phase-encode direction, this can result in stretching or compression of the image, with ensuing "dilution" or "piling up" of signal.

9.2.1.1 In-plane acceleration (parallel imaging)

The distortions in EPI images are directly proportional to the time it takes from start to end of the spatial encoding, i.e., the total readout time. The bandwidth per pixel is the reciprocal of the total readout time, so an obvious way of minimizing displacement is to read out faster. This can be achieved by utilizing the spatial information in multiple coils, as explained in Chapter 2.

9.2.2 Susceptibility-induced distortions

The magnetic susceptibility of a material determines the field in that material induced by an external field. Most materials will "resist" magnetization very slightly, and the field inside the material will be slightly lower (on the order of PPMs) than the external field. The human head can be broadly divided into tissue (water), bone, and air cavities (e.g., sinuses and ear canals), which all have slightly different susceptibility. In a "complicated" geometry like that, there is not a simple relationship between a map of the susceptibility and the resulting field, and it can be quite non-intuitive, in particular around the air cavities (Jenkinson et al., 2004). Therefore it is often easier to measure the field, using, for example, a dual echo-time gradient-echo sequence, than to attempt to calculate it.

Because this off-resonance field is generated by the object (head) itself, it can be treated as constant throughout a diffusion protocol. Even in the presence of subject movement, the field can, as a first approximation, be used as a constant field that follows the object in a rigid body sense.

Fig. 9.1 explains how a susceptibility off-resonance field translates to distortions for different acquisition parameters and also exemplifies what the resulting distortions look like.

9.2.3 Eddy current-induced distortions

A current will be generated in any conductor that experiences a changing magnetic field, be it a conductor that physically moves through a static field (e.g., a dynamo) or a static conductor in a changing field. That current will in turn generate a magnetic field.

9.2 Distortions 125

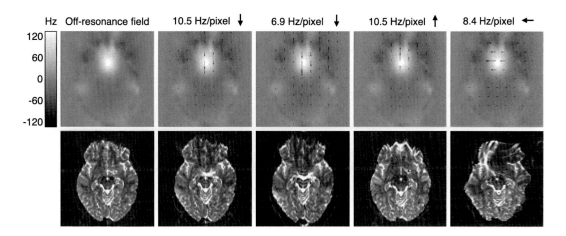

FIGURE 9.1

The leftmost panel in the top row shows a susceptibility-induced field (from a 3T scanner) at a level a little above the nasal cavities, demonstrating the relatively higher field in that area. The subsequent four panels show that field translated into displacement fields by knowledge of the relevant acquisition parameters. The first parameter is bandwidth per pixel (in the phase-encode direction), where a bandwidth of X Hz/pixel means that an off-resonance value of X leads to signal being displaced by one pixel. The other parameter is direction and polarity of the phase encoding. This is demonstrated by arrows above the images that show the direction, pointing towards higher field strength (in the gradient field created by the phase-encoding blip). The interpretation of the arrows overlaid on the fields is that the signal that *should* be at the origin of the arrow ends up at the head. A lower bandwidth per pixel means longer arrows for a given off-resonance field. The direction of the arrows is the same as the PE-direction for positive off-resonance values and in the opposite direction for negative ones. The image in the leftmost bottom row is a spin-echo EPI image (i.e., a $b = 0$ image) that has been corrected for distortions. The subsequent panels show the (actual) distorted images acquired with the parameters shown above.

When a gradient, such as a diffusion encoding gradient, in an MR scanner is rapidly switched, it leads to a temporally changing magnetic field. That in turn leads to currents in any conductors in the scanner, such as the magnet dewar, shim coils, RF coils, and the gradient coils themselves, and those currents induce a magnetic field. This is the field that is referred to as an "eddy current-induced off-resonance field". It usually has a substantial component that opposes the field that has just changed, for example if it is caused by the turning off of a diffusion gradient, it would act so as to try to restore that gradient field. This is demonstrated in Fig. 9.2, which shows some examples of distorted images, the eddy current-induced fields that caused the distortions, and the diffusion gradients that caused the eddy currents. But there are typically also other components with a less obvious relationship to the preceding gradient.

Because the eddy current-induced field is created by currents in conductors that are located well outside, and some distance away from, the object (head) these fields are necessarily smooth inside the object. In the seminal paper by Jezzard et al. (1998), the resulting distortions were, in a single 2D slice, characterized as a zoom, shear, and translation along the phase-encode direction (see Fig. 9.3 for a graphical explanation). This corresponds to linear gradients in the x- and y-directions and a con-

126 Chapter 9 Diffusion MRI artifact correction

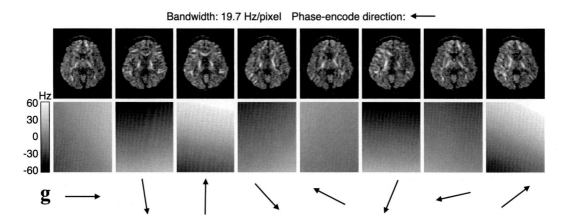

FIGURE 9.2
This figure shows actual estimates of eddy current-induced off-resonance fields in one of the pilot scans from the Human connectome project. The top row shows diffusion-weighted images that have been corrected for susceptibility-induced distortions, but which still have those caused by eddy currents. The second row shows the eddy current-induced fields that were estimated from the images. The third row shows the directions of the diffusion gradients that the images were acquired with. The images were selected from a data set with 150 volumes based on having a small (absolute value <0.1) z-component of the diffusion gradient, and the arrows in the third row ignore the z-component. It can be seen clearly that there is a close, albeit not one-to-one, relationship between the diffusion gradient direction and the resulting eddy current-induced field. It is also possible to discern the distortions in the images. These images were acquired with phase encoding in the x-direction, so an off-resonance field with a strong linear component in the y-direction would cause an xy-shear in the images (see Fig. 9.3). If one looks at the second and sixth panels, one can see that they both have a strong y-component with higher field towards the bottom, and the corresponding images looks like they are "leaning to the right". Conversely, Panels 3 and 8 have y-components with higher field towards the top, and the images look like they "lean to the left".

stant offset, and in 3D it corresponds to linear gradients along the three principal axes. Though the geometry of the situation dictates a field that changes more smoothly in space than is the case for the susceptibility-induced field, it is not obvious that it is limited to a superposition of linear gradients. Especially given that modern (short) gradients have sacrificed linearity for slew rate such that even the encoding gradients are significantly non-linear, which has to be compensated for in the reconstruction. The exact form of the eddy current-induced field is discussed further in Section 9.5.3.1.

9.2.4 Distortions are back in vogue
Until relatively recently, advances in acquisition meant that distortions were becoming less and less of a problem. Parallel imaging had a large impact on both susceptibility- and eddy current-induced distortions. An in-plane acceleration factor of 4 is realistic with modern coil arrays, and reduces all distortions by the same factor. Novel diffusion encoding schemes, aimed at nulling eddy currents, emerged to replace the Stejskal–Tanner scheme and were able to achieve very substantial reductions in eddy

9.2 Distortions

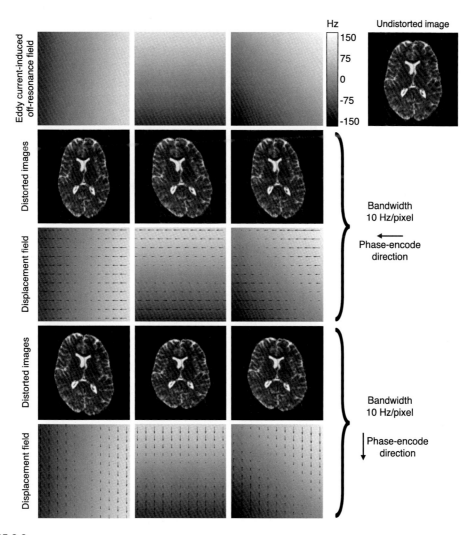

FIGURE 9.3

This schematic is intended to explain the basic eddy current-induced distortions, shear, and zoom. It is predicated on the idea that any eddy current-induced field is a linear combination of linear gradients in the three principal directions. The top row shows three off-resonance fields: a linear gradient in the x-direction, in the y-direction, and along the xy-diagonal. Rows two and three show these fields translated into displacement fields (see Fig. 9.1 for details) and into distorted images for phase encoding in the x-direction. Rows four and five show the same for the case where the phase encoding is in the y-direction. It can be seen that when the eddy current-induced field has a gradient in the same direction as the phase encoding, it causes a zoom (in or out) of the image in that direction. Conversely, when it has a gradient that is orthogonal to the phase encoding, it causes a shear, where the translation along the phase-encode direction depends linearly on the location along the orthogonal axis. The third column of rows two to five shows how oblique field gradients cause linear combinations of shear and zoom. Though not shown in the figure, an off-resonance field with a gradient along the z-axis causes a shear in the plane given by the phase-encoding direction and z. This is completely equivalent to the shears that are shown here.

128 **Chapter 9** Diffusion MRI artifact correction

current-induced distortions (Reese et al., 2003). This meant that in the clinic doctors could get close to distortion-free images straight off the scanner.

But more recently this has started to change again, not least because of the impact of the Human Connectome Project (HCP) (Uğurbil et al., 2013). The HCP developed an acquisition protocol aimed at high contrast-to-noise data with high resolution and dense angular sampling. To achieve these goals, it was decided to use a standard Stejskal–Tanner acquisition pulse sequence, and to sacrifice a high in-plane acceleration factor (see Chapter 2) for a higher multi-band (MB, also known as simultaneous multi-slice (SMS)) factor (see Chapter 3). A consequence of that decision was that both eddy current- and susceptibility-induced distortions got worse.

For clinical scanning, where getting a usable image immediately is important, eddy current-nulled sequences with high in-plane acceleration are still the norm. But owing to the substantial impact that the HCP has had, an increasing number of scans for research purposes have adopted similar acquisition protocols to theirs. Therefore distortions will be present and need to be corrected.

9.3 **Subject movement**

Subjects will move in the scanner, and movement is always a problem for any type of imaging protocol. This is especially true for scans, such as BOLD-fMRI and diffusion MRI, where a protocol can last for tens of minutes, and can be particularly bad for certain populations, such as babies, children, or patients with dementia.

9.3.1 Gross movement

This is what we typically mean when we talk about subject movement. The subject has moved between the acquisition of two volumes, and the brain appears in a slightly different location within the "box" that constitutes the reconstructed FOV. It is also the effect of movement that is the most crucial to accurately detect and correct (see also Chapters 4 and 6). Diffusion-weighted images have very strong contrast, and subject's movement by as little as 2 mm can cause a change in signal of 50% or more in a given voxel.

9.3.1.1 Movement within a volume (deck of slices)

Many motion correction methods for diffusion MRI implicitly assume that any movement occurs between volumes, i.e., that the subject remains completely still during the few seconds it takes to acquire a volume, and then moves in the fraction of a second it takes to go from the last slice of volume i to the first slice of volume $i + 1$. This is of course not an entirely realistic model, and in reality movement tends to occur within a volume. Consider an acquisition where the slices are acquired sequentially, and where the subject slowly rotates their head around the z-axis throughout the acquisition of one volume. It would have an effect similar to spreading a deck of cards, and naively stacking the slices on top of each other will not result in a consistent 3D representation of the subject's brain. In diffusion, the slices are typically sampled in interleaved order, e.g., $1, 3, 5, \ldots, 2, 4, 6, \ldots$, which means that movement within a volume results in a telltale jagged pattern that is particularly apparent at the edges of the brain. This is demonstrated in Fig. 9.4.

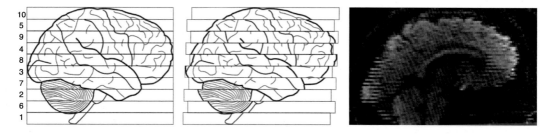

FIGURE 9.4

This figure illustrates intra-volume subject movement. On the left-hand side is shown how a brain is sampled by ten slices. The subject remains still throughout, and when stacked on top of each other, the brain is faithfully reproduced. The numbers to the far left indicate the interleaved order in which the slices are acquired, something that is typical for diffusion acquisitions. In the middle section, the same brain is shown, but now the subject has "moved" with a constant velocity during the acquisition of the volume such that each slice is translated by an equal amount compared to its (temporal) predecessor. Because each slice is spatially adjacent to two slices acquired half a repetition time ago, these end up being translated by a substantial amount relative to each other. This causes the "telltale" jagged edge that is typical for intra-volume movement in diffusion data. The rightmost panel shows an example of actual data showing exactly this effect.

Given how obviously "wrong" the volume-wise model is, it is surprising how effective it almost always is in correcting for movement effects. This indicates that for the majority of subjects, movement is "slow" compared to the time between acquiring consecutive volumes. But for particular groups that have difficulty in cooperating and lying still in the scanner, it can be important to consider a slice-wise movement model.

9.3.2 Movement-induced signal loss

The diffusion contrast is created by signal loss caused by the miniscule movement of water molecules during the diffusion encoding portion of the pulse sequence, so it comes as no surprise that gross subject movement during the diffusion encoding will cause signal loss. Perhaps more surprising is that this is not the case for all types of movement. It is only rotations that cause signal loss, and for a given rotation angle the amount of signal loss will depend on the axis of rotation in relation to the diffusion gradient direction.

A rotation will cause a linear phase roll in image space, which is equivalent to a translation of the signal in k-space. If the signal is translated sufficiently far from the center of (the acquired) k-space, part, or all, of the signal is outside the acquisition window and will not be sampled. If the acquisition is performed with partial k-space sampling, the distance that the signal needs to be translated in the partially sampled direction to be lost is shorter, which can aggravate the problem. At the same time, partial k-space acquisition allows for shorter echo time, and can hence be an important tool to maximize SNR.

Once the k-space has been acquired without the signal, that signal is forever lost and no processing can bring it back. At that stage the best that one can do is to detect the signal loss and make sure

130 **Chapter 9** Diffusion MRI artifact correction

that it doesn't affect the subsequent processing. An example of how signal dropout manifests itself in the data is described later in Section 9.6.3, which demonstrates how to detect and correct for the problem.

9.3.2.1 Special considerations for multi-band/simultaneous multi-slice

MB/SMS affects both signal dropout and within-volume movement in the way those effects manifest themselves. As explained above, signal dropout is caused by a rotational component in subject movement, and that component is of course identical for all slices within a multi-band group. Therefore, it is actually easier to detect even small/moderate dropout in multi-band data since the decision is based on more data than if one only has a single slice. The same is true for detecting within-volume movement, where in multi-band the movement/location is identical for all slices within an MB group. Similarly, it is an easier problem to find the movement parameters for a group of slices than for a single slice.

In later paragraphs when the term "slice-wise" is used, it is short for slice- or MB-group-wise, depending on the details of the acquisition.

9.3.3 Movement interacting with other factors

In addition to its direct effects, movement can also affect data through the way it interacts with other factors. It should be pointed out that the effect of these interactions is small compared to the direct effects, and is typically only a problem when the range of movement is very large.

9.3.3.1 Susceptibility-induced field

As described above, the susceptibility-induced field is caused by the object (head) disrupting the main static field in a way that is determined by the shape of the head and the exact configuration of tissue, bone, and air within it. It is also determined by how the magnetic flux, flowing along the bore, intersects the junctions between the surrounding air and the object, and also any internal junctions between tissue, bone, or air. That means that if the object is rotated around any axis that is not parallel to the flux, the angle of incidence with the junctions will change and so will the effect that they have on the field. Hence, the off-resonance field caused by a rotated object is *not* identical to a rotated field, and is not trivial to deduce from knowing the unrotated field and the angle of rotation.

9.3.3.2 Receive coil inhomogeneity

A single coil in a coil array "sees" mainly a small area adjacent to it, and has a very limited sensitivity to signals arising from outside that area. Even when considering all coils in an array and combining their sensitivity profiles, the resulting total sensitivity has a highly inhomogeneous "salad bowl" shape with a reasonably flat bottom and "half parabola" sides. Depending on what type of parallel imaging/reconstruction method is used, that inhomogeneity can be propagated as a multiplicative bias to the images, resulting in higher intensities near the surface of the brain, which are closer to the coils, than in the center of the brain. This is not in itself a problem for diffusion imaging if a given voxel has the same sensitivity in all volumes, in which case the effect cancels out in the subsequent processing. However, if there is considerable subject movement, a given location in the brain can move between regions with high and low sensitivity leading to artifactual signal variation.

9.4 Gradient non-linearities

Both the spatial and diffusion encoding of images are based on applying strong magnetic field gradients that are typically not perfectly linear. Usually the impact of any gradient non-linearity on the spatial encoding is corrected as part of the image reconstruction.

But there is an often overlooked aspect of the gradient non-linearities, which is that they will also have an effect on the diffusion weighting (Bammer et al., 2003). Gradients with significant non-linearities are typically stronger towards the edges, which means that the local gradient will increase as one moves outwards from the center such that the strength of the diffusion encoding will increase towards the edges. Not only will this lead to higher b-values towards the edges, but also to different diffusion gradient directions in different parts of the image. If one knows the gradient profiles, one can solve this by estimating and using separate b-values and gradient directions for each voxel (Sotiropoulos et al., 2013).

9.5 Correcting the distortions

If one has full knowledge of the off-resonance field, i.e., a superposition of the susceptibility- and the eddy current-induced fields, undistorted images can be reconstructed directly from the k-space data by modifying the Fourier basis functions to take into account the off-resonance field. However, for pragmatic reasons, such as the need to save the raw data and perform an offline reconstruction, it is often not practical. Therefore, the rest of this section will assume that distorted images have been reconstructed with no knowledge of the off-resonance field.

Many of the methods described below are registration based. Readers who are unfamiliar with registration are referred to Chapter 6, and in particular to the concept of a "similarity measure" (and the related concept of "cost function", which is the negation or reciprocal of a "similarity measure").

9.5.1 Difficulties specific to diffusion-weighted images

All registration problems have their own set of difficulties, but there are some difficulties specific to diffusion images that are especially problematic. These include

- The images within a diffusion data set are inherently different, which makes it non-trivial to define a useful cost function. This is especially true for data acquired with high b-values. Existing cost functions for "dissimilar images", such as mutual information, are not necessarily a good match since they tend to assume that images contain the same/similar information, only encoded differently. This is not really the case for high b-value diffusion images.
- All the images in a diffusion data set are distorted by eddy currents, sometimes severely. That means that there isn't an obvious "fixed" image to register the other images to.
- There are other, non-spatial, artifacts, such as the signal loss described in Section 9.3.2 and demonstrated in Section 9.6.3, that will affect the estimation of the spatial transform parameters if not included in the model.
- High b-value diffusion images suffer from poor SNR.

132 **Chapter 9** Diffusion MRI artifact correction

These are the reasons that specialized registration algorithms have been developed specifically for diffusion data.

9.5.2 How to estimate the susceptibility-induced field

A number of suggestions for how to find the susceptibility-induced field have been published, but at the present time there are two main strategies in common use.

9.5.2.1 Dual echo-time fieldmaps

One strategy is to use a dual echo-time sequence, where two (non-EPI) gradient-echo images are acquired with different echo times (Jezzard and Balaban, 1995). The two distortion-free images are reconstructed separately and the difference in phase between the two is a measure of how the phase has evolved as a consequence of the off-resonance field in the time interval Δt, i.e., the difference in echo-time between the acquisitions. Hence the fieldmap, in undistorted space and units of Hz, is calculated by subtracting the two phase images and dividing the resulting image by $2\pi \Delta t$. However, it is not quite as straightforward as it might appear.

- It cannot distinguish between a phase difference of ϕ and one of $n2\pi + \phi$, where n is any integer. So indirect, and non-trivial, methods have to be used to deduce what n should be.
- The phase is undefined in areas with no or little signal, such as the sinuses, the ear canals, or cranial bone. Hence the field has to be extrapolated/deduced in precisely those areas where the field changes rapidly.
- The fieldmap needs to be in exact register with the (EPI) image it is used to correct. This is not trivial if there is any subject movement between the acquisition of the fieldmap and the EPI image, as the two images are difficult to register with sufficient accuracy.
- Each of the two gradient-echo images takes on the order of a minute to acquire, and if there is any subject movement in that time it will "break" the volume in a way that is hard to repair and recover from.

Because of these difficulties, the method below for acquiring fieldmaps has become increasingly used.

9.5.2.2 Blip-up-blip-down fieldmaps

"Blip-up-blip-down" is the slightly irreverent name for a method of acquiring fieldmaps, also known as the "reversed gradient method" (Chang and Fitzpatrick, 1992). This uses two spin-echo EPI images (effectively a $b=0$ image from a diffusion protocol) acquired with different phase encodings such that the off-resonance field yields different distortions in the two images. The most common, and arguably the best, combination is two images with opposing (reversed) phase-encode directions, though other combinations, such as orthogonal directions, or more than two images are possible. Fig. 9.5 explains how these two images can be used to estimate an off-resonance field.

Different implementations of the method differ in whether they include a rigid body movement model or not, and in the way the field is represented and updated.

Compared to the dual echo-time method it has the following advantages:

- By a judicious choice of regularization and a model that includes signal modulation due to stretching/compression, one is guaranteed a field that is smooth, defined everywhere, and invertible.

9.5 Correcting the distortions

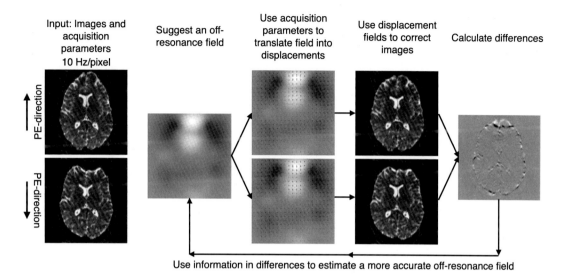

FIGURE 9.5

A schematic of how a susceptibility-induced field can be estimated from two images with different acquisition parameters. The process is typically initialized with an off-resonance field that is zero everywhere, and then updated at each iteration until the sum-of-squared difference between the corrected images is minimized. The "trick" is how to use the information in the difference image to take as good an update step as possible to find a (near) global minimum as quickly as possible. The implementation in topup (part of FSL) uses a multi-resolution pyramid to increase the chances of finding the global minimum and a Gauss–Newton update step for speed.

- The input images can, and should, be part of the data set that one intends to correct. That way the estimated field is guaranteed to be in perfect register with the data to which it is applied.
- The acquisition of each image is very fast (a few seconds), which reduces the risk of a corrupted volume because of subject movement. And because it is so fast, one can afford to acquire, for example, three volumes for each phase-encode direction, thereby ensuring that one has at least one serviceable volume for each direction.
- If the estimation algorithm includes a rigid body registration model, it is also robust to movement between the acquisition of the two different directions. Though to avoid second-order effects of movement, (see Section 9.3.3.1), it is best to acquire the two images closely in time.

A disadvantage of this method is that the execution time for estimating the field can be longer than for the dual echo-time method.

9.5.2.3 Estimating susceptibility-by-movement interaction

The off-resonance field caused by an object at location $\mathbf{p}_1$ is, as a *first approximation*, the field caused by the same object at location $\mathbf{p}_0$ resampled with the rigid body movement parameters $\mathbf{r}_1$ that map $\mathbf{p}_0$ onto $\mathbf{p}_1$. However, as described above (Section 9.3.3.1), that is not the whole truth, and any rotation component in $\mathbf{r}_1$ around an axis non-parallel to the magnetic flux will change the field such that it no longer simply follows the object. Therefore for N volumes, where the field is known for volume 0, with movement parameters $\mathbf{r}_1 \rightarrow \mathbf{r}_{N-1}$ relative to volume 0, there are potentially $N-1$ distinct fields, which would seem an insurmountable task to calculate.

Luckily, it turns out that in any given voxel/location, there is a close-to-linear relationship between field strength and rotation angles θ and ϕ around the x- and y-axes, respectively (i.e., the axes orthogonal to the magnetic flux). That means that a first-order Taylor approximation expanded with respect to θ and ϕ around a point $\mathbf{p}_0$, where the field was measured, can be a good approximation. Therefore, instead of having to estimate one field per volume, the problem has been reduced to the more manageable task of estimating two "derivative fields", $\partial\omega/\partial\theta$ and $\partial\omega/\partial\phi$. An example to aid in understanding these derivative fields is that the value at a given voxel in $\partial\omega/\partial\theta$ specifies the linear change of the field (in Hz/degree) when the subject rotates his/her head around the x-axis. Note that this is the field change in a voxel that is fixed in a coordinate system that follows that subject.

Perhaps surprisingly it is possible to estimate the derivative fields directly from the diffusion data, with no need for any additional measurements (Andersson et al., 2018). A forward model is used that predicts the "true" images based on an estimate of the movement parameters, derivative fields, and the observed images. This model is then used to interleave the estimation of the movement parameters with the estimation of the derivative fields, by minimizing the non-diffusion-related variance across the full data set. A schematic of the model is shown in Fig. 9.6.

9.5.3 How to estimate the eddy current-induced field

9.5.3.1 How to represent the field

As already discussed in Section 9.2.3, it has been suggested that the eddy current-induced fields can be approximated by a linear combination of linear gradients in the three principal directions. However, empirical tests have demonstrated that a second-order polynomial field performs better (Andersson and Sotiropoulos, 2016).

It is also important to model a constant offset, regardless of what order polynomial one uses. If we take an example where the phase-encode direction is in the y-direction, a linear gradient in the y-direction will cause a pure y-zoom, and linear gradients in the x- and z-directions will cause pure shears in the xy- and yz-planes *only if* the zero-crossing of the gradients coincide exactly with the center of the imaged volume. If not, it will additionally have a constant offset.

9.5.3.2 How to estimate the field

Because of the low-order variation over space, it is potentially much faster and better conditioned to actually measure the eddy current-induced field than is the case for the susceptibility-induced field. But it nevertheless requires a bespoke sequence that is not readily publicly available.

Another strategy is to estimate the fields directly from the data using image registration methods. A difficulty with that is to find a suitable cost function, whose minimization would indicate that the images are in register.

However, these days most diffusion data is HARDI (high angular resolution diffusion imaging), which means that the signal is sampled "densely" in the diffusion gradient direction-(Q)-space. Exactly what constitutes densely depends on the b-value, so HARDI does not really have a strict definition. But it is nevertheless the case that diffusion data in research tends to have a high level of redundancy. In other words if, for a given voxel, we know the signal in all diffusion-weighted images except one,

9.5 Correcting the distortions

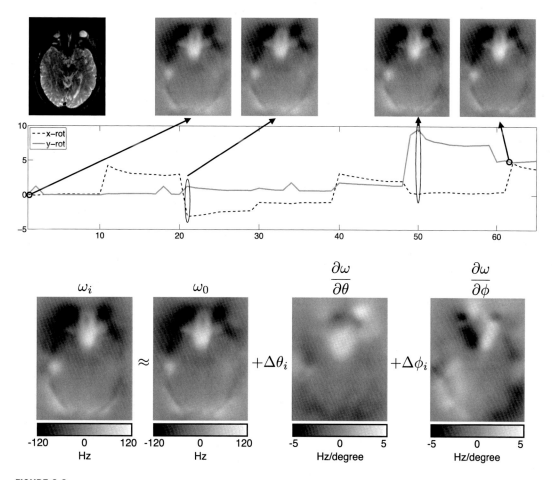

FIGURE 9.6

This figure shows the model for the susceptibility-by-movement interaction. The lower row shows how the field for the ith volume is given by the field (B_0) for the zeroth volume, plus the difference in θ (rotation around the x-axis) between volumes i and 0, multiplied by the rate-of-change with respect to rotation around the x-axis. And similarly for the rotation around the y-axis. The rate of change fields can be estimated directly from the data by inverting the model. The top row shows the x- and y-rotation for a data set with deliberate large movements and the resulting field for selected volumes. These were calculated using the model described and the pertinent rotation parameters for each volume. It can be seen that the differences in the field are quite subtle, even for relatively large movements.

we would be able to predict the signal in the unknown image with very high accuracy. This points to a strategy, where we could use $N-1$ of our N diffusion-weighted images to make a prediction for the missing image, and then use sum-of-squared-differences to align the missing image with the prediction. One iteration of a full algorithm could then be to step through all N images, and align each of them to a prediction based on the remaining $N-1$ images. Such an algorithm has been implemented in the `eddy` software (Andersson and Sotiropoulos, 2016), that is, part of `FSL`, and is explained in Fig. 9.7.

136 Chapter 9 Diffusion MRI artifact correction

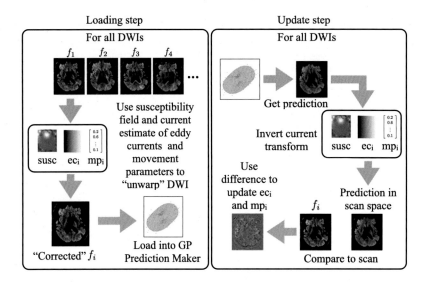

FIGURE 9.7

Schematic of the algorithm that `eddy` (a part of `FSL`) uses to estimate eddy currents and subject movement. It is divided into a "loading step" and an "update step", and one iteration of the algorithm consists of both steps. The algorithm typically runs for 5–10 iterations. The "loading step" consists of correcting each diffusion-weighted volume for susceptibility (a constant) and the current estimates of eddy currents and motion parameters, and then "loading" them into a Gaussian process. Once all volumes have been loaded, the "hyper-parameters" of the Gaussian process are estimated, and it is ready to make predictions. The update step consists of making a prediction for each of the diffusion-weighted volumes and "uncorrecting it" using the inverse of the transform given by the susceptibility and the current estimate of the eddy currents and motion parameters. This returns it to "scan space" and can be compared to the observed volume. The difference is used to update the estimates of eddy currents and motion parameters. It might seem a strange choice to inverse transform the prediction back to "scan space", but Section 9.6.3 explains why that might be a good idea. Also, it might not seem intuitive that there should be any difference to drive the registration after the volume has been corrected, and then "uncorrected". The important point is that the prediction is not just based on that volume, but on all volumes, with a higher weight for neighboring and antipodal volumes on the Q-sphere. That means that the location, in a position and distortion space, of the prediction is an average location of all the scans.

A crucial assumption here is that the prediction based on the N-1 images is not affected by the same distortions as the ith (left out) image, because then there would be no difference that can drive the registration. When using the N-1 images to predict an image acquired with the diffusion gradient $\mathbf{g}_i$, that prediction will be dominated by those images that were acquired with a gradient $\mathbf{g}_j$ that is close to parallel or antiparallel to $\mathbf{g}_i$. An image acquired with a gradient $\mathbf{g}_j$ close to parallel to $\mathbf{g}_i$ is likely to exhibit similar distortions to that acquired with $\mathbf{g}_i$, so a prediction dominated by $\mathbf{g}_j$ is likely to differ only slightly from the ith image, and each iteration would only "nudge" the ith image a short distance. In contrast, if the image was acquired with a gradient $\mathbf{g}_j$ close to antiparallel to $\mathbf{g}_i$, the distortions are likely to be very different (close to opposite) and a prediction dominated by $\mathbf{g}_j$ would generate a strong error signal, allowing the algorithm to take a much larger step towards the solution. It should be clear from the reasoning above that to facilitate estimating the eddy current-induced field, it is advantageous to sample the Q-space on the whole sphere. Concretely, this means that one should *not* choose one's diffusion gradients such that they all have the same sign along one of the principal directions, which has been very common in the past.

9.5.3.3 How to make the predictions

There are many possible ways in which to predict a diffusion-weighted image, given knowledge of the other images in a data set of N images. The immediately obvious way would be to fit a model, such as the diffusion tensor or spherical harmonics, to the remaining $N-1$ images. However, there are disadvantages to that strategy. The most serious one is that any distortion-induced variance that lies within that model space is "invisible" to such a strategy, which will potentially lead to distortions being left uncorrected.

It has therefore been suggested to use a Gaussian process that only assumes that the signal varies smoothly on a Q-sphere as parameterized by a covariance function (Andersson and Sotiropoulos, 2015). The Gaussian process is able to accommodate a wide range of signal variation on the sphere (e.g., three-way crossing fibers), while at the same time always favoring a maximally smooth (in Q-space) solution. The degree to which it will favor a smooth solution is determined from the data itself using cross-validation, so there are no "fudge factors" that need to be predefined. Because it will always favor a smooth solution, there is no variance that is "invisible" to it.

9.5.3.4 How to combine the two fields

To combine the two off-resonance fields, one simply has to superpose (add) them, but one does need to take subject movement into account. The eddy current-induced field is stationary in a scanner framework, whereas the susceptibility-induced field is stationary (to a first approximation) in a subject framework. If the derivative fields, which describe the rate of change of the susceptibility field with respect to subject movements (rotations), are estimated (see Section 9.5.2.3), those are stationary in a subject framework also.

9.5.4 "Causal" modeling of the eddy currents

The eddy currents are caused by the diffusion encoding gradient, so it follows that there is some mapping $f : \mathbb{R}^3 \to \mathbb{R}^n$ from the diffusion gradient to its off-resonance field (as defined over the n voxels in the FOV). When, such as in our case, the off-resonance field is represented using a low-order polynomial so that it is determined by a small number of coefficients, then that mapping can be broken down into a small number of $\mathbb{R}^3 \to \mathbb{R}$ mappings, where the co-domain of each is one of the coefficients. If one could find the general form and the pertinent parameters, one could represent the eddy current-induced fields of a whole data set with many fewer parameters, and potentially improve the robustness of the estimation.

The eddy current-induced field is, in general, relatively well-estimated by virtue of its low spatial order (only 4 parameters are estimated per volume for a first-order polynomial and 10 for a second-order) so it is not necessarily always a good idea. This is especially since the general form of the mapping cannot be inferred from first principles, and "true" information (distortions) could be lost from attempting to shoehorn the data into an assumed form. But there are situations where it can be useful to attempt to estimate the mapping from diffusion gradients to fields.

138   Chapter 9 Diffusion MRI artifact correction

One situation is when the diffusion gradients have been sampled on the half sphere, i.e., where one of the x-, y-, or the z-components of the gradients are all positive or all negative (see top part of Fig. 9.8). When registering all diffusion-weighted images to each other using an internal generative model to make predictions, the final space for the registered images is the "average distorted space". This average space will be identical, or very close to identical, to the undistorted space provided that each (x-, y-, or z-) component of the diffusion gradients add up to approximately zero across all volumes (this is equivalent to saying that the diffusion gradients have been sampled on the whole sphere). But if, for example, all the z-components of the gradients are positive, then all the images will be distorted in the way that is associated with a positive z-gradient (though to different degrees, depending on the size of the z-component for each volume). That means that the "average distorted space" will also be "positive z-component distorted" and that is the space where all the "corrected" images will end up. But if there is a parametric model, even a simple linear model, one can extrapolate from the non-zero point in the z-component direction to zero, and thereby bring corrected space closer to the true undistorted space. This is explained graphically in Fig. 9.8.

Note that although Fig. 9.8 represents real data and estimates, it has been simplified a little for the sake of clarity. In reality, the shear-parameters are caused by all three (x-, y-, and z-) components of the diffusion gradients; therefore the mapping from gradient to shear is a $\mathbb{R}^3 \to \mathbb{R}$, and the model is a 3D hyper-surface. In the figure, the dependence on the x- and z-components has already been regressed out of the estimates.

9.6 Correcting subject movement

In principle, the method for correcting subject movement is the same as that used for estimating the eddy current-induced off-resonance fields, but instead of estimating a set of parameters pertaining to the EC-field for each volume, one now estimates six rigid body movement parameters. In practice, it is highly recommended to simultaneously estimate eddy currents and movement (as in Fig. 9.7). One reason for this is that a shear is a "half rotation", so if one, for example, estimates eddy currents first, then a subject rotation will be interpreted as a shear, and the subsequent movement correction will not be able to rectify that.

9.6.1 Rotating "*b*-vecs"

There is a known and fixed relationship between the principal axes of the imaging matrix and the directions along which the diffusion weighting has been applied, colloquially known as *b*-vecs. But when processing the images in certain ways, for example when rotating an image as part of motion correction, that known relationship is disrupted. However, the transform that was applied to the image is known, and by applying the same rotation to the *b*-vec the correct relationship is re-established.

It has been shown that tractography can be seriously derailed by ignoring this correction (Leemans and Jones, 2009). It is easy to see why that would be the case; if in a set of diffusion images the *b*-vec is "wrong" by 1 degree on average (around some axis), then each step of the tractography will veer off course by a similar amount (1 degree), which will soon add up to a large error. What is perhaps less obvious is that it is mainly the *average* error that matters. A non-zero average (average over time/diffusion-gradient) error will cause a rotation of the orientation distribution function by the same

9.6 Correcting subject movement   139

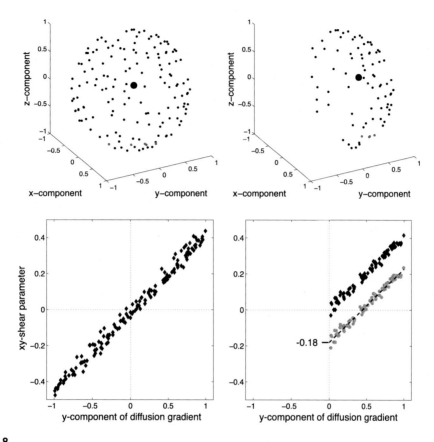

FIGURE 9.8

This figure shows the utility of causal modeling of the eddy current-induced fields when Q-space has been sampled only on a half sphere. The top left panel shows the Q-sphere pattern for a data set sampled on the whole sphere. The large marker is the center-of-mass of the samples, and it can be seen that it is located close to the [0 0 0] point. The lower left panel shows the estimated in-plane shear-parameters versus the y-component of the diffusion gradient (acquired with phase encoding in the x-direction) for the whole sphere data set. Note that each point corresponds to one image volume. It can be seen that the shear-parameter takes on both positive and negative values, and that the parameters cross the zero-line approximately at the point where the y-component of the diffusion gradient is zero. This indicates that all the volumes have been transformed towards a point where there are no shear distortions, i.e., the [0 0 0] point. The top right panel shows the Q-sphere sampling of a subset of the data on the left, those acquired with diffusion gradients with a positive y-component. In the lower right panel, indicated by gray circles, are the estimated shear-parameters for that subset. It can be seen that the relative values are very similar to when all the data were included, but that there are still positive and negative values. But now the crossing of the zero line has been translated to a point where the y-component of the diffusion gradient is approximately 0.5, i.e., the center-of-mass point in the top right panel. This indicates that the differences in shear between the volumes have been corrected to a space where the shear is no longer zero, but rather a point that corresponds to the average shear of the data. By fitting a linear causal model to the data (dashed line), it is possible to estimate what "shear-point" corresponds to zero y-component (-0.18 in these data), and hence zero shear. This can then be subtracted from the estimates (black diamonds), which means that the volumes can now be transformed to the zero shear point, despite this point not being present in the sample.

140 **Chapter 9** Diffusion MRI artifact correction

amount, and it is this that causes problems for the tractography. In contrast, errors around a zero mean will only result in a slight widening of orientation distribution function, which is a considerably smaller problem.

9.6.2 Correcting movement within a volume (deck of slices)

In particular populations, such as very young children or patients with dementia, there can be repeated sudden movements such that the volumetric movement model may not be sufficient. In that case, it can be useful to move to a model where the six movement parameters are estimated on a finer time scale than once per volume. This can be once per slice/multi-band group, or one can choose to use a continuous movement model, for example, parameterized by some set of basis functions. The principle of estimating the movement is essentially the same as for the volumetric case. Given a reference volume (which is assumed to have no movement) and another volume, for which one wants to find the movement, one can test candidate movement parameters for each slice and use these to resample and restack the reference volume and compare the resulting stack to that of the other volume.

Once the movement-over-time trajectory is known, the more difficult part is to recreate the "image that would have been obtained if there had been no movement". This is because intra-volume movement leads to "gaps" in the data, where parts of the brain have not been sampled, as can be seen in Fig. 9.9. It is a non-trivial problem, and means that "normal" interpolation methods, which are designed for data that have been acquired on a regular grid, are not applicable. In the implementation in eddy, this problem is solved by a two-step process that starts with a 2D regular interpolation (each slice is still acquired on a regular grid). This is followed by a non-equidistant 1D fitting of B-splines to the data in the slice direction, which is complemented with predictions (*cf.* the outlier replacement in Fig. 9.11), where data are missing (Andersson et al., 2017).

9.6.3 Correcting movement-induced signal loss

When signal has been lost because it was translated outside the k-space window that was acquired, there is no way of getting it back. The best one can do is to detect it and make sure that the loss of signal does not impact the subsequent analysis/modeling.

One way to detect signal loss is to compare the observed signal in the image to the "expected" signal. That expectation can be based on the signal in adjacent slices, or it can be based on what the signal is in the same voxel/slice in the other diffusion-weighted volumes. When using the signal from the same voxel in the other diffusion-weighted volumes to make a prediction about what to expect, one can fit a model, such as the diffusion tensor model, to the signal from the other volumes. Another option is to use the Gaussian process, as discussed above, to make that prediction. One can then compare the predicted signal to the observed signal, and if the difference is greater than some threshold (for example n standard deviations), then it is deemed to be an outlier, and hence affected by signal loss. Fig. 9.10 attempts to explain this in an intuitive way.

Another choice that has to be made is the spatial granularity in which one attempts to detect the dropout. As explained above, the dropout is caused by a rotation that coincides in time with the diffusion encoding part of the acquisition. If that rotation is a consequence of the subject moving, the whole slice will be affected by the signal loss. On the other hand, if only part of the brain is rotated, the signal loss will only affect parts of the brain. That may sound strange, but is something that can be seen in the

9.6 Correcting subject movement 141

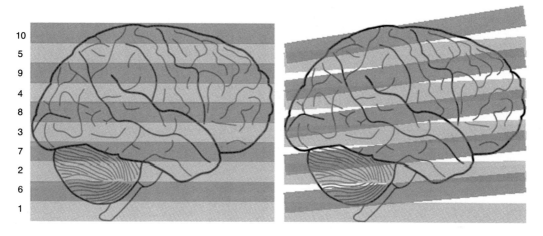

FIGURE 9.9

This figure illustrates the sampling problem caused by intra-volume movement. The left hand side shows the same brain and slice ordering as in Fig. 9.4, but this time the odd slices have been colored light gray and the even slices medium gray. On the right hand side, a situation is shown where the subject is performing a constant velocity nodding movement (rotation around the x-axis) such that at each consecutive slice they have nodded one degree forward compared to the previous slice. This is equivalent to rotating each sampled slice in the opposite direction in a stationary brain. We can see how this leads to a pattern of "wedges" that have been sampled twice (the "dark" gray areas). But more importantly, it also leads to unfilled white wedges that have not been sampled at all.

midbrain, where the arterial blood from each heartbeat pushes it up and forward (causing a rotation of upper parts of the midbrain around the left-right axis).

One can chose to define outliers on a slice or multi-band group of slices (Andersson et al., 2016) or on a voxel basis (Chang et al., 2005). Both strategies have been used, and they represent different choices of a trade-off between sensitivity and spatial specificity.

If it truly is only a subset of voxels in a slice that are affected by drop-out, then discarding the whole slice means throwing out good data. This can potentially be avoided by detecting outliers on a voxel basis. But the disadvantage is that the sensitivity is quite poor, and the relative signal loss needs to be quite large for it to be detected. The lack of sensitivity is further exacerbated if using the diffusion tensor model for the predictions, since in regions of crossing fibers the model is already a poor fit, and the threshold for outliers needs to be set high so as not to reject good data points.

If, on the other hand, outliers are defined on a slice/multi-band group basis, one compares jointly all voxels in the slice against their expectation. This gives very high sensitivity, and because the sensitivity is so high, one can set the threshold such that there are very few false positives and still expect to detect even very small signal dropouts. However, after motion correction, the original slices will have been rotated away from their original locations, potentially spreading a drop-out slice across several slices through the interpolation model. That means that any slicewise outlier detection has to be performed before, or ideally as part of, the spatial pre-processing. It also means that when detecting an outlier, it cannot "just be labeled and ignored", because it will be needed in combination with good data when interpolating across slices. This is explained graphically in Fig. 9.11.

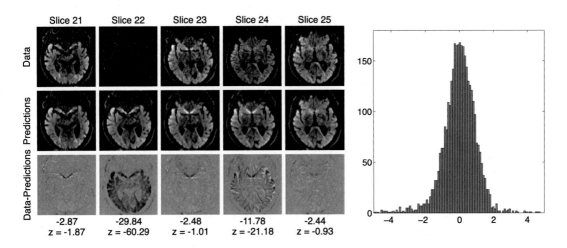

FIGURE 9.10

This figures demonstrates how outliers caused by movement-induced signal loss can be corrected. The three rows of images show 5 consecutive slices of one diffusion-weighted volume from a data set acquired in an elderly subject who moved significantly. The first row shows the raw data, and it is immediately clear that Slice 22 has had a complete loss of signal. The second row shows the predictions. Note that these predictions were made in "corrected" space, and then inverse transformed into scan space based on the current estimate of distortion and movement for this volume. The third row shows the data minus the predictions, and the number immediately below is the slice average of that subtraction. For a given data set, the number of such differences is the number of diffusion-weighted volumes times the number of slices per volume, so in the example data set, that number is 60 diffusion-weighted volumes × 64 slices, i.e., 3840. Thus even in a fairly standard data set, such as this, there is a large enough sample from which to assess the statistics, and hence outliers. Those differences can trivially be converted to z-scores, and those are shown in the rightmost part of the figure. Note that the histogram has a very long negative tail; the smallest numbers are more than 90 standard deviations away, but for clarity only the central part is shown. In the bottom left row, the differences have been converted to z-scores, i.e., how many standard deviations away they are from the mean. A threshold of -4 standard deviations means that Slices 22 and 24 are deemed as outliers, and replaced by the predictions.

9.7 What matters?

There is a very natural desire to stress the importance of our own contributions, and if one has, for example, developed a method for tracking the changes of the susceptibility field with subject movement, one might be inclined to promulgate the significance of that. This can make it a little difficult for a user to orient him-/herself and understand which of these corrections are crucial and which are less so. There is of course nothing wrong with "doing it all", just to be safe. But from a practical perspective, not all software packages will provide all corrections, and it is not always straightforward to combine multiple software implementations into a processing pipeline. The following is therefore an attempt to outline a hierarchy of corrections in order of importance. Such a list will not be 100% unequivocal, as the importance of the different corrections will be somewhat dependent on what the subsequent analysis will be.

9.7 What matters? 143

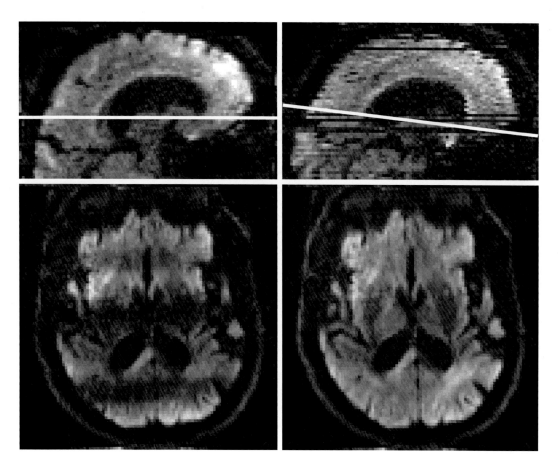

FIGURE 9.11

Illustration of the difficulty of outlier detection in the presence of subject movement. The top left panel shows a sagittal slice through the first diffusion-weighted volume, which is used as the reference position for subsequent motion correction. The white line shows the location of Slice 29. The top right panel shows the 12th diffusion-weighted volume from the same data set. At this stage, the subject has rotated his/her head by approximately 6.5 degrees around the left-right axis, which means that the location of Slice 29 in the reference now goes along the oblique white line. It can also be seen that there are several outlier slices with signal loss (dark bands) and intra-volume movement (jagged brain outline; see Fig. 9.4). The lower left panel shows the 12th volume resampled along the oblique line in the upper right panel so as to be in register with Slice 29 in the reference volume. It can be seen that it has cut through three slices with varying degree of signal loss, evident as three wide, dark bands. Due to the interpolation, the outliers that were previously well-defined have now "leaked" into many more voxels, representing varying mixtures of good data and data with signal loss. Finally, the lower right panel shows the same resampled slice, but where the outliers were detected and replaced by predictions in their original scan space prior to resampling the slice.

144 Chapter 9 Diffusion MRI artifact correction

1. In first place there is a split decision.
   (a) Gross volume-to-volume movement: Subjects will move, they may move a lot, and it will introduce a lot of unwanted variance that will affect the estimation of diffusion-related model parameters. Even a basic volume-to-volume motion correction method will remove the vast majority of that variance. If one has high b-value data, one needs to make sure that the method one uses is capable of dealing with that.
   (b) Susceptibility-induced distortions: Unlike many of the other effects, these will not introduce additional variance or affect the estimation of voxel-wise model parameters. But they *will* distort the fabric on which those are estimated. For tractography, that means that a voxel pointed to by a model-derived "arrow" (unaffected by the distortion) will not be the right one (Embleton et al., 2010). For other (non-tractography) types of analysis, it means that the estimates are in the wrong place, upwards of 10 mm in the worst affected areas.
2. Eddy current-induced distortions: The severity of the eddy current-induced distortions will depend crucially on whether an "eddy current-nulled" diffusion weighting has been used or not. If not, the distortions can be quite severe and introduce unwanted variance, similar to that of subject movement.
3. Rotation of "b-vecs": This is true when the subsequent analysis includes tractography, and with the caveat that the crucial part is to ensure that there is no average rotation.
4. Correction of b-values and "b-vecs" for gradient non-linearities: The effect of this can be substantial on modern scanners with short bores and fast gradient systems. The true diffusion weighting can be more than ten percent greater towards the edges of the brain, and oblique gradients will be rotated relative to the tentative ones.
5. Movement-induced signal loss: These artifacts can look dramatic, but luckily they are not very frequent for cooperative subjects and tend to occur randomly (i.e., not preferentially for some diffusion gradient directions). For subjects who move a lot, it can be more of an issue.
6. Intra-volume movement: Another artifact that looks very dramatic, but which rarely affects data from typical, cooperative subjects.
7. Susceptibility field changing with subject movement: This is mainly an issue if there are very large subject rotations. And even then it mainly affects only certain parts of the brain, such as the temporal poles.

A caveat to note is with regard to the last three items on the list. Their placing is predicated on data from typical subjects, i.e., motivated and cooperative adults. If one is working with categories of subjects who move a lot more, such as babies, small children, or patients with dementia, they can make the difference between getting useful data and having to discard it.

9.8 What have we not corrected?

This chapter has tried to outline the artifacts encountered in diffusion images, and how they can be corrected. So, is there anything left out?

The effect that I personally believe would be most important to find a method to correct for is "spin-history" effects (Yancey et al., 2011). This refers to the fact that the signal we can obtain after excitation of a set of spins depends on how long ago they were previously excited. The longer ago they were previously excited, the greater the signal, up to a couple of tens of seconds, after which the spins can again be considered pristine. When a slice gets excited, it was previously excited one repetition time ago (typically a few seconds ago), and this determines the signal available from the present excitation. For a subject who lies still, an equilibrium is reached after the first excitation, and all subsequent excitations of the same slice will have the same signal available. However, this can change substantially if the subject moves.

Imagine a case where slices are acquired sequentially, and where the subject makes a sudden movement (translation in the z-direction) immediately after a slice was acquired such that the same slice gets excited again. Because that slice was now excited such a short time ago, the signal in that slice will be severely reduced.

Similarly, in Fig. 9.9, it can be seen how parts (wedges) of the volume were never excited because the subject moved during the acquisition of that volume. That means that when these regions are excited as part of acquiring the subsequent volume, they were last excited two repetition times ago, and will now have more signal available. Hence, the effects are not restricted to loss of signal, but will be a spatially heterogeneous mix of hypo- and hyperintensities.

It can be easily realized that a prerequisite for correcting this is to know the exact location of each part of the object at all times. This remains an open area of research.

Acknowledgments

I would like to thank Frederik Lange for very helpful comments on the manuscript.

References

Andersson, J.L.R., Sotiropoulos, S.N., 2015. Non-parametric representation and prediction of single- and multi-shell diffusion-weighted MRI data using Gaussian processes. NeuroImage 122, 166–176. https://doi.org/10.1016/j.neuroimage.2015.07.067.

Andersson, J.L.R., Sotiropoulos, S.N., 2016. An integrated approach to correction for off-resonance effects and subject movement in diffusion MR imaging. NeuroImage 125, 1063–1078. https://doi.org/10.1016/j.neuroimage.2015.10.019.

Andersson, J.L.R., Graham, M.S., Zsoldos, E., Sotiropoulos, S.N., 2016. Incorporating outlier detection and re-placement into a non-parametric framework for movement and distortion correction of diffusion MR images. NeuroImage 141, 556–572. https://doi.org/10.1016/j.neuroimage.2016.06.058.

Andersson, J.L.R., Graham, M.S., Drobnjak, I., Zhang, H., Filippini, N., Bastiani, M., 2017. Towards a comprehensive framework for movement and distortion correction of diffusion MR images: within volume movement. NeuroImage 152, 450–466. https://doi.org/10.1016/j.neuroimage.2017.02.085.

Andersson, J.L.R., Graham, M.S., Drobnjak, I., Zhang, H., Campbell, J., 2018. Susceptibility-induced distortion that varies due to motion: correction in diffusion MR without acquiring additional data. NeuroImage 171, 277–295. https://doi.org/10.1016/j.neuroimage.2017.12.040.

Bammer, R., Markl, M., Barnett, A., Acar, B., Alley, M.T., Pelc, N.J., Glover, G.H., Moseley, M.E., 2003. Analysis and generalized correction of the effect of spatial gradient field distortions in diffusion-weighted imaging. Magnetic Resonance in Medicine 50, 560–569.

Chang, H.J., Fitzpatrick, J.M., 1992. A technique for accurate magnetic resonance imaging in the presence of field inhomogeneities. IEEE Transactions on Medical Imaging 11, 319–329.

Chang, L.-C., Jones, D.K., Pierpaoli, C., 2005. RESTORE: robust estimation of tensors by outlier rejection. Magnetic Resonance in Medicine 53, 1088–1095.

Embleton, K.V., Haroon, H.A., Morris, D.M., Lambon Ralph, M.A., Parker, G.J.M., 2010. Distortion correction for diffusion-weighted MRI tractography and fMRI in the temporal lobes. Human Brain Mapping 31 (10), 1570–1587.

Jenkinson, M., Wilson, J., Jezzard, P., 2004. A perturbation method for magnetic field calculations of non-conductive objects. Magnetic Resonance in Medicine 52, 471–477.

Jezzard, P., Balaban, R.S., 1995. Correction for geometric distortions in echoplanar images from B_0 field variations. Magnetic Resonance in Medicine 34, 65–73.

Jezzard, P., Barnett, A.S., Pierpaoli, C., 1998. Characterization of and correction for eddy current artifacts in echo planar diffusion imaging. Magnetic Resonance in Medicine 39, 801–812.

Leemans, A., Jones, D.K., 2009. The B-matrix must be rotated when correcting for subject motion in DTI data. Magnetic Resonance in Medicine 61, 1336–1349.

Reese, T.G., Heid, O., Weisskoff, R.M., Vedeen, V.J., 2003. Reduction of eddy-current-induced distortion in diffusion MRI using a twice-refocused spin echo. Magnetic Resonance in Medicine 49, 177–182.

Sotiropoulos, S.N., Jbabdi, S., Xu, J., Andersson, J.L., Moeller, S., Auerbach, E.J., Glasser, M.F., Hernandez, M., Sapiro, G., Jenkinson, M., Feinberg, D.A., Yacoub, E., Lenglet, C., Van Essen, D.C., Ugurbil, K., Behrens, T.E.J., WU-Minn HCP Consortium, 2013. Advances in diffusion MRI acquisition and processing in the human connectome project. NeuroImage 80, 125–143.

Uğurbil, K., Xu, J., Auerbach, E.J., Moeller, S., Vu, A.T., Duarte-Carvajalino, J.M., Lenglet, C., Wu, X., Schmitter, S., de Moortele, P.F.V., Strupp, J., Sapiro, G., Martino, F.D., Wang, D., Harel, N., Garwood, M., Chen, L., Feinberg, D.A., Smith, S.M., Miller, K.L., Sotiropoulos, S.N., Jbabdi, S., Andersson, J.L., Behrens, T.E., Glasser, M.F., Essen, D.C.V., Yacoub, E., 2013. Pushing spatial and temporal resolution for functional and diffusion MRI in the human connectome project. NeuroImage 80, 80–104.

Yancey, S.E., Rotenberg, D.J., Tam, F., Chiew, M., Ranieri, S., Biswas, L., Anderson, K.J.T., Baker, S.N., Wright, G.A., Graham, S.J., 2011. Spin-history artifact during functional MRI: potential for adaptive correction. Medical Physics 38 (8), 4634–4646.

CHAPTER

Diffusion MRI analysis methods

10

Szabolcs David[a,b], Joost Verhoeff[b], and Alexander Leemans[a]

[a]*PROVIDI Lab, Image Sciences Institute, University Medical Centre Utrecht, Utrecht, The Netherlands*
[b]*Department of Radiation Oncology, University Medical Centre Utrecht, Utrecht, The Netherlands*

10.1 Introduction

Early studies of the human brain were based on various invasive procedures (Klingler and Ludwig, 1956), such as dissection or tracer studies, but investigating the living brain with a high level of detail remained challenging until the early 1990s. This gap in knowledge was expressed in a commentary by Crick and Jones (1993) in a *Nature* article on how little is known about the human brain as compared to the macaque brain, which is widely used even nowadays to understand neuronal mechanisms. At that time, magnetic resonance imaging (MRI) was mainly a static technique and positron emission tomography (PET) was the dominant available dynamic technique able to monitor the whole brain, but was considered rather slow and was limited in spatial resolution. Their finishing words were: "*Clearly what is needed for a modern human brain anatomy is the introduction of some radically new techniques, but unless there is a general awareness of the need for them they are not likely to arise. [..] We wish we had more concrete suggestions for new techniques. Although we have not, we feel we should make a wide audience aware of this pressing need, especially as most neuroanatomists seem scarcely to have noticed it*". Just one year later, Basser and colleagues (Basser et al., 1994) developed such radically new technique called diffusion tensor (DT) MRI (DT-MRI or DTI), which measured the diffusion of water and which could indirectly map the axonal connections of the living human brain. With the proliferation of new diffusion MRI (dMRI) methods in recent years we can now start to unravel the brain's circuitry with an unprecedented level of detail.

Over the past several decades, dMRI has become the preferred method to investigate microstructural properties of neuronal tissue and to virtually reconstruct the structural connections of the brain. Diffusion MRI provided a novel way of studying brain anatomy. For example, Catani et al. (2012) described the short, frontal lobe connections in the human brain and validated this at the same with (Klingler) dissection. A wide range of neuroscience and clinical applications utilized dMRI including, but not limited to, investigations in neurodegenerative diseases (such as Alzheimer's disease or dementia), developmental processes, or even pre-surgical planning. During the research question formulation, experts make choices not only on which dMRI parameters they wish to study, but also on how to compare them. There are multiple strategies available, each with its own benefits and drawbacks. For example, the effect of local lesions may be overshadowed if overly gross atlas labels are used to extract diffusion parameters, whereas a voxel-wise comparison may yield striking differences. Several academic software packages have been built by the scientific community to ensure the transparency and reproducibility of data preparation and the extraction of parameters. Readers are encouraged to discover the data analysis potential of DIPY (dipy.org), DSI Studio (dsi-studio.labsolver.org), ExploreDTI (exploredti.com), FreeSurfer (surfer.nmr.mgh.harvard.edu), FSL (fsl.fmrib.ox.ac.uk/fsl), and MRtrix (mrtrix.org), among others. Though the common interest of dMRI studies is biology, or pathology-related, some researchers are interested in grading the performance of image processing pipelines too. The same data set can be prepared many times with different processing settings, from which pipeline-induced effects are measured via differences in, for example, the propagation of fiber pathways from the same seed point (Mesri et al., 2019). In the following sections, we will review the most common methods in dMRI analysis, along with their strengths and limitations: (a) histogram; (b) region-of-interest (ROI); (c) voxel-based; (d) fiber tractography-based; (e) along-the-tract; (f) connectomics; (g) fixel-based, and (h) shape-based (Fig. 10.1).

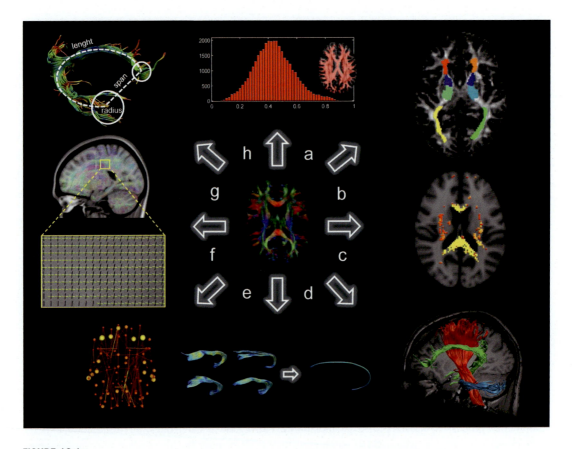

FIGURE 10.1

Overview of diffusion MRI data analysis methods: (a) histogram-based; (b) region-based; (c) voxel-based; (d) fiber tractography; (e) along-the-tract; (f) connectomics; (g) fixel-based, and (h) tract geometry analysis.

10.2 Analysis methods
10.2.1 Histogram analysis
Histogram-based analysis (Fig. 10.1a) may be preferred when the disease or condition of interest is analyzed as a global effect on the whole brain (Giulietti et al., 2018). Several statistical descriptors can be extracted from the histogram, for example: mean, median, peak location, etc., which are subjects of further analysis. Since comparison is performed on the whole brain, it can be very sensitive, and also operator-independent. The main drawback is that it cannot provide the location where any differences may occur. One way to improve the method's spatial specificity is to combine it with other analysis techniques, for example, region-based, or even voxel-wise analysis to investigate other properties than only the mean and standard variation and appreciate the skewness of the data (Rousselet et al., 2017).

10.2.2 Region-of-interest analysis
When one wishes to study specific parts of the brain, different flavors of region-based or region-of-interest (ROI)-based methods (Fig. 10.1b) are the primary tools. Manual delineations are often hand-drawn by a researcher or clinician on 2D slices for the full 3D volume, or *a priori* information is used in the form of atlases, which are matched to the data via image registration. Both a manual solution and an atlas-based registration can be applied to the diffusion data or on co-registered modalities, such as the T_1- or T_2-weighted scans of the same subject. Nowadays, the main applications of manual delineations are clinical cases or hypothesis-driven studies, where the required anatomical expertise is justified. For example, delineation of brain tumors is usually defined on contrast-enhanced T_1-weighted MR images, where the hypersignal areas are an indicator of tumor infiltration. The very same regions of interest can be used to extract diffusion property changes as compared to unaffected tissues. Defining the tumor areas directly on the diffusion data might be challenging because of secondary reactions to tumor and prior surgery (e.g., edema, inflammation, necrosis). Fig. 10.2 shows an example of a patient where the gross tumor volume (GTV, in red) before radiation therapy (RT) has been contoured based on the contrast-enhanced T_1-weighted image.

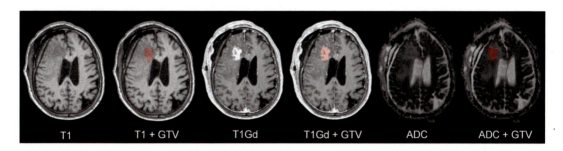

FIGURE 10.2

Images of a glioblastoma patient after debulking surgery, scanned prior to radiation treatment for radiation therapy planning purposes. From left to right: non-enhanced T_1-weighted image with and without the gross tumor volume (GTV) area (in red); gadolinium-based contrast enhanced T_1-weighted image (T_1Gd) with and without the GTV; and apparent diffusion coefficient (ADC) map with and without the GTV.

150 **Chapter 10** Diffusion MRI analysis methods

To automate the ROI definition process and to ensure anatomical fidelity among subjects, atlas-based ROI analysis is the preferred method. Atlases are parcellations, which cover the whole or part of the brain and are created by averaging together anatomical images and their individual parcellations from a large sample of subjects. Such atlases and their associated templates are commonly available in stereotaxic MNI (Montreal Neurological Institute) space. The templates are used as a moving image when the atlas is registered to the subject-specific space. Once the atlas labels are transformed to the individual subjects, diffusion measures can be calculated at the corresponding locations, e.g., average mean diffusivity (MD) from the left thalamus. Notable examples of volumetric atlases developed for diffusion MR analysis are the "JHU DTI-based white-matter atlas" (Wakana et al., 2007) from the Mori lab (cmrm.med.jhmi.edu) and the "Atlas of Human Brain Connections" from the BCB lab (www.bcblab.com). Surface templates are created for cortex-only analysis, such as the Desikan–Killiany, the Destrieux, or the multi-modal Glasser atlas (balsa.wustl.edu/study/show/RVVG).

10.2.3 Voxel-wise analysis

Explorative research is performed when there is no prior knowledge available or no hypotheses have been formulated on the expected location of the disease. In this scenario, it is recommended to analyze the whole brain. While histogram-based methods do incorporate metrics from the whole brain, they cannot provide any detail as to the location of the region in which the potential differences occur. Region-based analysis can cover the whole brain, but the results might be driven by the choice of atlas. To detect the smallest differences, it seems natural to use the smallest region for comparison, which is the elementary building block of the images: the voxel. During a voxel-wise or voxel-based analysis (VBA, Fig. 10.1c), microstructural properties among subjects are compared in every voxel. Considering that different subjects can have various brain shapes and sizes, the images-of-interest must be spatially transformed to a common coordinate system prior to VBA to ensure anatomical fidelity among subjects and brain regions. Popular templates of population-averaged T_1w, T_2w, or fractional anisotropy (FA)-based images are available in the aforementioned MNI space. Alternatively, one may consider creating a population-specific template by registering all subjects' images to an MNI template, and then calculating the mean image. Precise non-linear image registration is a challenging task, especially in the case of noisy FA maps, and the diseased brain can also affect the performance of the normalization. To eliminate artifactual findings which originate from possible misalignment, Smith et al. (2006) proposed the tract-based spatial statistics (TBSS) framework as a complementary method to VBA. Briefly, after the registration of FA maps to MNI space, a study-template is calculated from the whole cohort. Next, an FA skeleton image is created from the study-template, which represents the center of the white matter tracts by searching for the local perpendicular (or non-dominant) directions and truncating the FA values in that direction. This procedure will preserve the locally maximum FA, assuming that voxels with the highest FA identify as the center of the pathways. Following this skeletonization step, all realigned subjects' locally maximum FA perpendicular to the skeleton is projected back to the skeleton. Finally, voxel-wise statistics are calculated on the individual skeletonized FA images. Optionally, instead of the FA, other diffusion MRI metrics, such as MD, can be also projected back to the template FA-skeleton.

Regardless of the details of different flavors amongst VBA methods, for instance TBSS-style or not, or the amount of smoothing before computing voxel-wise statistics, VBA is an increasingly popular technique for full brain analysis in both basic neuroscience and clinical studies. Among the many examples, a notable one is the work of Deprez et al. (2012), who investigated the longitudinal, neural changes in breast cancer patients treated with chemotherapy and the relation of such changes to cognitive impairment. They showed that white matter pathways involved in cognition, like the superior longitudinal fasciculus (SLF) or corpus callosum (CC), are heavily affected by chemotherapy. The well-localized clusters of decreased FA also correlate with the diminished performance of attention and verbal memory tests, meaning that the exposure to chemotherapy may explain cognitive decline in breast cancer patients.

10.2.4 Fiber tractography: tract-based analysis

Fiber tractography (FT) or fiber tracking (Fig. 10.1d) is an ensemble of techniques aiming to reconstruct the white matter pathways in the brain. The estimated streamlines do not represent individual axons, but rather the averaged trajectory of macroscopic entities. These so called "bundles" are depicted as continuous, smooth curves and are calculated based on the integration of the underlying diffusion orientation information. In its most general form, a single path is generated from a seed point, which follows consecutively the local fiber orientation until predefined termination criteria are met. The procedure is repeated for multiple seed points throughout the whole brain. Details of the various settings, such as seeding strategy, integration method, how uncertainty of the orientation is incorporated, termination criteria, *post-hoc* clean-up of the false positive results, to mention only a few, can influence the resulting streamlines. To a large extent, the diffusion-weighted image quality descriptors, such as spatial or angular resolution and signal-to-noise ratio, among others, can also affect FT results.

The reconstructed full brain "tractograms" are the summary of all bundles. Prior to *in vivo* diffusion MRI, researchers could only investigate these building units of brain connections through invasive methods, such as post-mortem studies of human or animal brains, the results of which cannot always be translated to living humans. To investigate selected pathways, one popular solution is to define additional spatial constraints or gateways, similar to the Boolean logic operators, which the bundles must (or cannot) pass. The individual bundles can act as special ROIs, because they are anatomically more specific compared to when the bundle masks are acquired via atlas registration. Selecting different bundles allows one to investigate mechanisms that may have a tract-specific effect. A good example is the seminal work of Lebel et al. (2008) on showing how microscopic characteristics in different tracts reach their peak maturation at different ages. They analyzed a large cohort (n = 202) of healthy volunteers between age 5 and 30, and showed that development in numerous white matter fibers continues beyond infancy, and extends up to even age 25 in the case of the cingulum and corticospinal tract, whereas other tracts, such as the fornix, appear to be completely developed by age 5. Recent developments allow for the selection of a wide range of well-recognized bundles in a fully automated fashion (Warrington et al., 2020) as compared to the semi-automated solution in Lebel et al. (2008), in which the gateways are defined on a single reference subject manually.

In addition to tractography being able to provide bundle-specific microstructural measures, tracts can also be used to extract metrics from other modalities. Fig. 10.3 shows an example patient due to undergo radiation therapy for a brain tumor. Prior to therapy, a planning CT scan and a gadolinium-based contrast-enhanced T_1-weighted image (T_1Gd) were acquired for tumor delineation and to design the treatment, as well as DWIs to reconstruct the pathways. The CT scan and all other RT-related data sets, such as the local radiation or RT dose map, were rigidly registered to the MRI scan for spatial

152   **Chapter 10** Diffusion MRI analysis methods

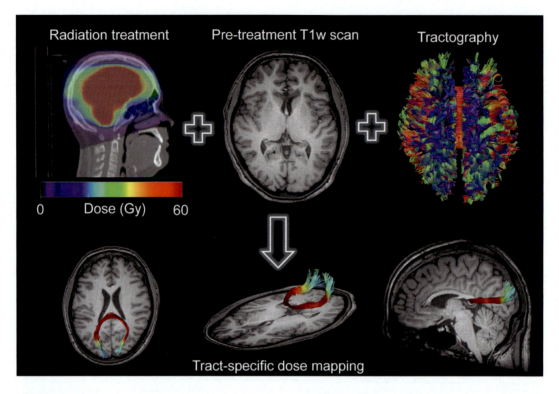

FIGURE 10.3

Fusion of radiation therapy (RT) and fiber tractography. The CT image and the RT dose plan are rigidly co-registered to the T_1w MRI scan to acquire delineations based on the excellent soft-tissue contrast. Meanwhile, diffusion MR images are non-linearly registered to the same T_1w scan to correct for motion and distortion artifacts, and also to be anatomically informed about fiber tractography (FT). Since RT and FT information are co-localized, it is possible to map the dose distribution on fiber bundles, as shown in the bottom of the figure. The color of the tractography (top right) represents the orientation of the underlying fiber tissue: red, green, and blue colors indicate left-right, anterior-posterior (front-back), and inferior-superior (up-down), respectively.

overlap, whereas the DWI were also registered to the T_1w scan for motion and distortion correction. Considering that all image modalities are aligned to the same coordinate system, a joint analysis is possible. We can use the T_1w scan to include anatomical priors to reconstruct the splenium of the corpus callosum, while at the same time estimate the radiation dose within that pathway. Hence, the effect of radiation can be investigated not just based on a structural T_1w scan, but also from selected white matter pathways. This approach can be easily extended to any number of additional imaging techniques.

The ability to reconstruct white matter bundles *in vivo* opened up new forms of analysis. Tracts can provide novel insights in localizing the effects of diseases (along-the-tract and fixel-based). In addition, they can reveal details about how different brain regions are connected (connectome), and their 3D geometrical properties (shape analysis) can also be considered as biomarkers.

10.2.5 Along-the-tract analysis

During the analysis of selected fiber bundles, all information is summarized into a couple of metrics, usually a mean and a standard deviation, for all tracts per subject. However, differences between groups of bundles are not necessarily driven by a global alteration in the microstructural properties, but perhaps disease-related changes are present within a well-localized region of the bundle. Furthermore, diffusion measures naturally vary within a bundle in healthy volunteers, simply by passing through different areas of the brain. As such, the summary of whole-bundle measures into a handful of estimates may ignore potential local features.

To accommodate the need to investigate more localized changes and features within the streamlines, an "along-the-tract" analysis (Colby et al., 2012) framework has been developed (Fig. 10.1e). For this approach, first, individual bundles are selected from all subjects, for example, with the aforementioned techniques. Next, the bundles and their underlying metrics need to be resampled to the same number of "building units" or points to match the same anatomical locations between subjects. The length of a pathway can vary between subjects, which requires a reparameterization step. Finally, the bundles with an identical number of points along the tract can be used for further statistical testing. Focal lesions, for example, lacunar infarcts in white matter, may cause local changes in the structural properties of the affected bundle, whereas such abnormalities are swamped when complete pathways are analyzed and compared to the unaffected bundles in the other hemisphere (Reijmer et al., 2013).

10.2.6 Connectome-based analysis

The brain is a highly interconnected organ, in which functions are spatially distributed to various systems, such as motor and language, and their normal operation is determined by the integrity of these systems. Until recently, white matter was analyzed as the medium of interest, which could directly represent changes due to disease. One of the more recent and popular approaches in brain dMRI analysis is to consider all fiber bundle connections between brain regions (Fig. 10.1f), also called the connectome. The field of graph theory studies the properties of networks, which has two components: "nodes" and "edges". For the brain, the nodes are the cortical and deep-gray matter regions, whereas the edges are the fiber bundles, connecting the nodes. Numerically, the connections are represented with connectivity (or adjacency) matrices (CMs), in which rows and columns are the brain regions and the values within the matrices are connection properties. CMs in dMRI are undirected, meaning that the connection between Region A and Region B is the same as between Region B and Region A. The simplest CMs are binary: if two regions are connected, then it is signified with a 1 (or yes), if not then a 0 (or no). More information about the connections can be gathered with weighted links, for example, the average FA of the connection, or from another co-registered modality. Once the CMs have been constructed, a wide range of network properties can be calculated. Among the many metrics, mean network degree or network density, which captures information about the wiring cost of the network, is often used. The degree is calculated per node and denotes the number of connections to other nodes. To learn about the extensive possibilities of connectivity measures, readers are referred to the work of Rubinov and Sporns (2010).

A special case of connectivity analysis is when the absence of connections is under investigation, also coined as a "disconnectome" analysis. A brain tumor or a lesion disrupts local tissue, which can also disconnect distant regions. Therefore any neurological symptoms are not only the consequence of the diseased gray matter regions (i.e., the location of the lesion), but also the provoked disconnections.

154 **Chapter 10** Diffusion MRI analysis methods

For instance, a disconnectome analysis of 1,333 stroke patients resulted in a new, highly reproducible atlas, which assigns functionality to the underlying white matter (Thiebaut de Schotten et al., 2020).

10.2.7 Fixel-based analysis

Though there are numerous examples of methodological leaps in the development of FT, the ability to model crossing fibers is a particularly important one. DTI is a straightforward method, but has the conceptual limitation that it cannot resolve multiple fiber populations within a voxel. Among the many solutions, one of the most notable methods is called constrained spherical deconvolution (CSD) by Tournier et al. (2007). In CSD, the diffusion MR signal is modeled with a set of spherical harmonics to calculate the voxel-wise fiber orientation distributions (FODs). The use of spherical harmonics proved to be efficient in detecting multiple fiber populations in a voxel, revealing that nearly all white matter voxels in the brain contain multiple fiber orientations with the exception of a few areas, such as the corpus callosum. However, the advent of CSD and similar methods did not change the process of VBA-type techniques, since information from all pathways was still summed up into a single metric per voxel. To address this limitation, a new framework called fixel-based analysis (FBA, Fig. 10.1g) has been proposed (Raffelt et al., 2017), in which the fixel (combination of "fiber" and "voxel") signifies a new concept: fiber population element within a voxel. The novelty of FBA lies in its ability to compare fiber-wise metrics within a voxel among multiple fiber populations, which results in increased specificity over traditional voxel-wise methods. Therefore diseases affecting certain pathways can be investigated in isolation from other fibers with high spatial specificity, which was not possible with previous methods. During an FBA analysis, FODs are calculated in the original coordinate system of the subject, and then normalized to a common template to calculate a study-specific white matter FOD template. A fixel template is then derived, which will serve as the basis for statistical analysis. Common metrics used in an FBA are the amplitude of the FODs, called fiber density (FD), and fiber-bundle cross-section (FC), the latter of which is obtained by incorporating the local volume changes of the subject into a template non-linear registration step (warp) into the fixels as well. It is also possible to combine FD and FC into a single metric by a simple multiplication, resulting in the fiber density and cross-section (FDC) metric.

10.2.8 Tract geometry analysis

Diffusion MRI and fiber tractography can provide useful metrics and tools to describe microstructural properties and connections in the brain. However, the previously discussed analysis methods do not consider the 3D geometrical properties of the tracts, which may provide further insights into the etiology of diseases and conditions. Shape or morphological analysis (Fig. 10.1h) is a common tool in structural MR image analysis and has been used to investigate, for instance, the deep gray matter nuclei (hippocampus, thalamus, etc.) and potential differences between Alzheimer's disease (AD) and control volunteers. Notable metrics of bundle shape analysis are volume, length, surface area, and span (the absolute measure between the two ends of a bundle), among many others. Shape analysis of large cohorts can reveal laterality differences between bundles from both hemispheres. For example, Yeh (2020) showed that the diameter of the left arcuate fasciculus is nearly 50% larger on average than the right arcuate fasciculus.

10.3 Conclusion

Investigating microstructural properties of the brain with diffusion MRI can be done in many ways. This chapter provided an overview of the most common analysis methods and discussed their advantages and disadvantages. There is no single "best analysis approach" for all dMRI applications. Readers are encouraged to inform themselves about the assumptions, requirements, and limitations of the different analysis methods to make the best decision for their own specific research question.

References

Basser, P.J., Mattiello, J., Le Bihan, D., 1994. Estimation of the effective self-diffusion tensor from the NMR spin echo. J. Magn. Reson., Ser. B 103, 247–254. https://doi.org/10.1006/jmrb.1994.1037.

Catani, M., Dell'Acqua, F., Vergani, F., et al., 2012. Short frontal lobe connections of the human brain. Cortex 48, 273–291. https://doi.org/10.1016/j.cortex.2011.12.001.

Colby, J.B., Soderberg, L., Lebel, C., et al., 2012. Along-tract statistics allow for enhanced tractography analysis. NeuroImage 59, 3227–3242. https://doi.org/10.1016/J.NEUROIMAGE.2011.11.004.

Crick, F., Jones, E., 1993. Backwardness of human neuroanatomy. Nature 361, 109–110.

Deprez, S., Amant, F., Smeets, A., et al., 2012. Longitudinal assessment of chemotherapy-induced structural changes in cerebral white matter and its correlation with impaired cognitive functioning. J. Clin. Oncol. 30, 274–281. https://doi.org/10.1200/JCO.2011.36.8571.

Giulietti, G., Torso, M., Serra, L., et al., 2018. Whole brain white matter histogram analysis of diffusion tensor imaging data detects microstructural damage in mild cognitive impairment and Alzheimer's disease patients. J. Magn. Reson. Imaging 48, 767–779. https://doi.org/10.1002/jmri.25947.

Klingler, J., Ludwig, E., 1956. Atlas Cerebri Humani: The Inner Structure of the Brain. Little, Brown & Co, Boston, USA.

Lebel, C., Walker, L., Leemans, A., et al., 2008. Microstructural maturation of the human brain from childhood to adulthood. NeuroImage 40, 1044–1055. https://doi.org/10.1016/j.neuroimage.2007.12.053.

Mesri, H.Y., David, S., Viergever, M.A., Leemans, A., 2019. The adverse effect of gradient nonlinearities on diffusion MRI: from voxels to group studies. NeuroImage, 116127. https://doi.org/10.1016/j.neuroimage.2019.116127.

Smith, S.M., Jenkinson, M., Johansen-Berg, H., et al., 2006. Tract-based spatial statistics: voxelwise analysis of multi-subject diffusion data. NeuroImage 31, 1487–1505. https://doi.org/10.1016/j.neuroimage.2006.02.024.

Raffelt, D.A., Tournier, J.D., Smith, R.E., et al., 2017. Investigating white matter fibre density and morphology using fixel-based analysis. NeuroImage 144, 58–73.

Reijmer, Y.D., Freeze, W.M., Leemans, A., Biessels, G.J., 2013. The effect of lacunar infarcts on white matter tract integrity. Stroke 44, 2019–2021. https://doi.org/10.1161/STROKEAHA.113.001321.

Rousselet, G.A., Pernet, C.R., Wilcox, R.R., 2017. Beyond differences in means: robust graphical methods to compare two groups in neuroscience. Eur. J. Neurosci. 46, 1738–1748. https://doi.org/10.1111/ejn.13610.

Rubinov, M., Sporns, O., 2010. Complex network measures of brain connectivity: uses and interpretations. NeuroImage 52, 1059–1069. https://doi.org/10.1016/j.neuroimage.2009.10.003.

Thiebaut de Schotten, M., Foulon, C., Nachev, P., 2020. Brain disconnections link structural connectivity with function and behaviour. bioRxiv 11, 5094. https://doi.org/10.1101/2020.02.27.967570.

Tournier, J.D., Calamante, F., Connelly, A., 2007. Robust determination of the fibre orientation distribution in diffusion MRI: non-negativity constrained super-resolved spherical deconvolution. NeuroImage 35, 1459–1472. https://doi.org/10.1016/j.neuroimage.2007.02.016.

Wakana, S., Caprihan, A., Panzenboeck, M.M., et al., 2007. Reproducibility of quantitative tractography methods applied to cerebral white matter. NeuroImage 36, 630–644. https://doi.org/10.1016/j.neuroimage.2007.02.049.

Warrington, S., Bryant, K.L., Khrapitchev, A.A., et al., 2020. XTRACT - standardised protocols for automated tractography in the human and macaque brain. NeuroImage 217, 116923. https://doi.org/10.1016/j.neuroimage.2020.116923.

Yeh, F.C., 2020. Shape analysis of the human association pathways. NeuroImage 223, 117329. https://doi.org/10.1016/j.neuroimage.2020.117329.

CHAPTER 11

Diffusion as a probe of tissue microstructure

Yaniv Assaf[a,b,c] and Daniel Barazany[c]

[a]School of Neurobiology, Biochemistry and Biophysics, Faculty of Life Science, Tel Aviv University, Tel Aviv, Israel
[b]Sagol School of Neuroscience, Tel Aviv University, Tel Aviv, Israel
[c]The Strauss Center for Computational Neuroimaging, Tel Aviv University, Tel Aviv, Israel

11.1 Diffusion MRI: sensitivity vs specificity

Diffusion MRI is based on the Stejskal–Tanner "pulsed gradient spin-echo" pulse sequence (PGSE, Fig. 11.1), in which the sensitivity for diffusion or motion of water molecules is achieved by applying a pair of gradient pulses separated by the 180° pulse of a spin-echo sequence (Stejskal and Tanner, 1965). Within the jargon of diffusion MRI, the time separation between the gradients is called the diffusion time (Δ). Other important factors are the gradient duration (δ) and its amplitude (G or g), together with the diffusion time. These factors are used to compute the "q" value in some formalisms and the "b" value in others. Providing an expression that relates the obtained dMRI signal in a PGSE experiment to the diffusion process is complicated, and includes integrating over all possible random motions and positions that an ensemble of molecules may execute, and estimating the net phase shift of their magnetization (Table 11.1, Eq. (11.1)). Yet, by assuming the abovementioned Gaussian approximation

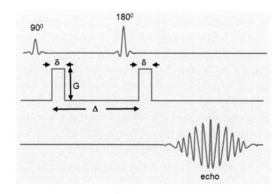

FIGURE 11.1 The pulsed gradient spin echo (PGSE) sequence

Based on a regular spin-echo (90°–180°) sequence with the addition of a pair of gradient pulses of duration δ, amplitude G, and separation Δ, the obtained echo is attenuated proportionally to the displacement, and hence diffusion of water molecules.

158 **Chapter 11** Diffusion as a probe of tissue microstructure

(Table 11.1, Eq. (11.2)), it is possible to formulate Eq. (11.1) into the well-known Stejskal–Tanner relationship, describing signal decay in dMRI versus the imposed b-value (Table 11.1, Eq. (11.3)).

Table 11.1 The Stejskal–Tanner Formalism.	
General Description[a]	$$E(q) = \int \rho(x_1) \int P(x_1, x_2, \Delta) e^{-iq(x_2-x_1)dx_2dx_1} \qquad (11.1)$$
Assumptions[b]	$$P(x_1, x_2, \Delta) = \frac{1}{\sqrt{4\pi D \Delta}} e^{\left(-\frac{(x_2-x_1)^2}{4D\Delta}\right)} \qquad (11.2)$$
Final Equation[c]	$$E(q) = e^{-q^2 D(\Delta - \frac{\delta}{3})} = e^{-bD} \qquad (11.3)$$

[a] *Where $q = \gamma \delta G$, $E(q)$ is the measured signal decay for specific g and G, $\rho(x_1)$ is the spin density at the application of the first gradient pulse, $P(x_1, x_2, \Delta)$ indicates the probability of a spin originally located at point x_1 to be found at point x_2 after time Δ.*
[b] *We assume that $P(x_1, x_2, \Delta)$ has a Gaussian form.*
[c] *Using Eq. (11.2) to solve Eq. (11.1): replace all positions (x_1, x_2) in Eq. (11.1) with the diffusion coefficient (D) to obtain the well-known Stejskal–Tanner relation, where b is the b-value.*

The framework presented in Table 11.1 (Eqs. (11.1)–(11.3)) and Fig. 11.1 was the starting point for the first application of dMRI in neuroscience: calculating the diffusion coefficient from a series of diffusion-weighted images and variable b-values. It became quickly apparent that the measured diffusion coefficient appears to have lower values when the b-value increases (Fig. 11.2). This was the first indication that the Gaussian approximation of diffusion in neural tissue does not hold. Despite the incompatibility of the model with experimental data, the diffusion MRI neuroscience community continued to use this framework by using the linear part or the relation between the diffusion coefficient and the b-value (assuming that for this b-value range the Gaussian assumption is more valid). However, the term "diffusion coefficient" (which is defined by the flux of water molecules across surfaces per time unit) was replaced by "apparent diffusion coefficient" (ADC) to indicate the inaccuracy of the model. Even the generalization of the Stejskal–Tanner framework from measuring the diffusion coefficient to measuring the diffusion tensor (diffusion tensor imaging, DTI) still assumed a Gaussian form of diffusion (Basser et al., 1994). The main reason for this is that if the diffusion experiment is done in a b-value range where it appears to follow the Gaussian assumption (see Fig. 11.2), the incompatibility of the model is expected to be negligible. More importantly, the extracted parameters of this model— the ADC (and the mean diffusivity, MD, and fractional anisotropy, FA, from the DTI model)—were found to be highly sensitive to the microstructure of tissue, providing new quantitative measures of an uncharted property in neuroscience (Basser and Pierpaoli, 1996).

There are two examples that are frequently used to emphasize the high sensitivity of dMRI for elucidating tissue microstructure. One is the use of ADC for early detection of stroke, and the other is the measurement of diffusion anisotropy as a proxy for white matter organization (Fig. 11.3).

The first clinical application of dMRI revealed that ADC measurements could identify ischemic stroke minutes after its induction (Moseley et al., 1990). This discovery revolutionized the management of stroke patients and opened a therapeutic window opportunity that was impossible before the use of dMRI. Now, 30 years after its discovery, this application of dMRI is in routine practice in diagnostic

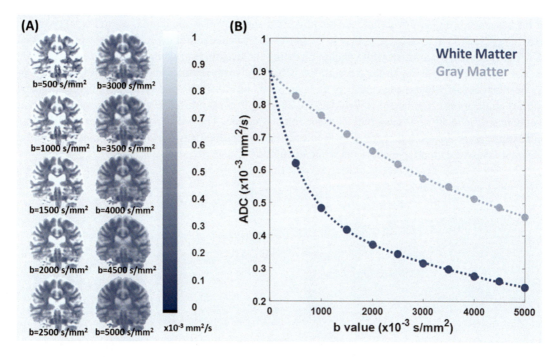

FIGURE 11.2 Apparent diffusion coefficient (ADC) as a function of b

(A) ADC maps computed for different b-values. The ADC seems to become slower as the b-value increases (B) ADC values from two ROIs (in the gray matter and white matter), showing that the reduction in ADC (or ADC values) in white matter is more pronounced than in gray matter. Moreover, whereas the dependency of ADC vs b value in gray matter is nearly linear, in white matter it deviates from linearity and starts to level off at $b>1500$ s/mm^2.

imaging of suspected stroke patients and has surely saved the lives of myriad of patients worldwide. In the late 1990s and early 2000s, a significant research effort was invested to reveal the source of this high sensitivity. Although the cellular and physiological processes that occur after ischemic stroke are complicated, it is well accepted today that cell swelling (cytotoxic edema) is the main source for ADC reduction immediately after stroke (Fig. 11.3A). This application was the first to underscore the utility of dMRI as a microstructural probe.

In parallel to the development of dMRI and ADC as markers of early stroke, first indications of anisotropy in diffusion measurements emerged in the 1990s (Chenevert et al., 1990; Basser and Pierpaoli, 1996; Pierpaoli et al., 1996). These observations promoted the development of DTI that enabled the quantification of anisotropy by estimating the full diffusion tensor, rather than a single ADC (Basser and Pierpaoli, 1998). From DTI, two main parameters are commonly extracted: MD and FA. Though MD is similar in concept to ADC, but more accurately computes the diffusion coefficient in regions with high anisotropy (providing a rotationally invariant measure), the FA offered a new contrast highlighting regions with high anisotropy that co-localized with the brain's white matter tracts (Fig. 11.3B). FA maps provided a quantitative measure of white matter, and when combined with directionally color-coded maps, the neuroanatomy of white matter became visible and vivid (Catani et al., 2002). Measurement of FA has since been used to explore the healthy neuroanatomy of white matter, white matter development, degeneration in ageing, as well as in a handful of clinical conditions. Rapidly, FA was identified as a highly sensitive marker of white matter, revealing the dynamics of white matter and its active role in brain physiology and cognition. Though FA is not free from artifacts and pitfalls, it is still one of the best markers of white matter integrity and one of the most widely used parameters in research and clinical applications. Similar to stroke/ADC application, it is also the case with white matter/FA that the main source of its high sensitivity is tissue microstructure. The ordered alignment of neural fibers and axons causes the motion of water molecules to be macroscopically anisotropic, providing the first ever non-invasive method to explore the white matter.

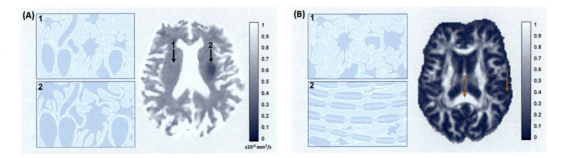

FIGURE 11.3 The effect of microstructure on diffusion indices

(A) ADC in stroke: Region 1 demonstrates healthy neural tissue (dark blue are cells and light blue is the extracellular matrix), whereas Region 2 represents tissue following stroke, indicated by swollen cells. On the right of (A) is a mean diffusivity map of a subject 3 hours following stroke, where Region 2 shows marked reduction in ADC. (B) FA in white matter: Regions 1 and 2 depict cellular arrangement in gray matter (1) and white matter (2). The white matter tissue is fibrously arranged, whereas the gray matter tissue is more heterogeneous. These microstructural differences in arrangement are reflected in the FA maps (right side of B), where high intensity is shown in the WM and low intensity in the GM.

Though the uses of dMRI in stroke and white matter mapping are the most reported studies that highlight its sensitivity to tissue microstructure, there are many more uses that will be described in this chapter, including the measurement of axon diameter, the mapping of structural neuro-plasticity, the revealing of complicated fiber system arrangement, up to characterizing the entire wiring diagram of the brain: the structural connectome.

Why is dMRI so sensitive to tissue microstructure? The answer to this is embedded in Fig. 11.2: the non-Gaussianity of diffusion in tissue. Although there could be several biophysical reasons for deviation from Gaussianity (e.g., flow effects), it was shown over the years that the geometry of the microstructure dramatically affects the dMRI signal. At long enough diffusion times, the effect of geometry (either membranes or the arrangement of dense organelle/cellular-structures) will affect the Gaussian displacement of water molecules, causing them to be hindered or even restricted, as will be described in the following section. However, the main message to take from this observation is that dMRI measures the displacement of water molecules, which on the time scale of diffusion MRI experiments can cover distances of a few microns. This is the source for the high sensitivity of dMRI: it enhances the sensitivity of MRI information on the micron scale while retaining the ability to image the entire organ.

11.2 Restricted diffusion

Whereas exploring dMRI signal over its "linear portion" (see Fig. 11.2, the b-value region that corresponds to Gaussian behavior) provides the means to explore tissue microstructure and reveal new discoveries, obviously the leveling of the ADC at higher b-value reflects a different order of dependency of the dMRI signal on tissue microstructure. At the simplest level, this deviation from linearity of the curve reflects significant disturbance to the natural Gaussian desire of water molecules to diffuse. Such disturbances may occur when the diffusion is restricted. This phenomenon is frequently reported in porous material studies (see Callaghan, 1991). Trying to put this observation into an empirical formulation reveals some difficulties. The main difficulty has to do with the modeling approach: if a Gaussian model is not suitable, what is an appropriate model? To answer that, one should try to reveal what is the source for restricted diffusion in neural tissue. From a biological perspective, there is no definite answer. Yet, it is well accepted that water molecules should be able to pass across the cell membrane relatively easily (either through the membrane itself or through designated water channels). In theory, the membrane of a neuron or glial cell should not be dramatically different from that of a liver or muscle cell. However, one structure in the nervous system may significantly affect membrane permeability: the myelin. Myelin constitutes multiple wraps of cellular membrane around the axon to increase its conduction capacity. The probability of a water molecule passing through a membrane depends on the cell type. For example, in red blood cells water can diffuse across the membrane easily with an exchange lifetime of $\sim$20 ms (Gianolio et al., 2016). Other experiments suggest that neural cell membranes may impose more barriers on water molecules, increasing their exchange lifetimes to about 500 ms (Yang et al., 2018). Moreover, adding multiple lamellae of these membranes, one on top of the other as in myelin, will probably decrease the exchange rate to much longer time periods. Thus from a biological perspective it appears that neural cells are less permeable than other body cells, and within neural tissue, myelinated axons are distinctively impermeable compared to other cellular components.

Indeed, the fact the non-Gaussian nature of white matter is more prominent than in gray matter seems to be in line with this biological interpretation (Assaf and Cohen, 2000). Moreover, the fact that it is possible to observe both Gaussian-like and non-Gaussian behavior in neural tissue (Fig. 11.2) suggests that two pools of water exist. The first, with a Gaussian-like behavior, probably reflects free or slightly hindered diffusion, whereas the second non-Gaussian component arises from restricted diffusion. It can also be assumed that the main source for the restricted diffusion component is myelinated axons residing dominantly in the white matter. This is the theoretical basis for the composite hindered and restricted model of diffusion (CHARMED; Assaf et al., 2004) and consequent related methods (e.g., NODDI; Zhang et al., 2012). The CHARMED model assumes that the two pools of water (hindered and restricted) reside in different compartments, and thus the obtained signal can be represented as a linear combination of those (Eq. (11.4)). Although the hindered part of Eq. (11.4) can be expressed mathematically using a conventional DTI formula (Eq. (11.5)), the restricted component cannot be described by conventional dMRI equations.

$$ E(q, \Delta) = f_h \cdot E_h(q, \Delta) + f_r \cdot E_r(q, \Delta) \tag{11.4} $$

162 **Chapter 11** Diffusion as a probe of tissue microstructure

Where $E\,(q,\Delta)$ is the signal decay, E_h the signal decay of the hindered component, E_r the signal decay of the restricted component, and f_h, f_r the volume fractions of each component.

$$E_h\,(q,\Delta) = e^{-4\pi^2(\Delta-\frac{\delta}{3})q^T Dq} \tag{11.5}$$

When dealing with any model that is intended to characterize/imitate biological tissue (including the case of restricted diffusion in white matter), some constraints and assumptions need to be imposed. All of them relate to the time we let the molecules diffuse and the compartments they are diffusing in. Let's start with the latter. If we accept the biological interpretation of restricted diffusion under dMRI conditions, then these water molecules will be found within the axons; thus we can assume that the limiting geometry for water motion will have a cylindrical arrangement (as opposed to spherical arrangements in cells, for instance). This assumption will allow the solving of Eq. (11.1), taking into account that the possible displacement of the molecules is constrained to known geometry (Assaf et al., 2004). However, as the geometry is extremely small ($\sim$1–2 μm), the definition of start/end locations (x_1, x_2) is critical. To recap, x_1 is the position of the molecule at the time of the first gradient pulse, x_2 is its location at the time of the second gradient pulse, and R (the displacement) is the Euclidean distance between these locations. For R to be well-defined with respect to the geometry, the tagging period (δ) should be short, short enough that the diffusion during the gradient pulse will be negligible compared to the compartment size. This is the basis for the main assumption when trying to find a solution for restricted diffusion within impermeable compartments: the so-called narrow pulse approximation. In this approximation, the diffusion during the gradient pulse should be minimal, whereas the diffusion during the diffusion time (Δ) should allow the molecules to reach the boundaries of the cell (or axon), thus $\delta \ll \Delta$. This assumption simplifies mathematically the solution of Eq. (11.1). Using the narrow pulse approximation, analysis of restricted diffusion can be done either using a parametric or non-parametric approach.

In the non-parametric approach, using the narrow pulse approximation, Eq. (11.1) becomes a Fourier expression that relates the signal decay in dMRI and the displacement probability function or the diffusion propagator (Eq. (11.6)). Simply, by measuring dMRI signal within the narrow pulse approximation limits, it is possible to obtain the propagator by Fourier transformation of the signal. This is the basis for the q-space approach that allows the extraction of geometrical information from diffusion data without any empirical modeling (Assaf and Cohen, 1999, 2000). Such analyses revealed that the diffusion of water molecules in white matter is restricted to a cylindrical geometry with dimensions of roughly $\sim$2 μm (Assaf and Cohen, 2000). Moreover, the extraction of mean displacement for the q-space analysis was shown to be highly sensitive in distinguishing various neuroanatomical structures and pathological conditions.

$$E\,(q,\Delta) = \int_{-\infty}^{\infty} P\,(R,\Delta)\,e^{iq\cdot R} d^3 R \tag{11.6}$$

The parametric approach requires the development of a mathematical expression that describes the dependency between the dMRI signal decay and restricted diffusion. Several solutions for this problem exist that differ in their assumption regarding the gradient pulse. If the narrow pulse approximation holds ($\Delta \gg \delta$), one may use Callaghan's formula (Eq. (11.7); Callaghan, 1995). However, as most experimental setups (especially in clinical scanners) cannot reach such conditions, other expressions were developed for condition where $\Delta > \delta$ (finite pulse length) (Eq. (11.8); van Gelderen et al., 1994) and where $\Delta \sim \delta$ (Eq. (11.9); Neuman, 1974).

From the equations, it can be noted that the dependency of the signal decay in dMRI for restricted water diffusion within impermeable cylinders is far from being simple. Moreover, these expressions are only approximations of the (ill-posed) solution that fits the real experimental conditions. Fig. 11.4 shows the signal decays in dMRI experiments of rat corpus callosum with dMRI conditions that approximate the limitations of each framework and a corresponding estimation of each of the abovementioned models. It should be noted that the results shown in Fig. 11.4 are not model fits, but rather model estimations of the signal decay given an "initial guess" of the free parameters (mainly the diffusion coefficient, which was taken as 1 μm^2/ms). This figure emphasizes the crucial need to fit the right model to its corresponding dMRI conditions. Though the most suitable model appears to represent appropriately the signal decay, using an inappropriate model might fit the data, but will over- or under-estimate the free parameters (either the diffusion coefficient or the volume fraction). Interestingly, the Neuman model predicts a slower signal decay when the conditions are not suitable to the model (Fig. 11.4C and 11.4D). One explanation for this observation is the center of mass theory originally provided by Mitra et al. (Mitra and Halperin, 1995). They suggested that if the diffusion during the pulse is significant, then the position x_1 will become the average of all positions during the pulse (center of mass) that eventually will be at the center of the cylinder; in this way the phase shift due to the gradient pulses will be smaller or effectively zero leading to predicted slow signal decay. However, regardless of the accuracy of these models, it is evident that the signal decay will depend on several factors, including the diffusivity within the cylinder, but more interestingly its diameter (a in Eq. (11.7) and R in Eqs. (11.8) and (11.9)). This sensitivity to the cylinder (axon) diameter is the basis for another framework called

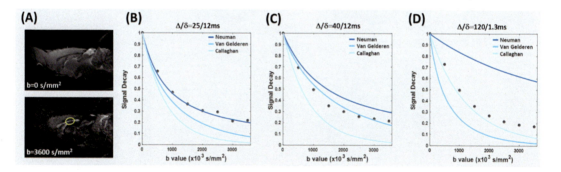

FIGURE 11.4 δ, Δ and diffusion modeling

(A) shows two diffusion-weighted images with $b=0$ (upper) and $b=3600$ s/mm^2 (lower) with the gradients applied exactly perpendicular to the corpus callosum (CC). The region of interest at the body of the corpus callosum used for further analysis in (B–D) is circled. (B–D) signal decays from the body of the CC for three experiments measured at different combinations of Δ/δ (25/12 ms, 40/12 ms, and 120/1.3 ms) that fit the assumptions of the 3 models given in Eqs. (11.7)–(11.9). The lines represent each equation's predicted signal decay when taking D=1 μm^2/ms and typical axon diameter distribution in the corpus callosum (see Assaf and Basser, *NeuroImage*, 27, 48–58, 2005). It appears that each of the models better predicts the data when the experimental conditions are similar to the model's assumptions.

AxCaliber, which extracts the axon diameter properties from diffusion MRI experiments (Assaf et al., 2008, see below).

Assumption	Model
$\Delta \gg \delta$	$E_r = \sum_k 4e^{-\beta_{0k}^2 D_r \Delta/a^2} \times \frac{(2\pi qa) J_0'(2\pi qa)}{(2\pi qa)^2 - \beta_{0k}^2} + \sum_{nk} 8e^{-\beta_{0k}^2 D_r \Delta/a^2} \times \frac{\beta_{nk}^2}{\beta_{nk}^2 - n^2} \times \frac{(2\pi qa) J_n'(2\pi qa)}{(2\pi qa)^2 - \beta_{nk}^2}$ (11.7)
$\Delta > \delta$	$E_r = \exp(-2\gamma^2 g^2 \sum_{m=1}^{\infty} \frac{2D_f \alpha_m^2 \delta - 2 + 2e^{-D_f \alpha_m^2 \delta} + 2e^{-D_f \alpha_m^2 \Delta} - e^{-D_f \alpha_m^2 (\Delta-\delta)} - e^{-D_f \alpha_m^2 (\Delta+\delta)}}{D_f^2 \alpha_m^6 (R^2 \alpha_m^2 - 1)}$ (11.8) where $J_1'(\alpha_m R) = 0$
$\Delta \sim \delta$	$E_r = e^{-(\frac{4\pi^2 R^2 q^2}{D_r \tau})(\frac{7}{296})(2-(\frac{99}{112})(\frac{R^2}{D_r \tau}))}$ (11.9) where τ is the TE/2

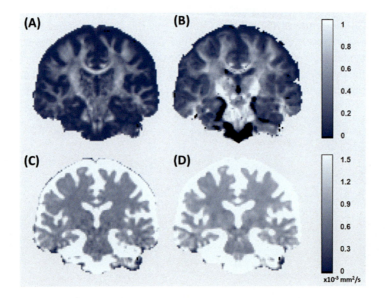

FIGURE 11.5 DTI vs CHARMED

(A) and (C) are conventional FA (A) and MD (C) of a healthy subject. (B) and (D) represent the f_r (estimated axonal density) and hindered diffusivity extracted from a CHARMED analysis. Comparing (A) with (B) shows that contrast given by CHAMRED shows significant differences from FA, and hence represents a different water population. Similarly, the high MD values in CHARMED indicate that these maps represent water diffusion in the extra-axonal space.

The CHARMED model (Eq. (11.4)) used both Neuman and van Gelderen equations to compute maps of restricted diffusion (Fig. 11.5), including the volume fraction of the restricted component, which may be assigned as an estimation of axonal density. These maps were the basis for several studies that showed that the separation of the dMRI signal into its microstructural components increases sensitivity towards various processes and conditions. It was argued in the early days of DTI that MD and FA merely provide the powder average of all water compartments, yet CHARMED (and similar models) allow one to disentangle sub-voxel compartmentation and increase accuracy, sensitivity, and specificity of the modeling.

11.3 Applications in resolving complex fiber architecture

The increase in sensitivity and specificity of restricted diffusion to the intra-axonal compartment became useful in another application of dMRI that suffers from averaging artifacts: tractography. In the process of fiber tracking, partial volume effects, whether caused by mixed white/gray matter tissues or multiple fiber systems, causes major miscalculation of fiber trajectories. For instance, this can occur where different fiber systems unite, end prematurely, or reach non-relevant regions. Such artifacts cause a major confound when performing global connectivity analysis, where some of the connections are either not represented or are connected to the wrong location. Among the most notable locations that demonstrate such a problem are the intersection of the forceps minor with the corona radiata and other association fibers (Fig. 11.6) and the fanning of the corticospinal tracts, which intersect with the superior longitudinal fasciculus (Fig. 11.6).

The use of high b-values dMRI (in the non-Gaussian regime) combined with advanced orientation density function (ODF) estimation procedures, such as constrained spherical harmonics deconvolution (Tournier et al., 2004), allows better definition of the multiple fiber orientations in a complex, heterogenic area. Fig. 11.7 shows the b-value effect on ODF estimation in the region of the forceps minor and cortico-spinal tract in human brain. Evidently, when tracking is done with the non-Gaussian part of dMRI signal decay, the embedded information appears to be more accurate, despite the lower signal-to-noise ratio.

Fiber-tracking analysis is commonly associated with white matter in the human brain, but this ignores the axonal origin, which resides in the cerebral cortex and has a complicated fiber architecture of its own. The arrangement of neuronal layers in the cortex has an interwoven and heterogeneous fiber organization, especially at layers adjacent to the white matter, where fibers appear to pass both in a radial orientation (with respect to the white matter), but also along the surface line of the cortex to provide intra-cortical connectivity (Fig. 11.8A). This phenomenon is difficult to demonstrate in human brain due to insufficient spatial resolution (conventional dMRI voxel resolution is in the range of 1.5–2 mm, whereas the cortex thickness is 2–4 mm). However, in the rodent brain, where high voxel resolution can be obtained and the cortex defined by ~10–15 voxels, the distinction between parallel and radial fibers is apparent (Fig. 11.8B). Obviously, tractography analysis based on high b-value dMRI could benefit from reaching the real end location of the fiber in the cortex, for which the accuracy of connectome analysis is increased substantially (Fig. 11.9 compares DTI-based connectome analysis with high-b-value CSD-based connectome analysis).

166 Chapter 11 Diffusion as a probe of tissue microstructure

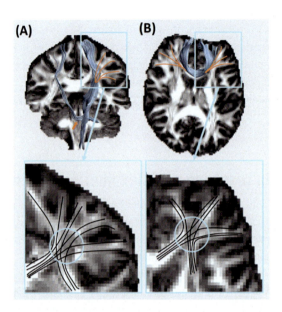

FIGURE 11.6 Tensor-based tractography type 1 and 2 errors

(A) reconstruction of the cortico-spinal tract (blue) from conventional DTI analysis. The orange arrow indicates false positive connections, where the fibers appear to diverge and pass to contralateral areas. Orange lines represent true negative connections, where part of the cortico-spinal tract fanning into the cortex was not reconstructed. The enlarged sections show the area of reduced FA due to crossing fibers that causes some of errors shown in (A). (B) Similar to (A), but for fibers passing through the forceps major.

11.4 Application in plasticity and functional imaging

The use of high b-values is essential for more accurate characterization of the white matter yet, as evident from Fig. 11.2, in the gray matter this phenomenon is less significant. Consequently, in gray matter MD will be an excellent marker of tissue microstructure and a proxy of tissue density. Indeed, studies have shown that MD in the cortex is sensitive to subtle microstructural changes that occur following neuronal activity at various time scales (from seconds to days). These studies found a reduced MD in areas that underwent significant functional activity and exhibit long-lasting remodeling of the tissue (plasticity). The length and magnitude of this reduction relates to the intensity and duration of the activity and most likely to the initiation of neuroplasticity processes (e.g., synaptogenesis).

What is the biological process behind this observation? Though there is no definite answer, some studies suggested that several processes accompanying neuronal activity (action potential) may lead to cell swelling that lead to MD reduction (Johansen-Berg et al., 2012). Such cell swelling was suggested to cause MD reduction transiently following neuronal activity (called functional diffusion MRI). In functional dMRI, MD reduction is transient and tends to normalize when activity ends. Other studies have shown that prolonged neural activity in a specific region leads to increase in synaptic plasticity (a process that may happen within few minutes) that is co-localized with pronounced and long-lasting MD reduction (Blumenfeld-Katzir et al., 2011). This observation may be related to astrocyte remodeling

11.5 AxCaliber   167

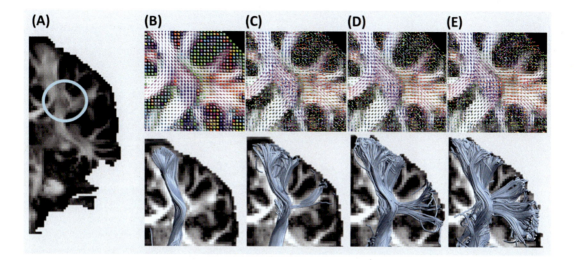

FIGURE 11.7 The effect of b-value on fiber tracking

(A) FA coronal slice in an area of complicated fiber architecture (crossing fibers) is marked by a circle. (B) ODF maps of the areas shown in (A) and corresponding fiber tracts of the cortico-spinal tract. As indicated in Fig. 11.6, the fanning of cortico-spinal fibers into the cortex is not reconstructed due to the crossing fibers' partial volume effects. (C–D) similar to (B), but with constrained spherical harmonics ODF calculation of high-angular resolution diffusion imaging acquired at $b=1000$ (C), $b=2000$ (D), and $b=4000$ (E) s/mm^2. It is evident that as the b-value increases the ability of CSD ODF to resolve the crossing fibers' PVE artifact and reconstruct the cortico-spinal tract, fanning increases significantly.

that occurs following plasticity to maintain the reformed network during activity (Fig. 11.10). This remodeling was shown to sustain days after the activity had ended.

Such studies underscore the dynamics of brain microstructure and the ability of dMRI to capture this phenomenon. Measuring MD provides a tool to probe plasticity, a process that was previously confined to invasive microscopy. A series of studies were able to show that MD reduces within minutes in multiple locations in the human brain following various cognitive tasks, including spatial navigation, motor sequence learning, new lexical learning, and an object recognition task. Such experiments are complementary to fMRI and provide additional means to explore the dynamics of brain microstructure in relation to learning and cognition (Assaf, 2018).

11.5 AxCaliber

The non-Gaussian component of dMRI signal is sensitive to intra-axonal geometry and, consequently, to the axon diameter (as shown in Section 11.3 and by Eqs. (11.7)–(11.9)). The CHARMED model used a predefined axon diameter distribution (average from histological studies) to account for the variance in axon diameters in the tissue (Assaf et al., 2004). In an expansion of CHARMED, the AxCaliber framework uses a gamma-variate function to fit the axon diameter distribution (Assaf et al., 2008).

168   Chapter 11 Diffusion as a probe of tissue microstructure

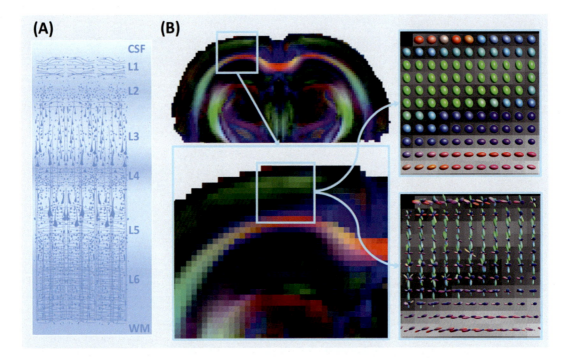

FIGURE 11.8 Diffusion imaging in the cortex

(A) a scheme of cyto- and myelo-architecture in the cortex showing fibers that pass radially to the cortex, but also parallel at the layers adjacent to the white matter (sketch is based on Palomero-Gallagher and Zilles, *NeuroImage*, 197, 716–741, 2019). (B) Color-coded FA maps of the cortex computed from a multi-shell HARDI acquisition of the rat cortex with part of the somato-sensory cortex enlarged. On the right are shown two ODF reconstructions: conventional tensor (top) and CSD for $b=4000$ s/mm^2 (bottom). The CSD reconstruction shows the fiber arrangement running both parallel and radially to the cortex, providing meaningful information on the inner architecture of the cortex.

The CHARMED model uses a multi *b*-shell diffusion data set to fit a relatively high number of free parameters (12–14 parameters: 3 volume fractions, 6 diffusion tensor elements, 2–4 fiber orientations, intra-axonal diffusivity). Obviously, introducing another level of complexity to the model (axon diameter distribution modeled by a gamma function) entails additional optimization difficulties that may lead to overfitting (i.e., the number of free parameters allows multiple possible solutions). To overcome this fitting problem, the original AxCaliber framework degenerated its complexity by imposing that the acquisition must measure diffusion exactly perpendicular to the fiber orientations. This way, the number of free parameters reduces to 6 (3 volume fractions, hindered diffusivity, intra-axonal diffusivity and 2 gamma function parameters). Consequently, AxCaliber can be implemented on very specific cases, where the fiber orientation could be predetermined (e.g., the corpus callosum at the mid-sagittal plane).

The 1D-AxCaliber framework was validated on excised optic and sciatic nerves, spinal cord specimens, and *in-vivo* on rat corpus callosum. Yet, a slight discrepancy between the obtained axon diameters from AxCaliber and the known diameters from histology was observed. The histological values tended

11.5 AxCaliber   169

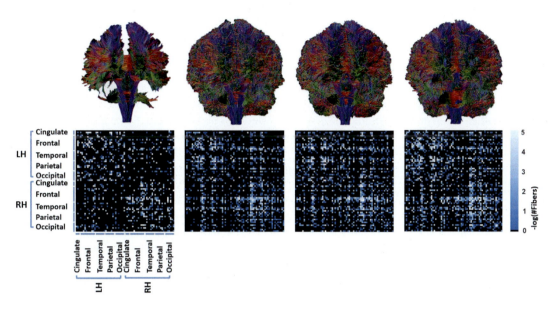

FIGURE 11.9 The effect of b-value on connectome reconstruction

Fiber tracts following DTI-based reconstruction (A), and CSD-based reconstruction for $b=1000$ (B), $b=2000$ (C), and $b=4000$ s/mm^2 (D). Below each reconstructed tract map is the connectome. Evidently, with CSD and higher b-value, the number of extracted connections increases significantly.

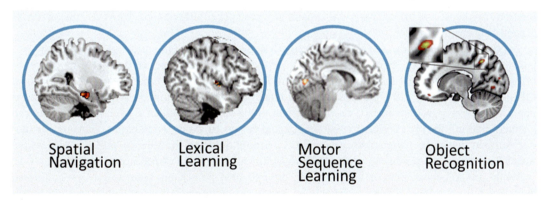

FIGURE 11.10 Using MD to explore neuroplasticity

Mean diffusivity reduction following different cognitive tasks highlights areas that underwent microstructural remodeling in spatial navigation, lexical learning, motor sequence learning, and object recognition tasks. Colored areas represent pixels where MD reduction was significant enough to reject the null hypothesis.

to be smaller from the AxCaliber ones by a factor of 2–3 (especially when AxCaliber was measured *in-vivo*). This inconsistency was attributed to shrinkage of the *ex-vivo* tissue caused by histology preparation procedures. It was also argued that AxCaliber cannot accurately model small-diameter axons, and

170   Chapter 11 Diffusion as a probe of tissue microstructure

therefore the technique may be biased towards higher values. This inaccuracy relates to the insensitivity of dMRI to small displacements (see Section 11.2).

The insensitivity to small axons is determined by two factors: the magnitude of the q-value and the length of the gradient pulse (δ). The q-space theory defines $1/q$ as the resolution of the reciprocal displacement space, which in conventional diffusion experiment will be around ~ 1 μm, suggesting that smaller axons cannot be distinguished. This issue is even more severe in clinical scanners, where the limited gradient strength suggests that the q-space resolution is about 2–3 μm. Some histologists would argue that most axons in the CNS are smaller than 1 μm, decreasing the relevance of these methods or confining them to large axons only. However, whereas the q-space resolution limits can be calculated for the Fourier relation between the signal decay and the displacement distribution function (Eq. (11.6)) using the $1/q$ factor, for the parametric modeling (Eqs. (11.7)–(11.9)) this resolution argument is less definite, suggesting that smaller axons (<1 μm) could be measured, at least theoretically.

Obviously, the ability to separate smaller axons will depend on the gradient strength (G) and gradient duration (δ). The stronger and shorter the gradients are, the more accurately small axonal separation can be estimated. Yet, the exact effect of the gradient strength on axon diameter estimation is still under investigation. Axon diameter estimation is more susceptible to the diffusion time (Δ) and gradient pulse duration (δ). The diffusion time should satisfy the condition, whereby water molecules experience the entire axonal space during that time, typically Δ of at least 30–40 ms should be sufficient. The effect of the gradient pulse length (δ) is more cumbersome. As discussed above, Mitra has suggested the center of mass explanation (Mitra and Halperin, 1995) when lengthy diffusion pulses are used (and in a clinical setup this is always the case). Consequently, a significant diffusion is expected during the gradient pulse, which should theoretically reduce the sensitivity to smaller axons (as no matter what the axon diameter size is, the center of mass will be the same: the center of the axon). As the gradient pulse duration lengthens, this insensitivity will expand to include ever larger axons. However, this matter is currently under investigation.

Another confound on the AxCaliber modeling framework is the high correlation between the signals that originate from different compartments. Novikov et al. have suggested that hindered/restricted diffusion that occurs in the extra-axonal space will have similar signal characteristics to intra-axonal diffusion (Novikov et al., 2019). In that case, the model will be unable to separate these two compartments and may assign, erroneously, one component to the other. This effect is even more pronounced when considering the high correlation between signal decays of axons with similar diameter. Simulations suggest that these correlations are extremely strong, reducing the validity and relevance of the model. This issue is ill-posed and appears to be a significant limitation of AxCaliber modeling.

While AxCaliber accuracy is under debate, the extracted parameters seem to provide additional and meaningful information that can accompany neuroscience research in various manners. For example, the first demonstration of AxCaliber in rodents replicated the known neuroanatomical variation of axonal diameter distribution (ADD) along the corpus callosum (smaller in the genu and splenium of the CC and larger at the body of the CC), providing the first method that can extract such information *in-vivo*. This demonstration led to the implementation of AxCaliber on clinical scanners. The main challenge here is the limited gradient strength that clinical scanners have. Despite this, with the newest generation of MRI scanners with relatively strong gradient systems (even up to 300 mT/m for specialist human scanners), AxCaliber may become more applicable (Fig. 11.11). The first study that implemented AxCaliber on a clinical scanner equipped with an 80 mT/m gradient unit also correlated its results with conduction velocity measurements, reproducing the known relation between the two

(Horowitz et al., 2014). Additional studies with even stronger gradient systems have shown the sensitivity of this method to the anatomy of the corpus callosum and to pathological conditions. Recent AxCaliber studies expanded the methodology to 3D to allow examination of axon diameter for any fiber orientations, thus increasing its relevance to neuroscience. Despite the fact that these studies are in their early stages, and the above inherent theoretical and modeling issues of AxCaliber, the information embedded in the high b-value signals and the high sensitivity towards the intra-axonal space allows characterization of axon diameter properties with an accuracy that depends on the experimental setup.

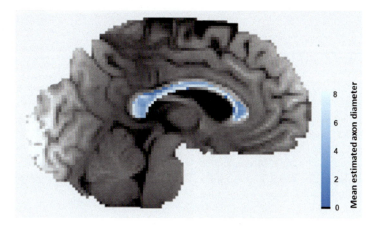

FIGURE 11.11 AxCaliber on the corpus callosum (CC) of the human brain

Axon diameters were computed with the van Gelderen model (Eq. (11.8)), depicting the well-known pattern of small estimated ADD in the genu and splenium of the CC, and larger ADD in body.

11.6 Summary

Diffusion MRI is a valuable microstructural probe. As such, it fills a gap between invasive microscopy and conventional MRI. Whereas the former probes only a small number of cells in a specific area, the latter obtains microstructural measures of the whole organ, but indirectly and with poor specificity. The incredible sensitivity and specificity of dMRI on such a large span of scales is unprecedented. It is no wonder that dMRI has become popular in neuroscience and has been incorporated as a basic imaging sequence alongside T_1 anatomic scanning and functional MRI. The influence and uses of dMRI in neuroscience are expected to grow. The ability to follow neuroplasticity, to explore the connectome with ever-higher accuracy, and estimate conduction velocity via axon diameter measures, were considered as science fiction 15 years ago. Although dMRI suffers from many artifacts, pitfalls, and inherent limitations, its advantages and the novel information it provides makes it a valuable tool nevertheless.

As dMRI provides new approaches to explore microstructural information *in-vivo*, the need for validation of the obtained indices appears to be critical. Yet, over the years, we have learned that validating *in-vivo* measures of microstructures by *ex-vivo* histological and physiological measures does not always provide the ground truth. This is mainly because histology and physiological measures suffer

172 **Chapter 11** Diffusion as a probe of tissue microstructure

from artifacts and pitfalls themselves and, more importantly, once tissue is excised and is no longer in an "*in-vivo*" state, there are dramatic microstructural changes that affect the credibility of direct comparison between the two. Thus while the search to validate dMRI measures is important, maybe reassurance in the extracted parameters should come by gaining experience with the various parameters over a wide range of applications.

Presently, dMRI is central in neuroimaging mainly due to the extensive use of DTI. Yet, we anticipate that with the unique and unequivocal information that microstructural dMRI provides, its applications in neuroscience will increase and eventually will parallel that of fMRI.

References

Assaf, Y., Cohen, Y., 1999. Structural information in neuronal tissue as revealed by q-space diffusion NMR spectroscopy of metabolites in bovine optic nerve. NMR Biomed. 12, 335–344.

Assaf, Y., Cohen, Y., 2000. Assignment of the water slow-diffusing component in the central nervous system using q-space diffusion MRS: implications for fiber tract imaging. Magn. Reson. Med. 43, 191–199.

Assaf, Y., Freidlin, R.Z., Rohde, G.K., Basser, P.J., 2004. New modeling and experimental framework to characterize hindered and restricted water diffusion in brain white matter. Magn. Reson. Med. 52, 965–978.

Assaf, Y., Blumenfeld-Katzir, T., Yovel, Y., Basser, P.J., 2008. AxCaliber: a method for measuring axon diameter distribution from diffusion MRI. Magn. Reson. Med. 59, 1347–1354.

Assaf, Y., 2018. New dimensions for brain mapping. Science 362, 994–995.

Basser, P.J., Mattiello, J., LeBihan, D., 1994. MR diffusion tensor spectroscopy and imaging. Biophys. J. 66, 259–267.

Basser, P.J., Pierpaoli, C., 1996. Microstructural and physiological features of tissues elucidated by quantitative-diffusion-tensor MRI. J. Magn. Reson., Ser. B 111, 209–219.

Basser, P.J., Pierpaoli, C., 1998. A simplified method to measure the diffusion tensor from seven MR images. Magn. Reson. Med. 39, 928–934.

Blumenfeld-Katzir, T., Pasternak, O., Dagan, M., Assaf, Y., 2011. Diffusion MRI of structural brain plasticity induced by a learning and memory task. PLoS ONE 6, e20678.

Callaghan, P.T., 1995. Pulsed-gradient spin-echo NMR for planar, cylindrical, and spherical pores under conditions of wall relaxation. J. Magn. Reson., Ser. A 113, 53–59.

Catani, M., Howard, R.J., Pajevic, S., Jones, D.K., 2002. Virtual in vivo interactive dissection of white matter fasciculi in the human brain. NeuroImage 17, 77–94.

Chenevert, T.L., Brunberg, J.A., Pipe, J.G., 1990. Anisotropic diffusion in human white matter: demonstration with MR techniques in vivo. Radiology 177, 401–405.

Gianolio, E., Ferrauto, G., Di Gregorio, E., Aime, S., 2016. Re-evaluation of the water exchange lifetime value across red blood cell membrane. Biochim. Biophys. Acta 1858, 627–631.

Horowitz, A., et al., 2014. In vivo correlation between axon diameter and conduction velocity in the human brain. Brain Struct. Funct.

Johansen-Berg, H., Baptista, C.S., Thomas, A.G., 2012. Human structural plasticity at record speed. Neuron 73, 1058–1060.

Mitra, P.P., Halperin, B.I., 1995. Effects of finite gradient-pulse widths in pulsed-field-gradient diffusion measurements. J. Magn. Reson., Ser. A 113, 94.

Moseley, M.E., et al., 1990. Early detection of regional cerebral ischemia in cats: comparison of diffusion- and T2-weighted MRI and spectroscopy. Magn. Reson. Med. 14, 330–346.

Neuman, C.H., 1974. Spin-echo of spins diffusing in a bounded medium. J. Chem. Phys. 60, 4508–4511.

Novikov, D.S., Fieremans, E., Jespersen, S.N., Kiselev, V.G., 2019. Quantifying brain microstructure with diffusion MRI: theory and parameter estimation. NMR Biomed. 32, e3998.

Pierpaoli, C., Jezzard, P., Basser, P.J., Barnett, A., Di Chiro, G., 1996. Diffusion tensor MR imaging of the human brain. Radiology 201, 637–648.

Stejskal, E.O., Tanner, J.E., 1965. Spin diffusion measurements - spin echoes in presence of a time-dependent field gradient. J. Chem. Phys. 42, 288–292.

Tournier, J.D., Calamante, F., Gadian, D.G., Connelly, A., 2004. Direct estimation of the fiber orientation density function from diffusion-weighted MRI data using spherical deconvolution. NeuroImage 23, 1176–1185.

van Gelderen, P., DesPres, D., van Zijl, P.C., Moonen, C.T., 1994. Evaluation of restricted diffusion in cylinders. Phosphocreatine in rabbit leg muscle. J. Magn. Reson., Ser. B 103, 255–260.

Yang, D.M., et al., 2018. Intracellular water preexchange lifetime in neurons and astrocytes. Magn. Reson. Med. 79, 1616–1627.

Zhang, H., Schneider, T., Wheeler-Kingshott, C.A., Alexander, D.C., 2012. NODDI: practical in vivo neurite orientation dispersion and density imaging of the human brain. NeuroImage 64, 1000–1016.

Further reading

Callaghan, P.T., 1991. Principles of Nuclear Magnetic Resonance Microscopy. Clarendon Press/Oxford University Press, New York/Oxford.

Johansen-Berg, H., Behrens, T.E.J., 2009. Diffusion MRI: From Quantitative Measurement to In-Vivo Neuroanatomy. Elsevier/Academic Press, Amsterdam/Boston.

Jones, D.K., 2010. Diffusion MRI: Theory, Methods, and Application. Oxford University Press, New York.

Jones, D.K., Cercignani, M., 2010. Twenty-five pitfalls in the analysis of diffusion MRI data. NMR Biomed. 23, 803–820.

Le Bihan, D., 1995. Diffusion and Perfusion Magnetic Resonance Imaging: Applications to Functional MRI. Raven Press, New York.

PART 4

Perfusion MRI

CHAPTER

12

Non-contrast agent perfusion MRI methods

Matthias Günther[a,b,c]
[a] Fraunhofer MEVIS, Bremen, Germany
[b] University Bremen, Bremen, Germany
[c] mediri GmbH, Heidelberg, Germany

12.1 Introduction

In contrast to structural imaging, physiological imaging is an area that can shed light on the function of tissues and organs, instead of simply providing morphological information. In this way, it can provide complementary information for assessing the human body. In several diseases, physiological changes in tissue are expected to occur at a much earlier time compared to structural changes. However, assessment of physiological processes and parameters can be challenging to measure with MRI due to several reasons:

- physiology can change over short time scales (even during the measurement process itself)
- several confounders (in fact 100s) are known to influence and modify physiology in the short and long term (see Fig. 12.1)
- the effect that most physiological processes have on the MR signal is typically small (usually on the order of a few percent). Although the effects may be larger if exogenous contrast media are used.

Physiology covers a lot of processes in the human body, with many MR techniques having been developed to assess them. In this chapter, we will concentrate on the very important (yet not the only) physiological parameter describing the transport of blood to the tissue, namely microvascular perfusion.

Perfusion is a measure which describes the delivery of blood to the capillaries. Here, at the capillary exchange site, the transition of water, oxygen, nutrients and other substances into the surrounding tissue takes place, as well as the removal of waste products from tissue into the blood. The physical measure has units of (blood) volume flow per supplied (tissue) volume, or (blood) volume per unit time per (tissue) volume. In the case of perfusion of the brain, the term cerebral blood flow (CBF) is commonly used, although this is an over-simplification from a physical point of view. Perfusion is also not to be mistaken as a (blood) velocity nor as a (blood) volume. It simply describes the amount of blood delivered to a certain tissue volume per unit time. In SI units, this perfusion is measured as $[m^3/s/kg]$, but since perfusion values in the human body tend to be relatively small, the unit is most often used is [ml blood/min/100g tissue]. For example, the typical perfusion of gray matter in young healthy adults is about 60 [ml blood/min/100g tissue], as only a small fraction of the brain volume consists of vessels ($\approx$1–3% in white matter, $\approx$3–5% in gray matter).

Due to its very nature, perfusion is not a constant parameter, but adapts and changes at rather short time scales to react to external or internal stimuli and requirements (Clement et al., 2018). Fig. 12.1 lists several such stimuli and provides a rough idea of the amount of change in perfusion associated with it as reported in the literature. From this figure it can be seen that global perfusion can change by 30% and more due to, e.g., intoxication or exercise. It is also well known that brain perfusion in adults decreases with age. For meaningful interpretation of absolute global perfusion values, all potential confounders would have to be considered or controlled.

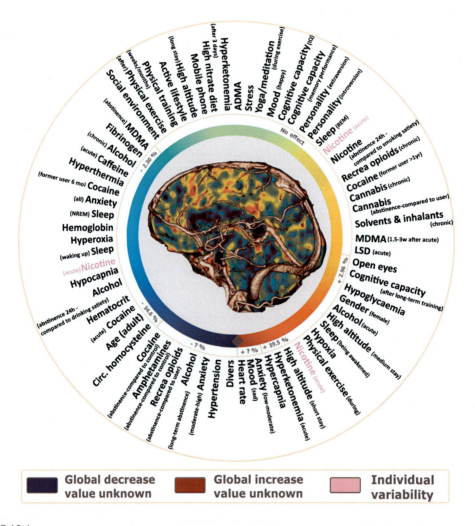

FIGURE 12.1

Effects of modifiers on global brain perfusion summarized as a color gradient: factors in the green area induce no effect, the blue and red areas represent global decrease and increase, respectively. All factors are classified both according to their effect and the corresponding magnitude on global perfusion changes. Other factors, whose value is still unknown, are grouped around the gray diamond [reprinted with kind permission: (Clement et al., 2018)].

The ability to measure perfusion relies on the capability of distinguishing the blood compartment from the surrounding tissue compartment. All methods described in the remainder of this chapter make, in one or the other way, use of the fact that blood is flowing compared to stationary tissue. Either the approach is used to magnetically tag blood such that it serves as an endogenous tracer to a different location, where the imaging takes place, and make use of transport phenomena, or the specific properties of flowing blood within the imaging region is used to selectively modify blood water magnetization.

12.2 Arterial spin labeling

The basic idea behind arterial spin labeling (ASL) is to separate blood water signal from tissue signal by acquiring two data sets with different preparation of the blood water magnetization, while tissue magnetization is prepared identically in both data sets. These two data sets are typically termed label and control images. By subtracting these two data sets, the tissue signal (actually all signal arising from static components) will cancel out, and only the signal which has moved from the location where the blood signal was labeled to the image location remains. The highest difference between label and control images can be achieved by tag inversion, which is the most common approach, whereas other constraints (simplicity of implementation, robustness or practicality) might favor a tag saturation approach. Regardless of the exact flavor of preparation, the process of tagging blood water spins is denoted "labeling". All variants of ASL rely on the assumption that blood is moving during the experiment. A delay between labeling and image readout is utilized to allow for the assessment of different phases of the inflow of blood into the vasculature (as visualized in Fig. 12.2). This delay is either called the inflow time (TI) or post-labeling delay (PLD), depending on the nature of ASL preparation. It is important to note that since labeling is performed by inversion of the longitudinal magnetization, the label will decay with the local T_1, which effectively leads to a loss of ASL signal over time (the half-life time of the ASL "tracer" is typically only slightly above one second, and the ability to detect an ASL signal in the tissue therefore "disappears" over the course of a few seconds).

12.2.1 Labeling variants

In the late 1990s and the following decade, a huge and confusing number of preparation schemes were published. It became fashionable to create new acronyms (as it seems to be an unwritten law in the whole field of MRI) even for very small, sometimes irrelevant changes. Cautious estimates put the figure at "30 different arterial blood labeling schemes, combined with at least six different methods of encoding the labeled information during the inflow time and as many readout strategies" (Golay and Guenther, 2012). As an example, in the supplementary material of their review on ASL studies in 2009–2014, Wong and Maller (2016) list a subset of 24 of the most commonly used acronyms.

Nonetheless, all published ASL variants can be placed into three categories:

- Pulsed ASL: label shape spatially defined: labeling of blood water magnetization is performed by a short inversion module ($\sim$10–15 ms duration) at a given point in time within a larger area ($\sim$100 mm) completely outside and upstream relative to the imaging region.
- Continuous ASL (including pseudo-continuous ASL): label shape temporally defined: labeling by flow-driven adiabatic inversion in a small region ($\sim$20 mm) upstream relative to the imaging region over a long period of time (typically one to a few seconds).

180 Chapter 12 Non-contrast agent perfusion MRI methods

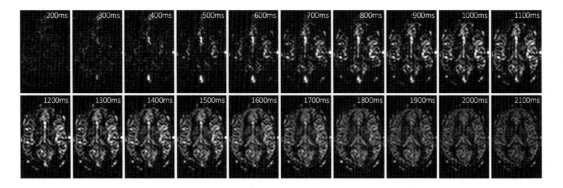

FIGURE 12.2

Inflow phases of labeled blood into a single brain slice of a healthy 34-year-old subject. The ASL variant FAIR was used for labeling with a 3D-GRASE image readout. The inflow time TI is indicated for each inflow phase. Due to the symmetric labeling region of the FAIR scheme, blood above the imaging plane is also labeled, and therefore the sagittal sinus vein lights up early on in the posterior part of the brain.

- Velocity- or acceleration-selective ASL: labeling of blood water magnetization, slowing down within the imaging region by saturation or inversion at a given point in time.

The small signal difference arising from different states of blood water magnetization makes all ASL variants sensitive to small erroneous differences of tissue signal between label and control data sets created during the ASL preparation. Unwanted residual signal will arise in the ASL image if the signal of stationary magnetization does not fully cancel, and can incorrectly mimic perfusion. A common problem in this regard is magnetization transfer effects (see Chapter 24) varying in the label and control phases due to differences in RF power, asymmetric slab positions and/or gradient switching. Another problem can arise from B_1 inhomogeneities and off-resonance issues, which could manifest as inhomogeneous saturation and/or inversion. To provide the maximum robustness against off-resonance and B_1-field inhomogeneities, most ASL variants utilize adiabatic processes to manipulate the magnetization. In this context, adiabatic describes the property of the RF pulse to "lock" the magnetization vector and change its direction slowly enough so that the magnetization vector follows tightly. This is typically achieved by a frequency sweep of the RF pulse, e.g., starting at negative off-resonance frequencies and ending at positive off-resonance frequencies. Provided the amplitude of the RF pulse is high enough and the rate of frequency sweep (yielding the orientation change of the RF pulse) is slow enough, the magnetization vector will follow independent of off-resonances and B_1-field inhomogeneities.

12.2.2 Pulsed ASL (PASL)

In pulsed ASL (PASL) blood is tagged in a region upstream of the imaging site. For the labeling phase, a single pulse with a duration of typically 10–15 ms is played out to invert the magnetization in a slab with a thickness in the range of 50–100 mm. For control purposes, the magnetization in this preparation slab is left unchanged. During the inflow time, this will eventually result in either unperturbed blood water magnetization (control) or inverted magnetization (label) to flow into the imaging slab. For a long time during the 1990s and early 2000s, a number of variants of pulsed ASL were developed to cope with magnetization transfer confounds, and symmetric and asymmetric labeling schemes were proposed. The FAIR (Flow-sensitive Alternating Inversion Recovery; symmetric scheme with slab-selective and global inversion) approach (Kim and Tsekos, 1997) and the STAR (Signal Targeting with Alternating Radiofrequencies; asymmetric scheme with well-defined inversion slab below and above imaging region) approach (Edelman et al., 1994) are representatives of each class and are often employed for pulsed ASL measurements (see Fig. 12.3). In recent years, another approach to deal with magnetization transfer effects became more popular: namely, applying robust and reliable saturation of the imaging region immediately after the ASL preparation. This results in a complete history deletion of the magnetization and establishes a well-defined magnetization state ($M(t = 0) = 0$).

For robust inversion, adiabatic full passage RF pulses are used that incorporate either a hyperbolic-secant pulse or a so-called FOCI-pulse (Frequency-Offset Corrected Inversion pulse). These pulses can be (easily) implemented on clinical systems, and therefore provide a well-tested basis for almost all PASL sequences. An excellent review of adiabatic pulses and pulse design is provided in (Tannus and Garwood, 1997).

Neither the length of the labeled blood bolus (as a spatial measure) nor the bolus duration (as a temporal measure) are well defined in pulsed ASL, due to the labeling process. As labeling is performed in a spatially defined region over a short point in time, the exact length depends on vessel tortuosity and inversion profile (e.g., due to limited transmit RF field coverage). Bolus duration is an essential parameter to allow quantification of CBF and depends, in addition to the unknown bolus length, on blood velocity. Techniques have been developed to temporally define bolus duration by using additional saturation pulses directly upstream of the imaging region starting from an inflow time that equals the desired bolus duration. These methods are called QUIPSS (Wong et al., 1998) and Q2TIPS (Luh et al., 1999) and are used often in single-TI PASL measurements. However, these techniques only allow definition of a maximum bolus duration, but they cannot guarantee the exact temporal width. This can lead to significant underestimation of perfusion. Another way to deal with the initially unknown bolus length is to acquire multi-TI data sets and include these in the biophysical modeling (see below).

12.2.3 Continuous ASL (CASL) and pseudo-continuous ASL (pCASL)

One drawback of all pulsed ASL schemes is the large spatial extent of the labeling region. This leads to a range of arterial transit times with the front boundary of the labeled blood bolus taking less time to reach the imaging region than the rear part of the bolus. As the whole bolus was created at the same time in PASL, the rear part of the labeling will decay with T_1 relaxation more than the front part upon arrival in the imaging slice.

In contrast to PASL, continuous ASL (CASL) approaches tag the blood at a well-defined position over a long period of time so that each part of the labeled blood bolus will experience the same travel time to the imaging slab (assuming constant flow velocity). The time the blood is allowed to flow into the imaging slab (i.e., the time from the end of labeling to the start of imaging) is called the post-labeling delay (PLD). It compares to the inflow time TI used in pulsed ASL in that the sum of labeling time (bolus duration) and PLD equals TI.

In CASL, the frequency of the RF pulse is not changed as for the case of the adiabatic RF pulses described above, but the frequency sweep is achieved by using a magnetic field gradient along the flow

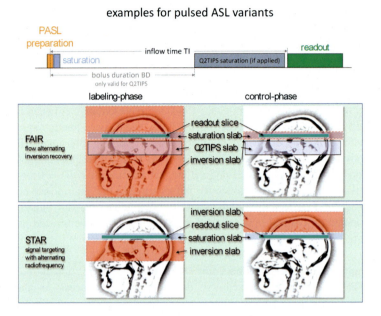

FIGURE 12.3

Examples of pulsed ASL variants. The label and control phase of the symmetric FAIR labeling scheme and the asymmetric STAR scheme are shown. With proper slice-selective saturation, the inversion pulses in the control phase could be omitted without experiencing magnetization transfer artifacts. The exact location of the labeling regions might vary for multi-slice and whole-brain imaging.

direction. With this gradient, blood water magnetization flowing along this gradient will experience an increasing (or decreasing) net magnetic field. Thus the resonance frequency of the blood water magnetization will increase (decrease) while it is flowing. With a continuous B_1 transmit field at a constant frequency, blood water magnetization will thus experience a frequency sweep from higher (lower) to lower (higher) off-resonance frequency, with on-resonance exactly in the middle of the labeling region. As in the case of adiabatic RF-pulses described above, the magnetization will become inverted. This is the so-called flow-driven adiabatic inversion, which is employed in all CASL experiments. Historically, the continuous B_1-field was applied over a period of 1–2 seconds, either by using a regular transmit coil or by using a second local coil, dedicated only to the labeling. Use of a second coil has the benefit of only locally affecting magnetization, and not extending into the imaging region, so that magnetization transfer effects can be neglected. However, additional technical equipment is necessary for this, which hampered the use in a clinical setting (and in most research sites). This might change in future, because more and more modern MR-scanners are equipped with multiple transmit capabilities.

To control magnetization effects without a dedicated labeling coil, several techniques have been developed, with the amplitude-modulated approach being the most used. Here, the amplitude of the continuous B_1-field is changed periodically for the control image, which essentially yields two inversion slices next to each other instead of one (see Fig. 12.4). Using this scheme, blood water magnetization is inverted twice, which results in (almost) undisturbed magnetization for the control case. However,

12.2 Arterial spin labeling   183

these CASL approaches were difficult to use on clinical scanners due to their high demand on continuous RF-power. Therefore a new approach was developed, where instead of a long continuous RF-field, many short RF-pulses are applied in such a rapid manner that the conditions for flow-driven adiabatic inversion are still fulfilled. A typical setting uses 0.5 ms-long RF-pulses with a pause of 0.4–0.5 ms between consecutive RF-pulses. Stronger gradients are used to confine the effect of the RF-pulses to a small region. The gradient switching during the application of the RF-pulses has to be partially refocused to yield a similar net gradient as in the classical CASL experiments. This technique is called pseudo-continuous ASL (pCASL, originally named pulsed-continuous; it was soon adapted to pseudo-continuous). The pCASL variant turned out to provide better labeling efficiency and less magnetization transfer effect (due to the strong field gradients) than the previously used CASL variants and became quasi-standard for ASL measurements. It is part of the recommendations in the ASL consensus-paper published in 2015 (Alsop et al., 2015).

However, the flow-driven adiabatic inversion process used in CASL, and especially in pCASL, is more sensitive to off-resonances compared to adiabatic RF pulses used for PASL. Therefore special care has to be taken to ensure that the inversion process at the labeling slice takes place as intended.

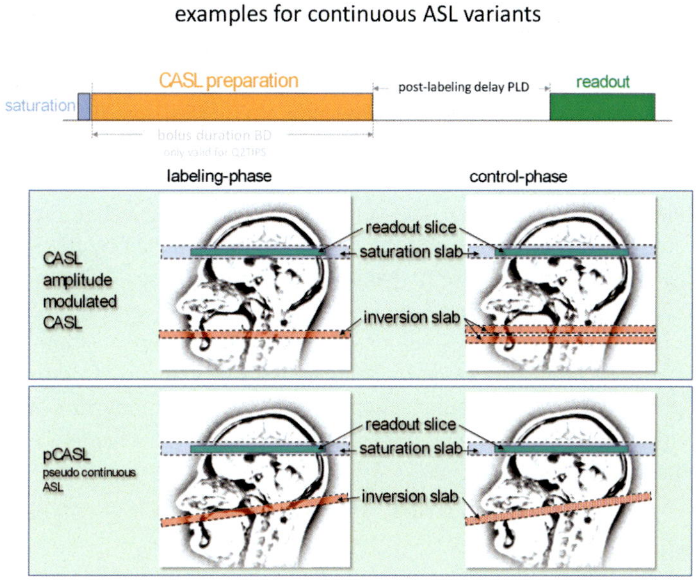

FIGURE 12.4

Examples of continuous ASL variants. The amplitude-modulated CASL scheme is shown together with today's quasi-standard pseudo-continuous ASL (pCASL).

12.2.4 Velocity, acceleration-selective ASL

Pulsed and continuous ASL techniques, as described above, have in common the fact that the inversion of blood water magnetization takes place outside the imaging region. The basic idea of both groups of

184 **Chapter 12** Non-contrast agent perfusion MRI methods

ASL variant is to modify magnetization outside the imaging plane and use the fact that only the blood will travel from the preparation site to the imaging site. This has the advantage that the inversion process does not have to take the static tissue compartment at the labeling location into account, which will also be affected by the adiabatic inversion process, and is therefore also tagged during ASL preparation. This is also true for flow-driven adiabatic inversion, where the static tissue magnetization in the labeling region also gets disturbed, although it will not be properly inverted. The separation of the location of tagging and the location of imaging allows the application of robust and (mostly) reliable inversion pulses. However, this comes with a price tag as well. The labeled blood has to travel from the labeling site to the imaging site, which requires a certain amount of time, depending on blood flow velocity (the so-called arterial transit time, ATT). In patients with impaired hemodynamics, this can pose a problem (and does so on a regular basis), because the label may not have reached the brain tissue and can still reside in the larger arteries at the moment of readout, leading to vascular artifacts.

The basic idea of velocity- and acceleration-selective ASL is different (Wong et al., 2006). Here, the labeling takes place within the imaging region itself, and thus removes the arterial transit time almost completely. An RF and gradient pulse train is utilized, which selectively saturates or inverts magnetization moving no faster than a given cut-off velocity (velocity-selective). Alternatively, the echo train can saturate magnetization that is speeding up or slowing down (acceleration-selective). The threshold velocity and acceleration for the label and control case are different so that a certain range of velocities/accelerations can be tagged. Most often, the threshold value for the control phase tends to very large values, essentially leaving all existing magnetization untouched. As stated above, since the labeling occurs much closer to the capillary exchange site than in the pulsed and continuous ASL variants, the arterial transit time is greatly reduced. This helps to improve perfusion assessment in cases where blood delivery is delayed (e.g., in stroke). The velocity/acceleration-selective preparation train is applied in a spatially non-selective manner, i.e., the whole volume reached by the RF transmit coil will undergo the velocity/acceleration-selective preparation. Adiabatic pulses, such as the BIR-4 or BIR-8 pulses (Tannus and Garwood, 1997) are used to increase the robustness against off-resonances and eddy currents. Originally being implemented as velocity-/acceleration-selective saturation, schemes allowing for inversion have been published recently. With its main advantage of cutting down the arterial transit time, it is of great value for those clinical applications where hemodynamics are modified. However, perfusion quantification is challenging with velocity/acceleration-selective ASL, due to the very specific velocity-dependent labeling efficiency.

12.2.5 Background suppression

As mentioned above, ASL relies on small signal changes in the label and control image of a few percent at most. This makes the technique very sensitive to small differences between the two data sets not arising from perfusion. This could be bulk motion, breathing or signal fluctuations due to RF inconsistencies. If one assumes a measurement with a signal-to-noise ratio of 100 for each label and control data set, the normal fluctuation (noise) of the tissue signal would be of the same order as the complete blood signal! For typical 2D image readout strategies, it typically suffices to average a large number of measurements, but for 3D acquisition approaches, the noise contamination and signal instability is higher. Therefore strategies were developed to reduce the (unwanted) static tissue signal at the time of readout, while preserving the (almost) full blood signal. These background suppression (BS) schemes typically consist of well-placed inversion pulses along with an additional saturation pulse in the beginning of the sequence. The idea behind this is to (almost) null the tissue magnetization at the time of readout. Perfect nulling can be achieved for signal components with certain T_1 relaxation times by proper placement of inversion pulses, where the number of different components will equal the number of inversion pulses used. Signal components that don't exactly match one of these T_1 relaxation times will still be attenuated, but not as perfectly nulled. This does not pose a problem, since, typically, some residual tissue signal is needed anyway, to avoid an unclear sign (positive or negative residual signal) for non-fully-nulled tissue signal. This is usually achieved by arranging for the null time of the magnetization to be well before the time of readout (e.g., 50 ms), or by positioning the inversion pulses so that a certain wanted fraction is achieved (e.g., 5% residual signal).

The magnetization after N inversion pulses of a component with a T_1 relaxation rate of R_1 at time TI can then be calculated as follows:

$$M\left(\text{TI}, R_1\right) = 1 + \left(M\left(0\right) - 1\right) \cdot \left(-1\right)^N \cdot e^{-R_1 \cdot \text{TI}} + \sum_{n=1}^{N} \left(-1\right)^{N-n+1} \cdot e^{-R_1 \cdot \left(\text{TI} - ti_n\right)} \tag{12.1}$$

Here, the magnetization is assumed to be normalized (-1...+1), and the nth inversion pulse is played out at time ti_n.

For the proper timings of the N inversion pulses to achieve the desired residual signal for K tissue components, the following system of equations has to be solved:

$$
\begin{aligned}
M\left(\text{TI}, R_1^1\right) &= M_{\text{res}}^1 \\
\vdots \quad &\vdots \quad \vdots \\
M\left(\text{TI}, R_1^K\right) &= M_{\text{res}}^K,
\end{aligned}
\tag{12.2}
$$

where M_{res}^k is the targeted residual magnetization of component K with a T_1 relaxation rate R_1^K.

For $K > N$, the system is underdetermined and an optimization algorithm can be used along with a target measure (e.g., minimal overall residual magnetization) to deduce the positions of the inversion pulses. The typical behavior of magnetization after two inversion pulses is shown in Fig. 12.5 for different T_1 components.

12.2.6 Image acquisition

For almost all cases, ASL preparation can be viewed completely independently from the image acquisition part. In general, any readout technique can be used; however, some are more suited and efficient than others. Most often, the preparation is the most time-consuming part of the ASL measurement. Typically, arrival of labeled blood at the capillary exchange site is expected not much earlier than 1.5 s, or even later after the start of labeling. Exceptions are velocity-selective and related ASL variants, where the arrival time is much smaller. However, the same delivery time dictates the measurement duration, albeit this time with a delay that is needed after image readout to allow for refreshing of blood magnetization within the imaging region. Overall, the required minimum repetition time of a few seconds will, in general, be the same for all ASL variants (note: there are some "short TR" ASL variants, which mix different states of magnetization preparation, but they have not yet caught on for quantitative perfusion imaging). Due to these time constraints, image acquisition techniques, which acquire

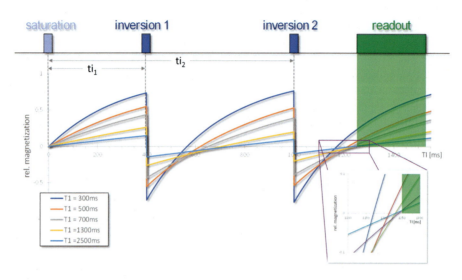

FIGURE 12.5

Background suppression scheme with two inversion pulses. Components with different T_1 relaxation times are shown. Only two of them are nulled at the beginning of readout.

only a small portion of the imaging data in one repetition period, are not very efficient (e.g., such as turbo-spin-echo (TSE) with a small number of refocusing pulses (turbo factor)). Therefore single-shot or few-shot readout techniques are usually employed.

Echo-planar imaging (EPI) was used early on due to its fast imaging capabilities, which allowed the acquisition of several slices after one ASL preparation (Edelman et al., 1994; Edelman and Chen, 1998). However, due to the subsequent acquisition, each slice will have a slightly different inflow time. This can be corrected for in the modeling and processing step and is typically minimized by utilizing modern speedup approaches, such as parallel imaging and simultaneous multi-slice. With this, EPI is still an often-used imaging technique with ASL, especially for cerebral perfusion measurements. Nonetheless, 3D imaging variants are replacing 2D EPI due to several benefits.

3D imaging approaches (Gunther et al., 2005; Talagala et al., 2004) have the advantage of providing full-brain coverage and of acquiring the whole imaging volume at the same inflow time, TI. This allows for easier implementation of background suppression, especially with respect to having uniform levels of background suppression in the slice-direction. Furthermore, it has been shown that 3D imaging can significantly increase the signal-to-noise ratio (SNR) compared to EPI (Gunther et al., 2005), thus reducing acquisition time accordingly. Typically, a combination of multiple spin-echoes and EPI is used for fast 3D imaging in ASL. The echo-planar imaging train can be performed along different trajectories, such as Cartesian (Gunther et al., 2005) or spiral (Ye et al., 2000; Dai et al., 2008). Segmentation is often used to improve image quality and reduce blurring, but also increases motion sensitivity.

Other readout options, such as HASTE (half Fourier turbo spin echo imaging), balanced Steady-State Free Precision (bSSFP), and others, have been published, but most find their application in measurements in non-neuro regions. More details on image acquisition and comparison between 2D and 3D imaging strategies in the neuro-context can be found in Alsop et al. (2015) and Vidorreta et al. (2013).

12.2.7 Efficient acquisition of multiple inflow times

The dynamics of the inflow of the labeled blood into the imaging region can vary between subjects and can have tremendously different characteristics for some diseases. Therefore, in both PASL and CASL, it is beneficial to use not one measurement with a fixed inflow time (or post-labeling delay in CASL variants), but capture the whole inflow of the labeled blood at various inflow times. However, this can be very time-consuming. Therefore speed-up techniques were sought to reduce scan time for the acquisition of multiple inflow timepoints.

The most time-consuming part of ASL sequences is the waiting time to allow labeled blood to reach the imaging region and ultimately to reach the capillary exchange site. To speed this up, more than one data set can be acquired after the ASL preparation. This is the idea of the so-called Look–Locker readout (Gunther et al., 2001), whereby multiple data sets at different inflow times are acquired after a single preparation. To achieve this, the readout of the images at earlier inflow times have to retain some of the labeled blood water magnetization for later readouts. This is done by reducing the excitation flip angle. Originally developed for PASL variants, it has also been used successfully for pCASL, even though no images can be acquired at early inflow times, where the labeling process is still active. This technique works well for gradient-echo sequences, but less well for spin-echo sequences, as the refocusing pulses frequently disturb the label magnetization. See Fig. 12.6.

FIGURE 12.6

Look–Locker ASL readout technique, which acquires several different inflow timepoints after one ASL preparation.

For spin-echo readouts, another approach to efficiently sample the inflow of labeled blood was developed, which turns out to also be efficient for all readout approaches, whether spin-echo or gradient-echo based. In the time-encoded pCASL technique, the period of continuously labeled blood bolus that lasts several seconds in duration is split up into so-called sub-boli by alternating between label and control conditions within one acquisition (i.e., over the course of a single pCASL preparation). Instead of using purely label or control conditions for preparing the blood water magnetization, label and control states are mixed. Each sub-bolus experiences a distinctive signature, which allows separation of its signal from all others, once a series of such acquisitions is combined in appropriate subtraction pairings. The order in which label and control condition is varied is defined by a certain matrix, which underlies some constraints:

- For maximum efficiency, only two states (reflecting label and control) are allowed.
- For a given sub-bolus, the number of label and control conditions has to be identical.

188 Chapter 12 Non-contrast agent perfusion MRI methods

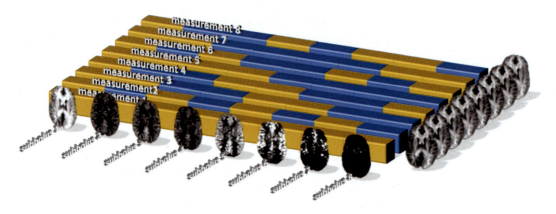

FIGURE 12.7

Pictorial description of time-encoded ASL with a Hadamard encoding pattern. Blue and yellow blocks represent label and control phases, which are mixed in a different pattern for each of the eight measurements. Each sub-bolus has a distinctive signature, which allows reconstruction of the corresponding image. The eight measurements have to be added (blue) and subtracted (yellow) according to each sub-bolus' signature. As the same label/control patterns were used during measurement, only the signal of the sub-bolus will remain, canceling out all other sub-boli's contributions.

A pattern which fulfills these constraints is the Hadamard pattern, which is used most often for time-encoded pCASL. Fig. 12.7 shows the application of a Hadamard pattern for an 8×8 matrix. Eight measurements are required to encode 7 different inflow times (one "sub-bolus" (sub-bolus 1 in the figure) does not fulfill the second constraint and is not considered). The same matrix used for labeling is used to decode the sub-boli. All eight measurements are used to reconstruct each of the 7 inflow times. This makes this approach highly efficient for sampling the inflow. However, this method is also sensitive to motion and other artifacts, which might affect one or more of the measurements, as all measurements are required for proper decoding. Using the Walsh/Hadamard-reordering scheme, instead of Hadamard, helps to make the measurement more robust by acquiring the low-frequency patterns first. Further improvements can be achieved on a post-processing level.

12.2.8 Consensus on ASL variants

To provide a clear guidance for clinical applications, a majority of the ASL community published a recommendation, which provides a consensus of what sequence to use as a workhorse for clinical application, especially for users without the support of local ASL-experts (Alsop et al., 2015). In this white paper the use of pseudo-continuous ASL (pCASL) is proposed for standard applications (if available), and the use of FAIR (a pulsed ASL variant, see below) as an alternative. Furthermore, 3D imaging is favored, compared to 2D imaging and values for important timing parameters (PLD, inflow time, and for pCASL the labeling duration) are recommended for different subject groups (children, elderly, patients with vascular disease, etc). Background suppression is shown as a prerequisite for 3D ASL flavors and optional for 2D ASL. Nonetheless, other ASL variants are appreciated and can be of high value for special applications and challenges.

12.2 Arterial spin labeling   **189**

Given the relatively long interval since the consensus-paper was published, it is unsurprising that new techniques have been developed and are becoming ready for more clinical use. These include multi-PLD pCASL measurements, either sequential or as time-encoded variants, velocity-selective ASL, and advanced post-processing approaches, such as partial volume correction. However, the challenge of finding a proper ASL protocol for a given patient for robust and reliable perfusion quantification still requires a lot of experience.

12.2.9 Biophysical modeling

Quantification of perfusion is not possible without properly modeling the biophysical processes of the measurement. For this, several biophysical models have been proposed and discussed for extracting quantitative perfusion values. One has to keep in mind that models are always simplifications, and sometimes the relationship to reality is opaque. Nonetheless, models have their range of validity and are useful and indispensable tools for estimating certain parameters, such as perfusion. The models differ in their basic assumptions and the number of aspects being modeled. In general, the more properties of the object that are incorporated, the more free parameters the model will have. These parameters either have to be measured, estimated, or taken from the literature. The latter two approaches pose the risk of providing misleading results, as the specific patient could have unexpected parameter values due to his or her disease process. Though measuring these parameters empirically seems to be the preferred approach, this can turn out to be very time-consuming and not feasible for a clinical setting.

The general kinetic model (Buxton et al., 1998) describes the behavior of the labeled magnetization (i.e., the difference magnetization $\Delta M(t) = M_{\text{control}}(t) - M_{\text{label}}(t)$) in a voxel of the imaging region over time. It is not suited for the description of the magnetization of the individual measurements M_{label} and M_{control}, which usually is not required anyway. The general kinetic model assumes that a certain amount of magnetization is delivered to the voxel by arterial blood and that venous outflow will drain the voxel. During the experiment, labeled magnetization will be reduced by longitudinal relaxation. Essentially, there are three functions governing this process:

- A delivery function $c(t)$, which describes the amount of labeled magnetization arriving in the voxel at time t in a normalized manner.
- A residue function $r(t,t')$ describing the remaining part of the labeled magnetization having flowed in at time t' and still present at time t. For rapid exchange with the tissue one can assume that the ratio of total tissue concentration and venous contribution is constant and equals the so-called tissue/blood partition coefficient of water λ. With the overall concentration being proportional to perfusion f, $r(t,t') = e^{-f/\lambda \cdot t}$.
- And a magnetization relaxation function $m(t,t')$, which describes whatever processes are affecting the labeled magnetization within the voxel. In the simplest case only longitudinal relaxation with the relaxation rate R_1^t of tissue is modeled, yielding an exponential $m(t,t') = e^{-R_1^t(t-t')}$.

These three functions govern the general kinetic model description:

$$\Delta M(t) = 2M_0^b f \int_0^t c(t') r(t-t') m(t-t') dt', \tag{12.3}$$

190 **Chapter 12** Non-contrast agent perfusion MRI methods

where M_0^b is the equilibrium value of the magnetization of a voxel completely filled with blood and f is the desired perfusion parameter. Eq. (12.3) is essentially a convolution of the delivery function with a response curve, which is the product of the magnetization relaxation and the residue function.

In the general kinetic model approach, pulsed and continuous ASL variants differ only in the delivery function $c(t)$. For PASL the delivery function is

$$c_{PASL}(t) = \begin{cases} 0 & 0 < t \leq \text{ATT} \\ \alpha \cdot e^{-R_1^b \cdot t} & \text{ATT} < t \leq \text{ATT} + \text{BD} \\ 0 & t > \text{ATT} + \text{BD} \end{cases} \tag{12.4}$$

with α being the labeling efficiency of the inversion process, whereas for CASL (this also includes pCASL, which is to all intents and purposes equivalent to CASL) the delivery function is

$$c_{CASL}(t) = \begin{cases} 0 & 0 < t \leq \text{ATT} \\ \alpha \cdot e^{-R_1^b \cdot \text{ATT}} & \text{ATT} < t \leq \text{ATT} + \text{BD} \\ 0 & t > \text{ATT} + \text{BD} \end{cases} \tag{12.5}$$

For PASL, Eq. (12.4) along with Eq. (12.3), and the simplest assumption for the tissue response curve, yields the following equation:

$$\Delta M(t) = \frac{2M_0^b \alpha f}{\delta R} \cdot \begin{cases} 0 & 0 < t \leq \text{ATT} \\ e^{-R_1^b \cdot t}\left(1 - e^{\delta R \cdot (t - \text{ATT})}\right) & \text{ATT} < t \leq \text{ATT} + \text{BD} \\ e^{-R_1^b \cdot (\text{ATT} + \text{BD})}\left(1 - e^{\delta R \cdot \text{BD}}\right) \cdot e^{-(R_1^t + f/\lambda) \cdot (t - (\text{ATT} + \text{BD}))} & t > \text{ATT} + \text{BD} \end{cases} \tag{12.6}$$

$$\text{with } \delta R = R_1^b - (R_1^t + f/\lambda).$$

For CASL, the following equation results:

$$\Delta M(t) = \frac{2M_0^b \alpha f}{\delta R} \cdot \begin{cases} 0 & 0 < t \leq \text{ATT} \\ e^{-R_1^b \cdot \text{ATT}}\left(1 - e^{\delta R \cdot (t - \text{ATT})}\right) & \text{ATT} < t \leq \text{ATT} + \text{BD} \\ e^{-R_1^b \cdot \text{ATT}}\left(1 - e^{\delta R \cdot \text{BD}}\right) \cdot e^{-(R_1^t + f/\lambda) \cdot (t - (\text{ATT} + \text{BD}))} & t > \text{ATT} + \text{BD} \end{cases} \tag{12.7}$$

$$\text{with } \delta R = R_1^b - (R_1^t + f/\lambda).$$

For quantitative perfusion estimation, arterial transit time ATT, labeling efficiency α and M_0^b are crucial parameters, which should ideally be measured on an individual basis. Although the first parameter, ATT, is easily assessed by the acquisition of multi-TI and multi-PLD data, different approaches are feasible for the latter two. More details can be found in (Alsop et al., 2015). See Table 12.1.

Table 12.1 Summary of symbols and parameters used for biophysical modeling.

Symbol	Description	Unit	Comment
ATT	Arterial transit time	[s], [ms]	Time taken for the labeled blood to travel from the labeling site to the imaging site
BD	Bolus duration	[s], [ms]	Temporal duration of labeled blood bolus
$R_1^b = 1/T_1^b$	T_1 relaxation rate of blood	$[s^{-1}]$	Often taken from the literature, but can be important to be measured in some patients, feasible measurement options for clinical setups exist
$R_1^t = 1/T_1^t$	T_1 relaxation rate of tissue	$[s^{-1}]$	Often taken from the literature, but can be important to be measured in some patients, feasible measurement options for clinical setups exist
f	(microvascular) perfusion	SI: $[m^3/s/kg]$ [ml/min/100g]	
λ	Blood/brain partition coefficient	Dimensionless	Almost always taken from the literature, measurement is challenging in a clinical setting
M_0^b	Equilibrium magnetization of blood	In this context considered to be dimensionless	Essentially, this parameter is the equilibrium value of the magnetization of a voxel completely filled with blood, i.e., the maximum signal one expects in an ASL experiment. For normalized considerations, this parameter is 1
ΔM	Difference magnetization	In this context considered to be dimensionless	The difference of label and control measurement, sometimes called the "ASL signal", although it refers to magnetization
α	Labeling efficiency	Dimensionless, ranges from 0 to 1	This parameter accounts for the amount of magnetization, actually inverted (1=perfect inversion)

A tutorial describing perfusion measurement in clinical routine and highlighting some example with potential pitfalls is provided in Ferre et al. (2013).

12.2.10 Comments on ASL post-processing

The different ASL variants can make post-processing cumbersome, especially when working with data from different scanners, sites, and vendors. An effort to streamline this is the initiative of the ASL community to define an exchange file format, which takes care of all the different variants. This format is an extension of the brain imaging data structure (BIDS, https://bids.neuroimaging.io/) and is logically called ASL-BIDS. Although very new, the use of this format is recommended for future work.

An extensive approach to post-processing ASL data is ExploreASL (Mutsaerts et al., 2020). Features of this powerful tool (http://www.ExploreASL.org) include WM/GM segmentation, spatial normalization, motion correction, quantification, partial volume correction, and statistical analysis of the data. At this time, it only supports single-TI and single-PLD data, but an extension is planned to support multi-TI/PLD as well.

For the post-processing of multi-TI/PLD data, the BASIL toolbox (https://fsl.fmrib.ox.ac.uk/fsl/fslwiki/BASIL) of the FSL package can be used.

12.3 Other non-contrast perfusion methods

Although ASL is by far the most popular method for perfusion measurement without the use of contrast agents in general, there are other approaches for assessing perfusion. One method, published in 1986, well before the first ASL publication in 1992, was introduced along with diffusion MRI. For very weak diffusion-weightings, this method becomes sensitive to motion of blood water within small vessels. At a capillary level the vasculature resembles a network of small vessels in various random directions, with only piecewise bulk motion along a short capillary or arteriole vessel. Summing over a voxel, the motion appears random with specific characteristics (at different scales as the stochastic nature of diffusional motion). Thus it was observed that diffusion-weighted measurements will deviate from the pure diffusional exponential decay for weak diffusion weightings due to the apparent randomness of micro-vascular perfusion (which appear as a high pseudo-diffusivity component). Biophysical modeling allows for the separation of the true tissue diffusion signal from the microvascular perfusion signal. Quantifying perfusion remains challenging, though. This so-called intravoxel incoherent motion (IVIM) approach has seen a renaissance in recent years. The main field of application for perfusion assessment is in the field of oncology. Further details can be found in the excellent review of Le Bihan (2019).

Finally, it is worth noting that there are additional parameters that ASL can provide information on, including an ability to separately label major feeding vessels, thus allowing vascular territory maps to be visualized, and the ability for ASL to depict the vasculature itself. The latter is possible if high-resolution control and label images are taken while the blood is still in the major vessels (i.e., if the TI and PLD values are sufficiently short that the blood remains in the vessels, usually considered an unwanted artifact in tissue perfusion imaging). Yet another area of active research is in the use of ASL principles to report on alterations in blood-brain barrier function, by extracting permeability values from the ASL data.

References

Alsop, D.C., Detre, J.A., Golay, X., Gunther, M., Hendrikse, J., Hernandez-Garcia, L., Lu, H., Macintosh, B.J., Parkes, L.M., Smits, M., Van Osch, M.J., Wang, D.J., Wong, E.C., Zaharchuk, G., 2015. Recommended implementation of arterial spin-labeled perfusion MRI for clinical applications: a consensus of the ISMRM perfusion study group and the European consortium for ASL in dementia. Magn. Reson. Med. 73, 102–116.

Buxton, R.B., Frank, L.R., Wong, E.C., Siewert, B., Warach, S., Edelman, R.R., 1998. A general kinetic model for quantitative perfusion imaging with arterial spin labeling. Magn. Reson. Med. 40, 383–396.

Clement, P., Mutsaerts, H.J., Vaclavu, L., Ghariq, E., Pizzini, F.B., Smits, M., Acou, M., Jovicich, J., Vanninen, R., Kononen, M., Wiest, R., Rostrup, E., Bastos-Leite, A.J., Larsson, E.M., Achten, E., 2018. Variability of physiological brain perfusion in healthy subjects - a systematic review of modifiers. Considerations for multicenter ASL studies. J. Cereb. Blood Flow Metab. 38, 1418–1437.

Dai, W., Garcia, D., De Bazelaire, C., Alsop, D.C., 2008. Continuous flow-driven inversion for arterial spin labeling using pulsed radio frequency and gradient fields. Magn. Reson. Med. 60, 1488–1497.

Edelman, R.R., Chen, Q., 1998. EPISTAR MRI: multislice mapping of cerebral blood flow. Magn. Reson. Med. 40, 800–805.

Edelman, R.R., Siewert, B., Darby, D.G., Thangaraj, V., Nobre, A.C., Mesulam, M.M., Warach, S., 1994. Qualitative mapping of cerebral blood flow and functional localization with echo-planar MR imaging and signal targeting with alternating radio frequency. Radiology 192, 513–520.

Ferre, J.C., Bannier, E., Raoult, H., Mineur, G., Carsin-Nicol, B., Gauvrit, J.Y., 2013. Arterial spin labeling (ASL) perfusion: techniques and clinical use. Diagn. Interv. Imaging 94, 1211–1223.

Golay, X., Guenther, M., 2012. Arterial spin labelling: final steps to make it a clinical reality. MAGMA 25, 79–82.

Gunther, M., Bock, M., Schad, L.R., 2001. Arterial spin labeling in combination with a look-locker sampling strategy: inflow turbo-sampling EPI-FAIR (ITS-FAIR). Magn. Reson. Med. 46, 974–984.

Gunther, M., Oshio, K., Feinberg, D.A., 2005. Single-shot 3D imaging techniques improve arterial spin labeling perfusion measurements. Magn. Reson. Med. 54, 491–498.

Kim, S.G., Tsekos, N.V., 1997. Perfusion imaging by a flow-sensitive alternating inversion recovery (FAIR) technique: application to functional brain imaging. Magn. Reson. Med. 37, 425–435.

Le Bihan, D., 2019. What can we see with IVIM MRI? NeuroImage 187, 56–67.

Luh, W.M., Wong, E.C., Bandettini, P.A., Hyde, J.S., 1999. QUIPSS II with thin-slice TI1 periodic saturation: a method for improving accuracy of quantitative perfusion imaging using pulsed arterial spin labeling. Magn. Reson. Med. 41, 1246–1254.

Mutsaerts, H., Petr, J., Groot, P., Vandemaele, P., Ingala, S., Robertson, A.D., Vaclavu, L., Groote, I., Kuijf, H., Zelaya, F., O'Daly, O., Hilal, S., Wink, A.M., Kant, I., Caan, M.W.A., Morgan, C., De Bresser, J., Lysvik, E., Schrantee, A., Bjornebekk, A., Clement, P., Shirzadi, Z., Kuijer, J.P.A., Wottschel, V., Anazodo, U.C., Pajkrt, D., Richard, E., Bokkers, R.P.H., Reneman, L., Masellis, M., Gunther, M., Macintosh, B.J., Achten, E., Chappell, M.A., Van Osch, M.J.P., Golay, X., Thomas, D.L., De Vita, E., Bjornerud, A., Nederveen, A., Hendrikse, J., Asllani, I., Barkhof, F., 2020. ExploreASL: an image processing pipeline for multi-center ASL perfusion MRI studies. NeuroImage 219, 117031.

Talagala, S.L., Ye, F.Q., Ledden, P.J., Chesnick, S., 2004. Whole-brain 3D perfusion MRI at 3.0 T using CASL with a separate labeling coil. Magn. Reson. Med. 52, 131–140.

Tannus, A., Garwood, M., 1997. Adiabatic pulses. NMR Biomed. 10, 423–434.

Vidorreta, M., Wang, Z., Rodriguez, I., Pastor, M.A., Detre, J.A., Fernandez-Seara, M.A., 2013. Comparison of 2D and 3D single-shot ASL perfusion fMRI sequences. NeuroImage 66, 662–671.

Wong, E.C., Buxton, R.B., Frank, L.R., 1998. Quantitative imaging of perfusion using a single subtraction (QUIPSS and QUIPSS II). Magn. Reson. Med. 39, 702–708.

Wong, E.C., Cronin, M., Wu, W.C., Inglis, B., Frank, L.R., Liu, T.T., 2006. Velocity-selective arterial spin labeling. Magn. Reson. Med. 55, 1334–1341.

Wong, W.H.E., Maller, J.J., 2016. Arterial spin labeling techniques 2009–2014. J. Med. Imaging Radiat. Sci. 47, 98–107.

Ye, F.Q., Frank, J.A., Weinberger, D.R., Mclaughlin, A.C., 2000. Noise reduction in 3D perfusion imaging by attenuating the static signal in arterial spin tagging (ASSIST). Magn. Reson. Med. 44, 92–100.

CHAPTER

Contrast agent-based perfusion MRI methods

13

Laura C. Bell[a], Sudarshan Ragunathan[a], and Anahita Fathi Kazerooni[b]

[a]*Division of Neuroimaging Research, Barrow Neurological Institute, Phoenix, AZ, United States*
[b]*Department of Radiology, Perelman School of Medicine, University of Pennsylvania, Philadelphia, PA, United States*

13.1 Introduction

Contrast agent-based perfusion MR methods provide measurements of perfusion and vascular permeability, which are altered in various neurological diseases, such as cancer, and cerebrovascular and neurodegenerative diseases. The most common methods are dynamic susceptibility contrast (DSC) and dynamic contrast-enhanced (DCE) acquisitions, which depend on dynamically measuring T_2/T_2^*-weighted and T_1-weighted changes, respectively, due to intravenous injection of a contrast agent passing through the capillary system. First introduced in the 1990s, these techniques have been extensively researched and used in multi-site clinical trials, proving clinical relevance for diagnosis, progression, and treatment response; however, clinical adoption has been slow due to concerns about reproducibility. To address this, several initiatives have focused on standardization of imaging protocols and analysis methods, which are coming to fruition almost 30 years later, to ensure reproducibility (Boxerman et al., 2020; Kaufmann et al., 2020; Thrippleton et al., 2019).

Although consensus recommendations are now being published, they primarily focus on acquisition protocols. A 2018 survey was conducted by the Perfusion Study Group within the International Society for Magnetic Resonance in Medicine (ISMRM) assessing current interest in an open-source initiative for perfusion imaging (OSIPI). Though popular feedback revealed prevailing confusion regarding analysis, one particular comment resonated the most "...there needs to be a clear recipe for perfusion analysis, from theory to code, that produces measurements of perfusion in common physiological units". That is the driving motivator for this chapter. Section 13.2 discusses the biophysical properties that influence the MR signal in contrast agent-based MRI. Section 13.3 reviews the tracer kinetic theories for perfusion and vascular permeability, and their application to acquired MR data. To accompany this section, a "cookbook" recipe and a worked example with code are provided to demonstrate the connection of theory to analysis. Lastly, Sections 13.4 and 13.5 briefly cover imaging protocols and emerging areas of research.

13.2 Signal derivation in contrast-based perfusion MRI

When perfusion is measured by computed tomography (CT) and positron emission tomography (PET), the contrast agent concentration through the capillary system is measured directly and quantified (i.e.,

Hounsfield units in CT and Becquerels in PET). However, MR perfusion indirectly measures the contrast agent concentration by measuring the change in MR signal due to the contrast agent bolus. This change in MR signal is predominantly driven by the properties of the contrast agent (i.e., amount injected and its intrinsic magnetic properties) and its biodistribution within tissue compartments (e.g., water exchange across cellular membranes and water diffusion) and the biophysical properties within the tissue environment (e.g., cellular and vascular architecture). This section will cover these driving factors for MR signal generation and the relationship between MR signal change and contrast agent concentration. Lastly, concerns regarding contrast dosing will be covered briefly as well as how to potentially decrease this dose in perfusion acquisitions.

13.2.1 Biophysical properties of perfusion imaging

Paramagnetic gadolinium-based chelates are the most commonly used contrast agents for clinical MR perfusion. When injected intravenously, the passage of a gadolinium-based contrast agent (GBCA) shortens the tissue's transverse (T_2 and T_2^*) and longitudinal (T_1) relaxation times via both the through-space mesoscopic susceptibility effects induced by gadolinium's compartmentalization and the direct microscopic, dipole-dipole interaction of gadolinium with water, respectively (Quarles et al., 2019). Specific to brain perfusion, gadolinium's compartmentalization is typically restricted to the intravascular compartment when the blood-brain-barrier (BBB) is intact. In this scenario, the MR signal is dominated by the through-space mesoscopic magnetic field gradients that are perturbed as the GBCA intravascularly transverses the capillary bed, creating predominantly T_2/T_2^*-weighted changes in MR signal (see Fig. 13.1). When the BBB is disrupted, the GBCA will cross into the interstitial compartment and interact with water molecules creating microscopic gradient fields in the extravascular space. This interaction effectively decreases the tissue's T_1 properties leading to predominately T_1-weighted changes in the MR signal (Fig. 13.1).

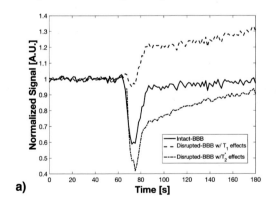 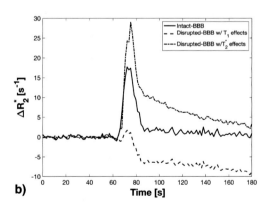

FIGURE 13.1

DSC-MR line profile examples of normalized signal time curves (Fig. 13.1a) and their corresponding $\Delta R_2^*(t)$ curves (Fig. 13.1b) for an intact-BBB (no leakage effects; solid line) and disrupted-BBB (leakage effects present) scenario. Predominately T_1 (dash-dash) and T_2^* (dash-dot) leakage effects are illustrated. The over- and underestimation of DSC-derived CBV ($\propto \int R_2^*(t)\,dt$) is easily observed when T_2^* and T_1 leakage effects are present.

13.2.2 MR signal derivation

Measured MR signal changes are quantified by the computation of relaxation rates (i.e., $R_i = 1/T_i$) assuming fast water exchange:

$$R_i(t) = r_i C(t) + R_{i0} \tag{13.1}$$

where R_i is the relaxation rate (s^{-1}) after gadolinium injection, r_i is the contrast agent relaxivity ($mM^{-1} s^{-1}$), $C(t)$ is the concentration of gadolinium (mM) at a given time, and R_{i0} is the native relaxation rate (s^{-1}). These relaxation rates are transverse (when $i = 2$ or 2^*) or longitudinal (when $i = 1$), depending on the biophysical properties of the contrast agent as it travels through the capillary system. Note that how these changes are measured with MRI depends on the imaging acquisition method chosen (as covered in Section 13.4).

In DCE-MRI, the longitudinal relaxivity (r_1) is typically known *a priori* from *in-vitro* studies and is unique for the GBCA used (Pintaske et al., 2006). However, in DSC-MRI, the transverse relaxivity is typically not known *a priori* and is dependent on more than just the gadolinium agent itself. Previous, *in-silico* simulations and preclinical studies have shown that the transverse relaxivity is highly dependent on vascular architecture, which varies both across the brain and for different neurological pathologies (Kim et al., 2019; Semmineh et al., 2014). Differences in the vascular architecture will directly impact the gadolinium concentration, which also varies dynamically between the intra- and extra-vascular space, creating differences in the susceptibility gradient. In practice for DSC-MRI, the precise value of the transverse relaxivity is usually ignored or assigned a value based on simulations (Willats and Calamante, 2013). In terms of absolute quantification, the known longitudinal relaxivity in DCE-MRI is what allows this method to provide absolute quantification, whereas relative quantification is typically used for DSC-MRI.

Despite the more complex quantification of DSC-MRI compared to DCE-MRI, DSC-MRI is still the most commonly used method in the clinic for brain perfusion (e.g., brain cancer, stroke) for two reasons. First, when the BBB is intact and slow water exchange across the endothelial wall is assumed, changes in the longitudinal relaxation will only depend on protons within the blood; which is only ~2% and ~5% by volume for white and gray matter, respectively. Second, for GBCAs used clinically, r_1 is about 1.5–2 times less than r_2 and an order of magnitude less than r_2^* (Kim et al., 2019; Pintaske et al., 2006). To reliably detect perfusion in healthy cerebral tissue with DCE, the longitudinal relaxivity would need to be much higher than current GBCAs. However, DCE is almost ubiquitously implemented outside of the brain, where the absence of a BBB heavily favors T_1 relaxation effects.

13.2.3 Current gadolinium concerns and dosing recommendations

Clinically available GBCAs are chelated (i.e., bonded by a ligand) as when left in its natural state as free ions gadolinium is highly toxic. Currently, there is only one known adverse effect of GBCA use in MRI. Nephrogenic system fibrosis (NFS) was first observed in patients with renal failure in 2006. However, since this observation, glomerular filtration rate guidelines have been used to determine the safety prior to administration and no new cases have been reported (Willats and Calamante, 2013). In 2013, concerns regarding GBCA safety rose again in response to a study that hypothesized that long-term gadolinium deposition was occurring in the brain, and many studies have followed (Guo et al., 2018). It is now clear that even with an intact BBB and normal renal function, gadolinium is retained in the brain with repeat doses; and that linear chelated GBCAs result in more gadolinium deposition for longer periods of time than macrocyclic GBCAs (Guo et al., 2018). However, at the present time the clinical significance and associated risks of gadolinium deposition are still unknown.

Due to the uncertainty regarding gadolinium deposition in the brain, there has been a push towards reducing the amount of GBCA during contrast-enhanced perfusion imaging, specifically for brain cancer. Prior to 2013, a typical dose of GBCA for perfusion imaging was in the range of 0.1 mmol/kg ("single dose") to 0.2 mmol/kg ("double dose") across neuropathologies (Willats and Calamante, 2013), where the "double dose" was primarily used for brain cancer applications. As of 2020, the brain tumor perfusion recommendation reduces the amount of gadolinium administered by half through optimization of pulse sequence parameters (Boxerman et al., 2020). This new consensus recommendation brings the total dose administered for brain cancer imaging to a single dose, which is the typical amount given for other neuropathologies, such as stroke.

13.3 Quantification of perfusion and permeability parameters

The pathophysiological properties of the tissue microvasculature are altered in different neuro diseases and during various stages of the disease, potentially allowing for perfusion parameters to serve as biomarkers for disease diagnosis, progression, and response to therapy. The classical quantitative perfusion parameters are cerebral blood flow (CBF), cerebral blood volume (CBV), and mean transit time (MTT). Perfusion, denoted by CBF, is the process of arterial blood flow (mL of blood per minute) passing through the capillary system of an organ (gram of tissue) generating units of mL/min/g. The microvascular blood volume, CBV, represents the total amount of CA within the tissue (mL of blood per gram of tissue, mL/g). Lastly, MTT (min) is a measure of the time that CA particles reside within the capillary bed.

Several neuropathologies are associated with compromised or dysfunctional BBB, such as malignant tumors, traumatic brain injury (TBI), and some neurodegenerative diseases, leading to permeability of the vessels. Quantitative permeability analysis yields the transfer constant, K^{trans} (min^{-1}), volume of the vascular plasma, v_p (dimensionless), and volume of the extravascular extracellular space (EES), v_e (dimensionless), which are representative of capillary permeability, angiogenesis, and cellularity, respectively (Tofts et al., 1999).

This section is dedicated to the discussion of the tracer kinetic and permeability theories alongside analysis steps required to apply these theories to MR data. These discussions are accompanied by a "cookbook" of post-processing steps that need to be considered for a perfusion or permeability study (see Fig. 13.2). Supplementary code is provided in a Jupyter notebook (see Section 13.6) to illustrate each step.

13.3.1 Quantitative perfusion parameters (CBF/CBV/MTT)

13.3.1.1 Theory

The primary quantitative cerebral perfusion hemodynamic parameters, i.e., CBF, CBV, and MTT, are based on the tracer kinetic theory of linear and stationary systems. Tracer kinetic theory assumes that the CA particles enter the vascular bed with negligible contrast extravasation out of the vascular (plasma) space, and can take different paths to transit through the system during the first pass (Østergaard et al., 1996). This model further assumes a conservation of mass principle, implying that the amount of CA

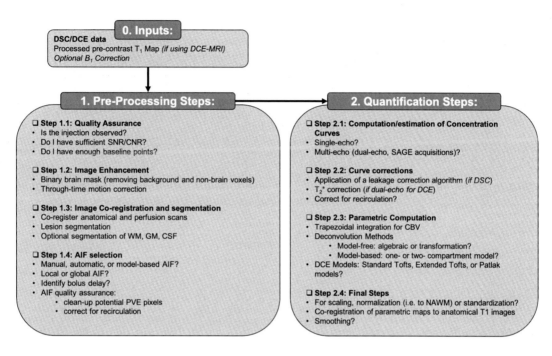

FIGURE 13.2

An overview of the general analysis summarized for perfusion quantification with steps categorized as 0) Inputs, 1) Pre-processing, and 2) Quantification. Suggested software for steps that involve segmentation (1.3) and registration (1.2, 1.3, 2.4) are the following: FMRIB Software Library (FSL) (https://fsl.fmrib.ox.ac.uk/fsl/fslwiki/), Statistical Parametric Mapping (SPM) (https://www.fil.ion.ucl.ac.uk/spm/), Cancer Imaging Phenomics Toolkit (CaPTk) (https://www.med.upenn.edu/cbica/captk/), and Advanced Normalization Tools (ANTs) (http://stnava.github.io/ANTs/). Recommended further reading for Step 1.1 (Willats and Calamante, 2013), Step 1.4 (Calamante, 2013), Steps 2.1 and 2.2 (Quarles et al., 2019), and Step 2.3 (Sourbron et al., 2007; Sourbron and Buckley, 2012). For more general DSC and DCE analysis, please see citations (QIBA MR Biomarker Committee, 2012, 2020).

volume at a constant rate of flow entering the system is preserved until it exits the system. Depending on the tracer's velocity and the undertaken paths, the mean transit time (MTT) will vary. The model's input is defined as the arterial input function (AIF) and is the CA concentration as a function of time measured from the main carotid artery that feeds into the vascular space within the capillaries (Calamante, 2013). As the AIF passes through the system, the tissue residue function $R(t)$ characterizes the properties of the tissue vasculature and is the basis of both CBF and CBV measures.

The tracer (indicator) dilution theory is commonly used to determine blood flow and volume based on total concentration of CA within the brain tissue. Total CA concentration within the cerebral tissue is defined by the amount of flow into the tissue and the duration that it stays within that voxel:

$$C_t(t) = \frac{\rho}{H_f} \cdot \text{CBF}[C_{\text{AIF}}(t) \otimes R(t)], \tag{13.2}$$

200 Chapter 13 Contrast agent-based perfusion MRI methods

where $\otimes$ denotes the convolution between $C_{AIF}(t)$ and the residue function, $R(t)$. The residue function, $R(t)$, represents the fraction of CA residing in the tissue at time t after the CA injection and is scaled by CBF. This convolution is scaled by the density of the brain tissue ρ (g/mL), and the hematocrit factor $H_f = \frac{1-H_{LV}}{1-H_{SV}}$, accounting for the differences of hematocrit levels between large vessels (H_{LV}) and small vessels or capillaries (H_{SV}). Regional CBV is calculated by integrating the concentration of CA within the cerebral tissue over time normalized to the time-integrated tracer concentration within the AIF:

$$\text{CBV} = \frac{H_f}{\rho} \frac{\int_0^\infty C_t(t)dt}{\int_0^\infty C_{AIF}(t)dt}. \tag{13.3}$$

Finally, based on the central volume theorem for a non-diffusible indicator that remains within the intravascular space (a valid assumption when there is an intact BBB), the MTT is determined by

$$\text{MTT} = \frac{\text{CBV}}{\text{CBF}}. \tag{13.4}$$

13.3.1.2 Analysis

To apply perfusion theory to MR data, the analysis using either DSC- or DCE-MRI generally consists of the following steps: (a) inspection of image enhancement (Fig. 13.2, Step 1.2); (b) conversion of signal intensity-time curves (SITC) to concentration-time curves (CTC) (Fig. 13.2, Step 2.1); (c) AIF selection (Fig. 13.2, Step 1.4); (d) deconvolution using transformation or algebraic methods (Fig. 13.2, Step 2.3). Apart from the AIF selection (which is covered in Section 13.3.3 since it pertains to both perfusion and permeability computation); these steps are described below.

The conversion of SITC to CTC will depend on the type of acquisition chosen. For a DSC-MRI acquisition, the CTC for the commonly used single-echo acquisition can be estimated by the following equation (Fig. 13.2, Step 2.1):

$$C(t) \propto k\Delta R_2^* = -\frac{k}{\text{TE}} \ln(\frac{S(t)}{S_0}), \tag{13.5}$$

where $C(t)$ is the concentration time function, ΔR_2^* is the change in T_2^* relaxation rate, $S(t)$ is the intensity time signal, S_0 is the mean baseline signal before the arrival of CA, k is a proportionality constant (in practice assumed to be unity), and TE is the echo time. For dual or multi-echo sequences, the T_1 effects can be removed (see Fig. 13.2, Step 2.1). For a DCE-MRI acquisition, the CTC for the commonly used spoiled gradient recalled echo (SPGR) acquisition can be estimated by the following equation (Fig. 13.2, Step 2.1):

$$C(t) = \frac{\Delta R_1}{r_1} = \frac{1}{\text{TR}.r_1} \ln\left(\frac{1 - \cos(\alpha).E.\frac{S(t)}{S_0}}{1 - E.\frac{S(t)}{S_0}}\right) - \frac{1}{T_{1,0}.r_1}, \tag{13.6}$$

$$\text{where } E = \frac{1 - e^{-\text{TR}/T_{1,0}}}{1 - \cos(\alpha).e^{-\text{TR}/T_{1,0}}},$$

where TR is the repetition time of the sequence, r_1 is the longitudinal relaxivity of the CA, $T_{1,0}$ is the T_1 of the tissue in the absence of CA, α is the flip angle used, $S(t)$ is the intensity-time signal, and S_0 is the intensity of the signal prior to the arrival of the CA.

13.3 Quantification of perfusion and permeability parameters

Once the C_{AIF} (see Section 13.3.3 for more details) and C_t curves are estimated, the perfusion parameters can be quantified. CBV is computed by Eq. (13.3) by approximating the discretized CTC by a trapezoidal integration. In practice, H_f and ρ are assumed to be 0.733 and 1 (g/mL), respectively (Willats and Calamante, 2013). In a DSC-MRI scan, CBV is usually normalized to normal-appearing-white-matter (NAWM) instead of the AIF (due to the challenges of AIF determination as covered in Section 13.3.3). In a DCE-MRI scan, CBV will be normalized to the AIF since whole-brain analysis is difficult in intact BBB regions. Computation of CBF in either DSC- or DCE-MR is a bit more complex because of the required deconvolution to determine the $R(t)$ (Eq. (13.2)) for estimation of CBF. Proposed deconvolution methods must take into account that the deconvolution is inherently a differentiation method: an inverse problem that is mathematically ill-posed and sensitive to noise, especially with the low contrast-to-noise (CNR) of perfusion scans. Deconvolution in tracer kinetic studies can be carried out by model-based (parametric) deconvolution or model-free (non-parametric) approaches (see Fig. 13.2, Step 2.3).

In model-based deconvolution methods, a parametric model is assumed for $R(t)$ such that several parameters form the residue function (Sourbron and Buckley, 2012). By assuming an analytic form with few degrees of freedom for $R(t)$, a stable fitting of Eq. (13.2) with reasonable parameter values may be achieved. These techniques are desirable in practical application, as dynamic MRI scans usually have a low contrast-to-noise ratio (CNR) and insufficient temporal resolution; the latter complicates the accurate sampling of the actual AIF. The most common model-based deconvolution methods are the one-compartment or two-compartment pharmacokinetic models. One-compartment models only consider the intravascular or plasma space, with the assumption that the EES and intravascular spaces are combined into a single distribution volume. A two-compartment model will separate the EES into its own compartment.

Model-free approaches adopt a non-parametric deconvolution operator, either algebraic or transform-based, without any presumptions about the functional form of $R(t)$ (which may introduce errors in CBF and MTT measurements) and provide tissue-specific insights about the characteristics of the underlying architecture of the tissue vasculature. Model-free approaches are performed using either transformation, e.g., Fourier transformation, or algebraic, e.g., singular value decomposition (SVD) deconvolution methods (Sourbron et al., 2007). To achieve a robust and stable solution using model-free techniques for perfusion quantification, two important post-processing steps need to be adopted: AIF discretization and regularization. The first step in deconvolution is discretization of the continuous data, i.e., assuming that the arterial and tissue concentration-time curves are measured at discrete and equally spaced time intervals. The choice of the AIF discretization method influences the deduced residue function (Sourbron et al., 2007). Furthermore, to account for noise sensitivity and to diminish spurious high-frequency components in the resulting residue function, a regularization term, as a function of $R(t)$, should be considered with the discrete equations (for further reading see: (Sourbron et al., 2007)). With a proper choice of regularization term, the solution for $R(t)$ can be constrained to a mathematically and physiologically meaningful "well-behaved" function (Østergaard et al., 1996). The most common nonparametric deconvolution method in perfusion quantification for clinical applications is block-circulant SVD (due to its robustness when a bolus delay is present) with standard-form Tikhonov-regularization. This technique has been shown to be accurate even for echo-planar perfusion scans with lower SNR (Quarles et al., 2019).

13.3.2 Quantitative permeability parameters ($K^{trans}/v_e/v_p$)

13.3.2.1 Theory

Classical quantification of DCE-MRI is carried out using a pharmacokinetic 2-compartment model, commonly referred to as the Tofts model (Tofts et al., 1999). Assuming a well-mixed two-compartment capillary-tissue model, the low-weight particles of CA that enter the vascular space by a constant blood plasma flow, F_p, pass out of the intravascular plasma space and diffuse into the EES with a rate determined by the permeability-surface area product, PS. Therefore the total tissue concentration is a summation of the concentration of particles inside the plasma and the EES:

$$C_t(t) = v_p C_p(t) + v_e C_e(t) \tag{13.7}$$
$$= v_p C_p(t) + K^{trans} C_p(t) \otimes e^{-k_{ep}t},$$

where K^{trans} is a physiological quantity, also referred to as the volume transfer constant depending on flow- ($K^{trans} = F_p$) or permeability-limited ($K^{trans} = PS$) transport regimes. The rate constant for the outflow or efflux of the EES is summarized as $k_{ep} = \frac{K^{trans}}{v_e}$.

To simplify the quantification, it may be assumed that $C_p(t) = C_{AIF}(t)/(1 - H_{LV})$ to obtain:

$$C_t(t) = v_p \frac{C_{AIF}(t)}{(1 - H_{LV})} + K^{trans} \frac{C_{AIF}(t)}{(1 - H_{LV})} \otimes e^{-k_{ep}t} \tag{13.8}$$

This model may be interpreted as a two-compartment model with three parameters, v_p, v_e, K^{trans} (for further reading see: (Sourbron and Buckley, 2012)).

13.3.2.2 Analysis

To apply the pharmacokinetic theory to DCE data, a model-based deconvolution is generally assumed for Eq. (13.7) and is carried out through the following steps: (a) estimating baseline T_1 values based on T_1-mapping or assuming a predefined constant T_1 value; (b) conversion of SITC to CTC (Fig. 13.2, Step 2.1); (c) selection of an AIF (Fig. 13.2, Step 1.4); (d) approximating the pharmacokinetic model (Fig. 13.2, Step 2.3) with a least-squares fitting approach.

Analysis for (a) and (d) are considered out of scope for this chapter, with further reading provided within Fig. 13.2; (b) and (c) are the same steps as outlined above in Section 13.3.1.2.

13.3.3 Special considerations

The models described above rely on assumptions that do not necessarily hold when data are acquired with MRI; in particular, the assumptions that the tracer remains intravascular and that the AIF is the feeding artery to the voxel. For these reasons, DCE and DSC perfusion analysis should incorporate two special considerations.

The AIF represents the concentration of CA in the arterial supply to the brain as a function of time, and accurate measurement of an AIF is essential for robust quantification of both perfusion and permeability parameters. Theoretically, the AIF should be measured from the small vessels that supply the voxel, and are therefore located in its proximity, defined as a *local* AIF. However, with the coarse spatial resolution of the dynamic scans, selected local AIFs may be severely affected by partial volume effects (PVEs), leading to errors in quantification. Alternatively, a *global* AIF selected from a major artery can minimize the problems caused by PVE. But it introduces additional errors due to bolus delay (the temporal difference between the arterial and tissue arrival) and dispersion (widening of the bolus). To this end, multiple solutions may be adopted (more details can be found in (Calamante, 2013)). Bolus dispersion refers to a distorted and spread shape of the bolus due to its transit through a vascular system. It can be considered as a convolution of the bolus with the residue function of the arterial system, which is unknown. Bolus dispersion imposes errors in quantification of DSC-MRI data and leads to an underestimation of CBF and an overestimation of MTT. There is no perfect solution for correcting the dispersion (see (Calamante, 2013)), but it may be avoided by considering a local AIF. When reliable measurement of an AIF is difficult to obtain due to acquisition constraints, such as limited spatial or temporal resolution, or a lack of a suitable artery inside the acquisition coverage, a model-based AIF can be approximated by fitting the plasma CA from a major vessel to a function (Fig. 13.2, Step 1.4). This is particularly beneficial in quantification of DCE-MRI scans with low temporal resolution.

A fundamental assumption in indicator-dilution theory in DSC-MRI is intravascular compartmentalization of the CA. However, in many neuropathologies CA extravasation occurs due to the breakdown of the BBB and is known to alter the measured perfusion time curves (Fig. 13.2). This means that the post-contrast SI time points may either increase (due to T_1 effects) or decrease (due to T_2^* effects) relative to the pre-contrast time points. If left uncorrected, CBV measures will either be over- or underestimated, depending on the type of leakage effect. To mitigate these effects, two points must be considered: fine tuning of the image acquisition to decrease T_1 sensitivity (Section 13.4) and an application of a post-processing leakage correction method (Fig. 13.2, Step 2.2). A widely accepted and recommended leakage correction method is the Boxerman–Schmainda–Weiskoff (BSW) method (Boxerman et al., 2006, 2020). More advanced leakage correction methods exist, but their accuracy and benefits require further validation at this time (Quarles et al., 2019).

13.4 Acquisition strategies

To achieve robust perfusion biomarkers of interest, the choice of acquisition method and its subsequent optimization will depend on the perfusion theory and the known biophysical properties associated with the underlying tissue microenvironment. Regardless of the target neuropathology and/or desired biomarkers, all ideal acquisition strategies necessitate full brain coverage to properly assess disease heterogeneity, and a fast sampling rate to accurately capture the first pass of GBCA. Conventionally, contrast-enhanced acquisitions are split into either DSC or DCE strategies, depending on the desired relaxation changes, T_2/T_2^* or T_1, respectively, to be measured. However, it is well known that these relaxation changes can simultaneously compete with each other and introduce biases into the perfusion measurements (Boxerman et al., 2006; Kleppestø et al., 2014).

For the most part, conventional DSC and DCE acquisition strategies have remained unchanged in the last decade and are designed to minimize these competing effects. However, in recent years, there has been a push towards standardization of both these methods to ensure reproducibility. These acquisition strategies will be briefly reviewed below with a primary focus on the current clinical recommendations for each. Outside of the current clinical recommendations, there has been increased attention to the development of more advanced acquisition methods focused on enabling multi-echo acquisitions and incorporating improved acceleration methods. Though currently limited in their use, these methods will be discussed next.

204 **Chapter 13** Contrast agent-based perfusion MRI methods

13.4.1 DSC acquisitions

DSC-MRI is typically acquired with a T_2/T_2^*-weighted acquisition dictated by long TR and TE choices. The selection of a spin-echo (SE) or gradient-recalled-echo (GRE) sequence will drive the image contrast to be T_2- or T_2^*-weighted, respectively, and the echo time (TE) is commonly chosen to be similar to the pre-contrast T_2/T_2^* values (Bell et al., 2017). The difference in image contrast between these two may be subtle, but there are distinct differences in their measurement and image quality. When the GBCA arrives into the imaging region, an MR signal loss will be observed due to proton dephasing caused by both diffusional motion through microscopic field gradients and the local tissue static field inhomogeneities. With a SE acquisition, the dephasing due to the static field inhomogeneities will be refocused, leaving the derived image contrast to depend on the diffusional motion of water within and around the cerebral microvasculature. On the other hand, a GRE acquisition will not refocus either dephasing contributions, and therefore is more sensitive to all blood vessel sizes, including larger arteries typically used for AIF selections (Calamante, 2013). Consequently, the GRE acquisition will have greater contrast-to-noise ratio (CNR) compared to a SE acquisition, because of the marked increase in signal drop at the time of GBCA arrival, favoring GRE acquisitions to be chosen over a SE acquisition. These differences indicate that perfusion parameters, such as CBV/CBF/MTT, will reflect arterial hemodynamics if acquired with a GRE or tissue hemodynamics if acquired with a SE.

In 2020, consensus recommendations for DSC-MRI were released (Boxerman et al., 2020; QIBA MR Biomarker Committee, 2020). All recommend a 2D GRE-based single-shot echo-planar imaging (EPI) acquisition. The temporal resolution will be dictated by TR of 1000–1500 ms and TE of 25–35 ms with a standard dose of GBCA for the injection dose. Historically, a higher flip angle of 60–70 degrees was used. With this high flip angle, significant T_1 effects were inevitable, with a disrupted BBB necessitating a standard dose of GBCA before the start of the acquisition (referred to as the preload). This protocol is considered the reference for DSC-MRI and many studies used these for validation purposes. If a double dose is not tolerated by the patient or desired by the institution, a low flip angle of 30 degrees can be utilized in the absence of a preload without sacrificing accuracy (Semmineh et al., 2018).

13.4.2 DCE acquisitions

DCE-MRI is typically acquired with a T_1-weighted acquisition dictated by short TR and TE times, and fine tuning of parameters that depend on the clinical application (Thrippleton et al., 2019; QIBA MR Biomarker Committee, 2012). For absolute DCE quantification, the clinical protocol consensus comprises two separate 3D fast SPGR acquisitions: the pre-contrast T_1 measurement acquired with a variable flip angle followed by the DCE acquisition (Fig. 13.2, input). Current recommendations aim for a TR of 3–5 ms and a TE of 1.5–2.0 ms with a relatively high flip angle of 25–35 degrees to minimize signal saturation effects (QIBA MR Biomarker Committee, 2012).

Unlike the relatively fast temporal resolution and ~3 min scan length in a DSC-MRI scan, the temporal resolution in DCE-MRI is a bit more forgiving, especially when AIF determination is not necessary (see Section 13.3.3). If permeability measurement is desired, the total scan length will be around 5 min, a reasonable clinical scan duration for brain cancer, but some neuropathologies, such as aging and multiple sclerosis, may require longer scan times (~15 minutes) due to their slower extravasation processes when compared to brain cancer (Thrippleton et al., 2019). The temporal resolution of a DCE-MRI scan should be less than the average transit time through the capillary and will depend on the neuropathology of interest.

When a patient-specific AIF is required, careful consideration must be made to ensure a major artery lies along the in-plane position of the imaging slab to minimize inflow effects. Additionally, temporal resolution should be sufficient to accurately capture the AIF. At the moment, it is advised that parallel imaging not be used as it has shown to be different across vendors, therefore potentially reducing the reproducibility of K^{trans} (QIBA MR Biomarker Committee, 2012). Instead, partial Fourier techniques are recommended to meet temporal resolution requirements.

13.4.3 Advanced acquisition methods

Parameters derived from T_2/T_2^* DSC and T_1 DCE MRI, in addition to being complementary, also provide unique hemodynamic measures. For this reason, there has been increased interest in multi-parametric mapping and radiogenomics. Multi-echo acquisitions allow for simultaneous acquisition of DSC/DCE parameters in a single scan, and may enable more robust leakage correction methods (Paulson et al., 2016) or mitigate EPI-related artifacts by using non-Cartesian trajectories (Fig. 13.3) (Ooi et al., 2020). Hybrid multi-echo gradient- and spin-echo acquisitions of T_2/T_2^* provide sensitivity to both micro- and macro-vasculature to allow for estimation of relative vessel size (Schmiedeskamp et al., 2012).

An important challenge that multi-echo acquisitions for simultaneous perfusion and permeability quantification face is to achieve comparable spatial and temporal resolution to prevailing clinical single echo acquisitions, while maintaining whole brain coverage. Modern acceleration techniques (e.g., parallel imaging, simultaneous multi-slice, compressed sensing, non-Cartesian trajectories, and deep learning reconstruction) can all potentially be applied.

13.5 Emerging methods

With the increasing popularity of artificial intelligence (AI) in radiology, machine learning (ML) methods have recently emerged as novel solutions for model-free quantification of dynamic MRI. These techniques use the parametric maps that are generated by a standard deconvolution method as a reference or ground truth data. Regression analysis is carried out to approximate the reference parametric maps from tissue CTCs and build a predictive model that may substitute the standard deconvolution method for any given tissue CTCs (Mckinley et al., 2018; Meier et al., 2019) (Fig. 13.4). As these techniques utilize the parametric maps generated by standard deconvolution techniques as the ground truth, they perform only as well as their training data, which could be an erroneous approximation of the true physiological parametric values. Alternatively, an end-to-end learning approach can be employed based on native information from raw dynamic MRI curves to realize specific patterns of CTCs (Choi et al., 2019).

Common quantification methods for DSC- or DCE-MRI attempt to resolve the underlying properties of the tissue based on temporal changes and do not account for spatial interrelationship of the voxels. Once the pixel-wise parametric maps are obtained, the mean or maximum values within an ROI are calculated and fed into statistical analysis or ML algorithms. Nonetheless, several diseases exhibit significant heterogeneity, which may be overlooked by summary statistics. Over the recent decade, a

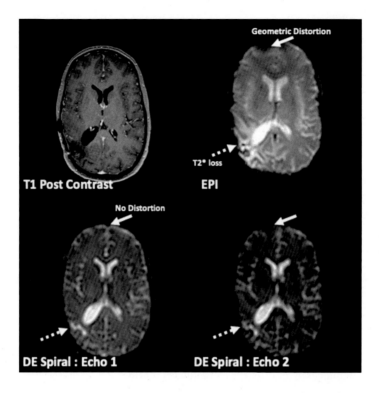

FIGURE 13.3

Benefits of improved image quality in a 3D dual-echo spiral acquisition (TE = 1.4 and 20 ms) compared to a conventional 2D EPI acquisition (TE = 30 ms) are observed in a glioblastoma patient with a surgical implant (see T_2 FLAIR box). The spiral trajectory's shorter echo times minimize susceptibility-related signal loss near the shunt (dotted arrows), while also minimizing geometric distortions (solid arrows) that arise from field inhomogeneities related to the EPI trajectory. Additional advantages of a dual-echo spiral acquisition are the possibility for simultaneous DSC/DCE analysis and removal of T_1 leakage effects due to a disrupted BBB.

growing body of research has focused on high-throughput analysis, called "radiomics", to assess the underlying heterogeneity of cancers. In radiomics, a large set of features, including texture, shape, volume, and edge measures, which quantify the tumorous region in an objective and reproducible manner, are extracted and then combined using ML methods to predict patient outcome (survival, treatment response, etc.) or to reveal the tumor or tumor habitat genomics (Fathi Kazerooni et al., 2020; Sala et al., 2017). In this context, DSC/DCE-MRI scans incorporated with other imaging contrasts in a radiomic study, provide unique information about tumor ecology, neo-angiogenesis and blood flow, adaptation to the environmental forces, and therefore response or resistance to standard therapies. Radiomic approaches in DSC/DCE-MRI studies increase objectivity (removing reliance on subjective segmentations) and account for tissue heterogeneity in estimations, both of which contribute to generating reproducible results. Nonetheless, the impact of radiomics in multi-center studies remains to be proven (Fathi Kazerooni et al., 2020).

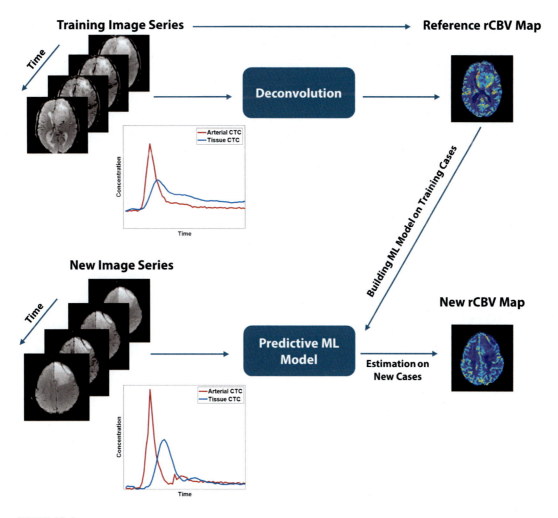

FIGURE 13.4

An illustration of an ML method for substituting standard deconvolution in a DSC-MRI quantification problem: The arterial and tissue CTCs from the training image series are used as the input, with reference parametric maps (CBV map in this example) that have been generated by a standard deconvolution method as the output. The ML method (a regressor) learns the associations between the input and output data to build a predictive ML model. This predictive model can then be used for new scans, which are unseen by the ML model, to approximate a corresponding parametric map, and therefore to replace the standard deconvolution method for prospective cases.

Appendix 13.6 Supplementary material

Supplementary material related to this chapter can be found online at https://www.elsevier.com/books-and-journals/book-companion/9780128224793.

References

Bell, L.C., Does, M.D., Stokes, A.M., Baxter, L.C., Schmainda, K.M., Dueck, A.C., Quarles, C.C., 2017. Optimization of DSC MRI echo times for CBV measurements using error analysis in a pilot study of high-grade gliomas. American Journal of Neuroradiology 38, 1710–1715. https://doi.org/10.3174/ajnr.A5295.

Boxerman, J.L., Quarles, C.C., Hu, L.S., Erickson, B.J., Gerstner, E.R., Smits, M., Kaufmann, T.J., Barboriak, D.P., Huang, R.H., Wick, W., Weller, M., Galanis, E., Kalpathy-Cramer, J., Shankar, L., Jacobs, P., Chung, C., van den Bent, M.J., Chang, S., Al Yung, W.K., Cloughesy, T.F., Wen, P.Y., Gilbert, M.R., Rosen, B.R., Ellingson, B.M., Schmainda, K.M., 2020. Consensus recommendations for a dynamic susceptibility contrast MRI protocol for use in high-grade gliomas. Neuro-Oncology. https://doi.org/10.1093/neuonc/noaa141.

Boxerman, J.L., Schmainda, K.M., Weisskoff, R.M., 2006. Relative cerebral blood volume maps corrected for contrast agent extravasation significantly correlate with glioma tumor grade, whereas uncorrected maps do not. American Journal of Neuroradiology 27, 859–867.

Calamante, F., 2013. Arterial input function in perfusion MRI: a comprehensive review. Progress in Nuclear Magnetic Resonance Spectroscopy. https://doi.org/10.1016/j.pnmrs.2013.04.002.

Choi, K.S., Choi, S.H., Jeong, B., 2019. Prediction of IDH genotype in gliomas with dynamic susceptibility contrast perfusion MR imaging using an explainable recurrent neural network. Neuro-Oncology 21, 1197–1209. https://doi.org/10.1093/neuonc/noz095.

Fathi Kazerooni, A., Bakas, S., Saligheh Rad, H., Davatzikos, C., 2020. Imaging signatures of glioblastoma molecular characteristics: a radiogenomics review. Journal of Magnetic Resonance Imaging 52, 54–69. https://doi.org/10.1002/jmri.26907.

Guo, B.J., Yang, Z.L., Zhang, L.J., 2018. Gadolinium deposition in brain: current scientific evidence and future perspectives. Frontiers in Molecular Neuroscience 11, 335. https://doi.org/10.3389/fnmol.2018.00335.

Kaufmann, T.J., Smits, M., Boxerman, J., Huang, R., Barboriak, D.P., Weller, M., Chung, C., Tsien, C., Brown, P.D., Shankar, L., Galanis, E., Gerstner, E., Van Den Bent, M.J., Burns, T.C., Parney, I.F., Dunn, G., Brastianos, P.K., Lin, N.U., Wen, P.Y., Ellingson, B.M., 2020. Consensus recommendations for a standardized brain tumor imaging protocol for clinical trials in brain metastases. Neuro-Oncology 22, 757–772. https://doi.org/10.1093/neuonc/noaa030.

Kim, J., Moestue, S.A., Bathen, T.F., Kim, E., 2019. R2* relaxation affects pharmacokinetic analysis of dynamic contrast-enhanced MRI in cancer and underestimates treatment response at 7 T. Tomography 5, 308–319. https://doi.org/10.18383/j.tom.2019.00015.

Kleppestø, M., Larsson, C., Groote, I., Salo, R., Vardal, J., Courivaud, F., Bjørnerud, A., 2014. T_2*-correction in dynamic contrast-enhanced MRI from double-echo acquisitions. Journal of Magnetic Resonance Imaging 39, 1314–1319. https://doi.org/10.1002/jmri.24268.

Mckinley, R., Hung, F., Wiest, R., Liebeskind, D.S., Scalzo, F., Mckinley, R., 2018. A machine learning approach to perfusion imaging with dynamic susceptibility contrast MR 9. https://doi.org/10.3389/fneur.2018.00717.

Meier, R., Lux, P., Jung, B.M.S., Fischer, U., Gralla, J., 2019. Neural Network – derived Perfusion Maps for the Assessment of Lesions in Patients with Acute Ischemic Stroke.

Ooi, M.B., Li, Z., Robison, R.K., Wang, D., Anderson, A.G., Zwart, N.R., Bakhru, A., Nagaraj, S., Mathews, T., Hey, S., Koonen, J.J., Dimitrov, I.E., Friel, H.T., Lu, Q., Obara, M., Saha, I., Wang, H., Wang, Y., Zhao, Y., Temkit, M., Hu, H.H., Chenevert, T.L., Togao, O., Tkach, J.A., Nagaraj, U.D., Pinho, M.C., Gupta, R.K., Small, J.E., Kunst, M.M., Karis, J.P., Andre, J.B., Miller, J.H., Pinter, N.K., Pipe, J.G., 2020. Spiral T1 spin-echo for routine postcontrast brain MRI exams: a multicenter multireader clinical evaluation. American Journal of Neuroradiology 41, 238–245. https://doi.org/10.3174/ajnr.A6409.

Østergaard, L., Weisskoff, R.M., Chesler, D.A., Gyldensted, C., Rosen, B.R., 1996. High resolution measurement of cerebral blood flow using intravascular tracer bolus passages. Part I: mathematical approach and statistical analysis. Magnetic Resonance in Medicine 36, 715–725. https://doi.org/10.1002/mrm.1910360510.

Paulson, E.S., Prah, D.E., Schmainda, K.M., 2016. Spiral perfusion imaging with consecutive echoes (SPICE) for the simultaneous mapping of DSC- and DCE-MRI parameters in brain tumor patients: theory and initial feasibility. Tomography 2, 295–307. https://doi.org/10.18383/j.tom.2016.00217.

Pintaske, J., Martirosian, P., Graf, H., Erb, G., Lodemann, K.-P., Claussen, C.D., Schick, F., 2006. Relaxivity of Gadopentetate Dimeglumine (Magnevist), Gadobutrol (Gadovist), and Gadobenate Dimeglumine (MultiHance) in human blood plasma at 0.2, 1.5, and 3 Tesla. Investigative Radiology 41, 213–221. https://doi.org/10.1097/01.rli.0000197668.44926.f7.

Quarles, C.C., Bell, L.C., Stokes, A.M., 2019. Imaging vascular and hemodynamic features of the brain using dynamic susceptibility contrast and dynamic contrast enhanced MRI. NeuroImage 187, 32–55. https://doi.org/10.1016/J.NEUROIMAGE.2018.04.069.

Sala, E., Mema, E., Himoto, Y., Veeraraghavan, H., Brenton, J.D., 2017. Unravelling tumour heterogeneity using next-generation imaging: radiomics, radiogenomics, and habitat imaging. Clinical Radiology 72, 3–10. https://doi.org/10.1016/j.crad.2016.09.013.

Schmiedeskamp, H., Straka, M., Newbould, R.D., Zaharchuk, G., Andre, J.B., Olivot, J.M., Moseley, M.E., Albers, G.W., Bammer, R., 2012. Combined spin- and gradient-echo perfusion-weighted imaging. Magnetic Resonance in Medicine 68, 30–40. https://doi.org/10.1002/mrm.23195.

Semmineh, N.B., Bell, L.C., Stokes, A.M., Hu, L.S., Boxerman, J.L., Quarles, C.C., 2018. Optimization of acquisition and analysis methods for clinical dynamic susceptibility contrast MRI using a population-based digital reference object. American Journal of Neuroradiology 39. https://doi.org/10.3174/ajnr.A5827.

Semmineh, N.B., Xu, J., Boxerman, J.L., Delaney, G.W., Cleary, P.W., Gore, J.C., Quarles, C.C., 2014. An efficient computational approach to characterize DSC-MRI signals arising from three-dimensional heterogeneous tissue structures. PLoS ONE. https://doi.org/10.1371/journal.pone.0084764.

Sourbron, S., Luypaert, R., Morhard, D., Seelos, K., Reiser, M., Peller, M., 2007. Deconvolution of bolus-tracking data: a comparison of discretization methods. Physics in Medicine and Biology 52, 6761–6778. https://doi.org/10.1088/0031-9155/52/22/014.

Sourbron, S.P., Buckley, D.L., 2012. Tracer kinetic modelling in MRI: estimating perfusion and capillary permeability. Physics in Medicine and Biology. https://doi.org/10.1088/0031-9155/57/2/R1.

Thrippleton, M.J., Backes, W.H., Sourbron, S., Ingrisch, M., van Osch, M.J.P., Dichgans, M., Fazekas, F., Ropele, S., Frayne, R., van Oostenbrugge, R.J., Smith, E.E., Wardlaw, J.M., 2019. Quantifying blood-brain barrier leakage in small vessel disease: review and consensus recommendations. Alzheimer's & Dementia. https://doi.org/10.1016/j.jalz.2019.01.013.

Tofts, P.S., Brix, G., Buckley, D.L., Evelhoch, J.L., Henderson, E., Knopp, M.V., Larsson, H.B., Lee, T.Y., Mayr, N.A., Parker, G.J., Port, R.E., Taylor, J., Weisskoff, R.M., 1999. Estimating kinetic parameters from dynamic contrast-enhanced T(1)-weighted MRI of a diffusable tracer: standardized quantities and symbols. Journal of Magnetic Resonance Imaging 10, 223–232. https://doi.org/10.1002/(SICI)1522-2586(199909)10:3<223::AID-JMRI2>3.0.CO;2-S.

Willats, L., Calamante, F., 2013. The 39 steps: evading error and deciphering the secrets for accurate dynamic susceptibility contrast MRI. NMR in Biomedicine 26, 913–931. https://doi.org/10.1002/nbm.2833.

QIBA MR Biomarker Committee, 2012. MR DCE quantification, quantitative imaging biomarkers alliance. Profile stage: consensus profile. August 8. Available from: http://qibawiki.rsna.org/index.php/Profiles.

QIBA MR Biomarker Committee, 2020. MR DSC quantification, quantitative imaging biomarkers alliance. Profile stage: consensus profile. Available from: http://qibawiki.rsna.org/index.php/Profiles.

CHAPTER

Perfusion MRI: clinical perspectives

14

Kevin Yuqi Wang, Eric K. van Staalduinen, and Greg Zaharchuk
Department of Radiology, Stanford University, Stanford, CA, United States

14.1 Introduction

Perfusion abnormalities are a hallmark of many neurological diseases. Given the remarkable progress in MR methods to assess blood flow and permeability changes, perfusion imaging has begun to play an important role in diagnosis. The most common use is, not unexpectedly, in acute stroke, where perfusion is the primary abnormality. However, changes in perfusion accompany many other abnormalities, particularly brain neoplasms, where increased blood flow and permeability are associated with the presence of viable tumor, allowing radiologists to distinguish this from other non-neoplastic changes related to treatment. Arterial spin labeling (ASL), a non-contrast perfusion technique described more fully in Chapter 12, is valuable for quantitation, which can be used to measure cerebrovascular reserve. More surprisingly, its ability to identify arteriovenous shunting in a very sensitive way makes it incredibly valuable in the assessment of vascular malformations. Other conditions where perfusion imaging is helpful include the assessment and diagnosis of dementia, epilepsy, hypercarbia, and brain death. In this chapter, we will explore how perfusion MR imaging is changing how we evaluate clinical neurological conditions.

14.2 Cerebrovascular diseases

14.2.1 Acute ischemic stroke

14.2.1.1 Core and penumbra

The increasing role of noninvasive angiographic imaging to identify anterior circulation occlusions contributed tremendously to the success of the endovascular thrombectomy trials within the last decade (MR CLEAN, EXTEND-IA, REVASCAT, SWIFT PRIME), allowing endovascular reperfusion therapy to proceed at an unprecedented rate (Zerna et al., 2016). Since then, the same may be said for the increasing role of perfusion imaging and its impact on subsequent trials evaluating the efficacy of endovascular reperfusion therapy in later stroke time windows, most prominently in the DAWN trial (Nogueira et al., 2018) and the DEFUSE-3 trial (Albers et al., 2018). Indeed, with fully automated software that can process perfusion maps rapidly and with relative robustness to common artifacts, imaging has now become a mainstay in routine acute stroke management, aiding in target identification and in functional outcome prognostication. This reflects the paradigm shift from uniform, time-based treatment to individualized, tissue status-based treatment of acute stroke. Correspondingly, this is reflected

Advances in Magnetic Resonance Technology and Applications, Volume 4, ISSN 2666-9099. https://doi.org/10.1016/B978-0-12-822479-3.00025-7 **211**
Copyright © 2021 Elsevier Inc. All rights reserved.

in the study by Lansberg et al. (2017) that reported good functional outcomes in imaging-selected patients, regardless of stroke onset to imaging time. Both MRI and CT can readily perform perfusion imaging, and have different advantages and disadvantages, as will be discussed later. The goal is to identify and select patients who would respond best to reperfusion therapy and those who are at increased risk of more detrimental outcomes (e.g., symptomatic intracranial hemorrhage). Such individualized treatment begins by determining the brain tissue status on perfusion imaging, specifically by distinguishing critically hypoperfused tissue that is likely to infarct in the absence of reperfusion (penumbra) from tissue that is already irreversibly infarcted (core). See Fig. 14.1.

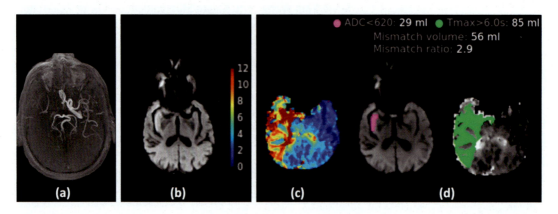

FIGURE 14.1

88-year-old male who was last known normal 4 hours prior presented with acute left-sided weakness and facial droop. (a) MRA demonstrates complete lack of flow-related enhancement in the right anterior circulation due to right ICA occlusion. (b) DWI demonstrates high diffusion signal in the right insula. (c) DSC perfusion imaging demonstrates a large region of critical hypoperfusion in the vascular territory, corresponding to the inferior division of the right MCA. (d) Automated perfusion software calculated a penumbra of 56 mL, core infarct of 29 mL, and a mismatch ratio of 2.9. As the patient met the target mismatch profile, they were treated with intravenous tPA, followed by mechanical thrombectomy.

The most common method to measure perfusion in acute stroke MRI is with dynamic susceptibility contrast (DSC), which assesses the transit of injection gadolinium-based contrast agents through the brain parenchyma (see Chapter 13). Commonly used perfusion parameters include cerebral blood flow (CBF), measuring the volume of blood flow per minute per 100 mL of brain tissue; cerebral blood volume (CBV), measuring the fraction of the voxel composed of blood; mean transit time (MTT), measuring the average transit time of a tracer through a region of brain tissue; and time-to-peak to the maximum of the residue function (Tmax), roughly measuring the time between peak contrast density through a region of brain tissue and that in a more central artery. MTT and Tmax are the most sensitive markers for hypoperfusion. Decreased CBF in relation to normal brain tissue (relative CBF [rCBF]) is the most consistent and accurate surrogate marker for the core infarct on CT, with a threshold of rCBF <30% having been validated extensively (Demeestere et al., 2020). With MR, the core infarct is directly assessed on diffusion-weighted imaging (DWI), rather than indirectly inferred based on perfusion changes. An apparent diffusion coefficient (ADC) threshold of 600 to 625×10^{-6} mm^2/s has been reasonably robust in highlighting the core (Purushotham et al., 2015). The penumbra is then derived by subtracting the core volume from the total tissue volume that is critically hypoperfused, which is typically defined as a threshold of Tmax >6 seconds. A threshold with sufficiently high specificity is needed to reasonably discriminate critical hypoperfusion from benign oligemia, and Tmax >6 seconds has been shown to provide a reasonable estimate of a completed infarct volume when no reperfusion is performed. Moreover, it may be the most concordant perfusion parameter between CT and MR.

14.2.1.2 Target mismatch

With these aforementioned parameters, a mismatch ratio (MMR) can be calculated, which is defined as the ratio between the total hypoperfusion volume and the core volume (see Fig. 14.1). A higher MMR indicates a disproportionally larger volume of salvageable "tissue at risk" when compared to the core. The target mismatch (TMM) criteria were introduced to identify patients at high likelihood to benefit from endovascular thrombectomy, and was ultimately refined in the DEFUSE-2 trial (Lansberg et al., 2012) to be MMR>1.8, penumbra >15 mL, core <70 mL, and Tmax >10 seconds volume <100 mL. Since then, the DAWN and DEFUSE-3 randomized controlled trials utilizing TMM criteria for patient selection in the later time windows (between 6 and 16 to 24 hours after stroke onset) showed significantly improved outcomes for patients receiving medical therapy, plus endovascular thrombectomy, when compared to medical therapy alone. Limited studies have also shown improved functional outcomes of using perfusion imaging in selecting patients with TMM for intravenous thrombolysis outside the conventional time window (Ma et al., 2019) from 4.5 to 9 hours after onset.

In addition to the MMR, the severity of the perfusion deficit may also predict the fate of brain tissue and likelihood to benefit from reperfusion therapy. Tissue at risk with poor collateral circulation is more likely to progress rapidly to infarct. The extent of collateralization among patients may partly explain why there is such high variability in pace of progression to infarct observed, and is partly influenced by the extent to which chronic hypoperfusion is present, which reduces the potential for collateralization. The extent of poorly collateralized tissue can be inferred by tissue with Tmax >10 seconds. Specifically, the hypoperfusion intensity ratio, which is the ratio between Tmax >10 seconds and Tmax >6 seconds, is a good predictor of collateral circulation and rapid infarct growth (Olivot et al., 2014). The higher the ratio, the larger the relative volume of Tmax >10 seconds, suggesting a larger volume of poorly collateralized ischemic tissue that will rapidly progress to infarct. Such patients who are predicted to respond poorly to reperfusion therapy are often referred to as having a malignant perfusion profile.

14.2.1.3 Computed tomography vs magnetic resonance

The advantages and disadvantages with both modalities in other applications are similarly true here (see Fig. 14.2). CT is readily available and more rapid, but comes at the expense of lower signal-to-noise and contrast-to-noise ratios, radiation exposure, and an indirect estimation of the core infarct. By comparison, MR provides a direct visualization of the core infarct on DWI, which is generally considered the gold standard for core volume estimation. Moreover, DWI allows detection of ischemic changes within minutes of stroke onset and visualization of acute lacunar or small subcortical infarcts, for which CT perfusion demonstrates lower sensitivity (Demeestere et al., 2020). MR rapid stroke protocols can also provide comparable door-to-groin times to that of CT. However, there are more contraindications to MR in certain patient populations (e.g., pacemakers, metallic foreign bodies), and one also has to consider the unknown long-term effects of gadolinium deposition. Additionally, MRI utilizes DSC for most stroke perfusion imaging, which has its own drawbacks associated with this technique. Both modalities

214 Chapter 14 Perfusion MRI: clinical perspectives

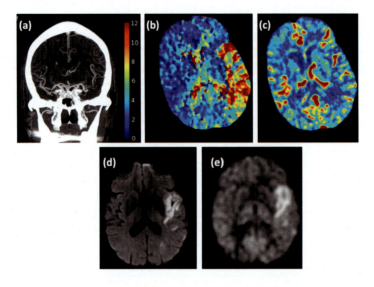

FIGURE 14.2

69-year-old male who was last known normal 9 hours prior presented with acute right-sided weakness and aphasia. (a) CT angiography demonstrates abrupt cut-off of the dominant division of the left post-bifurcation M1. CT perfusion demonstrated a large region of critical hypoperfusion based on Tmax (b), but did not identify any core infarct based on the CBF map (c). The patient underwent successful mechanical thrombectomy. (d) MRI performed the following day demonstrated high diffusion signal in the left frontal operculum and left parietal lobe on DWI, consistent with regions of completed infarct. (e) ASL cerebral blood flow imaging demonstrates elevated signal in these regions consistent with luxury perfusion.

demonstrate low sensitivity for perfusion changes in the posterior fossa. In the setting of renal insufficiency, gadolinium or iodinated contrast allergy, or lack of intravenous access, arterial spin labeling (ASL) may serve a reasonable substitute. The ability of ASL to measure quantitative CBF may also yield prognostic information in acute stroke, as suggested by a study showing that the absolute CBF in the contralateral hemisphere is a strong predictor of outcome; patients with low contralateral CBF actually did not benefit significantly, even from successful reperfusion.

14.2.1.4 Pitfalls and caveats

Though there may be consensus on the thresholds for perfusion parameters that define penumbra and ischemic core, the processing of such parameters is not standardized. Different software products calculate perfusion parameters differently (e.g., variation in vascular input function placement, deconvolution method, scan length, and field-of-view), and values calculated using one software package cannot directly be compared to those from another. Indeed, values from commercially available software show significant differences in core and penumbra volume estimations. It therefore may be best to utilize software that has been validated in the landmark randomized controlled trials of DAWN and DEFUSE-3, as those estimated volumes were the ones acted upon that ultimately resulted in significantly favorable

14.2 Cerebrovascular diseases **215**

outcome in those studies, and are therefore more clinically meaningful. Despite this, it is likely that calibrating other software packages probably produces similar performance.

One should be mindful of visually interpreting perfusion maps in isolation, as those with a lack of visual mismatch sometimes did actually fulfill quantitative mismatch criteria (Bivard et al., 2015). Most, if not all, software now provides thresholding to allow more objective and consistent estimations, and to prevent the tendency to qualitatively overestimate the core and to help distinguish regions of critical hypoperfusion that are likely to progress to infarction from regions with benign oligemia.

In patients with chronic hypoperfusion (e.g., those with hemodynamically significant stenosis of the carotid bulbs or a moyamoya pattern), Tmax is already delayed to varying degrees at baseline, which if it exceeds set hypoperfusion thresholds will cause overestimation of the perfusion deficit. One must be mindful of interpreting perfusion maps in these patients presenting acutely with suspected ischemic stroke, and comparison with prior perfusion imaging and relatively benign clinical presentation may be valuable clues to accurately identify acute or chronic components of hypoperfusion.

Lastly, one must keep in mind that ischemic strokes are dynamic processes that evolve in time. Although an ADC threshold of 600 to 625×10^{-6} mm^2/s has been robust in depicting the core, a single ADC threshold may nevertheless result in different estimations of core volume, depending on the time of stroke onset. In later time windows, it is also not uncommon to see *increased* blood flow in what would eventually be infarcted tissue, often termed luxury perfusion, and is partly due to increased collateral flow and/or spontaneous recanalization (see Fig. 4.2). Such increased blood flow will not be identified as core on CT perfusion maps if rCBF thresholds are exceeded, resulting in core volume underestimation. Therefore vigilance on non-contrast CT for cytotoxic edema within these regions is required, particularly for patients presenting in the later time windows, as these regions of core infarct should be readily visualizable at this juncture. This problem is obviated with MRI, where DWI changes will persist in dead tissue, despite spontaneous recanalization.

14.2.2 Cerebrovascular reserve

Cerebrovascular reserve (CVR) can be defined as the brain's capacity to increase perfusion through vasodilatation when responding to a vasodilatory challenge. This assessment may prove to be more informative than traditional risk stratifications for stroke, which historically relied on the degree of arterial stenosis and does not take into account collateralization and potential autoregulation by the brain to maintain blood flow in response to severe stenosis. Reduced CVR suggests the brain's autoregulatory mechanism to compensate is close to exhaustion, and has been shown to be significantly associated with increased risk of stroke and poorer outcomes following extracranial-to-intracranial carotid bypass for patients with Moyamoya disease. Moreover, Moyamoya disease patients may even demonstrate reduced CBF following vasodilatory challenges in certain regions due to steal phenomenon, evidence of particularly poor hemodynamics.

Positron emission tomography (PET), single-photon emission CT (SPECT), and transcranial Doppler ultrasound have been the gold standard in assessing CVR. More recently, CT and MR perfusion (DSC and ASL) have also been developed to assess CVR. In the case of MR, blood oxygenation level-dependent (BOLD) effects can be exploited to infer information related to CVR. BOLD MR measures the local susceptibility secondary to the amount of paramagnetic deoxyhemoglobin present within a voxel. Blood flow that is augmented from vasodilatation will result in increased tissue oxygenation (without substantial increased tissue metabolism), thereby decreasing overall deoxyhemoglobin within

216   **Chapter 14** Perfusion MRI: clinical perspectives

the voxel and consequently the local susceptibility. The change before and after the vasodilatory challenge may then be quantified to infer CVR. An alternative MR technique that can be utilized is ASL. Similar to BOLD, ASL can be performed both before and after a vasodilatory challenge to infer CVR, and has the advantage of being able to directly quantify the CBF changes pre- and post-vasodilation.

There are several options available when performing a vasodilatory challenge. These include increasing arterial CO_2 partial pressure, either by breath holding, and thereby reducing ventilation and CO_2 exchange at the alveoli, or by breathing hypercarbic gas mixtures. Increases in arterial CO_2 partial pressures induce vasodilation of the cerebral vasculature, and thereby CBF. Alternatively, intravenous administration of acetazolamide (ACZ), a carbonic anhydrase inhibitor, results in carbonic acidosis and considerably increases CBF (30%–60% increase in the normal brain). Use of ACZ may mitigate inter-patient variability when compared to breath-hold techniques or breathing hypercarbic gas, given differences in patient respiratory rates and tidal volumes.

However, the large number of studies with differing patient populations, vasodilatory stimuli, imaging techniques, region-of-interest (ROI) placement, and post-processing algorithms has made it difficult to create consensus definitions for expressing CVR, which have included ΔCBF, %CBF change, and %BOLD change. The methodological variability precludes establishment of reliable reference values for hypoperfused and normal brain tissue. For example, one of these differences is post-label delay in ASL, which ranged from 1 to 2.5 seconds, depending on the study. Yet, despite these differences, Gupta et al. (2012) reported that the association between CVR reduction and stroke is significant, regardless of modality or vasodilatory stimuli.

14.3 Vascular malformations and other shunting lesions

Vascular malformations are a heterogeneous group of disorders that exhibit a broad spectrum of biologic behaviors, traditionally classified by histopathology into four major types: arteriovenous malformations (AVMs), developmental venous anomalies (DVAs), capillary telangiectasias, and cavernous malformations. Though these lesions have traditionally been classified by histopathology, many neuro-interventionalists and neurosurgeons group them by function. With this functional classification, there are two basic categories: malformations with and without arteriovenous shunting. Malformations in the first functional group include AVMs, arteriovenous fistulas, and transitional DVAs, whereas non-shunting malformations include typical DVAs, capillary telangiectasias, and cavernous malformations. This functional classification of vascular malformations is important for clinical perfusion MRI, because this function, that is, arteriovenous shunting, helps us accurately visualize and characterize these lesions. It also helps us predict whether ASL or DSC techniques will be more helpful in the assessment of these lesions.

AVMs are congenital abnormalities of vascular development that demonstrate tightly packed tangles of thin-walled vessels without an intervening capillary bed, thus allowing for arteriovenous shunting. Although traditional MRI techniques enable visualization of the classic imaging findings of feeding arteries, a central nidus, and draining veins, small lesions may remain occult on structural imaging. The presence of arteriovenous shunting can be characterized with perfusion MRI, most reliably with ASL techniques. The characteristic finding of arteriovenous shunting on ASL is high signal in the venous system, so-called venous ASL signal, which occurs due to the absence of a normal capillary bed. Typically, the capillaries extract the vast majority of labeled spins, so it is only when the capillary bed is missing that venous ASL signal is seen. This results in the appearance of intraluminal hyperintensities within the AVM nidus and draining veins, a finding that is not normally present (Le et al., 2012). DSC and DCE perfusion techniques demonstrate nonspecific findings in the setting of AVM, which can include mildly increased CBF and CBV. See Fig. 14.3.

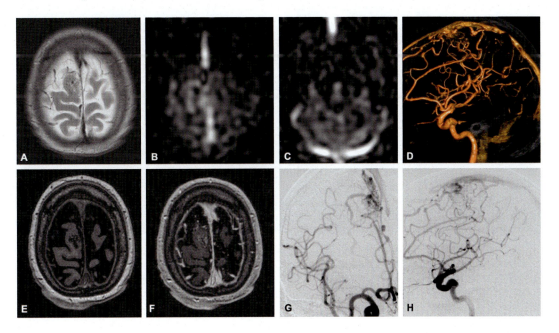

FIGURE 14.3

77-year-old male with a Spetzler–Martin Grade 1 arteriovenous malformation (AVM). (a) Axial T_2-weighted, (b–c) ASL, (e) T_1-weighted pre-contrast, and (f) T_1-weighted post-contrast images demonstrate a small tangle of vessels in the right superior frontal gyrus. There is venous ASL signal in the superior sagittal sinus (b), which indicates superficial venous drainage. There is also venous ASL signal in the transverse and sigmoid sinuses (c). (g, h) DSA and (d) 3D reconstructed images demonstrate the nidus in the right superior frontal gyrus with arterial supply from pericallosal branches of the right anterior cerebral artery and distal branches of the right middle cerebral artery. The presence of venous ASL signal is very sensitive for arteriovenous shunting.

Dural arteriovenous fistulas (dAVFs) are the second major type of cerebrovascular malformation that exhibits arteriovenous shunting. A dAVF is a network of tiny vessels that shunt blood between meningeal arteries and small venules within the wall of a dural venous sinus or cortical vein. They are usually acquired and secondary to thrombosed dural venous sinuses. Though they may involve any dural venous sinus, they are most commonly found in the posterior fossa and skull base, with greatest involvement at the transverse/sigmoid sinus junction. Perfusion imaging is especially useful in their identification due to the presence of arteriovenous shunting, which is best appreciated with ASL as the identification of venous signal (Le et al., 2012). This technique can be useful in assessing known dAVFs and in the workup of a suspected lesion. It can also help to classify the type of dAVF by determining the presence or absence of cortical venous drainage (Amukotuwa et al., 2016). See Fig. 14.4.

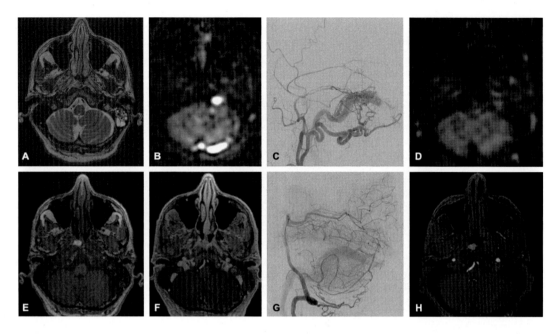

FIGURE 14.4

71-year-old male with a left transverse-sigmoid sinus Cognard Type III dural arteriovenous fistula (dAVF). (a) Axial T_2-weighted, (b) ASL, (e) T_1-weighted pre-contrast, and (f) T_1-weighted post-contrast images demonstrate venous ASL signal in the left transverse and sigmoid sinuses. There is no other appreciable MR signal abnormality. (c, g) Digital subtraction angiography demonstrates the dAVF at the left transverse-sigmoid sinus junction. Early draining veins are visualized extending into the transverse-sigmoid sinus junction, consistent with the venous signal on ASL. After treatment with embolization, (d) ASL and (h) 3D TOF MR angiography images demonstrate resolution of the previously visualized venous ASL signal, consistent with angiographic cure.

Although AVMs and dAVFs demonstrate arteriovenous shunting and are well assessed with ASL techniques, developmental venous anomalies (DVAs), capillary telangiectasias, and cavernomas do not usually demonstrate arteriovenous shunting, and subsequently show a different imaging appearance with perfusion MRI. Developmental venous anomalies are umbrella-shaped congenital cerebrovascular malformations composed of mature venous elements, with dilated, thin-walled venous channels within, and separated by normal brain parenchyma. These dilated medullary veins converge into large central venous channels that drain into either superficial or deep venous systems. Though the majority of lesions are found in the deep white matter adjacent to the frontal horn of the lateral ventricle, they may occur anywhere in the brain. Although these lesions are not classically described as demonstrating arteriovenous shunting, ASL signal abnormality has been described in up to 8% of lesions, suggesting possible small AV shunts in some of these lesions (Iv et al., 2015). Additionally, the nature of these anomalies, namely a prominent venous structure with multiple collecting venous channels, predisposes them to the susceptibility effects of deoxyhemoglobin that are accentuated with DSC. As such, perfusion abnormalities are noted in up to 79% of lesions, with elevated CBF, elevated CBV, and mildly delayed MTT in and around DVAs (Iv et al., 2015). Capillary telangiectasias may also demonstrate

14.4 Neoplasms

elevated CBV without associated ASL signal abnormality. Cavernous malformations are not known to demonstrate perfusion signal abnormalities.

14.4 Neoplasms
14.4.1 Tumor grading

DSC has been widely used for tumor grading. Using ROI-based techniques, grading can be performed by assessing the ratio of rCBV between tumor and the unaffected contralateral tissue. There was significant correlation between maximum rCBV ($rCBV_{max}$) and tumor grade in gliomas, with cutoff of 1.75 providing a sensitivity and specificity of 0.95 and 0.81 in discriminating between low-grade and high-grade gliomas, respectively (Law et al., 2007) (see Fig. 14.5). Further evaluation with histogram analysis demonstrated even higher specificities without sacrificing sensitivity depending on the histogram parameter used (e.g., median, 25th percentile, and standard deviation). This may be because a histogram analysis better accounts for tumor heterogeneity. Indeed, oligodendrogliomas commonly

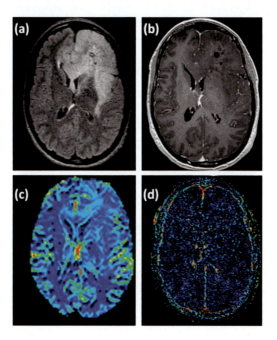

FIGURE 14.5

Pretreatment MRI of a 39-year-old female with WHO Grade II diffuse astrocytoma (IDH-mutant) demonstrates a left frontal infiltrative mass on (a) T_2 FLAIR, with mild patchy enhancement and cystic changes on (b) T_1 postcontrast imaging. Both (c) rCBV and (d) K^{trans} maps from DSC and DCE, respectively, did not demonstrate elevated values.

exhibit higher rCBV$_{max}$ irrespective of grade, and histogram analysis has been shown to provide increasing discriminatory power between oligodendrogliomas and high-grade gliomas.

Dynamic contrast-enhanced (DCE) may also provide an indication of tumor grade of gliomas. Elevated K^{trans} and V_e, parameters in DCE, indicating the contrast efflux into the extracellular space and markers for vascular permeability, were significantly associated with higher grade gliomas, with V_e being more sensitive and K^{trans} being more specific (Zhao et al., 2015). V_e was also significantly higher in metastases and primary CNS lymphoma than in high-grade gliomas. Histogram analysis can similarly be applied (Yan et al., 2019) and has demonstrated superior discriminatory power (using the area under curve [AUC] metric of up to 0.84) when compared to ASL CBF (AUC of 0.66). See Fig. 14.6.

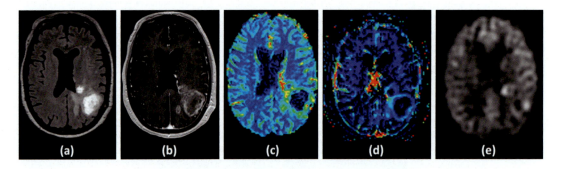

FIGURE 14.6

79-year-old female with two left parietal hyperintense lesions with surrounding white matter signal abnormality on (a) T_2 FLAIR and thick nodular ring enhancement on (b) T_1 post-contrast. Both (c) rCBV and (d) K^{trans} maps from DSC and DCE, respectively, as well as (e) ASL, demonstrated elevated values, suggesting increased perfusion and vascular permeability in the regions of enhancement. The findings are consistent with a high-grade glioma, in this case an IDH-wildtype glioblastoma.

14.4.2 Molecular markers

Imaging biomarkers predicting tumor grade may become increasingly less relevant as the paradigm shift in the understanding and classification of brain tumors moves toward a stronger molecular underpinning. Prognoses of certain tumors often correlate more with molecular markers (e.g., IDH mutation and 1p19q codeletion) than with tumor grade. For instance, astrocytomas with IDH mutations are prognostically more favorable when compared to their wildtype counterparts. With ASL, wildtype glioblastomas (GB) demonstrate significantly higher absolute and relative CBF than IDH-mutants. Using ROI-based techniques on DSC, rCBV can discriminate between IDH-mutant and wildtype astrocytomas (AUC between 0.83 and 0.94), regardless of tumor grade (Tan et al., 2017). Similarly, GBs frequently harbor the EGFR variant III mutation, which carries a worse prognosis and is associated with significantly higher rCBV, K^{trans}, and V_e compared to their wildtype GB counterparts. MGMT methylation is also commonly seen in GB but, in contrast, carries a more favorable prognosis. On DSC, this is significantly associated with a lower rCBV, with an optimized threshold allowing for a sensitivity of 0.73 and specificity of 0.86 (Jung et al., 2013). Interestingly, on DCE, increasing vascular permeability, as reflected by a higher K^{trans}, was associated with the presence of this molecular marker.

Oligodendroglioma can now be confidently diagnosed by the presence of 1p/19q codeletion, a mainstay molecular marker of adult oligodendroglioma (less true in the pediatric counterpart). The presence of 1p/19q codeletion is also prognostically more favorable, irrespective of tumor grade. However, to our knowledge, since the 2016 World Health Organization classification, whereby oligodendrogliomas can be diagnosed purely on the basis of molecular markers, very few studies have reported significant associations between 1p/19q status and perfusion changes. This is not surprising, as such association would essentially imply discriminating between oligodendrogliomas and other gliomas by perfusion parameters alone.

14.4.3 Treatment response assessment

14.4.3.1 Pseudoprogression

Since the landmark study by Stupp et al. (2005), the standard of care treatment for GB is maximal safe tumor resection, followed by radiation therapy (RT) and concomitant and adjuvant temozolomide (TMZ) chemotherapy. MRI is widely used for assessing post-treatment response, and the extent of the contrast enhancing and non-enhancing components of the tumor have been used as surrogates for tumor progression. However, since the standardization of GB treatment with RT with concomitant and adjuvant TMZ, there has been increasing recognition of a phenomenon known as pseudoprogression (PsP), whereby early post-treatment MRI demonstrates increased contrast enhancement, which eventually subsides without changes to therapy. PsP most commonly occurs within the first 3 months following chemoradiation, may or may not be accompanied by clinical deterioration, and is thought to be partly due to transiently increased vascular permeability from RT. The increasing awareness of PsP following standardization of treatment with TMZ has implicated TMZ in the role of potentiating RT-associated PsP. Specifically, PsP is widely believed to be more frequent following concomitant RT-TMZ compared to RT alone, although the limited available evidence remains equivocal. Interestingly, PsP has been occasionally associated with an increased survival rate, not only when compared to those with true early progression, but also to those with uneventful stable disease, who do not develop PsP following chemoradiation. These studies altogether have suggested that PsP may reflect a prognostically favorable, enhanced inflammatory response against the tumor, although evidence among all studies remains inconsistent. Lastly, PsP appears to be more commonly seen in treated GB with MGMT promoter methylation.

From a diagnostic standpoint, the biggest dilemma presented by PsP is arguably the inability of anatomic imaging to reliably differentiate tumor recurrence and progressive disease from PsP. Differentiation is of considerable importance as progressive disease implies treatment failure and a transition to a salvage therapy. Mistaking PsP for progressive disease may lead to premature termination of effective treatment, unnecessary debulking surgeries, and re-irradiation. The lack of reliable imaging findings on conventional MRI to differentiate true progression from PsP has resulted in the diagnosis of PsP being made only retrospectively based on subsequent changes on serial imaging and clinical features.

Given the limitations of anatomic imaging, the diagnostic performance of multiple perfusion imaging techniques, including DSC, DCE, and ASL, have been investigated, as well as other imaging techniques, such as DWI, diffusion tensor imaging (DTI), and magnetic resonance spectroscopy (MRS) with sensitivities ranging from 0.71–0.92 and specificities ranging from 0.86–0.95, depending on the technique (van Dijken et al., 2017). However, a recurrent theme related to advanced perfusion imaging is the lack of standardization and its use in assessing PsP is no exception, precluding universally accepted cut-off values with high sensitivity and specificity. Patients on corticosteroids and bevacizumab, who are not excluded from studies, further confound results. Nevertheless, decreased K^{trans}, V_e, and V_p on DCE and rCBV on DSC have been significantly associated with PsP. Given that findings on imaging (and even on pathology) often represent a continuum of both treatment effect and residual tumor, a single cut-off value or an averaged perfusion parameter from ROI-based methods may oversimplify an interpretation to what is often a complex, heterogeneous mix of both processes. Histogram analysis may provide more meaningful analysis, with skewness and kurtosis on normalized rCBV histograms as predictors. Lastly, though both DCE and DSC may have similar sensitivities and specificities in distinguishing tumor from PsP, DCE may be preferable in certain scenarios, given DSC's demerits in the setting of hemorrhage, postsurgical blood products, and calcification. The intent of further improving the discriminatory power of advanced MRI techniques has led to the investigation of multiparametric MRI, whereby a combination of two or more parameters, often from advanced MRI techniques, are analyzed in tandem. For example, Seeger et al. (2013) demonstrated a sensitivity and specificity of 0.74 and 0.94, respectively, when using a multiparametric assessment with DCE, DSC, ASL, and MRS. A recent meta-analysis of multiparametric MRI demonstrated a pooled sensitivity and specificity of 0.84 and 0.95, respectively (Suh et al., 2018).

14.4.3.2 Pseudoresponse

The use of anti-angiogenic agents, such as bevacizumab, can lead to a substantial decrease in contrast enhancement and peritumoral edema, which may or may not also be accompanied by improvement in clinical symptoms. However, these improvements are not believed to be associated with a true decrease in tumor burden or improvement in survival, and these ostensible improvements on conventional MRI have been termed pseudoresponse. Indeed, randomized controlled trials of anti-angiogenic agents, excluding pseudoresponse patients, have failed to show improvement in overall survival (Song et al., 2018). Perfusion imaging may distinguish those with pseudoresponse from true response, as the former tends to continue to demonstrate increased perfusion parameters, despite improvement on conventional imaging. Those with an increased standardized rCBV demonstrated significantly shorter progression-free and overall survival on DSC, whereas, by comparison, another study failed to find a significant association between DSC parameters and outcome.

14.4.3.3 Radiation necrosis

Imaging manifestation of radiation necrosis most frequently occurs 3 to 12 months following RT, but occurrences many years following RT are also not uncommon. Similar to PsP, findings on conventional MRI may be indistinguishable from tumor recurrence or progressive disease. A strong awareness and understanding of the radiation field during treatment will aid in imaging interpretation. Both DSC and DCE have demonstrated significantly increased rCBV and K^{trans} in GB when compared to radiation necrosis, respectively. Receiver operating characteristic analysis demonstrated the highest AUC of 0.92 for rCBV with a threshold of 2.2, providing sensitivity of 0.80 and specificity of 0.92 (Nael et al., 2018). Similar use of multiparametric analysis by combining the assessment rCBV and K^{trans} improves the diagnostic accuracy with an AUC of 0.96.

14.4.4 Other brain tumors
14.4.4.1 Metastases

A history of underlying malignancy and lesion multiplicity are some of the most helpful criteria in differentiating brain metastases from GB. However, when presented with a solitary lesion, differentiating a single brain metastasis from GB becomes more challenging. Both may exhibit enhancement, hemorrhage, restricted diffusion, and peritumoral signal abnormality. The peritumoral signal abnormality is one region that can be exploited on perfusion imaging to aid in differentiation. The peritumoral area in GB is often a combination of vasogenic edema, neoplastic capillaries, and infiltrating tumor, whereas it is typically pure vasogenic edema in metastasis. This is partly due to the complete lack of blood-brain-barrier in the latter, resulting in uncontrolled leakage of blood plasma into the interstitial space. Consequently, the higher rCBV and K^{trans} reported in the peritumoral region of high-grade gliomas may be differentiated from similar-appearing metastasis. In concordance with these findings, when assessing the T_2^* relaxivity curve on DSC, the maximal signal intensity drop from first pass contrast was reported to be higher in the peritumoral region of GBs when compared to that of metastasis (Cha et al., 2007).

Assessment of the perfusion characteristics of lesion itself is less straightforward, given the myriad of origins and tumor biology of metastasis. Indeed, Jung et al. (2016) did not find significant differences in K^{trans} or V_p between GB and hypovascular metastasis, GB and melanoma (hypervascular) metastasis, or hypovascular and melanoma metastasis—even without adjusting for multiple comparisons. Similarly, Hatzoglou et al. (2017) found no significant differences in K^{trans} between hypovascular non-small cell lung cancer and melanoma metastasis, but did for V_p, albeit with a relatively low AUC of 0.66.

14.4.4.2 Primary CNS lymphoma

Primary CNS lymphoma and GB may be indistinguishable on anatomic imaging, given their similar infiltrative pattern, enhancement, and predilection for the corpus callosum. On DCE, primary CNS lymphoma is known to have increased vascular permeability and is reported to have significantly higher K_2 (leakage coefficient) than that of GB. Moreover, rCBV was significantly lower in primary CNS lymphoma, regardless of whether the underestimation by the leakage effect was corrected for or not (Toh et al., 2013), and demonstrated superior discriminatory power when compared to K_2 (AUC 0.94 vs 0.78).

14.5 Miscellaneous conditions

Perfusion MRI is also valuable in the assessment of numerous miscellaneous conditions, including dementia, epilepsy, brain death, and hypercarbia.

Dementia is an acquired impairment in intellectual ability that affects multiple cognitive domains, including memory, thinking, language, judgment, and behavior. Dementia has many causes, but the three most common types are Alzheimer's disease, dementia with Lewy bodies, and vascular dementia. It can be difficult to distinguish between the various dementia syndromes; therefore imaging has played an increasing role in diagnosis, with efforts to distinguish different types from potentially reversible non-dementing disorders. Since brain metabolic alterations precede structural abnormalities during cognitive decline, perfusion MRI is useful in the assessment of dementia due to perfusion-metabolism coupling.

Alzheimer's disease is associated with gray matter volume loss in the mesial temporal and parietal lobes. ASL studies have consistently shown a reduction in CBF in a posterior parietal distribution, including the precuneus, posterior cingulate, angular gyrus, and superior parietal gyrus, which is remarkably similar to the pattern of hypometabolism observed with 18F-fluorodeoxyglucose-PET. Though less is known about the potential of ASL in other forms of dementia, hypoperfusion patterns that correlate with described hypometabolic patterns in dementia with Lewy bodies and vascular dementia have been reported. These include hypoperfusion of the posterior cingulate and visual association areas in dementia with Lewy bodies, and widespread decreases in CBF, especially in the bifrontal and parietal areas in patients with vascular dementia.

Epilepsy is a complex neurological disorder characterized by abnormal electrical activity in the brain resulting in seizures. Although many tests are used in the evaluation of patients with epilepsy, the main interest for perfusion MRI is to locate the potential epileptogenic focus. Conventional methods, such as ictal and interictal SPECT and PET, are often performed to evaluate for metabolic changes related to epileptic activity. Due to perfusion-metabolism coupling, there is good correlation between areas of ASL hypoperfusion and hypoperfusion measured on interictal PET images. Additionally, during the acute peri-ictal period, CBF is typically elevated due to pathologic neuronal activity, a phenomenon that can be effectively demonstrated with ASL. While this imaging appearance may not be diagnostic in isolation, it provides a complementary assessment in the evaluation of epilepsy and correlates well with other measures, including electrophysiologic data. See Fig. 14.7.

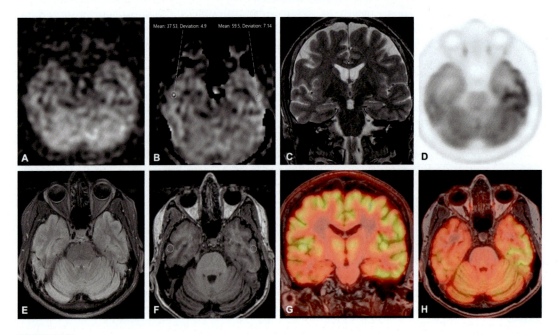

FIGURE 14.7

53-year-old female with a history of medically intractable epilepsy. (a) ASL, (b) transit-corrected CBF map, (c) coronal T_2-weighted, (e) axial FLAIR, and (f) axial T_1-weighted images at the level of the temporal lobes demonstrate subtle ASL hypoperfusion throughout the right temporal lobe. No apparent structural abnormality is present. Regions of interest are annotated, with corresponding CBF values. (d) FDG PET and (g, h) fused FDG PET/MR images demonstrate pronounced hypometabolism throughout the right inferolateral temporal lobe, which corresponds with the ASL hypoperfusion pattern.

14.5 Miscellaneous conditions

Other conditions that can be appreciated with perfusion MRI include the assessment of brain death and hypercarbia. Brain death is defined as irreversible loss of brain and brainstem function, with clinical findings of coma, absence of brainstem reflexes, and apnea. As it is sometimes difficult to arrive at a clinical diagnosis of brain death, ancillary confirmatory tests may be used, including those that demonstrate loss of bioelectrical activity and those that show absence of CBF. Perfusion MRI is an excellent option for this evaluation, with both DSC and ASL being useful candidates. Specifically, ASL demonstrates extremely decreased whole-brain cerebral perfusion, bright vessel signal intensity at the skull base, patent external carotid artery circulation, and a "hollow" skull sign, akin to that visualized with perfusion SPECT imaging. See Fig. 14.8.

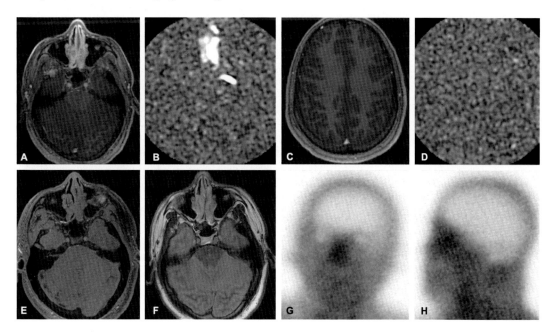

FIGURE 14.8

51-year-old male with a history of cardiac arrest. (a) Axial T_1-weighted post-contrast, (b) ASL, (e) 3D TOF MR angiography, (f) T_2-weighted images at the level of the skull base, (c) T_1-weighted post-contrast, and (d) ASL images at the centrum semiovale level demonstrate absence of intracerebral perfusion. There is minimal enhancement (a) and flow-related enhancement (e) along the petrous internal carotid arteries with corresponding loss of the normal flow voids (f), and tubular ASL signal (b). There is no appreciable intracranial contrast enhancement (c) or evidence of intracranial ASL perfusion (d). (g, h) Cerebral perfusion SPECT imaging confirms an absence of cerebral blood flow, with intact extracranial circulation, characteristic of brain death.

Hypercarbia, or elevated pCO_2, is a condition that is often clinically underrecognized, but has a distinct perfusion pattern that can be elucidated with perfusion MRI. As carbon dioxide is a potent stimulator of CBF through its vasodilatory effect on cerebral vasculature, even small changes in the partial pressure of CO_2 are capable of generating appreciable changes on perfusion imaging (Pollock et al., 2009). As such, patients with hypercarbia demonstrate global ASL hyperperfusion,

226 **Chapter 14** Perfusion MRI: clinical perspectives

involving both gray and white matter, whereas patients with hypocarbia show marked global hypoperfusion.

14.6 Conclusions

Perfusion imaging with MRI allows better diagnosis and treatment for a wide range of commonly-encountered neurological diseases. Though DSC and DCE have played a large role in stroke and tumor imaging, ASL is becoming increasingly used for these indications and others due to its unique contrast in the presence of arteriovenous shunts and its quantitative nature. Continued basic research and clinical translation will be crucial to reap the benefits of perfusion imaging for neurological diseases.

References

Albers, G.W., Marks, M.P., Kemp, S., Christensen, S., Tsai, J.P., Ortega-Gutierrez, S., et al., 2018. Thrombectomy for stroke at 6 to 16 hours with selection by perfusion imaging. The New England Journal of Medicine 378, 708–718.

Amukotuwa, S.A., Heit, J.J., Marks, M.P., Fischbein, N., Bammer, R., 2016. Detection of cortical venous drainage and determination of the borden type of dural arteriovenous fistula by means of 3D pseudocontinuous arterial spin-labeling MRI. American Journal of Roentgenology 207, 163–169.

Bivard, A., Levi, C., Krishnamurthy, V., McElduff, P., Miteff, F., Spratt, N.J., et al., 2015. Perfusion computed tomography to assist decision making for stroke thrombolysis. Brain 138, 1919–1931.

Cha, S., Lupo, J.M., Chen, M.H., Lamborn, K.R., McDermott, M.W., Berger, M.S., et al., 2007. Differentiation of glioblastoma multiforme and single brain metastasis by peak height and percentage of signal intensity recovery derived from dynamic susceptibility-weighted contrast-enhanced perfusion MR imaging. American Journal of Neuroradiology 28, 1078–1084.

Demeestere, J., Wouters, A., Christensen, S., Lemmens, R., Lansberg, M.G., 2020. Review of perfusion imaging in acute ischemic stroke: from time to tissue. Stroke 51, 1017–1024.

Gupta, A., Chazen, J.L., Hartman, M., Delgado, D., Anumula, N., Shao, H., et al., 2012. Cerebrovascular reserve and stroke risk in patients with carotid stenosis or occlusion: a systematic review and meta-analysis. Stroke 43, 2884–2891.

Hatzoglou, V., Tisnado, J., Mehta, A., Peck, K.K., Daras, M., Omuro, A.M., et al., 2017. Dynamic contrast-enhanced MRI perfusion for differentiating between melanoma and lung cancer brain metastases. Cancer Medicine 6, 761–767.

Iv, M., Fischbein, N.J., Zaharchuk, G., 2015. Association of developmental venous anomalies with perfusion abnormalities on arterial spin labeling and bolus perfusion-weighted imaging. Journal of Neuroimaging 25, 243–250.

Jung, S.C., Choi, S.H., Yeom, J.A., Kim, J.H., Ryoo, I., Kim, S.C., et al., 2013. Cerebral blood volume analysis in glioblastomas using dynamic susceptibility contrast-enhanced perfusion MRI: a comparison of manual and semiautomatic segmentation methods. PLoS ONE 8, e69323.

Jung, B.C., Arevalo-Perez, J., Lyo, J.K., Holodny, A.I., Karimi, S., Young, R.J., et al., 2016. Comparison of glioblastomas and brain metastases using dynamic contrast-enhanced perfusion MRI. Journal of Neuroimaging 26, 240–246.

Lansberg, M.G., Straka, M., Kemp, S., Mlynash, M., Wechsler, L.R., Jovin, T.G., et al., 2012. MRI profile and response to endovascular reperfusion after stroke (DEFUSE 2): a prospective cohort study. The Lancet Neurology 11, 860–867.

Lansberg, M.G., Christensen, S., Kemp, S., Mlynash, M., Mishra, N., Federau, C., et al., 2017. Computed tomographic perfusion to predict response to recanalization in ischemic stroke. Annals of Neurology 81, 849–856.

Law, M., Young, R., Babb, J., Pollack, E., Johnson, G., 2007. Histogram analysis versus region of interest analysis of dynamic susceptibility contrast perfusion MR imaging data in the grading of cerebral gliomas. American Journal of Neuroradiology 28, 761–766.

Le, T.T., Fischbein, N.J., Andre, J.B., Wijman, C., Rosenberg, J., Zaharchuk, G., 2012. Identification of venous signal on arterial spin labeling improves diagnosis of dural arteriovenous fistulas and small arteriovenous malformations. American Journal of Neuroradiology 33, 61–68.

Ma, H., Campbell, B.C.V., Parsons, M.W., Churilov, L., Levi, C.R., Hsu, C., et al., 2019. Thrombolysis guided by perfusion imaging up to 9 hours after onset of stroke. The New England Journal of Medicine 380, 1795–1803.

Nael, K., Bauer, A.H., Hormigo, A., Lemole, M., Germano, I.M., Puig, J., et al., 2018. Multiparametric MRI for differentiation of radiation necrosis from recurrent tumor in patients with treated glioblastoma. American Journal of Roentgenology 210, 18–23.

Nogueira, R.G., Jadhav, A.P., Haussen, D.C., Bonafe, A., Budzik, R.F., Bhuva, P., et al., 2018. Thrombectomy 6 to 24 hours after stroke with a mismatch between deficit and infarct. The New England Journal of Medicine 378, 11–21.

Olivot, J.M., Mlynash, M., Inoue, M., Marks, M.P., Wheeler, H.M., Kemp, S., et al., 2014. Hypoperfusion intensity ratio predicts infarct progression and functional outcome in the DEFUSE 2 cohort. Stroke 45, 1018–1023.

Pollock, J.M., Deibler, A.R., Whitlow, C.T., Tan, H., Kraft, R.A., Burdette, J.H., et al., 2009. Hypercapnia-induced cerebral hyperperfusion: an underrecognized clinical entity. American Journal of Neuroradiology 30, 378–385.

Purushotham, A., Campbell, B.C., Straka, M., Mlynash, M., Olivot, J.M., Bammer, R., et al., 2015. Apparent diffusion coefficient threshold for delineation of ischemic core. International Journal of Stroke 10, 348–353.

Seeger, A., Braun, C., Skardelly, M., Paulsen, F., Schittenhelm, J., Ernemann, U., et al., 2013. Comparison of three different MR perfusion techniques and MR spectroscopy for multiparametric assessment in distinguishing recurrent high-grade gliomas from stable disease. Academic Radiology 20, 1557–1565.

Song, J., Xue, Y.Q., Zhao, M.M., Xu, P., 2018. Effectiveness of lomustine and bevacizumab in progressive glioblastoma: a meta-analysis. OncoTargets and Therapy 11, 3435–3439.

Stupp, R., Mason, W.P., van den Bent, M.J., Weller, M., Fisher, B., Taphoorn, M.J., et al., 2005. Radiotherapy plus concomitant and adjuvant temozolomide for glioblastoma. The New England Journal of Medicine 352, 987–996.

Suh, C.H., Kim, H.S., Jung, S.C., Choi, C.G., Kim, S.J., 2018. Multiparametric MRI as a potential surrogate endpoint for decision-making in early treatment response following concurrent chemoradiotherapy in patients with newly diagnosed glioblastoma: a systematic review and meta-analysis. European Radiology 28, 2628–2638.

Tan, W., Xiong, J., Huang, W., Wu, J., Zhan, S., Geng, D., 2017. Noninvasively detecting isocitrate dehydrogenase 1 gene status in astrocytoma by dynamic susceptibility contrast MRI. Journal of Magnetic Resonance Imaging 45, 492–499.

Toh, C.H., Wei, K.C., Chang, C.N., Ng, S.H., Wong, H.F., 2013. Differentiation of primary central nervous system lymphomas and glioblastomas: comparisons of diagnostic performance of dynamic susceptibility contrast-enhanced perfusion MR imaging without and with contrast-leakage correction. American Journal of Neuroradiology 34, 1145–1149.

van Dijken, B.R.J., van Laar, P.J., Holtman, G.A., van der Hoorn, A., 2017. Diagnostic accuracy of magnetic resonance imaging techniques for treatment response evaluation in patients with high-grade glioma, a systematic review and meta-analysis. European Radiology 27, 4129–4144.

Yan, L.F., Sun, Y.Z., Zhao, S.S., Hu, Y.C., Han, Y., Li, G., et al., 2019. Perfusion, diffusion, or brain tumor barrier integrity: which represents the glioma features best? Cancer Management and Research 11, 9989–10000.

228 Chapter 14 Perfusion MRI: clinical perspectives

Zerna, C., Hegedus, J., Hill, M.D., 2016. Evolving treatments for acute ischemic stroke. Circulation Research 118, 1425–1442.

Zhao, J., Yang, Z.Y., Luo, B.N., Yang, J.Y., Chu, J.P., 2015. Quantitative evaluation of diffusion and dynamic contrast-enhanced MR in tumor parenchyma and peritumoral area for distinction of brain tumors. PLoS ONE 10, e0138573.

PART

Functional MRI

5

CHAPTER

Functional MRI principles and acquisition strategies

15

Martina F. Callaghan[a] and Nadège Corbin[a,b]

[a]*Wellcome Centre for Human Neuroimaging, UCL Queen Square Institute of Neurology, UCL, London, United Kingdom*
[b]*Centre de Résonance Magnétique des Systèmes Biologiques, UMR5536, CNRS/University Bordeaux, Bordeaux, France*

15.1 Introduction

Functional MRI (fMRI) offers a non-invasive window into the workings of the human brain in health and disease. fMRI is an indirect measure, and therefore relies on the impact that cerebrovascular and metabolic responses, which occur in concert with neural activity, have on magnetic relaxation properties in the brain. With carefully designed experiments, data sensitive to these alterations can be acquired and used to identify which brain regions, or even which discrete computational units, such as cortical layers, columns or stripes, are involved in eliciting particular human behaviors, as well as to probe their temporal dynamics.

Relative to other imaging modalities, MRI offers comparatively high spatial resolution, potentially reaching sub-millimeter dimensions in each spatial direction. Although equivalent to less than a microliter, such a voxel will still contain approximately 100,000 neurons (Logothetis, 2008). The temporal resolution of MRI is somewhat limited, and typically comes at the cost of spatial coverage and/or resolution. As a result, fMRI relies on rapid imaging techniques, most notably the echo-planar imaging (EPI) scheme, which is the predominant means of acquiring fMRI data today. However, this speed comes at the cost of increased sensitivity to hardware imperfections, as well as participant-driven field perturbations and signal variance that can obscure the neuronally-driven signal changes of interest. The resultant loss, or mis-localization, of the MRI signal reduces the sensitivity and specificity of fMRI unless mitigation strategies are adopted.

MRI is generally a very flexible imaging modality, which can be exploited in fMRI to sensitize the acquisition to different aspects of the tissue microstructure by varying the acquisition scheme. For example, gradient-echo EPI offers high sensitivity to alterations in venous blood and extra-vascular tissue, whereas greater specificity to microvasculature can be obtained using spin-echo EPI. A more quantitative approach is to probe alterations in cerebral blood flow (CBF) or volume (CBV) via arterial spin labeling (ASL), or using vascular space occupancy (VASO) techniques, respectively. The appeal of increased spatial specificity has led to the VASO technique being increasingly used at ultra-high magnetic field strengths ($\geq$ 7T), which can compensate for VASO's reduced sensitivity.

232 **Chapter 15** Functional MRI principles and acquisition strategies

15.2 The effect of neural activity on MR properties
15.2.1 Cerebrovascular response to neural activity

Glucose and oxygen consumption, the latter described by the cerebral metabolic rate of oxygen, $CMRO_2$, are both increased by neural activity, which triggers a vasoactive signal that ultimately results in a disproportionately large increase in CBF, which in turn causes vessels to dilate, increasing CBV. The amount of oxygen bound to hemoglobin, i.e., oxyhemoglobin, which is transported to the active brain cells via the arterial branch of the cerebrovascular system, increases as a result of these effects. Metabolic exchange occurs within the capillary bed and the deoxygenated hemoglobin, i.e., deoxyhemoglobin, exits via the venous branch. Consequent to neural activity, the oxygen delivery exceeds demand, leading to a net increase in oxyhemoglobin in the capillaries and veins. These dynamic effects and their impact on the MRI signal are often described by the balloon model (Buxton et al., 1998), which aims to describe the physiological and biomechanical response of the venous "balloon", though capturing the full complexity of these relationships is challenging (Buxton, 2012; Logothetis, 2008).

15.2.2 Impact on relaxation properties

Magnetic susceptibility is a fundamental property of all matter, dictating the degree to which it is magnetized by an externally applied magnetic field. The magnetic susceptibilities of oxy- and deoxy-hemoglobin differ. Oxyhemoglobin is diamagnetic, more akin to tissue, whereas deoxyhemoglobin has a larger, paramagnetic susceptibility. Changes in the balance between oxy- and deoxy-hemoglobin in the vasculature of the brain lead to spatially and temporally varying magnetic susceptibility distributions, and therefore magnetic field gradients, which alter the detectable MRI signal. This phenomenon is termed the blood-oxygenation-level-dependent (BOLD) signal and underpins fMRI.

Extravascularly, the field induced by a vessel, of radius r, decreases quadratically with distance from the vessel, d, according to $(r/d)^2$ (Fig. 15.1). In MRI, images are created by manipulating the magnetization of endogenous water (specifically the constituent protons) within the body. Any component of the magnetization that is orthogonal to the main magnetic field will experience a rotational force, causing it to rotate, or precess, with a frequency dictated by the instantaneous magnetic field. The phase accrued will depend on the history of the magnetic field that was experienced over the timescale of the measurement. The water molecules giving rise to the MRI signal are not stationary. They undergo random motion governed by a diffusion process. Although motion can occur preferentially in certain directions depending on the tissue's microstructure, for simplicity we can consider a characteristic length scale, L, for a three-dimensional diffusion process to be $\sqrt{(6.D.\tau)} \approx 10\text{--}20$ µm (Ogawa et al., 1993). Here D is the diffusion coefficient of water in tissue measured in $m^2\,s^{-1}$, and τ is the relevant timescale for the measurement. The net signal from any given volume, e.g., all or part of a voxel, is proportional to the vector sum of the constituent magnetization and will have an amplitude and phase (respectively denoted by the length and orientation of the arrows in Fig. 15.1). Given that it is a vector sum, phase dispersion across these constituents reduces the net signal.

First let us consider the effects over the characteristic diffusion length scale. This will depend on the proximity of the water molecules to vessels and on the size of the vessels. If the field is highly inhomogeneous, as is the case close to vessels, and more particularly close to small vessels, extensive phase dispersion occurs as a result of dynamic averaging of the experienced magnetic fields. The greater

15.2 The effect of neural activity on MR properties

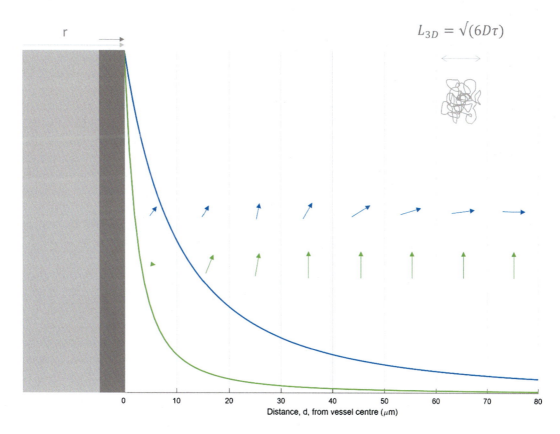

FIGURE 15.1

Two vessels with radius, r, of 5 and 20 μm are depicted in gray. The susceptibility difference between a vessel and the surrounding tissue leads to a spatially varying extra-vascular magnetic field that decreases quadratically with distance, d, from the vessel (green and blue curves for the small and large radius vessels, respectively.) The field around large vessels retains an appreciable amplitude over a much greater spatial extent. The variation of the induced magnetic field over the typical diffusion length scale (depicted by the vertical lines) dictates the balance between dynamic and static dephasing. This characteristic length depends on the diffusion coefficient, D, and on the time, τ, during which diffusion can occur, e.g., the echo time (TE). The net effect of constituent magnetization sampling the environment over such length scales, as a function of distance from the vessel, is denoted for both the small (green arrows) and large (blue arrows) vessels. Irreversible dynamic averaging reduces the amplitude of the signal (length of arrows), increasing R_2, whereas reversible static dephasing leads to a distinct, but coherent, phase accrual per length-scale interval (orientation of arrows) thereby increasing R_2'. In the vicinity of small vessels dynamic (R_2) dephasing dominates, whereas static (R_2') dephasing dominates in the vicinity of large vessels. The MRI signal is measured over the much larger length scale of a voxel. Gradient-echo imaging is sensitive to the combined effects of static and dynamic dephasing, whereas spin-echo imaging can refocus the static dephasing component, and therefore has greater sensitivity to microvasculature.

234 **Chapter 15** Functional MRI principles and acquisition strategies

the distance from small vessels, the less impact they have because they will no longer perturb the field. The extra-vascular field gradients induced by larger vessels will extend further in space, but may be comparatively homogeneous over the diffusion length scale. In this case, the phase dispersion of the constituent magnetization will be relatively small, leading to a lesser reduction in amplitude, but a variable net phase over space. This is referred to as static dephasing. These scenarios are depicted by the arrows in Fig. 15.1 for a small (green) and a large (blue) vessel.

Now let us consider the net signal over the length scale of an entire voxel, typically two orders of magnitude larger than the diffusion length scale. This is akin to summing over many diffusion length scales such that the phase accrued over each of these sub-scales can lead to a signal loss over the spatial scale of the voxel. The net signal, which is measured at the echo-time, TE, will depend on the acquisition scheme. A gradient-echo acquisition is sensitive to both dynamic and static dephasing effects, whereas a spin-echo acquisition utilizes a 180° refocusing RF pulse at time TE/2 to invert the phase of the magnetization. In the period TE/2 to TE, the same phase is accrued due to static dephasing, leading to its refocusing. Since phase dispersion, due to dynamic averaging, is the result of a random diffusion process, it is time-irreversible and still contributes to a reduction in the spin-echo signal. As a result, gradient-echo acquisitions are sensitive to vessels of all sizes, whereas spin-echo acquisitions are particularly sensitive to the microvasculature. For this reason, spin-echo acquisitions are sometimes favored to increase spatial specificity. However, this is at the cost of a lower effect size relative to a gradient-echo acquisition.

Increasing the echo time, TE, at which the signal is sampled, will increase the characteristic length scale and the degree of phase dispersion, leading to an ever greater attenuation of the signal, regardless of acquisition scheme. For a spin-echo, the rate of signal loss is described by the transverse relaxation rate, $R_2 = 1/T_2$. The gradient-echo signal decays more rapidly, according to the effective transverse relaxation rate, $R_2^* = 1/T_2^* = R_2 + R_2'$, where R_2' is the rate of signal decay due to static dephasing.

Intravascularly, a magnetic field offset will be induced, which depends on the balance between oxy- and deoxy-hemoglobin, and on factors such as the orientation of the vessel with respect to the main magnetic field. However, within the vessels, water exchanges rapidly between intracellular and plasma environments, leading to time-irreversible dynamic averaging of the environment-specific magnetic fields that are experienced. This leads to phase dispersion and a shorter T_2. Both intravascular and extravascular sources contribute to the fMRI signal by an amount determined by their volume fractions and T_2 times. The weighting from the extra-vascular compartment increasingly dominates at higher field strengths because of further intravascular T_2 shortening (Uludağ et al., 2009).

The greater spatial extent of field inhomogeneities induced by larger vessels also leads to the "draining vein effect", whereby the signal change induced by activation is biased towards larger vessels, which may be more spatially separated from the location of true neural activity. This is particularly problematic for laminar fMRI, which seeks to distinguish effects over very short spatial scales. The site of activity is biased towards the pial surface, where larger vessels exist (Turner, 2002). Explicit modeling, careful paradigm design, and additional pre-processing are typically used to mitigate or minimize this confound. It is less problematic at more typical spatial resolutions due to dilution with unperturbed blood as the distance from activity increases. Choosing a TE that is long compared to the $T_2^{(*)}$ of the intravascular compartment can serve to minimize one source of this effect. However, a longer TE additionally leads to a reduction in signal-to-noise ratio (SNR).

15.3 Imaging the consequences of neural activity
15.3.1 Imaging altered relaxation properties

Now we examine how the MRI signal changes as a result of alterations in the rate of transverse relaxation. The baseline signal, S_b, decays exponentially according to the (effective) transverse relaxation rate $R_2^{(*)}$ and is given by

$$S_b = S_o e^{-\text{TE}.R_2^{(*)}}.$$

The coherence of the signal is typically increased upon activation due to the larger contribution of diamagnetic oxyhemoglobin, in which case the magnetic field inhomogeneity and $R_2^{(*)}$ are decreased. In general, if the rate of decay of the transverse magnetization is altered by an amount $\Delta R_2^{(*)}$ as a consequence of neural activity in a fraction of the voxel volume, v, the altered signal upon activation, S_{act}, can be written as

$$S_{\text{act}} = v S_o e^{-\text{TE}.(R_2^{(*)} - \Delta R_2^{(*)})} + (1 - v) S_b.$$

The signal change is given by the difference between these two conditions:

$$\Delta S = S_{\text{act}} - S_b = v S_o e^{-\text{TE}.(R_2^{(*)} - \Delta R_2^{(*)})} - v S_b = v S_b \left(e^{\text{TE}.\Delta R_2^{(*)}} - 1 \right).$$

We see that the signal change depends on the amount by which the rate of signal decay is altered and on the volume fraction in which the change occurs. The voxel fractions and relaxation changes can be further broken down into intra- and extra-vascular contributions, as detailed thoroughly elsewhere (e.g., Buxton et al., 1998; Stephan et al., 2007). Given that susceptibility effects increase with field strength, altering the balance between different compartments, the choice of field strength and imaging technique differentially sensitizes the measurement to small vessels (e.g., spin-echo imaging via ΔR_2), all vessels (e.g., gradient-echo imaging via ΔR_2^*), or the change in fractional volume (e.g., vascular space occupancy, VASO, imaging via v) (Huber et al., 2017).

Regardless of imaging technique, it is of crucial importance that there be sufficient contrast relative to noise to robustly detect the consequences of neural activity. For example, in a gradient-echo acquisition, the sensitivity of the baseline signal to small perturbations in R_2^*, i.e., to ΔR_2^*, can be written as

$$\frac{dS_b}{dR_2^*} = -\text{TE} S_b.$$

Our aim is to choose an imaging parameter, in this case a TE, which maximizes sensitivity to these perturbations:

$$\frac{d^2 S_b}{d\text{TE}\, dR_2^*} = -S_b + \text{TE}.R_2^* S_b = S_b \left(\text{TE}.R_2^* - 1 \right) = 0.$$

This occurs when TE is equal to T_2^* (i.e., $1/R_2^*$) for gradient-echo imaging. Similarly, TE = T_2 is optimal for spin-echo imaging, and an inversion or inflow time, TI, that is chosen to null blood is optimal for measuring CBV via VASO (Lu et al., 2013).

Though we aim to maximize our sensitivity to the signal perturbation of interest, it is also crucial that any other source of signal fluctuation, or noise, is minimized. Noise sources include random (white) thermal noise, system instabilities, and patient motion at the bulk or physiological (cardiac pulsation/breathing) level (Liu, 2016). Although thermal noise is spatially uncorrelated and independent of signal, participant- or system-driven fluctuations may be correlated in space and/or time and depend on the signal amplitude. It is crucial for detection that the small functionally-driven fluctuations exceed these spurious fluctuations. A common assessment metric of a data acquisition scheme is therefore the temporal signal-to-noise ratio (tSNR). This is defined as the mean signal over time divided by its temporal standard deviation. If spurious signal fluctuations dominate, then the increase in tSNR and functional sensitivity that can be achieved by increasing image SNR will decrease (Fig. 15.2, Triantafyllou et al., 2005; Krüger and Glover, 2001). Another important source of variability arises from the inter-individual variability in key factors, such as the physiology or attention of the study's participants (Kirilina et al., 2015).

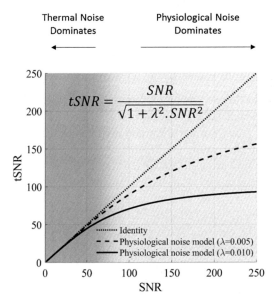

FIGURE 15.2

Ideally, increases in SNR will lead to concurrent increases in tSNR (identity line). However, the variance of physiological sources of signal fluctuation are proportional to the signal intensity and limit the gains that can be made by increasing image SNR. This behavior is characterized by the parameter λ such that the ultimate tSNR that can be achieved is $1/\lambda$. For example, λ is larger for 3D than for 2D acquisitions because of the larger number of k-space points that must retain phase coherence to form an image volume (via 3D iDFT). When $(\lambda.SNR)^2 \gg 1$, physiological noise dominates, whereas when $(\lambda.SNR)^2 \ll 1$ thermal noise dominates.

15.3.2 Key aspects of image formation

To be used as a functional brain mapping technique, the signal reflecting neuronal activity must be localized within the brain. We can denote this signal, $S(r)$, to capture its dependence on spatial location, r, within 3D space. MRI relies on detecting the precession of magnetization about the main magnetic field, B_0. Detectable precession occurs when the magnetization is orthogonal to B_0, i.e., in the transverse plane. In equilibrium conditions, the magnetization is aligned with the main magnetic field, termed longitudinal magnetization. Transverse magnetization orthogonal to the B_0 field is generated by the transient application of a magnetic field rotating in the transverse plane at the resonance frequency of the B_0 field in a process referred to as "excitation". The flip angle of the excitation denotes the degree of rotation of the longitudinal magnetization away from alignment with B_0 and into the transverse plane. Subsequently, the signal undergoes a characteristic decay caused by the loss of phase coherence that results from the distinct intra-voxel microenvironments, as described in the section on "Impact on relaxation properties" above.

The signal is spatially localized by making the precessional frequency spatially specific in a well-defined manner by applying magnetic field gradients in each spatial direction x, y, z, to modulate the B_0 field. A gradient, G_r, applied along arbitrary spatial direction $\vec{r}$ in 3D space, causes the precessional frequency, $\omega(r)$, and therefore the phase accumulated, $\varphi(r)$, to be spatially-dependent:

$$\omega(r, t) = \gamma G_r(t).r \rightarrow \varphi(r) = \gamma \int G_r(t).rdt.$$

We can write this more succinctly by introducing the variable k_r such that

$$k_r = \gamma \int G_r(t) dt \rightarrow \varphi(k_r, r) = k_r.r.$$

By varying the amplitude and/or duration of G_r, which is equivalent to varying k_r, differential phase distributions in space can be generated. Data, $s(k_r)$, are acquired from the entirety of space for each value of k_r to fill "k-space":

$$s(k_r) = \int S(r) e^{ik_r.r} dr.$$

These k-space data represent the Fourier transform of the spatial distribution of the signal of interest, $S(r)$, which can therefore be recovered by inverse discrete Fourier transform (iDFT):

$$S(r) = \sum_{k_r} s(k_r) e^{-ik_r.r}.$$

What is important to note here is that deviations from our expected k_r values, which can result from hardware imperfections or endogenous gradients caused by varying susceptibilities throughout the brain, lead to errors in our image encoding that manifest as artifacts in the reconstructed image, most notably ghosting and distortion.

Like any Fourier representation, important determinants of the reconstructed image are the extent $(\pm k_r^{max})$ and separation (Δk) of the Fourier terms. These dictate the resolution and spatial coverage (field of view, FoV) of the image, respectively. Multiple k-space points can be acquired under the application of a single gradient by repeatedly sampling the signal at regular time intervals. However,

238 **Chapter 15** Functional MRI principles and acquisition strategies

the application of a gradient will only spatially resolve the signal in that direction. Therefore additional gradients are required to move to separate k-space locations in orthogonal directions to be able to fully reconstruct the image in two or three spatial dimensions. Whereas all k-space encoding schemes rely on varying the integral of a gradient in a particular direction over time, sampling repeatedly under a continuous gradient is termed frequency-encoding, whereas moving to separate locations through repeated application of gradients is termed phase-encoding (Fig. 15.3a).

An alternative encoding scheme that can be used in one direction is slice-selection. In this case, a detectable transverse magnetization component is generated only for a certain spatial extent, termed a "slice" (Fig. 15.3). This is done by ensuring the resonance condition is only satisfied for these spatial locations through concurrent application of a gradient in this direction while the transient RF magnetic field is applied with a narrow bandwidth. In this case, an image volume is reconstructed, not by a 3D iDFT, but by slice-wise application of a 2D iDFT.

Regardless of adopting a 3D or slice-selective approach, the need to repeatedly excite the MRI signal to sample multiple unique k-space locations in multiple dimensions leads to a trade-off between image resolution, spatial coverage, and acquisition time, which for fMRI determines the temporal resolution.

15.3.3 Echo planar imaging (EPI)

Whereas the temporal dynamics of neural activity occur rapidly over periods of milliseconds, changes in blood flow take place over the course of several seconds, leading to a temporally smooth and extended hemodynamic response function (HRF) (Siero et al., 2013). Signal sampling needs to be sufficiently rapid to adequately sample this response, while also obtaining images with sufficient spatial resolution and brain coverage. This makes EPI the signal sampling scheme of choice, because it, typically, acquires all necessary k-space locations in two distinct spatial directions following a single excitation (Fig. 15.3b). As before, all k-space points in one direction, denoted k_{FE}, are acquired by continuously sampling the signal while a gradient, G_{FE}, is applied. A gradient is then briefly applied in the orthogonal direction, G_{PE}, before repeating the acquisition of a full line of data points in the first direction, but now using an inverted gradient polarity, $-G_{FE}$. The brief G_{PE} gradient is again applied to move to a new location in this direction before the signal is again sampled under the application of G_{FE}. This procedure is repeated until a sufficient number of k-space points are acquired to fill 2D k-space and reconstruct an image.

Additional means of accelerating data acquisition can be used in conjunction with an EPI readout. Most commonly, these exploit the fact that array coils are used for signal reception. These coils have spatially varying sensitivity that decreases with distance from the individual elements. Since they each receive signal from the same source, a degree of data redundancy is introduced. This redundancy can be exploited to acquire multiple slices concurrently, using a technique referred to as simultaneous multi-slice or multi-band imaging (see Chapter 3), or to sample the signal below the Nyquist rate, which is particularly efficient for 3D acquisitions that have two "slow" phase-encoded directions. Signal aliasing results from these types of acceleration, which has to be resolved as part of the image reconstruction process (see Chapter 2). These acceleration techniques are particularly vulnerable to motion during the acquisition of necessary coil calibration information. Independent of acceleration, the use of such array coils leads to spatially varying functional sensitivity that will be greater in the cortex than in the brainstem, or in deep gray matter structures, and can also be a source of signal variance if the participant moves.

15.3 Imaging the consequences of neural activity

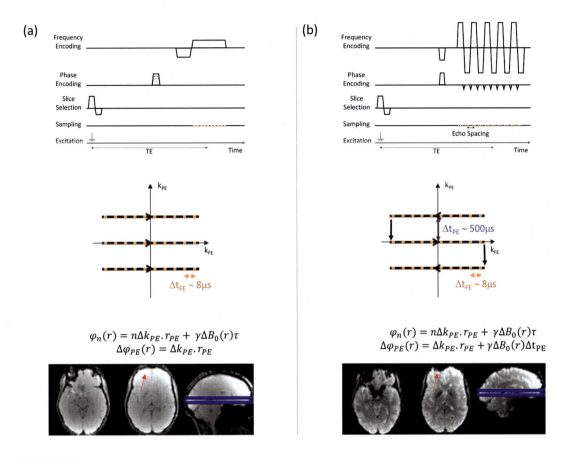

FIGURE 15.3

Sequence diagram (top), k-space traversal (middle), phase accrued and resulting images (bottom). The phase accrued is spatially-specific and dependent on the k-space location (determined by gradient amplitude and duration), field inhomogeneity, $\Delta B_0(r)$, and the time, τ, post excitation. (a) Multi-shot gradient-echo imaging acquires each of N lines of k-space sequentially ($n=1..N$; note that only three lines are shown for simplicity, but many more are typically acquired.) Since each phase-encoded (PE) line is acquired at the same time post excitation, only the k-space encoding term remains in the phase difference, $\Delta\varphi_{PE}$, between lines. This results in faithful image reconstruction. (b) In single-shot EPI all PE lines are acquired after a single excitation. However, the sampling interval is two orders of magnitude longer, e.g., 500 µs, in the slow PE direction. This leads to an appreciable effect as a result of field inhomogeneity remaining in the phase difference. This additional phase leads to spatially variable mis-localization of the signal in the image, cf. the inferior frontal cortex in the vicinity of field inhomogeneity caused by the sinuses (red arrows). In both cases, the sampling interval is very short in the rapid frequency-encoded (FE) k-space traversal direction, e.g., 8 µs, leading to a negligible impact on the phase difference between points in this direction.

The speed of EPI does not come without cost. It is demanding on gradient performance and highly sensitive to deviations from the ideal imaging conditions, which result from both hardware imperfec-

240 **Chapter 15** Functional MRI principles and acquisition strategies

tions and the insertion of the participant into the scanner, which most notably degrades the homogeneity of the main static magnetic field.

15.3.3.1 EPI artifacts

Susceptibility-induced image distortion & signal dropout

A particular difficulty for the EPI technique arises from endogenous magnetic field gradients caused by air cavities, which are particularly problematic when imaging the inferior frontal cortex and temporal lobes. As previously described in the context of blood vessels, spatially-varying susceptibility, and therefore magnetic fields, lead to more rapid signal decay. The variation induced by air cavities is of much greater amplitude and can lead to gross signal loss (Fig. 15.3b). Since the integral of the gradient over time is now spatially-specific, the effective k-space locations are also variable. This leads to *locally* distorted signal encoding, and therefore mis-localization of its origin upon iDFT to the image domain (Figs. 15.3 and 15.4C, D).

The degree of spatial mis-localization can be quantified. Consider the case where either the duration or strength of the applied image encoding gradient is altered between k-space locations to achieve an expected interval of Δk_r, dictating the target FoV in that direction. The differential phase between these points, in the presence of magnetic field inhomogeneity, $\Delta B_0(r)$, will be given by

$$\Delta \varphi_{PE}(r) = \Delta k_r . r + \gamma \Delta B_0(r) \Delta t_{PE},$$

where Δt_{PE} is the time interval between sample points in the phase-encoded direction. The first term imparts the desired image encoding, whereas the second term, which is not accounted for in the reconstruction (via iDFT), leads to an undesired mis-localization of signal in the image. The k-space interval, Δk_r, imparts 2π phase over the FoV. In this case, the spatial mis-localization relative to a FoV of N voxels, can be quantified by the voxel displacement, Δr_{VD}, measured in voxels:

$$\Delta r_{VD}(r) = \frac{\gamma \Delta B_0(r) \Delta t_{PE}}{2\pi} N.$$

In the direction of rapid sampling (the so-called frequency-encoded direction), Δt_{FE} is so small that the accumulated phase due to field inhomogeneity is negligible. However, the longer interval between samples in the slow phase-encoded direction leads to an appreciable effect (see timings in Fig. 15.3). The effect can be decreased by reducing this time interval, often referred to as the echo spacing. However, this is demanding on the gradients and also reduces SNR. Alternatively, the matrix size, N, can be reduced, e.g., through the use of parallel imaging techniques discussed above. However, this requires knowledge of the receiver coil sensitivities, and a more intricate image reconstruction scheme, with increased vulnerability to motion, and leads to an inherent loss of SNR due to the reduced number of data points acquired.

With 2D imaging approaches, geometric distortions can be partially compensated for by acquiring the EPI plane with an angulation that partitions the spurious, endogenous gradients across different spatial dimensions. So-called z-shim gradients can additionally be applied to compensate for the endogenous susceptibility-induced gradients. This is most commonly done in the through-slice direction. A toolbox to aid robust acquisition design at the group level, which can be used with the popular functional neuroimaging analysis software Statistical Parametric Mapping (SPM, https://www.fil.ion.ucl.ac.uk/spm/), is described in (Volz et al., 2019) and available for download from https://github.com/boast-group/BOAST.

Various post-processing schemes can be used to, at least partially, correct distortions if the field inhomogeneity that led to the voxel displacement is known. Recall that the net phase of the gradient-echo signal serves to characterize the macroscopic frequency offset, or effective local field strength. A separate multi-echo gradient-echo calibration scan can therefore be used to spatially map the magnetic field inhomogeneity at the spatial scale of a voxel. The B_0 field can also be deduced from the acquisition of data with inverted phase encoding gradient polarity, commonly referred to as "blip-up, blip-down".

The increased field inhomogeneity, owing to complex susceptibility distributions, will also incur signal loss in gradient-echo images, often referred to as "dropout". This effect can be mitigated by reducing the characteristic diffusion length, L_{3D}, of the acquisition by shortening the relevant measurement time, i.e., the echo time, TE. However, optimizing the TE for a location with greater susceptibility-induced inhomogeneity will come at a cost of reduced BOLD sensitivity elsewhere (recall that the optimal TE is equal to the T_2^* of the tissue). Acquiring the data at higher spatial resolution reduces the degree of intra-voxel phase dispersion since the field becomes comparatively more homogeneous, but the longer readout (higher N) will increase image distortion, unless a segmented approach is adopted.

Phase-based trajectory correction

The EPI technique is demanding on scanner hardware, because it requires rapid switching of comparatively high amplitude gradients. Ramp sampling, whereby data points are acquired before the readout gradient has reached its maximum amplitude (i.e., is still ramping to this amplitude), allows the echo-spacing to be shortened. However, this leads to a non-uniform k-space interval (since $k_r = \gamma \int G_r(t)\,dt$ and $G_r(t)$ is now variable). If not taken into account this will also lead to substantial image artifact (Fig. 15.4A). Since echoes are sampled under both positive and negative gradients, the EPI technique is highly sensitive to even the smallest discrepancies that make $|G_r| \neq |-G_r|$. Any differential modulation of adjacent lines in k-space, arising from these imperfections, for example caused by eddy currents, leads to an $N/2$ Nyquist ghost in the reconstructed image (Fig. 15.4A, B). "Navigator" echoes, which are projections through the imaged region without phase encoding, can be acquired to measure and compensate for k-space trajectory imperfections (Zhang et al., 1998). Often, three such echoes are acquired under alternating gradient polarity. Taking the average of the two navigator echoes acquired with the same gradient polarity provides an equivalent effective TE as the acquisition with opposite gradient polarity (Heid, 1997). Since the phase corresponds to the k-space location, the phase difference between the opposing polarity measures captures the trajectory differences (cf. Fig. 15.4B, C). The navigators can also be used to quantify frequency offsets that occur over time, e.g., due to breathing, from the phase difference between navigators with equivalent polarity scaled by the echo time difference. Although the acquisition of navigators increases the minimum TE, they are often incorporated into the ongoing data acquisition and image reconstruction to improve image quality. Alternatively, pre-scan calibration data can be acquired for trajectory correction.

Spatial specificity

As highlighted previously, the choice of acquisition scheme will play a role in determining the spatial specificity of the signal (Fig. 15.1), as will the field strength by altering the balance between intra- and extra-vascular signal contributions (Uludağ et al., 2009; Ogawa et al., 1993), and any post-processing steps. During the EPI readout, the signal continually decays according to $R_2^{(*)}$. This modulation has a filtering effect that causes spatial blurring. This becomes an increasingly important factor to consider when seeking to obtain data with high resolution, which require long readouts. The impact of such

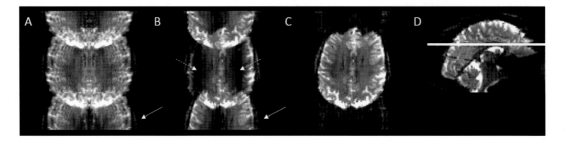

FIGURE 15.4

(A) Reconstructing EPI data with a simple iDFT results in significant artifact. High spatial frequency artifact is visible at the periphery of the brain, because high $|k_{FE}|$ points were sampled with ramp-sampling. (B) Incorporating knowledge of the trapezoidal readout gradient, via a non-uniform FT, removes this artifact. However, Nyquist ($N/2$) ghosts (solid arrows) and interference fringes (dashed arrows) are still visible, because this does not account for differential amplitude or time delays between the positive and negative polarity readout gradients (e.g., eddy currents, gradient or analogue-to-digital onset times). These imperfections affect navigator echoes in an equivalent manner. The navigators can therefore be used to measure and account for the trajectory errors and further improve image quality (C). Distortions and signal dropout caused by endogenous magnetic field gradients remain, e.g., in frontal cortex (D; white line indicates axial slice in A–C). The artifacts are particularly prominent in these images, because these data were acquired at 2 mm resolution using a comparatively long, unaccelerated readout at a field strength of 7T, where susceptibility effects are proportionately higher.

effects can be characterized through the estimation of the imaging point-spread-function (PSF), which provides a measure of the true, as opposed to the nominal, spatial resolution (Chaimow and Shmuel, 2016). Post-processing steps, such as co-registering images, to compensate for participant motion, or correcting for susceptibility-induced voxel displacement, require image interpolation that can introduce further smoothing. This is less problematic for group studies, where dedicated smoothing steps are often employed after spatial normalization to a common group space. Though this serves to improve sensitivity, and account for residual misalignment in group space, it is at the cost of spatial specificity.

Advanced Box: Alternatives to EPI

The main advantage of EPI is its rapidity. Spiral k-space sampling can provide greater flexibility for the choice of TE and TR, given that the center of the k-space can be acquired at the beginning, the end, or the middle of the readout. However, like EPI, spiral imaging is also very sensitive to imperfect magnetic field dynamics that lead to blurring and image distortion.

Approaches less sensitive to spatio-temporal field fluctuations have also been investigated. The phase-encoding gradient of the linear k-space trajectory can be replaced by a spatio-temporal encoding (SPEN) trajectory that requires a frequency-swept excitation pulse, but does not involve a Fourier transform to recover the image (Goerke et al., 2011). The phase-encoding gradients and the size of the FoV are then decoupled, providing flexibility to minimize the sensitivity to spurious magnetic field gradients. However, advanced image reconstruction methods are required to reach acceptable image resolution while maintaining reasonable energy deposition and scan time (Ben-Eliezer et al., 2012).

To maintain temporal resolution in EPI while using a TE of tens of milliseconds, multiple k-space lines must be acquired in one TR, which results in high sensitivity to B_0 inhomogeneity that manifests as distortion and dropout artifacts.

A relatively long TE ($\approx T_2^{(*)}$) is required to achieve sensitivity to variation of the decay rate of the transverse magnetization. One alternative is to encode the functionally-relevant T_2 variability in the longitudinal magnetization by using a T_2 preparation module prior to the volume acquisition (Solana et al., 2016). The TE is no longer constrained, enabling very rapid acquisition schemes (e.g., radial combined with parallel imaging) with short TE and TR to be adopted. Only one line or projection of k-space is acquired per TR, resulting in images that are effectively distortion-free. The sensitivity of this approach is comparable to SE-EPI strategies, but drawbacks are blurring, resulting from T_1 recovery during the readout, and the high k-space undersampling required to maintain a reasonable scan time.

With the same benefit of no longer requiring TE equal to $T_2^{(*)}$, one can instead target the frequency shift induced by the neural activity. As reviewed in Miller (2012), this can be done by taking advantage of the sensitivity to off-resonance frequencies of the balanced steady-state free precession (bSSFP) signal. The TE is no longer constrained, but the TR dictates the sensitivity to the frequency shift, which increases with decreasing TR. This rapid distortion-free approach can provide high functional sensitivity, but is also very sensitive to any physiologically- or hardware-driven fluctuation of the magnetic field, which can result in fluctuating banding artifacts.

15.4 Applications

Since its inception in the early 1990s, fMRI has been used to improve our understanding of functional organization at many spatial scales. With the advent of ultra-high field imaging, these insights are increasingly extending to the mesoscopic scale of discrete computational units, such as layers, columns, and stripes (Ugurbil, 2016). However, the translation of fMRI to the clinical environment has remained limited. This can be attributed to a number of factors, ranging from the complexity of the acquisition, particularly for task-based fMRI, to the sophisticated analyses required, but also stemming from the complexity of interpreting the underlying cause of observed changes because of the indirect consequence of neurovascular responses, which are likely to be altered in patient groups. For more detail see Chapters 17, 18, and 20, as well as Chapters 36 and 37.

15.5 Challenges and future directions

Many aspects of fMRI remain active areas of research. A continuing driver of innovation is the target of characterizing discrete units of neuronal computation to illicit mechanisms underpinning feedforward and feedback information processing and inter-regional message transmission. The demanding spatiotemporal requirements of such investigations necessitate advances in acquisition schemes, sophisticated biophysical modeling, and advanced hardware, such as ultra-high field MRI scanners, bespoke receivers, and parallel transmit technology. On the other hand, the reproducibility of fMRI and its ability to identify meaningful differences at the individual level will dictate the degree of translation into the clinical environment that will be achieved.

Given that fMRI is an indirect measure of neural activity, it is crucial that we continue to progress our understanding of the caveats, the true specificity, and the neural correlates of our acquisitions if we are to appropriately interpret our findings (Logothetis, 2008). As such, the spatiotemporal dynamics of the fMRI signal, the optimum functional contrast, and the most anatomically faithful means of mapping the brain's functional organization remain active areas of research.

244   Chapter 15 Functional MRI principles and acquisition strategies

15.6 Summary

Though it should be borne in mind that fMRI does not provide a direct measure of neural activity, it does provide a means of detecting the consequent effects of the hemodynamic response to such activity with remarkable spatial resolution that is now approaching the intra-cortical level. Rapid imaging is required to capture the temporal dynamics of these effects, but introduces vulnerability to image artifacts. Careful paradigm design and the integration of artifact mitigation strategies maximize functional sensitivity, allowing high resolution *in vivo* mapping of human brain function using fMRI.

References

Ben-Eliezer, N., et al., 2012. Functional MRI using super-resolved spatiotemporal encoding. Magnetic Resonance Imaging 30 (10), 1401–1408.

Buxton, R.B., 2012. Dynamic models of BOLD contrast. NeuroImage 62 (2), 953–961 Available at:. https://doi.org/10.1016/j.neuroimage.2012.01.012.

Buxton, R.B., Wong, E.C., Frank, L.R., 1998. Dynamics of blood flow and oxygenation changes during brain activation: the balloon model. Magnetic Resonance in Medicine 39 (6), 855–864.

Chaimow, D., Shmuel, A., 2016. A more accurate account of the effect of k-space sampling and signal decay on the effective spatial resolution in functional MRI. bioRxiv, 097154.

Goerke, U., Garwood, M., Ugurbil, K., 2011. Functional magnetic resonance imaging using RASER. NeuroImage 54 (1), 350–360.

Heid, O., 1997. Robust EPI phase correction. In: Proceedings of the International Society for Magnetic Resonance in Medicine 1. Vancouver, p. 2014.

Huber, L., et al., 2017. High-resolution CBV-fMRI allows mapping of laminar activity and connectivity of cortical input and output in human M1. Neuron 96 (6). 1253–1263.e7.

Kirilina, E., et al., 2015. The quest for the best: the impact of different EPI sequences on the sensitivity of random effect fMRI group analyses. NeuroImage 126, 49–59 Available at:. http://www.sciencedirect.com/science/article/pii/S105381191500988X.

Krüger, G., Glover, G.H., 2001. Physiological noise in oxygenation-sensitive magnetic resonance imaging. Magnetic Resonance in Medicine 46 (4), 631–637.

Liu, T.T., 2016. Noise contributions to the fMRI signal: an overview. NeuroImage 143, 141–151.

Logothetis, N.K., 2008. What we can do and what we cannot do with fMRI. Nature 453 (7197), 869–878. Available at: http://www.ncbi.nlm.nih.gov/pubmed/18548064. (Accessed 19 July 2012).

Lu, H., Hua, J., van Zijl, P.C.M., 2013. Noninvasive functional imaging of cerebral blood volume with vascular-space-occupancy (VASO) MRI. NMR in Biomedicine 26 (8), 932–948. Available at: http://doi.wiley.com/10.1002/nbm.2905.

Miller, K.L., 2012. FMRI using balanced steady-state free precession (SSFP). NeuroImage 62 (2), 713–719. Available at: https://doi.org/10.1016/j.neuroimage.2011.10.040.

Ogawa, S., et al., 1993. Functional brain mapping by blood oxygenation level-dependent. Biophysical Journal 64 (3), 803–812.

Siero, J.C.W., et al., 2013. BOLD specificity and dynamics evaluated in humans at 7 T: comparing gradient-echo and spin-echo hemodynamic responses. PLoS ONE 8 (1), 1–8.

Solana, A.B., et al., 2016. Quiet and distortion-free, whole brain BOLD fMRI using T2-prepared RUFIS. Magnetic Resonance in Medicine 75 (4), 1402–1412.

Stephan, K.E., et al., 2007. Comparing hemodynamic models with DCM. NeuroImage 38 (3), 387–401. Available at: https://doi.org/10.1016/j.neuroimage.2007.07.040.

Triantafyllou, C., et al., 2005. Comparison of physiological noise at 1.5 T, 3 T and 7 T and optimization of fMRI acquisition parameters. NeuroImage 26 (1), 243–250.

Turner, R., 2002. How much codex can a vein drain? Downstream dilution of activation-related cerebral blood oxygenation changes. NeuroImage 16 (4), 1062–1067.

Ugurbil, K., 2016. What is feasible with imaging human brain function and connectivity using functional magnetic resonance imaging. Philosophical Transactions of the Royal Society of London. Series B, Biological Sciences 371 (1705).

Uludağ, K., Müller-Bierl, B., Uğurbil, K., 2009. An integrative model for neuronal activity-induced signal changes for gradient and spin echo functional imaging. NeuroImage 48 (1), 150–165.

Volz, S., et al., 2019. Maximising BOLD sensitivity through automated EPI protocol optimisation. NeuroImage 189, 159–170.

Zhang, Y., et al., 1998. A novel k-space trajectory measurement technique. Magnetic Resonance in Medicine 39 (6), 999–1004.

Further reading

Bernstein, Matt A., King, Kevin F., Zhou, Xiahong J. (Eds.), 2004. Handbook of MRI Pulse Sequences. This is a key text for implementing data acquisition schemes. It provides the underlying mathematical principles and the practical implementation considerations.

Schmitt, Franz, Stehling, Michael K., Turner, Robert, 1998. Echo-Planar Imaging. This book specifically focuses on the EPI acquisition technique, covering hardware requirements, technical challenges, and mitigation strategies. It is particularly insightful for revealing the perspective of early developments overcoming hardware limitations.

Frackowiak, Richard S.J. (Ed.), 2004. Human Brain Function. This book provides a comprehensive guide to the understanding, analysis, and interpretation of functional brain mapping.

CHAPTER

Functional MRI analysis

16

Wei Zhang and Janine Bijsterbosch

Department of Radiology, Washington University School of Medicine, Washington University in St. Louis, St. Louis, MO, United States

16.1 Types of fMRI

There are two conventional types of functional MRI: task-based and resting-state fMRI. The latter is sometimes also referred to as task-free fMRI.

Task-based fMRI (tfMRI) studies focus on conditions or events of interest that researchers use to probe localized brain activation or connectivity. The fMRI recordings are continuous and indirect measures of neuronal activity (Logothetis, 2008). The absolute value of the BOLD signal is therefore meaningless. Instead, differences in the BOLD signal between two or more conditions are utilized to infer meaningful neural correlates or substrates that are associated with the task. Such contrasts (i.e., comparisons between two or more conditions) can also help reduce noise arising from non-specific sources, since random noise will partly cancel when subtracting two conditions. A simple example of a tfMRI study would be to investigate the brain activation associated with face image representations. To identify which regions of the brain are active when we view a face, a contrast between the condition of interest (e.g., trials presenting face images) and a control condition (e.g., trials or intervals without presenting any stimuli) can be compared. See also Chapter 5.

The two most commonly used experimental paradigms for tfMRI studies are block design and event-related design. Block designs consist of "on" and "off" periods, where the "on" block represents a period of stimulus presentations (e.g., 30-second presentation of face images) and the "off" block refers to the baseline (e.g., 10-second intervals in the absence of face image presentation). As a comparison, event-related designs separate the experiment into discrete events, which allow for independent investigation of brain processes associated with event types. Importantly, both block and event-related designs require randomization (e.g., of block or trial order) to ensure proper signal detection (see Chapter 15 for more details about efficient fMRI study design). Fig. 16.1 shows examples of block designs and event-related designs, and their associated design matrices (see later for details of design matrices).

In contrast to tfMRI studies, resting-state fMRI (rsfMRI) studies do not impose explicit task demands (i.e., not requiring behavioral or cognitive engagement) and are conducted to study spontaneous brain activity in the fMRI BOLD signal. During the acquisition, participants are usually instructed to relax and stay awake with their eyes open or closed. For eyes open settings, a fixation cross or naturalistic viewing (e.g., movie) can be used to prevent drowsiness and minimize potential head motion caused by drowsiness. Unlike tfMRI, rsfMRI studies do not focus on contrasts, as there are no specific stimuli or events of interest. Instead, measures indicating spontaneous brain activity are investigated, among which, functional connectivity (i.e., temporal correlation between the BOLD signals measured

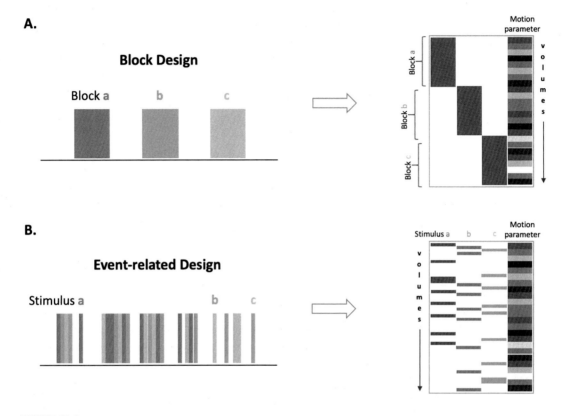

FIGURE 16.1

A sketch of block and event-related designs in task-evoked fMRI. A block design consists of several discrete epochs or blocks of "on-off" periods, with "on" blocks representing continuous stimulus presentation (e.g., Block a, b, and c) and "off" blocks representing the state of rest or baseline (e.g., flat lines between blocks (A). An event-related design separates stimuli presentation into discrete trials or events in a randomized sequence (B). Whereas the block design allows for measurement of a task block-related total neural activity (i.e., activity magnitude), the event-related design enables modeling of transient responses to different trials or event types. Design matrices for these two task designs are shown on the right side indicating that both contain regressors for block a–c or stimuli a–c, and a covariate of motion parameter.

from different brain regions) is the most commonly studied one. As such, research questions of tfMRI studies are largely focused on the task-related brain activity or connectivity, whereas rsfMRI studies investigate more general system-level patterns of connectivity among brain regions.

16.2 Preprocessing

The BOLD signal measured by the MRI scanner captures an indirect measure of neuronal activity that is mediated by metabolic and vascular processes. It is known to be sensitive to motion-related artifacts and

16.2 Preprocessing **249**

physiological noise, and instability of the equipment resulting from random processes, such as thermal fluctuations or hardware instabilities. De-noising fMRI data is therefore essential to not only increase data quality, but also to help promote reproducibility and reliability of research. Below we briefly introduce several typical preprocessing steps. The exact order and steps included in a preprocessing pipeline may vary depending on the data type, acquisition protocols, and research questions. To ensure high data quality, researchers are encouraged to perform visual inspection on the output images from each individual preprocessing step. Example measures for data quality control can be found below.

16.2.1 Slice timing correction

Echo-planar-imaging (EPI) is the most commonly employed fMRI acquisition sequence in the field. It typically acquires the brain images once every repetition time (TR) by sequentially exciting and reading out signals (i.e., frequency and phase encoding) from individual slices (see Chapter 15). As the statistical analyses are mainly about the time-course of the BOLD signal, slice timing correction is crucial for task and resting-state fMRI acquired with a long TR (>1 sec) to align the timing of BOLD signals across the brain. For example, if the TR was set to 2 seconds for acquiring 50 slices, the acquisition time of each individual slice will be 2000 ms/50=40 ms, sampled at different signal phase. Slice timing correction can compensate for this sampling shift in signal phase by selecting one slice as the reference—usually the middle slice—and aligning the remaining slices temporally by a given amount with regard to the acquisition time of the reference slice. An alternative is to include temporal derivatives in the analysis of tfMRI. These model regressors address slice timing effects, while bypassing temporal interpolation that occurs in the "resampling" stage when using slice timing correction. It is noteworthy that the time difference between slices is greatly reduced in recent fMRI studies using simultaneous multi-slice (multi-band) acquisition sequences (TRs<1 sec, see Chapter 3) such that slice timing correction becomes less necessary, given the slow nature of the hemodynamic response function. However, some new challenges are introduced in such corrections with the non-trivial nature of slice acquisition in simultaneous multi-slice/multi-band protocols (see also a similar problem when using simultaneous multi-slice/multi-band protocols in diffusion MRI, described in Chapter 9).

16.2.2 Motion correction

In the scanner, participants will always move during the acquisition, which causes a mismatch of the location of subsequent images in the time courses. This type of motion artifact can be partly corrected by simple rigid body transformation. Using a reference volume (e.g., usually the first or the middle one), this transformation aligns each individual volume to the reference volume by estimating six realignment parameters with three translations in the X, Y, Z directions and three rotations around the X, Y and Z axes. Motion correction accounts for the spatial mismatch between volumes, but does not correct for secondary effects of motion (e.g., partial volume effects, where the proportion of various brain tissue types in a voxel fluctuates over the period of head movement). To reduce the influence of residual head motion effects, the realignment parameters can be used for further correction at a later stage (i.e., in subject-level statistical analysis). Please see Chapters 4 and 6 for more information on motion correction.

16.2.3 Spatial smoothing

Spatial smoothing is achieved by applying a blurring (e.g., Gaussian) kernel to the data that performs a weighted averaging of intensities across a few adjacent voxels to reduce the noise. The number of voxels being smoothed or blurred is determined by the size of the kernel, defined by the full-width-half-maximum (FWHM) of the Gaussian kernel. Although there is no gold standard amount of smoothing, a rule of thumb is to set the size of the FWHM to be 1.5–2 times the size of the voxel from the raw data. Spatial smoothing can increase the signal-to-noise ratio (SNR) and enhance the validity of statistical assumptions underlying Gaussian random field theory. It can also accommodate between-subject functional and anatomical variations, thus promoting the discovery of commonalities across individuals. It is important to note, however, that spatial smoothing will lead to reduced spatial specificity of the data and may influence some downstream statistical measures due to compromised spatial accuracy.

16.2.4 Distortion correction

Similar to motion correction and spatial smoothing, distortion correction is also applicable to both task and resting-state fMRI data. Geometric distortions arise from inhomogeneities in the magnetic field. These distortions can further interact with head movement, making registration difficult between, e.g., functional images and high-resolution structural images. To account for these undesired effects, various methods that make use of acquired field maps have been developed to map the spatial distribution of field inhomogeneities (as more fully described in Chapter 9). Alternative approaches are also available, including point spread function, reversed gradient and non-linear registration using T_1-weighted images (Zeng and Constable, 2002; Morgan et al., 2004).

16.2.5 Temporal filtering

The aim of temporal filtering is to increase the SNR of the data by filtering out data from frequency bands of no interest. One example is to apply high-pass filtering (i.e., removing frequencies below a cut-off) to capture and remove slow scanner drifts. In contrast, low-pass filtering (i.e., removing frequencies above a cut-off, for example, 0.1 Hz) can be used in rsfMRI to focus on low-frequency fluctuations that are likely of neural origin. However, note that intrinsic brain fluctuations may be broadband in nature and spurious correlations can be introduced due to band-pass filtering. Furthermore, temporal filtering may affect the effective temporal degrees of freedom available in the data, and thus impacts the statistical tests. In general, whereas high-pass filtering is recommended, low-pass filtering is often not considered as an effective denoising step.

16.2.6 Physiological confounds

In addition to aforementioned motion artifacts and geometric distortion, physiology is another major source of confounds in the BOLD signal. The resulting noise usually occurs at the edge of the brainstem and around the major vessels, veins, and ventricles. To control for such effects and reduce brain signal fluctuations related to physiology, cardiac and respiratory response functions can be included as covariates in the fMRI analysis. Caution is required when performing such analyses as typical linear modeling on physiological processing may also remove the true signals that are associated with neural activity of interest (e.g., task-related changes in arousal). Alternatively, physiological noise can be reduced in fMRI studies acquired with a short TR of less than 1 second, and can be eliminated with a TR below roughly 400 milliseconds, because respiratory and heartbeat frequencies are not aliased (i.e., into lower frequencies of interest in the rsfMRI) and can be pinpointed in the frequency spectrum of the signal timecourse.

16.2.7 Further data denoising

In addition to six realignment parameters derived from rigid body transformation, additional parameters can be computed and included in the model (e.g., the temporal derivatives, the squared realignment parameters) as nuisance regressors to further account for motion artifacts. In the case of excessive motion, censoring or scrubbing (i.e., removing volumes where the subject moved by more than a set threshold) can be applied. When using such a strategy, it is very important to report the criteria and threshold used for censoring or scrubbing and the percentage of the timepoints that are affected. Whether the data of identified scans are zeroed, excluded from subsequent analyses, or interpolated with new data, should also be reported.

Alternatively, more advanced models can be employed to better characterize the pattern of motion and/or physiological confounds in the data, and thus reduce their impact optimally. For instance, the component-based noise correction (CompCor) method uses principal component analysis (PCA) to extract the timeseries from a referential noise region-of-interest (ROI), for example by using areas of white matter, ventricles, or large vessels. The assumption is that the fluctuations in the noise ROI are unlikely to be relevant to neural signals, and thus can be used as covariates to account for the noise effects in the BOLD signals from the gray matter. Additionally, data-driven methods based on independent component analysis (ICA) are often used for data denoising. Apart from the careful hand classification of noise components (Griffanti et al., 2017), researchers can also make use of automated removal methods, such as ICA-AROMA (Pruim et al., 2015) and FSL-FIX (Salimi-Khorshidi et al., 2014; Ciric et al., 2017).

16.2.8 Registration and normalization

The final step in the preprocessing pipeline that is required for group-level statistical analysis is registration and normalization. In addition to individual differences in brain size and shape, the positioning of each individual participant in the scanner can vary, and thus leads to further mismatch in the acquired brain data. To minimize these differences and make each individual data set comparable, we need to resample the denoised individual data to a common or standard template through linear and non-linear algorithms. For generic volume-based registration and normalization, individual high-resolution structural (T_1-weighted) images and standard brain templates (e.g., the MNI152 template) are typically used. Depending on the research question and the characteristics of the study sample, the group average map can be produced and used as the template as well. Cortical correspondence across participants can be further improved with surface-based registration, as it addresses the geometrical characteristics of the cerebral cortex as a highly folded sheet (Brodoehl et al., 2020). For surface-based registration, structural T_1- and T_2-weighted scans (of sufficiently fine-grained spatial resolution) can be used to segment the gray-white matter interface and represent the resulting cortical sheet as a triangular tessellated mesh.

Many of the aforementioned steps are included in default preprocessing pipelines for fMRI studies, with variations in the order of implementation and the exact approach taken to serve the purpose. Re-

252   **Chapter 16** Functional MRI analysis

searchers can make use of well-established preprocessing pipeline packages or software (e.g., Fmriprep, HCP workbench, FSL, FreeSurfer, and SPM) to implement image preprocessing and analysis.

16.2.9 Quality control

To ensure proper data quality, researchers are encouraged to check their data in a timely manner (i.e., during/immediately after acquisition). Additionally, visual inspection of the raw data and the preprocessing output images is recommended. Data quality control (QC) measures can be computed for further inspection, among which are temporal signal-to-noise ratio (tSNR) maps and motion-related parameters. In fMRI, tSNR is defined for each voxel as the ratio of mean signal intensity to the standard deviation of signal intensity over time; the latter is a crucial metric to evaluate the fMRI data quality. In general, high tSNR values indicate good data quality, with variations across different brain areas. Head motion-related parameters are also commonly used metrics for quality control. Some examples are root-mean-squared (RMS) motion, relative or absolute displacement, frame-wise displacement and DVARS (the spatial root-mean-square of the data after temporal differencing). More details for data quality control for fMRI can be found in (Lu et al., 2019). Data quality should be considered when designing the study and sequences, for example, by allowing sufficient data points for each condition (in tfMRI) or for the overall acquisition length (in rsfMRI).

16.3 Statistical analysis

16.3.1 Hypothesis vs data-driven analysis

Research questions can be largely considered as hypothesis-driven, data-driven or a hybrid of both. Different approaches and analyses are needed to address different individual research questions. Broadly speaking, hypothesis-driven research questions involve analyses to examine specific effects that are speculated prior to the analyses, whereas data-driven research questions relax such specific speculations and allow relatively free detections of patterns or effects of interest. Given the nature of task-related and resting-state fMRI studies, hypothesis testing is predominantly applied in tfMRI studies, whereas rsfMRI studies can promote the use of more data-driven approaches.

16.3.2 Univariate vs multivariate analysis

From the perspective of variable numbers, statistical analysis for fMRI studies can also be regarded as univariate or multivariate. In the context of fMRI research, voxel-wise analyses are considered as mass univariate, as the same test is repeated in a large number of voxels (mass), with each single voxel being tested individually for the given hypothesis or research question (univariate). This type of analysis is forced to employ very stringent corrections for multiple comparisons (i.e., correcting for all voxels that were tested). In contrast, multivariate approaches consider information from multiple voxels at the same time, which can result in comparably greater statistical power without the need for such corrections (Habeck, 2010; also see Chapter 5). Taking the example of face representations in the brain, a simple mass univariate analysis can be used to test which brain regions or clusters of voxels become activated in the presence of face images. To evaluate whether certain brain regions correlate or co-activate in such a task setting, however, requires a multivariate approach (i.e., testing the covariance pattern of face feature-related brain areas).

16.3.3 Whole-brain vs regional analysis

Depending on research questions and acquisition protocols, analysis may focus on the entire brain or on specific brain structures or regions. Regions-of-interest (ROIs) can be utilized to address the latter question by restricting the search area for examining specific neural effects. In most cases, the selection of ROIs is based on the prior knowledge of researchers about specific brain areas, or on the patterns that emerge from the data. Importantly, such practices should be approached with caution to avoid circularity in analyses (Vul et al., 2009). Regardless of the search area definition, analysis can be conducted at different levels or scales, ranging from individual voxels (in the case of volume-based analysis) or vertices (in the case of surface-based analysis) to summary quantities (e.g., mean coefficients).

16.3.4 Subject-level vs group-level analysis

In fMRI studies, analyses are conducted at two levels: subject and group level. With example research questions below we will introduce these analysis steps in more detail. As tfMRI and rsfMRI address different research questions, and employ different analytical approaches, we will provide separate examples for each modality. In essence, subject-level analysis involves model fitting for the estimation of within-subject effects, and subsequent group-level or second-level analysis requires statistical thresholding to infer about between-subject effects.

16.3.4.1 Task fMRI

o Example research question: Across participants, which brain areas are associated with face or place representations, and which brain areas show stronger activation for face representation in contrast to place representations, or vice versa?
o Experimental task: Presenting face and place images using a block design.
o Subject-level analysis: A general linear model (GLM, see Chapter 5) is used, where each regressor captures one condition (i.e., one regressor for face image blocks and one regressor for place image blocks). The combined set of regressors is known as the design matrix. As the fMRI data are time-series, the regressors in the design matrix specify the timestamps of each event or trial (e.g., the onset time and duration of a face image block relative to the start of the scan). All events or trials should be included as regressors in the design matrix, including events that may be of less interest, such as trials requiring responses to keep participants engaged. In addition to task regressors, regressors of confounds (i.e., head motion, physiological artefacts) can be specified as covariates in the model. The idea is to include as many as possible reasonable regressors in the model that can maximize the explained variance in the data and increase the model fit (see design matrix examples in Figs. 16.1 and 16.2). Once the design matrix is set, the preprocessed individual data can be fed into the model as the input and beta values for each regressor in the model will be estimated. Importantly, as the BOLD signal is a product of the unmeasured neural signal that is convolved with the hemodynamic response function (HRF), the regressors specified in the GLM should be convolved with a canonical HRF before fitting to the timeseries data (i.e., BOLD signal plus noise; see Chapter 5 for more details). Note that each individual data set contains a large number of voxels and the model will be fit separately to the timeseries measured in each voxel, resulting in an image of beta values for each regressor. With the estimated beta weights, contrasts can be made to test, for instance, the difference of beta weights for face presentations versus place presentations. If the research question was to test

brain areas associated with stronger face representation than place representation (face>place), a contrast of [1 -1] can be made for the estimated beta image for face presentation, and that for place presentation, respectively. If the sign was reversed in the contrast (i.e., [-1 1]), then the areas associated with stronger place representation will be tested (place>face). Similarly, the contrast estimation will be performed at the voxel level for each participant, and the resulting contrast images are the linear combination of beta values.

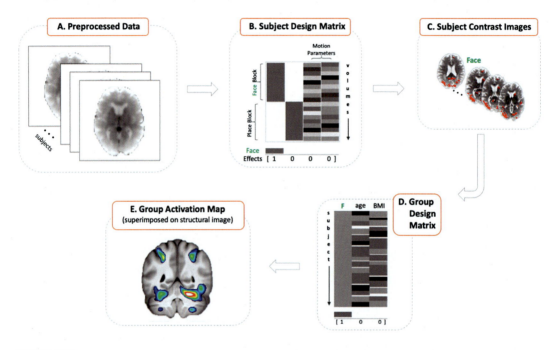

FIGURE 16.2

Overview illustration of data analysis to test brain activations related to face representation in the brain, from a block-design task. The preprocessed data are used as input for this analysis (A). Before fitting the data to a general linear model (GLM), a design matrix containing regressors for blocks of face images (first column) and place images (second column), as well as covariates of motion parameters (third and fourth columns) is generated (B). Subsequently, these regressors will be convolved with a canonical HRF, and beta weights of each regressor (including covariates) will be estimated at the voxel level for each individual participant. Using the estimated beta weights from the model, a contrast of [1 0 0 0] can be specified to estimate face effects at subject level (B). This will result in a contrast image of face effects for each individual participant (C), which can then be used as the input for subsequent group-level analysis. Similarly, a group design matrix is created to test the average face effects across all participants, while accounting for the influences of covariates of no interest, such as age and BMI (D). A simple contrast of [1 0 0] can be used for this test and the resulting group activation map can be superimposed on a high-resolution structural image for visualization (E). Note, only two blocks and few covariates are included in the current illustration for simplicity. In the real task and analysis design, more blocks of trials are needed for sufficient statistical power, and more covariates may be included. Please see Chapter 5 for more information about neuroimaging statistics.

o Group-level analysis: The contrast images estimated from the subject-level analysis are the input for the group-level analysis. Similar to the previous analysis, a GLM and design matrix are specified. At this stage, however, the regressors represent information about the participants rather than the stimulus timing. For example, the simplest group-level analysis is a one-sample t-test on face representation effects in the brain across all participants. In the design matrix for this analysis, a single regressor containing a series of [1] needs to be specified. Alternatively, a between-sample t-test can be used to test the differences across participants from two different groups (e.g., patients vs controls). Here, the first regressor would contain a series of [1]s for patients and a series of [0]s for controls, and the second regressor a series of [1]s for controls and a series of [0]s for patients. The group-level contrast for the two-sample unpaired t-test would be [1 -1] for [patients>controls] or [-1 1] for [controls>patients] effects. Additionally, covariate variables can be added in the model to test the effects of interest adjusted for other relevant factors, such as sex and age. To account for the fact that the same analysis is repeated across many voxels, an appropriate threshold is required to control for multiple comparisons. The two most commonly employed methods are family-wise error (FWE) correction and false discovery rate.

o Alternative approaches: In addition to GLM analyses, computational approaches can be used to address more sophisticated research questions. Some commonly used approaches include the following: multivoxel pattern analysis (MVPA), which can be used to discriminate patterns of activation pertaining to, for example, faces and places; representational similarity analysis (RSA), which can detect response similarity in BOLD signal for pairwise comparisons of stimuli; and dynamic causal modeling (DCM), which uses a Bayesian framework to infer hidden neuronal dynamics from brain activity measurements.

16.3.4.2 Resting-state fMRI

o Example research question: What is the difference in functional connectivity between patients suffering from anxiety and healthy controls?

o Experimental tasks: Although the rsfMRI studies do not use external tasks, participants may be required to keep their eyes open and look at a fixation cross presented on the screen during data acquisition.

o Subject-level analysis: After preprocessing and denoising, whole-brain time-series data for each individual can be used to derive statistical quantities. There are a variety of different analyses that can be performed using rsfMRI data. Here, we will briefly introduce the full/partial connectivity matrix as an example. First, one should subdivide the brain into a set of regions (also known as "nodes"). These brain regions can be defined by using existing functional parcellation templates or by generating sample-specific templates from the data (e.g., using ICA). An anatomical atlas may also be used to address specific research questions (e.g., with regard to the subdivision of the amygdala). Subsequently, the average BOLD timeseries of each node can be extracted, which then can be used to calculate node-to-node connectivity strength (also referred to as edge) for each possible pair of nodes. For example, the connectivity strength can be calculated using Pearson's correlation. Connectivity strength for all possible pairs can be combined to form a "full" connectivity network matrix. In the case that the coefficient of each pair has been calculated while controlling for effects of all other nodes (i.e., partial correlation), then it is known as a partial connectivity network matrix. These matrices for each participant can then be fed into a subsequent group-level analysis (Fig. 16.3).

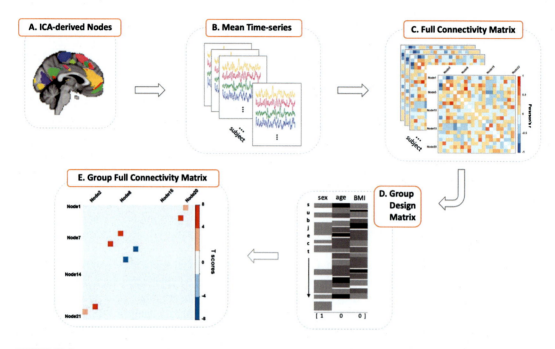

FIGURE 16.3

Overview illustration of data analysis to investigate group differences in resting-state network connectivity strength. A template containing multiple nodes or networks, such as the one generated from independent component analysis (ICA) can be used as the network masks, with different colors indicating different brain networks or nodes (A). Using these network masks, the mean time-series of each node can be extracted for every individual participant (B). A full network connectivity matrix can be generated by calculating Pearson's correlation coefficients for each pair of the nodes, per participant (C). To test the difference in connectivity strength (or edge) between e.g., males and females, a group design matrix with the regressor of interest "sex" and the covariates of "age" and "BMI" can be specified (D). Fitting the data with this design matrix in a GLM will return a group-level connectivity matrix that shows the differences in certain edges (after thresholding and correction for multiple comparisons), as indicated in non-ivory colors, between males and females (E). Note that Fisher's R to Z transformation should be applied to the full connectivity matrices prior to parametric statistical testing. Please see Chapter 5 for more information about neuroimaging statistics.

- Group-level analysis: Given the full or partial connectivity matrix, differences in connectivity patterns between, for instance, patient and control groups can be investigated. Similar to tfMRI, a group-level GLM can be used to determine whether edges differ between patients and controls. Here, the group-level design matrix and regressors are identical to those used in tfMRI and the model is fit separately to each edge in the connectivity network matrix. The approaches to correct for multiple comparison (across all edges) and thresholding are identical as for tfMRI. To further understand the meanings of between-group differences, one can link such differences to cognitive and/or behavioral outcomes and test whether the differences in connectivity patterns can explain variance in behavioral observations.

o Alternative approaches: Resting-state fMRI data allow for flexibility of data mining, and thus are particularly suitable when employing exploratory approaches. For example, independent component analysis (ICA) has been widely used to reduce data dimensionality by identifying important nodes and networks that are either spatially or temporally independent from each other. Another example is the graph theory approach that can be used to estimate local and global summary measures from network matrices. Besides the analytical approaches for studying static functional connectivity (i.e., averaged across time), methods to model time-varying connectivity (i.e., dynamics over time) have been increasingly employed in recent studies, such as sliding window analysis, point process analysis, and hidden Markov modeling. Whereas connectivity is typically used to address functional connections based on correlation coefficients, amplitude of low frequency fluctuations (ALFF) and regional homogeneity (ReHo) can quantify the amplitudes of low frequency oscillations (measured as the power in the frequency domain), and the similarity or synchronization between the given time-series (e.g., voxel-wise) and that of the nearest neighbors, respectively. Computational approaches, machine learning or deep learning-based methods are also increasingly utilized in rsfMRI analysis.

16.4 Communicating results

To convey the results to the scientific community and to the public, researchers need to interpret their results in a concise and understandable way, preferably with acknowledgment of limitations. Complementary to describing results in plain text, having results visualized is often a powerful and efficient way to summarize the core messages from the results. Below, we briefly discuss the caveats or challenges when interpreting fMRI results and introduce several packages and tools that can help achieve visualization of the fMRI results. Lastly, we address the necessity of participation in open science for efficient communication.

16.4.1 Interpretations

Functional MRI aims to measure neuronal activity using the BOLD signal, which is an indirect indicator and can be influenced by various factors irrelevant to neuronal activity. Caution is therefore required when it comes to the explanation of results that are derived from such signals.

More specifically, interpretations concerning the results of activation in tfMRI are mainly made in the context of contrasts. In the example of face image representation, the observation of either increased or decreased activation in certain brain areas is always relative to the contrast condition (e.g., relative to baseline inter-trial intervals or to place image representations). It is also important to note that such results are typically associative or correlational, and do not provide causal inference. Again, taking the face representation example, the observed activation increases in specific brain areas, such as the fusiform gyrus, cannot tell whether the activation is necessary or sufficient for the face representation. As for the results of functional connectivity, the correlation coefficient is typically interpreted as an index of connection strength, with greater values indicating stronger connections between, for instance, two regions. Importantly, apparent correlation-based functional connectivity and other similar measures can be influenced by various factors. Therefore the interpretation of neural coupling or communication should be made with caution.

258 **Chapter 16** Functional MRI analysis

16.4.2 Visualization

In recent decades, a great variety of methods have been developed to visualize the fMRI results, including overlaying of brain activation or connectivity images onto 2D or 3D brain volumes, or surface images. The use of brain image-based visualization can provide clear representation on brain anatomy and allows accommodation of multiple elements of the results with just one image or only a very few images. Currently, many fMRI analysis software packages also offer visualization features. For example, SPM has an anatomy toolbox that allows the overlay of imaging results on available brain atlases with anatomical labels. Similar utilities are also featured in FSL (i.e., FSLEYES). Whereas these tools primarily provide the rendering on a volumetric atlas, some software packages, such as AFNI's SUMA tool, the HCP connectome workbench, and FreeSurfer, have options to visualize the results on cortical surface images. Additionally, 3D or surface rendering can be achieved by specialty programs, such as Mango (http://ric.uthscsa.edu/mango), 3DSlicer (https://www.slicer.org), MIRcroGL (https://www.mccauslandcenter.sc.edu/mricrogl), and Pycortex (https://gallantlab.github.io/pycortex/).

Besides the generic brain image-based visualization, there is also a great variety of graphical methods to represent functional connectivity at a detailed scale (i.e., connectomics). To give an example, a circular connectogram (for example, see https://www.fmrib.ox.ac.uk/ukbiobank/netjs_d25/) can be used to show the number of connections between each node, whereas a sketch of dots and lines that can be superimposed on a glass brain template to demonstrate more system-level anatomical connections and their strengths among nodes. Additionally, figures and diagrams that are typically used for statistical results can be employed as well. A simple scatter plot, for instance, can clearly illustrate the relationship between the observed brain activation or connectivity and behavioral traits, whereas a heatmap can be useful to demonstrate the connectivity strength among brain nodes of interest.

16.4.3 Open science

To promote transparency and reproducibility of fMRI studies, researchers are encouraged to share source data, analysis pipelines and code, as well as results. Such practice is of great importance, for it can accelerate science discovery. For example, openly sharing data and results will not only encourage other researchers to replicate findings, but can also allow for meta-analyses across multiple studies. Additionally, practicing open science in general can help facilitate inclusivity of science for people with little or very limited access to expensive fMRI-related resources. Detailed guidelines for open science practice can be found in (Gorgolewski and Poldrack, 2016).

References

Brodoehl, S., Gaser, C., Dahnke, R., Witte, O.W., Klingner, C.M., 2020. Surface-based analysis increases the specificity of cortical activation patterns and connectivity results. Scientific Reports.

Ciric, R., Wolf, D.H., Power, J.D., Roalf, D.R., Baum, G.L., Ruparel, K., Shinohara, R.T., Elliott, M.A., Eickhoff, S.B., Davatzikos, C., Gur, R.C., Gur, R.E., Bassett, D.S., Satterthwaite, T.D., 2017. Benchmarking of participant-level confound regression strategies for the control of motion artifact in studies of functional connectivity. NeuroImage.

Gorgolewski, K.J., Poldrack, R.A., 2016. A practical guide for improving transparency and reproducibility in neuroimaging research. PLoS Biology.

Griffanti, L., Douaud, G., Bijsterbosch, J., Evangelisti, S., Alfaro-Almagro, F., Glasser, M.F., Duff, E.P., Fitzgibbon, S., Westphal, R., Carone, D., Beckmann, C.F., Smith, S.M., 2017. Hand classification of fMRI ICA noise components. NeuroImage.

Habeck, C.G., 2010. Basics of multivariate analysis in neuroimaging data. Journal of Visualized Experiments.

Logothetis, N.K., 2008. What we can do and what we cannot do with fMRI. Nature.

Lu, W., Dong, K., Cui, D., Jiao, Q., Qiu, J., 2019. Quality assurance of human functional magnetic resonance imaging: a literature review. Quantitative Imaging in Medicine and Surgery.

Morgan, P.S., Bowtell, R.W., McIntyre, D.J.O., Worthington, B.S., 2004. Correction of spatial distortion in EPI due to inhomogeneous static magnetic fields using the reversed gradient method. Journal of Magnetic Resonance Imaging.

Pruim, R.H.R., Mennes, M., van Rooij, D., Llera, A., Buitelaar, J.K., Beckmann, C.F., 2015. ICA-AROMA: a robust ICA-based strategy for removing motion artifacts from fMRI data. NeuroImage 112, 267–277. https://doi.org/10.1016/j.neuroimage.2015.02.064.

Salimi-Khorshidi, G., Douaud, G., Beckmann, C.F., Glasser, M.F., Griffanti, L., Smith, S.M., 2014. Automatic denoising of functional MRI data: combining independent component analysis and hierarchical fusion of classifiers. NeuroImage 90, 449–468. https://doi.org/10.1016/j.neuroimage.2013.11.046.

Vul, E., Harris, C., Winkielman, P., Pashler, H., 2009. Puzzlingly high correlations in fMRI studies of emotion, personality, and social cognition. Perspectives on Psychological Science 4 (3), 274–290.

Zeng, H., Constable, R.T., 2002. Image distortion correction in EPI: comparison of field mapping with point spread function mapping. Magnetic Resonance in Medicine.

Further reading

Bijsterbosch, J., Smith, S.M., Beckmann, C.F., 2017. An Introduction to Resting State fMRI Functional Connectivity.

Fornito, A., Zalesky, A., Bullmore, E.T., 2016. Fundamentals of Brain Network Analysis.

Jenkinson, M., Chappell, M., 2017. Introduction to Neuroimaging Analysis.

Jenkinson, M., Bijsterbosch, J., Chappell, M., Winkler, A., 2020. Short Introduction to the General Linear Model for Neuroimaging.

Poldrack, R.A., Nichols, T., Mumford, J., 2011. Handbook of Functional MRI Data Analysis.

CHAPTER 17

Neuroscience applications of functional MRI

Essa Yacoub[a] and Luca Vizioli[a,b]

[a]*Center for Magnetic Resonance Research (CMRR), Department of Radiology, University of Minnesota, Minneapolis, MN, United States*
[b]*Department of Neurosurgery, University of Minnesota, Minneapolis, MN, United States*

17.1 Introduction

Since the discovery of the blood-oxygenation-level-dependent (BOLD) contrast in the early 1990s (Ogawa et al., 1992) functional MRI (fMRI) has taken the world of human neuroscience by storm, quickly becoming one of the most, if not the most, widely used tool to study the brain non-invasively. This incredible success can be partly attributed to the concomitant ability of achieving relatively high spatial and temporal resolutions. Though other brain imaging techniques, such as positron emission tomography (PET), have allowed powerful insights into brain function, even the early days of fMRI afforded higher spatial and temporal resolution, allowing sampling of activity from multiple conditions within a single experimental run, on the scale of a few millimeters, without the cumbersome need for endogenous radioactive contrast agents. Faster sampling, which translates into higher statistical power in the estimation of neural responses, is also a highly desirable feature for clinical applications, permitting critical shortening of the total acquisition time. However, like all hemodynamic-based signals, the temporal resolution achievable with fMRI, which spans the range of a couple of seconds to several seconds (Fig. 17.1), is too slow to accurately sample true neuro-temporal dynamics, which occur within a few hundred milliseconds.

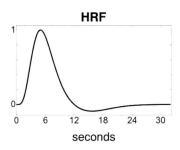

FIGURE 17.1

Schematic of the hemodynamic response function, showing how the BOLD signal evolves following an instantaneous neuronal firing.

262 Chapter 17 Neuroscience applications of functional MRI

The temporal sluggishness of fMRI is a direct consequence of the source of its signal. Functional MRI infers cortical activity by exploiting the coupling between blood flow (and specifically oxygenated blood for BOLD-based contrast) and neuronal firing. It builds on the metabolic demands of neuronal firing, requiring a directed and relatively localized flux of blood to supply the energy needed by a cell to fire. The sluggishness of this hemodynamic-based signal has traditionally led to neglecting fMRI's temporal dimension in favor of maximizing the accuracy of its spatial measurements.

Given these features, fMRI has qualitatively changed the way we study the brain non-invasively, allowing investigation of questions that had long remained elusive. In light of its non-invasive nature, for example, neuroscientists have been able to use fMRI to study neuronal processes that are specific to humans, such as high-level cognition, executive functions, speech, the impact of socio-cultural values on neural responses, and complex logic.

Here, we will look at how neuroscientists exploit fMRI to study neural processes. Rather than solely providing a review of recent findings which, taking into account the publication rate, is likely to become obsolete by the time any book is published, the goal of this chapter is to elucidate the main experimental strategies and approaches used in fMRI, highlighting their pros and cons to provide the reader with a solid understanding of how to best apply this incredible tool to study the brain non-invasively. The bulk of the chapter will focus on task-based fMRI and its main strength—namely, its spatial resolution— but we will also briefly touch upon resting-state fMRI and some of the advantages of increasing the temporal sampling of the hemodynamic signal.

17.2 fMRI and neuroscience

Functional MRI infers neural activity indirectly by measuring changes in regional hemodynamic metabolic demands consequent to neuronal firing. That is, firing neurons require additional "fuel", which is carried to the neural locus of interest in the blood stream. Though the coupling between fMRI signal and neuronal activity remains a subject of debate, it has been shown that the BOLD signal primarily reflects local field potentials (Logothetis, 2010).

As such, early studies were of a confirmatory nature, demonstrating the ability to replicate what we had already learned over decades of invasive measures of direct neuronal activity. In one such example, Sereno et al. (1995) exploited visual retinotopic organization, one of the most studied organizational principles of early visual cortices, which is shared across species. Leveraging responses to phase-encoded retinal stimulation, they demonstrated the ability to non-invasively generate retinotopic maps (e.g., in visual areas V1–V4) in human visual cortex with a precision that was comparable to that obtainable via invasive animal studies. Functional MRI has since moved on from replication of electrophysiological results to investigating uncharted organizing principles of human neurofunctional organization.

17.2.1 Historical perspective: brain damaged patients

Historically, neuroscientists have sought to parcellate the brain into specific regions, functional hubs and/or networks subserving specific cognitive processes. This view partly stems from the observations gathered through brain damaged patients. Localized cortical injuries, in fact, lead to specific cognitive impairments. One such example is the case of individuals with prosopagnosia.

The term prosopagnosia (from the ancient Greek *prospon* = face, the prefix *privative a* (alpha) indicating a negation; and *gnosia* = knowledge) refers to a disorder characterized by a specific deficit in face recognition abilities, often related to focal damage to a portion of the fusiform gyrus and/or the inferior occipital gyrus. Due to the spatial specificity of such damage, and the consequent loss of the ability to identify faces, brain damage studies of these kinds have fueled a belief in the existence of functionally dedicated cortical areas and networks.

However, localized brain damage associated with specific cognitive impairments represents a small minority of the population and are thus not only difficult to study, but once studied also become difficult to generalize in relation to the wider, healthy population. Moreover, the likelihood of encountering highly localized brain damage affecting a single cortical region is extremely low, as is the existence of patients with highly specific and isolated cognitive impairments. In total, the use of brain injuries in understanding functional organization is limited.

To this end, PET, followed by fMRI, have been instrumental in furthering the study of the brain and its function. Functional MRI, specifically because it can non-invasively monitor spatially localized hemodynamic changes and how these changes relate to specific tasks, experiences, or behaviors, is well suited to continue this endeavor.

17.3 Functional localization

Generally speaking, fMRI experiments can be categorized broadly into task-based (or stimulus locked) and resting-state studies (see also Chapter 16). As the names indicate, the former refers to evaluating signal changes following the presentation of a stimulus, such as the image of a face or the sound of a voice, while participants perform a specific task; the latter instead examines what is considered to be "spontaneous" neural activity of the brain "at rest" or, in other words, while participants in the scanner passively stare at a fixation cross projected on a screen, or simply keep their eyes closed.

Exploiting diverse analytical strategies and properties of the hemodynamic signal allows the computation of maps of neural activation geared towards the spatial identification of specialized functional areas or networks. This precise localization of neuro-cognitive functions and/or of dedicated cortical networks, achievable using, e.g., subtractive methodology and correlational approaches, represents fMRI's main contribution to neuroscience.

17.4 Task-based fMRI
17.4.1 Subtractive logic

Most task-based (tfMRI) studies rely on the idea of *cognitive subtraction*. Cognitive subtraction refers to the presumption that if the mental state of the participant differs only by a single feature or dimension, which can be precisely altered by the experimenter, one can subtract images acquired during one condition/state from the other, and the corresponding difference image identifies the cortical area associated with that stimulus/state dimension.

One example of this is the idea of functional localizers, as shown in Fig. 17.2.

Kanwisher et al. (1997) published what is considered a classic study in human neuroscience, using cognitive subtraction to identify the fusiform face area (FFA). Kanwisher et al. presented several stimuli

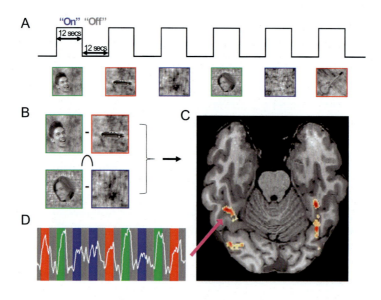

FIGURE 17.2

Cognitive subtraction. The figure portrays an example of cognitive subtraction in a functional localizer (block design; 12 seconds of visual stimulation alternated with 12 seconds of baseline periods: Panel A). Participants viewed visual stimuli belonging to three conditions: faces (green); phase-scrambled noise (blue); and non-face objects (red). The visual stimuli are from Stigliani et al. (2015). By subtracting the activity elicited by all face stimuli with that elicited by all noise stimuli in conjunction with all non-face stimuli (Panel B), we obtain the resultant functional map in Panel C, representing four face preferential regions (right and left FFA and right and left occipital face areas) in a representative subject. Panel D shows the time-course for a single run (gray bars indicate rest periods) of raw pre-processed BOLD responses computed by averaging all voxels within one of the FFAs (as indicated by the purple arrow).

to the participants in the scanner, including faces and other objects. When they contrasted the activity elicited by the face stimuli against all others, they observed a relatively confined locus of activation located in a portion of the fusiform gyrus. They concluded that this area (FFA) was a hub dedicated to face processing. In this example, to maintain the participant's attention, they are asked to perform a task throughout the experiment. However, while the presented stimuli change during the scan, the task does not.

The response profile of the FFA—namely, the larger activation to face stimuli compared to any other object category—has been observed for a variety of face stimuli, including full frontal and profile images, Mooney faces, line drawings, and schematic faces (for a review see Kanwisher and Yovel, 2006). The consistency of these results, in spite of the considerable differences in the low-level visual properties across the stimuli used, indicates that the larger response observed in the FFA for faces compared to non-face stimuli is genuinely related to a degree of "face preferentiality" of this region.

Another example of cognitive subtraction is when participants are presented with *identical* stimuli, but are asked to perform *different* tasks. Task instructions are either primed by a cue (usually preceding the stimulus presentation), or by instructing participants to perform a specific task in one experimental run and another task in a different experimental run.

By keeping the presented stimuli unchanged, and then manipulating the participants' behavior via a task, one can study top-down modulations and cognitive processes associated with the task. Dowdle et al., for example, presented degraded images of faces to healthy volunteers in the scanner, instructing them to perform either a stimulus relevant (i.e., face detection) or a stimulus irrelevant fixation task (Dowdle et al., 2020). By subtracting the activity elicited by one task to that elicited by the other, they identified a number of cortical areas, including the face-specific FFA, which responded more during the face detection task. In light of the fact that the stimuli were in fact identical across tasks, the authors concluded that these differences reflected top-down cortical modulations.

Although the idea of cognitive subtraction has proven extremely useful in advancing our understanding of the brain's functional organization, there are concerns with the approach. One concern is that of "pure insertion". That is, whether a single cognitive process can be inserted into a task without affecting the remaining processes. Complex non-linear interactions are likely to follow the insertion of cognitive processes. In addition to the debated assumption of linear additivity of cognitive processes (e.g., see Sidtis et al., 1999), there are also concerns about the validity of "rest conditions" or the physiological state of an individual during so-called "baseline conditions" (e.g. Binder et al., 1999).

Lastly, another complication of cognitive subtraction is that the conditions or cognitive states studied often differ across several dimensions, many of which may not be of interest to the researchers, but still modulate neural responses, resulting in a major limitation when interpreting the results.

Relating this concern back to the aforementioned face localizer experiment, for example, it had been argued that those sets of results could be explained by expertise, rather than face specificity: the FFA responds with greater activation to categories where participants are experts, and virtually all humans are face experts. This was the argument put forward and tested by Gauthier (for a review see Kanwisher and Yovel, 2006), who showed larger FFA responses to car experts than novices. Though, due to conflicting results, the "expertise" hypothesis has fallen from contention and it is now generally accepted that the FFA is in fact a face preferential cortical region, this example illustrates the need for caution when interpreting results via cognitive subtraction logic.

17.4.2 Parametric designs

Unlike cognitive subtraction which, as we have seen before, relies on a number of assumptions, parametric designs are relatively more assumption free. As the name suggests, the studies aim to examine the relationship between stimuli parameters (such as, for example, stimulus contrast or phase coherence) and/or behavioral measures (e.g., response accuracy, reaction time, or perceptual state) and brain activity. Though originally implemented in PET studies, parametric designs imply the employment of a multitude of experimental conditions and, as such, are more suited to fMRI, especially in light of its superior temporal efficiency.

These designs can be useful in studying the nature of neural responses, allowing the testing of specific hypotheses about the processes subserved by specific cortical regions. For example, they can shed light on whether neural responses to the parameters of interest are linear or non-linear and/or whether these response properties differ across regions.

The value of these observations can be crucial in our understanding of the brain. As an example, a given experiment may employ identical visual stimuli that only linearly vary according to image contrast, and which require subjects to report their percept. The relationship between stimulus parameters, behavioral responses, and neural activations can provide meaningful insights into the response properties of a given cortical region and, specifically, whether these follow the subjects' perceptual state, the stimulus properties, or a mixture of both. With this in mind, one can imagine that early visual regions will display a linear increase in the magnitude of BOLD responses as a function of image contrast. Conversely, a higher-level region involved in perceptual processing might exhibit a dichotomous response profile as a function of subjects' percepts (i.e., low response amplitudes when no percept is reported and high response amplitudes when a percept is reported).

As an example, in Dowdle et al. (2020) the authors showed degraded face stimuli that varied in their visibility based on the images' phase coherence (varying from 0% to 40% in steps of 10%) and asked the subjects to perform either a fixation task (respond when the fixation turns red), or a face detection task. They examined BOLD responses across a number of face preferential areas as a function of phase coherence and related these to participants' perceptual reports. They found that during the fixation task, a number of regions (including the FFA) responded in a pseudo-linear fashion, following the stimulus "faceness" (i.e., phase coherence). During the face detection task, the BOLD response instead varied non-linearly relative to image properties, according to participants' perceptual state and task difficulty. In examining the differences in BOLD responses across tasks, they observed that the largest response was for the most perceptually ambiguous condition (i.e., the most difficult percept to categorize). This experiment highlights one assumption of parametric studies, namely the fact that the magnitude of the hemodynamic response change is a function of cognitive "load" or task difficulty.

Parametric designs can be invaluable in studying the functional response profile of high-level regions, such as the frontal lobes, or processes that are specific to humans, such as executive functions, speech, working memory, or abstract thinking. One potential limitation to parametric designs, however, is that they are prone to being SNR-starved. Most parametric designs, such as the one cited above, tend to require a behavioral and neural response to every stimulus. This is in contrast to most localizer studies (relying on cognitive subtraction) that tend to model BOLD or behavioral responses to a series of stimuli.

17.4.3 Adaptation studies

Due to limitations in both spatial and temporal resolution, the ability to measure the firing patterns of individual neurons is a feat that goes well beyond the capabilities of fMRI. However, exploiting the principle of *neural adaption*, neuroscientists can use fMRI to indirectly infer neuronal firing properties. Neural adaptation refers to the observation that category-specific neurons will display a decrease in activity to the subsequent presentation of two or more stimuli of the category of interest. For example, studies in monkey neurophysiology have shown that the repeated presentation of the same stimulus results in a reduction of single-unit neural response (for a review see Grill-Spector et al., 2006).

A similar adaptation effect observed across a number of fMRI experiments may stem from this same neuronal mechanism. In such cases, repeated stimuli led to a lower overall MR signal. Evaluating fMRI response amplitudes to a "new" stimulus therefore allows determination of whether a neural region "sees" the stimulus as different from the previous one, and thus describes the area's functional profile (for a review see Grill-Spector et al., 2006).

In one of the first fMRI adaptation studies, Grill-Spector and colleagues used the principle of neural adaptation to study some high-level stimulus dimensions (such as size and viewpoint invariance) that had previously proven elusive. They found that higher-level regions, such as the posterior fusiform gyrus, exhibited significantly attenuated amplitude response to repetition of the same object that varied in size and position, relative to the object-selective posterior section of lateral occipital cortex (LO). The authors concluded that, unlike LO, the posterior fusiform gyrus encoded high-level information about a given stimulus, regardless of size and position. They further argued that their results demonstrated the utility of adaptation in determining the functional characteristics of neurons using fMRI.

17.5 Local vs focal

Although fMRI is generally recognized for the high precision of its spatial measurements, such spatial precision falls short when compared to invasive electrophysiological recordings. For example, at 3 tesla (one of the most widely available magnetic field strengths for MRI), the typical fMRI voxel size is around 2 mm isotropic. An fMRI voxel of this dimension can enclose hundreds of thousands of neurons, whereas electrophysiological measurements can record neural activity from a single cell.

At first, this untenable comparison can be interpreted as a major limitation of fMRI's main strength, namely, its ability to precisely localize a site of activity. The brain, however, is an extremely complex organ, in which, on a much larger scale, different areas work in concert more or less synchronously to produce a given sensory or cognitive state, something that can be captured with whole-brain fMRI. As such, to understand the intricacy of neuronal processes, scientists must be able to study the interactions of distally located functional hubs and how these relate to, for example, subjective experience.

Within this context, the unprecedented precision of electrophysiological recordings can be seen as a curse rather than a blessing, since such a high spatial precision is greatly limited in the extent of its coverage. As such, the ability to sample the whole brain at once represents one of fMRI's most appealing features, providing the unique possibility of studying the function of entire cortical networks simultaneously.

17.6 Block vs event-related designs
17.6.1 Block designs

Like most neuroimaging tools, fMRI lives in a relatively starved signal-to-noise ratio (SNR) regime, where many brain volumes acquired over time need to be averaged together to provide a reliable picture of neuronal activity.

In spite of its celebrated supremacy in the temporal domain relative to its predecessors (e.g., PET), early neuroscientific studies carried out with fMRI involved the presentation of stimuli blocked in long epochs, lasting from several dozens of seconds to minutes (e.g., Ogawa et al., 1992). This is extremely valuable for increasing sensitivity in fMRI and is made possible because, for stimulations ≥ 1 second, multiple repeated stimuli add together in an approximately linear fashion (Boynton et al., 1996). Furthermore, when a long train of repeated stimuli is presented, the resultant hemodynamic response is a peak that is broad and sustained and doesn't return to baseline until the stimulation presentation ends.

The continuous presentation of experimental stimuli over sustained periods of time therefore leads to greater and more reliable extents of activations, significantly improving the sensitivity and associated statistical power in functional measurements with fMRI. Such continuous presentation of stimuli is referred to as a block design (see also Chapter 16). Block designs are instrumental in fMRI applications to neuroscience and, by means of cognitive subtraction, successfully and efficiently identify regions of

268   Chapter 17 Neuroscience applications of functional MRI

interest that preferentially respond to a specific stimulus category. For example, the functional localization of the FFA (e.g., Dowdle et al., 2020; Kanwisher et al., 1997; Kanwisher and Yovel, 2006) is generally achieved using block designs.

17.6.2 Event-related designs

Block designs are an indispensable tool for most cognitive neuroscientists. However, they only allow quantification of neural activity to a train of stimuli. This feature can represent a limitation if one is interested in behavioral and neural responses to individual stimuli (as is the case for most parametric studies). As such, event-related designs, following hardware improvements in achievable SNR, along with the development of more efficient acquisition protocols (e.g., multi-band/simultaneous multi-slice methods, see Chapter 3, and also Moeller et al., 2010), have risen in popularity amongst neuroscientists using fMRI. They can be broadly categorized as slow and fast event-related designs on the basis of the inter-trial stimulus interval (ISI). Traditionally, slow designs refer to those contexts in which the ISI is longer than the duration of the hemodynamic response function, or HRF (requiring 5–6 seconds to peak and another 5–6 seconds to return to baseline; Fig. 17.1), whereas fast designs refer to an ISI that is shorter (Buckner et al., 1998). Dowdle et al. (2020), for example, used a fast event-related design with a 2 seconds "on" 2 seconds "off" paradigm, where face stimuli were presented for 2 seconds, followed by a 2-second fixation period.

Whereas block designs allow evaluation of the amplitude of a sustained neural response, event-related designs can tackle transient hemodynamic modulations. Moreover, since they are intrinsically SNR-starved compared to blocked experiments (Fig. 17.3), event-related designs allow stacking many stimuli in a relatively short amount of time, increasing the statistical power of neuroimaging inference.

In addition, event-related designs keep participants engaged rather than bored, augmenting their ability to cognate and sustaining their attention. Also, a randomized trial presentation order can be used, which avoids undesirable habituation and adaptation effects.

Due to closely spaced events and the sluggishness of the hemodynamic signal, the resulting functional responses can overlap substantially. Building on the linearity of hemodynamic responses (see Boynton et al., 1996), an estimate of the HRF can be retrieved using deconvolution analysis. A crucial aspect of event-related designs is the jittering of the ISI. Dale (1999) demonstrated that, with short ISIs, jittering the ISI duration leads to a 10-fold increase in the design efficiency (related to the ability to detect an effect of interest), relative to fixed ISI experiments.

17.7 Resting-state fMRI

One of the most popular (in recent years) fMRI applications to neuroscience is resting-state fMRI (rsfMRI) (e.g., Biswal et al., 1995; Glasser et al., 2016; Lv et al., 2018). Unlike for tfMRI, rsfMRI images are acquired in the *absence* of a stimulus or a task, referred to as a "resting" state. As such, rsfMRI focuses on spontaneous, rather than time-locked or evoked, neural activity. Because of this, specific analytical approaches are used to derive resting-state functional maps (e.g., seed-based con-

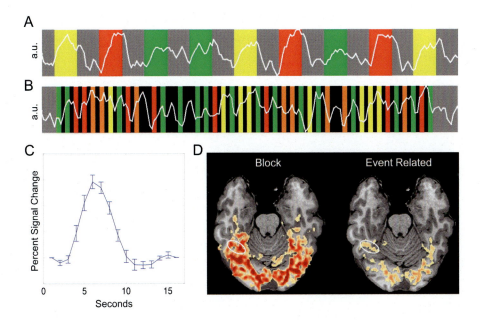

FIGURE 17.3

Block vs event-related designs. Panel A portrays the raw, pre-processed BOLD time-course for a single run of a typical visual block design (in this case, 12 seconds on/off) for all voxels within a given region of interest (white oval in Panel D). Different colors indicate different visual conditions, and gray bars indicate baseline or rest periods. Panel B portrays the raw, pre-processed BOLD time-course for a single run of a fast event-related design (in this case, 2 seconds on/off with a number of blank trials, effectively jittering the ISI) for all voxels within the same region of interest (white oval in Panel D) in the same subject. Whereas in Panel A we can clearly see the temporal characteristics of the hemodynamic response function (not how voxels in the region show preferential activity towards the "red" condition), these same temporal properties are not easily detectable in Panel B. The HRF, however, can be deconvolved, and thus "recovered" by exploiting the linear and additive properties of the hemodynamic signal (as shown in Panel C). Panel D shows mean activation of all conditions vs baseline for block and event-related designs. In spite of both experimental runs lasting a comparable amount of time (with the fast event-related experiment involving more trials), SNR advantages are clearly seen for the maps elicited by the block design experiment.

nectivity or independent component analysis (ICA)). Furthermore, unlike tfMRI, which tends to tackle questions about specific cortical regions, rsfMRI examines interactions across the entire brain at once. Resting-state functional connectivity research has revealed a number of networks (Fig. 17.4) which are consistently found in healthy subjects through different stages of consciousness, across species, and which represent specific patterns of synchronous activity.

The lack of need for a task makes rsfMRI particularly attractive for patients or vulnerable populations, such as children, who may have difficulty with task instructions. What makes rsfMRI even more appealing is its ease of implementation. It doesn't require additional devices for stimulus presentation or the recording of behavioral responses.

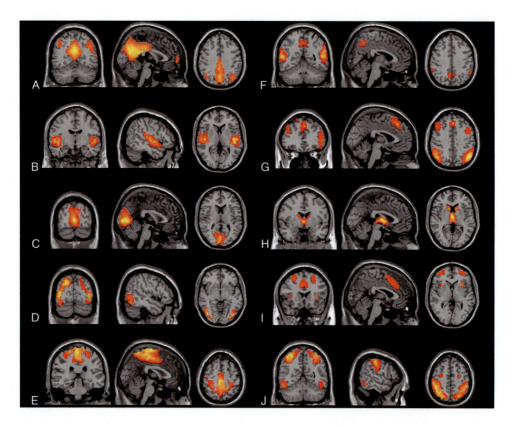

FIGURE 17.4

Resting-state networks. Example of the main resting-state networks computed on 200 participants. A) Default mode network; B) Auditory network; C) Medial visual network; D) Lateral visual network; E) Sensorimotor network; F) Precuneus network; G) Dorsal visual stream; H) Basal Ganglia network. (from Lv et al., 2018).

However, unlike tfMRI, rsfMRI does not allow assessing local changes in hemodynamic responses and, in light of the absence of a controlled task or instructions, is characterized by a lack of experimental control over the cognitive processes in which participants engage.

Conventional rsfMRI approaches do not possess enough power to carry out single-subject analyses, relying heavily on pooling across many participants. As such, rsfMRI relies on assumptions of anatomical and functional correspondence across subjects. A participant's brain is first spatially morphed into a normalized space (e.g., MNI or Talairach), and timeseries are then concatenated before the computation of resting-state maps. Though a degree of anatomical correspondence exists across individual brains, this is generally a very coarse and crude assumption and, as such, rsfMRI is limited in the spatial precision of its measurements. Just as subject averaging is also common practice in tfMRI, in task-based analyses one can move from averaging individual brains to averaging, for example, responses within a functionally defined ROI, mitigating the anatomical correspondence problem.

Even with these limitations, rsfMRI has proven to be powerful and, accordingly, widely used.

17.8 Temporal resolution

As noted, the popularity of fMRI is traditionally related to the precision of its spatial measurement and the large volume coverage with which functional images can be noninvasively recorded. However, due to the sluggishness of the hemodynamic response, exploring temporal features of neuronal events with fMRI has historically been assumed to be unreliable, if not impossible. With the advent of ultra-high field MRI (7 tesla or higher) and fMRI, and the development of more SNR-efficient parallel accelerations (Moeller et al., 2010), it is now possible to record BOLD signals across the brain with unprecedented spatial-temporal resolutions (<1 second). It remains to be determined, however, whether the gains from these ultra-fast measurements will be primarily from statistical power, or whether fast sampling rates can be exploited to unravel fast temporal dynamics of neural processing. Recently, a number of studies have reported that the BOLD signal carries neural information on a timescale faster than previously conceived (e.g., up to 1 Hz., Lewis et al., 2016); and that using fast repetition times (TR) (e.g., ~500 ms), it is possible to extract more precise information about stimulus dimensions coded by a specific cortical region (e.g., see Vu et al., 2016). Furthermore, the possibility of measuring such fast processes with fMRI, while also maintaining a relatively high spatial resolution over a large volume, could shed light on a number of neuroscience questions that remain largely unresolved, such as inter- and intra-area communication related to feedforward and feedback signals. Other strategies that may benefit from fast temporal sampling are correlational-based analyses, such as functional connectivity, which allows inferences to be made about the communication across areas, or dynamic causal modeling, which allows inferences to be made about causality or directionality of activation between regions.

Regardless of whether high temporal resolution allows access to faster neuro-temporal dynamics, or whether it is only useful for increasing statistical power, and therefore the precision of hemodynamic estimates, it has proven fruitful in a variety of fMRI applications.

17.9 Ultra-high field (UHF) fMRI

With the growing availability of ultra-high field scanners (i.e., ≥7 tesla), researchers have begun trading the gains in SNR that accompany UHF to record BOLD images with high spatial resolutions (e.g., 0.8 mm isotropic). These highly precise measurements can, at least in principle, provide the means for scientists to tackle research questions that have thus far proven elusive. Specifically, the study of the functional organization of some of the most fundamental units of neural computations—cortical layers and columns—has only recently begun to seem a worthwhile scientific endeavor (for a review, see De Martino et al., 2018, and also see Chapter 36). A number of studies to date have already successfully utilized UHF sub-millimeter fMRI to study the functional organization of layers and columns (Fig. 17.5; e.g., Yacoub et al., 2008).

Unfortunately, however, doubts still exist as to whether the achievable resolution of the images and the fMRI hemodynamic contrast of choice are sufficient to draw meaningful conclusions in terms of cortical columns and layers. The nominal image resolution (in this case, 0.8 mm isotropic) is in fact compromised by a number of factors—including the image readout time or the proximity to large draining vessels—which blur the ultimate resolution of the functional images and their correspondence with the underlying neuronal organizations and computations.

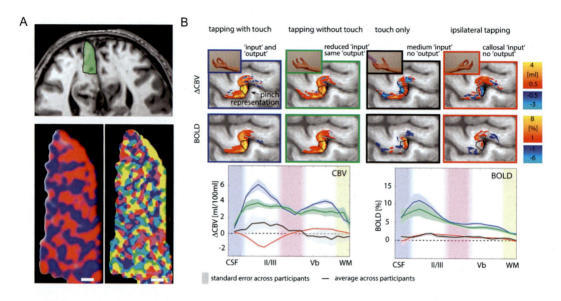

FIGURE 17.5

Columnar and laminar fMRI. Panel A shows an example of ocular dominance (lower left) and orientation preference (lower right) columnar maps from a flat portion of gray matter (shown in the top panel in green) obtained using sub-millimeter BOLD fMRI (scale bar 1 mm, from Yacoub et al., 2008). Panel B shows maps and cortical depth activation profiles for BOLD and CBV VASO to different finger tapping conditions (from Huber et al., 2017). Though BOLD fMRI possesses higher SNR, it is also compromised by large vessels, which blur its functional precision and lead to increases in response magnitude in proximity to the pial surface, where most large vessels reside, leading to the typical ramping profile of gradient-echo BOLD. Conversely, CBV VASO, though SNR-starved relative to gradient-echo BOLD, is instead less impacted by the influence of large vessels.

A number of strategies exist to circumvent this problem. The nominal resolution of functional images can be exploited by clever analytical approaches (e.g., multivariate pattern analyses, computational models, or differential mapping). Alternatively, the choice of acquisition protocol, which can alter the sensitivity to different aspects of the hemodynamic response, can be used to maximize the functional resolution of hemodynamic signals. This is, however, not a trivial problem. As laminar applications of fMRI are intrinsically SNR-starved, it is attractive to use a sequence that maximizes contrast-to-noise ratio, such as gradient-echo BOLD, which unfortunately suffers from reduced spatial specificity due to its sensitivity to large draining vessels (this also increases the magnitude of responses; Fig. 17.5). On the other hand, acquisition protocols that are less impacted by the blurring effects of large vessels (such as spin-echo, cerebral blood flow, or volume-weighted approaches, e.g., see Huber et al., 2017) tend to be SNR-starved. As such, when deciding on which acquisition strategy is optimal, one usually has to weigh up trade-offs between SNR efficiency and spatial specificity.

A challenge with sub-millimeter measurements, even at UHF, is the dominance of zero-mean Gaussian-distributed noise arising from electronics or hardware, which poses a major limitation in pushing the limits of the achievable image spatial resolution. To this end, denoising algorithms tackling this specific noise source may be crucial in facilitating our ability to acquire such high-resolution images. Recently, one such denoising method, noise reduction with distribution corrected (NORDIC) principal component analysis (PCA) published by Vizioli et al. (2021), has been shown to significantly increase the SNR of activation maps and/or permit shorter acquisition times (see Fig. 17.6). Such a technique can potentially bring sub-millimeter fMRI into clinical, rather than just research, settings where acquisition times represent a major impediment.

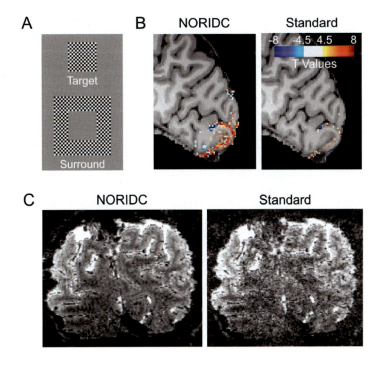

FIGURE 17.6

Example of NORDIC denoising on block design stimulation for 7T 2D gradient-echo 0.8 mm isotropic images. The experiment involved a 12 seconds on/off presentation of two visual conditions: a target and a surround checkerboard (Panel A). Both are checkerboard flickered in counterphase at 6 Hz. Panel B shows t-maps for a single run (i.e., 2.5 minutes of data) of NORDIC and Standard (i.e., no denoising) obtained for the contrast target > surround, superimposed on a T_1-weighted image (sagittal slice). The activity is confined within visual area V1 (calcarine sulcus). In red is the activation to the target condition and, in blue, activation to the surround condition. Note the dramatic effect of NORDIC denoising in estimating the extent of activation in V1. Panel C shows a single slice for a single volume of a 7T 3D gradient-echo EPI data set with a spatial resolution of 0.5 mm isotropic voxels for NORDIC and standard images. The removal of thermal noise via NORDIC, prominent in the medial portion of the image, dramatically improves image quality, which, for this specific resolution, would be otherwise unattainable.

Thus far, there is no one-size-fits-all answer to a protocol choice for fMRI, and different applications may choose different strategies. As hardware and software developments—including the development of analytical strategies, acquisition protocols and denoising algorithms—continue to grow, sub-millimeter fMRI in humans is concurrently gaining momentum, showing more and more promise towards bridging the gap between invasive electrophysiology and human neuroimaging with non-invasive fMRI (Fig. 17.7), potentially leading to another transformative wave in our understanding of the human brain.

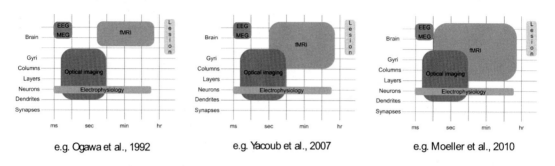

FIGURE 17.7

Spatio-temporal resolutions of some of the main neuroimaging techniques. Note how fMRI's resolution dramatically improves over the years, coming closer and closer to invasive neuroimaging tools, such as optical imaging and electrophysiology.

17.10 Conclusion

Despite providing an indirect measure of neuronal activity, fMRI has revolutionized the way we study the human brain, providing qualitatively and quantitatively different avenues for how neuroscientists investigate the relationship between brain and behavior and delivering novel insights into the functional organization of the human brain. The non-invasive nature of fMRI, along with its relatively high spatial and temporal resolution, has played a major part in its rise to stardom as the primary technique employed by cognitive neuroscientists.

Even so, at least for now, fMRI fails to provide a complete picture of neural processes, with its main limitations residing in the sluggishness of its temporal dimension and coarse features of the hemodynamic response. Neuroscientists must complement fMRI with other tools, such as electroencephalography (EEG) or magnetoencephalography (MEG), to comprehensively address spatial and temporal questions concerning cortical and subcortical processes.

The fast-paced technological advances in the MRI industry, along with some of the most recent developments pushing the spatial and temporal capabilities of UHF fMRI, will continue to provide novel avenues for studying the human brain; potentially even one day evolving the technique into a complete tool for systems neuroscience.

References

Binder, J.R., Frost, J.A., Hammeke, T.A., Bellgowan, P.S., Rao, S.M., Cox, R.W., 1999. Conceptual processing during the conscious resting state. A functional MRI study. J. Cogn. Neurosci. 11, 80–95.

Biswal, B., Yetkin, F.Z., Haughton, V.M., Hyde, J.S., 1995. Functional connectivity in the motor cortex of resting human brain using echo-planar MRI. Magn. Reson. Med. 34, 537–541.

Boynton, G.M., Engel, S.A., Glover, G.H., Heeger, D.J., 1996. Linear systems analysis of functional magnetic resonance imaging in human V1. J. Neurosci. 16, 4207–4221.

Buckner, R.L., Goodman, J., Burock, M., Rotte, M., Koutstaal, W., Schacter, D., Rosen, B., Dale, A.M., 1998. Functional-anatomic correlates of object priming in humans revealed by rapid presentation event-related fMRI. Neuron 20, 285–296.

Dale, A.M., 1999. Optimal experimental design for event-related fMRI. Hum. Brain Mapp. 8, 109–114.

De Martino, F., Yacoub, E., Kemper, V., Moerel, M., Uludag, K., De Weerd, P., Ugurbil, K., Goebel, R., Formisano, E., 2018. The impact of ultra-high field MRI on cognitive and computational neuroimaging. NeuroImage 168, 366–382.

Dowdle, L., Ghose, G., Ugurbil, K., Yacoub, E., Vizioli, L., 2020. Clarifying the role of higher-level cortices in resolving perceptual ambiguity using ultra high field fMRI. NeuroImage, 117654.

Glasser, M.F., Coalson, T.S., Robinson, E.C., Hacker, C.D., Harwell, J., Yacoub, E., Ugurbil, K., Andersson, J., Beckmann, C.F., Jenkinson, M., Smith, S.M., Van Essen, D.C., 2016. A multi-modal parcellation of human cerebral cortex. Nature 536, 171–178.

Grill-Spector, K., Henson, R., Martin, A., 2006. Repetition and the brain: neural models of stimulus-specific effects. Trends Cogn. Sci. 10, 14–23.

Huber, L., Handwerker, D.A., Jangraw, D.C., Chen, G., Hall, A., Stuber, C., Gonzalez-Castillo, J., Ivanov, D., Marrett, S., Guidi, M., Goense, J., Poser, B.A., Bandettini, P.A., 2017. High-resolution CBV-fMRI allows mapping of laminar activity and connectivity of cortical input and output in human M1. Neuron 96, 1253–1263. e7.

Kanwisher, N., Mcdermott, J., Chun, M.M., 1997. The fusiform face area: a module in human extrastriate cortex specialized for face perception. J. Neurosci. 17, 4302–4311.

Kanwisher, N., Yovel, G., 2006. The fusiform face area: a cortical region specialized for the perception of faces. Philos. Trans. R. Soc. Lond. B, Biol. Sci. 361, 2109–2128.

Lewis, L.D., Setsompop, K., Rosen, B.R., Polimeni, J.R., 2016. Fast fMRI can detect oscillatory neural activity in humans. Proc. Natl. Acad. Sci. USA 113, E6679–E6685.

Logothetis, N.K., 2010. Neurovascular uncoupling: much ado about nothing. Front. Neuroenergetics 2, 11.

Lv, H., Wang, Z., Tong, E., Williams, L.M., Zaharchuk, G., Zeineh, M., Goldstein-Piekarski, A.N., Ball, T.M., Liao, C., Wintermark, M., 2018. Resting-state functional MRI: everything that nonexperts have always wanted to know. Am. J. Neuroradiol. 39, 1390–1399.

Moeller, S., Yacoub, E., Olman, C.A., Auerbach, E., Strupp, J., Harel, N., Ugurbil, K., 2010. Multiband multislice GE-EPI at 7 tesla, with 16-fold acceleration using partial parallel imaging with application to high spatial and temporal whole-brain fMRI. Magn. Reson. Med. 63, 1144–1153.

Ogawa, S., Tank, D.W., Menon, R., Ellermann, J.M., Kim, S.G., Merkle, H., Ugurbil, K., 1992. Intrinsic signal changes accompanying sensory stimulation: functional brain mapping with magnetic resonance imaging. Proc. Natl. Acad. Sci. USA 89, 5951–5955.

Sereno, M.I., Dale, A.M., Reppas, J.B., Kwong, K.K., Belliveau, J.W., Brady, T.J., Rosen, B.R., Tootell, R.B., 1995. Borders of multiple visual areas in humans revealed by functional magnetic resonance imaging. Science 268, 889–893.

Sidtis, J.J., Strother, S.C., Anderson, J.R., Rottenberg, D.A., 1999. Are brain functions really additive? NeuroImage 9, 490–496.

Stigliani, A., Weiner, K.S., Grill-Spector, K., 2015. Temporal processing capacity in high-level visual cortex is domain specific. J. Neurosci. 35 (36), 12412–12424.

Vizioli, L., Moeller, S., Dowdle, L., et al., 2021. Lowering the thermal noise barrier in functional brain mapping with magnetic resonance imaging. Nat. Commun. 12, 5181. https://doi.org/10.1038/s41467-021-25431-8.

Vu, A.T., Phillips, J.S., Kay, K., Phillips, M.E., Johnson, M.R., Shinkareva, S.V., Tubridy, S., Millin, R., Grossman, M., Gureckis, T., Bhattacharyya, R., Yacoub, E., 2016. Using precise word timing information improves decoding accuracy in a multiband-accelerated multimodal reading experiment. Cogn. Neuropsychol. 33, 265–275.

Yacoub, E., Harel, N., Ugurbil, K., 2008. High-field fMRI unveils orientation columns in humans. Proc. Natl. Acad. Sci. USA 105, 10607–10612.

CHAPTER

Clinical applications of functional MRI

18

Natalie L. Voets

Wellcome Centre for Integrative Neuroimaging (FMRIB-WIN), John Radcliffe Hospital, University of Oxford, Oxford, United Kingdom

18.1 Introduction

Throughout the 19th to mid-20th centuries, huge strides were made in our understanding of brain function. Fascinating case studies identified patterns of brain injury that had resulted in loss of specific cognitive or neurological abilities. Similar evidence of functional specialization was emerging from the pioneering work of neurosurgeons newly armed with electrical stimulation techniques that induced clear and repeatable behavioral change when applied directly to certain areas of the brain.

The development of fMRI, however, offered a bridge between purely neurological observations and spatially limited neurosurgical observations by providing a detailed reflection of a patient's entire brain, functioning in (semi-)real time. Given its safe, non-invasive nature and ability to probe even deep brain nuclei in great detail, fMRI has increasingly taken up a prime position in mapping human brain functions. By measuring—albeit indirectly—aspects of brain activity, fMRI has uncovered huge variety in functional "re-mappings" after similarly-appearing pathology. Information gained in this way about the spatial distribution of functions currently helps to guide neurosurgical treatment decisions. Usefully, fMRI can probe not just the location of evoked neural activity, but also its magnitude, offering a tool to link amounts of functionally-induced signal change to variations in performance. In this way, fMRI offers a mechanism to study and monitor the effects of treatment interventions on dysfunctional networks. In this emerging field, fMRI holds potential to inform the choice between treatments, and their further refinements, to achieve maximal individual benefit.

18.2 Surgical planning

The unique spatial sensitivity of fMRI motivates its primary clinical application: to produce maps showing which regions in the brain "activate" when patients engage in a specific task. The value of such maps is most obvious in the domain of neurosurgery. Certain pathological processes affect the brain in a localized manner. Removing the pathological site often offers a successful treatment for the condition. This applies to epilepsy, tumors, and vascular abnormalities most commonly.

18.2.1 Non-lesional epilepsy

In the case of drug-resistant epilepsy, seizure control can be achieved by surgically removing the brain tissue from which seizures arise. Controlling seizures is a clinical priority not just for a patient's quality of life, but also because some patients are at high risk of sudden unexpected death in epilepsy (SUDEP). An incomplete but meaningful reduction in seizures can therefore have a deep impact on a patient's ability to lead a full, independent life. On the other hand, the risks of surgery in some cases outweigh the benefits.

Most drug-resistant epilepsies arise from the temporal lobe, and the medial temporal structures in particular. The seminal work of Penfield and Ojemann demonstrated that lateral (predominantly left) temporal lobe cortical areas play central roles in speech and language. Parallel discoveries by Scoville and Milner highlighted the indispensable contribution of the medial structures to memory. Consequently, the primary surgical concern in temporal lobe epilepsy (TLE) surgery is the potential for causing amnesia, followed by the risk of decline in verbal and/or non-verbal aspects of memory.

Fortunately, amnestic syndromes following TLE surgery are extremely rare. Such concerns arise mainly when bilateral structures are implicated in, or affected by, epilepsy. Risks of global amnesia cannot currently be adequately determined from fMRI. This is in part because of uncertainty around the processing performed by medial temporal lobe structures, due to difficulties in designing fMRI experiments that measure those processes, and because of statistical considerations discussed in Section 18.5.1 below. At present, therefore, assessment of the risks of amnesia are based on the results of clinical data and invasive Wada testing. During the Wada test, each hemisphere is temporarily anesthetized to assess residual language and memory abilities in the contralateral side. However, interpretation is not straightforward. Cases are reported both of amnesia, despite adequate Wada test results, and of good memory outcomes, despite "failing" a Wada test.

Due to the rarity of this complication and the limitations of the Wada test, efforts have been directed at predicting more specific memory declines using fMRI. Converging, though still small-scale, evidence indicates that fMRI is superior for predicting post-surgical memory decline compared to neuropsychology, structural MRI, and Wada. At present, these results are based mostly on studies of language lateralization. Increasingly, tasks are being designed to probe lateralized memory functions, inasmuch as these are lateralized. Optimal experiments for memory "mapping" are therefore not yet established. Nonetheless, fMRI is cautiously recommended by the American Academy of Neurology to predict risks of material-specific memory decline in TLE surgery (Szaflarski et al., 2017). Furthermore, fMRI has all but substituted the Wada test to establish language dominance (Binder, 2011).

18.2.2 Lesional pathologies

In the case of neurosurgery targeting a defined lesion, fMRI is also called upon to provide a specific evaluation of functional risks that vary according to the location of pathology.

The main motivation for cortical mapping around surgically-accessible lesions is the unpredictability of functional localization in the brain. For example, the primary visual and primary motor cortices are well-established as the neural substrates for their name-sake functions in the healthy brain. In a brain containing pathology or that has been previously injured, however, the normally tight coupling between anatomy and function can be lost. Consequently, functional risks from surgery cannot be fully predicted by the anatomical location of a lesion alone. In this context, fMRI offers complementary information to identify which anatomical regions contribute to core functions, relevant to inform patient discussions and treatment planning, as illustrated in Fig. 18.1.

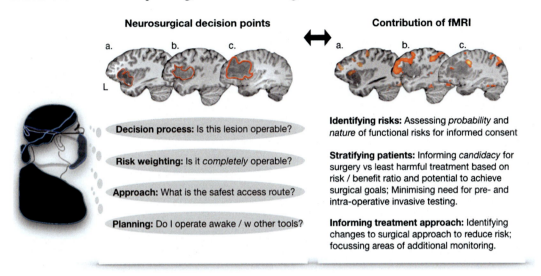

FIGURE 18.1

The brain-behavior conundrum. Faced with three brain tumors (top left) each overlapping "Broca's area", challenges arise in predicting risks from anatomy. Symptoms are informative, but cannot determine if first-line neurosurgical treatment is possible, and how. FMRI activation (top right) during a silent word generation task (versus rest) was left-hemisphere lateralized in each case, but revealed important distinctions between them. Patient (a) had a radiologically stable but multifocal lesion involving the striatum. Given the fMRI-determined risks and uncertain lesion nature (glioma or dysembryoplastic neuroepithelial tumor), the patient opted against surgery. Patients (b) and (c) had suspected gliomas. FMRI found no activation lateral to the tumor, suggesting surgical access was possible, but indicating risks to speech functions along the superior (b) and posterior (c) margins. Each underwent awake surgery, with direct brain stimulation confirming the fMRI results. Complete resection, with intact neuropsychological results, was achieved in both of these tumors classically considered inoperable.

For the most common primary brain tumors (gliomas), surgery aims to curb tumor growth. When tumors are slow-growing, surgery also aims to delay conversion into aggressive brain cancer. Extensive surgery, going beyond the anatomically visible tumor borders, can significantly extend survival. But, if surgery causes permanent new neurological symptoms, survival benefits are reversed (Rahman et al., 2017). Preserving quality of life has therefore taken center stage in glioma surgery. It is in this domain that fMRI offers the most concrete clinical benefits, provided that the surgical question can be explicitly defined and the functions of concern can be adequately "mapped" (discussed below). The functions most often mapped involve primary sensory (sensorimotor, visual) and core language processes (speech production, comprehension, reading, naming, and semantic access or association). Two such cases are illustrated in Fig. 18.2. An important caveat is that tumors recruit pathological vessels. In some cases, the assumptions underlying BOLD fMRI may therefore be affected. Negative fMRI results (i.e., no activation when activation is expected from performance) should therefore be interpreted with caution. Breath-hold calibration of the BOLD signal has been advocated as a potential practical indicator of neurovascular uncoupling in these and other lesions (Pak et al., 2017).

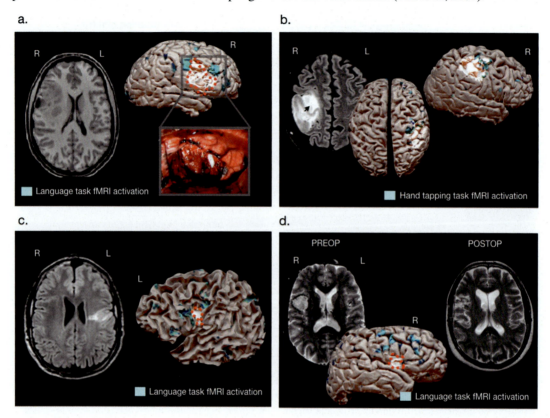

FIGURE 18.2

Neurosurgical Case Illustrations. Pre-surgical fMRI mapping in patients with glioma (a, b), focal cortical dysplasia (c), and cavernoma (d). A 24-year-old (a) experienced a seizure affecting speech and mouth control due to a right frontal lobe glioma. Given the symptoms and left-handedness, fMRI was performed using two language tasks, confirming atypical right hemisphere language. Access appeared possible, and awake surgery was performed, producing speech arrest at the fMRI-identified anterior cortical site and in the resection cavity, where tractography indicated the superior longitudinal fasciculus (not shown). In contrast, (b) hand-tapping fMRI indicated extensive activation within a suspected glioma spanning the right central sulcus. The 39-year-old patient opted for biopsy and imaging surveillance. Similarly, high risks to speech were identified in a patient with chronic epilepsy around the inferior frontal focal cortical dysplasia (c). Direct stimulation through implanted grids confirmed the inoperability of this lesion. Finally, unexpected language lateralization was observed in a patient initially referred for motor mapping in the context of a right frontal cavernoma (d). The patient had no speech symptoms, but was left handed. Language mapping revealed right hemisphere dominance and the surgical approach was revised to achieve safe complete resection.

Functional concerns also arise in the context of lesional epilepsy and vascular lesions, such as cavernomas (Fig. 18.2). Cavernomas are abnormal clusters of blood vessels that may bleed, thereby damaging healthy neighboring tissue or causing seizures. The role for fMRI in these cases also is predominantly to map the proximity of "eloquent" tissue in and around the surgical target zone. Of note, cavernomas that have bled can limit the sensitivity of fMRI in the zone affected by hemosiderin; discussed in Section 18.4.1.

A different clinical problem is encountered in the case of arteriovenous malformations (AVMs). AVMs are (usually) congenital abnormalities, consisting of pathological direct connections between veins and arteries. AVMs may rupture, with potentially catastrophic consequences. Treatment poses a conundrum, since the risk of spontaneous bleeding is <4% per year, and the risk of treatment is non-negligible. Treatment need not be surgical, but when it is, often the clinical question is whether to operate, embolize (inject material to block a pathological artery) or both. The risk in both cases is vessel rupture and/or occlusion, the latter of which could result in ischemic stroke. FMRI can be used to map functions of adjacent tissue territories to predict the consequences of such an event. Additional uses of fMRI here are to advise the safest treatment approach and, for combination treatment, to inform the order of treatment (i.e., which vessel(s) to embolize first). Given the complexity of AVMs and their treatment, there is limited data around the added benefits of fMRI. Only one study randomized patients to fMRI or no fMRI before microsurgery (Lin et al., 2017). The results showed no difference in deficit rates, although patients were not specifically selected based on their AVM involving territories that pose higher functional risks.

18.2.3 Localizing seizure activity

Many patients with drug resistant epilepsy have no identified structural abnormality. Identifying the surgical target can pose a huge problem in its own right. The mainstay of seizure localization is scalp-EEG. However, EEG suffers from limited sensitivity to seizures arising from deep structures, such as the frequent culprit comprising the medial temporal lobe. Here, in select patients, the enhanced spatial sensitivity of fMRI can be combined with the precise temporal resolution of EEG to better localize the seizure onset region. Surgery that includes areas of abnormal activity identified with simultaneous EEG-fMRI has been associated with better seizure control than surgery performed based on established criteria alone (Coan et al., 2016). Promisingly, this combined approach has shown potential to inform which patients might not be amenable to surgery at all, possibly sparing them from further invasive procedures before reaching a decision on surgical suitability (Chaudhary et al., 2012). And, conversely, EEG-fMRI provided newly localizing information in other patients, highlighting clinical potential to guide the best placement of intracranial electrodes (Pittau et al., 2012).

18.3 Non-neurosurgical applications
18.3.1 Stroke outcome prediction

Among the most famous cases in the history of neuroscience are patients Leborgne and Lelong. Aged 31, Leborgne had become progressively aphasic as a result of long-standing epilepsy, while still being able to understand and articulate. When he later lost sensation, and then movement on the right side, Leborgne, in a critical condition having developed gangrene requiring amputation, came to the attention of surgeon Paul Broca. Upon the patient's death, Broca identified the focus of trouble in the left hemisphere inferior frontal gyrus. Around the same time, Lelong suffered a stroke leaving him profoundly

282   Chapter 18 Clinical applications of functional MRI

aphasic. The autopsy revealed a similar site of damage, leading Broca to propose this area's essential role in speech. Crucially, new cases surfaced of a disorder presenting with the opposite problem (intact speech without comprehension) arising elsewhere in the brain. These cases indicated that language is an intricate skill, which relies not on any single area, but on a network of connected brain regions (Hickok and Poeppel, 2007) that can now be routinely observed with fMRI.

While invaluable neurological cases facilitated the identification of consequences of focal brain damage, fMRI has offered insight into the mechanisms of recovery. By allowing any number of re-peat observations in the same patients, longitudinal fMRI studies have contributed several clinically important findings (Cramer et al., 2011; Hartwigsen and Saur, 2019). Firstly, that other brain regions within (and to a lesser extent outside of) the conventional task-relevant network are recruited to support damaged functions. Secondly, the contribution of wider network regions varies in different phases of recovery. Thirdly, recruitment of specific brain structures appears to reflect the efficiency of recovery. Finally, task fMRI signals collected after the initial hyper-acute stroke phase are independently predictive of longer-term performance outcomes.

These latter findings are of particular clinical interest, since they indicate a potential application for fMRI to monitor and predict the impact of interventions. Rehabilitative treatments can boost recovery post-stroke, but vary widely in their efficacy. FMRI has uncovered patterns of neural activation that correlate with behavioral improvements, as well as non-specific or even counter-productive adaptations post-injury (Cramer et al., 2011). It remains unclear which patterns of reorganization lead to optimal outcomes. This makes for a challenging search, since such patterns will likely vary according to the site of injury, stage of recovery, functional process affected, ongoing or collateral pathological processes, and other factors unique to each patient. Research is underway exploring the prospect for fMRI to reveal why some patients respond better to treatment than others. If transcranial magnetic stimulation or real-time "neurofeedback" prove effective treatments, fMRI offers a means to measure how much these techniques enhance or suppress activity in target brain regions in each individual. Such applications extend beyond stroke to a range of neurological and psychiatric conditions.

18.3.2 Drug development

A corollary to interventional treatments post-injury is the use of pharmacological agents in the treatment of disease. There is a vast literature using pharmacological fMRI to explore treatment effects that were intended, as well as those that were not. Specific uses of fMRI include the following: to inform mechanisms of action of pharmacological agents, to select (or reject) candidate compounds, measure their efficacy, tailor drug dose-escalation regimens, and differentiate patients who will likely respond from those who will not. An excellent recent review comprehensively outlined the promise and directions for pharmacological fMRI (Carmichael et al., 2018).

Pain, in particular, chronic pain, poses unique challenges for the development of effective treatments. The highly subjective nature of the pain experience makes it challenging to evaluate objectively. In addition, patients show a strong placebo effect, which clouds the development of treatments targeting the underlying cause. Studies using fMRI have proven helpful, particularly to confirm modulation of relevant brain networks by analgesic agents over and above placebos. In this way, new compounds could be put directly to the test. Perhaps most excitingly, fMRI read-outs may index the extent to which networks are susceptible to modulation, or predict pain states at an individual level. If so, fMRI results could have profound implications for the treatment of patients unable to communicate their pain

(Mouraux and Iannetti, 2018). Its multifaceted nature does, however, highlight a need for caution when interpreting fMRI signals as reflecting neural signatures specific to pain and its relief (Mouraux and Iannetti, 2018).

18.4 Considerations for clinical fMRI

Few techniques are without limitation. The ability of fMRI to probe networks of brain regions working in concert is also, in clinical terms, its main limitation. The complex relationship between observable behavior and measurable neural processes is incompletely understood. Since the clinical application of fMRI revolves around "mapping" select processes onto their brain substrates, a crucial concept is how well the sub-components of any complex behavior can be teased apart. To a large extent, the answers obtained from fMRI depend on what behavior the patient was asked to perform, what the patient actually did, and how accurately we can separate fMRI responses that are clinically of interest from those that are not. A few key practical and theoretical limitations that influence fMRI's clinical interpretability are considered next.

18.4.1 Patient selection

Very anxious or claustrophobic patients, and children, often require extensive preparation to attempt a scan. fMRI can also prove very challenging in patients with substantial performance impairments. Careful team review of symptoms and diagnostic data can establish the minimal answers that would be clinically useful, what tasks could provide them, and how to tailor tasks to accommodate pre-existing deficits. Resorting to purely visual or auditory task administration may, for example, be necessary for patients with hearing or vision impairments. Common other adaptations include adjusting the difficulty level or task speed to elicit strong and sustained fMRI signals by making the task neither too difficult (if patients have an impairment) nor too easy (if they do not).

Additional challenges arise when pathology or previous treatment causes artifacts in the fMRI echo planar images. Examples include metallic implants from previous surgery, hemosiderin staining from a bleed, and fixed metal braces. Two examples are illustrated in Fig. 18.3. Depending on the clinical question, fMRI may not be suitable, or alterations to the acquisition techniques may be necessary to obtain interpretable data. Possible adaptations include changing the slice angle of acquisition (to "avoid" image artifacts), or using an arterial spin labeling perfusion sequence (in the case of hemosiderin staining). See Chapter 12 for details of the arterial spin labeling method.

18.4.2 Sensitivity and task design

A common clinical misconception is that fMRI data are radiologically "read" in the same way as diagnostic anatomical scans. fMRI provides information about dynamic changes occurring in the brain measured every few seconds (or less) in time. To "map" a brain process, we therefore need to evoke that process in an experimentally controlled way, and detect these signals of interest among ongoing "background" activity. Consequently, the choice of task and comparison conditions, and how precisely data are captured in time, are crucial determinants of fMRI "success".

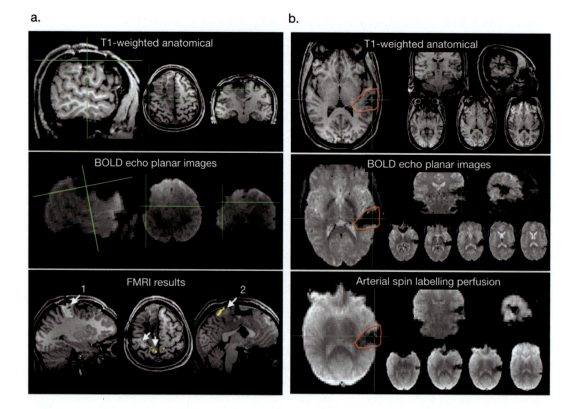

FIGURE 18.3

Pathological artefacts in clinical fMRI. Metallic plates from previous implants can cause substantial distortions in the echo planar images on which fMRI is based. In case (a), the clinical question concerned the proximity of motor cortical activations to the posterior margins of this recurrent tumor. The lateral artifact precluded mapping of the lips and mouth. However, contralateral hand- (arrow 1) and foot-tapping (arrow 2) tasks were successful in partially identifying the (intact) motor cortex. The second case (b) shows the potential for hemosiderin staining from a previous lesion bleed to cause peri-lesional signal loss far greater than apparent on anatomical imaging. Careful inspection of the raw fMRI data is essential to decide whether conventional gradient-echo echo-planar imaging is likely to underestimate relevant task activation, and to implement an alternative sequence, such as arterial spin labeling perfusion-based fMRI. In this case, language activations were observed only in the lesional left hemisphere. Further probing of the functionality of the immediate peri-lesional cortex was not possible given the large extent of signal artifact in both sequences.

If the clinical question is to establish left- versus right-hemisphere language dominance, a battery of widely used tasks could be used (Black et al., 2017). If the results are to be used further to decide the surgical feasibility or approach, entirely different tasks might be better to map processes most relevant, given the lesion location. A clear, precise, and testable clinical question is therefore essential.

During fMRI, the primary aim is to identify brain regions that are *more* active when the patient performs a clinically relevant behavior than when they are not, or are engaged in another activity. To do so, most clinical fMRI tasks are presented in a "block design". In these tasks, patients are engaged in an activity of interest (e.g., "tap your left hand") for sustained periods of around 20–30 s, which alternate with a "control" activity, such as rest. BOLD signal changes (determined by the hemodynamic response) are slow. By repeating the behavior, the associated signals should build up and plateau. This maximizes the signal during each task condition, making it statistically easier to capture the biggest possible *difference* between them. The trade-off is that we lose power to detect variations in performance within each block. If it is clinically important to localize activity for individual task items (for example only accurately named pictures), an alternative "event-related" task design is usually preferable. Because it is more difficult to capture the signal of individual task responses, a lot more trials are needed, making event-related tasks often impractically long.

18.4.3 Specificity: choosing the "baseline"

The clinical question naturally guides the selection (or creation) of a task with a suitable active condition. What is less frequently appreciated is the impact of the comparison condition. Most often, fMRI is criticized for not isolating a cognitive process specifically enough. Usually, this criticism arises from differences obtained with fMRI compared with intra-operative brain stimulation. However, neither fMRI nor intraoperative tasks are currently standardized, and only rarely do they overlap.

As an example, stimulating the ventral premotor cortex while a patient counts out loud reliably causes speech arrest by disrupting articulation. The vast majority of fMRI tasks used to map "speech" are performed silently, because overt speech causes head motion. If head motion occurs systemically during the task period of interest, the large confounding signals caused by head motion can be impossible to separate from neural processes associated with the task. Covert speech does engage regions involved in articulatory planning, but much less than overt speech. If the clinical aim is to identify *all* regions involved with speech generation and execution, for example to establish overall risk, then a widely activating overt task with a low baseline (rest) might be favored, or orofacial tasks could be added. In this context, there is no attempt to separate the roles performed by sub-components of the "speech" network.

Instead, if the question is whether specific aspects of language are close to lesion borders, then well-chosen task-control conditions are important to narrow down the observed activations. The control condition is designed to engage generic processes involved in task performance, but that are not specific to the process we wish to isolate. Fig. 18.4 shows the substantial difference in activation obtained during a semantic association task using a single "active" task condition, but varying the "control". Of course, not all cognitive processes can be appropriately isolated. But often the specificity of task activation maps can be improved with deeper consideration of non-specific processes that are automatically engaged by a task.

18.4.4 To activate or not to activate... what is the question?

FMRI relies on patients performing a task as instructed. This is a strong assumption. One reason for "failed" fMRI studies is lack of patient compliance, often due to impaired performance.

Resting-state fMRI, without any active manipulations, robustly identifies brain networks that spatially overlap with those engaged during tasks. Resting-state-derived networks also appear to correlate

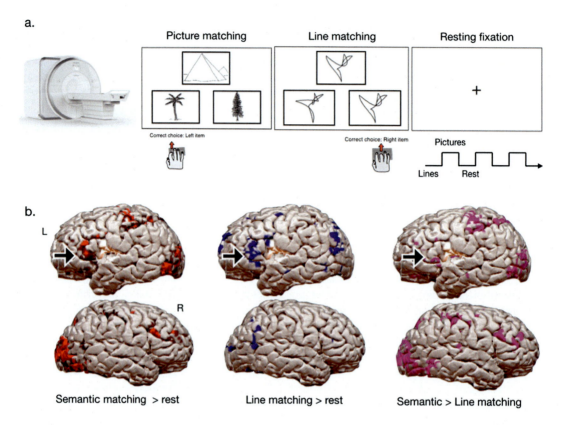

FIGURE 18.4

Impact of task "control" conditions on the specificity of activation maps. Illustration a block-design semantic association task adapted from the Pyramids and Palm trees test for fMRI (a). During active task blocks, the patient chooses between picture items that are conceptually linked. Two control conditions are included: resting fixation and line-matching, during which the patient performs similar processes (view pictures, select a match, make a response), but the images are un-nameable, meaningless lines. The bottom row (b) shows the activation maps associated with the semantic condition of interest when compared separately to each control condition. Compared to "rest", semantic association blocks generated extensive activation (arrow) anterior to this patient's tumor. However, line-matching, compared to rest, activates many similar brain regions. Unsurprisingly therefore, directly comparing "semantic-matching" against "line-matching" yielded much more focused activation, identifying sub-regions within the inferior frontal gyrus more specifically involved in semantic association.

with some types of behavior. This approach therefore offers appealing advantages over task fMRI. Resting-state fMRI is often faster to acquire, since multiple brain networks can be extracted from a single resting-state scan. It is also easier for patients, whose active role is reduced to lying still and staying awake (although, arguably, tasks are better for that!). The major disadvantage is uncertainty about the functional relevance of signal correlations between brain regions at rest. This is a concern not just for resting-state networks that are easily detected, but also those which might not spontaneously "emerge" at rest (for example, areas involved in reading). In terms of large-scale functional networks, such as the sensorimotor network, promising results comparing resting-state networks to intraoperative stimulation suggest a potential application in patients unable to reliably perform tasks. In this context, the acquisition protocol for resting-state fMRI may be an important determinant of network sensitivity, as illustrated in Fig. 18.5. Since there are fundamental questions about network specificity, the choice be-

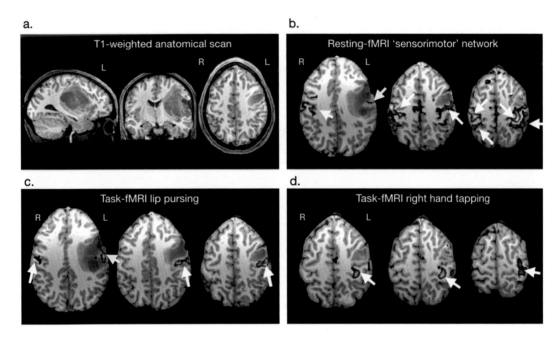

FIGURE 18.5

Identifying (sensori)motor cortex from task- and resting-state fMRI. In healthy participants, resting-state fMRI reliably identifies networks of brain networks that spatially co-localize with established functional systems, such as the sensorimotor network. The sensitivity and specificity to detect these networks in individual patients with pathology is less well known. In a 23 year-old patient with a tumor invading the precentral gyrus (a), a 5-minute resting-state fMRI sequence (repetition time (TR): 3.5 s, echo time: 30 ms, voxel resolution: 2 × 2 × 2 mm) readily identified a network that spatially overlapped with the anatomically-expected sensorimotor cortex (b). The resting-state network was much more expansive, but intersected with, task-fMRI activation maps corresponding to active mouth (c) and contralateral hand (d) movements. Advanced acquisition protocols using simultaneous multi-slice acquisitions that enable very fast temporal sampling rates (e.g., TRs of 1.5 s or less), more often produce finer-grained subdivisions that better resemble task-activation maps. However, these rely on high anatomical confidence to identify the most plausible maps, conflicting with the indication for motor fMRI mapping, which is greatest when anatomical landmarks are displaced or effaced by pathology. Conversely, task-fMRI to localize motor sub-regions requires acquisition of multiple tasks, and is not always successful when patients have extensive pre-existing weakness. In this (performance-intact) patient, direct brain stimulation during awake surgery confirmed the task-identified site for lip movements, which was more prominent in the task activation map than in the resting network component. Histopathological analysis diagnosed a Grade III anaplastic astrocytoma.

tween resting-state versus task fMRI comes down to whether the clinical question can be answered by identifying a network-level (sensory) map, or based on anatomical criteria (for region-of-interest signal correlations). If the patient is able to engage actively, task-fMRI is preferable for the higher behavioral confidence it provides.

18.5 Analyzing fMRI for clinical applications
18.5.1 Single-subject analyses

Most established image analysis approaches were developed for group-based analyses. Unique considerations arise for fMRI data analysis in individual subjects. Neuroscientific imaging studies aim to establish general principles about brain function and are, therefore rightly, concerned that findings should be authentic and generalizable. FMRI "mapping" is essentially a signal detection problem, testing every voxel of the brain to determine if it shows an expected signal. Crucially, *the answers are never all-or-nothing*. FMRI activation maps generally reflect the *probability* that a detected signal is related to the task, based on statistical testing. When searching over the whole brain, we perform a vast number of statistical tests, raising the probability of detecting an activation purely by chance. To minimize the risk that a major discovery about brain function was an unfortunate statistical false alarm, neuroscientific studies focus on controlling this false positive rate by limiting the probability that detected "activations" are due to chance to no more than, say, 5% ($p < 0.05$).

Clinical concerns, however, are usually *the opposite*. To minimize harm, such as before surgically removing brain tissue on the basis of fMRI results, it is more crucial that *no true areas of activation are missed*. This shifts the focus onto minimizing false negatives (Haller and Bartsch, 2009). There is no standard way to select the "right" balance for individual patients, and some commercial fMRI analysis packages do not offer the user control over these settings.

This discussion may seem pedagogical, but the clinical implications run deep. Consider applications of fMRI to determine levels of awareness in patients with disorders of consciousness. Monti and colleagues showed that some patients considered clinically to be in a vegetative state have the ability to voluntarily modulate their brain activity in response to fMRI task instructions (Monti et al., 2010). Cases remain exceptionally rare, but one patient could answer "yes" or "no" questions by either imagining hitting a tennis ball, or visualizing "walking" around a familiar place. These tasks activate different brain regions, and in this way, consistent "answers" were obtained in response to easily-verified autobiographical questions. The team could therefore next pose new, medically relevant questions, such as if the patient was in pain. Since such ground-breaking applications might influence decisions to continue patient life-support, as the authors highlight (Peterson et al., 2015), it raises profound medical and ethical questions as to the readiness of fMRI as a diagnostic test.

The main difficulty is to establish with high certainty what a detected fMRI signal measures, and how reliably that signal is detected in a single patient. An inability to detect activation does not necessarily mean the patient cannot (willfully) generate it. Their attention may have lapsed, or perhaps activation was present, but too small or variable to reach statistical significance.

18.5.2 Impact of processing choices

Methods to analyze fMRI at the single patient level remain far from standardized. Yet, seemingly innocuous choices in data pre-processing can dramatically alter activation maps. This is an important consideration, since some surgical teams reportedly use fMRI to define a radius around fMRI as a "safe" resection margin (Benjamin et al., 2018). The impact of one such choice, spatial smoothing, is illustrated in Fig. 18.6, highlighting that "localization" by fMRI is not absolute, and attempts to guide surgery based on distances from the borders of "activation" are misinformed. Further factors are highlighted in Box 18.1.

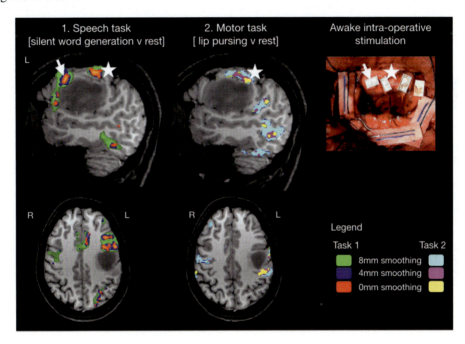

FIGURE 18.6

Impact of smoothing on spatial "precision" of fMRI. Spatial smoothing is a common pre-preprocessing step used to improve statistical signal-to-noise. There is no hard rule as to whether to apply spatial smoothing and how much. The "optimal" level of smoothing reflects a balance between the brain region being studied and the resolution that the fMRI data were acquired at. The impact is shown of varying smoothing between 0, 4 and 8 mm on two tasks in a patient with a left frontal glioma. For "speech", the "activation" at 8 mm smoothing extends along the anterior border of the tumor, overlapping with it, while also producing extensive activation contralaterally. At 0 and 4 mm smoothing, the activations (at the same statistical threshold) are more focused and confined to the left hemisphere. Similar results are seen for the motor task. Intraoperative stimulation identified an anterior site for speech arrest (arrow). Stimulation also confirmed posterior sites associated with mouth movements (motor arrest and tongue sensations, star), where a small amount of tumor was left behind. Spatial extents of fMRI activations are not categorical measures of the underlying (and indirectly sampled) neural activity. Selecting "safe" resection margins based on distances from "activations" is not an intended nor indicated use.

290 **Chapter 18** Clinical applications of functional MRI

Box 18.1

Registration

FMRI results are often aligned with anatomical images for neuronavigation. However, prominent artifacts in EPI data affect the accuracy of registration. The algorithm used to register fMRI, and the inclusion of static field inhomogeneity maps to correct for EPI deformations, substantially influence registration accuracy. Additionally, no matter the accuracy achieved for pre-operative plans, the surgical process of opening the skull can cause substantial brain shift. Intra-operative confirmation of functional margins remains essential whenever possible.

Confound modeling

It is important to minimize head motion at the time of image acquisition. Still, some movement is inevitable and can cause substantial artifactual "activation". Similarly, cardiac pulsations and breathing contribute noise to fMRI signals, more often apparent in data acquired at very fast sampling rates. Variance associated with these parameters can be removed from the task fMRI signal if physiological recordings are available, or using data-driven analysis approaches. User experience guides whether and how to deal with these possible confounds, but the outcome is difficult to evaluate objectively.

Statistical thresholding

Individuals vary hugely in the magnitude of BOLD response they produce during a task. This variance can be functionally meaningful (e.g., mirroring behavioral performance) or not (e.g., reflecting head motion). Choosing a threshold at which to display results is a difficult problem. Different approaches include selecting a very low (even sub-)threshold to maximize detection of *any* activation, or the opposite: selecting a high threshold to increase the likelihood that those activations are robust. A third—popular—option is to make a subject-specific choice, tailoring the threshold to a proportion of the maximum seen in that patient.

Analysis technique

Many approaches exist to analyze task-fMRI, including general linear modeling, time-course correlation and independent component analysis. Each has advantages and disadvantages. The choice is sometimes best informed by the post-task interview of the patient and by visually examining the time-course of their responses. Patients may show a delay in their task responses, fall asleep, or other unexpected issues may occur. Data-driven analyses can provide a helpful complement to model-driven approaches to build confidence in the interpretation of a noisy or unexpected activation map, since structured noise (head motion, respiration, etc.) is typically segregated into separate components.

18.5.3 A note on laterality

Issues with calculating a language "laterality index" are well-established (Seghier, 2008), but biases also arise during visual inspection of activation maps. When an activation map appears "bilateral", it is tempting to conclude that the risk of surgery in the dominant hemisphere is lower than it would be in a patient with a strongly left-lateralized activation map. This interpretation *may* be true. However, greater activity in the supposedly non-dominant hemisphere can also reflect heightened attention, effort, working memory, error monitoring, or other processes not directly sustaining language. Consequently, task-relevant activation close to a surgical target should be presumed to denote a risk to that function, irrespective of how much activation is present elsewhere. In other words, *where* task-related activation occurs is almost always more useful than *which hemisphere's* activation looks greatest.

18.5.4 Validating fMRI

Numerous studies have compared the performance of fMRI to stimulation techniques, including (navigated) transcranial magnetic stimulation and electrocortical stimulation mapping. Though these are important comparisons, the aims of the techniques are quite distinct. Since the unifying purpose is to improve outcomes, the most relevant comparison is how accurately each predicts post-treatment performance. As mentioned, fMRI in general outperforms the Wada test (Binder, 2011; Szaflarski et al., 2017). Preliminary studies in small case series suggest that removing tissue showing fMRI-detected activity during surgery results in worse outcomes, even when intraoperative stimulation was used. However, very little data exist and crucial prospective studies are lacking. Since no technique prevents a decline in performance completely, a combination of methods may be superior in this respect than any that is used in isolation (Rolinski et al., 2019).

18.6 Conclusion

The primary neurosurgical application of fMRI developed out of the traditional view that essential functions arise from separate and delineated parts of the brain. The underlying assumption is that behaviors arise from neural processes that are consistent, serial, and localized. There are cases where this is evidenced, but also instances where these assumptions break down. Clearly, fMRI, like other techniques, is not without limitations. Additionally, there are conceptual limits to how well we can condense rich behavioral experiences into single spatial maps to navigate around. FMRI is one of the surgeon's many tools, and essential complementary information is provided by diffusion tractography and brain stimulation techniques. With cautious consideration of what signals are measured, and how, fMRI has made direct contributions to clinical problems of functional network preservation. In neurosurgery, fMRI has a now well-established role in assessing neurosurgical risks and revising plans to maximize performance outcomes, while reducing invasive clinical testing. Additional applications have emerged in the field of monitoring pharmacological and interventional treatment effects to distinguish effective from ineffective mechanisms of action. Unifying these applications suggests the tangible potential for fMRI to predict treatment outcomes in single subjects, and hence to derive customized treatment plans. The real challenge is generally not what fMRI *can* do, but defining a precise, testable hypothesis based on detailed understanding of what fMRI measures. At least in neurosurgical terms, the answer provided by fMRI is only as good as the question.

References

Benjamin, C.F.A., Li, A.X., Blumenfeld, H., Constable, R.T., Alkawadri, R., Bickel, S., Helmstaedter, C., Meletti, S., Bronen, R., Warfield, S.K., Peters, J.M., Reutens, D., Polczynska, M., Spencer, D.D., Hirsch, L.J., 2018. Presurgical language fMRI: clinical practices and patient outcomes in epilepsy surgical planning. Hum. Brain Mapp. 39, 2777–2785.

Binder, J.R., 2011. Functional MRI is a valid noninvasive alternative to Wada testing. Epilepsy Behav. 20, 214–222.

Black, D.F., Vachha, B., Mian, A., Faro, S.H., Maheshwari, M., Sair, H.I., Petrella, J.R., Pillai, J.J., Welker, K., 2017. American society of functional neuroradiology-recommended fMRI paradigm algorithms for presurgical language assessment. Am. J. Neuroradiol. 38, E65–E73.

Carmichael, O., Schwarz, A.J., Chatham, C.H., Scott, D., Turner, J.A., Upadhyay, J., Coimbra, A., Goodman, J.A., Baumgartner, R., English, B.A., Apolzan, J.W., Shankapal, P., Hawkins, K.R., 2018. The role of fMRI in drug development. Drug Discov. Today 23, 333–348.

Chaudhary, U.J., Carmichael, D.W., Rodionov, R., Thornton, R.C., Bartlett, P., Vulliemoz, S., Micallef, C., Mcevoy, A.W., Diehl, B., Walker, M.C., Duncan, J.S., Lemieux, L., 2012. Mapping preictal and ictal haemodynamic networks using video-electroencephalography and functional imaging. Brain 135, 3645–3663.

Coan, A.C., Chaudhary, U.J., Grouiller, F., Campos, B.M., Perani, S., De Ciantis, A., Vulliemoz, S., Diehl, B., Beltramini, G.C., Carmichael, D.W., Thornton, R.C., Covolan, R.J., Cendes, F., Lemieux, L., 2016. EEG-fMRI in the presurgical evaluation of temporal lobe epilepsy. J. Neurol. Neurosurg. Psychiatry 87, 642–649.

Cramer, S.C., Sur, M., Dobkin, B.H., O'Brien, C., Sanger, T.D., Trojanowski, J.Q., Rumsey, J.M., Hicks, R., Cameron, J., Chen, D., Chen, W.G., Cohen, L.G., Decharms, C., Duffy, C.J., Eden, G.F., Fetz, E.E., Filart, R., Freund, M., Grant, S.J., Haber, S., Kalivas, P.W., Kolb, B., Kramer, A.F., Lynch, M., Mayberg, H.S., Mcquillen, P.S., Nitkin, R., Pascual-Leone, A., Reuter-Lorenz, P., Schiff, N., Sharma, A., Shekim, L., Stryker, M., Sullivan, E.V., Vinogradov, S., 2011. Harnessing neuroplasticity for clinical applications. Brain 134, 1591–1609.

Haller, S., Bartsch, A.J., 2009. Pitfalls in FMRI. Eur. Radiol. 19, 2689–2706.

Hartwigsen, G., Saur, D., 2019. Neuroimaging of stroke recovery from aphasia - insights into plasticity of the human language network. NeuroImage 190, 14–31.

Hickok, G., Poeppel, D., 2007. The cortical organization of speech processing. Nat. Rev. Neurosci. 8, 393–402.

Lin, F., Jiao, Y., Wu, J., Zhao, B., Tong, X., Jin, Z., Cao, Y., Wang, S., 2017. Effect of functional MRI-guided navigation on surgical outcomes: a prospective controlled trial in patients with arteriovenous malformations. J. Neurosurg. 126, 1863–1872.

Monti, M.M., Vanhaudenhuyse, A., Coleman, M.R., Boly, M., Pickard, J.D., Tshibanda, L., Owen, A.M., Laureys, S., 2010. Willful modulation of brain activity in disorders of consciousness. N. Engl. J. Med. 362, 579–589.

Mouraux, A., Iannetti, G.D., 2018. The search for pain biomarkers in the human brain. Brain 141, 3290–3307.

Pak, R.W., Hadjiabadi, D.H., Senarathna, J., Agarwal, S., Thakor, N.V., Pillai, J.J., Pathak, A.P., 2017. Implications of neurovascular uncoupling in functional magnetic resonance imaging (fMRI) of brain tumors. J. Cereb. Blood Flow Metab. 37, 3475–3487.

Peterson, A., Cruse, D., Naci, L., Weijer, C., Owen, A.M., 2015. Risk, diagnostic error, and the clinical science of consciousness. NeuroImage Clin. 7, 588–597.

Pittau, F., Dubeau, F., Gotman, J., 2012. Contribution of EEG/fMRI to the definition of the epileptic focus. Neurology 78, 1479–1487.

Rahman, M., Abbatematteo, J., De Leo, E.K., Kubilis, P.S., Vaziri, S., Bova, F., Sayour, E., Mitchell, D., Quinones-Hinojosa, A., 2017. The effects of new or worsened postoperative neurological deficits on survival of patients with glioblastoma. J. Neurosurg. 127, 123–131.

Rolinski, R., Austermuehle, A., Wiggs, E., Agrawal, S., Sepeta, L.N., Gaillard, W.D., Zaghloul, K.A., Inati, S.K., Theodore, W.H., 2019. Functional MRI and direct cortical stimulation: prediction of postoperative language decline. Epilepsia 60, 560–570.

Seghier, M.L., 2008. Laterality index in functional MRI: methodological issues. Magn. Reson. Imaging 26, 594–601.

Szaflarski, J.P., Gloss, D., Binder, J.R., Gaillard, W.D., Golby, A.J., Holland, S.K., Ojemann, J., Spencer, D.C., Swanson, S.J., French, J.A., Theodore, W.H., 2017. Practice guideline summary: use of fMRI in the presurgical evaluation of patients with epilepsy: report of the guideline development, dissemination, and implementation subcommittee of the American Academy of Neurology. Neurology 88, 395–402.

PART 6
The brain connectome

CHAPTER

The diffusion MRI connectome

19

Michiel Cottaar[a] and Matteo Bastiani[a,b]

[a]*Wellcome Centre for Integrative Neuroimaging (WIN), Oxford Centre for Functional MRI of the Brain (FMRIB),*
University of Oxford, Oxford, United Kingdom
[b]*Sir Peter Mansfield Imaging Centre (SPMIC), University of Nottingham, Nottingham, United Kingdom*

19.1 Introduction

The average human brain contains tens of billions of neurons. These microscopic functional elements are organized in cortical layers and columns at the mesoscopic scale, and in cortical areas and subcortical structures at the macroscopic one. All these functional elements are not independent information processing units. Across the different scales, microscopic neurons and macroscopic brain areas are both embedded within complex networks, whose intrinsic and extrinsic structural connections mediate information transfer and functional integration. This wiring makes information traveling among different functional units possible, and its properties determine key functional aspects, such as propagation speed and efficiency. Therefore, to understand how the brain works it is necessary to map its circuitry, which ultimately determines individual behavioral differences and pathological states.

The field of connectomics aims at building and analyzing comprehensive maps of brain connectivity across all scales. A *connectome* is the network matrix, whose elements indicate whether and, in some cases, how strongly, each pair of nodes is connected. A microscopic connectome maps synaptic connections between individual neurons, whereas a macroscopic connectome delineates which brain regions are connected via interregional white matter pathways. Microscopic connectivity constrains the computations of individual neurons, whereas macroscopic white matter tracts enable brain systems to perform specific computations. The functional relevance of the structural connectome has been assessed in several studies, showing that synaptic weights in the mouse or whole white matter tract bundles play a key role in predicting the functional responses of the brain elements they connect.

The endeavor of mapping the brain connectome has been pursued since the 17th century using microscopy techniques, with detailed descriptions of white matter organization and cortical cyto- and myelo-architecture being published across the 19th and 20th centuries (Catani et al., 2013). Histological staining techniques and advanced serial electron microscopy have made a multi-labeled mapping of the brain microcircuitry possible in a semi-automated fashion. However, both the high data throughput of these techniques and the lack of fully automated analysis frameworks limit the exploration to small tissue samples. The first full microscopic connectome mapped using electron microscopy was obtained from a roundworm (i.e., Caenorhabditis elegans with 302 neurons) (White et al., 1986). Probing the microscopic structural connectome of bigger mammals poses several challenges. Currently, researchers

Advances in Magnetic Resonance Technology and Applications, Volume 4, ISSN 2666-9099. https://doi.org/10.1016/B978-0-12-822479-3.00032-4
Copyright © 2021 Elsevier Inc. All rights reserved.

296 **Chapter 19** The diffusion MRI connectome

are acquiring electron microscopy data to study 1 mm^3 of the mouse connectome, containing approximately 100,000 neurons (DeWeerdt, 2019).

The advent of chemical tracers has allowed researchers to map specific brain connections of different species at a larger scale. By combining the information obtained from multiple injection sites, researchers have obtained detailed macroscopic brain connectomes in animal models (Jbabdi et al., 2015). These are considered to be the current gold standard in connectomics and, in some cases, their edges can be weighted by measures of connectivity strength, such as the number of labeled cell bodies. However, despite offering high sensitivity and a low false positive rate, tracer studies also have some limitations. To build a normative connectome, it is necessary to combine results across animals, since only a few injections can be performed on a single brain, but the lack of well-defined cortical area boundaries makes standardizing injection sites very challenging. Since tracers can only be injected in animals and results can only be assessed *ex vivo*. Direct translatability to *in vivo* human settings is also difficult, especially when studying structural connections related to higher cognitive functions, such as language. Quantifying the "connectivity strength" is also still an open challenge. It is possible to count labeled cell bodies by injecting retrograde tracers, but axonal terminals, synaptic strength or number of terminal buttons are currently out of reach.

Magnetic resonance imaging (MRI) has proven to be a very effective tool to non-invasively map the macroscopic human brain connectome *in vivo* (Jbabdi et al., 2015). Diffusion MRI (dMRI) is the main contrast that researchers have extensively used to estimate macroscopic structural connections (Sotiropoulos and Zalesky, 2019) and to characterize their microstructural properties (see Chapter 11). Diffusion MRI-based tractography is currently the only tool to probe the structural organization of the human connectome *in vivo*, and it offers several advantages when compared to classical histology. Biopsy is no longer needed, and tissues can be studied through time (i.e., longitudinally) without the need to extract the brain, avoiding deformations and changes in their properties. Moreover, it is possible to map the whole brain connectome in a relatively fast (i.e., < hours) and automated way both at the single subject and group-wise levels. However, dMRI-based connectome mapping presents several challenges. The difference in scales between the typical voxel volume in dMRI (> 1 mm^3) and the average human axonal diameter ($\sim$ 1 µm), means that thousands of axons, glial, and other cells contribute to the signal sampled at each spatial location. Within a voxel, axons from multiple tracts can also cross or "kiss" each other, making the estimation of structural patterns very challenging. Moreover, dMRI does not directly measure the actual features of interest, such as axonal orientations or tract-specific myelination. The contrast in dMRI images is obtained by sensitizing the acquisition to the diffusion of water molecules. Therefore computational modeling approaches are needed to infer axonal orientations, which tractography algorithms use to reconstruct white matter tracts.

In this chapter, we describe the necessary steps to map the macroscopic human connectome using dMRI. We present different approaches to estimate its nodes and edges and discuss the implications of crucial methodological choices. Lastly, we cover the current limitations of *in vivo* connectomics. These are currently hindering our knowledge of the human brain and the potential for clinical translation of connectome mapping approaches. However, they also pose exciting new scientific endeavors that will generate new quantitative techniques to better understand the connectivity of the human brain and, ultimately, its function.

19.2 Mapping the structural connectome with diffusion MRI

A structural connectome is a graph representation of the wiring of the human brain, consisting of a set of *nodes* and *edges* (Sporns et al., 2005). Typically, a minimal connectome mapping pipeline requires two different types of acquisition (Fig. 19.1). A high-resolution anatomical scan, usually T_1-weighted, provides the necessary contrast to segment basic tissue types, i.e., white matter (WM) and gray matter (GM) and cerebrospinal fluid (CSF). These tissue maps can be used both to define relevant nodes, such as cortical area labels obtained from an atlas, and to constrain tractography results by, e.g., enforcing fiber tracking only through white matter regions. Diffusion MRI data provide the necessary contrast to estimate voxel-wise fiber orientation distributions (FODs), which are then used to estimate the connectome edges by using tractography. The following sections will provide the reader with more details on how to estimate nodes and edges using dMRI.

19.3 Inferring fiber orientations

Diffusion MRI is sensitive to the random movement (i.e., diffusion) of water within the brain. By changing the gradient orientation of the dMRI sequence, we change the direction along which we are sensitive to water diffusion. The anisotropy, i.e., the directional preference, of water molecules' diffusion allows us to estimate the FODs in each voxel, because the water can diffuse more freely along the axons than perpendicular to them. Several models have been developed to infer axonal orientations from the dMRI signal.

The first and most widely used model to characterize the anisotropic diffusive behavior of water molecules using dMRI is diffusion tensor imaging (DTI) (Basser et al., 2000). By modeling molecular displacement using a three-dimensional Gaussian function, DTI can estimate the principal diffusion direction (PDD), which is assumed to correspond to the underlying axonal orientations (top row in Fig. 19.2). Tractography approaches based on the diffusion tensor have been used to reconstruct many major white matter tracts. However, axons from multiple white matter fascicles are present in most voxels with complex sub-voxel geometries, leading to the necessity of more advanced diffusion MRI models that capture the full complexity of the FOD.

The main focus of these more advanced models has been on accurately resolving crossing fiber configurations, caused by white matter tracts crossing each other within the same voxel (second row in Fig. 19.2). Such crossing fiber configurations are very common in the human brain (Behrens et al., 2007), making it necessary to use a model that can estimate them, especially when doing virtual dissection of specific white matter tracts and structural connectome estimation. The diffusion tensor model can be extended to multiple crossing fibers by modeling the signal as the sum of multiple diffusion tensors, each corresponding to a different crossing fiber population. However, parameter inversion for this multi-tensor model is very ill-posed.

Parametric spherical deconvolution (SD) approaches, such as the ball & stick model (Behrens et al., 2007), aim at resolving this issue by adding some assumptions about the diffusion tensors. In this model, the signal is represented as the sum of an isotropic diffusion tensor, i.e., the "ball", and one or more purely anisotropic diffusion tensors, i.e., the "stick". Each stick models diffusion only along a single direction, which in this model corresponds to the orientation of a fiber population (Fig. 19.2). While such a model can deal with crossing fibers, it still cannot capture the full complexity of the

298 Chapter 19 The diffusion MRI connectome

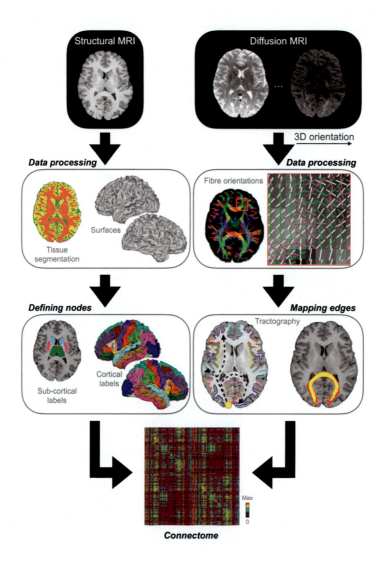

FIGURE 19.1

Structural connectome mapping pipeline. Two parallel processing streams are typically required to map a structural connectome. The structural MRI-based one is used to first segment tissue types and obtain surface meshes in each subject's native space. This information is used to define the nodes of the connectivity matrix, such as sub-cortical structures and cortical areas derived from atlases in standard space. The dMRI-based one is used to estimate the voxel-wise FODs. These and the tissue segmentation maps are then fed into tractography algorithms to map the edges of the connectome, i.e., estimate the fiber tracts that run from each node to the rest of the brain. By repeating tractography for all the nodes, it is possible to build a weighted connectivity matrix, whose weights quantify connectivity strength between, e.g., cortical areas and sub-cortical structures.

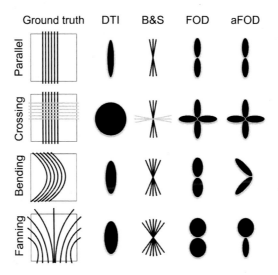

FIGURE 19.2

Estimated fiber orientations using different dMRI-based models. Across the four simulated ground truth sub-voxel fiber geometries, DTI can only accurately represent the first case, where a single bundle of parallel fiber is present. Using a Bayesian inference framework, the ball and stick (B&S) model can correctly estimate and disentangle the posterior distribution of up to three separate fiber populations crossing within a voxel, or of a single one running straight or fanning. Similarly, FOD estimation based on a non-parametric constrained spherical deconvolution (CSD) approach correctly captures most of the complex configurations, including the amount of fiber dispersion. However, neither the B&S nor CSD models correctly estimate the bending configuration nor the polarity of the fanning fibers. To achieve that, the spherical harmonic basis can be augmented, and information coming from the neighboring voxels can be incorporated in the estimation of the FOD, resulting in an asymmetric FOD (aFOD).

FOD. After all, not all axons within a single white matter tract will be perfectly aligned with each other. In other words, fiber dispersion around the estimated mean orientation needs to be accounted for. However, the ball & stick model cannot capture this, because it assumes that the FOD consists of a sum of discrete fiber orientations without any width. The ball & stick model can be expanded to account for dispersion by modeling the orientations of each crossing fiber population as a continuous distribution rather than a single, discrete orientation. The most common choices are the Watson distribution for isotropic dispersion of the Bingham distribution for anisotropic dispersion. Though such approaches are popular in microstructural mapping models (see Chapter 11), they still make fairly strong assumptions about the shape of the FOD.

Non-parametric constrained spherical deconvolution (CSD) approaches model the FOD as a set of basis functions, such as spherical harmonics. These techniques are typically model-free and can quickly estimate the FOD by using linear optimization techniques. These can lead to reliable FOD estimates as long as the optimization is constrained to ensure that it remains positive (Dell'Acqua and Tournier, 2019). However, these approaches typically assume a single fiber response function, i.e., the signal profile expected for perfectly aligned fibers. It has been shown that this assumption does not always work in every brain area (Howard et al., 2019), but this issue will mainly affect the width of the FOD,

300 **Chapter 19** The diffusion MRI connectome

i.e., the fiber dispersion, and will only have a minimal effect on the mean fiber orientations used in tractography.

The approach used to estimate the FOD parameters has strong implications for the choice of tractography method. They can be inferred using either a best-fit or a probabilistic approach. The former will result in a point estimate of the FOD, whereas the latter tries to estimate the full posterior distribution of the FOD's parameters. Whereas best-fit approaches are usually quicker, parametric or non-parametric probabilistic inference allows modeling the uncertainty of each parameter's estimate. The uncertainty may be caused both by hardware and modeling noise. This uncertainty can be used in tractography to model the uncertainty due to thermal noise in the dMRI data on the structural connectome. It has been shown that, for robust estimation of the FOD, acquiring multi b-value shells and high angular resolution diffusion imaging (HARDI) data, is very beneficial. Using such data lead to more robust crossing fiber configurations and allows decreasing the risk of overfitting (Jbabdi et al., 2012; Jeurissen et al., 2014). It is crucial that all diffusion data are well-aligned, and any artifacts and distortions have been corrected before estimating the FOD (see Chapter 9).

Many other models are available to estimate the FOD. In general, these different approaches provide estimates of the mean fiber orientations, which are in good agreement with each other and with corresponding information derived from histological slices, which offer sub-voxel resolution (Howard et al., 2019) (Fig. 19.3). However, there is substantially more variability between FOD reconstruction techniques in the estimated number of crossing fibers and in the amount of fiber dispersion. How to incorporate fiber dispersion into tractography algorithms is still an active area of research, as it requires properly accounting for complex fiber configurations, such as sharp bending and fanning (Fig. 19.2). Because of the underlying assumption that the dMRI signal is symmetric, i.e., diffusion along $+x$ is the same as diffusion along $-x$, most methods cannot resolve such configurations. This degeneracy can be broken by reconstructing an asymmetric FOD (aFOD) by adding information from the local neighborhood of each voxel (Bastiani et al., 2017).

19.4 From fiber orientations to the connectome

The aim of tractography is to estimate the edges of the connectome, i.e., the white matter tracts connecting cortical and sub-cortical structures with each other. The elements of a connectivity matrix only contain information about the tracts' termination points rather than their overall shapes. These elements can be either binary, reflecting whether a connection between two nodes exists, or weighted, trying to quantify the connectivity strength between nodes. However, a major strength of tractography is its ability to perform *virtual dissection*, which is the estimation of the overall shape, and not just the termination points, of a specific tract of interest. Such segmentation of white matter into its constituent white matter tracts has been shown for at least the major tracts to be very robust across large numbers of subjects and different data sets.

Fiber tracking algorithms integrate the information provided by the voxel-wise FODs to propagate virtual streamlines that approximate white matter bundles. Several tractography approaches have been developed, which can take advantage of the information provided by the different FOD estimation methods. Local tractography methods follow a step-wise propagation strategy from each seed voxel. Streamlines run tangentially to the voxel-wise fiber orientations extracted from the peaks of the FODs. User-defined rules determine when propagation stops and which streamlines to discard. For example, a

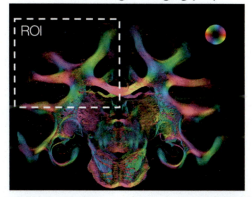
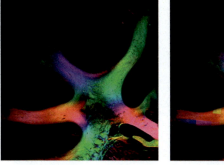
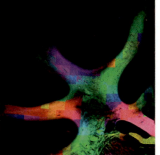

FIGURE 19.3

Validation of diffusion MRI fiber orientations with ground truth in BigMac data set, which is a large data set of a macaque with both *in-vivo* and *ex-vivo* MRI data and microscopy data. Polarized light imaging was used to estimate the in-plane fiber orientations, which has an excellent agreement with the fiber orientations from the ball & stick dMRI model when projected onto this plane (note that only the orientation of the most closely aligned stick is shown). Color coding shows in-plane fiber orientation according to the disc in the upper-most panel.

streamline stops propagating when it reaches a target region, or it gets discarded if it enters the ventricles (Smith et al., 2012). Surface or volume-based masks can also be used to guide tractography by, e.g., seeding and targeting vertices on the white/gray matter boundary surface, while enforcing propagation only within the segmented white matter volume.

Local fiber tracking approaches can be further subdivided into deterministic and probabilistic. Local deterministic approaches will propagate streamlines following the peaks of the voxel-wise FODs, resulting in point estimates of white matter tracts connecting two nodes. Local probabilistic approaches work similarly to the deterministic ones, but they account for the uncertainty in the estimation of the orientation of the peaks extracted from the FODs. Once the range of possible fiber orientations have been estimated, probabilistic tractography propagates the streamlines based on random samples from this range. To fully account for such uncertainty, local probabilistic approaches typically sample thousands of streamlines from the same seed voxel. This results in a spatial distribution of a given path, which quantifies the likelihood of any given voxel being connected with the seed one.

To obtain a connectome, the same tractography algorithm can be repeatedly seeded from each of its nodes. This procedure will generate a comprehensive map of the macroscopic structural connections of the brain (Fig. 19.1). The choice of tractography algorithm and FOD estimation approach influences the connectome mapping results, potentially biasing downstream results when analyzing the brain architecture using, e.g., network analysis (Bastiani et al., 2012). In general, probabilistic tractography approaches tend to have higher test-retest reliability in connectome reconstruction than deterministic ones. However, by exploring all possible paths probabilistic tractography is far more sensitive to false positives (Maier-Hein et al., 2017). Given enough streamlines, probabilistic tractography will eventually find some path between each pair of nodes. This means that to arrive at a binarized connectome indicating which nodes are connected, thresholding becomes a crucial issue in probabilistic tractogra-

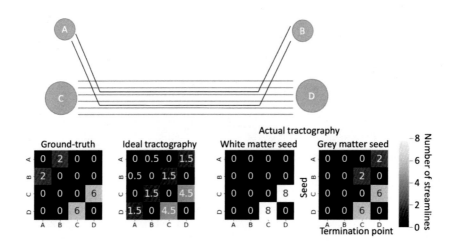

FIGURE 19.4

Illustration of the limitations of the tractography results when two pairs of regions (A–B & C–D) are connected through the same white matter tract. In such a case, there are two distinct issues in reconstructing the ground-truth connectivity matrix (left). Firstly, after streamlines from A and C mix together in the center "bottleneck" there is no way for any tractography algorithm to tell which ones should go to B or D (without adding prior anatomical knowledge). This inevitably leads to false positive connections between A and D, and between B and C. Note that this is only a false positive if there are indeed no fibers connecting A to D, and B to C. It is unknown how common it is in the human white matter for two tracts to merge, and then to cleanly separate like this without exchanging fibers, but it might be a large source of false positives (Maier-Hein et al., 2017). The second limitation comes from the tendency of streamlines to travel in straight lines (see Fig. 19.5), which means that most streamlines will terminate in C and D, rather than A and B. When seeding from the white matter tract, this will result in very low or no connectivity to A and B. When seeding from the gray matter, the streamlines seeded in A or B will result in some connectivity estimates for these regions, although nearly all such streamlines will end up in C or D.

phy. How high to set this threshold depends on the application and its sensitivity to either false positives or false negatives (Bastiani et al., 2012).

An overview of the many of the potential sources of false positives and negatives in tractography is provided by Rheault and colleagues (Rheault et al., 2020). The source of false positives is that streamlines going along one tract might switch to another adjacent or overlapping tract. For crossing tracts, the occurrence of such switches can be reduced by enforcing strict angular constraints when propagating streamlines. However, if two tracts overlap spatially and have a similar orientation, they will be represented in the FOD as a single fiber orientation. In such a "bottleneck", tractography has no way of keeping track of which streamline belongs to which tract, which leads to inevitable mixing of the streamlines (Fig. 19.4).

Enforcing strict angular constraints may prevent a lot of false positives, but it also contributes to false negative connections. Axonal bundles can bend very sharply, close to 90 degrees. One case of such sharp curvature can be found in cortical gyri, where axons projecting to the gyral wall tend to travel along the fundal white/gray matter boundary up the gyral crown, until they sharply turn into the gyral wall. Tractography streamlines are not allowed to take such sharp turns and end up preferentially connecting to the gyral crown (Fig. 19.5). Though these false negatives are mostly obvious in the gyri, they probably occur throughout the whole of white matter, wherever there are fibers branching off a white matter tract (Fig. 19.4).

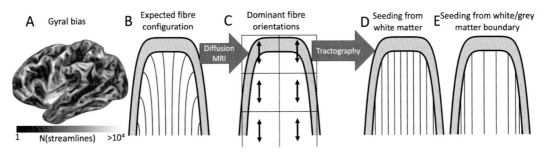

FIGURE 19.5

A) Tractography streamlines tend to terminate at the gyral crowns rather than in the sulci. This so-called "gyral bias" is very strong with some parts of the gyral crown receiving more than ten thousand streamlines, whereas some sulcal fundi do not get any streamlines. B) The expected fiber configuration in a simplified gyrus with roughly uniform distribution of fibers entering from the deep white matter and connecting uniformly to the convoluted gray matter. C) Due to the limited spatial resolution of diffusion MRI, we cannot capture the fibers branching off into the gyral wall, and only see the dominant upwards fiber orientation. This causes large difference in the streamline density, depending on the direction streamlines are traveling in with streamlines coming up from the deep white matter traveling parallel to the gyral walls up to the gyral crown (D), whereas streamlines seeded from the white/gray matter boundary remain stuck close to the gyral walls (E). Figure adapted from Cottaar et al. (2021).

To resolve some of these issues, it might be helpful to consider not just a single streamline at a time (as in local tractography), but try to estimate all streamlines, i.e., the whole structural connectome, at once. This is the idea behind global tractography approaches. Such an approach allows the user to not only put constraints on the shape of the streamlines, but also their density. For instance, one can reduce the gyral bias by finding a streamline configuration that is both smooth at the cortical surface and

304 **Chapter 19** The diffusion MRI connectome

throughout the underlying white matter while still following the fiber orientations (Cottaar et al., 2021). Another advantage of global tractography is that this results in paths that are not precisely tangent to the local FODs. Because of this, global approaches are thought to be less prone to local estimation errors due to, e.g., low data signal-to-noise ratio (SNR) or bad model fit. However, such global tractography approaches have the disadvantage that they are harder to implement and are far more computationally expensive than local tractography. One practical approach to global tractography is to take a pre-existing set of streamlines (e.g., from probabilistic local tractography) and assign weights to each of them. This allows one to put constraints on the density of streamlines using a linear optimization algorithm, which is far more efficient than generating the streamlines from scratch within the global tractography algorithm (Daducci et al., 2016).

19.5 **Quantifying connectivity strength**

All tractography algorithms discussed above return a streamline count between pairs of voxels, vertices, or regions of interest. The number of streamlines connecting two regions is often taken as 1) evidence of a connection existing and 2) a measure of "connectivity strength". Though comparisons with tracer studies have suggested that there is indeed a correlation between the number of streamlines and both the probability of a connection existing and the number of axons of that connection (Donahue et al., 2016), the number of streamlines will be confounded by many variables:

- Length: Trying to virtually dissect longer tracts will have more opportunities to deviate from the correct path, which leads to a lower number of streamlines reaching the other side of the tract (Fig. 19.6).
- Complex fiber configurations: It is easier to reconstruct a tract that mainly propagates through regions with low uncertainty and fiber dispersion, rather than a tract that crosses many other fiber bundles. This is particularly true for algorithms that only estimate a single fiber orientation in every voxel (such as the DT model), but will still hold for models that allow for crossing fibers (Fig. 19.6).
- Curvature: Nearly all tractography algorithms tend to avoid making sharp curves. If multiple fiber orientations are estimated in a voxel, these algorithms assume that they represent the crossing of two straight bundles, without any axons switching between the two orientations. Though many white matter tracts do indeed show little curvature, many individual axons and even some major tracts have sharp bends, such as in the Meyer's loop. Most streamlines will miss these curves, which leads to underestimation of the connectivity through these tracts.
- Alternative paths: If streamlines from region A normally travel to regions B and C, but in one subject the path from A to C is lost. In that subject all streamlines from region A might now travel to region B, which might lead to the potential misleading conclusion that the connection between A and B is now stronger, whereas in fact the change is in another unrelated tract between A and C. This is an example of the more general issue that streamlines have to go somewhere, so reductions or increases in the number of streamlines between two ROIs will inevitably have to be compensated for on some other route (Fig. 19.7).

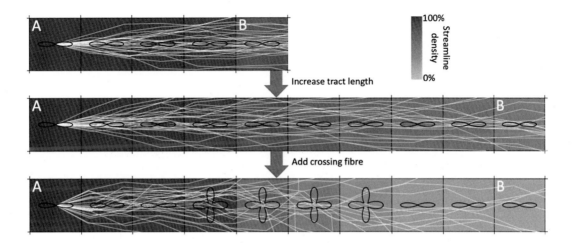

FIGURE 19.6

Illustration of confounds that mean streamline density is not a metric of connectivity strength. Streamlines (white) are drawn from the FODs (black). Darker background colors indicate larger streamline density (based on 1000 streamlines out of which 30 are pictured). This streamline density from voxel A to voxel B decreases if they are further apart (even if the diffusion data is identical in every voxel) or if there are crossing fibers, which reduces the accuracy with which the fiber orientation can be estimated in those voxels.

These limitations limit the usefulness of streamline count as a measure of connectivity strength. In particular, these confounds will probably dominate any comparison between different white matter tracts, which will in general have different lengths, crossing tracts, and curvature. However, most studies of the connectivity strength compare the number of streamlines of the same tract across subjects or between contralateral tracts in the same subject. In this case, the general morphology of the tract can be assumed to be similar enough that these confounding factors should play a smaller role.

Given these limitations, many researchers have proposed alternative approaches to quantify the strength of a fiber bundle. Most common among these approaches is to ignore the number of streamlines connecting two regions, but instead compute the average of some microstructural index along this tract. The idea here is that any damage along a tract will show up in these microstructural indices, which allows the researcher to identify which edges in the connectome get damaged in different disorders. When choosing a microstructural index, it is important to select one that is minimally affected by the FOD in each voxel, otherwise it is possible to get a similar bias as discussed above between solitary tracts and those tracts crossing other fiber populations. These indices can either be derived from the same dMRI data (see Chapter 11) or different modalities.

Some recent approaches can reduce these confounds. For example, by using the neighborhood information, aFODs (Fig. 19.2) might be able to distinguish between a white matter tract making a sharp bend versus two fibers crossing each other. Also, recent global tractography methods to upweight streamlines traveling through poorly sampled regions could increase the relative weight of any long, or otherwise particularly hard to track, fiber bundles (Daducci et al., 2016).

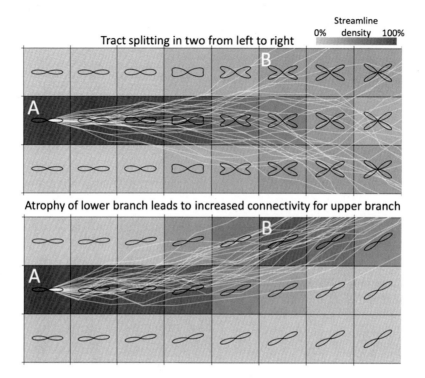

FIGURE 19.7

Illustration of how streamline density can increase in one tract, not because of any changes in that tract, but because of atrophy in an alternative route. The connectivity in the upward tract (e.g., between Voxels A and B) is greatly increased in the lower case, even though the FODs for this branch have remained identical. Color coding is the same as in Fig. 19.6.

19.6 Conclusions

Despite all the limitations discussed in this chapter, it is worth stressing that structural connectome mapping approaches and dMRI-based estimation of local and global microstructural properties represent the only tools to probe the neuroanatomy of the human brain *in vivo* and non-invasively (Lerch et al., 2017). If sufficient care is taken when acquiring and processing the dMRI data, several works have described strong correlations between the structural connectome from diffusion MRI and histological techniques, such as myelin-stained slices, polarized light imaging estimates of fiber orientations, and connectivity strengths from tracers. Notably, changes in the dMRI structural connectome across subjects do likely reflect changes in the white matter, even if one might not be able to pinpoint whether the difference is due to a change in the number of fibers or some other metric, for example demyelination or inflammation, along the tract.

Acknowledgments

The authors would like to thank Amy Howard for providing Fig. 19.3.

References

Basser, P.J., Pajevic, S., Pierpaoli, C., Duda, J., Aldroubi, A., 2000. In vivo fiber tractography using DT-MRI data. Magn. Reson. Med. 44 (4), 625–632. https://doi.org/10.1002/1522-2594(200010)44:4<625::aid-mrm17>3.0.co;2-o.

Bastiani, M., Cottaar, M., Dikranian, K., Ghosh, A., Zhang, H., Alexander, D.C., Behrens, T.E., Jbabdi, S., Sotiropoulos, S.N., 2017. Improved tractography using asymmetric fibre orientation distributions. NeuroImage 158, 205–218. https://doi.org/10.1016/j.neuroimage.2017.06.050.

Bastiani, M., Shah, N.J., Goebel, R., Roebroeck, A., 2012. Human cortical connectome reconstruction from diffusion weighted MRI: the effect of tractography algorithm. NeuroImage 62 (3), 1732–1749. https://doi.org/10.1016/j.neuroimage.2012.06.002.

Behrens, T.E.J., Johansen Berg, H., Jbabdi, S., Rushworth, M.F.S., Woolrich, M.W., 2007. Probabilistic diffusion tractography with multiple fibre orientations: what can we gain? NeuroImage 34 (1), 144–155. https://doi.org/10.1016/j.neuroimage.2006.09.018.

Catani, M., Thiebaut de Schotten, M., Slater, D., Dell'Acqua, F., 2013. Connectomic approaches before the connectome. NeuroImage 80, 2–13. https://doi.org/10.1016/j.neuroimage.2013.05.109.

Cottar M., Bastiani M., Boddu N., Glasser M.F., Haber S., van Essen D.C., Sotiropoulos S.N., Jbabdi S. 2021.

Cottaar, M., Bastiani, M., Boddu, N., Glasser, M.F., Haber, S., van Essen, D.C., Sotiropoulos, S.N., Jbabdi, S., 2021. Modelling white matter in gyral blades as a continuous vector field. NeuroImage 227, 117693. https://doi.org/10.1016/j.neuroimage.2020.117693.

Daducci, A., Dal Palú, A., Descoteaux, M., Thiran, J.-P., 2016. Microstructure informed tractography: pitfalls and open challenges. Front. Neurosci. 10, 247. https://doi.org/10.3389/fnins.2016.00247.

Dell'Acqua, F., Tournier, J.-D., 2019. Modelling white matter with spherical deconvolution: how and why? NMR Biomed. 32 (4), e3945. https://doi.org/10.1002/nbm.3945.

DeWeerdt, S., 2019. How to map the brain. Nature 571 (7766), S6–S8. https://doi.org/10.1038/d41586-019-02208-0.

Donahue, C.J., Sotiropoulos, S.N., Jbabdi, S., Hernandez-Fernandez, M., Behrens, T.E., Dyrby, T.B., Coalson, T., et al., 2016. Using diffusion tractography to predict cortical connection strength and distance: a quantitative comparison with tracers in the monkey. J. Neurosci. 36 (25), 6758–6770. https://doi.org/10.1523/JNEUROSCI.0493-16.2016.

Howard, A.F.D., Mollink, J., Kleinnijenhuis, M., Pallebage-Gamarallage, M., Bastiani, M., Cottaar, M., Miller, K.L., Jbabdi, S., 2019. Joint modelling of diffusion MRI and microscopy. NeuroImage 201, 116014. https://doi.org/10.1016/j.neuroimage.2019.116014.

Jbabdi, S., Sotiropoulos, S.N., Haber, S.N., Van Essen, D.C., Behrens, T.E., 2015. Measuring macroscopic brain connections in vivo. Nat. Neurosci. 18 (11), 1546–1555. https://doi.org/10.1038/nn.4134.

Jbabdi, S., Sotiropoulos, S.N., Savio, A.M., Graña, M., Behrens, T.E.J., 2012. Model-based analysis of multishell diffusion MR data for tractography: how to get over fitting problems. Magn. Reson. Med. 68 (6), 1846–1855. https://doi.org/10.1002/mrm.24204.

Jeurissen, B., Tournier, J.-D., Dhollander, T., Connelly, A., Sijbers, J., 2014. Multi-tissue constrained spherical deconvolution for improved analysis of multi-shell diffusion MRI data. NeuroImage 103, 411–426. https://doi.org/10.1016/j.neuroimage.2014.07.061.

Lerch, J.P., van der Kouwe, A.J.W., Raznahan, A., Paus, T., Johansen-Berg, H., Miller, K.L., Smith, S.M., Fischl, B., Sotiropoulos, S.N., 2017. Studying neuroanatomy using MRI. Nat. Neurosci. 20 (3), 314–326. https://doi.org/10.1038/nn.4501.

Maier-Hein, K.H., Neher, P.F., Houde, J.-C., Côté, M.-A., Garyfallidis, E., Zhong, J., Chamberland, M., et al., 2017. The challenge of mapping the human connectome based on diffusion tractography. Nat. Commun. 8 (1), 1349. https://doi.org/10.1038/s41467-017-01285-x.

Rheault, F., Poulin, P., Caron, A.V., St-Onge, E., Descoteaux, M., 2020. Common misconceptions, hidden biases and modern challenges of DMRI tractography. J. Neural Eng. 17 (1), 011001. https://doi.org/10.1088/1741-2552/ab6aad.

Smith, R.E., Tournier, J.-D., Calamante, F., Connelly, A., 2012. Anatomically-constrained tractography: improved diffusion MRI streamlines tractography through effective use of anatomical information. NeuroImage 62 (3), 1924–1938. https://doi.org/10.1016/j.neuroimage.2012.06.005.

Sotiropoulos, S.N., Zalesky, A., 2019. Building connectomes using diffusion MRI: why, how and but. NMR Biomed. 32 (4), e3752. https://doi.org/10.1002/nbm.3752.

Sporns, O., Tononi, G., Kötter, R., 2005. The human connectome: a structural description of the human brain. PLoS Comput. Biol. 1 (4), e42. https://doi.org/10.1371/journal.pcbi.0010042.

White, J.G., Southgate, E., Thomson, J.N., Brenner, S., 1986. The structure of the nervous system of the nematode caenorhabditis elegans. Philos. Trans. R. Soc. Lond. B, Biol. Sci. 314 (1165), 1–340. https://doi.org/10.1098/rstb.1986.0056.

CHAPTER

Functional MRI connectivity

20

Eugene Duff

Department of Paediatrics, and Wellcome Centre for Integrative Neuroimaging, University of Oxford, Oxford,
United Kingdom

20.1 The promise of fMRI functional connectivity
20.1.1 Defining functional connectivity

Functional neuroimaging studies gain understanding of the large-scale structure of neural processing by characterizing neural activity across the brain via perfusion-based surrogate markers, such as the fMRI blood-oxygenation-level-dependent (BOLD) signal. A direct analysis strategy for these studies is to determine how the level of this neural signal correlates with the performance of specific tasks, assessing the effects of different experimental manipulations, or how these responses vary across populations. However, the spatial coverage of functional neuroimaging techniques means that it is also possible to analyze the correlations of brain activity signals between different regions and assess how these correlations vary with experimental manipulations or across populations. This strategy can identify additional structure in the patterns of neural activity across the brain. An early demonstration of the functional connectivity approach in neuroimaging used regional cerebral blood flow measured from PET. The approach was soon translated to functional MRI, which is less invasive and provides higher spatial and temporal resolution (see Friston, 2011 for a historical review).

Functional connectivity (FC) is defined simply as correlations in the activity of neural measurements from distinct locations (Friston, 2011). In contrast, *effective connectivity* refers to quantifications of the causal influence of some brain regions on others: the *efficacy* of their connections. These concepts are relevant to spatially resolved neural recordings of all types and predate functional neuroimaging. Though FC is relatively straightforward to characterize if neural signals can be accurately identified, reliable estimation of effective connectivity from functional neuroimaging data is more challenging, as it requires stronger assumptions about the nature of signal generation, disentangling causal relationships between many correlated components of brain activity. This has led to a variety of different approaches to its estimation, making the integration of results across studies challenging.

The simplicity of FC has meant that it has become a major approach to characterizing functional neuroimaging data in a wide range of contexts. Though FC representations do not provide direct inferences relating to the causal roles of individual brain regions, they do provide an easily estimated measure of association that can be applied to a wide variety of functional neuroimaging data, and relatively easily combined across studies, with considerable promise as biomarkers in a variety of disease conditions.

A connectome is a comprehensive map of neural connections in the brain. The functional connectome identified by FC has the potential to extend the static structural connectome by identifying

Advances in Magnetic Resonance Technology and Applications, Volume 4, ISSN 2666-9099. https://doi.org/10.1016/B978-0-12-822479-3.00033-6
Copyright © 2021 Elsevier Inc. All rights reserved.

309

310   **Chapter 20** Functional MRI connectivity

how connectivity is modulated across different states, and how direct and indirect connectivity gives rise to networks of regions that co-activate to achieve specific functional outcomes. A comprehensive functional connectome is yet to be achieved. The range of states for which FC has been characterized remains incomplete; there has not been the standardization of analysis approaches needed to allow the integration of FC observations across studies; and the origin and specificity of FC remains uncertain. Nevertheless, FC-related measures are increasingly proving to be of value as putative biomarkers.

20.1.2 Experimental approaches

The study of correlations in data requires a source of variation. Some of the earliest FC approaches were applied to standard task-activation paradigms, which induce robust modulations of neural activity over a scan (Friston, 2011). Here, the study of inter-regional correlations in activity can reveal sets of regions that co-activate over task performance, expanding insight into the organization of the underlying processes, beyond that provided by voxel-wise mapping. Naturalistic stimuli, such as movies have been subsequently studied in a similar manner (Vanderwal et al., 2019).

A second type of experimental approach for FC analyses relies entirely on random, spontaneous fluctuations in brain activity to drive correlations during a steady-state condition. Often this state is "resting state", where participants are asked only to remain still and awake in the scanner. Though there was an awareness of spontaneous neural activity long before functional neuroimaging, it was not expected that large-scale mapping of the brain could be achieved from this activity. After a study by Biswal and colleagues observed that motor-related brain regions exhibited correlated activity during rest, many researchers began investigating the structure of resting-state brain activity correlations (Biswal, 2012). However, it wasn't until the development of methods to reliably extract the large-scale structure of resting-state signal, such as independent component analysis (ICA) and global signal regression techniques (see sections below), that the approach became a major experimental paradigm for functional neuroimaging. The FC structure of resting-state brain activity has now been extensively studied in a wide variety of species and clinical populations (Snyder and Raichle, 2012).

As the FC technique is sensitive to confounds, sequences need to have high spatial and temporal resolution to enable neural effects to be easily separated. For this reason, fast BOLD fMRI sequences are the most common functional imaging acquisition used for FC. However, FC is also applied to PET and ASL data (Jann et al., 2015). Multi-echo BOLD fMRI approaches, which can help to separate major sources of artifact, are another promising acquisition technique.

20.1.3 Interpreting functional connectivity

FC analyses aim to characterize correlations in brain activity, which is composed of a wide range of processes, at a variety of spatial and temporal scales. The neurovascular response to neural activity, measured by functional neuroimaging (e.g. perfusion (ASL) or blood oxygenation (BOLD)), is also complex and may have a regionally specific relationship to underlying neural activity (Mark et al., 2015). Some specificity has been identified: fMRI BOLD responses have been linked to input and intracortical processing via electrophysiological local field potentials, whereas certain band-limited power fluctuations have been linked to spontaneous BOLD signals (Leopold et al., 2003). Spontaneous fluctuations could reflect a mix of activity associated with uncontrolled changes in ongoing sensation, cognition, and motor activity, along with activity linked to more basal functions, such as those associated with memory consolidation or the general maintenance of neural tissue (Snyder and Raichle,

2012). As these fluctuations are likely at least in part to be driven by the same neural processes as stimulus-driven activity, ideal analysis approaches would simultaneously characterize stimulus-locked and spontaneous activity, but at present this remains a topic of research. In sum, observed FC cannot easily be translated to specific neural parameters.

A variety of non-neural sources also contribute to correlations in functional neuroimaging measurements, increasing interpretational challenges (Fig. 20.1). Confounding sources include non-neural physiological fluctuations linked to cardiac and respiratory cycles and head motion (Murphy et al., 2013). Careful preprocessing is required to ensure that correlations are not impacted by these noise sources (see section below, and Chapters 4 and 6).

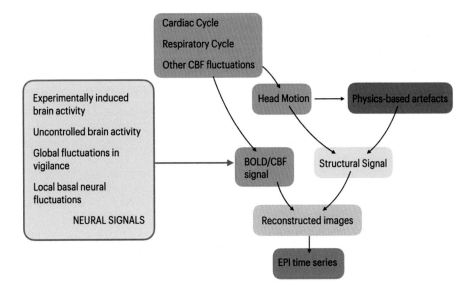

FIGURE 20.1

Schematic of elements contributing to the functional neuroimaging signals driving functional connectivity analyses. Each element will have a different spatio-temporal profile contributing to the measured FC.

20.2 Analysis and interpretation
20.2.1 The functional connectivity processing pipeline

Functional connectivity analyses largely utilize the same pre-processing pipelines as fMRI task-response analyses, surveyed in Chapter 16. However, rather than characterizing the association of individual brain signals with a gold standard external measure, functional connectivity methods assess associations between multiple artifact-impacted signals (and sometimes their interactions with external measures). Measures of associations between noisy signals can be both positively and negatively impacted by their noise components. As a result, FC analyses can be considerably more sensitive to

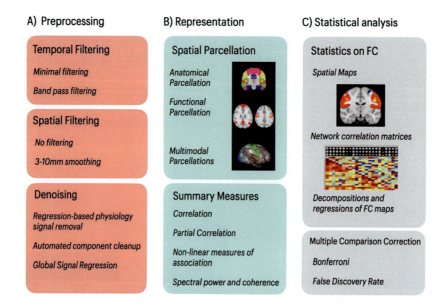

FIGURE 20.2

Analysis and representational choices for functional connectivity: A) Preprocessing: many aspects of preprocessing are not standardized across laboratories. B) Representation: spatial parcellation and between-time-series measures of association are key choices. C) Statistical analysis: once representation has been determined, there are further choices regarding how these associations are tested statistically.

artifacts than standard analyses (Murphy et al., 2013). We therefore focus on the processing stages that are most important for reducing the impact of signal confounds.

20.2.1.1 Temporal and spatial filtering

Functional connectivity measures are likely to be acutely sensitive to physiological fluctuations. Whereas they have a strong low-frequency component, the spontaneous neural fluctuations contributing to FC have a broad-band spectral range, and filtering parameters have not become fully standardized. High- or band-pass filtering is often employed to reduce the impact of frequencies where artifacts are most prominent, most notably high frequencies above 0.1–0.25 Hz. Heavy low-pass filtering (e.g., <0.08 Hz) can greatly limit the degrees of freedom available in typical scanning durations. Spatial smoothing and cortical surface projection approaches can also reduce the impact of these signal components.

20.2.1.2 Motion correction

Appropriate motion correction is another vital step for FC studies, with FC having been demonstrated to show a profound sensitivity to variations in motion. Studies comparing patient groups and distinct cognitive states can be acutely sensitive to differences in head motion (Power et al., 2015). Motion can affect images in a variety of ways, including image alignment, spin-history effects, and changes in distortions (see also Chapter 9 for similar issues in diffusion MRI). A combination of some or all of image-realignment, motion parameter regression, and motion-related component removal are required to minimize the effects of motion. Recent approaches that aim to remove time-varying distortions associated with head motion will be valuable for particularly challenging data sets, such as infant or elderly subjects.

20.2.1.3 Physiological noise regression

Physiological noise is another major confound that can differentially affect FC measures across different task conditions or patient groups (Murphy et al., 2013). Cardiac fluctuations, respiration, and their interactions have a substantial effect on BOLD signals through multiple mechanisms. As for head motion, a variety of techniques are likely to be required to adequately reduce the effects of these signals. Ideally, cardiac and respiratory recordings are made, which permit the removal of contributions via regression approaches. However, it is quite likely that there is a non-linear relationship between the recorded signals and their impact on the imaging data, which may reduce the value of the acquisition of these measurements when automated artifact detection methods can directly identify these artifacts.

20.2.1.4 Further denoising with ICA or global signal regression

Automated component identification approaches can remove substantial additional contributions from many unwanted sources of variance, including those described above. Independent components analysis (ICA) or other signal decomposition methods are used to separate the 4D functional series into spatio-temporal components. A variety of features can be estimated from these components (e.g., band-limited spectral power; spatial overlap with non-brain structures; correlation with respiration). Automated classifiers can then be built to identify artifacts from these features, either using a manually defined training set or hand crafting classifier parameters (Griffanti et al., 2014). This approach has the benefit that while associations with external confounds, such as physiology, can be used to identify the components, there are no strong assumptions regarding the specific impact of the confounds. However, it is vital that the decomposition methods adequately separate confounds from neural signal.

Often it is possible to identify an apparent "global" signal component contributing to measures across the brain. This signal may have contributions from a variety of signal sources, including spatially extended fluctuations in activity. Though the removal of a global signal component can be an important strategy to separate functional networks, it also risks removing true neural signal (Murphy and Fox, 2017).

20.2.2 Representing functional connectivity

Although measuring inter-regional correlations in the brain is conceptually simple, there are many choices involved in quantifying and representing FC within a data set (Fig. 20.2) (Bijsterbosch et al., 2020). These choices affect which aspects of the spatial and temporal structure of neural activity are highlighted, the sensitivity of the analysis to different background artefacts, and how comparable results are with bodies of existing work.

The voxel-based brain images acquired in functional neuroimaging provide spatial units that are arbitrary relative to the underlying activity. An important requirement of any functional connectivity analysis approach is to parsimoniously represent the associations between regions across the brain. Representations of brain FC often comprise of a set of "brain units", from which signal is extracted, and that form the *summary measure* that is applied to measure association between the signal from each of the units (see Bijsterbosch et al., 2020). The choice of representation can have a profound impact on the interpretation of results. We first describe these elements, and then discuss how these are combined in different ways to represent FC and the types of statistical analyses that can be performed.

20.2.2.1 Spatial representation

Brain units may be defined from binary or weighted-map parcellations of the brain and may consist of individual, spatially separated, regions or overlapping, spatially complex networks. They may be defined in volumetric space, or from projections to the cortical surface, and may be defined in standard space or uniquely for each subject of the study. The choice of brain units has significant implications for the results and interpretation of FC analyses. Inaccurately defined functional units will mix signals, distorting FC (Fig. 20.3), making results from different parcellation schemes difficult to compare. As functional neuroimaging is not able to resolve the full complexity of the spatial organization of brain activity, choices of spatial representations necessarily involve trade-offs. Fine-grained parcellations can achieve greater homogeneity of functional activity within nodes and more complete sampling of functional activity, but may result in lower SNR, less robustness to misalignments, and redundancy.

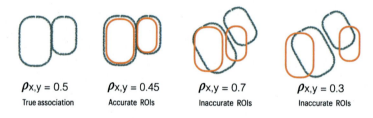

$\rho_{x,y} = 0.5$ $\rho_{x,y} = 0.45$ $\rho_{x,y} = 0.7$ $\rho_{x,y} = 0.3$
True association   Accurate ROIs   Inaccurate ROIs   Inaccurate ROIs

FIGURE 20.3

Spatial discrepancies in ROIs can increase and decrease apparent FC.

Inspired by Brodmann areal definitions, a natural and common choice for spatial units are discrete parcellations based on structural anatomy. Several widely used structural parcellations are available, including the Harvard-Oxford and AAL atlases. However, structural parcellations do not fully match functional organization, and tend not to perform well when tested for their ability to provide predictive features for functional data.

For this reason, approaches that incorporate the use of functional data to define parcellations or to register individuals, have become preferred. These approaches include clustering (e.g. K-fold), a variety of standard decomposition methods (e.g., principal component analysis (PCA), ICA) and approaches that directly align functional data across subjects. An important choice is whether to allow spatially non-contiguous node elements (e.g., the default mode network), which will be naturally produced by many of these approaches. Such network components can be conceptually problematic for representing FC, as they implicitly represent functional connectivity between the constituent regions of the network, requiring any changes in these associations to be represented with further overlapping nodes.

Multi-modal parcellations that utilize macro-structural, micro-structural, functional, and other data may provide the optimal ability to separate distinct populations of neurons, while avoiding voxels associated only through long-range connectivity, although arbitrary distinctions may be unavoidable (Glasser et al., 2016).

20.2 Analysis and interpretation   **315**

20.2.2.2 Functional connectivity summary measures

A variety of measures of association can be used to characterize FC. Pearson correlation, a linear measure of shared variance, is a common approach to characterize FC across two regions and a relatively robust marker of linear association. Alternative approaches aim for improved robustness to outliers (e.g., Spearman's correlation); sensitivity to non-linear associations (e.g., mutual information); and exclusion of associations mediated by other brain regions (e.g., partial correlation) (Smith et al., 2011).

Partial correlation characterizes the correlation of two signals once other regions are regressed out. When applied across a network of regions, partial correlation can highlight elements of relationships between pairs of regions that are not mediated by other regions (often interpreted as "direct" connections) and may also reduce the effects of confounds that influence multiple regions. However, partial correlation between two nodes is dependent on which other nodes are defined. For example, the inclusion of a node redundantly sampling the same activity as another will greatly affect their estimated connectivity. Partial correlation often requires regularization for reliable calculation and should be interpreted alongside full correlation to understand the impact of the partialling procedure.

Strategies that characterize multivariate relationships between spatially extended regions have also been employed. For example, multiple spatially extended signal components from each region may be identified and the overall shared variance across regions calculated.

fMRI and neural time series are intrinsically autocorrelated. This lack of independence between measurements made near in time means that standard statistical calculations associated with the strength or changes in FC need appropriate corrections for the reduced degrees of freedom. Even with corrected statistics, effects associated with FC are challenging to interpret. From a measurement perspective, differences or changes in FC may be produced by a wide variety of changes in signal properties (and underlying neural activity). For example, an increase in FC between two brain regions could either be produced by the increase in strength of some common signal component, perhaps involvement in a particular cognitive activity, or by the reduction of a component that is not shared (Fig. 20.4). This ambiguity may be reduced by assessing additional summary measures that complement FC. The amplitude or power of activity fluctuations within individual regions is a valuable measure of spontaneous functional activity. Assessing it alongside FC can help to identify whether changes in FC are likely to be linked to increases or decreases in the strength of different signal components (Duff et al., 2018).

More detailed investigations can assess uncontrolled, transient changes in FC within a session, "dynamic FC" (Hutchison et al., 2013). Analysis of these phenomena are challenging, as the complex autocorrelation structure of functional neuroimaging signals, with substantial low-frequency components, means that measurements of FC over short time periods will naturally fluctuate in a complex manner. This poses the questions of how to define the baseline state of FC and any alternative states it may enter. Ideally, such modeling would also accommodate experimentally induced activations and state changes. Approaches, such as autoregressive change models, hidden Markov models, and LSTM neural networks have been employed, but no widely employed standard approaches to dynamic FC have appeared.

20.2.2.3 FC representation and statistical analysis

The spatial parcellations and summary measures can be combined in a variety of ways to represent FC across the brain (Fig. 20.2). A simple approach is to produce a correlation matrix reflecting

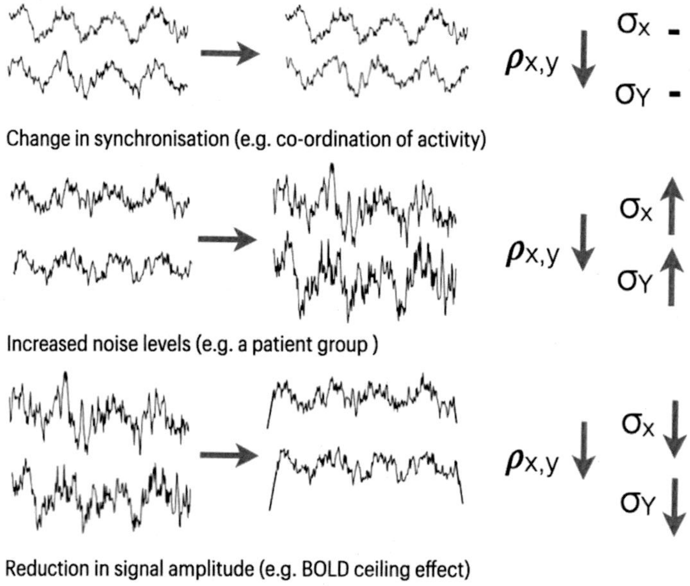

Change in synchronisation (e.g. co-ordination of activity)

Increased noise levels (e.g. a patient group)

Reduction in signal amplitude (e.g. BOLD ceiling effect)

FIGURE 20.4

Temporal ambiguities in functional connectivity. Distinct changes in signal properties can produce the same change in FC.

the FC between every node that results from a spatial parcellation. Alternatively, these elements can be used as targets to build connectivity profiles for every brain voxel. For example, seed-region or dual regression approaches map the connectivity of every voxel to a set of regions or networks. More recently, approaches have been used to identify major spatial modes of variation in connectivity patterns across the brain, often utilizing the connectivity of voxels to a set of brain units as the "connectivity fingerprint" for this decomposition. These approaches can identify gradients of connectivity within a region, where spatial patterns reflecting variation in connectivity fingerprints are identified.

Care is required when performing statistical analyses of these summary representations, for example comparisons across conditions: the elements of correlation and covariance matrices are not independent and have specific null distributions. The analysis of maps reflecting connectivity with sets of spatial nodes require careful multiple comparisons correction, both across space and across the multiple nodes under assessment.

It is important to be aware of the profound impact that representational choices can have on the statistical analysis and interpretation of results. For example, fine-grained parcellations will typically require stricter control for false positives. Moreover, the use of spatially extended brain units models in itself a component of the FC of brain activity. In particular, spatially non-contiguous brain units (e.g., canonical RSNs) implicitly model strong connectivity between the component regions, but do not quantify the extent of this connectivity (Fig. 20.5).

20.2 Analysis and interpretation

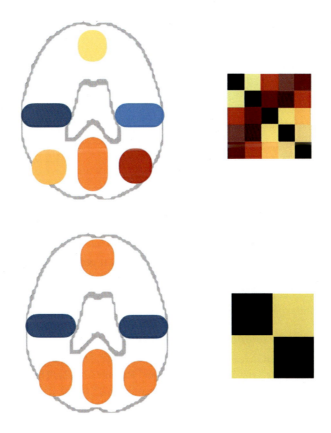

FIGURE 20.5

FC is often represented partly by the merging of related voxels to form Regions of Interest (ROIs) (left column), and partly by a network matrix representing FC between those ROIs (right column). A fine parcellation of the brain (e.g., upper row, six regions), results in a larger connectivity matrix, but may split homogeneous functional regions, reducing interpretability and SNR. A broader parcellation (e.g., lower row, two networks) can provide a simplified connectivity matrix, but important and potentially changing connectivity may be subsumed within the spatial representation.

20.2.2.4 Task manipulations

FC is commonly assessed in data where there is explicit experimental manipulation. The psychophysiological interactions analysis approach proposed in 1997 presents a general strategy for FC analyses in the context of experimental manipulations (Friston, 2011; O'Reilly et al., 2012). Here, correlates of the interaction term between activity from a seed region and a "psychological variable", such as a task design, are identified. Often, the canonical predicted hemodynamic responses are modeled out of the data in these analyses so that associations are driven by variability around these responses. Both consistent deviations from the canonical task response and trial-to-trial variability will drive measured associations. As a variety of sources associated within the stimulus response can drive associations, these analyses should not be assumed to reflect the same sources as resting-state analyses.

318 **Chapter 20** Functional MRI connectivity

20.2.2.5 Analyses derived from and extending functional connectivity

A variety of analysis approaches use functional connectivity as a starting point. For example, many approaches derive graph-theoretical measures from FC matrices to represent specific properties of the overall connectivity graph seen in the data, for example the extent to which particular regions form central hubs of connectivity (Fornito et al., 2016). Effective connectivity approaches, such as structural equation modeling or dynamic causal modeling, are often derived from covariance matrices and aim to extend FC to provide inferences regarding causal relationships between brain regions. However, all these approaches inherit the limitations and ambiguities inherent to FC (Smith et al., 2011).

20.3 Review of the functional connectome and its applications
20.3.1 Structure of functional correlations

Early functional imaging studies noted consistent correlations in activity across brain regions, first with task-induced activity, and then from spontaneous activity. It rapidly became clear that mining the correlational structure of functional neuroimaging data would provide insight. The simplicity of the paradigm also makes the technique popular for application to a wide variety of populations, including young children, older adults, patients with various diseases, and animals.

20.3.1.1 Spontaneous activity and resting state networks

The rich spatial structure of spontaneous activity was an unexpected finding, and this phenomenon has been extensively explored through the 2000s (Snyder and Raichle, 2012). The driving signals of spontaneous FC have strong low-frequency contributions between 0.02 and 0.15 Hz, but are fundamentally broad-band. The amplitude of these fluctuations is of similar magnitude to task-induced activations, so will substantially contribute to FC analyses of stimulus-driven functional data.

Independent component analysis proved to be one of the most effective techniques for parsimoniously identifying the structure of FC, decomposing activity patterns into a set of spatially independent networks that reflect major functional networks of the brain (Beckmann et al., 2005; Calhoun and Adalı, 2012). No canonical set of these networks exists, but around ten major networks of correlated activity can reliably be detected in adult human resting-state data. These networks, encompassing sensory, cognitive, limbic, and motor-related networks, can be identified in infant and even fetal subjects (Grayson and Fair, 2017), as well as in many animals. These networks are also identified in decompositions of databases of fMRI activation results. The consistent presence of resting-state networks (RSNs) has motivated the use of these networks as the spatial parcellation in many functional connectivity studies, despite the use of spatially extended networks bringing interpretational challenges.

The source of these resting-state networks has been extensively debated. Early concerns were that they may primarily reflect properties of the circulatory system or cardiac and respiratory artefacts. A variety of accumulated evidence now suggests a major neural contribution (Leopold et al., 2003; Mark et al., 2015). Though ICA and related techniques summarize activity in terms of discrete networks, this does not imply that discrete networks are intrinsic to the brain, and rather may reflect statistical properties of more complex and dynamic ongoing functional activity fluctuations.

Although most of these networks represent sets of brain regions with well-known functional roles and relationships, functional connectivity studies had a substantial role in defining and characterizing

20.3 Review of the functional connectome and its applications 319

the default-mode network (DMN). This network, comprising precuneus, lateral, and frontal components, was initially identified as a set of regions that consistently show higher activation during rest periods in PET and fMRI studies, but the unity of DMN components was confirmed by its consistent presence in the resting state (Raichle, 2015). Subsequently, hundreds of studies have investigated the DMN a major target of studies of clinical cohorts.

20.3.1.2 Variation in FC within individuals

Understanding the variation of FC within and across individuals is vital if this phenomenon is to have value as a probe for characterizing individual variability and disease. The RSN structure of FC persists during sensory stimulation, task performance, and mild anaesthesia. However, even subtle variations of state do affect FC. For example, consistent differences in the strength of FC can be identified across eyes-open and eyes-closed rest states, even for separate scans in a single session. Networks can be detected during sleep, where the strength of RSNs varies across different sleep stages. Caffeine, known to strengthen the SNR of fMRI activations, strengthens RSNs, whereas anaesthesia weakens them.

Ongoing stimulation or task performance can have a mixture of effects on FC, but these are poorly documented compared to population variation and effects of clinical interest. Activation of an individual region (increase in its mean BOLD signal) may increase or decrease connectivity with other regions. Strong, constant activation may produce a ceiling effect on the BOLD signal, reducing background fluctuations and FC. On the other hand, many ongoing states will involve fluctuations in cognitive activity, which may induce additional signal fluctuations, increasing measured FC.

FC structure changes over the lifespan, with machine learning approaches able to accurately predict an individual's age. Functional connectivity patterns are detectable before birth, with most major RSNs visible by birth and strengthening over early childhood (Grayson and Fair, 2017). Primary motor and sensory RSNs are reported to develop earlier than frontal and multi-sensory networks, reflecting known maturation of brain connections and microstructure over development. A variety of reductions in FC are reported with aging and aging-related disease conditions (Sala-Llonch et al., 2015).

20.3.1.3 Variability in FC across the population

A major focus of studies of FC has been investigation of inter-individual variation across populations. The simplicity of the resting-state paradigm has meant that large databases of resting-state studies can be compiled, making it a mainstay technique for large-scale population studies, such as the Human Connectome Project (HCP) and the UK Biobank. Sex differences in FC have been identified, along with a reliable genetic component, and modest associations with many health and lifestyle factors tracked in these large-scale studies. A major latent connectivity "signature" contributes to much of this predictive ability (Smith et al., 2015). Broadly, this dimension predicts positive and negative valance attributes, such as happiness and depression or addiction. Further studies have identified FC markers of IQ and other factors.

20.3.1.4 FC as a biomarker for disease-related brain changes

With its ability to characterize brain-wide changes in functional properties using easily tolerated resting state protocols, FC is a promising candidate in efforts towards identifying surrogate biomarkers for a variety of clinical applications, where they could be used for diagnosis and prognosis and the assessment of novel drug candidates. For biomarkers, accurate inferences regarding neural sources can be less important, so long as they can provide useful predictions.

320 **Chapter 20** Functional MRI connectivity

FC alterations have been extensively studied in clinical populations for the main neurodegenerative and psychiatric disorders, although reliable effects have been slow to emerge (Hohenfeld et al., 2018; Pievani et al., 2014). In Alzheimer's disease (AD), spatial and temporal disruptions in FC overlap disease-related changes in the DMN. DMN activity levels are reduced at rest and FC between anterior and posterior DMN nodes are compromised. FC alterations have been seen pre-symptomatically and may predict the age of onset in autosomal dominant AD (Smith et al., 2021). In Parkinson's disease, studies report disruptions of FC in corticostriatal-thalamic-cortical networks that underlie both motor and nonmotor symptoms (Baggio et al., 2015), and network-specific functional disruptions are reported in other forms of neurodegenerative diseases. Many other conditions have also been investigated. Schizophrenia is characterized by FC changes in the emotion-processing, reward, empathy, and action control networks. (Sheffield and Barch, 2016). FC-based markers of ongoing chronic pain have been shown to be reliable across studies and may help to track pain levels in an objective manner (Lee et al., 2021).

Care is required to understand the disease-related sources of FC changes. At sites of degeneration, FC may be affected directly by structural or physiological differences and may provide limited additional prognostic power. However, FC could additionally reveal downstream consequences of these changes. Given the ambiguities of FC discussed above, interpreting the mix of increases and decreases in FC often observed in disease states is not straightforward. Reduced FC is often taken to reflect reduced communication between brain regions due to disease-related dysfunction, whereas increased FC could reflect compensatory increases in communication. Multi-variate machine learning approaches that integrate multiple changes across different areas are vital to maximize the sensitivity and specificity of potential biomarkers.

20.4 Future directions

Though FC has become a mainstay technique for functional MRI and other functional modalities, it needs to evolve to increase its impact on neuroscience and clinical translation. Major concerns remain regarding its limited interpretability, lack of standardization, sensitivity to artifacts, and limited predictive ability. However, despite these challenges, FC has not been superseded in 25 years. Biophysical model-based approaches that model underlying neural and physiological parameters and their impact on acquisition sequences are the ideal, but adequately constraining models by data is a major challenge. FC may remain the de-facto standard until advanced multi-modal imaging data can be acquired to better constrain biophysical models. Before this, the development of simpler optimizations of FC techniques, for example to reduce structure-driven inter-subject variability and improve the ability to integrate results across studies, remains a vital area of research.

The different available processing pipelines for fMRI data vary in how they perform many of the processing steps. These differences have been shown to impact the results of both task-response and FC analyses. Differences in representation across studies add further challenges in determining how results compare across studies and can be combined in meta-analyses. With the uncertainty regarding underlying sources of FC leaving no gold-standard test data to identify optimal pipelines, standardization of analysis approaches is unlikely. This emphasizes the importance of sharing raw time series data of FC studies. Achieving standardized formats (e.g. https://bids.neuroimaging.io/), including representations of processed connectivity data will greatly enhance the field's ability to identify reliable patterns of FC and its variation across different contexts.

Acknowledgments

Roser Sala, University of Barcelona, for editing assistance.

References

Baggio, H.C., Segura, B., Junque, C., 2015. Resting-state functional brain networks in Parkinson's disease. CNS Neuroscience & Therapeutics 21, 793–801. https://doi.org/10.1111/cns.12417.

Beckmann, C.F., DeLuca, M., Devlin, J.T., Smith, S.M., 2005. Investigations into resting-state connectivity using independent component analysis. Philosophical Transactions of the Royal Society of London. Series B, Biological Sciences 360, 1001–1013. https://doi.org/10.1098/rstb.2005.1634.

Bijsterbosch, J., Harrison, S.J., Jbabdi, S., Woolrich, M., Beckmann, C., Smith, S., Duff, E.P., 2020. Challenges and future directions for representations of functional brain organization. Nature Neuroscience, 1–12. https://doi.org/10.1038/s41593-020-00726-z.

Biswal, B.B., 2012. Resting state fMRI: a personal history. NeuroImage 62, 938–944. https://doi.org/10.1016/j.neuroimage.2012.01.090. 20 YEARS OF fMRI.

Calhoun, V.D., Adalı, T., 2012. Multisubject independent component analysis of fMRI: a decade of intrinsic networks, default mode, and neurodiagnostic discovery. IEEE Reviews in Biomedical Engineering 5, 60–73. https://doi.org/10.1109/RBME.2012.2211076.

Duff, E.P., Makin, T., Cottaar, M., Smith, S.M., Woolrich, M.W., 2018. Disambiguating brain functional connectivity. NeuroImage 173, 540–550. https://doi.org/10.1016/j.neuroimage.2018.01.053.

Fornito, A., Zalesky, A., Bullmore, E., 2016. Fundamentals of Brain Network Analysis. Academic Press.

Friston, K.J., 2011. Functional and effective connectivity: a review. Brain Connectivity 1, 13–36. https://doi.org/10.1089/brain.2011.0008.

Glasser, M.F., Coalson, T.S., Robinson, E.C., Hacker, C.D., Harwell, J., Yacoub, E., Ugurbil, K., Andersson, J., Beckmann, C.F., Jenkinson, M., Smith, S.M., Van Essen, D.C., 2016. A multi-modal parcellation of human cerebral cortex. Nature 536, 171–178. https://doi.org/10.1038/nature18933.

Grayson, D.S., Fair, D.A., 2017. Development of large-scale functional networks from birth to adulthood: a guide to neuroimaging literature. NeuroImage 160, 15–31. https://doi.org/10.1016/j.neuroimage.2017.01.079.

Griffanti, L., Salimi-Khorshidi, G., Beckmann, C.F., Auerbach, E.J., Douaud, G., Sexton, C.E., Zsoldos, E., Ebmeier, K.P., Filippini, N., Mackay, C.E., Moeller, S., Xu, J., Yacoub, E., Baselli, G., Ugurbil, K., Miller, K.L., Smith, S.M., 2014. ICA-based artefact removal and accelerated fMRI acquisition for improved resting state network imaging. NeuroImage 95, 232–247. https://doi.org/10.1016/j.neuroimage.2014.03.034.

Hohenfeld, C., Werner, C.J., Reetz, K., 2018. Resting-state connectivity in neurodegenerative disorders: is there potential for an imaging biomarker? NeuroImage: Clinical 18, 849–870. https://doi.org/10.1016/j.nicl.2018.03.013.

Hutchison, R.M., Womelsdorf, T., Allen, E.A., Bandettini, P.A., Calhoun, V.D., Corbetta, M., Della Penna, S., Duyn, J.H., Glover, G.H., Gonzalez-Castillo, J., Handwerker, D.A., Keilholz, S., Kiviniemi, V., Leopold, D.A., de Pasquale, F., Sporns, O., Walter, M., Chang, C., 2013. Dynamic functional connectivity: promise, issues, and interpretations. NeuroImage 80, 360–378. https://doi.org/10.1016/j.neuroimage.2013.05.079.

Jann, K., Gee, D.G., Kilroy, E., Schwab, S., Smith, R.X., Cannon, T.D., Wang, D.J.J., 2015. Functional connectivity in BOLD and CBF data: similarity and reliability of resting brain networks. NeuroImage 106, 111–122. https://doi.org/10.1016/j.neuroimage.2014.11.028.

Lee, J.-J., Kim, H.J., Čeko, M., Park, B., Lee, S.A., Park, H., Roy, M., Kim, S.-G., Wager, T.D., Woo, C.-W., 2021. A neuroimaging biomarker for sustained experimental and clinical pain. Nature Medicine 27, 174–182. https://doi.org/10.1038/s41591-020-1142-7.

Leopold, D.A., Murayama, Y., Logothetis, N.K., 2003. Very slow activity fluctuations in monkey visual cortex: implications for functional brain imaging. Cerebral Cortex 13, 422–433. https://doi.org/10.1093/cercor/13.4.422.

Mark, C.I., Mazerolle, E.L., Chen, J.J., 2015. Metabolic and vascular origins of the BOLD effect: implications for imaging pathology and resting-state brain function. Journal of Magnetic Resonance Imaging 42, 231–246. https://doi.org/10.1002/jmri.24786.

Murphy, K., Birn, R.M., Bandettini, P.A., 2013. Resting-state fMRI confounds and cleanup. NeuroImage 80, 349–359. https://doi.org/10.1016/j.neuroimage.2013.04.001.

Murphy, K., Fox, M.D., 2017. Towards a consensus regarding global signal regression for resting state functional connectivity MRI. NeuroImage 154, 169–173. https://doi.org/10.1016/j.neuroimage.2016.11.052. Cleaning up the fMRI time series: Mitigating noise with advanced acquisition and correction strategies.

O'Reilly, J.X., Woolrich, M.W., Behrens, T.E.J., Smith, S.M., Johansen-Berg, H., 2012. Tools of the trade: psychophysiological interactions and functional connectivity. Social Cognitive and Affective Neuroscience 7, 604–609. https://doi.org/10.1093/scan/nss055.

Pievani, M., Filippini, N., van den Heuvel, M.P., Cappa, S.F., Frisoni, G.B., 2014. Brain connectivity in neurodegenerative diseases—from phenotype to proteinopathy. Nature Reviews Neurology 10, 620–633. https://doi.org/10.1038/nrneurol.2014.178.

Power, J.D., Schlaggar, B.L., Petersen, S.E., 2015. Recent progress and outstanding issues in motion correction in resting state fMRI. NeuroImage 105, 536–551. https://doi.org/10.1016/j.neuroimage.2014.10.044.

Raichle, M.E., 2015. The brain's default mode network. Annual Review of Neuroscience 38, 433–447. https://doi.org/10.1146/annurev-neuro-071013-014030.

Sala-Llonch, R., Bartrés-Faz, D., Junqué, C., 2015. Reorganization of brain networks in aging: a review of functional connectivity studies. Frontiers in Psychology 6. https://doi.org/10.3389/fpsyg.2015.00663.

Sheffield, J.M., Barch, D.M., 2016. Cognition and resting-state functional connectivity in schizophrenia. Neuroscience and Biobehavioral Reviews 61, 108–120. https://doi.org/10.1016/j.neubiorev.2015.12.007.

Smith, R.X., Strain, J.F., Tanenbaum, A., Fagan, A.M., Hassenstab, J., McDade, E., Schindler, S.E., Gordon, B.A., Xiong, C., Chhatwal, J., Jack, C., Karch, C., Berman, S., Brosch, J.R., Lah, J.J., Brickman, A.M., Cash, D.M., Fox, N.C., Graff-Radford, N.R., Levin, J., Noble, J., Holtzman, D.M., Masters, C.L., Farlow, M.R., Laske, C., Schofield, P.R., Marcus, D.S., Morris, J.C., Benzinger, T.L.S., Bateman, R.J., Ances, B.M., 2021. Resting-state functional connectivity disruption as a pathological biomarker in autosomal dominant Alzheimer disease. Brain Connectivity 11, 239–249. https://doi.org/10.1089/brain.2020.0808.

Smith, S.M., Miller, K.L., Salimi-Khorshidi, G., Webster, M., Beckmann, C.F., Nichols, T.E., Ramsey, J.D., Woolrich, M.W., 2011. Network modelling methods for FMRI. NeuroImage 54, 875–891. https://doi.org/10.1016/j.neuroimage.2010.08.063.

Smith, S.M., Nichols, T.E., Vidaurre, D., Winkler, A.M., Behrens, T.E.J., Glasser, M.F., Ugurbil, K., Barch, D.M., Van Essen, D.C., Miller, K.L., 2015. A positive-negative mode of population covariation links brain connectivity, demographics and behavior. Nature Neuroscience 18, 1565–1567. https://doi.org/10.1038/nn.4125.

Snyder, A.Z., Raichle, M.E., 2012. A brief history of the resting state: the Washington University perspective. NeuroImage 62, 902–910. https://doi.org/10.1016/j.neuroimage.2012.01.044.

Vanderwal, T., Eilbott, J., Castellanos, F.X., 2019. Movies in the magnet: naturalistic paradigms in developmental functional neuroimaging. Developmental Cognitive Neuroscience 36, 100600. https://doi.org/10.1016/j.dcn.2018.10.004.

CHAPTER

Applications of MRI connectomics

21

Jessica S. Damoiseaux[a]**, Andre Altmann**[b]**, Jonas Richiardi**[c]**, and Sepideh Sadaghiani**[d]

[a]*Institute of Gerontology, Department of Psychology, Wayne State University, Detroit, MI, United States*
[b]*Centre for Medical Image Computing (CMIC), Department of Medical Physics and Biomedical Engineering, University College London (UCL), London, United Kingdom*
[c]*Department of Radiology, Lausanne University Hospital and University of Lausanne, Lausanne, Switzerland*
[d]*Psychology Department, Beckman Institute for Advanced Science and Technology, University of Illinois at Urbana-Champaign, Urbana, IL, United States*

21.1 Introduction

How can magnetic resonance imaging (MRI) connectomics be applied to study typical brain structure and function, and be used in a clinical setting to inform diagnosis, prognosis, or treatment of patients? In the current chapter we will discuss possible applications of MRI connectomics as assessed with functional and structural connectivity. Chapters 19 and 20 of this book detail multiple techniques to assess functional and structural (diffusion-based) brain connectivity. In short, functional connectivity is a measure of the association of functional MRI (fMRI) derived blood-oxygenation-level-dependent (BOLD) fluctuations across brain regions, commonly expressed as correlation coefficients. As BOLD is an indirect measure of neuronal function, functional connectivity is considered to reflect system-level neuronal signaling between brain regions. Brain regions with higher measures of functional connectivity are interpreted as having more synchronous neuronal signaling, and therefore as more likely belonging to the same neural network. The extant literature has identified about 7–10 canonical intrinsic connectivity networks (ICNs), including sensory, motor, and higher cognitive systems (cf. Chapter 20 on functional connectivity). When comparing functional connectivity measures within and between individuals, e.g., based on features such as behavior, age, physical health etc., it is tempting to assume that higher connectivity indicates better brain function. However, the interpretation of connectivity differences is not as straightforward; depending on the specific brain regions involved, and other circumstances, lower connectivity can also be considered advantageous.

Structural connectivity, as described in this book in Chapter 19, is derived from diffusion-weighted imaging (DWI). Structural connectivity "strength" can be assessed in multiple ways, such as an average diffusion measure per tract of interest (e.g., fractional anisotropy, mean diffusivity, neurite density etc.), or as the number of streamlines between brain regions of interest using probabilistic tractography. Diffusion-derived structural connectivity measures are considered to reflect white matter pathways (i.e., the direction of axons). Brain regions with higher structural connectivity are presumed to have more dense white matter tracts and/or higher white matter integrity, and therefore more intact or stronger anatomical connections. This interpretation is not without controversy, though, as discussed by (Jones

Advances in Magnetic Resonance Technology and Applications, Volume 4, ISSN 2666-9099. https://doi.org/10.1016/B978-0-12-822479-3.00034-8
Copyright © 2021 Elsevier Inc. All rights reserved.

323

324 Chapter 21 Applications of MRI connectomics

et al., 2013), and careful consideration of the actual measures extracted is warranted when interpreting the results.

A common approach to examine whole-brain or system-level connectomics is the use of brain graphs (see Box 21.1 for a brief primer on brain graph analyses). A brain graph approach allows us to determine specific network properties and can be applied similarly to connectivity measures extracted from multiple imaging modalities. Therefore, in both the functional and structural connectomics literature, similar network properties are discussed.

Connectivity signatures are heritable to some degree, and therefore represent a conserved biological property rather than a mere temporary snapshot of brain activity. Connectivity patterns are expected to relate to cognitive function, and deviations from normative connectivity patterns can be an indicator of disease processes and consequently serve as disease biomarkers. There is currently limited direct clinical application of brain connectivity measures for diagnostics or treatment. Nevertheless, there are multiple fundamental and clinical research applications that increase our understanding of typical and atypical brain structure and function. In the following sections, we will provide examples of our current understanding of (1) the impact of the connectome on cognitive processes and behavior, (2) the connectome across the lifespan, and (3) clinical research applications of connectomics.

21.2 Impact of the connectome on cognitive processes and behavior

Ultimately, the functional significance of the connectome lies in its role in healthy cognition and, by extension, in cognitive consequences of connectome aberrations. Associations with cognitive abilities and behavioral outcomes are further important for demonstrating that neuroimaging-derived structural and functional connectomes reflect genuine neural connectivity rather than noise (cf. discussion of methodological limitations in Section 21.5). Several general approaches have been taken to establish and describe such impact on cognitive processes and behavior (Fig. 21.1). Specifically, differences in behavioral measures have been associated with differences in the connectome *across* individuals (Section 21.2.1) or, alternatively, *within* individuals (21.2.2). In both of these approaches, behavioral associations have been explored for the DWI-derived structural connectome, the fMRI-derived "static" (i.e., time-averaged) functional connectome, and the fMRI-derived "dynamic" (i.e., time-varying) re-configurations of the functional connectome (cf. Chapter 20 for definitions of static and dynamic connectivity). In the following, we will discuss examples of each of these approaches.

21.2.1 Association of connectome features with cognitive abilities *across* subjects

An important avenue for understanding the cognitive relevance of the connectome is to study how cognition and connectome features co-vary across individuals. For inter-individual comparisons, cognitive abilities are commonly assessed by self-report questionnaires or by performance in standardized neuropsychological tests or other cognitive tasks. The following examples explore which specific structural and functional connectome features are behaviorally relevant. This section focuses on inter-individual studies of relatively homogeneous populations; for age- and disease-related differences refer to the Sections 21.3 and 21.4 of this chapter, respectively.

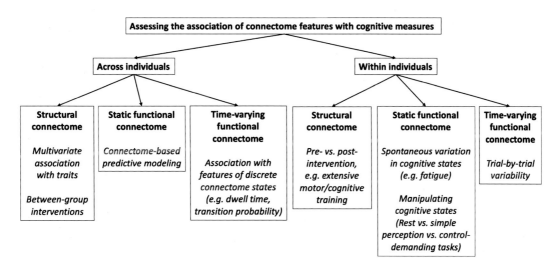

FIGURE 21.1

Overview of recent research approaches to characterize the association of connectome features with cognitive and behavioral processes. The approaches range from between- to within-group designs and from association to intervention studies. The highlighted approaches are not exhaustive, but provide examples from studies that have proven informative.

21.2.1.1 Structural connectome across individuals

Structural connectivity reflects the cumulative effect of genes combined with the impact of the environment, the latter including life-long experience and learning. This representation extends from individual synapses to the macroscale connectome observable with DWI. Consequently, it is expected that specific features of the DWI-derived structural connectome are linked to individuals' cognition. Though the relationship of targeted single connections to specific cognitive abilities has long been studied, recent imaging and analysis advances have enabled association studies of the distributed structural connectome at once. Specifically, cognitive associations have been assessed concurrently for all edges or nodes of the DWI-derived connectome using multivariate analyses, and for global topological measures using network science (see Box 21.1). By applying these approaches, associations with higher-order control and executive functions were identified. These associations involve (often sparse sets of) structural connections widely distributed across anatomical space, rather than being, e.g., confined to connectivity within specific canonical ICNs.

21.2.1.2 Phenotyping individuals based on their static functional connectome

All humans share a common level of spatial organization of the static functional connectome, most notably the presence of the previously mentioned set of so-called canonical ICNs or resting-state networks, each comprising a specific group of distributed brain regions (cf. Chapter 20). However, the exact instantiation of this spatial organization differs across individuals in characteristic ways similar to an individual's fingerprint. The characteristic differences, distributed throughout the brain, can be used to identify an individual from others. Given the success of such identification or functional con-

326 Chapter 21 Applications of MRI connectomics

nectome "fingerprinting", one might expect that individuals' cognitive abilities could be predicted from relevant connectome features (e.g., using connectome-based predictive modeling (Shen et al., 2017)). Indeed, despite the close dependence of functional connectivity on anatomy (the way traffic patterns depend on roads), certain functional connectome features are uniquely associated with cognitive abilities beyond structural connectivity. Such features from resting-state fMRI are associated with a person's cognitive abilities, such as fluid intelligence (the ability of abstract reasoning and problem-solving), sustained attention, and performance on perception tasks.

It should be noted that while studies into inter-individual differences most commonly use fMRI data from a task-free resting state, individuals' characteristic functional connectome features are largely stable within individuals irrespective of cognitive state. Further, the functional connectome's prediction of cognitive traits may improve when fMRI is acquired during targeted cognitive states that enhance relevant connectome idiosyncrasies. For example, the level of global integration of the functional connectome (i.e., the extent to which densely connected clusters of are interconnected; cf. Box 21.1) during a demanding working memory and cognitive control task is associated with individuals' task performance (Shine et al., 2016).

21.2.1.3 Time-varying dynamics of the functional connectome as traits

Many everyday cognitive processes, such as task-switching and multitasking, require cognitive flexibility. It has been suggested that time-varying changes in the functional connectome permit new alliances to form and dissolve between brain regions, described as "connectome flexibility". These different configurations of the functional connectome are suggested to constitute different "cognitive architectures", each supporting a different type of cognitive process. In line with this view, one approach to functional connectome dynamics is to define multiple, relatively discrete connectome *states* and characterize how their spatial, topological, and temporal features affect cognition. For example, individuals with more frequent occurrence of a certain connectome state (characterized by high variability of connectivity strength) during resting state perform better in common measures of task-switching and working memory (Nomi et al., 2017). It should be noted that due to technical limitations (see Section 21.5), fMRI typically captures functional connectome dynamics only on the temporal order of tens of seconds. Many cognitively relevant connectivity changes therefore will require methods other than MRI.

21.2.2 Association of connectome features with cognitive states *within* subjects

Beyond comparing individuals with each other, a second window into the cognitive significance of connectome features is to study how such features co-vary with changes in behavior *within* an individual. This approach commonly takes advantage of spontaneous variability of behavior and cognitive performance or, alternatively, changes in such functions due to interventions and training. Changes in large-scale structural connectivity can be observed upon relatively long-term and extensive learning. Conversely, static *functional* connectivity can additionally capture more rapid reorganization, for example upon switching cognitive states (e.g., across resting state and different task paradigms). Finally, even within a task paradigm, trial-to-trial variability in behavior can be linked to dynamic changes in the functional connectome. In the following, we explore examples of associations of structural, static functional, and dynamic functional connectome features with cognition and behavior within individuals.

21.2.2.1 Structural connectome and learning

A straightforward intervention to study the behavioral impact of structural connectome changes within an individual is to induce learning. For example, two months of working memory training enhances efficiency of information flow (a network science measure, cf. Box 21.1) in a structural network of frontal and parietal nodes (Caeyenberghs et al., 2016). Importantly, subjects in the training group (but not a control group) showed cognitive transfer in terms of improved performance on other tasks involving working memory post-training compared to pre-training.

21.2.2.2 Static functional connectome and cognitive states

Though the spatial organization of the functional connectome is extremely stable over cognitive contexts, the subtle changes that occur between such contexts can be meaningfully linked to cognitive processes. A robust example of such subtle changes is the level of global topological integration (see Box 21.1) increasing gradually with the level of cognitive demands from resting state and simple motor tasks to cognitive control-demanding paradigms. Here, the relevance to cognition is either assessed by a between-subject association with performance (see Section 21.2.1, e.g., (Shine et al., 2016)), or indirectly inferred from the expectation that cognitively demanding tasks require information exchange across an especially large number of regions, and thus would benefit from topological integration. In addition to experimentally controlled changes in cognitive/mental state, spontaneous fluctuations, e.g., of levels of vigilance and fatigue, have been associated with subtle changes in the functional connectome.

21.2.2.3 Time-varying dynamics of the functional connectome and behavioral variability

Cognitive processes are often highly variable within an individual, even when stimuli and external conditions are held constant. The association of this variability with changes in the momentary state of the connectome sheds light into the cognitive significance of the latter. As discussed above, analyzing task-based fMRI data in a continuous manner similar to resting-state approaches, e.g., (Shine et al., 2016), provides important information about task-dependent functional connectivity. However, intrinsically driven changes in the functional connectome may remain non-dissociable from task-evoked co-activation. To dissociate the two and understand how the former affects the latter, connectivity has been studied during prestimulus time periods. These studies use stimuli that are identical or directly comparable from trial to trial, yet cause different behavioral outcomes each time, such as threshold-level or ambiguous stimuli. For example, a machine learning approach (cf. Box 21.1) applied to prestimulus functional connectivity can predict (with above-chance accuracy) the participant's success or failure to detect a faint sound on a given trial (Sadaghiani et al., 2015). Furthermore, the subject is more likely to hear the sound when the functional communities are more segregated (measured as high modularity, cf. Box 21.1) just prior to the sound. It is likely that the connectome switches between more globally segregated states optimal for simple perception or motor output on the one hand, and more globally integrated states for cognitive control-demanding tasks on the other. Together with investigations of continuous task periods and task-free resting state, as discussed in the previous sections, evidence is converging for the cognitive importance of global topological segregation/integration of functional connectome states.

21.3 The connectome across the lifespan

Even though general brain network organization is largely consistent across individuals, as discussed above, differences between individuals have been observed. One important modifier of brain connectomics, which affects us all, is an individual's age. The observed age-related differences across the lifespan suggest that the connectome undergoes structural and functional changes during development and aging.

21.3.1 Age-related within- and between-network connectivity changes

Based on decades of research, we know that our cognitive abilities change with age. Typically, the trajectory of age-related cognitive changes shows an improvement during development, which peaks in early adulthood, and then gradually declines with older age. A similar pattern of developmental maturation followed by gradual age-related decline is observed in the brain connectome (see Fig. 21.2). A particularly consistent observation, mostly from cross-sectional studies, indicates that functional connectivity within the so-called default mode network, one of the canonical ICNs, increases with development and declines throughout older adulthood. The default mode network consists of some of the brain's main cortical hubs, such as the posterior cingulate cortex and medial prefrontal cortex, and is generally involved in self-referential processes, emotional processes, and memory function. It plays a central role in supporting our cognitive abilities, and its age-related connectivity changes are reflected in the observed cognitive changes. The extant literature on structural connectivity reveals a similar pattern, where rich club organization (encompassing brain regions that overlap with the default mode network) shows an age-related decline. Most studies that examined functional and structural connectivity in the same sample reveal that these measures are closely aligned (although functional connectivity can exist between brain regions in the absence of direct structural connectivity), and that they are similarly affected by aging. See Damoiseaux (2017) for a review on this topic.

In addition to the specific changes in the default mode network, the brain's global network organization also changes across the lifespan. Several studies indicate that across the adult lifespan within-network connectivity decreases, whereas between network connectivity increases. These brain changes indicate neural network dedifferentiation, meaning a reduction in functional network specialization with older age. Such network dedifferentiation implies less optimal brain function, possibly reflecting a compensation mechanism to maintain cognitive performance. To do so, additional brain regions are recruited to compensate for signal loss within specialized networks. However, it could also reflect noisy signal propagation due to age-related pathology that in turn leads to a reduction of neural selectivity. Either way, the observation of age-related differences in MRI-derived brain network measures provides us with an understanding of typical brain aging across the lifespan.

It has to be noted that our current understanding of age-related changes is mostly based on cross-sectional studies. Some of the relatively few longitudinal studies done appear to align with the cross-sectional findings; however, others show no change over time. More longitudinal studies, spanning longer periods of time, are needed to assess the actual trajectory of age-related brain changes.

21.3.2 Typical brain aging informs identification of pathological brain aging

As outlined above, the existing literature on age-related connectivity changes provides evidence in support of the applicability of connectomics to reveal individual differences in brain structure and

21.4 Clinical research applications of connectomics

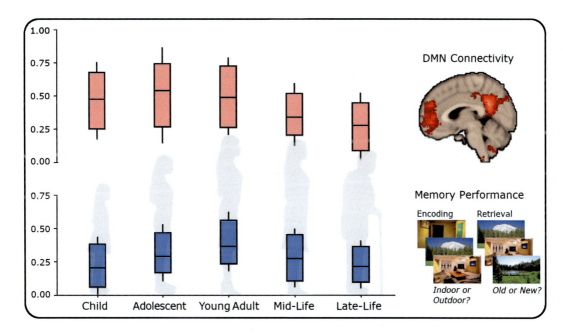

FIGURE 21.2

Illustration of the differences in connectomics and memory performance across the lifespan. Default mode network (DMN) functional connectivity (top) and memory performance (retrieval accuracy) for scenes (bottom) both show developmental maturation, peak during young adulthood, and gradually decline during mid-life and older adulthood. Based on unpublished data.

function. One potential application of connectomics as a biomarker for an individual's brain health is the "brain-age" approach (Cole and Franke, 2017). In this approach an individual's biological brain age can be estimated based on their brain network measures and compared to their chronological age. If, for example, an adult's brain age is higher than their chronological age, this indicates accelerated aging, which in turn may indicate potential neurodegenerative disease. Our knowledge of typical brain aging can thus inform the identification of possible pathological brain processes. How connectomics may aid in the diagnosis, prognosis, and treatment of clinical disorders will be discussed in the next section.

21.4 Clinical research applications of connectomics

Analyzing brain connectivity is mainly still an academic research tool to better understand brain function and organization. However, since the very beginning of connectome-based research, researchers have recognized the potential of connectivity-based measures in clinical settings. The following sections demonstrate examples of connectomics applications to aid diagnosis, disease prognosis, and clinical intervention.

330   Chapter 21 Applications of MRI connectomics

21.4.1 Connectomics reflects biology and therefore probably disease pathways

Both structural and functional connectivity exhibit a substantial degree of heritability, i.e., a person's genetic markup controls features of the connectome. Likewise, many disorders of the nervous system have been linked to genetic risk factors. One pertinent question is whether disease associated genetic risk variants exercise their effect on features of the connectome in healthy individuals, which would afford a better characterization of people at an increased disease risk. Indeed, in Alzheimer's disease (AD), the most common form of dementia, the $\varepsilon 4$ allele of the apolipoprotein E (*APOE*), the strongest common risk factor for AD, showed altered connectivity with regions participating in the default mode network in healthy adults across various studies (e.g., (Damoiseaux et al., 2012); Fig. 21.3). Similarly, in a cohort of typically developing children, carriers of a risk variant in the autism risk gene *CNTNAP2* were found to have altered connectivity with the medial prefrontal cortex (Fig. 21.3; (Scott-Van Zeeland et al., 2010)).

A different approach, used in schizophrenia research, found that increased polygenic risk (a score incorporating many hundreds of possibly weak genetic effects) was associated with reduced connectivity in a cluster primarily encompassing the visual, default mode, and frontoparietal systems (Cao et al., 2020).

Taken together across various studies, it seems that healthy people who carry genetic variants that increase their risk for developing a brain disorder exhibit changes in their structural and/or functional connectome that precede clinical symptoms.

21.4.2 Connectomics as tool for (differential) diagnosis

There is evidence from numerous diseases (neurodegenerative, autoimmune, psychiatric, and others) that there are differences in connectomics between patient and control groups that are comparable to differences across subjects with varying levels of cognitive abilities (cf. Section 21.2.1). Thus a strand of research has focused on eliciting sensitive and specific connectomics-derived quantities that can be used as diagnosis biomarkers. These endophenotypes of the disease typically do not rely on symptomatology, but for many of them good statistical relationships are shown with established diagnostic criteria or clinical scales. For some diseases, such as multiple sclerosis (MS), there has been a frustrating lack of correlation between imaging semiology and clinical scales, a phenomenon known as the "clinico-radiological paradox". One tenet of proponents of connectomics-derived biomarkers is that these biomarkers could pick up more subtle disease associations and help bridge this gap.

White matter lesions in MS cause demyelination and subsequent axonal transection, thereby causing important alterations in white matter connectivity. There is a well-known spatial distribution preference for white matter lesions, in particular around the ventricles, meaning that specific tracts, such as the cortico-spinal tract, are often impacted. Such white matter lesions impact not only the structural connectome, but also the large-scale organization of the functional connectome, which displays decreases in the network science measures (Box 21.1) of efficiency (Liu et al., 2017) and small-worldness (Faivre et al., 2016). These large-scale changes can be used as biomarkers enabling diagnosis of MS patients, although the specificity has not been fully established for use in a clinical context, in particular for differential diagnosis.

A challenging clinical problem is the differentiation between distinct but related clinical syndromes that share a range of symptoms. Imaging biomarkers, including structural and functional connectivity, are being explored to assist with differential diagnosis. In an early work, Seeley et al. (2009) reported

21.4 Clinical research applications of connectomics

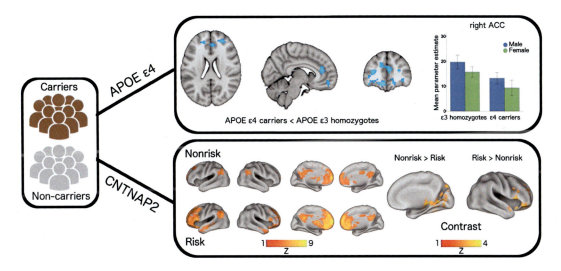

FIGURE 21.3

Genetic effects on functional connectivity. Healthy older adults carrying the APOE ε4 allele show decreased functional connectivity in the anterior default mode network when compared to APOE ε3 homozygotes (top panel). The statistical maps are thresholded using TFCE and p < 0.05 familywise error corrected. Adapted from (Damoiseaux et al., 2012) with permission from the author. Functional connectivity with the medial prefrontal cortex is associated with *CNTNAP2*: non-risk subjects show relatively greater long-range anterior-posterior connectivity than risk carriers and relatively greater right frontal connectivity in risk carriers compared to the non-risk group (bottom panel). Color scales indicate Z-scores of connectivity strength with the medial prefrontal cortex (left part) and the contrast between carriers of the *CNTNAP2* risk allele and non-carriers (right part). Adapted from (Scott-Van Zeeland et al., 2010) with permission from the American Association for the Advancement of Science.

that different neurodegenerative disorders exhibit characteristic patterns of gray matter loss that spatially overlap with canonical ICNs. For instance, AD imaging signatures tend to appear first in the default mode network, whereas frontotemporal dementia (FTD) imaging signatures are first located in the so-called salience ICN. Connectivity-based biomarkers are being investigated to better understand and discriminate between subtypes of syndromes. In post-traumatic stress disorder (PTSD), for example, functional connectivity between the periaqueductal gray and regions associated with emotion processing was increased in patients compared to controls. However, only in patients with the dissociative PTSD subtype was there also increased connectivity between the ventrolateral periaqueductal gray and brain regions known to be involved in passive coping strategies (Harricharan et al., 2016).

21.4.3 Connectomics for prognosis and relationship with clinical scales

Typically, prognosis for brain disease is established on a combination of demographic factors, comorbidities, neurological findings, including specialized clinical scales, radiological findings (mostly based

332 **Chapter 21** Applications of MRI connectomics

on structural imaging with various contrasts), and laboratory tests. With connectomics, the relationships between brain regions and large-scale changes in connectomics caused by the disease, can be leveraged to offer new perspectives on the possible future evolution of the patient's brain reorganization through adaptive or maladaptive plasticity.

For example, in stroke there is evidence that ischemic lesions cause changes in both structural and functional connectomes, leading to disconnection and reconfiguration of brain networks distal to the lesion (Carrera and Tononi, 2014). Observing brain networks that are either still intact, impacted by stroke, or at future risk can have important implications for the rehabilitation potential of specific patients and guiding therapy. Indeed, it has been reported that larger topology changes were associated with larger residual symptom burden several months after the acute phase (Schlemm et al., 2020).

Another example is FTD, which has been characterized by frontolimbic connectivity disruption leading to unconstrained prefrontal connectivity. Research showed that in patients with the behavioral variant or semantic dementia, the extent of prefrontal hyperconnectivity and frontolimbic disconnection reflected apathy and disinhibition scores, respectively (Farb et al., 2013).

21.4.4 Connectomics for treatment planning and response prediction

Choosing treatment options is based on assumptions about the patient's response to a specific treatment course. This can for example be a choice between either drug treatment or surgical intervention, several types of psychological therapy, or several types of drugs available for a particular condition. There has been increasing research about the use of connectomics to guide treatment choice, sometimes focusing on the connectivity between very specific brain regions, with several promising results in neuropsychiatric disorders (as illustrated in Fig. 21.4).

For example, in depression, several studies aimed to predict the response to electro-convulsive therapy based on functional connectivity. These studies show that a decrease in depressive symptoms after electro-convulsive therapy was correlated with pre-intervention connectivity of the subcallosal cingulate cortex (Argyelan et al., 2016).

Another example is Parkinson's disease, for which deep brain stimulation (DBS) is an established treatment option. However, clinical response is highly variable and may depend on the connectivity profile of the simulated brain region. Horn et al. (2017) identified the volume of tissue activated by DBS in a given patient and combined this information with a group-level structural connectome to identify affected fiber tracts. Moreover, they used the volume of tissue activated as a seed in a large cohort to establish the functional connectivity profile. Using these group-level structural and functional connectomes improved the prediction of motor scores (as measured with the unified Parkinson disease rating scale-III) in response to DBS treatment, and may be used to revise or guide DBS.

Brain surgery may be needed to treat refractory epilepsy and brain tumors. Detailed planning is required to avoid damage to critical brain regions (e.g., those involved in memory, language, and motor functions) and to maintain acceptable quality of life post-surgery. Traditionally, a personalized mapping of relevant brain regions, such as the eloquent cortex, is conducted using task-based fMRI or intraoperative electrocortical stimulation (see Chapter 18). Recent advances use functional connectivity to better predict treatment outcomes and to fine-map critical cortical regions (Sair et al., 2016).

21.5 Limitations for research and clinical translation

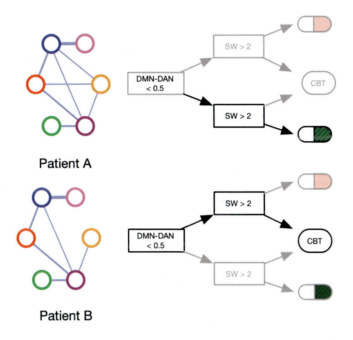

FIGURE 21.4

Illustration of the use of connectomics for treatment planning in psychiatric disorders. Based on strength of connections between certain ICNs, or specific network science metrics (see Box 21.1), each patient can be oriented towards the most appropriate pharmacological (striped green pill or filled red pill) or psychological treatment (CBT, cognitive behavioral therapy). DMN: default-mode network. DAN: attention network. SW: Small world index.

21.5 Limitations for research and clinical translation

Given all the promising results we have mentioned in this chapter thus far, one may wonder: where are these tools used in actual clinical settings? There are in fact a number of obstacles in bringing these results to use, some of which are shared by other modalities, such as structural MRI. Here, we focus on those issues that are more specifically preventing MRI connectomics from being used clinically, and that also pose problems for non-clinical research.

A perennial problem for fMRI-based connectomics, but also DWI-based connectomics, is head motion. Connectivity is modulated by motion in a spatially-dependent fashion, with differing effects in long- and short-range estimates. This is particularly problematic when two groups are compared, such as patients and controls, as group differences in motion alone can cause considerable group differences in connectivity patterns, affecting all analysis methods outlined in Box 21.1. Possible mitigation strategies include prospective motion correction, embedded cameras for head motion tracking, or a posteriori motion compensation, including independent component analysis (ICA)-based approaches, such as ICA-FIX or motion "scrubbing" for fMRI. Other unwanted physiological signals, such as breathing or heart rate variability, can also impact the BOLD signal, in large part due to the low sampling frequency, which causes aliasing into the frequency bands of interest for resting-state analysis. Mitigation strategies include low TR acquisition, or retrospective correction using various algorithms (Caballero-Gaudes and Reynolds, 2017).

There are additional confounds for functional connectivity concerning the cognitive states of the subjects. Among those, sleep (practically the loss of consciousness) imposes a drastic reorganization of the connectome, such as the breakdown of thalamo-cortical coupling (as illustrated in Fig. 21.5 by the functional connectivity difference between subcortical regions (SC) and the rest of the brain). Some diseases or medications may affect the participants' vigilance and render them more prone to doze off during the MRI session. Seemingly harmless events, such as enjoying a cup of coffee, may alter functional connectivity. The sensitivity of the functional connectome to pathological emotional states (such as anxiety disorders) renders it susceptible to the "normal" range of emotional states and affects its utility as a biomarker. Lastly, the seemingly simple instruction to "lie still in the MRI scanner and to not think of anything in particular" may be difficult to follow for some patient groups (e.g., AD, ADHD, PD).

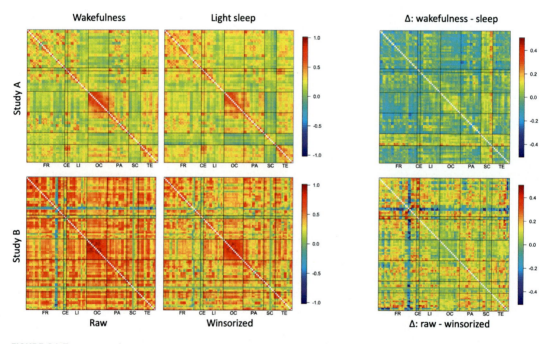

FIGURE 21.5

Effect of vigilance states and movement artifacts on functional connectivity. Matrices display regional connectivity using Spearman correlation (left and middle columns) or their difference (right column). Top row: Transitioning from wakefulness to light sleep reduces thalamo-cortical connectivity (as part of the SC regions) with group difference showing an absolute change in correlation of around 0.3; based on data from (Spoormaker et al., 2010). Bottom row: Movement (or head motion) causes structured noise in the fMRI time series that can lead to widespread artificially increased connectivity estimates (about 0.4 in the example). The use of robust connectivity estimates, such as winsorizing (or "clipping") the regional fMRI time series (e.g., measurements below the 5th percentile or above the 95th percentile are set to the 5th percentile or 95th percentile, respectively), can reduce movement artifacts. FR=Frontal; CE=Central; LI=Limbic; OC=Occipital; PA=Parietal; SC=subcortical; TE=Temporal lobe.

A further complication is that connectomics measures are modulated by demographic factors, such as age (see Section 21.3), sex, and genetic ancestry. Some of these factors, such as sex and genetic ancestry, are known to exercise a strong influence on measures such as intra cranial volume and regional brain morphology. It is still the subject of ongoing research to properly adjust for these factors in connectivity analyses. However, functional connectivity may be more subtly influenced by differences such as the native language or bilingualism (Ge et al., 2015).

One of the main issues in bringing fMRI and high-quality DWI to the clinic is acquisition time. Whereas around 5 minutes is sufficient to acquire a high resolution T_1-weighted MRI, which is used for almost all brain diseases, adding an fMRI acquisition will typically add 6–7 minutes at the minimum, and adding a DWI of sufficient quality to permit tractography (e.g., multishell imaging) will add at least 7 minutes of scan time. Though these acquisition times are steadily decreasing with the widespread adoption of techniques such as compressed sensing, multi-band imaging, or deep learning-based reconstruction, fMRI and DWI must compete for acquisition time with other well-established sequences, such as FLAIR or perfusion imaging, which have clearly demonstrated their clinical utility. For radiology departments, adding more sequences means decreasing patient throughput, at a time when clinical imaging exams are more and more requested by other medical specialties.

Finally, an important issue is that fMRI and DWI data acquired on different machines (in multiple sites) can differ very importantly in terms of technical parameters, such as spatial and temporal resolution, contrast, number and distribution of diffusion directions, diffusion b-values, etc. These differences will lead to vastly different connectomics, even for the same patient. Two trends offer hope that site differences can be overcome: 1) several initiatives, notably in the radiomics field, are attempting to standardize specific biomarkers; 2) post-acquisition harmonization is progressing rapidly, driven by progress in deep learning (Tax et al., 2019).

Box 21.1 Analysis and inference with brain graphs

Once they are constructed, brain graphs can be analyzed at the whole-graph level, subgraph level, vertex level, or connection level, depending on the goal of the analysis. Mathematical tools to analyze and model brain graphs can be roughly grouped into four fuzzy categories: statistical approaches, machine learning approaches, network science approaches, and graph signal processing approaches (see Fig. 21.6). In statistical approaches, the goal is to perform hypothesis testing on groups of graphs, subgraphs, vertices, or edges. Several techniques developed specifically for graphs exploit subgraphs to gain power, such as the network-based statistics (Zalesky et al., 2010), or two-step (screening-filtering) testing (Meskaldji et al., 2015). Machine learning approaches focus instead on prediction using individual graphs, making them particularly suitable for clinical applications. There has been tremendous progress in graph-based machine learning in the last few years, especially in representation learning, either with graph embeddings (representing a graph as a vector) or with graph neural networks (end-to-end learning). Though these approaches typically have very good predictive ability, they can be difficult to interpret in terms of specific brain regions or their interactions. Network science approaches, instead, propose various graph topological metrics that can be readily interpreted to yield neuroscientific insights. Notably, the notions of modularity (representing integration versus segregation of function), hubs (representing parts of the brain which play a central role in information exchange), or efficiency can be expressed and estimated compactly. These network metrics help place analysis results within a systems-oriented frame of reference; however, readers should be cautious, because mathematical definitions often differ between authors. Lastly, graph signal processing approaches have gained traction recently in the neuroimaging community, and propose to translate common concepts in signal processing, such as filtering, downsampling, or Fourier analysis to the domain of brain graphs.

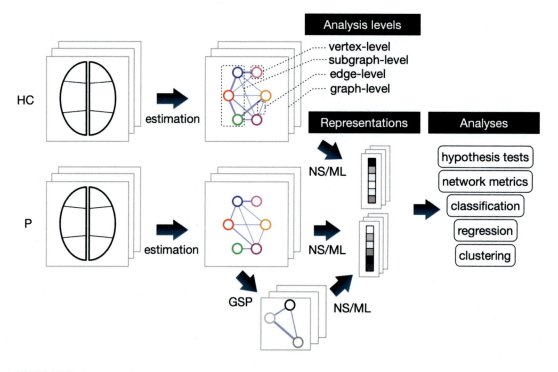

FIGURE 21.6

Overview of analysis and inference. HC: healthy controls. P: patients. GSP: graph signal processing. NS: network science. ML: machine learning. In end-to-end approaches, such as graph convolutional networks or graph autoencoders, representations are learned implicitly, with the goal of minimizing prediction or reconstruction errors.

21.6 Concluding remarks

Over the last decade, MRI-derived connectivity investigations have made rapid progress towards studying the whole-brain connectome simultaneously and harnessing its multivariate information using mathematical tools, such as machine learning and network science. This progress has been enabled by advances in imaging technology and, more importantly, the discovery of the intrinsic nature of connectome organization, especially in functional MRI. Connectome approaches have revealed associations with cognitive processes, development and aging, genetic makeup and neurological and psychiatric disorders. These associations have not yet been harnessed for clinical diagnosis, prognosis, and treatment response prediction. Such translational impact is expected to become attainable as studies advance from the group level to characterizing functionally consequential individual differences. Both basic brain research and precision medicine are likely to benefit strongly from this development over the next decade.

References

Argyelan, M., Lencz, T., Kaliora, S., Sarpal, D.K., Weissman, N., Kingsley, P.B., Malhotra, A.K., Petrides, G., 2016. Subgenual cingulate cortical activity predicts the efficacy of electroconvulsive therapy. Transl. Psychiatry 6, e789. https://doi.org/10.1038/tp.2016.54.

Caballero-Gaudes, C., Reynolds, R.C., 2017. Methods for cleaning the BOLD fMRI signal. NeuroImage 154, 128–149. https://doi.org/10.1016/j.neuroimage.2016.12.018. Cleaning up the fMRI time series: Mitigating noise with advanced acquisition and correction strategies.

Caeyenberghs, K., Metzler-Baddeley, C., Foley, S., Jones, D.K., 2016. Dynamics of the human structural connectome underlying working memory training. J. Neurosci. 36, 4056–4066. https://doi.org/10.1523/JNEUROSCI.1973-15.2016.

Cao, H., Zhou, H., Cannon, T.D., 2020. Functional connectome-wide associations of schizophrenia polygenic risk. Mol. Psychiatry. https://doi.org/10.1038/s41380-020-0699-3.

Carrera, E., Tononi, G., 2014. Diaschisis: past, present, future. Brain 137, 2408–2422. https://doi.org/10.1093/brain/awu101.

Cole, J.H., Franke, K., 2017. Predicting age using neuroimaging: innovative brain ageing biomarkers. Trends Neurosci. 40, 681–690. https://doi.org/10.1016/j.tins.2017.10.001.

Damoiseaux, J.S., 2017. Effects of aging on functional and structural brain connectivity. NeuroImage 160, 32–40. https://doi.org/10.1016/j.neuroimage.2017.01.077.

Damoiseaux, J.S., Seeley, W.W., Zhou, J., Shirer, W.R., Coppola, G., Karydas, A., Rosen, H.J., Miller, B.L., Kramer, J.H., Greicius, M.D., 2012. Gender modulates the APOE ε4 effect in healthy older adults: convergent evidence from functional brain connectivity and spinal fluid tau levels. J. Neurosci. 32, 8254–8262. https://doi.org/10.1523/JNEUROSCI.0305-12.2012.

Faivre, A., Robinet, E., Guye, M., Rousseau, C., Maarouf, A., Le Troter, A., Zaaraoui, W., Rico, A., Crespy, L., Soulier, E., Confort-Gouny, S., Pelletier, J., Achard, S., Ranjeva, J.-P., Audoin, B., 2016. Depletion of brain functional connectivity enhancement leads to disability progression in multiple sclerosis: a longitudinal resting-state fMRI study. Mult. Scler. 22, 1695–1708. https://doi.org/10.1177/1352458516628657.

Farb, N.A.S., Grady, C.L., Strother, S., Tang-Wai, D.F., Masellis, M., Black, S., Freedman, M., Pollock, B.G., Campbell, K.L., Hasher, L., Chow, T.W., 2013. Abnormal network connectivity in frontotemporal dementia: evidence for prefrontal isolation. Cortex 49, 1856–1873. https://doi.org/10.1016/j.cortex.2012.09.008.

Ge, J., Peng, G., Lyu, B., Wang, Y., Zhuo, Y., Niu, Z., Tan, L.H., Leff, A.P., Gao, J.-H., 2015. Cross-language differences in the brain network subserving intelligible speech. Proc. Natl. Acad. Sci. USA 112, 2972–2977. https://doi.org/10.1073/pnas.1416000112.

Harricharan, S., Rabellino, D., Frewen, P.A., Densmore, M., Théberge, J., McKinnon, M.C., Schore, A.N., Lanius, R.A., 2016. fMRI functional connectivity of the periaqueductal gray in PTSD and its dissociative subtype. Brain Behav. 6, e00579. https://doi.org/10.1002/brb3.579.

Horn, A., Reich, M., Vorwerk, J., Li, N., Wenzel, G., Fang, Q., Schmitz-Hübsch, T., Nickl, R., Kupsch, A., Volkmann, J., Kühn, A.A., Fox, M.D., 2017. Connectivity predicts deep brain stimulation outcome in Parkinson disease. Ann. Neurol. 82, 67–78. https://doi.org/10.1002/ana.24974.

Jones, D.K., Knösche, T.R., Turner, R., 2013. White matter integrity, fiber count, and other fallacies: the do's and don'ts of diffusion MRI. NeuroImage 73, 239–254. https://doi.org/10.1016/j.neuroimage.2012.06.081.

Liu, Y., Wang, H., Duan, Y., Huang, J., Ren, Z., Ye, J., Dong, H., Shi, F., Li, K., Wang, J., 2017. Functional brain network alterations in clinically isolated syndrome and multiple sclerosis: a graph-based connectome study. Radiology 282, 534–541. https://doi.org/10.1148/radiol.2016152843.

Meskaldji, D.-E., Vasung, L., Romascano, D., Thiran, J.-P., Hagmann, P., Morgenthaler, S., Van De Ville, D., 2015. Improved statistical evaluation of group differences in connectomes by screening–filtering strategy with application to study maturation of brain connections between childhood and adolescence. NeuroImage 108, 251–264. https://doi.org/10.1016/j.neuroimage.2014.11.059.

Nomi, J.S., Vij, S.G., Dajani, D.R., Steimke, R., Damaraju, E., Rachakonda, S., Calhoun, V.D., Uddin, L.Q., 2017. Chronnectomic patterns and neural flexibility underlie executive function. NeuroImage 147, 861–871. https://doi.org/10.1016/j.neuroimage.2016.10.026.

Sadaghiani, S., Poline, J.-B., Kleinschmidt, A., D'Esposito, M., 2015. Ongoing dynamics in large-scale functional connectivity predict perception. Proc. Natl. Acad. Sci. USA 112, 8463–8468. https://doi.org/10.1073/pnas.1420687112.

Sair, H.I., Yahyavi-Firouz-Abadi, N., Calhoun, V.D., Airan, R.D., Agarwal, S., Intrapiromkul, J., Choe, A.S., Gujar, S.K., Caffo, B., Lindquist, M.A., Pillai, J.J., 2016. Presurgical brain mapping of the language network in patients with brain tumors using resting-state fMRI: comparison with task fMRI. Hum. Brain Mapp. 37, 913–923. https://doi.org/10.1002/hbm.23075.

Schlemm, E., Schulz, R., Bönstrup, M., Krawinkel, L., Fiehler, J., Gerloff, C., Thomalla, G., Cheng, B., 2020. Structural brain networks and functional motor outcome after stroke—a prospective cohort study. Brain Commun. 2. https://doi.org/10.1093/braincomms/fcaa001.

Scott-Van Zeeland, A.A., Abrahams, B.S., Alvarez-Retuerto, A.I., Sonnenblick, L.I., Rudie, J.D., Ghahremani, D., Mumford, J.A., Poldrack, R.A., Dapretto, M., Geschwind, D.H., Bookheimer, S.Y., 2010. Altered functional connectivity in frontal lobe circuits is associated with variation in the autism risk gene CNTNAP2. Sci. Transl. Med. 2, 56ra80. https://doi.org/10.1126/scitranslmed.3001344.

Seeley, W.W., Crawford, R.K., Zhou, J., Miller, B.L., Greicius, M.D., 2009. Neurodegenerative diseases target large-scale human brain networks. Neuron 62, 42–52. https://doi.org/10.1016/j.neuron.2009.03.024.

Shen, X., Finn, E.S., Scheinost, D., Rosenberg, M.D., Chun, M.M., Papademetris, X., Constable, R.T., 2017. Using connectome-based predictive modeling to predict individual behavior from brain connectivity. Nat. Protoc. 12, 506–518. https://doi.org/10.1038/nprot.2016.178.

Shine, J.M., Bissett, P.G., Bell, P.T., Koyejo, O., Balsters, J.H., Gorgolewski, K.J., Moodie, C.A., Poldrack, R.A., 2016. The dynamics of functional brain networks: integrated network states during cognitive task performance. Neuron 92, 544–554. https://doi.org/10.1016/j.neuron.2016.09.018.

Spoormaker, V.I., Schröter, M.S., Gleiser, P.M., Andrade, K.C., Dresler, M., Wehrle, R., Sämann, P.G., Czisch, M., 2010. Development of a large-scale functional brain network during human non-rapid eye movement sleep. J. Neurosci. 30, 11379–11387. https://doi.org/10.1523/JNEUROSCI.2015-10.2010.

Tax, C.M.W., Grussu, F., Kaden, E., Ning, L., Rudrapatna, U., John Evans, C., St-Jean, S., Leemans, A., Koppers, S., Merhof, D., Ghosh, A., Tanno, R., Alexander, D.C., Zappalà, S., Charron, C., Kusmia, S., Linden, D.E.J., Jones, D.K., Veraart, J., 2019. Cross-scanner and cross-protocol diffusion MRI data harmonisation: a benchmark database and evaluation of algorithms. NeuroImage 195, 285–299. https://doi.org/10.1016/j.neuroimage.2019.01.077.

Zalesky, A., Fornito, A., Bullmore, E.T., 2010. Network-based statistic: identifying differences in brain networks. NeuroImage 53, 1197–1207. https://doi.org/10.1016/j.neuroimage.2010.06.041.

PART

Susceptibility MRI

7

CHAPTER

Principles of susceptibility-weighted MRI

22

Sagar Buch[a], Yongsheng Chen[b], and E. Mark Haacke[a,b]

[a]*Department of Radiology, Wayne State University School of Medicine, Detroit, MI, United States*
[b]*Department of Neurology, Wayne State University School of Medicine, Detroit, MI, United States*

22.1 Introduction

Several sources of magnetic field variation can be found in the human body. These magnetic sources can cause signal distortion and unwanted loss of signal (local reduction in T_2^*). There are three main sources, the local tissues themselves, the air/tissue interfaces in the body, and extra-corporeal objects. Examples of extracorporeal objects include surgically implanted objects, iron-based tattoos, and certain cosmetic products, such as eye shadows (Bellon et al., 1986; Sacco et al., 1987). Both the air/tissue interface fields and those associated with extracorporeal objects are large enough to create local distortion artifacts. Generally, the deleterious effects of these fields should be removed. In comparison, the field changes associated with biological tissues are small, and are generated from the magnetic susceptibility differences between the tissues. The fields arising from the local tissues are based on their magnetic properties of being either diamagnetic or paramagnetic and on the shape of the structure. These non-zero susceptibilities lead to non-local phase effects and can be visualized once the background fields from the air/tissue interfaces and any extracorporeal objects have been removed (Haacke et al., 2004; Reichenbach et al., 1997). Therefore local tissue susceptibility change creates a new contrast mechanism, which can be helpful in distinguishing abnormal from healthy tissue. The ability to visualize local changes in phase was originally accomplished by performing a high-pass filter on the phase (Haacke et al., 1995), and then enhancing the susceptibility effects in the magnitude image using a specially designed phase mask, leading to the development of susceptibility-weighted imaging or SWI as we know it today (Haacke et al., 2004; Reichenbach et al., 1997).

22.2 What is magnetic susceptibility?

Magnetic susceptibility is a material property that measures the ability of a given material to be magnetized when it is placed within an external uniform magnetic field. In this magnetized state, the object alters the surrounding local magnetic field in a way that is determined in part by its tissue properties and in part by its shape (geometry).

The magnetic susceptibility of an object can be classified under either diamagnetism, paramagnetism or ferromagnetism based on the macroscopic influence of the external magnetic field. This implies that the magnetization depends on the magnetic susceptibility, χ, of the object. For empty

Advances in Magnetic Resonance Technology and Applications, Volume 4, ISSN 2666-9099. https://doi.org/10.1016/B978-0-12-822479-3.00036-1
Copyright © 2021 Elsevier Inc. All rights reserved.

space, the value of χ is zero, whereas a negative value of χ represents a diamagnetic material, such as water. Human tissues contain a significant amount of water, making most of the soft tissues diamagnetic in nature, especially white matter fiber bundles, such as the optic radiation. Bone, on the other hand, is much more diamagnetic than most soft tissues in the body since it is made predominantly of calcium. Similarly, if the value of χ is positive or slightly greater than zero, the material is paramagnetic. Iron is strongly paramagnetic, so that even small amounts can be detected as in microbleeds, for example. Gadolinium is another good example of a paramagnetic substance. It is combined with a chelating agent to reduce its toxicity, so it can be used in MRI as a contrast agent to depict the vascular network. For typical applications, its effect is predominantly not one of high susceptibility, but rather as a T_1 reducing contrast agent for the most part. For ferromagnetic materials, the value of χ is much larger than 1, and these materials can achieve constant magnetization even at a room temperature. Most of the ferromagnetic signals in MRI originate from an external source rather than a biological tissue. Generally, the relevant information for human tissue imaging comes from susceptibility values, which are relatively small, being on the order of parts per billion (ppb) to a few parts per million (ppm). However, iron in ferritin, when the ferritin is heavily loaded, is on the order of several thousand ppm.

22.3 SWI pulse sequence considerations

Susceptibility variations from tissue to tissue lead to spatial variations in the magnetic field, which affects both phase (via local frequency changes) and magnitude (via T_2^* decay) data, and both of these can be measured with gradient-echo (GRE) sequences. The resonance frequency shifts occurring in response to these magnetic field variations offer the possibility to extract information about the magnetic properties of the tissues in the form of field variations, as seen in the MRI phase data. The problem is complicated by the fact that usually, depending on the shape of the object, the phase generated from a given tissue is non-local, that is, there is a spatial variation of the field induced by a given structure. Nevertheless, phase itself plays a major role in producing contrast, particularly in small structures such as veins and microbleeds.

SWI combines a T_2^*-weighted magnitude image with a filtered phase image acquired using a GRE sequence to enhance image contrast. The magnitude image already provides some susceptibility contrast via the dephasing effect that occurs in the presence of locally varying fields across a voxel. SWI enhances the contrast between tissues of differing susceptibility by applying a phase mask to the original magnitude image. For this reason, SWI has become established in the neuroimaging field, as it highlights small structures, such as veins and microbleeds that are otherwise difficult to detect by conventional MRI. Since the first description in 1997 (Reichenbach et al., 1997), SWI has been proven useful in a multitude of clinical applications, including high-resolution MR venography, imaging of traumatic intracranial hemorrhage, visualizing blood products, and vascularization of tumors, or assessing iron deposits in the brain (Haacke et al., 2009; Mittal et al., 2009). More recently, the application of diamagnetic SWI (or dSWI) has been applied to visualize white matter tracts, particularly the optic radiation (Jella et al., 2021).

For SWI data acquisition, a 3D, radiofrequency (RF)-spoiled, velocity-compensated, GRE sequence is utilized (Haacke et al., 2004; Wu et al., 2016). A 3D acquisition is preferred (as opposed to 2D), allowing thinner slices and smaller voxel sizes to be obtained, yielding excellent contrast between tissues of differing susceptibility. With high resolution imaging, it is possible to reduce the macroscopic effects

22.4 Phase information   **343**

of dephasing across voxels that can occur in lower resolution imaging. Flow-compensating gradients are used (ideally in all three spatial directions) to prevent artifacts caused by blood flow, particularly the artifacts caused by the rapid and pulsatile flow of blood. This leaves the pristine susceptibility-induced field variations from just the local tissues themselves. Low flip angles (FAs) also reduce the inflow pulsation-based aliasing artifacts and make SWI safe for high field imaging (due to the dramatically reduced specific absorption rate of low FAs). The use of both phase-encoding and partition-encoding flow compensation eliminates the shift artifacts that otherwise occur in vessels that make an angle to the readout direction. However, the presence of background field gradients (particularly near the sinuses and, hence, near the middle cerebral arteries) may cause a failure in flow compensation, even with the ideal, theoretically designed first-order gradient moment nulling (Wu et al., 2016). To accomplish this phase/partition flow compensation, these gradients are rewound after sampling a given echo signal in preparation for the next echo acquisition (Haacke et al., 2009; Wu et al., 2016). This way every echo is flow compensated.

22.4 **Phase information**

The phase accrual ($\varphi\,(\vec{r}, t)$) for a GRE sequence at time (t) depends on the Larmor frequency (ω) and the local variations in the main magnetic field ($B(\vec{r})$). For a right-handed system, a positive rotating spin has $\omega = -\gamma B$, and, in the rotating reference frame, the phase can be written as

$$\varphi\,(\vec{r}, TE) = -\gamma\,(B\,(\vec{r}) - B_0) \cdot TE = -\gamma \cdot \Delta B\,(\vec{r}) \cdot TE, \tag{22.1}$$

where $\Delta B(\vec{r})$ is the local field variation about the main field B_0. SWI uses a relatively high spatial resolution, and the tissue magnetic susceptibility difference is ideally the only source to affect the local magnetic field across two neighboring voxels. Due to the high spatial resolution, the background field inside a voxel can be regarded as homogeneous and the magnetic field variations ($\Delta B(\vec{r})$) can be represented as the product of the magnetic susceptibility difference ($\Delta\chi$) between the two voxels and the main magnetic field. Hence, Eq. (22.1) becomes

$$\Delta\varphi = -\gamma \cdot (\Delta\chi B_0) \cdot TE. \tag{22.2}$$

The above expression shows the phase variation between two voxels, but for a larger region of interest at a macroscopic level, the field variations and the local phase differences are given as

$$\Delta B\,(\vec{r}) = g\,(\vec{r}) \cdot \Delta\chi B_0 \tag{22.3}$$

and

$$\Delta\varphi\,(\vec{r}, TE) = -\gamma \cdot (g\,(\vec{r}) \cdot \Delta\chi B_0) \cdot TE, \tag{22.4}$$

where, $g(\vec{r})$ is dependent on the geometry of the object.

344 **Chapter 22** Principles of susceptibility-weighted MRI

22.5 Phase aliasing and background fields

In reality, these macroscopic fields also include global field changes ($\Delta B_{global\ geometry}$) caused by the tissues with strong susceptibility differences, such as the air-tissue interface around the sinuses in the head, and by inhomogeneities in the main magnetic field ($\Delta B_{main\ field}$). The effective phase behavior can be written as the summation of these fields:

$$\varphi \alpha \Delta B_{main\ field} + \Delta B_{cs} + \Delta B_{global\ geometry} + \Delta B_{local\ field}, \tag{22.5}$$

where, ΔB_{cs} represents the field variations due to the chemical shift. These sources of field variation dominate the local field variations across the tissues ($\Delta B_{local\ field}$), making it difficult to directly utilize the phase images for their susceptibility-based contrast.

Due to the linear relationship between the phase signal and TE, higher TEs are ideal for enhancing the contrast for local tissues (at least up to TEs on the order of T_2^* of the tissue). However, as phase continues to increase, it will alias and remain between the bounds of $[-\pi, \pi]$. In the presence of a macroscopic field (Eq. (22.5)), this phase wrapping increases as TE increases, as shown in Fig. 22.1. To remove the field variations due to the inhomogeneities in the main magnetic field and the global geometries, processing techniques, such as the conventionally used homodyne high-pass (HP) filter or other background removal methods, such as the sophisticated harmonic artifact reduction for phase data (SHARP) (Schweser et al., 2011), can be applied to the original phase images.

22.5.1 Homodyne high-pass filter

A high-pass filtered image, $\rho'(\vec{r})$, is obtained by complex dividing of the original phase data, $\rho(\vec{r})$, by a low-pass filtered complex image ($\rho_m(\vec{r})$), which is generated from truncating the central n×n pixels from the original complex image and zero-filling the elements outside the central n×n elements to get the same dimensions as the original image.

$$\rho'(\vec{r}) = \rho(\vec{r})/\rho_m(\vec{r}) \tag{22.6}$$

The central part of k-space, or spatial frequency domain, of the complex acquired data contains the low spatial frequency changes of the main magnetic field (Haacke et al., 2004). By generating an image based on the central part of the k-space and complex dividing it into the original complex data, the main field global inhomogeneity effects are reduced leaving only the high spatial frequency components. This removes most of the unwanted field variations due to global geometries that obscure the local inter-tissue phase differences of interest (Fig. 22.1).

The filtered-phase images remove most of the background field from the sinuses and make it possible to differentiate one tissue from another. However, apart from removing the background field effects, the HP filter also tends to remove the physiologically relevant low spatial frequency phase information from larger anatomic structures. This trade-off between the phase unwrapping nature of this filter and the preservation of low spatial frequencies limits the use of filter size to 96×96 in the case of the data shown in Fig. 22.1. On the other hand, the alternative background removal methods, such as SHARP, preserve the low spatial frequencies better than the HP filtered results. However, these methods require an additional step of phase unwrapping, which makes them less time efficient compared to the HP filter approach. Moreover, the enhancement of the high-frequency terms, caused by the HP filter,

22.6 Phase mask and SWI processing   **345**

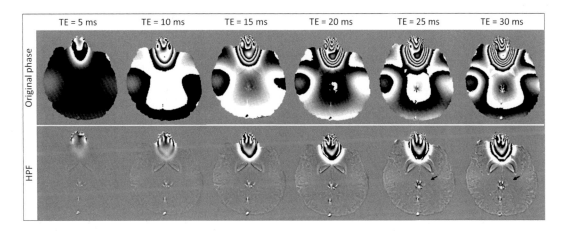

FIGURE 22.1

Studying the evolution of the phase behavior as a function of echo time (TE) using numerical simulations. The simulated phase images (top row) were generated by applying the forward dipole filter (as explained in Koch et al., 2006; Salomir et al., 2003) onto a 3D susceptibility model of the human brain (matrix size = 512^3) at 3T. The phase aliasing caused by the global or background phase makes it impossible to study the local structures. Hence, the original phase is high-pass filtered (filter size = 96×96, bottom row) to reduce this background field. The remnant contrast is mostly generated by variations in the magnetic field caused by local susceptibility sources only. Although this contrast is heightened at higher TEs (black arrows), the global field effects near the air-tissue interfaces still remain.

can be considered an advantage when the primary application of the SWI images is to be used as a venogram. Another important consideration while preparing the HP filtered phase is to vary the filter size as a function of the FOV. For example, for an FOV of 256×256 mm² and an in-plane resolution of 0.67×0.67 mm², the matrix size is 384×384. By using a HP filter size of 96×96, this is equivalent to filtering out tissues with a diameter greater than 256/96 mm or slightly less than 3 mm. If the FOV is changed to FOV′, then the filter size should be changed according to 96×FOV′/FOV to keep the same spatial frequency effect on the image. For example, if FOV′ is 128×128 mm², the filter size should be 48×48. Newer techniques have utilized spatial high-pass filters to avoid the filtering artifacts at the edge of the brain (Eckstein et al., 2021).

22.6 Phase mask and SWI processing

The multiplication of the magnitude image by a phase mask is used in the SWI output to create enhanced contrast; this basically deepens the usual attenuation caused by T_2^* shortening. The phase mask is designed according to whether one is looking for enhancement of diamagnetic or paramagnetic tissues. For example, for a right-handed system, suppressing tissues with calcium or white matter fiber bundles, would use a mask with unity for negative phase and linearly scale the mask to zero, as the phase varies

346   **Chapter 22** Principles of susceptibility-weighted MRI

from 0 to π (Eq. (22.7)).

$$\varphi_M(\vec{r}) = \begin{cases} 1 - \frac{\varphi(\vec{r})}{\pi}, & \text{if } 0 < \varphi < \pi \\ 1, & \text{else.} \end{cases} \tag{22.7}$$

This mask is used to create the dSWI data. On the other hand, suppressing paramagnetic substances would use a mask with unity for positive phase and linearly scale the mask to zero, as the phase varies from 0 to $-\pi$ (Eq. (22.8)).

$$\varphi_M(\vec{r}) = \begin{cases} 1 - \frac{|\varphi(\vec{r})|}{\pi}, & \text{if } -\pi < \varphi < 0 \\ 1, & \text{else.} \end{cases} \tag{22.8}$$

This mask is used to create the usual paramagnetic SWI data. In the final step, the phase mask ($\varphi_M(\vec{r})$) is multiplied several times (multiplication factor = n) with the original magnitude data (mag) to generate the SWI images (see Fig. 22.2):

$$\text{SWI} = \text{mag} \cdot \left[\varphi_M(\vec{r})\right]^n. \tag{22.9}$$

Earlier work has shown that multiplying the mask four times (n = 4) with the magnitude produces an optimum contrast-to-noise ratio between venous vessels and surrounding tissue (Haacke et al., 2004).

22.7 Imaging parameters and acquisition time

To obtain the SWI data with optimum contrast and signal-to-noise for the tissue of interest, the imaging parameters, such as FA, TE, resolution and readout bandwidth need to be chosen carefully. For a GRE sequence, the peak signal occurs when the FA is equal to the Ernst angle $\theta_E = \arccos(e^{-\text{TR}/T_1})$, or an approximation for TR $\ll T_1$, $\theta_E \approx \sqrt{2\text{TR}/T_1}$, where TR is the repetition time and T_1 is the longitudinal relaxation time of the tissue of interest (Brown et al., 2014). For instance, for a tissue with a T_1 value of 900 ms (e.g., white matter at 3T) and a TR of 25 ms, the FA of the SWI sequence should be chosen close to $\theta_E = 13°$. Similarly, to get a strong cancellation effect, and to generate good susceptibility images, a TE around 20–25 ms at 3T provides good contrast for SWI in terms of cancelling venous signal and for susceptibility in terms of signal-to-noise ratio. Although more T_2^* dephasing will occur for longer TEs, echo times that are too long lead to a loss of SNR and phase aliasing, making it difficult to study areas adjacent to air-tissue interfaces (Fig. 22.1). Depending on the susceptibility of the object of interest, a short TE might give better SNR and CNR and true object size than a longer TE. This is especially true for strongly paramagnetic objects such as cerebral microbleeds.

On the other hand, too high a resolution will reduce the T_2^* effects. Therefore choosing an in-plane resolution on the order of 0.5×0.5 mm^2 does an excellent job of highlighting medullary veins as small as 250 microns in diameter, whereas keeping the slice thickness to 1–2 mm keeps the signal loss still significant for veins that are on the order of 1–2 mm in diameter. Luckily, SWI data can be acquired with multiple echoes, providing flexibility in choosing the lower and higher limits of the desired echoes to best visualize one or more structures-of-interest. Additionally, it is possible to simultaneously obtain an angiogram (using the first echo data, without the use of a contrast agent) and SWI (using the second or later echo data), which both necessary to depict the cerebral vascular system (Chen et al., 2018a; Ye et al., 2013).

22.7 Imaging parameters and acquisition time

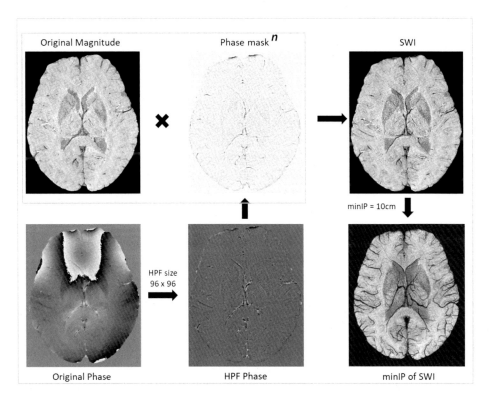

FIGURE 22.2

Process of generating SWI images using the original magnitude data and the homodyne high-pass (HP) filtered phase. The original magnitude data are multiplied with the phase mask generated from the HP filtered phase, where the multiplication factor (n) is usually 4, to produce SWI images. The SWI data are minimum intensity projected (minIP) over several slices to better visualize the venous network.

Our recommendation is that the minimally acceptable resolution for an SWI scan be set at 0.5 (readout) $\times 1$ (phase encoding) $\times 2$ (partition) mm^3 for a number of reasons. First, the veins and microbleeds that are of interest are on the order of 1–2 mm in size, and often much smaller such as the medullary veins, which are useful for monitoring oxygen saturation changes in stroke (these veins are only a few hundred microns in diameter). Second, the ability to visualize the vessels clearly is also limited by the in-plane resolution. Twenty years of experience with SWI suggests the above resolution is sufficient for most clinical applications at both 1.5T and 3T, with the former taking 6 to 8 minutes and the latter 3 to 4 minutes for full brain coverage. From a research perspective or special applications perspective this could be increased to $0.5 \times 0.5 \times 2$ mm^3 or $0.5 \times 0.5 \times 1.5$ mm^3 for sharper images, but this will take twice as long to acquire. Our own efforts in studying iron and the nigrosome-1 sign in Parkinson's disease have used a resolution of $0.67 \times 1 \times 1.34$ mm^3 with echo times of 7.5 ms, 15 ms and 22.5 ms and a TR of 29 ms in just under 5 minutes at 3T. These times assume a parallel imaging factor of 2, a partial Fourier factor of 7/8 in both phase, and partition encoding directions and elliptical sampling.

Recent advances using Wave-CAIPI (controlled aliasing in parallel imaging) SWI can cut these times down by another factor of 2 to 4, making high resolution whole-brain SWI viable in 3 minutes or less (Bilgic et al., 2015; Conklin et al., 2019).

22.8 Non-contrast SWI vs MICRO SWI

Microvascular or small vessel (e.g., less than 500 µm in internal diameter) abnormalities, in particular in the arterial system, contribute to fundamental physiological processes and pathological events in a number of neurovascular and neurodegenerative disorders. The ultra-small superparamagnetic iron oxide (USPIO) agent, Ferumoxytol, can be administered to induce an increase in susceptibility in both arteries and veins (Fig. 22.3). This makes it possible to visualize the cerebral microvasculature using high-resolution SWI. This method has been termed MICRO for "Microvascular In-vivo Contrast Revealed Origins" (Buch et al., 2020b; Liu et al., 2018). MICRO beautifully shows the small vessels throughout the brain for both arteries and veins. Using MICRO, it should be possible to see the entire

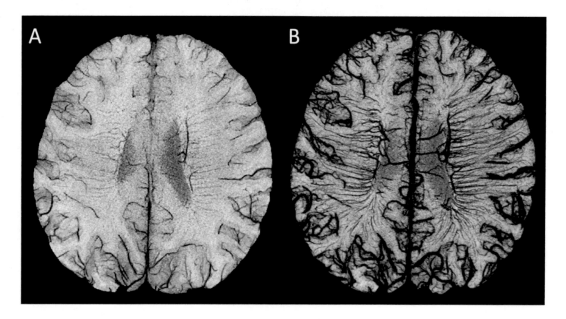

FIGURE 22.3

High-resolution SWI (A) before and (B) after Ferumoxytol administration (dose = 4 mg/kg) demonstrate the ability of USPIOs to reveal the cerebral microvasculature on a healthy volunteer. The pre-contrast SWI data were acquired using a conventional TE of 22.5 ms with TR = 36 ms, bandwidth = 100 Hz/pixel and FA = 20°, whereas the post-contrast SWI data were acquired using a TE of 15 ms with TR = 27 ms, bandwidth = 181 Hz/pixel and FA = 15°. Both the images were acquired with a resolution of $0.22 \times 0.44 \times 1$ mm^3 (interpolated to $0.22 \times 0.22 \times 1$ mm^3 data) and minimum intensity projected over 9 slices or 9 mm.

vascular tree and study neurovascular diseases, such as multiple sclerosis to examine white matter lesions for the presence of vascular abnormalities (Buch et al., 2020a), or to study vascular dementia by looking for microvascular disease.

22.9 Pitfalls of SWI

The phase, despite reflecting the actual magnetic field locally, is affected by tissue geometry and orientation relative to the main magnetic field and is basically non-local in nature. For example, the intravascular phase for veins perpendicular to the field has the opposite sign compared to those parallel to main magnetic field. Nevertheless, it turns out that the final phase of small veins sitting in a thick slice (e.g., medullary veins sitting in a 2 mm thick slice) integrates to the opposite of the expected phase, effectively possessing the same sign as those parallel to the main field. This is why the SWI phase mask works so well on these small veins perpendicular to the field as well (Xu and Haacke, 2006). Additionally, the HP filtered phase, which is used instead of the original phase to avoid phase wraps due to the background global field, may still possess remnant aliased voxels (as seen in Fig. 22.1 and Fig. 22.4D and 22.4E). This leads to the idea of using quantitative susceptibility mapping (QSM) to create a source image, which has no dependence on geometry. Instead of the phase images being used to create a mask to enhance contrast, the QSM results can be used to create what is referred to as true SWI (tSWI) or susceptibility map-weighted imaging (Gho et al., 2014; Liu et al., 2014). These images suffer less from frontal aliasing artifacts and enhance the contrast of the neuromelanin-iron complex of the substantia nigra, as seen in Fig. 22.4C and 22.4G. However, care should be taken using tSWI, since the aliasing artifacts near the sinuses were largely removed by the brain mask used in QSM reconstruction, which also eliminates the edge of the brain, and so may lose the ability to visualize microbleeds at the edge of the brain. Nevertheless, these variants of SWI have demonstrated their merit, and their use will depend on the purpose of the application.

22.10 Differentiating calcium from iron

SWI images can detect iron and calcium deposits within tissue using HP filtered phase data. However, the calcium that is found in the body in the form of calcium phosphates ($Ca_3(PO)_4$) is diamagnetic, whereas the iron deposits or blood products are paramagnetic; and both these types of susceptibility sources will create a hypointense region on the SWI data. This means that although SWI images are highly sensitive to the presence of iron or calcium products, they have low specificity in being able to distinguish one from the other, unless the phase information is used. To take advantage of the phase data, one can take a minimum intensity projection (minIP) of the HP filtered phase, in sagittal or coronal view, to study the phase dipole behavior and to distinguish the calcium (diamagnetic) and the iron (paramagnetic) deposits. In addition, although the suppression of the signal on the SWI magnitude images is highly sensitive to the presence of veins, hemorrhage or iron storage, it cannot be used directly to quantify the iron deposition. Both these limitations can be addressed using QSM.

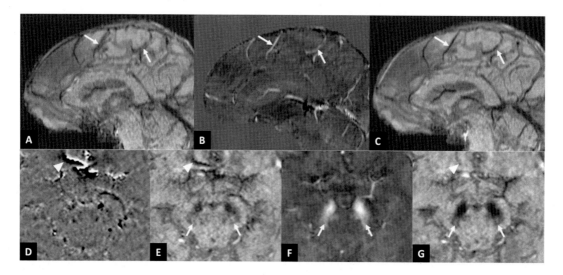

FIGURE 22.4

Comparison of the SWI magnitude and true SWI (tSWI) magnitude data. (A, E) SWI data, (B, F) susceptibility maps generated after applying the SHARP process on the unwrapped original phase and (C, G), the tSWI data. These images demonstrate the limitations of SWI in accurately delineating the presence of the pial veins (arrows in A–C), uniformly enhancing the high susceptibility structures, such as the substantia nigra (arrows in E–G) and the remnant aliased voxels that were present on the high-pass filtered phase (D) and introduced to the SWI data through the phase mask (arrowheads in D, E, G). These shortcomings can be addressed using tSWI shown in (G). The imaging parameters for these data were the following: B_0 = 3T, TE/TR = 22.5 ms/29 ms, flip angle = 27°, bandwidth = 220 Hz/pixel, resolution = 0.67×0.67×1.34 mm³.

22.11 High field SWI

All sequences at high field are subject to finite wavelength effects in the RF transmit field, which only worsen as the field strength increases. Although phase images remain uniform, the signal-to-noise ratio will vary spatially as the magnitude signal changes. These effects are fairly small at 1.5T, becoming evident at 3T and much worse at 7T. These RF field effects can be corrected with a multi-echo, gradient echo method referred to as STAGE (strategically acquired gradient echo) imaging, which helps in generating uniform images for the original data and for SWI, as shown in Fig. 22.5 (Chen et al., 2018b, p. 1; Haacke et al., 2020, p. 3; Wang et al., 2018, p. 2). STAGE can also correct for RF receive coil spatial variations.

22.12 New approaches to SWI

Although there are many new methods for rapid imaging, such as parallel imaging and compressed sensing, one particularly practical method is wave-CAIPI SWI or wave-SWI for short. This approach makes it possible to speed up data acquisition by a factor of 6 to 8 when combined with parallel imaging.

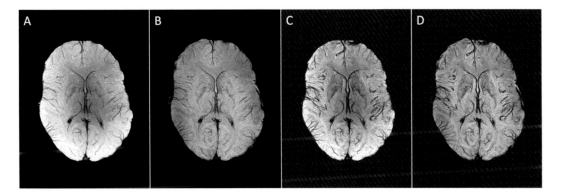

FIGURE 22.5

Representative 7T SWI images with and without radiofrequency (RF) corrections. These SWI images without (A and C) and with (B and D) RF corrections were from a double-echo SWI sequence acquired on a 7T scanner (Siemens, investigational device). Both the SWI images from the first echo (A) and the second echo (C) suffer severe RF inhomogeneities, in which the contrast of white matter and cortical gray matter at the peripheral of the brain were over-exposed at the typical window and level settings, making visualization of the venous system difficult. In contrast, the RF corrected SWI images of the first (B) and second echo (D) now present with uniform background and veins can be easily seen throughout the brain. The key imaging parameters of the double-echo SWI sequence were TR = 22 ms; TEs = 7.5 and 15 ms; flip angle = 12°; bandwidth = 170 Hz/pixel; resolution = $0.25 \times 0.25 \times 1.0$ mm^3; number of slices = 128; parallel imaging acceleration factor = 2; scan time = 14 min 15 sec. Images were minimum intensity projection over 10 slices (showing a 10 mm thick region). Data courtesy of Dr. Yulin Ge, Department of Radiology, NYU Langone Health, New York City.

The ability to image the entire brain with good resolution is key to the correct application and use of SWI. The results shown in Fig. 22.6 demonstrate that a total brain imaging time of 3 minutes is feasible at 3T and 5 minutes at 1.5T.

Another ignored area in the venue of SWI is dSWI (Jella et al., 2021). Although calcium will appear highlighted in this case, the magnitude signals from calcium are already dark. The main use of dSWI may be in the enhancement of dense white matter fiber tracts, such as the optic radiation. The enhanced contrast clearly shows the different layers of the optic radiations (Fig. 22.7).

22.13 Quantitative susceptibility mapping (QSM)

As mentioned earlier, SWI has proven to be useful in a multitude of clinical applications, but it does not allow for a direct quantification of the tissue susceptibility. On the other hand, a technique commonly referred to as quantitative susceptibility mapping (QSM), can be used to uncover local tissue magnetic properties by deconvolving the local field (via the image phase data). This local field is obtained from the same raw phase signal that is used in the generation of the SWI data. Hence, the process of QSM does not require any additional scan information, and the resultant susceptibility maps are naturally co-registered to the conventional SWI, as they are obtained from the same data.

352 Chapter 22 Principles of susceptibility-weighted MRI

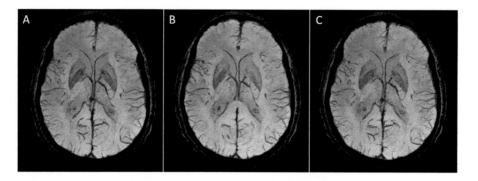

FIGURE 22.6

A comparison of Siemens wave-CAIPI SWI averaging first (TE = 13 ms) and second (TE = 28 ms) echo SWI data rather than using just the long echo time. (A) 2×2 acceleration, TA = 2 min 33 sec: resolution 0.5×1×2 mm^3; (B) 2×2 acceleration, TA = 3 min 2 sec: 0.5×1×1.5 mm^3; and (C) 3×2 acceleration, TA = 1 min 45 sec: 0.5×1×2 mm^3. TA = acquisition time. Images courtesy of Drs. Yu Liu and Youmin Zhang from Ruijin Hospital and Caixia Fu, Qing Li and Wei Liu from Siemens. The veins show slightly better with the 1.5 mm thick slice compared to the 2 mm thick slice, but overall the images are very similar in showing the veins and have good signal-to-noise ratio.

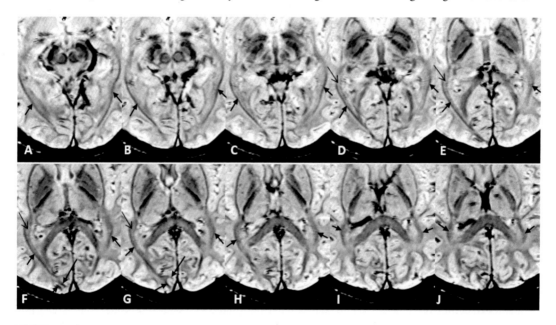

FIGURE 22.7

Ten consecutive slices (A to J) of dSWI images showing the extent of the optic radiations. Some slices show the three bundles particularly well (D to G, long thin arrows). The external sagittal striatum appears to be the darkest bundle in all these images (short thick sold arrows). Both F and G show penetration into the visual cortex (long thick solid arrows).

22.13 Quantitative susceptibility mapping (QSM)   353

In general, quantitative susceptibility maps are generated by performing the following steps: estimating the global magnitude field by unwrapping the raw phase signal, eliminating the unwanted global background field that originates from air-tissue and bone-tissue interfaces (such as near the sinuses), and then calculating the local susceptibility distributions from the field perturbations using the inverse process (Fig. 22.8A). These three steps can be optimized based on the application and tissue-of-interest. The resultant QSM data will provide a direct measure of tissue susceptibility, where paramagnetic structures, such as deoxyhemoglobin in veins and iron deposition in basal ganglia and midbrain structures, will appear hyperintense (Fig. 22.8B); and diamagnetic structures, such as myelin in white matter and calcium deposits, will appear hypointense.

As mentioned earlier, the phase behavior is non-local; i.e., the phase value in a given voxel is dependent not only on the magnetic susceptibility of the tissue present within that voxel, but also on the magnetic susceptibility distribution of surrounding tissues. Assuming the susceptibility-induced magnetization is induced from a magnetic dipole, then the field perturbation caused by a known susceptibility distribution can be obtained by convolving the susceptibility distribution with a unit dipole kernel. The resultant field perturbations can be obtained from a pointwise multiplication in the frequency domain (or k-space domain) using the following expression:

$$\Delta B_z(k) = B_0 \cdot D(k) \cdot \chi(k), \tag{22.10}$$

where, $D(k) = \left(\frac{1}{3} - \frac{k_z^2}{k^2}\right)$ is the Fourier transform of the dipole kernel: $d(r) = \frac{1}{4\pi} \cdot \frac{3\cos^2\theta - 1}{r^3}$; k_x, k_y and k_z are the x-, y- and z-components in k-space; $k^2 = k_x^2 + k_y^2 + k_z^2$; B_0 is the applied magnetic field; $\Delta B_z(k)$ is the z-component of the magnetic field perturbation in the frequency domain; and $\chi(k)$ is the Fourier transform of the magnetic susceptibility distribution. Hence, the susceptibility distribution in the image domain is calculated by inverting the dipole kernel ($D^{-1}(k)$) as

$$\chi(r) = FT^{-1}\left\{D^{-1}(k) \cdot \Delta B_z(k)\right\}. \tag{22.11}$$

Although this deconvolution of the field perturbations with the dipole kernel is meant to resolve the non-local property of the phase signal, this inversion process is ill-posed, because of zeros in the k-space dipole kernel along the conical surface at an angle of 54.7° with respect to the main magnetic field (i.e., when $3\cos^2\theta - 1 = 0$). Hence, the inverse kernel is unreliable along this cone, and a simple kernel division causes strong artifacts (also known as streaking artifacts) in the reconstructed susceptibility map.

Fortunately, a reasonably accurate susceptibility map can be obtained using regularization to minimize or replace the region where the dipole kernel is small, or by using iterative methods to estimate the data in the unreliable regions for structures with high susceptibility, such as veins, which help in reducing streaking artifacts as well as improving the accuracy of the structures-of-interest (Shmueli et al., 2009; Tang et al., 2013). Additionally, there are several fitting algorithms that calculate the susceptibility distribution as a solution to a minimization problem and estimate the missing k-space data through L1- and L2-norm (Haacke et al., 2015; Liu et al., 2015). This way, the regularized QSM data reduces the artifacts from the inversion kernel and becomes an essential metric in providing new insights into tissue composition and organization due to its more direct relationship to the actual physical tissue magnetic properties.

354 **Chapter 22** Principles of susceptibility-weighted MRI

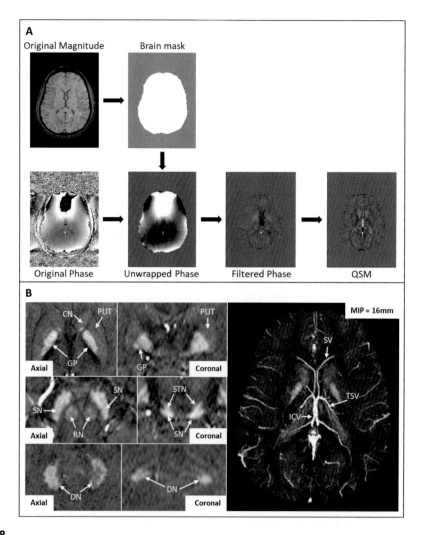

FIGURE 22.8

(A) QSM processing pipeline. Left-most column shows the original magnitude and phase images of the long TE (19.5 ms) data. The imaging parameters used for this acquisition were TE1/TE2/TR = 7.5/19.5/26 ms, FA = 24°, bandwidth = 241 Hz/pixel, resolution = 0.67×0.67×1.35 mm^3 at 3T. The magnitude image is used to obtain a brain mask, which is then applied to the unwrapped phase data to discard the unwanted voxels outside the brain tissues. The unwrapped phase is filtered (a sophisticated harmonic artifact reduction for phase data, or SHARP, algorithm was used for this figure) to reduce the background fields. The truncated k-space method for inverse filtering was applied to the filtered phase and an iterative algorithm with geometric constraint was used to obtain the QSM result for each echo (Tang et al., 2013). The QSM results from both TEs were combined to produce a higher quality QSM result. (B) QSM can highlight many structures with high susceptibilities, such as the structures of the basal ganglia (CN, PUT, and GP), midbrain (RN, SN, and STN), and cerebellum (DN) due to their high iron content; along with the veins due to the presence of deoxyhemoglobin. PUT = putamen; GP = globus pallidus; CN = caudate nucleus; RN = red nucleus; SN = substantia nigra; STN = sub-thalamic nucleus; DN = dentate nucleus; ICV = internal cerebral vein; TSV = thalamo-striate vein; SV = septal vein.

22.14 Conclusions

Although SWI has been in use for more than 20 years, it continues to find new clinical applications (Haller et al., 2021) and technical improvements (Eckstein et al., 2021). Surprisingly, new sequence developments, such as wave-CAIPI, open the door for not only faster imaging of SWI, but also the potential of acquiring SWI with higher resolution, reducing scan times from what might otherwise not be clinically viable durations to more reasonable durations. Advances in phase processing and image processing also continue to improve image quality, such as the true-SWI approach. Overall, it appears that SWI will continue to play a major role in clinical imaging, especially at high fields, where low flip angles make it a safe technology with low power deposition into the subject. Additionally, the phase information that is used for SWI processing can also be utilized to obtain local quantitative susceptibility via QSM methods. There appears to be a clinical role for QSM by measuring the changes in susceptibility caused by hemoglobin, ferritin, and calcifications, which can be essential in studying neurodegenerative and neurovascular pathologies.

References

Bellon, E.M., Haacke, E.M., Coleman, P.E., Sacco, D.C., Steiger, D.A., Gangarosa, R.E., 1986. MR artifacts: a review. Am. J. Roentgenol. 147, 1271–1281. https://doi.org/10.2214/ajr.147.6.1271.

Bilgic, B., Gagoski, B.A., Cauley, S.F., Fan, A.P., Polimeni, J.R., Grant, P.E., Wald, L.L., Setsompop, K., 2015. Wave-CAIPI for highly accelerated 3D imaging. Magn. Reson. Med. 73, 2152–2162. https://doi.org/10.1002/mrm.25347.

Brown, R.W., Cheng, Y.-C.N., Haacke, E.M., Thompson, M.R., Venkatesan, R., 2014. Magnetic Resonance Imaging: Physical Principles and Sequence Design, 2nd ed. Wiley, New York, NY.

Buch, S., Subramanian, K., Jella, P.K., Chen, Y., Wu, Z., Shah, K., Bernitsas, E., Ge, Y., Haacke, E.M., 2020a. Revealing vascular abnormalities and measuring small vessel density in multiple sclerosis lesions using USPIO. NeuroImage Clin. 29, 102525. https://doi.org/10.1016/j.nicl.2020.102525.

Buch, S., Wang, Y., Park, M.-G., Jella, P.K., Hu, J., Chen, Y., Shah, K., Ge, Y., Haacke, E.M., 2020b. Subvoxel vascular imaging of the midbrain using USPIO-enhanced MRI. NeuroImage 220, 117106. https://doi.org/10.1016/j.neuroimage.2020.117106.

Chen, Y., Liu, S., Buch, S., Hu, J., Kang, Y., Haacke, E.M., 2018a. An interleaved sequence for simultaneous magnetic resonance angiography (MRA), susceptibility weighted imaging (SWI) and quantitative susceptibility mapping (QSM). Magn. Reson. Imaging 47, 1–6. https://doi.org/10.1016/j.mri.2017.11.005.

Chen, Y., Liu, S., Wang, Y., Kang, Y., Haacke, E.M., 2018b. STrategically Acquired Gradient Echo (STAGE) imaging, part I: creating enhanced T1 contrast and standardized susceptibility weighted imaging and quantitative susceptibility mapping. Magn. Reson. Imaging 46, 130–139. https://doi.org/10.1016/j.mri.2017.10.005.

Conklin, J., Longo, M.G.F., Cauley, S.F., Setsompop, K., González, R.G., Schaefer, P.W., Kirsch, J.E., Rapalino, O., Huang, S.Y., 2019. Validation of highly accelerated wave-CAIPI SWI compared with conventional SWI and T2*-weighted gradient recalled-echo for routine clinical brain MRI at 3T. Am. J. Neuroradiol. 40, 2073–2080. https://doi.org/10.3174/ajnr.A6295.

Eckstein, K., Bachrata, B., Hangel, G., Widhalm, G., Enzinger, C., Barth, M., Trattnig, S., Robinson, S.D., 2021. Improved susceptibility weighted imaging at ultra-high field using bipolar multi-echo acquisition and optimized image processing: CLEAR-SWI. NeuroImage 118175. https://doi.org/10.1016/j.neuroimage.2021.118175.

Gho, S.-M., Liu, C., Li, W., Jang, U., Kim, E.Y., Hwang, D., Kim, D.-H., 2014. Susceptibility map-weighted imaging (SMWI) for neuroimaging. Magn. Reson. Med. 72, 337–346. https://doi.org/10.1002/mrm.24920.

Haacke, E., Mittal, S., Wu, Z., Neelavalli, J., Cheng, Y.-C.N., 2009. Susceptibility-weighted imaging: technical aspects and clinical applications, part 1. Am. J. Neuroradiol. 30, 19–30. https://doi.org/10.3174/ajnr.A1400.

Haacke, E.M., Chen, Y., Utriainen, D., Wu, B., Wang, Y., Xia, S., He, N., Zhang, C., Wang, X., Lagana, M.M., Luo, Y., Fatemi, A., Liu, S., Gharabaghi, S., Wu, D., Sethi, S.K., Huang, F., Sun, T., Qu, F., Yadav, B.K., Ma, X., Bai, Y., Wang, M., Cheng, J., Yan, F., 2020. STrategically Acquired Gradient Echo (STAGE) imaging, part III: technical advances and clinical applications of a rapid multi-contrast multi-parametric brain imaging method. Magn. Reson. Imaging 65, 15–26. https://doi.org/10.1016/j.mri.2019.09.006.

Haacke, E.M., Lai, S., Yablonskiy, D.A., Lin, W., 1995. In vivo validation of the bold mechanism: a review of signal changes in gradient echo functional MRI in the presence of flow. Int. J. Imaging Syst. Technol. 6, 153–163. https://doi.org/10.1002/ima.1850060204.

Haacke, E.M., Liu, S., Buch, S., Zheng, W., Wu, D., Ye, Y., 2015. Quantitative susceptibility mapping: current status and future directions. Magn. Reson. Imaging 33, 1–25. https://doi.org/10.1016/j.mri.2014.09.004.

Haacke, E.M., Xu, Y., Cheng, Y.-C.N., Reichenbach, J.R., 2004. Susceptibility weighted imaging (SWI). Magn. Reson. Med. 52, 612–618. https://doi.org/10.1002/mrm.20198.

Haller, S., Haacke, E.M., Thurnher, M.M., Barkhof, F., 2021. Susceptibility-weighted imaging: technical essentials and clinical neurologic applications. Radiology, 203071. https://doi.org/10.1148/radiol.2021203071.

Jella, P.K., Chen, Y., Tu, W., Makam, S., Beckius, S., Hamtaei, E., Hsu, C.C.-T., Haacke, E.M., 2021. Quantifying tissue properties of the optic radiations using strategically acquired gradient echo imaging and enhancing the contrast using diamagnetic susceptibility weighted imaging. Am. J. Neuroradiol. 42, 285–287. https://doi.org/10.3174/ajnr.A6897.

Koch, K.M., Papademetris, X., Rothman, D.L., de Graaf, R.A., 2006. Rapid calculations of susceptibility-induced magnetostatic field perturbations for in vivo magnetic resonance. Phys. Med. Biol. 51, 6381. https://doi.org/10.1088/0031-9155/51/24/007.

Liu, C., Wei, H., Gong, N.-J., Cronin, M., Dibb, R., Decker, K., 2015. Quantitative susceptibility mapping: contrast mechanisms and clinical applications. Tomogr. J. Imaging Res. 1, 3–17. https://doi.org/10.18383/j.tom.2015.00136.

Liu, S., Brisset, J.-C., Hu, J., Haacke, E.M., Ge, Y., 2018. Susceptibility weighted imaging and quantitative susceptibility mapping of the cerebral vasculature using ferumoxytol. J. Magn. Reson. Imaging 47, 621–633. https://doi.org/10.1002/jmri.25809.

Liu, S., Mok, K., Neelavalli, J., Cheng, Y.-C.N., Tang, J., Ye, Y., Haacke, E.M., 2014. Improved MR venography using quantitative susceptibility-weighted imaging. J. Magn. Reson. Imaging 40, 698–708. https://doi.org/10.1002/jmri.24413.

Mittal, S., Wu, Z., Neelavalli, J., Haacke, E.M., 2009. Susceptibility-weighted imaging: technical aspects and clinical applications, part 2. Am. J. Neuroradiol. 30, 232–252. https://doi.org/10.3174/ajnr.A1461.

Reichenbach, J.R., Venkatesan, R., Schillinger, D.J., Kido, D.K., Haacke, E.M., 1997. Small vessels in the human brain: MR venography with deoxyhemoglobin as an intrinsic contrast agent. Radiology 204, 272–277. https://doi.org/10.1148/radiology.204.1.9205259.

Sacco, D.C., Steiger, D.A., Bellon, E.M., Coleman, P.E., Haacke, E.M., 1987. Artifacts caused by cosmetics in MR imaging of the head. Am. J. Roentgenol. 148, 1001–1004. https://doi.org/10.2214/ajr.148.5.1001.

Salomir, R., de Senneville, B.D., Moonen, C.T., 2003. A fast calculation method for magnetic field inhomogeneity due to an arbitrary distribution of bulk susceptibility. Concepts Magn. Reson., Part B Magn. Reson. Eng. 19B, 26–34. https://doi.org/10.1002/cmr.b.10083.

Schweser, F., Deistung, A., Lehr, B.W., Reichenbach, J.R., 2011. Quantitative imaging of intrinsic magnetic tissue properties using MRI signal phase: an approach to in vivo brain iron metabolism? NeuroImage 54, 2789–2807. https://doi.org/10.1016/j.neuroimage.2010.10.070.

Shmueli, K., de Zwart, J.A., van Gelderen, P., Li, T.-Q., Dodd, S.J., Duyn, J.H., 2009. Magnetic susceptibility mapping of brain tissue in vivo using MRI phase data. Magn. Reson. Med. 62, 1510–1522. https://doi.org/10.1002/mrm.22135.

Tang, J., Liu, S., Neelavalli, J., Cheng, Y.C.N., Buch, S., Haacke, E.M., 2013. Improving susceptibility mapping using a threshold-based K-space/image domain iterative reconstruction approach. Magn. Reson. Med. 69, 1396–1407. https://doi.org/10.1002/mrm.24384.

Wang, Yu, Chen, Y., Wu, D., Wang, Ying, Sethi, S.K., Yang, G., Xie, H., Xia, S., Haacke, E.M., 2018. STrategically Acquired Gradient Echo (STAGE) imaging, part II: correcting for RF inhomogeneities in estimating T1 and proton density. Magn. Reson. Imaging 46, 140–150. https://doi.org/10.1016/j.mri.2017.10.006.

Wu, D., Liu, S., Buch, S., Ye, Y., Dai, Y., Haacke, E.M., 2016. A fully flow-compensated multiecho susceptibility-weighted imaging sequence: the effects of acceleration and background field on flow compensation. Magn. Reson. Med. 76, 478–489. https://doi.org/10.1002/mrm.25878.

Xu, Y., Haacke, E.M., 2006. The role of voxel aspect ratio in determining apparent vascular phase behavior in susceptibility weighted imaging. Magn. Reson. Imaging 24, 155–160. https://doi.org/10.1016/j.mri.2005.10.030.

Ye, Y., Hu, J., Wu, D., Haacke, E.M., 2013. Noncontrast-enhanced magnetic resonance angiography and venography imaging with enhanced angiography. J. Magn. Reson. Imaging 38, 1539–1548. https://doi.org/10.1002/jmri.24128.

CHAPTER

Applications of susceptibility-weighted imaging and mapping

23

Stefan Ropele
Department of Neurology, Medical University of Graz, Graz, Austria

23.1 Introduction

This chapter focuses on applications of susceptibility-weighted imaging (SWI) and quantitative susceptibility mapping (QSM). The chapter is not intended to be exhaustive, even for neuroimaging applications of these approaches (they have been used widely in other aspects of body imaging). Rather, the sections below focus on the main diseases that have benefited from these two new approaches. Whereas there has been good clinical implementation of SWI on modern scanners, it is worth noting that QSM remains less well disseminated as a clinical tool, and still remains more exclusively in the research domain.

23.2 Applications of susceptibility-weighted imaging

When SWI was first introduced in 1997, it was primarily proposed for use in high-resolution venography (Reichenbach et al., 1997). The success of SWI in the following decades is mostly due to its sensitivity to the oxygenation state of blood and its degradation products. The fact that SWI is based on a conventional spoiled gradient-echo sequence, which is readily available on modern clinical scanners, further contributed to the fast and widespread application of SWI in the brain and other organs. Though many radiological features seen on SWI images are also detectable on conventional T_2^*-weighted gradient echoes, SWI provides much better susceptibility contrast, and therefore has been fully established in clinical MRI.

23.2.1 Microbleeds (MBs)

Because of their high prevalence, MBs are probably the most frequent findings in SWI. The prevalence of MBs in normal subjects over 80 years of age is approximately 40% and is associated with small vessel disease and stroke. MBs present as small round hypointensities with a diameter of typically less than 5 mm and reflect clusters of hemosiderin-containing macrophages (often perivascular). MBs also contain other products of blood degradation, but the paramagnetic behavior is induced by the hemosiderin. Hemosiderin contains conglomerates of denatured lipids, protein, and ferritin, but it has no fixed composition. Since it also has no fixed size or size-limiting shell, such as for ferritin, it can become even larger than a ferritin molecule with a much stronger paramagnetic effect. Due to the blooming effect (dipole effect), MBs can appear larger than they are in reality. Compared to T_2^*-weighted images, SWI provides a much higher sensitivity for detecting MBs (Fig. 23.1). Several studies reported that when moving towards higher field strength and thinner slices, the sensitivity for detecting MBs increases by a factor of 3 when compared to SWI images at 1.5 tesla.

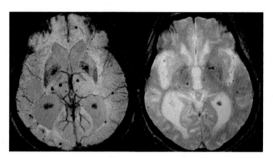

FIGURE 23.1

Corresponding SWI (left) and T_2^*-weighted (right) images from a patient with small vessel disease (75 years, male). SWI shows a higher sensitivity for MBs, which is due to the stronger susceptibility contrast and the minimum intensity projection.

23.2.2 Cerebral amyloid angiopathy (CAA)

CAA is a form of vasculopathy that is strongly associated with MBs and that accounts for approximately 10–20% of spontaneous intracerebral hemorrhages with higher proportions in the elderly population. CAA is caused by the accumulation of β-amyloid within the wall of small cortical arteries, leading to fibrinoid necrosis and vessel fragility. This is also the reasons why MBs are mostly restricted to lobar regions, i.e., cortex and subcortical white matter regions, as shown in Fig. 23.2.

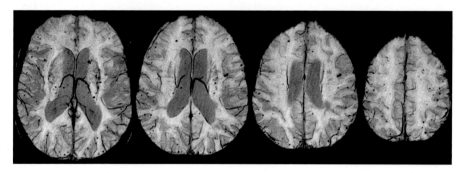

FIGURE 23.2

SWI of a patient with CAA, with typical cortical and subcortical MBs.

23.2.3 Cavernomas

Cavernomas, also known as cavernous venous malformations, are typically much larger than MBs and represent clusters of thin-walled capillaries with surrounding hemosiderin, because these capillaries can be leaky. The majority of cavernomas remain asymptomatic throughout life, and therefore they are detected incidentally, although they comprise 10%–20% of all cerebrovascular malformations (Lehnhardt et al., 2005). In particular, in familial cases, there is a higher risk of hemorrhage. The MRI findings of these lesions are variable, which is also due to the reoccurrence of hemorrhages. Cavernomas may represent mixtures of deoxyhemoglobin from acute hemorrhages and hemosiderin from older ones. Both of these cause a strong paramagnetic shift, which makes SWI the most sensitive technique to depict these lesions (Fig. 23.3).

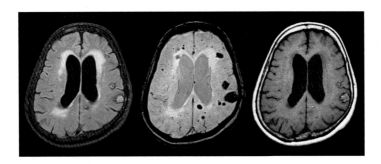

FIGURE 23.3

Patient with multiple cavernomas. Some of them show acute hemorrhages as evident from the post-contrast T_1w image (right). All cavernomas can be clearly detected on SWI (middle), whereas most of them remain undetected on FLAIR (left).

23.2.4 Traumatic brain injury (TBI)

Diffuse axonal injury (DAI) as a consequence of shearing forces is a frequent finding in traumatic brain injury. The most vulnerable regions are the gray–white matter junction, but also the splenium of the corpus callosum and the dorsolateral brain stem (Blitstein and Tung, 2007). SWI is the modality of choice to depict microbleeds that are associated with DAI. FLAIR and T_1w images remain largely unaffected by DAI (Fig. 23.4). The extent of parenchymal hemorrhages seen on SWI correlates with a poor prognosis. Brain stem involvement is a further predictor for poor long-term outcome.

23.2.5 Cerebral venous sinus thrombosis

Acute venous sinus thrombosis is usually identified by a prominent hypointense signal on SWI images (Fig. 23.5). This is due to venous stasis, which leads to an increased concentration of deoxyhemoglobin and often results in blooming artifacts. SWI is also helpful to show any associated hemorrhage, which occurs in approximately 70% of venous infarctions.

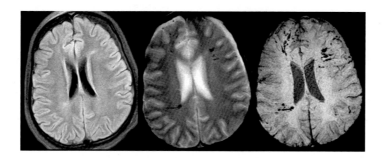

FIGURE 23.4

FLAIR, T_2^*-weighted, and SWI sequence (from left to right) of a 42 year old female, who had a car accident. Diffuse axonal injury is reflected by microhemorrhages, which are best seen on SWI (right).

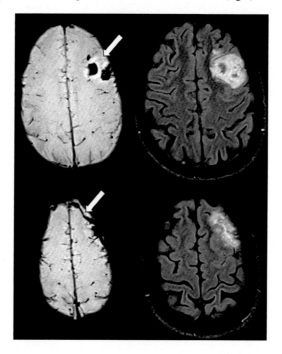

FIGURE 23.5

Patient with venous sinus thrombosis. The stasis in the cortical vein (arrow in lower row) has led to an increased intravascular pressure, which resulted in a hemorrhage. The hemorrhage and infarcted tissue can also be seen on FLAIR (right), but the stasis is seen on the SWI only (left).

23.2.6 Acute stroke

The prominent hypointense vessel sign (PHVS) is a characteristic finding in acute ischemic stroke and can be observed in draining veins in the affected hemisphere. The hypointensity in SWI can be explained by an increased oxygen extraction fraction following a sudden deficit in oxygen, which can occur as early as two hours after the onset of the stroke. Consequently, the increasing concentration of deoxyhemoglobin causes a paramagnetic shift in the affected veins. The PHVS can also be considered as an indicator for diffusion-perfusion mismatch, which represents penumbral brain tissue, because the oxygen extraction fraction is significantly increased in the penumbra. Since the PHVS often persists beyond the perfusion window period, its predictive ability with respect to clinical outcome remains unclear. More recent studies suggest that the PHVS beyond the reperfusion window period is a risk factor for poor clinical outcome (Wang et al., 2018). SWI may also help to identify hemorrhages within the infarct region, and therefore allow differentiation of a hemorrhagic stroke from an ischemic stroke. This differentiation can be achieved with an even higher sensitivity than with CT (Wycliffe et al., 2004).

23.2.7 Tumors

SWI provides high sensitivity to tumors, including glioma, the most common type of primary malignant brain tumor, and in this regard is considered equivalent or even better than post-contrast T_1w imaging. SWI can highlight several features of tumors, including neovascularization (venous blood), calcifications in the tumor, improved contrast at the tumor boundary, and tumor hemorrhage and microhemorrhage. A recent study has analyzed these features on SWI and related them to molecular tumor markers, including IDH1, MGMT, and 1p19q (Kong et al., 2019). It was found that the intra-tumoral signal intensity on SWI had a high predictive ability for glioma grade, IDH1 mutation, and MGMT methylation. This is also related to the observation that higher tumor grades show greater presence of small blood vessels and hemorrhage in the tumor. When performing SWI twice, before and after administration of contrast agent, blood vessels can be better identified, because they change their signal intensity, which is not the case for vessel-mimicking hemorrhages.

23.2.8 Central veins

Central veins in multiple sclerosis lesions have been known from histological studies for almost 100 years. It is believed that the perivascular space surrounding these veins is a privileged site for immune cells, which can then trigger the inflammatory cascade and lead to the formation of MS lesions around the veins. Most of these lesions are found in the periventricular space, which is not unexpected when considering that the density of small veins is highest there. The central vein is considered a biomarker of inflammatory demyelination, and therefore might be relevant for differentiation of MS lesions from other white matter lesions (Sinnecker et al., 2019). The central vein sign is usually assessed by "FLAIR*", which is actually a phase-filtered FLAIR image (Sati et al., 2012). The image composition is identical to SWI, but the magnitude image of the gradient echo is replaced by the FLAIR image, which provides a better contrast for white matter lesions (Fig. 23.6).

23.2.9 Iron rims

Another MS-specific signature that can be found with SWI scans are so-called iron rims, which appear as a black rim around MS lesions (Fig. 23.7). Only a small fraction of MS lesions show this feature. It was histopathologically validated that slowly expanding lesions have a rim of macrophages with myelin degradation products and iron from dying oligodendrocytes. Slowly expanding lesions represent a pathological concept, where the center of the lesion is inactive and demyelinated, and where the edge

364 **Chapter 23** Applications of susceptibility-weighted imaging and mapping

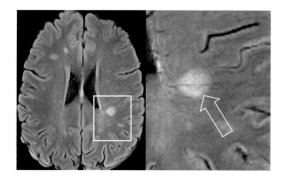

FIGURE 23.6

Periventricular MS lesion on conventional FLAIR (left) and corresponding FLAIR* with the central vein sign (inset right). Most of these lesions are found in the periventricular space, which is not unexpected when considering that the density of small veins is highest there.

is subject to continuous demyelination. This type of lesion is mostly found in progressive forms of MS and was proposed as a marker of disease activity. Iron rims have been mostly reported at 7 tesla, but they can also be seen on 3T SWI images, provided the spatial resolution is high enough.

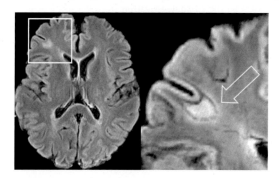

FIGURE 23.7

Iron rim surrounding a slowly expanding MS lesion on FLAIR (left) and FLAIR* (inset right) at 3T. Note that the in-plane resolution of the FLAIR image was 1×1 mm, whereas the resolution of the gradient-echo-derived phase image was 0.6×0.6 mm.

23.3 Applications of quantitative susceptibility mapping (QSM)

Current clinical SWI applications are based on phase filtering to better highlight paramagnetic or diamagnetic structures on an underlying magnitude image. In contrast, QSM displays the entire spectrum of magnetic susceptibilities in a quantitative manner. As such, QSM allows characterization and assessment of blood, calcium, bone, abnormal tissue, or even normal appearing tissue. This can make

23.3 Applications of quantitative susceptibility mapping (QSM)   365

QSM also very helpful where blood deposits and calcifications can be present in similar conditions (Deistung et al., 2013a). Most applications of QSM are based on paramagnetic shifts that are induced by ferritin or by differently oxygenated iron in blood and its degradation products. Paramagnetic shifts are counteracted by diamagnetic macromolecules and cell structures, which can provide a new contrast at very high resolution and also can match the contrast details of histological images (Deistung et al., 2013b). Many approaches have been proposed for the mathematical dipole inversion of phase images (see Chapter 22), but so far none of them has been implemented by manufacturers on the scanner console. This hinders an integration of QSM into the clinical workflow, because QSM reconstruction has to be done offline. So far, the most impressive QSM results have come from 7T, because the QSM effect benefits from two factors when moving to a higher field strength. Firstly, the susceptibility-induced frequency shift scales with field strength, and secondly the SNR or image resolution benefits.

23.3.1 Iron mapping

Iron mapping was one of the first applications of QSM. Iron is the most abundant trace element in the brain and is mostly stored in the form of ferritin, a storage protein that can bind up to 4500 Fe^{3+} ions as a nanocrystal underneath its globular shell. Ferric iron, with a spin of 3/2, has an effective magnetic moment of 3.87 Bohr magnetons. Though this is less than the magnetic moment for iron in deoxyhemoglobin or in iron-sulfur proteins, the ferritin concentration in the brain and in hepatic liver cirrhosis can reach considerable levels. It was demonstrated by a post-mortem correlation study that iron levels in gray matter structures can be reliably assessed by QSM over the entire physiological range, up to 250 mg iron per kg tissue wet weight (Langkammer et al., 2012). The latter corresponds to a susceptibility of approximately 0.2 ppm, which yields a net susceptibility of 0.9 ppb per mg iron in tissue. Ferritin is not equally distributed across the brain, with highest concentration found in the basal ganglia. Iron mapping in white matter is less reliable, because of its rather low concentration and the counteracting effect of diamagnetic myelin. Since the myelin can act as a diamagnetic hollow cylinder, orientational effects with respect to the main B_0 static field play an additional role. Iron accumulation has been observed in the liver and in brain deep-gray matter in many inflammatory and neurodegenerative diseases, and often scales with disease duration and severity. But it should be mentioned that disease-induced changes are usually much smaller than iron accumulation due to normal ageing (Li et al., 2014).

23.3.2 Multiple sclerosis (MS)

Iron accumulation in the basal ganglia as assessed by QSM can be observed at a very early stage of MS, and scales with disability and cortical atrophy (Langkammer et al., 2013). The latter suggests that iron accumulation in the basal ganglia is an epiphenomenon of tissue destruction and concomitant iron release, rather than a trigger of the inflammatory cascade. This may be different in white matter, where histological studies have reported iron deposits in and around MS lesions, in vessel walls, and also around veins. Explanations for these findings include disruption of the blood—brain barrier, reduced axonal clearing, attraction of iron-rich macrophages and microglia, and also chronic inflammatory damage to vein walls. Since changes in iron homeostasis are more directly related to the pathophysiology of MS, QSM in white matter has received increased attention (Fig. 23.8). When following up the susceptibility of acute enhancing lesions, it was observed that their susceptibility does not differ from surrounding normal appearing tissue. In the later and non-enhancing stage, the susceptibility becomes more paramagnetic and remains so for a couple of years (Chen et al., 2014). The increase in susceptibility is assigned to demyelination and iron deposition, because demyelination alone cannot explain the full extent of the paramagnetic shift. QSM therefore might help to identify acute enhancing lesions, without the administration of contrast media, and to estimate the age of lesions.

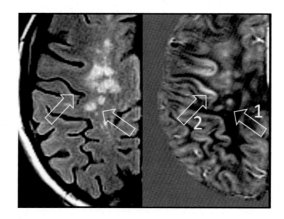

FIGURE 23.8

QSM (right) provides insights into MS-specific tissue changes not seen on conventional MRI, including T_2w FLAIR images (left). The increase of the perilesional susceptibility can be caused by demyelination and iron release (Arrow 1). Even the adjacent cortex seems to be affected by the pathology, despite looking normal on the corresponding FLAIR image (Arrow 2).

23.3.3 Neurodegenerative diseases

Amyotrophic lateral sclerosis (ALS) is a progressive neurodegenerative disease that affects the upper and lower motor neurons and that invariably results in death. The diagnosis of ALS is often difficult, because there is no specific biomarker. QSM could become a potential biomarker, because it allows for the assessment of a specific feature of the disease, which is iron accumulation in the deeper layers of the motor cortex. It was demonstrated that the amount of iron in the subregions corresponding to Penfield's areas of the hand and foot was scaled with impairment (Costagli et al., 2016). However, it remains unclear if the excess of iron is a consequence or a cause of the disease, and how much cortical microgliosis and demyelination contribute to the observed increase in susceptibility.

In Parkinson's disease, QSM allows a better visualization of the sub-thalamic nucleus (Alkemade et al., 2017). The visualization of this structure is relevant for correct targeting of deep brain stimulation (DBS), since DBS provides an effective treatment for patients in an advanced stage of the disease. In particular, the medial border of the substantia nigra is difficult to assess on conventional MRI. Based on the iron content in nigral and extranigral regions, QSM may also help to differentiate Parkinson's disease from atypical Parkinsonisms (Mazzucchi et al., 2019).

There is strong evidence from histological studies of Alzheimer's disease (AD) brains that iron is frequently co-localized with amyloid plaques, which are considered as one of the pathological hallmarks of AD. Imaging of cortical iron with QSM could therefore provide a means of assessing Aβ

load. Though amyloid plaques are far below the resolution of conventional MRI, the global assessment of iron in the cortex was demonstrated to highly correlate with $A\beta$-plaque load, as measured by 11-Carbon Pittsburgh-Compound-B PET (Van Bergen et al., 2016). Current studies on this topic are mostly performed at 7T to fully benefit from the increased susceptibility effect and resolution.

23.3.4 Mapping of oxygen saturation and extraction

The magnetism of hemoglobin offers the opportunity to assess oxygenation state in the veins with QSM. Hemoglobin consists of four heme-groups, each with a single iron atom in the center. The loading with oxygen therefore determines the bulk susceptibility of hemoglobin, which makes deoxyhemoglobin fully paramagnetic. When the iron atom is bound to oxygen, no unpaired electrons exist, and therefore oxyhemoglobin becomes diamagnetic. The dependency of the susceptibility on the degree of oxygen saturation can be utilized to study the physiology of oxygen extraction of the brain at rest and during functional activity. If the hematocrit is known, the oxygenation state can be estimated from the susceptibility difference between vessels and surrounding tissue, which is typically around 0.5 ppm. It has been proposed to use CSF as a reference, because the perivascular susceptibility varies across gray and white matter (Fan et al., 2014).

The oxygen extraction fraction (OEF) is an important metabolic parameter that informs on restricted oxygen consumption or perfusion deficits, which play a major role in cerebrovascular diseases. To estimate the OEF, the susceptibility of fully oxygenated blood and the partial volume effect for small veins have to be considered. If arterial blood is fully oxygenated and remains stable, the OEF can be estimated directly from the venous oxygen saturation (Fan et al., 2014). Mapping of the OEF is only possible for a larger volume of interest, but multiple volumes covering the entire brain can reveal OEF maps that are comparable to results from ^{15}O positron emission tomography (Kudo et al., 2016). It was recently demonstrated that OEF mapping also provides sensitive insights into the perfusion status in acute ischemic stroke. In regions with large perfusion-diffusion mismatch, the OEF is increased as a compensation for low cerebral blood flow (Fan et al., 2020).

23.3.5 Perfusion imaging

Standard dynamic susceptibility contrast perfusion MRI (see Chapter 13) is based on a first-pass analysis of a contrast agent bolus, usually a gadolinium (Gd) chelate. By assuming a linear relationship between Gd concentration and T_2^* shortening, the Gd concentration is usually derived from a T_2^*-weighted gradient-echo sequence with echo-planar readout. However, in particular for the arterial input function, this linear relationship does not hold true, which can introduce significant quantification errors in the perfusion maps. Other effects that additionally contribute to quantification errors are T_1 shortening effects and T_2^* saturation effects at very high Gd concentrations. QSM allows this problem to be solved, because the magnetic susceptibility in feeding arteries is directly proportional to the concentration of the paramagnetic contrast agent. QSM also does not need any assumption about the underlying vessel geometry. However, accelerated acquisition techniques with non-Cartesian readout are needed to sample the first pass with sufficient temporal resolution (Xu et al., 2015). The cerebral blood volume can also be estimated from the susceptibility change following steady-state distribution of the contrast agent, thus with fewer time constraints (Lind et al., 2017).

References

Alkemade, A., et al., 2017. Comparison of T2*-weighted and QSM contrasts in Parkinson's disease to visualize the STN with MRI. PLoS ONE 12 (4), 1–13. https://doi.org/10.1371/journal.pone.0176130.

Van Bergen, J.M.G., et al., 2016. Colocalization of cerebral iron with Amyloid beta in Mild Cognitive Impairment. Scientific Reports 6 (September), 1–9. https://doi.org/10.1038/srep35514.

Blitstein, M.K., Tung, G.A., 2007. MRI of cerebral microhemorrhages. American Journal of Roentgenology 189 (3), 720–725. https://doi.org/10.2214/AJR.07.2249.

Chen, W., et al., 2014. Quantitative susceptibility mapping of Multiple Sclerosis lesions at various ages. Radiology 271 (1), 183–192.

Costagli, M., et al., 2016. Magnetic susceptibility in the deep layers of the primary motor cortex in Amyotrophic Lateral Sclerosis. NeuroImage: Clinical 12, 965–969. https://doi.org/10.1016/j.nicl.2016.04.011.

Deistung, A., et al., 2013a. Quantitative susceptibility mapping differentiates between blood depositions and calcifications in patients with glioblastoma. PLoS ONE 8 (3), e57924. https://doi.org/10.1371/journal.pone.0057924.

Deistung, A., et al., 2013b. Toward in vivo histology: a comparison of quantitative susceptibility mapping (QSM) with magnitude-, phase-, and R2*-imaging at ultra-high magnetic field strength. NeuroImage 65, 299–314. https://doi.org/10.1016/j.neuroimage.2012.09.055.

Fan, A., et al., 2020. Elevated brain oxygen extraction fraction measured by MRI susceptibility relates to perfusion status in acute ischemic stroke. Journal of Cerebral Blood Flow and Metabolism 40 (3). https://doi.org/10.1177/0271678X19827944.

Fan, A.P., et al., 2014. Quantitative oxygenation venography from MRI phase. Magnetic Resonance in Medicine 72 (1), 149–159. https://doi.org/10.1002/mrm.24918.

Kong, L.W., et al., 2019. Intratumoral susceptibility signals reflect biomarker status in gliomas. Scientific Reports 9 (1), 1–9. https://doi.org/10.1038/s41598-019-53629-w.

Kudo, K., et al., 2016. Oxygen extraction fraction measurement using quantitative susceptibility mapping: comparison with positron emission tomography. Journal of Cerebral Blood Flow and Metabolism 36 (8), 1424–1433. https://doi.org/10.1177/0271678X15606713.

Langkammer, C., et al., 2012. Quantitative susceptibility mapping (QSM) as a means to measure brain iron? A post mortem validation study. NeuroImage 62 (3), 1593–1599. https://doi.org/10.1016/j.neuroimage.2012.05.049.

Langkammer, C., et al., 2013. Quantitative susceptibility mapping in multiple sclerosis. Radiology 267 (2), 551–559. https://doi.org/10.1148/radiol.12120707.

Lehnhardt, F.G., et al., 2005. Value of gradient-echo magnetic resonance-imaging in the diagnosis of familial cerebral cavernous malformation. Archives of Neurology 62 (4), 653–658. https://doi.org/10.1001/archneur.62.4.653.

Li, W., et al., 2014. Differential developmental trajectories of magnetic susceptibility in human brain gray and white matter over the lifespan. Human Brain Mapping 35 (6), 2698–2713. https://doi.org/10.1002/hbm.22360.

Lind, E., et al., 2017. Assessment of MRI contrast agent concentration by quantitative susceptibility mapping (QSM): application to estimation of cerebral blood volume during steady state. Magnetic Resonance Materials in Physics, Biology and Medicine 30 (6), 555–566. https://doi.org/10.1007/s10334-017-0637-9.

Mazzucchi, S., et al., 2019. Quantitative susceptibility mapping in atypical Parkinsonisms. NeuroImage: Clinical 24 (May), 101999. https://doi.org/10.1016/j.nicl.2019.101999.

Reichenbach, J.R., et al., 1997. Small vessels in the human brain: MR venography with deoxyhemoglobin as an intrinsic contrast agent. Radiology 204 (1), 272–277. https://doi.org/10.1148/RADIOLOGY.204.1.9205259.

Sati, P., et al., 2012. FLAIR*: a combined MR contrast technique for visualizing white matter lesions and parenchymal veins. Radiology 265 (3), 926–932. https://doi.org/10.1148/radiol.12120208.

Sinnecker, T., et al., 2019. Evaluation of the central vein sign as a diagnostic imaging biomarker in multiple sclerosis. JAMA Neurology 76 (12), 1446–1456. https://doi.org/10.1001/jamaneurol.2019.2478.

Wang, Y., et al., 2018. Prominent hypointense vessel sign on susceptibility-weighted imaging is associated with clinical outcome in acute ischaemic stroke. European Neurology 79 (5–6), 231–239. https://doi.org/10.1159/000488587.

Wycliffe, N.D., et al., 2004. Reliability in detection of hemorrhage in acute stroke by a new three-dimensional gradient recalled echo susceptibility-weighted imaging technique compared to computed tomography: a retrospective study. Journal of Magnetic Resonance Imaging 20 (3), 372–377. https://doi.org/10.1002/jmri.20130.

Xu, B., et al., 2015. Quantification of cerebral perfusion using dynamic quantitative susceptibility mapping. Magnetic Resonance in Medicine 73 (4), 1540–1548. https://doi.org/10.1002/mrm.25257.

PART 8

Magnetization transfer approaches

CHAPTER

Magnetization transfer contrast MRI

24

Seth A. Smith[a,b,c,d] **and Kristin P. O'Grady**[a,b]

[a]*Vanderbilt University Institute of Imaging Science, Vanderbilt University Medical Center, Nashville, TN, United States*
[b]*Department of Radiology and Radiological Sciences, Vanderbilt University Medical Center, Nashville, TN, United States*
[c]*Department of Biomedical Engineering, Vanderbilt University, Nashville, TN, United States*
[d]*Department of Ophthalmology, Vanderbilt University Medical Center, Nashville, TN, United States*

24.1 Summary

Many experiments in MRI rely on directly imaging protons associated with water. In fact, nearly all clinical MRI scans utilize signals that come from water protons, its interaction with its environment, its relaxation properties, diffusion along barriers, or flow. The rationale is that water 1) is abundant, 2) has relaxation times that are sufficiently long and accessible to conventional imaging methods, 3) is related to tissue environment and composition, and 4) is sensitive to many types of pathology. However, in tissue, there is another set of protons that is less accessible to conventional imaging: protons associated with solid-like macromolecules. The challenge to imaging these protons exclusively is that due to their relatively immobile composition they have relaxation times that are far too short to be readily imaged. However, the protons in macromolecules can (and do) interact with the surrounding water in such a fashion that selective saturation of these macromolecular protons can influence the signal of the surrounding water through the so-called magnetization transfer (MT) effect. This phenomenon can be exploited to derive contrast reflective of tissue macromolecular composition, and thus provide an indirect method for interrogating the properties of abundant macromolecules, such as myelin, in the central nervous system.

24.2 The magnetization transfer (MT) phenomenon and observations

In general terms, MT in MRI is the exchange of spin information between two (or more) populations of protons in distinct molecular environments. That is, protons within one milieu can exchange information with protons in another by 1) direct chemical exchange, and 2) dipole-dipole interactions (Edzes and Samulski, 1977). It should be cautioned that MT is often an umbrella term that captures any exchange of spin information whether by chemical exchange, dipole-dipole interactions, or cross-relaxation, which sometimes can confuse the discussion of the MT contrast (MTC) imaging that is performed on the MR scanner. In this chapter, we will focus solely on MTC, rather than chemical exchange saturation transfer (CEST), where the former is dominated by dipole-dipole interactions, and

Advances in Magnetic Resonance Technology and Applications, Volume 4, ISSN 2666-9099. https://doi.org/10.1016/B978-0-12-822479-3.00039-7
Copyright © 2021 Elsevier Inc. All rights reserved.

the latter by direct chemical exchange (Desmond and Stanisz, 2012). We will discuss the MT effect that generates MTC in two ways: phenomenologically and biophysically.

Wolff and Balaban demonstrated that by applying an off-resonance (with respect to water) radiofrequency (RF) irradiation in a rabbit kidney, the observed water signal was attenuated (Wolff and Balaban, 1989). They found that by providing an RF pre-saturation off-resonance with respect to water to a set of rotationally immobilized spins that are in communication with the surrounding water, the rotationally immobilized protons transfer the saturation to the water, which results in a signal attenuation. Water signal attenuation will occur if 1) the semi-solid spins are of sufficient concentration, 2) have exchange rates that are fast on the NMR time-scale, and 3) have a broad enough saturation spectrum to be able to be selectively saturated. The magnitude of the saturation after applying a saturation can be described by the MT ratio (MTR), which is discussed in Section 24.3.1.

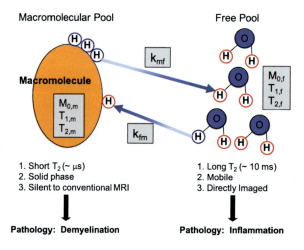

FIGURE 24.1

Cartoon demonstrating the two pools (Macromolecular (m) and Free (f)) existing in tissue. Each pool has its own relaxation times ($T_{1,fm}$, $T_{2,fm}$) and proton densities ($M_{0,fm}$) but, importantly, the protons in each pool are in exchange with one another with rate constants given by k_{mf}, k_{fm}. The macromolecular pool is not able to be imaged directly, because its protons have relaxation times too short for conventional MRI, whereas the free pool is that which is typically imaged and thought to represent free water. Through exchange, the macromolecular pool can influence the free water pool and provide an indirect way to measure effects in the central nervous system, such as demyelination.

To describe the MT effect and prepare for a discussion of quantitative magnetization transfer (qMT), we can employ a standard biophysical model. Let us consider two proton pools (extension to more protons pools is possible): a free water pool, and a macromolecular proton (also called rotationally immobilized, semisolid, or bound) pool (Fig. 24.1) (Henkelman et al., 2001). The free water pool has a long T_2 (~ms) and can be directly imaged and contrasts derived from the water pool include T_1-weighted, T_2-weighted, FLAIR, MPRAGE, diffusion, and others. The unprecedented sensitivity of water images allows for detecting and quantifying pathology of the central nervous system, most notably those pathologies that result in inflammation. The semi-solid proton pool has a long rotational correlation time, short T_2 (~μs) and cannot be directly imaged due to the micro-second dephasing of

24.2 The magnetization transfer (MT) phenomenon and observations 375

the transverse signal. A benefit of the short T_2 of the semi-solid proton pool is its broad absorption lineshape that spans hundreds of ppm, allowing it to be selectively saturated over a wide range of offset frequencies. The free pool, however, due to its long T_2, has a narrow lineshape and is only directly saturated when the saturation is either on-resonance or close to on-resonance ($\sim$10% direct water saturation at 1.5 kHz off-resonance at 3T, with a 10.5 μT pulse (Smith et al., 2006). Because of the different frequency ranges of responses of the saturation lineshape, the semi-solid pool can be selectively saturated by off-resonance RF irradiation over a large frequency range, while leaving the free pool virtually unsaturated. This fact was why MTC was originally used in the clinic. To improve the sensitivity to blood signals, MTC was used to selectively saturate the surrounding tissue, leaving the blood water signal relatively unaffected and improving sensitivity for MR time-of-flight angiography.

We know that applying a saturation off-resonance with respect to water will selectively saturate the semi-solid proton pool, and since the semi-solid proton pool is in communication with free water, the saturation is transferred to the water. However, it is important to note how the semi-solid protons are saturated and how they communicate with the surrounding water. An off-resonance selective saturation to the semi-solid pool undergoes intra-molecular dipole-dipole interactions (spin diffusion), whereby after a short period of time the saturation is transferred through the entire semi-solid proton pool (Koenig and Brown, 1993). The inter-molecular dipole-dipole interaction (between macromolecular protons and free water protons) then is a bulk dipole-dipole influence, rather than a direct chemical exchange of saturated protons as is seen in CEST (Guivel-Scharen et al., 1998; Stanisz et al., 1999).

To complete the model of the MTC effect, the observed magnitude of water signal attenuation after MT preparation depends on several factors: 1) parameters of the MT preparation, such as the duration (t_{sat}), magnitude (B_1), and offset frequency ($\Delta\omega$) of the MT saturation, 2) the relative size of the semi-solid proton pool (Fig. 24.1, $M_{0,m}$), 3) the rate of MT exchange between the semi-solid and free pools (Fig. 24.1, k_{mf}, k_{fm}), 4) the absorption lineshape of the semi-solid pool (impulse response function), and 5) the longitudinal and transverse relaxation of each proton pool ($R_{1f,m}$, $T_{2f,m}$). The details of this model are discussed in more depth in Section 24.3.

24.2.1 The MT experiment

A conventional MT experiment consists of a saturation (or, as discussed in Section 24.3.2.3, an inversion pulse), gradient spoiling, an excitation, and a readout. After the MT preparation, the MT effect on water can be read out through a variety of standard pulse sequences (gradient-echo, spin-echo, EPI, etc.). Here, we focus on how MT preparation is performed. Historically, an MT experiment consisted of performing a long ($\sim$seconds), high power MT saturation off-resonance with respect to water, followed by a rapid readout before the saturation relaxed (governed by R_1). This pulse sequence is termed continuous wave (CW) saturation (Henkelman et al., 2001) and remains the gold standard for animal systems. However, *in vivo*, CW saturation has two challenges: 1) it is time-consuming, and 2) human MRI systems do not typically have sufficient RF amplifier performance to sustain long, high power saturation pulse fidelity. To obviate the latter, a pulse-train approach has been used, whereby a series of smaller, shaped pulses are performed at a high duty cycle, which mimics the CW experiment when the interpulse delay is $\ll T_1$ (Helms and Piringer, 2005; Mougin et al., 2010). For the sake of this chapter, we will focus on experiments that are more rapid and can be deployed more easily on clinical MRI systems.

In vivo, MT experiments are typically of two sorts: 1) off-resonance, saturation-based MT and 2) on-resonance MT. For saturation-based MT, we have already discussed CW, however here we focus on pulsed MTC, which has transformed the ability to perform MT experiments *in vivo* through increasing imaging efficiency. Pulsed MT was introduced in (Pike, 1996) and is defined as a series of short (~ms), high power (>5 μT), shaped, off-resonance saturation prepulses repeated over many TRs to create a steady-state saturation. If the imaging TR is short, then a pulsed MT experiment is similar to a straightforward pulse train, however for pulsed MT, after each MT prepulse, some fraction of k-space is acquired. By timing the acquisition of the center of k-space to the time at which the saturation is in steady state, one can image the steady-state MT effect in a time-efficient manner. The pulsed MT approach has provided an opportunity to perform MT over a large field of view, or at higher resolution in a reasonable clinical scan time. Most saturation-based MT approaches in the literature currently use this approach.

The second method for generating MTC does not use saturation, but rather relies on the exchange between water and the semi-solid protons to alter the water relaxation properties. In previous literature, this has been seen as a negative side-effect of multi-slice MRI, whereby MT can affect the signal intensities on neighboring slices (Constable et al., 1992). However, it can be exploited to generate desired MT contrast, for example by selectively inverting the water signal, called selective-inversion-recovery (SIR) (Gochberg and Gore, 2003). On-resonance MT methods have several advantages, such as low power deposition (SAR) and the ability to tailor the inversion pulse to increase inversion efficiency. SIR MT will be discussed in Section 24.3.2.3.

Though we have discussed that the MT experiment, and its effect on the observed water signal, is defined by the MT saturation scheme and associated parameters, it should be pointed out that the MT experiment can be performed with only one set of imaging parameters (e.g., one set of saturation power or offset frequency) or using multiple MT saturation parameters. When performing a pulsed saturation MT experiment, the observed result is an MT-weighted image, which is a function of the MT pulse parameters and MR pulse sequence. Obtaining multiple MT-weighted images over a range of offset frequencies, and/or powers generates an MT spectrum and was termed the MT z-spectrum (Bryant, 1996). Importantly, obtaining MT z-spectra in a tissue-of-interest will allow fitting of those data to a biophysical model and deriving physiologically more specific indices, which is termed quantitative MT (qMT) (see Section 24.3).

24.2.2 Biochemical origin of the MT effect

For the purpose of this chapter, we will focus on the MT effect in nervous system tissue. However, it should be pointed out that any tissue with a semi-solid and exchanging spin population can generate an MT effect (cf. Wolff and Balaban, 1989). There continues to be debate in the literature about the sensitivity and specificity of the MT effect, yet the connection between the MT effect and myelin is undoubted. Myelin is present in white matter (and gray matter to a lesser extent) and is a lipid rich molecule, whose biochemical composition is roughly 70% lipid and 30% protein. Its primary purpose is to improve the speed of action potential transmission along the axon. Myelin is a modified plasma membrane composed of phospholipids (biased towards the intracellular face) and glycolipids (biased towards the extracellular face). It has been shown that glycolipids dominate the MT effect 3 times more than cholesterol or sphingomyelin, primarily due to their headgroups being rich in fast exchanging hydroxyl groups (exchange rate = 1000–10,000 s^{-1}) (Fralix et al., 1991; Koenig, 1991). The bias of glycolipids on the extracellular face allows efficient dipole-dipole interaction with the surrounding water.

Because of the biochemical structure and abundance in the nervous system, from the early 1990s the MT effect was ascribed to myelin. However, an MT experiment sensitized to the MT effect cannot discriminate among the origins of the exchanged saturation. Nevertheless, Schmierer and colleagues (Schmierer et al., 2004) ascribed 90% of the observed MTR in the nervous system to myelin. The pool size ratio derived from qMT (Section 24.3.2) has also been shown to be significantly associated with myelin concentration. Even though the specificity of the MT effect to myelin is debatable, using MT to survey diseases, where demyelination or remyelination is plausible, has provided unique understanding of pathological changes *in vivo*. To summarize this section, and to pay homage to the debate about sensitivity and specificity of the MT effect to myelination, the following quote by Arnold is relevant: "Although structures other than myelin contribute to MT, pathological changes in the MTR of white matter are largely determined by changes in myelin". (Myelin Imaging Meeting, Vancouver, BC 2006).

24.3 **Quantification of the MT effect**

24.3.1 **Part 1: the MTR**

When Wolff and Balaban first described the MT effect seen in their studies, they provided an easy, and still used, method for quantifying the MT effect, the magnetization transfer ratio (MTR) (Wolff and Balaban, 1989) defined as

$$\text{MTR}(\Delta\omega) = \frac{S_0 - S(\Delta\omega)}{S_0}, \tag{24.1}$$

the fraction of signal attenuation after an MT preparation, $S(\Delta\omega)$, compared to a reference image, S_0. The MTR typically requires MT saturation at only one offset frequency (1–4 kHz) and generates one value per voxel. An example of the MTR calculation and images used to derive the MTR are shown in Fig. 24.2. Note that in the $S(\Delta\omega)$ image, the white matter is saturated (darker) to a greater degree than is the CSF and gray matter, lending strength to the sensitivity of the MT effect to myelin. The resulting MTR shows CSF as dark, gray matter as intermediate, and white matter as bright.

Though the MTR is the most often used method of characterizing the MT effect, it has some limitations. The MTR is scanner/sequence dependent, and because of this, the MTR is not easily compared across sites, field strength, scanner vendors, and pulse sequences. Additionally, the MTR is sensitive to field inhomogeneity (B_0 and B_1), saturation preparation strategies (duration, amplitude, duty cycle), and T_1, especially in pathology that can alter T_1. Since the MTR is straightforward to use, there has been work performed to correct the MTR for B_0 and B_1 effects and standardize acquisitions across scanners. However, the sensitivity to non-physiological parameters has led to hesitancy in adopting the MTR as a method to characterize pathology, especially in larger multi-center trials. Nevertheless, the MTR has been shown to be useful in assessing pathology.

The MTR has been used in a variety of neuroimaging applications especially over many years in the study of multiple sclerosis. MTR has been shown to correlate with cognitive impairment in normal aging, to be altered in patients with treatment-resistant depression, and to provide complementary information to CEST for assessing brain tumors. MTR in the brain has also been applied as an endpoint for multi-site clinical drug trials for progressive multiple sclerosis, and for assessing migraine, lupus as well as schizophrenia. Pediatric applications of brain MTR include studies in children born very preterm, who demonstrate reduced MTR consistent with delayed myelination. MTR has also been

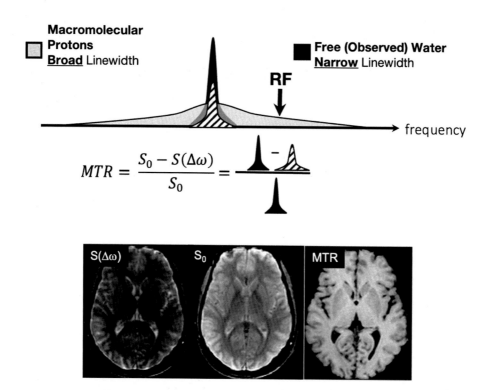

FIGURE 24.2

A schematic and example data in a standard MTR experiment. Typically, an RF irradiation is applied away from the water at a single off-resonance frequency to saturate the macromolecular pool (gray shade). The saturation exchanges with the free water (black) and attenuates the water signal (hashed lines). The MTR is the fraction saturated as a function of the signals obtained with (S(Δω)) and without (S₀) RF irradiation. In the bottom panel, a saturated and non-saturated 3T MRI are shown as well as the MTR. Note that in the S(Δω) image, white matter is saturated to a greater degree than the surrounding gray matter and CSF, which is due to higher concentration of macromolecules, in the WM.

applied to study pathologies of the cervical spinal cord, including adrenomyeloneuropathy, cervical spondylotic myelopathy, and multiple sclerosis. MTR studies have also been applied in the peripheral nervous system in Charcot–Marie–Tooth diseases and hereditary transthyretin amyloidosis with polyneuropathy.

24.3.2 Quantification of the MT effect – part 2: quantitative MT (qMT)

One way to interrogate the MT effect is to model the biophysical MT phenomenon using a two (or more) pool model (Henkelman et al., 2001; Stanisz et al., 1999). Each pool in the model shown in Fig. 24.1 has its own relaxation times ($T_{1f,m}$, $T_{2f,m}$), pool size ($M_{0f,m}$), and two rate constants (k_{fm}, k_{mf}) for the rate of MT exchange between the two pools. qMT affords the opportunity to minimize

24.3 Quantification of the MT effect

the dependencies of the MTR on non-physiological parameters, and using a model fit to MT z-spectra (Bryant, 1996), to derive indices reflective of physiological indices of tissue composition. Additionally, qMT utilizes information from B_1, B_0, and T_1 to correct the z-spectra for field inhomogeneities and remove confounds from T_1 effects. Two main quantitative MT methods will be discussed here: pulsed MT and selective inversion recovery.

24.3.2.1 Pulsed MT

Recall the two-pool model described above. Two pools (free water, F, and macromolecular, M) are in exchange with each other with rate constants k_{mf} and k_{fm} (forward and backward, respectively). Each pool has its own proton density (M_{0f}, M_{0m}) and relaxation times ($T_{1f,m}$, $T_{2f,m}$). In the qMT experiment, the semi-solid proton pool is saturated with a RF irradiation defined by offset frequency ($\Delta\omega$), saturation power B_1, and saturation duration. Therefore one can write the modified Bloch equations for exchange as follows:

$$\frac{dM_x^F}{dt} = -\frac{M_x^F}{T_2^F} - 2\pi\,\Delta\omega M_y^F$$

$$\frac{dM_y^F}{dt} = 2\pi\,\Delta\omega M_x^F - \frac{M_y^F}{T_2^F} - \gamma B_1(t)M_z^F \tag{24.2}$$

$$\frac{dM_z^F}{dt} = \gamma B_1(t)\,M_y^F - \left(R_1^F + k_{FM}\right)M_z^F + k_{MF}M_z^M + R_1^F M_0^F$$

$$\frac{dM_z^M}{dt} = -\left(R_1^M + k_{MF} + \pi\gamma^2 B_1^2(t)\,g\left(\Delta, R_2^M\right)\right)M_z^F + k_{FM}M_z^F + R_1^M M_0^M,$$

where $M_{x,y,z}^{F,M}$ are the x, y, and z components of the magnetization in the free (F) and macromolecular (M) pools. $M_0^{F,M}$ is the equilibrium magnetization of each pool (i.e., $M_{0f,m}$ from above); $\Delta\omega$ and $B_1(t)$ are the frequency offset and amplitude of the saturation RF pulse, respectively; $R_{1,2}^{F,M}$ is the longitudinal and transverse relaxation rate constant of the two pools; γ is the gyromagnetic ratio; k_{FM} and k_{MF} are the exchange rates from the free pool to the MT pool and vice versa (i.e, k_{fm} and k_{mf} from above); $g(\Delta, R_2^M)$ is the absorption lineshape of the semisolid pool, a function of bound-pool transverse relaxation time and offset frequency. The lineshape can be represented by several different shapes, though super-Lorentzian is considered the most accurate for MT representation *in vivo*.

In a pulsed MT experiment, the pulse sequence components are described by the following: 1) off-resonance irradiation, 2) delay for spoiling, 3) on-resonance excitation, and 4) a delay for SAR reduction and/or readout (Sled and Pike, 2000; Yarnykh, 2002). Using this formalism, the Bloch equations can be analytically solved for each pulse period and combined to represent a single signal equation for the MT pulse sequence. Sled and Pike (Sled and Pike, 2000) first introduced this pulsed MT signal equation, which can be fit voxel-by-voxel to derive 4 parameters: k_{mf}, pool size ratio, transverse relaxation times for the free, and bound pool ($T_{2f,m}$). Fitting to this model also requires a measurement of T_1 and assumes that R_{1f} can be fixed. However, this formalism requires a simulation to understand the direct effect of MT saturation on the water signal.

Yarnykh revised this formalism (Yarnykh, 2012), which proposes that if the MT saturation is performed sufficiently far off-resonance ($\Delta\omega > 1.5$ kHz), the direct water saturation can be effectively

380 Chapter 24 Magnetization transfer contrast MRI

ignored. Additionally, it is assumed that the MT saturation pulse can be accurately summarized by an effective rectangular pulse with the same duration and constant amplitude. Lastly, it assumes that $R_{1m} = R_{1f}$, and the product $T_{2f}*R_{1f}$ is roughly constant at 0.055. Using these assumptions, the signal equation immediately after on-resonance excitation can be written as

$$M_s = \left[I - e^{-\underline{R}(TR - t_{\text{delay}})} e^{\underline{W} t_{\text{sat}}} \cdot C \right]^{-1}, \tag{24.3}$$

where M_s is the signal after excitation, I is the identity matrix, $\underline{R}$ is a relaxation and exchange matrix (Yarnykh, 2002), t_{delay} is the delay after excitation to the next MT saturation pulse, $\underline{W}$ is the saturation matrix, t_{sat} is the duration of MT saturation, and C is a constant. The matrix $\underline{W}$ contains the saturation lineshape and T_{2b}, whereas the matrix $\underline{R}$ contains exchange rates and longitudinal/transverse relaxation rates. Thus, the parameters fit from this equation are reduced to T_{2f}, T_{2m}, k_{mf}, and pool size ratio (PSR). Note that in some qMT literature, substitutions are made, and the parameters that are fit are referred to with different names, but all are based on the Bloch equations given above.

To fit the model to MT data, an MT z-spectrum needs to be acquired over multiple offset frequencies and MT saturation powers. An example of this is shown in Fig. 24.3, where we show the spinal cord under two different MT saturation flip angles ($\alpha_{MT} = 360°$ and $820°$) and several offset frequencies. A voxel-wise MT z-spectrum for each power is shown in the bottom figure, and a fit to the data using the formalism shown above. The resulting PSR map for the spinal cord is shown in Fig. 24.3 right panel (Smith et al., 2014). Note the higher PSR in the white matter and lower PSR in the CSF (blue) and internal, butterfly-shaped gray matter (green).

qMT often requires very long scan times to obtain data from multiple offset frequencies and MT saturation powers at sufficient SNR to allow for robust fitting. However, due to its sensitivity to myelin, often the goal in a qMT experiment is to quantify the PSR. There are several data reduction strategies that have been employed. For example, the dependency of the MT z-spectrum on certain model parameters is limited over a particular range of offset frequencies, and thus a proposed method to characterize solely the PSR has been presented, which requires only one off-resonance saturation ($\Delta\omega$), and T_1, B_1, and B_0 maps (Yarnykh, 2012). In effect, this is a way to calculate the MTR using an MT saturation pulse at a single offset frequency and power, but using the two-pool model to correct the measurement for T_1, B_1, and B_0. The advantage of "single-point qMT" to derive the PSR is that fewer data points need to be collected, and the extra scan time can be used for increasing SNR and/or resolution. However, the single-point method does not model changes in the exchange rate, or bound pool transverse relaxation time. The single-point method has been applied in the brain, spinal cord, and brainstem (Trujillo et al., 2017; Yarnykh et al., 2015).

24.3.2.2 Application of pulsed qMT

Pulsed qMT has been applied in several clinical neuroimaging applications at 1.5T and 3T field strengths. The PSR has been reported in the whole brain (Yarnykh et al., 2015), small structures in the brain, such as the locus coeruleus and the substantia nigra pars compacta. In studies of patients with mild cognitive impairment, qMT at baseline shows potential to differentiate those who convert to Alzheimer's disease from those who remain stable. Additional studies in Alzheimer's disease have investigated differences in brain qMT indices that correspond with risk factors for late onset Alzheimer's disease, such as midlife obesity and genetic risk factors (APOE-ε4). In Huntington's disease, the macro-

24.3 Quantification of the MT effect

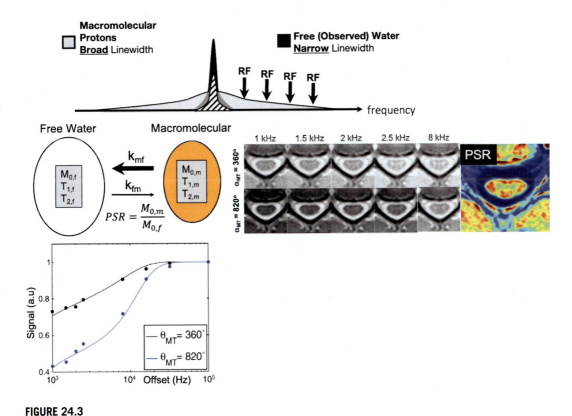

FIGURE 24.3

A schematic and example data of a pulsed qMT experiment. Top shows the same broad macromolecular lineshape (gray shade), free water signal (black), and attenuated water signal (hashed lines), however, for pulsed qMT, multiple RF irradiation pulses are played out at several offset frequencies and/or saturation powers, which generates an MT z-spectrum, as shown in the bottom panel. To perform qMT, a 2-pool model is fit (middle, left) to images obtained over multiple offsets and powers (middle, right). Fitting voxel-by-voxel (bottom left), the pool size ratio (PSR), and other qMT parameters can be estimated (middle far right).

molecular proton fraction derived from qMT has been shown to be reduced in white matter. Other applications of pulsed qMT in the brain include studies of normal appearing white matter in patients with glioblastoma, qMT indices as biomarkers for monitoring glioblastoma response to radiotherapy, and using qMT to differentiate between tumor types in patients with neoplastic and metastatic brain tumors.

Outside the brain, pulsed qMT has been used in the human cervical spinal cord *in vivo*, and the single-point method for making the qMT scan time more clinically feasible has been applied in the spinal cord of multiple sclerosis patients. Strategies have also been developed to apply qMT to an even smaller structure, such as the human optic nerve. This application required development of an approach to remove the fat component from the MT images since the optic nerve is surrounded by fatty connective tissue.

24.3.2.3 Selective inversion recovery (SIR)

Though saturation-based qMT has received the most attention in the MT literature, there are alternative methods for performing qMT. Saturation-based qMT has some limitations: 1) it requires additional measurements of B_1, B_0, and T_1, 2) it has sensitivity to assumptions about the macromolecular pool and lineshape, 3) it has a complicated data analysis, and 4) the power deposition (SAR) for saturation-based qMT is generally very high and at the FDA limit in most applications. The last point is especially difficult to obviate as the principle behind saturation-based qMT is to perform short, high-power saturation pulses multiple times to generate a saturation steady state in the tissue. The impact of SAR will be discussed in Section 24.4.

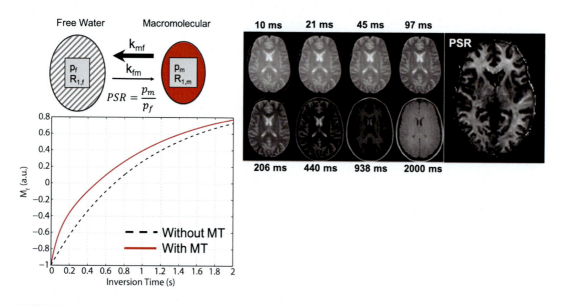

FIGURE 24.4

A schematic selective inversion recovery (SIR) qMT experiment. In the SIR qMT method, we assume two pools, each with their own longitudinal relaxation rates ($R_{1,fm}$) and pool sizes (p_{mf}), and in exchange with each other with rate constants k_{mf}, k_{fm}. Unlike pulsed qMT, the SIR assumes that the inversion pulse is longer than T_{2m} and shorter than T_{2f}, thereby selectively inverting the water signal, which in tissue is not mono-exponential at short TIs, but rather bi-exponential. Images of the brain at 8 TIs is shown in the right panel and fitting each voxel to a bi-exponential recovery curve, as presented in the text, can yield the pool size ratio (PSR), as shown on the right. Note that in the PSR, the white matter is brightest and GM and CSF are significantly lower intensity.

Selective inversion recovery (SIR) addresses some of these challenges. The SIR technique was first noted by Gochberg and colleagues (Gochberg and Gore, 2003) and utilizes an on-resonance inversion pulse with a conventional readout. Recalling the two-pool model presented before, when performing an inversion recovery sequence at short inversion times (TI) in tissue with an MT effect, the inversion recovery signal is bi-exponential, rather than mono-exponential as seen in a water phantom (see Fig. 24.4). Therefore one can write the inversion recovery signal under exchange using the following equations:

$$\frac{dM_f(t)}{dt} = -R_{1,f}\left(\frac{M_f(t)}{M_{f,\infty}} - 1\right) - k_{fm}\left(\frac{M_f(t)}{M_{f,\infty}} - \frac{M_m(t)}{M_{m,\infty}}\right),$$

$$\frac{dM_m(t)}{dt} = -R_{1,m}\left(\frac{M_m(t)}{M_{m,\infty}} - 1\right) - k_{mf}\left(\frac{M_m(t)}{M_{m,\infty}} - \frac{M_f(t)}{M_{f,\infty}}\right), \quad (24.4)$$

where $M_{f,m}$ is the magnetization of the free and bound pool, respectively, $R_{1f,m}$ is the longitudinal relaxation rate of each pool, and $M_{fm,\infty}$ is the equilibrium magnetization. The forward (macromolecular to free) and backward (free to macromolecular) exchange rates are denoted as k_{mf}, and k_{fm}, respectively. The solution to the above equations follows:

$$\frac{M_f}{M_{f,\infty}} = b_f^+ e^{-R_1^+ t} + b_f^- e^{-R_1^- t} + 1. \quad (24.5)$$

Details of the mathematical formalism of the amplitudes ($b_f^\pm$) and slow and fast recovery rates (R_1^- and R_1^+, respectively) can be found in (Dortch et al., 2011). The PSR is the ratio of the exchange rates, and macromolecular and free pool sizes ($p_{m,f}$, respectively):

$$\frac{k_{fm}}{k_{mf}} = \frac{p_m}{p_f} = PSR. \quad (24.6)$$

Therefore kmf and PSR can be determined by fitting the above equations to the inversion recovery curve at multiple TIs, however, an extra step is necessary: the bound-pool inversion efficiency needs to be simulated *a priori* using information about the inversion pulse.

SIR qMT requires that the inversion pulse is low power and has a duration that is longer than T_{2m}, and much shorter than T_{2f}. Under this assumption, ideally, the inversion pulse will invert the free pool magnetization with minimal influence on the bound pool, thereby maximizing the difference between the two pools after inversion. It has been shown that the selective inversion recovery preparation can be used in conjunction with either a turbo-field-echo or fast-spin-echo readout, but under the condition that the longitudinal magnetization after the readout is effectively zero.

Fig. 24.4 shows the two pool-model modified for the SIR experiment and a simulation of the inversion recovery curves in water vs in tissue (with MT). The images in the right panel show the contrast changes in the brain at 8 different TIs (10 ms–2000 ms) showing the contrast change with each TI and a resulting calculated PSR map. Note that in the PSR map, the white matter is bright, and CSF and GM are darker, which is in concert with pulsed qMT methods shown earlier.

One challenge with SIR qMT is that it can also be a long experiment, due to the need for multiple TIs and long delay times to assure the complete zeroing of the longitudinal magnetization before a repeat inversion. However, in a similar fashion to the pulsed qMT work, data reduction strategies can be employed by recognizing the sensitivity of the fitted parameters to the choice in TIs. That is, the TIs can be chosen (and thereby reduced) to minimize the influence of the exchange rate on the PSR. To that end, a reduced set of TIs can be used to estimate the PSR from a limited data set with similar PSR results. Further work at high field using SIR qMT will be discussed in Section 24.4.2.

384   Chapter 24 Magnetization transfer contrast MRI

24.3.2.4 Application of SIR qMT

Selective inversion recovery qMT has most recently been applied in several studies, largely due to the work of Gochberg, Gore, and Dortch. However, the use of SIR qMT as a method to provide robust estimates of the PSR in the presence of field inhomogeneities, its SAR demands, and its unknown lineshapes make it attractive for further study. SIR has been used in both animal and human studies. For human studies, SIR qMT has been utilized in the brains of patients with multiple sclerosis.

24.4 High field

There has been considerable interest in performing MRI at high field, due to the promise of improved SNR, increased spectral dispersion, and sensitivity to susceptibility. However, for MT imaging, higher field is somewhat problematic. Most MT experiments performed in the human utilizing pulsed MT are already at the FDA limit for power deposition (SAR). That is, the short, high amplitude, repeated MT saturation pulses result in a high-power pulse sequence. Importantly, the SAR scales with B_0^2, flip angle α^2, and linearly with the duty cycle (t_{sat}/TR). Additionally, at high field, B_0/B_1 inhomogeneities are prominent and must be accounted for. Thus, though the MT effect is not diminished at high field, the tools to measure it have faced challenges.

24.4.1 Pulsed MT

The pulsed MT experiments deployed at 3T and below are already high SAR. Therefore using the SAR equation as a guideline, there are only a few methods available to reduce SAR: 1) reduce the duty cycle of the saturation, or 2) reduce the power. For the former, Mougin and colleagues (Mougin et al., 2010) showed that by performing an MT saturation pulse train (in a similar fashion as CEST) and allowing the duty cycle to remain low, MTR imaging at high field can be obtained with excellent quality. Oh and colleagues (Oh et al., 2018) took a different approach and identified that not every excitation needs to have an MT pulse, and that selecting when to provide the MT saturation during a k-space sampling scheme can reduce the SAR. This was termed the variable density magnetization transfer (vdMT).

24.4.2 Selective inversion recovery

While pulsed MT is most prevalent and at high field can be challenging, the selective inversion recovery (SIR) sequence can potentially provide some relief. Unlike pulsed MT, where the duration, amplitude, shape, and offset frequency of the MT saturation needs to be set, controlled, and corrected for, the SIR sequence utilizes only a single inversion pulse. Importantly, at high field, expert pulse design can be employed to design an inversion pulse (that meets the requirement of being longer than T_{2b} and shorter than T_{2f}, and low power) that is relatively insensitive to the B_1 and B_0 effects seen at high field. Dortch and colleagues showed that a composite inversion pulse showed excellent inversion fidelity over a range of B_1 and B_0 and did not meet the same SAR challenges seen with pulsed MT. SIR could be applied to patients with multiple sclerosis at high resolution to assess cortical gray matter and showed that the SIR-derived exchange rate (rather than PSR) was correlated with cognitive impairment. Lastly, SIR qMT could also be used in post-mortem MS brains to assess myelination.

24.5 Conclusion

In this chapter, we highlighted the MT phenomenon, ways to measure the MT effect, as well as three methods to quantify the MT effect. The chapter closes with a forward-looking opportunity for high field MT MRI. Though the focus of this chapter was on magnetization transfer and the MRI contrast that can be generated with an MT experiment, there are many other current methods to measure the macromolecular content within nervous system tissue, such as myelin water imaging (O'Muircheartaigh et al., 2019; Zhang et al., 2015).

References

Bryant, R.G., 1996. The dynamics of water-protein interactions. Annu. Rev. Biophys. Biomol. Struct. 25, 29–53.

Constable, R.T., Anderson, A.W., Zhong, J., Gore, J.C., 1992. Factors influencing contrast in fast spin-echo MR imaging. Magn. Reson. Imaging 10, 497–511.

Desmond, K.L., Stanisz, G.J., 2012. Understanding quantitative pulsed CEST in the presence of MT. Magn. Reson. Med. 67, 979–990.

Dortch, R.D., Li, K., Gochberg, D.F., Welch, E.B., Dula, A.N., Tamhane, A.A., Gore, J.C., Smith, S.A., 2011. Quantitative magnetization transfer imaging in human brain at 3 T via selective inversion recovery. Magn. Reson. Med. 66, 1346–1352.

Edzes, H.T., Samulski, E.T., 1977. Cross relaxation and spin diffusion in the proton NMR or hydrated collagen. Nature 265, 521–523.

Fralix, T.A., Ceckler, T.L., Wolff, S.D., Simon, S.A., Balaban, R.S., 1991. Lipid bilayer and water proton magnetization transfer: effect of cholesterol. Magn. Reson. Med. 18, 214–223.

Gochberg, D.F., Gore, J.C., 2003. Quantitative imaging of magnetization transfer using an inversion recovery sequence. Magn. Reson. Med. 49, 501–505.

Guivel-Scharen, V., Sinnwell, T., Wolff, S.D., Balaban, R.S., 1998. Detection of proton chemical exchange between metabolites and water in biological tissues. J. Magn. Reson. 133, 36–45.

Helms, G., Piringer, A., 2005. Simultaneous measurement of saturation and relaxation in human brain by repetitive magnetization transfer pulses. NMR Biomed. 18, 44–50.

Henkelman, R.M., Stanisz, G.J., Graham, S.J., 2001. Magnetization transfer in MRI: a review. NMR Biomed. 14, 57–64.

Koenig, S.H., 1991. Cholesterol of myelin is the determinant of gray-white contrast in MRI of brain. Magn. Reson. Med. 20, 285–291.

Koenig, S.H., Brown, R.D. 3rd, 1993. A molecular theory of relaxation and magnetization transfer: application to cross-linked BSA, a model for tissue. Magn. Reson. Med. 30, 685–695.

Mougin, O.E., Coxon, R.C., Pitiot, A., Gowland, P.A., 2010. Magnetization transfer phenomenon in the human brain at 7 T. NeuroImage 49, 272–281.

O'Muircheartaigh, J., Vavasour, I., Ljungberg, E., Li, D.K.B., Rauscher, A., Levesque, V., Garren, H., Clayton, D., Tam, R., Traboulsee, A., Kolind, S., 2019. Quantitative neuroimaging measures of myelin in the healthy brain and in multiple sclerosis. Hum. Brain Mapp. 40, 2104–2116.

Oh, S.H., Shin, W., Lee, J., Lowe, M.J., 2018. Variable density magnetization transfer (vdMT) imaging for 7T MR imaging. NeuroImage 168, 242–249.

Pike, G.B., 1996. Pulsed magnetization transfer contrast in gradient echo imaging: a two-pool analytic description of signal response. Magn. Reson. Med. 36, 95–103.

Schmierer, K., Scaravilli, F., Altmann, D.R., Barker, G.J., Miller, D.H., 2004. Magnetization transfer ratio and myelin in postmortem multiple sclerosis brain. Ann. Neurol. 56, 407–415.

Sled, J.G., Pike, G.B., 2000. Quantitative interpretation of magnetization transfer in spoiled gradient echo MRI sequences. J. Magn. Reson. 145, 24–36.

Smith, A.K., Dortch, R.D., Dethrage, L.M., Smith, S.A., 2014. Rapid, high-resolution quantitative magnetization transfer MRI of the human spinal cord. NeuroImage 95, 106–116.

Smith, S.A., Farrell, J.A., Jones, C.K., Reich, D.S., Calabresi, P.A., Van Zijl, P.C., 2006. Pulsed magnetization transfer imaging with body coil transmission at 3 Tesla: feasibility and application. Magn. Reson. Med. 56, 866–875.

Stanisz, G.J., Kecojevic, A., Bronskill, M.J., Henkelman, R.M., 1999. Characterizing white matter with magnetization transfer and T2. Magn. Reson. Med. 42, 1128–1136.

Trujillo, P., Summers, P.E., Smith, A.K., Smith, S.A., Mainardi, L.T., Cerutti, S., Claassen, D.O., Costa, A., 2017. Pool size ratio of the substantia nigra in Parkinson's disease derived from two different quantitative magnetization transfer approaches. Neuroradiology 59, 1251–1263.

Wolff, S.D., Balaban, R.S., 1989. Magnetization transfer contrast (MTC) and tissue water proton relaxation in vivo. Magn. Reson. Med. 10, 135–144.

Yarnykh, V.L., 2002. Pulsed Z-spectroscopic imaging of cross-relaxation parameters in tissues for human MRI: theory and clinical applications. Magn. Reson. Med. 47, 929–939.

Yarnykh, V.L., 2012. Fast macromolecular proton fraction mapping from a single off-resonance magnetization transfer measurement. Magn. Reson. Med. 68, 166–178.

Yarnykh, V.L., Bowen, J.D., Samsonov, A., Repovic, P., Mayadev, A., Qian, P., Gangadharan, B., Keogh, B.P., Maravilla, K.R., Jung Henson, L.K., 2015. Fast whole-brain three-dimensional macromolecular proton fraction mapping in multiple sclerosis. Radiology 274, 210–220.

Zhang, J., Kolind, S.H., Laule, C., Mackay, A.L., 2015. Comparison of myelin water fraction from multiecho T2 decay curve and steady-state methods. Magn. Reson. Med. 73, 223–232.

CHAPTER

Chemical exchange saturation transfer (CEST) MRI as a tunable relaxation phenomenon

25

Moritz Zaiss[a,b], Felix Glang[b], and Kai Herz[b,c]

[a]*Department Neuroradiology, University Clinic Erlangen, Friedrich Alexander University Erlangen-Nürnberg, Erlangen, Germany*
[b]*Magnetic Resonance Center, Max Planck Institute for Biological Cybernetics, Tübingen, Germany*
[c]*Department of Biomedical Magnetic Resonance, University of Tübingen, Tübingen, Germany*

25.1 Introduction and theoretical background

Different relaxation rates of water protons in different environments are the origin of the unique soft matter contrast in MRI. Water content and macromolecular structures, together with molecular tumbling rates relative to the Larmor frequency, as well as magnetic susceptibilities, are the major influence on the relaxation rates R_1 and R_2 *in vivo*. But also diluted spin populations can affect the abundant water pool relaxation via inter– and intramolecular magnetization transfer (MT) processes mediated by scalar or dipolar spin–spin couplings or chemical exchange (Englander et al., 1972; Ward et al., 2000). Thus, the presence of a proton pool that exchanges magnetization with water affects both the R_2 relaxation rate described by the Swift–Connick equation (Swift and Connick, 1962)

$$R_{2,obs} = R_{2,w} + R_{2,exch} = R_{2,w} + f_s k_s \frac{R_{2s}^2 + R_{2s}k_s + \delta\omega_s^2}{(R_{2s} + k_s)^2 + \delta\omega_s^2} \tag{25.1}$$

and the R_1 relaxation rate (Edzes and Samulski, 1977),

$$R_{1,obs} = \frac{R_{1w} + R_{1s} + k_s(1 + f_s)}{2}$$
$$- \frac{1}{2}\sqrt{(k_s(1 + f_s) + R_{1w} + R_{1s})^2 - 4 \cdot (k_s \cdot R_{1w} + k_s f_s \cdot R_{1s} + R_{1w} \cdot R_{1s})}$$
$$= \frac{R_{1w} + f_s R_{1s}}{1 + f_s}, \tag{25.2}$$

as known, for example, from semi-solid MT influence or the use of paramagnetic contrast agents. In these equations, k_s is the exchange rate from a solute pool to water and f_s is the fraction of exchanging protons with respect to the water protons $f_s = \frac{n \cdot [s]}{2 \cdot [w]}$. These and all following equations can be derived from the Bloch–McConnell (BM) equations.

Advances in Magnetic Resonance Technology and Applications, Volume 4, ISSN 2666-9099. https://doi.org/10.1016/B978-0-12-822479-3.00040-3
Copyright © 2021 Elsevier Inc. All rights reserved.

387

388 **Chapter 25** CEST MRI as a tunable relaxation phenomenon

The influence of a contrast agent can even dominate the relaxation pathways. Thus, the normal situation in tissue is that many relaxation pathways exist, and when an exchanging agent is added, a new relaxation pathway for water protons opens up. But what happens if an existing relaxation pathway is blocked or enhanced? Again, the total relaxation rate of water will be altered. This selective alteration of a relaxation pathway by using radiofrequency (RF) irradiation is the underlying principle of chemical exchange saturation transfer (CEST) MRI.

In a CEST experiment, the chemical exchange relaxation pathway between a solute pool and the water pool is perturbed by RF irradiation at the solute pool resonance frequency. Thus, indirect detection of a solute pool is possible by observing changes in the water pool relaxation rate or the steady-state signal (Forsen and Hoffman, 1963; Ward et al., 2000).

This RF perturbation, here considered as continuous wave irradiation, introduces new degrees of freedom, most importantly the RF irradiation amplitude B_1 and the irradiation frequency offset $\Delta\omega$ from the water frequency. The new relaxation rate upon this irradiation $R_{1\rho}$ is a function of these parameters and the free relaxation rates and the exchange parameters $R_{1\rho}(\Delta\omega,B_1,R_1,R_2,f,k)$. Consequently, this forms a tunable relaxation rate, as we have external control over $\Delta\omega$ and B_1.

The irradiation frequency offset $\Delta\omega$ defines a new rotating frame of reference and $R_{1\rho}(\Delta\omega)$ depicts the longitudinal relaxation rate in this rotating reference frame (Trott and Palmer, 2002). This relaxation rate is actually well-known, as it is exactly the relaxation rate in off-resonance spin-lock experiments; in several studies it was shown that $R_{1\rho}$ describes the CEST dynamic as well (Jin et al., 2011; Zaiss and Bachert, 2013). $R_{1\rho}$ is an eigenvalue of the BM equation system that dominates the dynamic for long saturation. In CEST experiments, $R_{1\rho}$ is not measured directly; instead, the water Z-magnetization is acquired after RF preparation. The signal of the prepared Z-magnetization (S_{prep}), normalized by an unprepared scan S_0 as a function of the frequency offset $\Delta\omega$, forms the so called Z-spectrum, which can now be described by $Z(\Delta\omega) = S_{prep}(\Delta\omega)/S_0$:

$$Z(\Delta\omega, t) = \left(P^2 Z_i - Z^{ss}(\Delta\omega)\right) e^{-R_{1\rho}(\Delta\omega)t} + Z^{ss}(\Delta\omega); \tag{25.3}$$

$P^2 = \frac{\Delta\omega^2}{\Delta\omega^2 + \omega_1^2}$ results from the projection to the new longitudinal axis along the effective field $\vec{\omega}_{eff} = (\omega_1 = \gamma B_1, 0, \Delta\omega)$; P^2 is close to 1 for larger offsets. The initial Z–magnetization $Z_i = |M_{initial}|/M_0$ decays towards a steady–state given by

$$Z^{ss} = P^2 \frac{R_{1,obs}}{R_{1\rho}}. \tag{25.4}$$

The dynamic equation (25.3) is very similar to the standard longitudinal relaxation formula; however, also the steady-state Z-value, which is often measured in CEST experiments, is altered. Its frequency dependency is given by $R_{1\rho}(\Delta\omega)$. As often observed for relaxation rates, also for $R_{1\rho}$, different contributions simply add up in first order and $R_{1\rho}$ is given by:

$$R_{1\rho} = R_{1\rho,\text{wmt}} + R_{ex,\text{solute 1}} + R_{ex,\text{solute 2}} + \cdots \tag{25.5}$$

The background $R_{1\rho,\text{wmt}}$ of water and semi-solid MT can also be expressed analytically (Zaiss et al., 2015), which is not detailed here for brevity, but plotted as a function of the irradiation frequency offset in Fig. 25.1a. Most importantly, this term describes the direct water saturation around 0 ppm and the broad MT background (see more in Chapter 24), and it depends on R_1, R_2, and MT parameters. In the ideal case of no concomitant saturation, e.g., far off-resonance, the equality $R_{1\rho,\text{wmt}} = R_{1,\text{obs}}$ holds, which leads to Z=1 for large offsets.

The exchange-dependent relaxation term R_{ex} contains solely parameters of the exchanging pool. Essentially, the selective nature can be understood by the Lorentzian resonance around the resonance frequency of the exchanging pool $\delta\omega_s$ as it can be seen in Fig. 25.1a or directly here in the definition:

$$R_{\text{ex}}(\Delta\omega) \approx f_s k_s \underbrace{\frac{\omega_1^2}{k_s(k_s + R_{2s}) + \omega_1^2}}_{\alpha} \cdot \underbrace{\frac{\Gamma^2/4}{\Gamma^2/4 + (\Delta\omega - \delta\omega_s)^2}}_{\text{Lorentzian}}, \quad (25.6)$$

where $\delta\omega_s$ is the chemical shift relative to water protons, and the linewidth Γ of the Lorentzian peak is given by

$$\Gamma = 2\sqrt{\frac{R_{2s} + k_s}{k_s}\omega_1^2 + (R_{2s} + k_s)^2}. \quad (25.7)$$

If the saturation amplitude B_1 is altered, both the amplitude and the width of the peak are altered (Fig. 25.1d). The relative amplitude is given by α, which is the so-called labeling efficiency. It is also depicted as a function of the B_1 amplitude by the solid green line in Fig. 25.1e. The labeling efficiency α is close to zero for $\omega_1 \ll k$, 50% for $\omega_1 \approx k$, and would approach 100% for $\omega_1 \gg k$, without direct water saturation.

Now, we can understand CEST as a tunable relaxation phenomenon: If RF irradiation is applied at the center frequency of the Lorentzian, this additional exchange-dependent relaxation term increases, and the water relaxation, and thus the steady-state (Eq. (25.4)) is altered. Fig. 25.1 shows an example of $R_{1\rho,\text{wmt}}$ and R_{ex} as function of $\Delta\omega$ and the corresponding Z-spectrum emerging from this $R_{1\rho}$ distribution (Fig. 25.1b). Only upon irradiation at the CEST offset, the water relaxation is altered, and the exchange-dependent effect emerges. To isolate only one contribution, the concept of label and reference scans is used. The label scan has full CEST labeling and is often acquired on-resonance with respect to the CEST pool. The reference scan has minimal CEST labeling, but all other contributions of the label scan. For reference scans, background/baseline estimations or the opposite frequency (leading to MTR_{asym}) are used. In steady-state, the ideal label and reference values are given by

$$Z_{\text{ref}}^{\text{ss}} = P^2 \frac{R_{1\text{obs}}}{R_{1\rho,\text{wmt}}}, \qquad Z_{\text{label}}^{\text{ss}} = P^2 \frac{R_{1\text{obs}}}{R_{1\rho,\text{wmt}} + R_{\text{ex}}}. \quad (25.8)$$

With these values, also depicted in Fig. 25.1b, the CEST effect can be isolated from the background, leading to the effect in Fig. 25.1c and the MT ratio MTR, here indexed by LD, which is simply the linear difference:

$$\text{MTR}_{\text{LD}} = Z_{\text{ref}}^{\text{ss}} - Z_{\text{label}}^{\text{ss}} = \frac{R_{\text{ex}} \cdot R_{1,\text{obs}} P^2}{R_{1\rho,\text{wmt}}(R_{1\rho,\text{wmt}} + R_{\text{ex}})}. \quad (25.9)$$

This metric is the most direct and simple one, and it is to first order proportional to R_{ex}, and thus to the CEST pool concentration and the exchange rate. It still depends on $R_{1\rho,\text{wmt}}$, which explains the effect of spillover dilution, meaning that apparent CEST signals become diluted when background

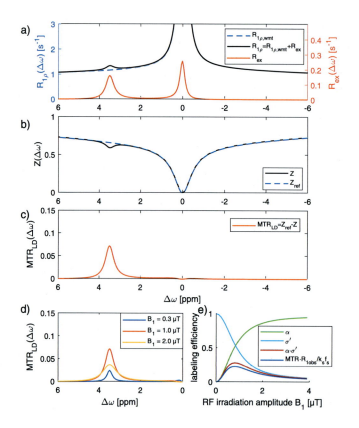

FIGURE 25.1

(a) The rotating frame relaxation of water and MT adds up with the exchange-dependent relaxation R_{ex} to the combined $R_{1\rho}$. This shows a strong direct water contribution on the order of $R_{2,water}$ ($\simeq 17$ Hz), a broad contribution from the semi-solid MT and a selective contribution at 3.5 ppm from an assumed amide pool, in this case, with parameters according to Table 25.1. The calculated Z-spectrum (black line in b) shows exactly these features in an inverse manner. Using a reference Z-spectrum without CEST pools (dashed line in b), the magnetization transfer ratio MTR_{LD} can be calculated (c), which is proportional to R_{ex}. The measurable effect size given by MTR_{LD} depends strongly on the saturation power, as both the labeling efficiency α and the spillover dilution σ' depend on B_1 in a complementary manner. The optimal CEST effects in a real situation can be found at a B_1 level that compromises between labeling and spillover dilution. This simulation can be reproduced with the code at https://github.com/cest-sources/Z-cw/tree/master/advanced_neuro_MR_Fig1 and also at https://www.elsevier.com/books-and-journals/book-companion/9780128224793.

effects are larger. Expressed with the labeling efficiency α and the approximated spillover term $\sigma' = Z_{ref}^2 = \left(\frac{R_{1,obs}P^2}{R_{1\rho,wmt}}\right)^2$, the CEST effect is given by:

$$MTR_{LD} \overset{R_{ex} \ll R_{1\rho,wmt}}{\approx} \frac{R_{ex} \cdot R_{1,obs}P^2}{R_{1\rho,wmt}^2} = \frac{R_{ex}}{R_{1,obs}} Z_{ref}^2 = \frac{f_s k_s}{R_{1,obs}} \cdot \alpha \cdot \sigma' \quad (25.10)$$

The terms α, σ', and $\alpha \cdot \sigma'$, and thus the maximal achievable effect, are highly B_1-dependent as displayed in Fig. 25.1e. The introduced σ' is an approximation of $(1 - \sigma)$, as described by Sun and colleagues (Sun et al., 2014), but also includes MT contribution. Other MTR metrics, e.g., inverse difference metrics, can even cancel out the spillover dilution term (Zaiss and Bachert, 2013).

In the ideal case of on-resonance CEST irradiation (and negligible direct water saturation and MT) the relaxation simplifies to $R_{1\rho,\text{wmt}} = R_1$, and the ideal CEST effect, including the dynamic part of Eq. (25.3), yields:

$$\text{MTR}_{\text{LS}}^{\text{lab}}(t_{\text{sat}}) = \frac{f_b k_b \cdot \alpha}{R_{1a} + f_b k_b \alpha}\left(1 - e^{-(R_{1a}+k_a \cdot \alpha)t}\right). \tag{25.11}$$

Thus, even on-resonance with respect to the CEST pool, the effect strength can be altered by the RF amplitude and the labeling efficiency, but also the saturation duration, which governs the build-up of the effect. Eqs. (25.10) and (25.11) are first-order signal equations for CEST, from which several important and general conditions can already be concluded:

1. Efficient labeling of a certain exchange rate requires a matched B_1, coarsely: $\omega_1 = \gamma B_1 \approx k_s$.
2. The saturation duration T_{prep} should be on the order of water $T_1 = 1/R_1$.
3. There is a trade-off between labeling α and spillover σ' of direct and MT saturation, which also depends on B_1 and T_{prep}. The optimum is given by $\alpha\sigma'$, which often has to be found experimentally.
4. The width of R_{ex} in Hz (Eq. (25.7)) does not depend on the static field strength, thus higher field strengths lead to better separability of CEST and water saturation effects, which can lead to lower spillover and higher observed effect strengths.

Thus, the external parameters $\Delta\omega$, T_{prep}, and B_1 allow tuning CEST experiments in many ways, aiming for different offsets, exchange regimes, and relative contributions, which is one reason why there are many different CEST protocols and achievable correlations at different B_0 fields.

To close the circle with conventional relaxation, $R_{1\rho}$ is actually the generalization of the above relaxation equations (25.1), (25.2), and when using the complete equations (Zaiss and Bachert, 2013), one can show that $\lim_{\Delta\omega\to\infty} R_{1\rho} = R_{1,\text{obs}}$ and $\lim_{\Delta\omega,\omega_1\to 0} R_{1\rho} = R_{2,w} + R_{2,\text{exch}}$ of Swift and Connick (1962).

25.1.1 Pulsed CEST

The above theory is derived for continuous wave (CW) saturation, which often cannot be played out on clinical scanners, due to safety or hardware limitations. Thus, pulse trains are used with n pulses of duration t_{p} and interpulse delay t_{d}. The total preparation time can then be adjusted by the number of pulses $T_{\text{prep}} = n \cdot (t_{\text{p}} + t_{\text{d}}) - t_{\text{d}}$.

It is generally helpful to define the duty-cycle-adjusted root-mean-squared B_1 of a pulse train

$$B_{1\text{rms}} = \sqrt{\frac{1}{t_p + t_d}\int_0^{t_p+t_d} B_1^2(t)dt}. \tag{25.12}$$

This leads to Z-spectra comparable to CW-Z-spectra (Sun et al., 2011; Zu et al., 2011) and decouples the influences of duty-cycle $DC = t_{\text{p}}/(t_{\text{d}} + t_{\text{p}})$, $B_{1\text{rms}}$ and pulse flip angles. Importantly, similar $B_{1\text{rms}}$ also leads to similar semi-solid MT contribution.

The above continuous wave theory also holds broadly in the case of pulse train preparation (Meissner et al., 2015). For a more accurate description of pulse train preparation, more eigenvalues are necessary to fully describe the dynamics (Gochberg et al., 2018). Especially the dynamics during the delay between pulses cannot be described by CW theory, but are relevant for, e.g., variable–delay multi–pulse (VDMP) approaches that vary the delay time between the pulses, or rotation transfer effects.

25.1.2 CEST sequence scheme

Fig. 25.2 shows a typical CEST sequence consisting of a relaxation delay, a CEST preparation period, and the subsequent water signal readout. Most importantly, the spectrum is not acquired in one shot as in MR spectroscopy, but every point of the Z-spectrum corresponds to a full 2D or 3D volume acquisition after preparation. Thus CEST data is actually 4D data, where the fourth dimension is the frequency dimension, and all evaluations, e.g., Eq. (25.9), have to be performed pixel- or voxel-wise, respectively.

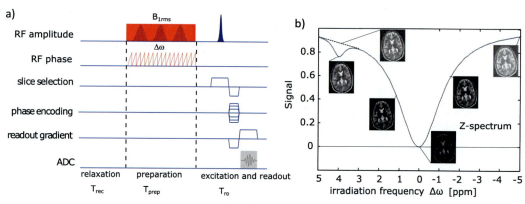

FIGURE 25.2

(a) A typical CEST sequence with relaxation delay (T_{rec}) before CEST preparation, i.e., CW or pulsed RF irradiation at a certain frequency offset $\Delta\omega$, at a certain RF amplitude B_1 or B_{1rms}, for a certain duration T_{prep}. Subsequently, the prepared magnetization is excited, spatially encoded, and one or more k–space lines are acquired; here a gradient echo readout of duration T_{ro}. This is repeated until the full k–space is sampled, if not acquired in a single snapshot. (b) To acquire a full Z–spectrum, the sequence of (a) is repeated for each offset frequency and/or B_1 level, leading to 4D data: an image for each offset $\Delta\omega$ or, equivalently, a Z–spectrum for each voxel. The Z–spectrum is further evaluated after normalization with an unsaturated image.

25.2 CEST effects in the human brain

Fig. 25.3 shows MTR_{LD} values similar to Fig. 25.1c, but acquired in the human brain at different field strengths. Obviously, compared to Fig. 25.1c, many more CEST effects occur. In addition to the amide CEST effect at 3.5 ppm, exchanging protons of amide, amine, guanidine, and hydroxyl groups lead to CEST effects in the range of positive ppm values. The exchange reactions are often base-catalyzed, thus the exchange rate increases with pH.

25.2 CEST effects in the human brain

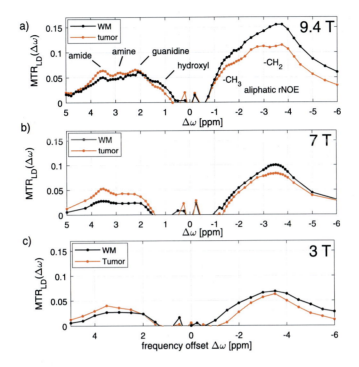

FIGURE 25.3

Real CEST effects in the human brain acquired with low saturation power ($B_{1rms} \approx 0.5\ \mu T$) evaluated using MTR_{LD} similarly to Fig. 25.1c by using a Lorentzian linear difference. a) 9.4T data of white matter (black line) and tumor region (red line). Due to the rather low saturation amplitude, slow exchanging species are dominant. In addition to amides at 3.5 ppm, amine (3 ppm) and guanidyl proton signals are visible (2 ppm). Hydroxyl protons would appear closer to water around 1–2 ppm, but are suppressed here due to the low B_1. In the negative frequency range, corresponding to covalently bound aliphatic protons, relayed nuclear Overhauser effects (rNOE) are present with a maximum at around -3.5 ppm. At -1.6 ppm another rNOE effect occurs associated with CH_3 groups of, e.g., PCho. The CEST effects at different field strengths of a) 9.4T, b) 7T, and c) 3T depict the increased separability of different effects, due to the increased Larmor frequency and lower spillover dilution. At all field strengths, chemical exchange effects in tumors are increased and rNOE decreased, consistently.

The best studied effect to date is amide CEST MRI, which originates from backbone amides of **endogenous proteins and peptides** (3.5 ppm), also known as amide proton transfer-weighted (APTw) CEST (Zhou et al., 2003). APTw CEST shows anti-correlation with **pH** (Heo et al., 2017) **in stroke** and elevated signals in brain tumor (Togao et al., 2014). Furthermore, it could be used to differentiate between radiation necrosis and progression of brain metastases, indicate histopathological grading of gliomas, predict isocitrate dehydrogenase (IDH) mutation status, and assess O^6-methylguanine-DNA methyltransferase (MGMT) status (Ladd et al., 2018). Early studies also showed that APTw MRI predicts radiotherapy response. Though APTw can be performed at clinical field strengths, further investigation at ultra-high fields of underlying contributions to the signal contrast yielded spatial coherence with Gd-enhanced MRI (see also Fig. 25.5), and correlations with early progression and tumor

394 **Chapter 25** CEST MRI as a tunable relaxation phenomenon

mutation (Ladd et al., 2018; van Zijl et al., 2018). APTw MRI also showed alterations in the spines of multiple sclerosis patients.

The **amine CEST** signal (2–3 ppm) yields an extra-cellular **pH-weighted MRI** and was shown to correlate with tumor regions (Harris et al., 2015) and to be altered in stroke affected regions (Jin et al., 2012). This pH sensitivity could be even enhanced by taking ratios of CEST effects at different saturation powers or by the combination of amine and amide CEST peaks. Depending on the saturation parameters, amine protons of **glutamate** also contribute to this CEST resonance (Cai et al., 2012).

The peak at 2 ppm was shown to be correlated with **creatine** guanidyl protons and to indicate tumor aggressiveness (van Zijl et al., 2018); in muscle this signal was successfully used for tracking of energy metabolism.

Closer to water (0.6–2 ppm), there are **hydroxyl CEST** signals expected. In other organs gly-cosaminoglycan, glycogen, and lactate were reported. In the human brain only injection-based methods were shown until now, such as dynamic glucose-enhanced CEST (van Zijl et al., 2018). Here, after a baseline CEST scan, additional glucose is injected, and the change in the CEST signal is detected dynamically. With this technique, uptake in brain tumors could be observed both at 7T and at 3T. Preliminary preclinical data show that this uptake is also altered upon neural activity, which opens a new path for neurophysiological approaches (Roussel et al., 2019).

Besides the physical transfer of protons through space, **relayed nuclear Overhauser effects (rNOE)**, mediated by dipolar interactions between close spins, provide further saturation pathways as dominant exchange–relayed NOEs and inter– and intramolecular NOEs.

The **rNOE CEST peak at -1.6 ppm** was until now only reported at 9.4T in animals and humans and attributed to be an NOE CEST effect of bound **Phospho-Cholines. Aliphatic rNOE CEST** (-3.5 ppm) is mainly attributed to mobile proteins, but was shown to correlate with changes of **protein conformation**, such as **unfolding** and **aggregation** (Zaiss et al., 2013; Goerke et al., 2017) as well. However, it remains to be clarified how strong this influence is *in vivo*. In cancer, the NOE CEST effect was shown to be decreased in the tumor area and, importantly, was shown to indicate radiation therapy response when it recovers to its normal value (Meissner et al., 2019). Another contributor at this frequency is the **lipid signal** that may indicate tumor necrosis as well as demyelination. Also, **aromatic NOE** contributions in the positive ppm range between 1 and 4 ppm were reported. Obviously, many different physiological and molecular correlations can be found in the CEST spectrum. Though parts of the signals overlap in the spectral domain, additional selectivity can be achieved by employing exchange rate and relaxation dependency of CEST effects on the saturation pulse amplitude, flip angle, and timing.

25.2.1 Quantitative model of CEST in the human brain

Having described the CEST theory and all the exchanging effects, a full analytical model for brain tissue seems to be in reach with Eqs. (25.5), (25.6), (25.7). Several methods, such as QUESP experiments, multi-B_1 Bloch–McConnell fitting, or CEST fingerprinting make quantification of *in vivo* CEST data possible. However, any quantification approach always assumes a certain pool model of a limited number of pools, and assumes that the Bloch–McConnell equations are sufficient. Furthermore, quantification results can depend on details of the employed fitting procedure, such as initial values and boundary conditions. It is of no surprise therefore that quantitative parameters determined *in vivo* show a variance between research groups, as can be seen in Table 25.1 and Fig. 25.4, which show parameters found in the literature (Perlman et al., 2020; Zaiss and Bachert, 2013).

25.2 CEST effects in the human brain

Table 25.1 Average values of quantitative CEST pool parameters in white brain matter and gray brain matter, calculated from data of Fig. 25.4 (equally weighted). As T_2 depends on field strength B_0, only studies performed at 7T are considered for the T_2 averages. To translate the resulting $T_{2,MT}$ values from Lorentzian lineshape to the commonly reported super-Lorentzian line shape, a correction factor of 0.25 was applied.

	White brain matter	Gray brain matter
k_{MT} (n=6)	(25 ± 22) Hz	(31 ± 20) Hz
k_{amide} (n=4)	(165 ± 98) Hz	(226 ± 140) Hz
k_{rNOE} (n=2)	(24.5 ± 4) Hz	(23 ± 2.4) Hz
k_{amine} (n=1)	1350 Hz $\pm$ 40%	1800 Hz $\pm$ 40%
f_{MT} (n=8)	(11.1 ± 4)%	(5.9 ± 2.2)%
f_{amide} (n=5)	(0.16 ± 0.12)%	(0.165 ± 0.13)%
f_{rNOE} (n=2)	(1.475 ± 1.29)%	(0.74 ± 0.62)%
f_{amine} (n=2)	(0.0775 ± 0.074)%	(0.0575 ± 0.046)%
$T_{2,MT}$ (7T: n=2)	(20.48 ± 0.67) µs	(26.79 ± 1.01) µs
$T_{2,amide}$ (7T: n=2)	(13.68 ± 12.76) ms	(18.47 ± 14.24) ms
$T_{2,rNOE}$ (7T: n=2)	(0.68 ± 0.52) ms	(1.05 ± 0.91) ms

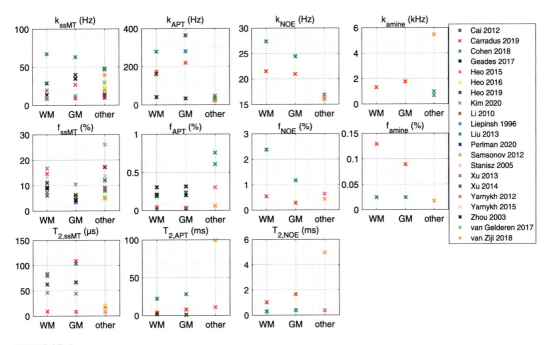

FIGURE 25.4

Comparison of CEST quantification results in the brain with values for exchange rates k, population fractions f, and transverse relaxation times T_2 of MT, amide (3.5 ppm), rNOE (-3.5 ppm) and amines (2 ppm) found in the literature (Perlman et al., 2020; Zaiss and Bachert, 2013). Values are plotted separately for human white matter (WM), human gray matter (GM), and other species. Mean values can be found in Table 25.1.

396 Chapter 25 CEST MRI as a tunable relaxation phenomenon

These differences in reported parameters can be due to various reasons from different field strengths B_0 and B_1, over different quantification methods, as well as different assumed models. However, microscopic parameters of the proton pools, such as relative fractions and exchange rates are intrinsic properties of the examined tissues and should therefore not depend on measurement parameters. Most importantly, these data show us that a final quantitative model for *in vivo* CEST is still needed, and that full quantification needs more efforts to achieve higher accuracy. Nevertheless, the mean values and standard deviations give us good estimations of the exchange regimes for the different proton pools, as summarized in Table 25.1. These regimes help a lot for finding optimal labeling parameters by Eqs. (25.10), (25.11), but also using simulations as performed for Fig. 25.1, which uses the parameters of Table 25.1, and can be reproduced using provided code, as given in the caption.

25.3 CEST sequences and contrasts of the healthy and diseased human brain

As shown above, many different CEST pools exist and their weighting depends strongly on the preparation parameters and the offset at which the CEST spectrum is evaluated. This leads to a vast number of different CEST preparation modules and protocols, of which a small selection is shown in Fig. 25.5. The parameters defining the preparation period, such as RF pulse shape, pulse duration (t_p), pulse train duty cycle (DC), and preparation duration (T_{prep}), have to be precisely defined. Reproduction of published protocols often remains a challenge; therefore, we follow here a recently proposed approach to define CEST preparation using the Pulseq format. Pulseq is a common, easy-to-use and vendor-independent file format, which is open source and allows sharing and comparing CEST preparations easily (Herz et al., 2021). All preparation modules shown in Fig. 25.5 can be found at https://pulseq-cest.github.io/, where also code for plotting and full simulation of the CEST preparations is shared. It is also available at https://www.elsevier.com/books-and-journals/book-companion/9780128224793.

Fig. 25.5a shows APT-weighted protocols, typically used for brain tumor studies. The B_{1rms} of 2 µT, together with the asymmetry analysis at ± 3.5 ppm, leads to a flat contrast in healthy brain. This allows the detection of pathological tissue, as seen by the elevated signals in a high grade tumor and hypointense ischemic regions in a stroke patient. Figs. 25.5c and d show glutamate and pH-weighted amine protocols, which use a higher B_1 field, due to the relative high exchange rate of both groups of labile protons. Fig. 25.5e shows the preparation of dynamic glucose-enhanced (DGE) imaging, where the measurements are repeated at the same frequency offset to acquire the dynamics before, during, and after the injection of glucose as a contrast agent. The DGE signal after injection indicates glucose uptake in the tumor area. A low-power multi-pool preparation is shown in Fig. 25.5f. Here, many frequency offsets are acquired at UHF, which makes it possible to isolate several CEST peaks by Lorentzian fitting. These CEST effects show different features in brain tumor tissue. In all of these protocols, the same preparation period is repeated over different frequency offsets. In contrast, CEST MR fingerprinting techniques, as visualized in Fig. 25.5g, employ preparation at different saturation powers, times, and offsets to generate unique signal trajectories for subsequent quantification using Bloch–McConnell simulations. This provides quantitative parameter maps for, e.g., amide proton concentration or exchange rate.

25.3 CEST sequences and contrasts of the healthy and diseased human brain 397

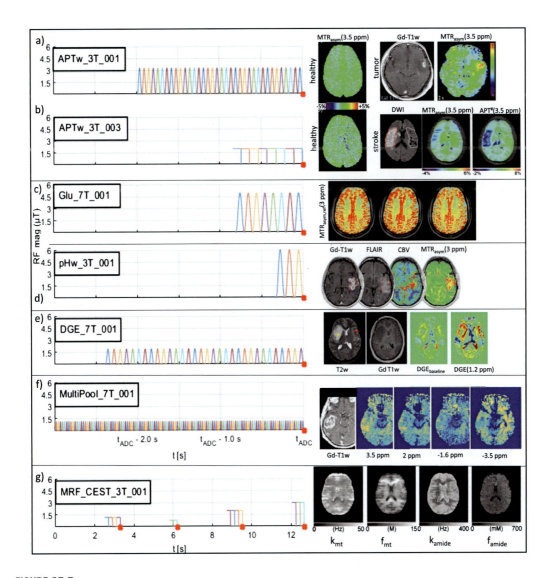

FIGURE 25.5

Different CEST preparations (left) in terms of saturation amplitude and duration lead to different CEST contrasts (right). (a, b) show different protocols for APTw imaging, evaluated at 3.5 ppm once applied in high grade tumor (a) and once in stroke (b). (c) shows glutamate-weighted amine CEST evaluated at 3 ppm. (d) shows pH-weighted amine CEST evaluated at 3 ppm. (e) shows dynamic glucose-enhanced imaging, where the offset 1.2 ppm is measured dynamically during glucose injection. (f) shows low-power multi-pool CEST at UHF (same as Fig. 25.2b) with several contrasts evaluated between -3.5 and + 3.5 ppm. (g) Shows a 3T CEST MR fingerprinting schedule yielding quantitative exchange rate and proton fraction maps. Reproduced with permission from a: doi.org/10.1371/journal.pone.0155925, b: doi.org/10.1002/mrm.26799, c: doi.org/10.1002/mrm.27362, d: doi.org/10.3174/ajnr.A6063, e: dx.doi.org/10.18383/j.tom.2015.00175, f: doi.org/10.1016/j.neuroimage.2018.06.026, g: doi.org/10.1016/j.neuroimage.2019.01.034.

25.3.1 Readout

After the CEST preparation modules, a fast MRI readout measuring the modulated water signals is played out, as shown in Fig. 25.2 and indicated by the red crosses in Fig. 25.5. If the preparation period is long enough or a relaxation delay is played out before the readout, the preparation is disentangled and the type of readout has a minor effect on the image contrast. Thus, many different readout modules from gradient-echo, EPI, to spin-echo sequences are in use in single-slice mode, segmented multi-slice or 3D mode, or 3D snapshot mode. When the preparation block is short and interleaved with a steady-state readout, the effects of the readout on the contrast are more complex, and more limitations with regard to duty-cycle occur. Both approaches are possible, though the first one with longer preparation is currently more common. Fig. 25.5d is an example for a multi-slice interleaved steady-state saturation approach.

25.4 Evaluation and artifacts – motion, normalization, B_0, B_1

25.4.1 Motion correction & temporal SNR

Even in the brain, CEST without motion correction is prone to false positive or false negative signals. A simple estimation of whether motion artifacts are a severe problem, even after correction, is to calculate the temporal SNR via a repeated measurement at, e.g., 3.5 ppm. If the generated normalized tSNR maps are below 1/(size of effect of interest), methodological improvements need to be performed first before any meaningful evaluation can be performed.

25.4.2 Normalization & reference values

Normalization by an unsaturated scan scales all CEST effects (Eq. (25.3)), thus it is as important as for the saturation scans to define, play out, and use this normalization scan consistently. Instead of an unsaturated scan, often a far off-resonance preparation, e.g., at -150 ppm to -300 ppm is played out to get consistent RF influences. Sometimes normalization is also acquired in the MT range to suppress MT influences.

The reference value of Eq. (25.9), which is the signal assumed to have no CEST contribution, is sometimes measured directly, e.g., for asymmetry-based approaches, the label scan at 3.5 ppm is subtracted from the reference scan measured at -3.5 ppm. Often it is also estimated from Bloch–McConnell or Lorentzian fits, or linear baselines, as well as different pre-saturation schemes. Again, it is important to be consistent and also take B_0 and B_1 inhomogeneities into account and correct for them if necessary.

25.4.3 B_0 and B_1 correction

A significant source of errors come from inhomogeneities of B_0 and B_1 fields. B_0 is crucial, in particular when asymmetry-based evaluation approaches are applied. When the position of the assumed symmetry axis deviates from the center of the water peak, direct water saturation is interpreted as CEST effect, especially near the water resonance. To compensate for this artifact, more than two offsets in the Z–spectrum must be acquired as well as an additional B_0 field map. Using this field map, the Z–spectrum data can be interpolated and registered pixel–by–pixel in the frequency dimension. To compensate for B_1 inhomogeneities, which are more problematic at ultra-high fields of $B_0 > 3T$, recently pTx approaches have been developed. In the case of insufficient B_1 field homogeneity, the same principle as for B_0 correction holds, and more than one B_1 saturation level must be acquired to perform a post-processing correction using a separately acquired B_1 field map.

25.4.4 CEST as the better MRS?

Herein we explained CEST as a water relaxation phenomenon; often CEST is also introduced as the cousin of MR spectroscopy and, of course, the chemical shift dependency and resonance frequencies of protons are the same, only shifted by -4.7 ppm in the case of CEST spectra, due to differently defined frequency scales. However, this comparison is often misleading for the following reasons: MRS works best for protons that do not exchange or only exchange very slowly. Then their linewidth is narrow and a peak is detectable. CEST works best when the exchange rate is rather high, then the CEST effects benefit from the built-up signal enhancement. Thus, MRS and CEST are actually complementary and due to the faster exchange rates and broader resonances in CEST, the specificity of CEST in the frequency domain is much lower compared to MRS, where individual groups and molecules can be distinguished.

25.4.5 Conclusion

CEST is often mentioned as a single MRI contrast. We hope to have shown herein that it is a whole zoo of different possible contrasts, with many different interesting correlations. Understanding CEST as a tunable relaxation phenomenon empowers the researcher to tune the relaxation in a way that a certain correlation dominates the contrast. For neuro-pathologies, CEST has already shown clinical relevance. For neuro-scientific approaches CEST shows early promising insights.

References

Cai, K., Haris, M., Singh, A., Kogan, F., Greenberg, J.H., Hariharan, H., Detre, J.A., Reddy, R., 2012. Magnetic resonance imaging of glutamate. Nat. Med. 18, 302–306. https://doi.org/10.1038/nm.2615.

Edzes, H.T., Samulski, E.T., 1977. Cross relaxation and spin diffusion in the proton NMR of hydrated collagen. Nature 265, 521–523. https://doi.org/10.1038/265521a0.

Englander, S.W., Downer, N.W., Teitelbaum, H., 1972. Hydrogen exchange. Annu. Rev. Biochem. 41, 903–924. https://doi.org/10.1146/annurev.bi.41.070172.004351.

Forsen, S., Hoffman, R.A., 1963. Study of moderately rapid chemical exchange reactions by means of nuclear magnetic double resonance. J. Chem. Phys. 39, 2892–2901. https://doi.org/10.1063/1.1734121.

Gochberg, D.F., Does, M.D., Zu, Z., Lankford, C.L., 2018. Towards an analytic solution for pulsed CEST. NMR Biomed. 31, e3903. https://doi.org/10.1002/nbm.3903.

Goerke, S., Milde, K.S., Bukowiecki, R., Kunz, P., Klika, K.D., Wiglenda, T., Mogk, A., Wanker, E.E., Bukau, B., Ladd, M.E., Bachert, P., Zaiss, M., 2017. Aggregation-induced changes in the chemical exchange saturation transfer (CEST) signals of proteins. NMR Biomed. https://doi.org/10.1002/nbm.3665.

Harris, R.J., Cloughesy, T.F., Liau, L.M., Prins, R.M., Antonios, J.P., Li, D., Yong, W.H., Pope, W.B., Lai, A., Nghiemphu, P.L., Ellingson, B.M., 2015. pH-weighted molecular imaging of gliomas using amine chemical exchange saturation transfer MRI. Neuro-Oncol. 17, 1514–1524. https://doi.org/10.1093/neuonc/nov106.

Heo, H.-Y., Zhang, Y., Burton, T.M., Jiang, S., Zhao, Y., van Zijl, P.C.M., Leigh, R., Zhou, J., 2017. Improving the detection sensitivity of pH-weighted amide proton transfer MRI in acute stroke patients using extrapolated semisolid magnetization transfer reference signals. Magn. Reson. Med. 78, 871–880. https://doi.org/10.1002/mrm.26799.

Herz, K., Mueller, S., Perlman, O., Zaitsev, M., Knutsson, L., Sun, P.Z., Zhou, J., van Zijl, P., Heinecke, K., Schuenke, P., Farrar, C.T., Schmidt, M., Dörfler, A., Scheffler, K., Zaiss, M., 2021. Pulseq-CEST: towards multi-site multi-vendor compatibility and reproducibility of CEST experiments using an open-source sequence standard. Magn. Reson. Med. 86 (4), 1845–1858. https://doi.org/10.1002/mrm.28825.

Jin, T., Autio, J., Obata, T., Kim, S.-G., 2011. Spin-locking versus chemical exchange saturation transfer MRI for investigating chemical exchange process between water and labile metabolite protons. Magn. Reson. Med. 65, 1448–1460. https://doi.org/10.1002/mrm.22721.

Jin, T., Wang, P., Zong, X., Kim, S.-G., 2012. Magnetic resonance imaging of the Amine-Proton EXchange (APEX) dependent contrast. NeuroImage 59, 1218–1227. https://doi.org/10.1016/j.neuroimage.2011.08.014.

Ladd, M.E., Bachert, P., Meyerspeer, M., Moser, E., Nagel, A.M., Norris, D.G., Schmitter, S., Speck, O., Straub, S., Zaiss, M., 2018. Pros and cons of ultra-high-field MRI/MRS for human application. Prog. Nucl. Magn. Reson. Spectrosc. 109, 1–50. https://doi.org/10.1016/j.pnmrs.2018.06.001.

Meissner, J.-E., Goerke, S., Rerich, E., Klika, K.D., Radbruch, A., Ladd, M.E., Bachert, P., Zaiss, M., 2015. Quantitative pulsed CEST-MRI using Ω-plots. NMR Biomed. 28, 1196–1208. https://doi.org/10.1002/nbm.3362.

Meissner, J.-E., Korzowski, A., Regnery, S., Goerke, S., Breitling, J., Floca, R.O., Debus, J., Schlemmer, H.-P., Ladd, M.E., Bachert, P., Adeberg, S., Paech, D., 2019. Early response assessment of glioma patients to definitive chemoradiotherapy using chemical exchange saturation transfer imaging at 7 T. J. Magn. Reson. Imaging 50, 1268–1277. https://doi.org/10.1002/jmri.26702.

Perlman, O., Ito, H., Herz, K., Shono, N., Nakashima, H., Zaiss, M., Chiocca, E.A., Cohen, O., Rosen, M.S., Farrar, C.T., 2020. AI boosted molecular MRI for apoptosis detection in oncolytic virotherapy. bioRxiv. https://doi.org/10.1101/2020.03.05.977793.

Roussel, T., Frydman, L., Le Bihan, D., Ciobanu, L., 2019. Brain sugar consumption during neuronal activation detected by CEST functional MRI at ultra-high magnetic fields. Sci. Rep. 9. https://doi.org/10.1038/s41598-019-40986-9.

Sun, P.Z., Wang, E., Cheung, J.S., Zhang, X., Benner, T., Sorensen, A.G., 2011. Simulation and optimization of pulsed radio frequency irradiation scheme for chemical exchange saturation transfer (CEST) MRI-demonstration of pH-weighted pulsed-amide proton CEST MRI in an animal model of acute cerebral ischemia. Magn. Reson. Med. 66, 1042–1048. https://doi.org/10.1002/mrm.22894.

Sun, P.Z., Wang, Y., Dai, Z., Xiao, G., Wu, R., 2014. Quantitative chemical exchange saturation transfer (qCEST) MRI - RF spillover effect-corrected omega plot for simultaneous determination of labile proton fraction ratio and exchange rate. Contrast Media Mol. Imaging 9, 268–275. https://doi.org/10.1002/cmmi.1569.

Swift, T.J., Connick, R.E., 1962. NMR-relaxation mechanisms of O17 in aqueous solutions of paramagnetic cations and the lifetime of water molecules in the first coordination sphere. J. Chem. Phys. 37, 307–320. https://doi.org/10.1063/1.1701321.

Togao, O., Yoshiura, T., Keupp, J., Hiwatashi, A., Yamashita, K., Kikuchi, K., Suzuki, Y., Suzuki, S.O., Iwaki, T., Hata, N., Mizoguchi, M., Yoshimoto, K., Sagiyama, K., Takahashi, M., Honda, H., 2014. Amide proton transfer imaging of adult diffuse gliomas: correlation with histopathological grades. Neuro-Oncol. 16, 441–448. https://doi.org/10.1093/neuonc/not158.

Trott, O., Palmer, A.G., 2002. R1rho relaxation outside of the fast-exchange limit. J. Magn. Reson. 154, 157–160. https://doi.org/10.1006/jmre.2001.2466.

van Zijl, P.C.M., Lam, W.W., Xu, J., Knutsson, L., Stanisz, G.J., 2018. Magnetization transfer contrast and chemical exchange saturation transfer MRI. Features and analysis of the field-dependent saturation spectrum. NeuroImage 168, 222–241. https://doi.org/10.1016/j.neuroimage.2017.04.045.

Ward, K.M., Aletras, A.H., Balaban, R.S., 2000. A new class of contrast agents for MRI based on proton chemical exchange dependent saturation transfer (CEST). J. Magn. Reson. 143, 79–87. https://doi.org/10.1006/jmre.1999.1956.

Zaiss, M., Bachert, P., 2013. Chemical exchange saturation transfer (CEST) and MR Z-spectroscopy in vivo: a review of theoretical approaches and methods. Phys. Med. Biol. 58, R221–R269. https://doi.org/10.1088/0031-9155/58/22/R221.

Zaiss, M., Kunz, P., Goerke, S., Radbruch, A., Bachert, P., 2013. MR imaging of protein folding in vitro employing nuclear-Overhauser-mediated saturation transfer. NMR Biomed. 26, 1815–1822. https://doi.org/10.1002/nbm.3021.

Zaiss, M., Zu, Z., Xu, J., Schuenke, P., Gochberg, D.F., Gore, J.C., Ladd, M.E., Bachert, P., 2015. A combined analytical solution for chemical exchange saturation transfer and semi-solid magnetization transfer. NMR Biomed. 28, 217–230. https://doi.org/10.1002/nbm.3237.

Zhou, J., Payen, J.-F., Wilson, D.A., Traystman, R.J., van Zijl, P.C.M., 2003. Using the amide proton signals of intracellular proteins and peptides to detect pH effects in MRI. Nat. Med. 9, 1085–1090. https://doi.org/10.1038/nm907.

Zu, Z., Li, K., Janve, V.A., Does, M.D., Gochberg, D.F., 2011. Optimizing pulsed-chemical exchange saturation transfer imaging sequences. Magn. Reson. Med. 66 (4), 1100–1108. https://doi.org/10.1002/mrm.22884.

CHAPTER

Clinical application of magnetization transfer imaging

26

Francesca Bagnato[a,b]

[a]*Neuroimaging Unit, Neuroimmunology Division, Neurology Department, Vanderbilt University Medical Center, Nashville, TN, United States*
[b]*Department of Neurology, Nashville VA Medical Center, TN Valley Healthcare System, Nashville, TN, United States*

26.1 Introduction

The use of magnetic resonance imaging (MRI) has revolutionized the way most neurological conditions are studied, diagnosed, and monitored, allowing for the identification of pathological changes even in the absence of clinical symptoms. T_2-weighted (T_2-w) sequences, e.g., T_2-w turbo-spin-echo (TSE) and fluid attenuated inversion recovery (FLAIR) methods, are sensitive to tissue damage. Two-dimensional (2D) and 3D T_1-w sequences permit delineation of anatomical structures and areas with increased water content due to edema. When obtained upon the injection of the contrast agent gadolinium (III) diethylenetriamine pentaacetate or Gd-DTPA, T_1-w sequences permit the identification of areas with increased blood-brain barrier permeability secondary to inflammation, infections, or cancer, for example. Using diffusion-based MRI to identify areas of restricted water diffusion indicative of, among others, early ischemic changes has transformed the treatment approach to ischemic stroke. Lastly, the routine utilization of susceptibility-based MRI has added sensitivity to small hemorrhagic foci, such as those seen in persons with amyloidosis or micro-traumatic brain injuries.

However, despite their sensitivity to disease processes, all the above-mentioned clinical sequences remain poorly specific to the identification and quantification of myelin and axonal injuries, both key pathologies of virtually any neurological condition. Because a healthy myelin fosters axonal health through structural and nutritional support (Pohl et al., 2011), imaging methods that accurately assess myelin integrity and capture early changes are crucial. Those methods would allow identifying pathological processes leading to irreversible clinical decline and measuring treatment effects in both day-to-day clinical practice and proof-of-concept clinical trials.

26.1.1 Magnetization transfer-based MRI to improve pathological specificity

Magnetization transfer (MT)-based methods have been optimized to overcome the limitations of clinical scans in probing myelin integrity and providing indirect estimates of its content. Such measurements add a layer of pathological specificity and accuracy to imaging of inflammatory-demyelinating diseases, dis-myelinating, and neurodegenerative conditions of the brain and the spinal cord and to the monitoring of developmental processes of the brain (Dubois et al., 2014).

The magnetization transfer ratio (MTR) derived from MT imaging has been introduced first in clinical studies. Due to its relatively simple and fast acquisition and postprocessing schemes, MT imaging

404 Chapter 26 Clinical application of magnetization transfer imaging

has been widely utilized to detect otherwise occult disease in seemingly healthy brain and spinal cord tissue. Clinically, MTR is viewed as the ratio between free water (expected to be seen in areas with vasogenic edema, such as, for example, in primary and metastatic brain cancers and in inflammatory diseases) and water with restricted motion (expected to be bound to macromolecules, such as proteins and lipids of an intact white or gray matter). Accordingly, any decrease in MTR is thought to reflect myelin loss, whereas any increase in MTR is viewed as myelin formation or repair. As detailed in Chapter 24, MTR suffers several limitations, which affect its degree of specificity to tissue pathology. These weaknesses are secondary to its semi-quantitative nature and its sensitivity to non-biological, experimental parameters (e.g., MT offset frequency, radiofrequency field amplitude variations, repetition time, MRI hardware, among others), and tissue relaxation time (Sled and Pike, 2000).

Quantitative MT methods (qMT) have been proposed as a possible solution to these MTR limitations. By fitting a series of MT-weighted images with a two-pool model of the MT effect, qMT methods remove the confounding influences associated with MTR (Sled and Pike, 2000). qMT yields tissue-specific indices, including the fraction of macromolecular protons, a metric sensitive to the relative quantity of macromolecules, and therefore total myelin content in the white matter. Clinically, the fraction of macromolecular protons is viewed as being more specific to myelin compared to MTR, given its selective sensitivity to protons in the macromolecular pool only. However, qMT methods typically require specialized sequences and complicated analysis pipelines that are unavailable at most sites. This requirement is a significant obstacle to their utilization.

To overcome the constraints of qMT, a qMT method known as selective inversion recovery (SIR) has been developed. SIR-qMT can provide qMT measures without the need for time-consuming measurements of the T_1, B_0, or B_1 (Li et al., 2010). This method uses conventional inversion recovery sequences and a user-friendly analysis based on a relatively simple biexponential signal model to estimate qMT parameters (see Chapter 24). Relative to myelin studies, SIR-qMT produces the macromolecular-to-free water pool-size-ratio (PSR), a metric comparable to the fraction of macromolecular protons generated by qMT.

In the present chapter, the clinical applications of MT imaging will be reviewed. In addition, the histopathologic counterparts of MT imaging-derived metrics will be described, along with highlighting the advances in clinical knowledge that the application of MT imaging has permitted. Finally, comment is made on possible barriers that continue to impede the adoption of MTI methods in clinical routine. Despite decades of effort and associated improved techniques, indeed, MT imaging has not made it to routine clinical practice.

26.2 Validation of MT imaging-derived metrics

Several combined MRI-histopathologic studies have been performed to assess the pathological sensitivity and specificity of MT imaging-derived metrics to myelin injury. Those studies are based upon either postmortem human samples or animal models of diseases. Most of these studies focus on demyelinating conditions, such as multiple sclerosis. As demyelination is a cardinal pathological feature of multiple sclerosis, this disease offers a suitable model to validate and implement MT methods. At the same time, scientists studying demyelinating diseases are mostly interested in myelin-sensitive techniques to understand disease pathology and evolution. Therefore multiple sclerosis-related studies will be predominently presented in this chapter to offer examples of the complexity of histopathologic validations of MTR- and qMT-derived metrics.

26.2.1 Histopathologic counterparts of MTR

26.2.1.1 Animal models

Early studies imaging mice affected by acute experimental allergic encephalomyelitis, one of the animal models of an inflammatory-demyelinating autoimmune white matter disease, proved that MTR values are slightly decreased in lesional areas featured by inflammation and edema, even in the absence of demyelination (Brochet and Dousset, 1999). The sensitivity of MTR to myelin loss was subsequently demonstrated in mice, whose demyelinating disease was induced by the experimental toxicant cuprizone and imaged at 7T (Fjaer et al., 2013), but not in those with myelin oligodendrocyte (MOG) 1–125 induced experimental autoimmune encephalomyelitis (Fjaer et al., 2015), where demyelination was, however, not observed.

It is important to highlight that there are substantial differences between demyelination induced by a myelin antigen or lipopolisaccaride immunization and that following the administration of cuprizone. The cuprizone-based diet induces a selective and reversible demyelination process secondary to both white matter and gray matter oligodendrocyte death. Spontaneous remyelination follows when cuprizone is no longer supplemented. Animals with cuprizone-induced demyelination have reduced levels of axonal loss and inflammation, thus less contaminants to MT imaging outputs relative to other animal models.

26.2.1.2 Postmortem human studies

Studies on humans obtained postmortem confirm data reported in investigations on animal models. MTR measurements differentiate white matter (Schmierer et al., 2004) and cortical (Chen et al., 2013) plaques, though axonal loss also affects MTR changes, a factor that lowers MTR specificity to myelin injury. MTR also detects differences in myelin content between demyelinated versus remyelinated plaques and the latter versus normal appearing tissue (Chen et al., 2013). Similarly, highly sensitive but poorly specific results were reported in the spinal cord of persons who died from multiple sclerosis (Mottershead et al., 2003).

26.2.1.3 Summary remarks

Overall histopathologic evidence supports the notion that MTR is reflective of myelin changes, but also shows that changes in this biometric are secondary to axonal loss and edema accumulation. This ambiguity can be resolved in the setting of histopathologic validations, but not necessarily in the context of *in vivo* applications. At this time, such ambiguity remains one of the most important limitations hindering pathological interpretation of *in vivo* findings.

26.2.2 Histopathologic counterparts of the fraction of macromolecular protons and PSR

26.2.2.1 Animal models

Work performed at 9.4T using an animal model system of Type III oligodendrogliopathy secondary to lipopolisaccaride immunization showed the ability of PSR to separate lesional versus non-lesional

406 Chapter 26 Clinical application of magnetization transfer imaging

tissue more accurately than radial diffusivity derived from diffusion tensor imaging and correlations between myelin content measured by luxol fast blue and PSR (Janve et al., 2013). The results parallel work performed on shiverer mice (Ou et al., 2009a) and on mice with retinal ischemia (Ou et al., 2009b).

Studies performed on cuprizone-treated animals confirmed significantly lower values of the macromolecular proton fraction in several white matter and cortical gray matter areas and significant associations between these values and the luxol fast blue intensity (Turati et al., 2015; Khodanovich et al., 2017).

Lastly, independent work using a 15.2T scanner to image mouse models of the tubero-sclerosis-complex-2 conditional knockout mouse (which exhibits extreme loss of myelin), the Rictor conditional knockout mouse (which displays less severe hypomyelination than the former) and the phosphatase and tensin homolog conditional knockout mouse (which presents with hypermyelination), has shown differences in PSR between different pairs of mice and a strong linear correlation between PSR and histologic measurements of myelin volume fraction.

26.2.2.2 Postmortem human studies

Combined MR-histopathological studies showed that both MTR and the fraction of macromolecular protons, correlate with myelin content in the brains of patients with multiple sclerosis, imaged using either 1.5T or 9.4T scanners. Significant associations were seen between myelin content, as measured by light transmittance on the luxol fast blue staining and the fraction of macromolecular protons. In addition, a larger effect size in the fraction of macromolecular protons compared to MTR was noted (Schmierer et al., 2007).

Work in our group has validated SIR-qMT at 7T against histopathology in human samples of multiple sclerosis (Bagnato et al., 2018). Fig. 26.1 shows the example of a lesion with demyelinating and remyelinating components; in this lesion, visible as a hyperintense area on a T_2-w gradient-echo spin-echo (GRASE) MRI at 7T (Fig. 26.1A), remyelination is seen only on the PSR maps (Fig. 26.1B, C), where one can appreciate differences in PSR values compared to the surrounding (yellow colored with PSR ~40%) normal white matter, and the luxol fast blue staining (Fig. 26.1D). In these samples, lesional PSR values were smaller than normal appearing white matter measurements (p=0.001 data not shown) and the two group values were distinctively separated.

26.2.2.3 Summary remarks

Growing evidence supports the sensitivity of the fraction of macromolecular protons and PSR to myelin integrity. More work is needed to untangle the effect of water accumulation, axonal injury, and myelin integrity, and that of the complicated interplay among these factors on those metrics.

It is in general important to emphasize that although histology is considered the gold-standard for the validation of MRI methods, there are many experimental challenges that impede histological validation of MRI in postmortem brain tissue, and these must be considered when interpreting these types of data. It is well known that the long-term fixation induces tissue chemical and structural changes and dehydration, which alters the T_2 relaxation time. These factors make direct postmortem to *in vivo* translations inaccurate. Ideally, postmortem work in humans should always be complemented by work on animal models. The latter, though not being biased by long-term fixation issues, suffers the limitations of presenting data related to animal diseases, which are notoriously similar, but not equivalent to the human illnesses.

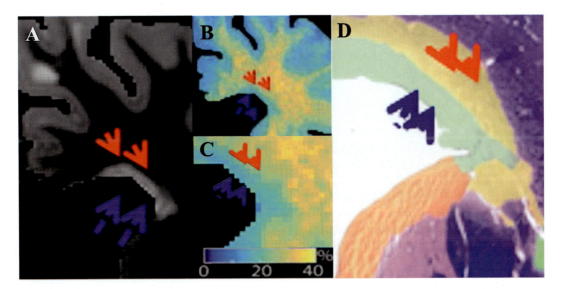

FIGURE 26.1 Histopathologic validation of PSR in postmortem human tissue (modified from Bagnato et al., 2018).

Example of a lesion (red and blue arrows) with demyelinating and remyelinating components; in this lesion, visible as a hyperintense area on a T_2-w gradient-echo spin-echo (GRASE) MRI (A), remyelination is seen only on the PSR map (B, C), where one can appreciate differences in PSR values, and on the luxol fast blue staining (D). In the color-coded luxol fast blue staining, green represents tissue with demyelination, and yellow indicates tissue with remyelination.

One may argue that the overall significance of the results showing changes in MTR or PSR as a function of myelin integrity is not affected as those measures reflect ratios (%) more than absolute values. Notwithstanding this consideration, a direct translation of absolute group-differences *in vivo* remains an inaccurate approach.

26.3 MT imaging to understand and monitor neurological disease evolution

A plethora of clinical studies have been performed using MT imaging to probe brain and spinal cord tissue integrity *in vivo*. Those studies have substantially enriched our knowledge of the evolution of several neurological conditions, and have improved our comprehension of patient disability.

The body of literature on clinical studies related to the use of MT imaging in patients with neurological conditions is virtually impossible to summarize. Therefore only representative examples of clinical applications of MT imaging will be provided here.

26.3.1 Lessons learned from multiple sclerosis

Multiple sclerosis is one of the diseases that has mostly exploited the advantages provided by MTR in identifying and characterizing tissue injury. In this condition, the use of MTR has allowed for the assessment and measurement of otherwise occult microstructural changes in the normal appearing white matter and normal appearing gray matter of the brain and spinal cord. Studies have shown that disease in normal appearing tissues in both brain (Inglese et al., 2003) and spinal cord (Combès et al., 2019) does insidiously occur and evolve over time. This progression likely contributes to accumulation of patient disability. The speed of disease progression is faster in progressive multiple sclerosis compared to earlier stages of the disease (Lommers et al., 2019), and it is likely affected by other clinical factors, such as aging (Newbould et al., 2014) and comorbidities. Those conclusions were reached by using both regions-of-interest-based analyses and whole normal appearing white matter/gray matter histogram analyses. Studies have also shown that disease in the normal appearing tissue, as measured by MTR changes, does explain part of the variance of both cognitive and physical impairment of patients with multiple sclerosis. The contribution that this measurable disease offers is often independent from that provided by the effect of lesion volume.

Moreover, MTR measurements have allowed for the assessment that the degree of tissue injury present in chronic lesions of patients with multiple sclerosis varies and may affect outcome (Lommers et al., 2019). This assessment adds pathological specificity to the identification of lesions on clinical scans. As demonstrated by histopathologic studies, chronic multiple sclerosis lesions visible on T_2-w images present a less destructive pathological process than those having a corresponding signal loss on T_1-w images, termed black holes. Similarly, MTR values of T_2-lesions have been reported to be higher than those measured in black holes. When these black holes are further characterized by their appearance on tissue-specific imaging, a technique that allows selective imaging of the three tissue compartments in the brain, i.e., white matter, gray matter, and cerebrospinal fluid (Riva et al., 2009), MTR aids our understanding that lesions visible on tissue-specific imaging show the greatest amount of tissue destruction. Accordingly, these lesions have signal intensity similar to that of the cerebrospinal fluid. Fig. 26.2 shows the example of two chronic black holes, one with appearance on tissue-specific imaging (Fig. 26.2A–C) and the other that does not correspond to a lesion on tissue-specific imaging (Fig. 26.2D–F). The box plots reported next to the MTR images show that chronic black holes with visibility on tissue-specific imaging have the lowest MTR values (Fig. 26.2G, Tissue 4). The box plots also represent typical MTR values measured in the brain tissue of patients with multiple sclerosis. Those values range between 0.40–0.50 in the seemingly healthy white matter, 0.30–0.35 in the normal appearing gray matter, and anywhere between 0.35 and 0.20 in lesions, depending upon the degree of tissue injury. Due to the presence of proteins, MTR values for the cerebrospinal fluid diverge somewhat from "zero".

Lastly, MTR measurements have shed light on disease changes occurring (1) prior to the appearance of an active lesion, (2) at the time of inflammatory activity, and (3) following the resolution of the acute phase. Contrast enhancing lesions have historically been regarded as the first recognizable pathological event in patients with multiple sclerosis. Those lesions are sustained by a relatively large blood-brain barrier breakdown, which promotes inflammation and recruitment of inflammatory cells from the periphery. Upon the resolution of the blood-brain barrier, some lesions undergo repair, whereas others evolve into chronic active or inactive lesions characterized by a core of profound myelin loss. Longitudinal MTR assessments have led to the description that tissue changes occur even before contrast-enhancing lesions become visible by showing measurable drops in MTR values, likely indicative of early inflammatory-demyelinating events. At the time of the acute disease activity, there is an additional drop in MTR, the depth of which is associated with the likelihood of recovery (Richert and Frank, 1999). Over time, MTR increases or remains unchanged, depending upon the ability of the in-

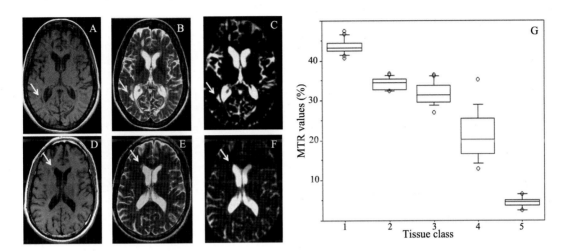

FIGURE 26.2 Differences in MTR between chronic black holes with different degrees of tissue injury (modified from Riva et al., 2009).

T_1-w (A, D) and T_2-w (B, E) spin-echo MRIs showing a chronic black hole with (white arrow in A, C) and without (white arrow in D, F), a corresponding lesion on tissue-specific imaging in two patients with multiple sclerosis. In G, box plots represent the mean MTRs of regions of interest placed in normal appearing white matter (Tissue 1), normal appearing gray matter (Tissue 2), chronic black holes without (Tissue 3) and with (Tissue 4) appearance on tissue-specific imaging and cerebrospinal fluid (Tissue 5). There was a highly significant difference ($F_{4,56} = 525.31$; $P < .0001$) among the MTR of the different brain components, with tissue differences (Bonferroni corrected $P < .0001$) found in each of the pairs analyzed except for between Tissues 2 and 3.

jured tissue to repair. Such heterogeneity can be measured even within lesions, on a voxel-by voxel basis, as shown in Fig. 26.3A–C (Ikonomidou et al., 2013). The importance of those studies stems from the fact that MTR changes over time provide an extremely valuable outcome measure to test the efficacy of medications in promoting repair. The discovery of a therapeutic with regenerative properties is the challenge for the next decades.

Motivated by the premise that, although sensitive to pathology, MTR may not be as specific as desired, a number of clinical studies using qMT methods have been performed. For example, work in our group compared PSR values among tissues expected to have different degrees of pathological injury. In 18 patients with multiple sclerosis, and 9 healthy controls, we analyzed how differences in PSR compared to those in the diffusion tensor imaging-derived radial diffusivity, and how both metrics explain patient disability. Similar 95% limits-of-agreement were found for PSR [−2.7, 3.0%] and radial diffusivity [−0.01, 0.014%], respectively, with no significant interscan bias for PSR (Scan 1: 10.4±4.2%; Scan 2: 10.5±4.2%) or radial diffusivity (Scan 1: 0.6±0.16%; Scan 2: 0.64±0.5%). Decrease in PSR and increase in RD were consistently seen for chronic black holes compared to T_2-lesions (Fig. 26.4A–D), and for the latter compared to normal appearing white matter (p<0.001 for all comparisons, data not shown). Histogram analysis for PSR and radial diffusivity across whole-brain normal white matter of healthy controls and normal appearing white matter of patients with multiple sclerosis with different degrees of physical disability, yielded interesting trends (Fig. 26.4E and 26.4F). From

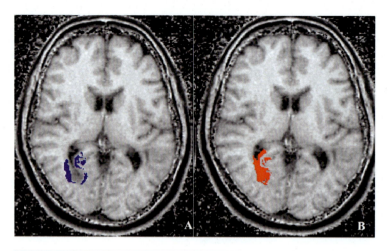

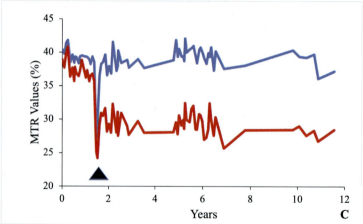

FIGURE 26.3 MTR changes preceding and following the resolution of the blood brain barrier.

MTR timecourse behavior heterogeneity within an active lesion in a patient with multiple sclerosis. An overall drop of MTR values preceded the acute phase and showed various degrees of recovery, with some of the voxels' MTR values returning to baseline values. Blue (A and C) indicates the peripheral region, and red (B and C) indicates the central core. A sharp decrease in MTR affected almost the entire enhancing area in the acute phase (black solid arrow). Smaller declines in MTR preceded the acute phase by 12 months. Signs of recovery were seen as early as 6 months after the lesion first appeared. The color-coded maps of the areas of lesion recovery are represented in A and B, showing in blue any voxel that recovered, and in red any voxel that did not recover over time.

visual inspection, peak histogram PSR values demonstrated a trend of decreasing values when comparing control subjects to patients with no disability (Expanded Disability Status Scale, EDSS, score $\leqslant 1$) and moderate disability (EDSS > 1). A smaller inverse trend was observed for radial diffusivity values. This agrees with quantitative analyses across cohorts, which indicated that mean histogram PSR values

26.3 MT imaging to understand and monitor neurological disease evolution **411**

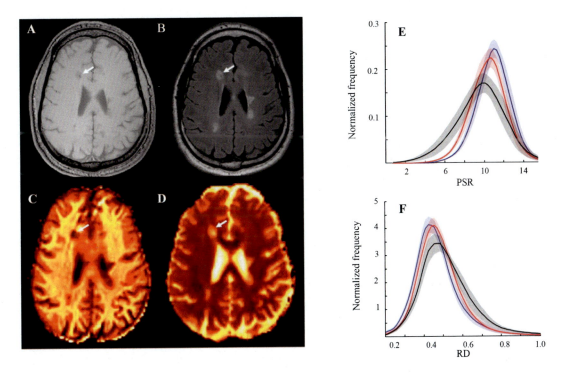

FIGURE 26.4 Differences in PSR and radial diffusivity between different lesion types and associations with clinical disability.

Black hole (white arrows in A–D) shows decreases in PSR (C) and increases in radial diffusivity (D). Histogram analysis for PSR (E) and RD (F) values derived from whole-brain normal appearing white matter of participants with an Expanded Disability Status Scale (EDSS) score > 1 (black line), EDSS ⩽ 1 (red line) and normal white matter from healthy controls (blue line). The solid dark lines and the surrounding shaded regions represent the mean values and the standard errors, respectively.

were reduced in patients with moderate disability relative to controls (p=0.05), whereas no significant difference was observed across cohorts for RD (p=0.08).

Other authors validated the use of the fraction of macromolecular protons *in vivo* (Davies et al., 2004; Yarnykh et al., 2015). It was observed that the fraction of macromolecular protons distinguished between normal appearing tissue of patients with secondary progressive multiple sclerosis and those with relapsing remitting multiple sclerosis, and between the latter group of persons and healthy controls. In the same study, MTR failed to distinguish between patients with relapsing remitting multiple sclerosis and healthy controls. Stronger correlations were seen between metrics of psychical and cognitive impairment and the fraction of macromolecular protons compared with MTR. The fraction of macromolecular protons was correlated to MTR in both gray matter ($r = 0.82$) and white matter ($r = 0.52$) regions. The authors concluded that the fraction of macromolecular protons may provide more clinically relevant information than MTR *in vivo*. This is in direct contrast to conclusions derived by other authors (Davies et al., 2004), who instead failed to detect improved

412 **Chapter 26** Clinical application of magnetization transfer imaging

associations between clinical and MRI data when using the fraction of macromolecular protons in lieu of MTR.

26.3.1.1 Summary remarks

It would be hard to refute that MT imaging has substantially improved upon the knowledge we currently possess regarding the pathogenesis and evolution of multiple sclerosis by yielding disease characterization and early detection. These are key elements for clinicians, scientists, and patients, as they ultimately inform on disease severity and lead to treatment personalization. It is also clear that the more advanced physics premise of both the fraction of macromolecular protons and PSR create a conceptually different framework for the assessment of myelin integrity in multiple sclerosis. The analyses on the discriminatory radiological capacity of these biometrics may at times overlap with that of MTR. It is important to note that similar sensitivity to disease, which one may or may not extrapolate from group-comparisons *in vivo*, does not equate to similar specificity to pathology. Such specificity is correctly expected to be superior for newly developed methodologies, e.g., qMT and SIRqMT, as they can clean some of the signal contaminants. Thus, similar sensitivity should not preclude the advancement of more pathologically specific imaging biometrics.

26.3.2 Lessons learned from normal brain development

Due to its safety characteristics and its noninvasive nature, MRI provides an excellent tool to measure brain changes during maturation. In particular, MT imaging has substantially enriched our knowledge on the processes leading to healthy human brain development (Dubois et al., 2014).

MTR computations of different white matter structures during the pre-term period, e.g., gestational age between 26 and 34 weeks, show that the genu and splenium of the corpus callosum increase MTR values before the periventricular white matter and the posterior limb of the internal capsule. It is believed that the corpus callosum is at this stage more densely packed, but not necessarily more myelinated. On the contrary, MTR grows exponentially during the first two years of a healthy child's life, reaching a plateau at around the 7th year of life, though such increases do not necessarily mirror brain volume changes. Post-term maturation of the white matter as monitored by changes in MTR does not follow a synchronous pattern across the brain. Occipital and frontal regions reach a mature stage earlier (between 12 and 15 months) than the splenium and genu of the corpus callosum (around 18 months).

MTR has allowed understanding that seemingly healthy basal ganglia and white matter structures may be significantly less myelinated (lower MTR) in children with developmental delay compared to healthy children, from the age of seven months old (Tang et al., 2020). Such differences are likely due to a defective myelination of the brain, which occurs in earlier developmental stages and would not be detectable using clinical scans.

26.3.2.1 Summary remarks

Much has been learned regarding brain maturation using MT imaging. It is to be noted, though, that fetal and infant MT imaging is limited due to specific, but at this time nearly insurmountable, challenges with fetal MRI. The most important difficulty is the presence of intra-uterine movements, which one cannot minimize. The same limitation applies to MRI of infants, as sedation is allowed only for clinical imaging. Clearly, research efforts must be devoted to implement fast protocols that do not penalize accuracy. Those MRI protocols must also deliver robust corrections for movement-related artifacts.

26.3.3 Exploiting the MT effect but not looking for myelin

The locus coeruleus is a thin nucleus located on the dorsal portion of the pons. Much has yet to be discovered regarding the physiology of the locus coeruleus, but it is nonetheless known that it is the major source of norepinephrine in the central nervous system. As such, the locus coeruleus plays an important role in arousal, memory, attention, pain modulation, and stress response via its widespread connections through the spinal cord, brain stem, cerebellum, and cerebral cortex. The importance of imaging the locus coeruleus is related to the unique MRI contrast exerted by the neuromelanin, a pigment contained in the neurons of the locus coeruleus. Loss of neuromelanin in the locus coeruleus is secondary to degeneration of the neuronal cells producing it, and has been found to be reflective of neuronal loss located elsewhere in the brain and ultimately linked to conditions such as Parkinson's and Alzheimer's diseases, multisystem atrophy, depression, and aging, among others (Liu et al., 2017). *In vitro* studies have shown that the neuromelanin-iron complex shortens the T_1 in a concentration-dependent manner. This shortening of the T_1 reduces the MT effect, likely due to an increase of the water protons interacting with any T_1-shortening paramagnetic intracellular ions. As a result, PSR maps offer superb visibility of the locus coeruleus (see Fig. 26.5), which presents with lower PSR compared to surrounding pontine tegmentum (Trujillo et al., 2019).

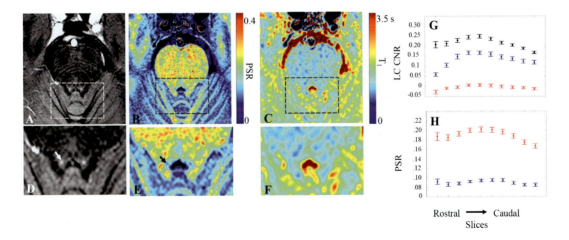

FIGURE 26.5 MT contrast of the locus coeruleus.

T_1-weighted high-resolution 3T MRI (A and D) color-coded PSR (B, E) and T_1 (C, F) maps of the pons with a representation of the locus coeruleus (white arrow in D and black arrow in E, the right locus coeruleus only is indicated). Contrast-to-noise ratio (CNR) between the locus coeruleus (LC) and the pontine tegmentum obtained from the MT-weighted (black), neuromelanin-sensitive turbo-spin-echo (blue), and reference (red) images (G). Differences are seen in PSR between the LC (blue line in H) and the pontine tegmentum, chosen as a reference surrounding tissue (red line in H). The values show the mean ± standard error of mean across 10 high-resolution MRI slices, where the locus coeruleus was identified.

414 **Chapter 26** Clinical application of magnetization transfer imaging

26.3.3.1 Summary remarks

Imaging of the locus coeruleus provides an example in which MT contrast is mostly exploited for its effect secondary to the free water molecules rather than that of macromolecules. This mechanism of contrast may form the basis for future investigations.

26.4 Why is MT imaging not part of routine clinical protocols?

Innumerable studies have shown the ability of MT imaging to identify and characterize microscopic disease changes in lesional and non-lesional areas of patients with various neurological conditions. Clinicians recognize the utility of MT imaging in adding pathological specificity to clinical MRI findings. Clinician-scientists are well aware that the discovery of therapeutics with neuroprotective or neuro-regenerative properties is *the challenge* of the 21st century in medicine. The identification of an MRI biomarker that can serve as a measure of outcome for proof-of-concept clinical trials to test the effect of experimental molecules plays a central role in this effort. Incorporating MTI as a measure of outcome in clinical trials has the potential to indirectly indicate the effectiveness of a given medication in restoring myelin integrity or preventing neurodegenerative changes.

Yet, despite this awareness and the body of literature available on the efficacy of MT imaging, none of the available MT imaging metrics has experienced a successful clinical translation in day-to-day clinical operations and in clinical trials.

Over the past decades, a tremendous effort has been made by MRI scientists to deliver different open source codes to promote immediate access to the scientific community. Easy propagation of this information has been crucial to permit study replications, ultimately strengthening the validity of the clinical findings reported from independent small studies. However, though this is a fundamental prerequisite for clinical translation, it is clearly not sufficient to achieve it.

The day-to-day clinical routine prioritizes features of an MRI protocol which may not necessarily parallel its strengths. First, in clinical practice, *time is of the essence*, as all radiology centers aim to perform the highest number of scans in the shortest time possible, to be able to serve as many patients as possible and meet the needs of the community. In addition, long acquisition scans may not always be feasible for patients, due to claustrophobia or uncontrollable movements. These factors indicate that protocols equipped with robust tools for motion correction are important for a successful translation.

Secondly, radiologists prefer qualitative over quantitative assessments, as those are quicker and easier to obtain. For example, the fundamental reason why diffusion-weighted images have become the most popular parametric modality in clinical practice is because the effect of water restriction on both mean diffusivity and apparent diffusion coefficient maps is visualized by the means of positive and negative signals. This factor makes findings on diffusion-weighted images easily identifiable and allows for fast interpretation, as it is anticipated to occur in the setting of an acute stroke.

One can certainly expect that a clinical radiologist could report quantitative measurements of a few regions of interest. To optimize the value of this information and facilitate the work of the radiologist, the referring neurologist should be very specific in the information that is required of them. Imaging protocols should also be equipped with robust registration methods such that one could easily register the scans of the same patients acquired at different time points and compare derived MT quantities.

Though this appears feasible and ideal, in reality patients do not undergo imaging in the same center consistently. Thus, quantitative assessments over time may not be comparable for patients traveling from site to site.

To this end, an important step toward clinical translation is a high degree of reproducibility and consistency across centers. Though studies have investigated and confirmed that MTR is likely a stable measure across different scanners and vendors (Schwartz et al., 2019), less is known regarding PSR and the fraction of macromolecular protons.

Last, but not least, normative reference values are lacking. Thus, even if MT imaging were to be available to clinicians on a regular basis, and even if quantities could be extrapolated and delivered routinely, it is unlikely that one would be able to derive meaningful information on individual patients at this stage, as normative reference values are not available.

All in all, while seemingly discouraging, the above-mentioned issues instead represent an opportunity for improvement and the next step on the pathway towards clinical translation.

26.5 Conclusions

Quantitative metrics derived from MT imaging have advanced the knowledge of neurological conditions by 1) providing pathological characterization of focal lesions visible on conventional T_1-w or T_2-w MRI; 2) depicting occult pathology in areas of otherwise normal appearing tissue; and 3) identifying changes indicative of reparative or developmental mechanisms. By providing a conceptually novel framework of improved specificity and reproducibility, advanced and more contemporary qMT methods have the potential to further improve our assessments and monitoring of neurological conditions, both in the clinic and at the site of clinical trials. However, despite decades of scientific effort, MT-based methods have not made it to clinical practice, due to a fundamental unresolved conflict between the scientific premise for excellence in imaging and practical clinical needs. As seen with therapeutics, Phase IV clinical studies should be implemented to further refine each newly developed MRI technique until the scientific needs meet those of the community clinician, and each method finds its niche in the clinic.

Declaration of conflicts of interest

Francesca Bagnato has received speaker or advisory-board-related honoraria from EMD-Serono, Janssen, Novartis, Sanofi. She serves/ed as site PI of multicenter studies sponsored by EMD-Serono and Novartis.

Funding

Francesca Bagnato receives research support from Biogen Idec, the National Multiple Sclerosis Society (RG-1901-33190), the National Institutes of Health (R21 NS116434-01A1), and the Veterans Health Administration (1T01 CX002160-01). Francesca Bagnato did not receive financial support for the research, authorship and publication of this article.

416 **Chapter 26** Clinical application of magnetization transfer imaging

References

Bagnato, F., Hametner, S., Franco, G., Pawate, S., Sriram, S., Lassmann, H., et al., 2018. Selective inversion recovery quantitative magnetization transfer brain MRI at 7T: clinical and post-mortem validation in multiple sclerosis. J. Neuroimaging 28, 380–388.

Brochet, B., Dousset, V., 1999. Pathological correlates of magnetization transfer imaging abnormalities in animal models and humans with multiple sclerosis. Neurology 53, S12–S17.

Chen, J.T., Easley, K., Schneider, C., Nakamura, K., Kidd, G.J., Chang, A., et al., 2013. Clinically feasible MTR is sensitive to cortical demyelination in MS. Neurology 80, 246–252.

Combès, B., Kerbrat, A., Ferré, J.C., Callot, V., Maranzano, J., Badji, A., et al., 2019. Focal and diffuse cervical spinal cord damage in patients with early relapsing-remitting MS: a multicentre magnetisation transfer ratio study. Mult. Scler. 25, 1113–1123.

Davies, G.R., Tozer, D.J., Cercignani, M., Ramani, A., Dalton, C.M., Thompson, A.J., et al., 2004. Estimation of the macromolecular proton fraction and bound pool T2 in multiple sclerosis. Mult. Scler. 10, 607–613.

Dubois, J., Dehaene-Lambertz, G., Kulikova, S., Poupon, C., Hüppi, P.S., Hertz-Pannier, L., 2014. The early development of brain white matter: a review of imaging studies in fetuses, newborns and infants. Neuroscience 276, 48–71.

Fjaer, S., Bø, L., Lundervold, A., Myhr, K.M., Pavlin, T., Torkildsen, Ø., Wergeland, S., 2013. Deep gray matter demyelination detected by magnetization transfer ratio in the cuprizone model. PLoS ONE 8, e84162.

Fjaer, S., Bø, L., Myhr, K.M., Torkildsen, Ø., Wergeland, S., 2015. Magnetization transfer ratio does not correlate to myelin content in the brain in the MOG-EAE mouse model. Neurochem. Int. 83–84, 28–40.

Janve, V.A., Zu, Z., Yao, S.Y., Li, K., Zhang, F.L., Wilson, K.J., et al., 2013. The radial diffusivity and magnetization transfer pool size ratio are sensitive markers for demyelination in a rat model of type III multiple sclerosis (MS) lesions. NeuroImage 74, 298–305.

Khodanovich, M.Y., Sorokina, I.V., Glazacheva, V.Y., Akulov, A.E., Nemirovich-Danchenko, N.M., Romashchenko, A.V., et al., 2017. Histological validation of fast macromolecular proton fraction mapping as a quantitative myelin imaging method in the cuprizone demyelination model. Sci. Rep. 7, 1–12.

Ikonomidou, V.N., Richert, N.D., Vortmeyer, A., Tovar-Moll, F., Bielekova, B., Cook, N.E., et al., 2013. Evolution of tumefactive lesions in multiple sclerosis: a 12-year study with serial imaging in a single patient. Mult. Scler. 19, 1539–1543.

Inglese, M., van Waesberghe, J.H., Rovaris, M., Beckmann, K., Barkhof, F., Hahn, D., et al., 2003. The effect of interferon beta-1b on quantities derived from MT MRI in secondary progressive MS. Neurology 60, 853–860.

Lommers, E., Simon, J., Reuter, G., Delrue, G., Dive, D., Degueldre, C., et al., 2019. Multiparameter MRI quantification of microstructural tissue alterations in multiple sclerosis. NeuroImage Clin. 23, 101879.

Li, K., Zu, Z., Xu, J., Janve, V.A., Gore, J.C., Does, M.D., et al., 2010. Optimized inversion recovery sequences for quantitative T1 and magnetization transfer imaging. Magn. Reson. Med. 64, 491–500.

Liu, K.Y., Marijatta, F., Hämmerer, D., Acosta-Cabronero, J., Düzel, E., Howard, R.J., 2017. Magnetic resonance imaging of the human locus coeruleus: a systematic review. Neurosci. Biobehav. Rev. 83, 325–355.

Mottershead, J.P., Schmierer, K., Clemence, M., Thornton, J.S., Scaravilli, F., Barker, G.J., et al., 2003. High field MRI correlates of myelin content and axonal density in multiple sclerosis - a post-mortem study of the spinal cord. J. Neurol. 250, 1293–1301.

Newbould, R.D., Nicholas, R., Thomas, C.L., Quest, R., Lee, J.S., Honeyfield, L., et al., 2014. Age independently affects myelin integrity as detected by magnetization transfer magnetic resonance imaging in multiple sclerosis. NeuroImage Clin. 31, 641–648.

Ou, X., Sun, S.W., Liang, H.F., Song, S.K., Gochberg, D., 2009a. The MT pool size ratio and the DTI radial diffusivity may reflect the myelination in shiverer and control mice. NMR Biomed. 22, 480–487.

Ou, X., Sun, S.W., Liang, H., Song, S., Gochberg, D., 2009b. Quantitative magnetization transfer measured pool-size ratio reflects nerve myelin content in ex vivo mice. Magn. Reson. Med. 61, 364–371.

Pohl, H.B.F., Porcheri, C., Mueggler, T., Bachmann, L.C., Martino, G., Riethmacher, D., et al., 2011. Genetically induced adult oligodendrocyte cell death is associated with poor myelin clearance, reduced remyelination, and axonal damage. J. Neurosci. 31, 1069–1080.

Richert, N.D., Frank, J.A., 1999. Magnetization transfer imaging to monitor clinical trials in multiple sclerosis. Neurology 53, 29–32.

Riva, M., Ikonomidou, V.N., Ostuni, J.J., van Gelderen, P., Auh, S., Ohayon, J.M., et al., 2009. Tissue-specific imaging is a robust methodology to differentiate in vivo T1 black holes with advanced multiple sclerosis-induced damage. Am. J. Neuroradiol. 2009 (30), 1394–1401.

Schmierer, K., Scaravilli, F., Altmann, D.R., Barker, G.J., Miller, D.H., 2004. Magnetization transfer ratio and myelin in postmortem multiple sclerosis brain. Ann. Neurol. 56, 407–415.

Schmierer, K., Tozer, D.J., Scaravilli, F., Altmann, D.R., Barker, G.J., Tofts, P.S., et al., 2007. Quantitative magnetization transfer imaging in postmortem multiple sclerosis brain. J. Magn. Reson. Imaging 26, 41–51.

Schwartz, D.L., Tagge, I., Powers, K., Ahn, S., Bakshi, R., Calabresi, P.A., NAIMS Cooperative, 2019. Multisite reliability and repeatability of an advanced brain MRI protocol. J. Magn. Reson. Imaging 50, 878–888.

Sled, J.G., Pike, G.B., 2000. Quantitative interpretation of magnetization transfer in spoiled gradient echo MRI sequences. J. Magn. Res. 145, 24–36.

Tang, X., Zhang, H., Zhou, J., Kang, H., Yang, S., Cui, H., et al., 2020. Brain development in children with developmental delay using amide proton transfer-weighted imaging and magnetization transfer imaging. Pediatr. Invetig. 4, 250–256.

Trujillo, P., Petersen, K.J., Cronin, M.J., Lin, Y.A., Kang, H., Donahue, M.J., et al., 2019. Quantitative magnetization transfer imaging of the human locus coeruleus. NeuroImage 200, 191–198.

Turati, L., Moscatelli, M., Mastropietro, A., Dowell, N.G., Zucca, I., Erbetta, A., et al., 2015. In vivo quantitative magnetization transfer imaging correlates with histology during de- and remyelination in cuprizone-treated mice. NMR Biomed. 28, 327–337.

Yarnykh, V.L., Bowen, J.D., Samsonov, A., Repovic, P., Mayadev, A., Qian, P., et al., 2015. Fast whole-brain three-dimensional macromolecular proton fraction mapping in multiple sclerosis. Radiology 274, 210–220.

PART 9

Quantitative relaxometry and parameter mapping

CHAPTER

Quantitative relaxometry mapping

27

Mark D. Does[a,b]

[a]*Department of Biomedical Engineering, Vanderbilt University, Nashville, TN, United States*
[b]*Institute of Imaging Science, Vanderbilt University Medical Center, Nashville, TN, United States*

27.1 Introduction

The quantitative characterization and interpretation of water proton relaxation rate/time constants (i.e., *relaxometry*) offers the potential to probe the composition and structure of tissue at the microscopic scale. When applied with MRI, quantitative relaxometry becomes a tool to generate 2D or 3D maps of relaxometry parameters and, potentially, tissue characteristics. Ideally, quantitative relaxometry provides measures that are independent of the measurement method, and thus provides absolute values that can be meaningfully compared between tissues, across time, or across individuals. Even better, these measures, or at least changes or variations in these measures, can potentially be interpreted in terms of changes or variations in specific tissue characteristics.

This chapter presents and discusses some ideas behind the most common types of water proton relaxometry mapping: MRI measures of T_1, T_2, and T_2^*. It focuses only on methods that treat the spatial encoding independently of the relaxation encoding, resulting in data that are analyzed in two steps: reconstruction of a series of relaxation-weighted images, followed by estimation of relaxation rates/time-constants and related signal parameters. MR fingerprinting, which is one approach that jointly inverts the spatial and relaxation encodings, is presented in the next chapter (Chapter 28). Likewise, this chapter primarily considers methods that report on one particular relaxation phenomenon at a time; methods that jointly report on multiple relaxation, and other quantitative parameters, are presented subsequently in Chapter 29.

Practical quantitative MRI relaxometry can be viewed in terms of two inter-related components: modeling and methods. In an ideal world, there is an additional step of experimentally validating both the methods and the model, but that challenge lies beyond the scope of this chapter.

27.1.1 Modeling

Strictly speaking, this component is not required. For a given objective, it may be sufficient to simply measure and report quantitative relaxation characteristics. However, if the ultimate objective is to gain insight into tissue characteristics, then a model relating relaxation to tissue characteristics is needed. In defining a model, one strives for a complexity that is sufficient to report relevant tissue characteristics with suitable accuracy, while also a simplicity that allows a suitable precision, given scan time and other acquisition constraints.

Advances in Magnetic Resonance Technology and Applications, Volume 4, ISSN 2666-9099. https://doi.org/10.1016/B978-0-12-822479-3.00043-9
Copyright © 2021 Elsevier Inc. All rights reserved.

422 **Chapter 27** Quantitative relaxometry mapping

27.1.2 Methods

A pulse-sequence is needed that suitably encodes both spatial and relaxation information to meet the requirements of the application and, potentially, the modeling. Given the pulse-sequence and the intended signal model, a signal equation can be defined. At this step, one must be careful to consider, and either avoid or account for, potential confounding factors, such as B_1 and B_0 variations. Generally, it is desirable to invert the observed signal into model parameters using a maximum-likelihood analysis, although a good approximation (such as using a linearization of the signal equation) may be acceptable. For the most part, consideration of different analysis algorithms falls outside the scope of this chapter.

27.2 Modeling

There is no comprehensive and general model explaining water proton relaxation in tissue, but effective models can relate longitudinal and/or transverse relaxation in brain to concentrations of iron and macromolecular protons and volume fractions of myelin, intra-axonal space, extra-axonal space, and cerebrospinal fluid. A good starting point for practical models of relaxation in tissue is a compartment model, in which all the protons within a given imaging voxel are ascribed to one or more different compartments. These compartments may be defined at a macroscopic (e.g., partial volume average of two tissues), microscopic (e.g., intra- and extra-cellular spaces), or molecular scale (e.g, water, macro-molecular protons).

Despite the known complexity of tissue, in many cases relaxation is approximately mono-exponential. In such cases, different compartments of protons are treated as one, with the reasoning that their relaxation rates are similar and/or that magnetization exchanges between these compartments rapidly enough to make them indistinguishable (the fast-exchange limit). Similarly, with the inclusion of paramagnetic materials into a water compartment, it is usually sound to assume that all the water interacts with the material equally through rapid mixing. Then, the observed relaxation rate, R, can be modeled as a linear combination of terms from each compartment and paramagnetic material, such as

$$R = f_a R_a + f_b R_b + f_c R_c + r[P], \tag{27.1}$$

where the f and R terms are the fractional sizes and relaxation rates from compartments 'a', 'b,' and 'c', while r and $[P]$ are the relaxivity and concentration, respectively, of some paramagnetic agent.

In cases where relaxation cannot be well described as a mono-exponential process, multi-compartment models with slow or intermediate rates of exchange models can be used. In the slow-exchange limit, the multi-compartment model is simply the sum of multiple single-compartment models. The net signal, $S(t)$, is described by a linear combination of functions, with the amplitude of each function being proportional to the size of its corresponding proton compartment. For example, a signal decay from three compartments in slow exchange is simply

$$S(t) = S(0) \left[f_a \exp(-R_a t) + f_b \exp(-R_b t) + f_c \exp(-R_c t) \right], \tag{27.2}$$

where the f and R terms are defined as above.

27.2 Modeling 423

With an intermediate rate of inter-compartmental magnetization exchange, this one-to-one correspondence between signals and compartments is lost, and coupled Bloch equations are needed to describe the net magnetization. For example, modifying Eq. (27.2) to include exchange between the three compartments results in this matrix algebra signal equation,

$$\mathbf{S}(t) = S(0) \exp(\mathbf{L}t) \mathbf{f}, \tag{27.3}$$

where $\mathbf{f}$ contains the compartment fractional sizes, $\mathbf{f} = [f_a, f_b, f_c]^T$, $\mathbf{L}$ contains the compartmental relaxation and exchange rate constants

$$\mathbf{L} = \begin{pmatrix} -R_a & & \\ & -R_b & \\ & & -R_c \end{pmatrix} + \begin{pmatrix} -(k_{a,b} + k_{a,c}) & k_{b,a} & k_{c,a} \\ k_{a,b} & -(k_{b,a} + k_{b,c}) & k_{c,b} \\ k_{a,c} & k_{b,c} & -(k_{c,a} + k_{c,b}) \end{pmatrix},$$

and $\exp(\mathbf{L}t)$ is a matrix exponential. Here, $k_{a,b}$ is the first-order exchange rate constant from compartment "a" to compartment "b", and likewise for similar k terms. The observed signal is the sum of the elements of $\mathbf{S}(t)$ (a 3×1 column matrix for any value t).

Similar equations can be worked out for systems and sequences of arbitrary complexity. In the particular case of modeling the exchange of longitudinal magnetization between water and macromolecular protons (i.e., magnetization transfer, see Chapter 24), the observed signal comes only from water (due to short T_2 of the macromolecular compartment) and is invertible into relative compartment sizes and an exchange rate. More generally, though, inverting such a signal into a multi-compartment model with intermediate exchange rates is either impossible, due to lack of information in the signal, or impractical, due to sampling and signal-to-noise ratio (SNR) requirements. Consequently, modeling of quantitative relaxometry in the brain generally relies on either a slow-exchange (multi-exponential relaxation) or fast-exchange (mono-exponential relaxation) assumption.

27.2.1 Transverse relaxation

Transverse relaxation in gray matter is close to mono-exponential, and the same may hold true in white matter if the echo time is long enough. Fast-exchange modeling is appropriate for these situations and linear models, such as Eq. (27.1), may be applied. For example, linear models have been used to relate increases in R_2 and R_2^* to increases in local iron content; however, increased myelin or macromolecular content will also cause the rate increases. Conversely, cell death or myelin loss will increase water content and, in-turn, decrease the relaxation rate. Consequently, a scalar measure of R_2 or R_2^* may be sensitive to a variety of tissue characteristics, but is inherently limited in specificity. In evaluating changes in pathological conditions, because the progression of various neurodegenerative diseases may involve competing influences on transverse relaxation, interpretation of a simple mono-exponential characterization of transverse relaxation is difficult.

Specificity can be improved with transverse relaxometry using multi-exponential models. For white matter, a suitable measurement of transverse relaxation reveals multi-exponential relaxation, which can be effectively modeled in terms of multiple water compartments. Myelin water is one of the compartments, and it has a relatively short transverse relaxation time of $T_{2,my} \approx 15$ ms (subscript "my" indicates "myelin"), but not too short that it cannot be measured. Myelin also serves as a physical barrier to separate and define two additional water compartments: the water inside myelinated axons ("intra-axonal")

424   Chapter 27 Quantitative relaxometry mapping

and the water outside myelinated axons ("extra-axonal"). In the brain, these two non-myelin compartments cannot easily be resolved by T_2 relaxometry, and so their signals are typically lumped together in the 40 ms $\lesssim T_{2,ie} \lesssim$ 500 ms domain, with a dominant component at $\approx$ 80 ms at 3T. If there exists partial-volume averaging of cerebrospinal fluid (CSF), then CSF becomes a fourth compartment to consider, which is easily distinguished by its long relaxation time ($T_{2,csf} \gtrsim$ 500 ms).

The transverse relaxation in white matter can be described by a spectrum of T_2 components, such as the spectra shown in Fig. 27.1. It is common to interpret the white matter T_2-spectrum with the slow-exchange assumption, which allows the definition of the so-called myelin water fraction (MWF) as the fraction of the signal within the myelin T_2 domain (5 ms $\lesssim T_{2,my} \lesssim$ 30 ms). However, there is evidence that inter-compartmental magnetization exchange in white matter is fast enough to violate the slow-exchange model. Exchange of magnetization between compartments results in a systematic shift of the spectral components to lower T_2 values and a decreasing amplitude of the shorter-lived component. Thus MWF, defined as the fraction of the signal in the short-T_2 domain, is likely an underestimation of the fraction of water in myelin, with a bias that depends also on factors that influence the exchange rate, such as axon diameter and myelin thickness. That being said, no other signal in the brain exhibits a T_2 similar to that of myelin water, which provides MWF a unique level of specificity amongst relaxometry measures, particularly in comparison to those results from a mono-exponential analysis. Also, comparison of MWF with various forms of histology have generally supported the conclusion that MWF is strongly correlated with myelin content.

For multi-exponential T_2^* relaxometry, a similar compartmental model can be used, with a few important differences. First, the model must now include the influence of macroscopic field variations. A first-order characterization of these field variations assumes that they are linear in space (i.e., field gradients in the X-, Y-, and Z-directions), which imparts a "sinc" function modulation on the net transverse magnetization. This signal variation must be mitigated or removed before the compartmental model can be considered. Second, compartment-level variations in magnetic susceptibility will create orientation-dependent resonance frequency differences among compartments and may need to be considered. Some previous work has ignored these effects and analyzed the magnitude signal as multi-exponential, identically to analysis of T_2 relaxation. However, the inclusion of frequency shift terms, ω, may help distinguish signals at the compartmental level, leading to a discrete, 3-compartment complex model, such as

$$S(t) = S(0) \left[f_{my} \exp\left(-R_{my}t + i\omega_{my}t\right) + f_{ax} \exp\left(-R_{ax}t + i\omega_{ax}t\right) + f_{ex} \exp\left(-R_{ex}t + i\omega_{ex}t\right) \right],$$

(27.4)

where subscripts "my", "ax", and "ex", indicate myelin, intra-axonal, and extra-axonal. This model has the added benefit of distinguishing the intra- and extra-axonal water compartments, providing a more detailed view of the white matter microstructure. Of course, T_2^* relaxometry is also subject to bias, due to inter-compartmental magnetization exchange. However, to the extent that $T_2^* < T_2$ at the compartment level (i.e., not simply due to meso- or macroscopic field variations), the compartmental model of T_2^* may be closer to the slow exchange limit than the T_2 model, and therefore less biased by the exchange.

27.2.2 Longitudinal relaxation

Due to the aforementioned effect of magnetization transfer, modeling longitudinal relaxation generally requires consideration of both water and macromolecular proton compartments. If one also considers

27.2 Modeling

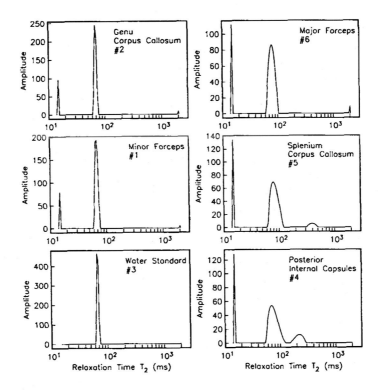

FIGURE 27.1

Representative T_2-spectra from human white matter, *in vivo*. The spectra show significant variation in the MWF and the long-lived component T_2 values across regions. With permission from Whittall et al. (1997).

two water compartments—myelin and non-myelin, as done for T_2—the inclusion of associated macromolecules brings the total number of proton compartments to four. On the time-scale of T_1, none of the associated exchange rates is likely in either the fast- or slow-exchange limit, resulting in four proton compartments with coupling between each water compartment and its associated macromolecular proton compartment, and between the two water compartments. This model is too complicated to be solved in almost all experimental situations, and so a simplified model is necessary.

In practice, with finite relaxation sampling and SNR, a bi-exponential model is often sufficient to describe longitudinal relaxation in the brain, which dictates a simplified two-compartment model. One such model is to consider all the water protons as one compartment and all the macromolecular protons as another. In this case, the fast-relaxing signal component is due to exchange of magnetization from the macromolecular to the water protons, and with sufficient relaxation sampling of the bi-exponential relaxation, the model can be solved to estimate the relative size of the macromolecular compartment. This compartment size is seen as a measure of myelin content, because of the relatively large macromolecular content of myelin. Alternatively, one can interpret the bi-exponential relaxation in terms of two water compartments, myelin and non-myelin, with the fast-relaxing component attributed to myelin water, while acknowledging that exchange between these compartments is likely fast enough to prevent

426 **Chapter 27** Quantitative relaxometry mapping

one-to-one association between signal components and water compartments. Regardless of the model, there is experimental evidence that the relative amplitude of the fast-relaxing signal component varies in relation to myelin content. This relationship remains empirical and the extent to which this signal is a consequence of magnetization transfer or myelin water is unclear, but bi-exponential T_1-relaxometry provides a measure of myelin content, nonetheless.

It is also possible to avoid the complexity of multi-exponential modeling by avoiding the fast-relaxing signal component during acquisition. In this case, a mono-exponential, fast-exchange model has been used to describe the slow-relaxing component of longitudinal relaxation in the brain. With this approach, the relaxation rate of the slow-relaxing T_1 component is modeled as the sum of two or more terms, such as an offset plus contributions from iron content and either myelin or macromolecular content. For example,

$$R_1 = R_0 + r_{\text{Fe}}[Fe] + r_{\text{M}}[M], \tag{27.5}$$

where r_{Fe} and r_{M} are relaxivities of iron and macromolecular protons, respectively, and $[Fe]$ and $[M]$ are corresponding concentrations. Similar models may include other paramagnetic substances, such as oxygen or various exogenous agents.

27.3 Methods

For each type of relaxometry covered in this chapter, the most common acquisition methods are presented and briefly discussed below. In all cases, the choice of pulse sequence parameters depends on a number requirements, including spatial resolution, volume of coverage, scan time, and expected relaxation characteristics (multi- or mono-exponential, in particular). It is important to note that the choice of relaxation weightings should be selected to provide the highest precision possible for a given application and scan time. For any given signal equation, acquisition parameters, and model parameters, the precision of the resulting relaxometry parameters can be computed using conventional propagation of error estimation (see inset). Analysis methods that denoise images and/or constrain or regularize solutions can enhance precision at the cost of (maybe negligible) inaccuracy. These methods should be considered for any quantitative relaxometry, however they are beyond the scope of this chapter.

Precision of parameter estimates

Define an observed signal, s, with a signal model, g, that depends on an independent parameter (α) and unknown relaxometry parameters (β), plus added noise, v,

$$s(\alpha) = g(\alpha, \beta) + v. \tag{27.6}$$

With N measurements of s, $\mathbf{s} = [s_1, s_2, \ldots, s_N]^{\text{T}}$, made unique by N independently adjusted values of α, assume that a maximum-likelihood estimate (MLE) of M unknown model parameters can be computed, $\widehat{\beta} = \left[\hat{\beta}_1, \hat{\beta}_2, \ldots, \hat{\beta}_M\right]^{\text{T}}$. When v is added Gaussian noise, the MLE is the least-squares solution

$$\widehat{\beta} = \text{MLE}[\mathbf{s}, g(\alpha, \beta)] = \underset{\beta}{\text{argmin}} \|\mathbf{s} - g(\alpha, \widehat{\beta})\|_2. \tag{27.7}$$

In this estimation process, the noise propagates from the signal to the estimated parameters. A first-order approximation of the resulting covariance matrix of the fitted parameters, $\Sigma_{\widehat{\beta}}$, is

$$\Sigma_{\widehat{\beta}} = \sigma^2 \left(\mathbf{J}^{\mathsf{T}}\mathbf{J}\right)^{-1}, \tag{27.8}$$

where the Jacobian ($\mathbf{J}$) is

$$\mathbf{J} = \begin{bmatrix} \partial g(\alpha_1)/\partial(\beta_1) & \partial g(\alpha_1)/\partial(\beta_2) & \cdots & \partial g(\alpha_1)/\partial(\beta_M) \\ \partial g(\alpha_2)/\partial(\beta_1) & \partial g(\alpha_2)/\partial(\beta_2) & \cdots & \partial g(\alpha_2)/\partial(\beta_M) \\ \vdots & \vdots & \ddots & \vdots \\ \partial g(\alpha_N)/\partial(\beta_1) & \partial g(\alpha_N)/\partial(\beta_2) & \cdots & \partial g(\alpha_N)/\partial(\beta_M) \end{bmatrix}. \tag{27.9}$$

Thus the standard error in the kth estimated parameter is

$$\sigma_{\beta_k} = \sigma \sqrt{\left[\left(\mathbf{J}^{\mathsf{T}}\mathbf{J}\right)^{-1}\right]_{kk}}, \tag{27.10}$$

with subscript kk indicating the kth diagonal element of this $M \times M$ matrix. This is also widely known as the Cramér–Rao lower bound of the error. Note that this type of analysis can be generalized to account for non-central χ-distributed noise and parameter constraints—see suggested readings—but this simple form is often suitable to define best choices of the independent acquisition parameter, α.

27.3.1 T_2 and T_2^*

The most common acquisition methods for T_2 and T_2^* relaxometry follow the direct approach—excite transverse magnetization, and then sample it at multiple time points while it decays. Fig. 27.2 shows both the multiple spin echo (MSE) and multiple gradient echo sequence (MGE) sequences, suitable for T_2 and T_2^* relaxometry, respectively. Imaging gradients are not included in these diagrams, because these sequences can be applied as 2D or 3D acquisitions and with various k-space sampling strategies.

For the MGE sequence and mono-exponential relaxation, the signal equation is simply $S(t_n) = S(0)\exp(-t_n/T_2^*)$, where $t_n = T_{E1} + (n-1)T_E$ for $n = 1$ to N_E. The excitation flip angle, θ_{exc} should be set at the Ernst angle, and the choice of the number of echoes (N_E) and echo spacing (T_{E1} and T_E) are not especially important, but the signal decay should be sampled to approximately two time constants, $t_{N_E} \gtrsim 2T_2^*$. For a multi-exponential analysis, a signal equation of the form of Eq. (27.2) or Eq. (27.4) is suitable, and echo spacing should be short enough to capture the myelin water signal. Because there is little wasted time between echoes, there is little cost to minimizing the echo spacing—the precision cost for increased receiver bandwidth is almost entirely recouped by the precision gain of more samples of the signal decay. Typically, $T_E \approx 2\,\text{ms}$ is used. Also, to avoid T_1-weighting of the myelin water signal, a relatively long repetition time, $T_R \approx 2\,\text{s}$, and near full excitation, $\theta \approx 85°$, are recommended. Note that this limitation undermines one of the benefits of the MGE compared with the MSE approach to measure transverse relaxation.

Transverse relaxometry with a MSE acquisition is primarily used for multi-exponential signals and has both advantages and disadvantages compared with the MGE approach. With RF refocusing, the effects of background field variations and inter-compartmental frequency difference can be ignored. The presence of refocusing pulses, though, brings two complications. First, time is needed between acqui-

428   **Chapter 27** Quantitative relaxometry mapping

sitions for RF refocusing and associated crusher gradients, which dictates that the echo spacing can be reduced only so much before the cost of increased receiver bandwidth limits the precision of the parameter mapping. For any given case scenario, optimal echo spacing can be determined using propagation of error calculations (see inset), but for many human scanner situations, $T_E \approx 8\,\text{ms}$ is nearly optimal.

A second consequence of RF refocusing is that, due to B_1^+ and B_0 variations, one cannot assume it is perfect or spatially uniform. The refocusing pulse flip angle can be incorporated into the signal equation, most commonly through the extended phase graph (EPG) model. Then the N_E signal magnitudes, $\mathbf{s} = [S(T_E), S(2T_E), \ldots, S(N_E T_E)]^T$, can be expressed in terms of a spectrum of K T_2 component amplitudes, $\mathbf{d} = [d_1, d_2, \ldots, d_K]^T$ as

$$\mathbf{s} = \mathbf{A}\mathbf{d}, \tag{27.11}$$

with

$$\mathbf{A} = \begin{pmatrix} \text{EPG}(T_E, T_{2,1}, \theta, T_1) & \text{EPG}(T_E, T_{2,2}, \theta, T_1) & \cdots & \text{EPG}(T_E, T_{2,K}, \theta, T_1) \\ \text{EPG}(2T_E, T_{2,1}, \theta, T_1) & \text{EPG}(2T_E, T_{2,2}, \theta, T_1) & \cdots & \text{EPG}(2T_E, T_{2,K}, \theta, T_1) \\ \vdots & \vdots & & \vdots \\ \text{EPG}(N_E T_E, T_{2,1}, \theta, T_1) & \text{EPG}(N_E T_E, T_{2,2}, \theta, T_1) & \cdots & \text{EPG}(N_E T_E, T_{2,K}, \theta, T_1) \end{pmatrix}.$$

Eq. (27.11) can be solved using a separable non-linear approach. Using assumed values for θ and T_1, the T_2 spectrum, $\hat{\mathbf{d}}$ can be estimated using a non-negative least squares algorithm. This can be repeated with varied θ to find the $\hat{\theta}$ and $\hat{\mathbf{d}}$, which provide the least square solution. To combat noise, additional spectral or spatial regularization can also be incorporated into this solution.

27.3.2 T_1

Methods for mapping of the longitudinal relaxation time constant, T_1 (or rate constant, $R_1 = 1/T_1$), tend to fall into one of two broad categories: variable-timing or variable-flip-angle. With variable timing, the longitudinal magnetization, M_z, is perturbed, and then allowed to relax for a (variable) delay before excitation and signal acquisition. This approach can be implemented with a two-pulse and two-delay pulse sequence, as shown in Fig. 27.2, and in various forms known as inversion-recovery (IR). The first pulse, labeled with flip angle θ_{inv}, prepares the longitudinal magnetization for relaxation weighting (usually, by inversion, although actual inversion is not required), and the second pulse, θ_{exc}, excites the magnetization for signal measurement. The sequence is repeated N_{IR} times with varied t_{inv} delay and a fixed sequence repetition time, T_R $(= t_{\text{inv}} + t_{\text{del}})$. (Note that this sequence can also be run with a fixed t_{del} or by independently varying both t_{inv} and t_{del}, but here we assume a constant T_R.)

At steady state, the solution to the Bloch equation for M_z for the IR sequence is

$$M_z(t_{\text{inv}}) = \frac{M_0 \left[1 - (1 - \cos\theta_{\text{inv}}) E_{\text{inv}} - \cos\theta_{\text{inv}} E_R\right]}{1 - \cos\theta_{\text{inv}} \cos\theta_{\text{exc}} E_R}, \tag{27.12}$$

where $E_{\text{inv}} \triangleq \exp(-t_{\text{inv}} R_1)$ and, similarly, $E_R \triangleq \exp(-T_R R_1) = \exp(-(t_{\text{inv}} + t_{\text{del}}) R_1)$. With $T_1 \sim 1\,\text{s}$, T_R must be relatively long (see below), and, consequently, the full longitudinal magnetization is usually excited every repetition. Thus with $\theta_{\text{exc}} \approx 90°$, the signal equation becomes

$$S(t_{\text{inv}}) = S_0 \left[1 - (1 - \cos\theta_{\text{inv}}) E_{\text{inv}} - \cos\theta_{\text{inv}} E_R\right], \tag{27.13}$$

27.3 Methods

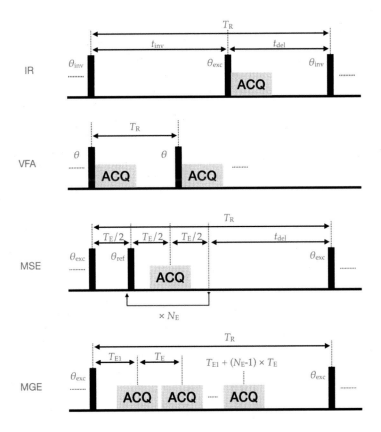

FIGURE 27.2

Four pulse sequence diagrams for relaxometry. The IR and VFA sequences are two different approaches for T_1 relaxometry, whereas MSE and MGE are used for T_2 and T_2^* relaxometry, respectively.

where S_0 includes a proportionality constant relating transverse magnetization to signal amplitude, and T_2 weighting after excitation is ignored. This signal equation is recommended, because it accounts for imperfect magnetization inversion, which is difficult to avoid. An adiabatic or composite pulse inversion pulse may allow the assumption that $\theta_{inv} \approx 180°$, reducing Eq. (27.13) to two unknowns, but one should be careful to ensure the performance of such a pulse. Note, for example, that a typical hyperbolic secant pulse on a clinical scanner will incur significant T_2-dependence and may provide only $\theta_{inv} \approx 150°$ for myelin water. When $t_d \gg T_1$ and $\theta_{inv} \approx 180°$, Eq. (27.13) reduces to the common (and commonly misused) $S(t_{inv}) = S_0 [1 - 2E_{inv}]$.

In contrast to IR, the variable-flip-angle (VFA) approach typically uses a one-pulse (θ), one-delay (T_R) sequence. At steady state, assuming complete spoiling of transverse magnetization prior to each excitation, the solution of the Bloch equation leads to a signal equation,

$$S(\theta) = \frac{S_0 \sin\theta \, (1 - E_R)}{1 - \cos\theta \, E_R}; \quad (27.14)$$

430 Chapter 27 Quantitative relaxometry mapping

again ignoring transverse relaxation after excitation. The sequence is repeated N_θ times with varied excitation flip angles. This approach accommodates short repetition times through low flip angle excitation and gradient echo readout; however, estimating T_1 requires independent knowledge of θ for each acquisition.

To compare these two very different looking approaches, consider the precision of their resulting estimated T_1 values. Assume that all images are corrupted with added Gaussian noise with variance σ^2, and that an unbiased and maximum-likelihood estimate of T_1 is generated by voxel-wise fitting of image data to Eqs. (27.13) or (27.14), for IR and VFA images, respectively. For both cases, the expected variance in this estimate, $\sigma_{T_1}^2$, can be computed by first-order propagation of error (see inset). To be more general, define $\zeta \triangleq \sigma/\sigma_{T_1}$ as a normalized measure of this precision, and then to account for scan time differences between the two methods, define $\eta = \zeta/\sqrt{T_{scan}}$ as a normalized measure of precision *efficiency*. Here, T_{scan} is the scan time per spatial encoding step: $T_{scan} = N_{IR} \times T_R$ for fixed-T_R IR sequence and $T_{scan} = N_\theta \times T_R$ for the VFA sequence.

For a quantitative example, consider a sample with $T_1 = 1$ s. For IR, use $N_{IR} = 3$ different t_{inv} values (the minimum required to estimate the three free parameters in Eq. (27.13)), and assume an actual inversion pulse flip $\theta = 180°$ (which does not limit the general conclusions, below). For VFA, use $N_\theta = 2$ (again, the minimum required). For each T_R over a wide range of possible T_R values, find the t_{inv} and θ values that maximize ζ for the IR and VFA methods, respectively. The resulting ζ and η values for both IR and VFA methods are plotted in Fig. 27.3. For a single scan, IR can provide $\approx 3\times$ greater precision in estimating T_1, but it comes at the cost of a much longer scan time ($T_R \gtrsim 10 \times T_1$ for IR, compared with $T_R \approx T_1$ for VFA). If repeated VFA scans are averaged, this precision can be recouped, which is what the precision efficiency, η, reports. In this case, we see that the peak precision efficiency is similar for the two methods, but VFA provides peak efficiency over a range of relatively short T_R values ($T_R \lesssim 0.4 \times T_1$), whereas similar efficiency with IR requires a longer scan ($T_R \approx 3.5 \times T_1$).

Thus, for whole brain coverage and high resolution, VFA is the more attractive of these two methods; however, it comes with its own challenges. As mentioned above, the VFA method is predicated upon independent knowledge of θ, which requires an additional mapping of the transmit field, B_1^+. For multi-slice acquisitions, this problem is exacerbated by slice profile variations across different flip angles. Also, the VFA signal equation (27.14) holds only when transverse magnetization is completely spoiled immediately prior to each excitation, which can be a challenge, particularly when operating at the shortest T_R values, as one might want for a whole-brain 3D measurement. These are not insurmountable problems, and VFA is widely used for mono-exponential T_1-relaxometry.

The conventional IR method, as used to calculate the precision efficiency plotted in Fig. 27.3, has plenty of time during the t_{inv} and t_{del} periods that is not used to acquire signal, which provides substantial opportunity for acceleration. One option is to interleave and shuffle multi-slice acquisitions, which extends coverage at no additional scan time cost. Another option is the Look-Locker method, in which M_z is sampled at multiple t_{inv} times following each inversion (much like the MSE sequence samples transverse magnetization multiple times after a given excitation). Alternatively or additionally, one can sample more of k-space during each acquisition, such as with a snapshot, echo-planar, or fast-spin-echo readout. One popular variation is the MP2RAGE method (magnetization-prepared rapid gradient echo), which acquires snapshots at two different effective t_{inv} times following each inversion. With the assumption of ideal adiabatic inversion, these two images are sufficient to estimate a mono-exponential T_1 relaxation time, with similar efficiency to the VFA method.

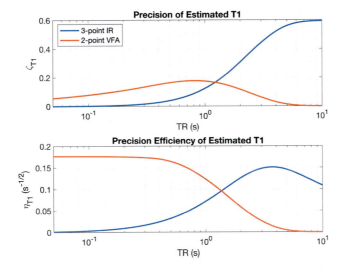

FIGURE 27.3

Normalized precision, ζ (top) and normalized precision efficiency, η (bottom) for example regarding IR and VFA measurements.

27.4 Conclusion and suggested readings

This chapter has briefly introduced the basic ideas behind the most common forms of relaxometry. Modeling the relationship between brain tissue microstructure and relaxometry requires assumptions and known simplifications; thus, interpretation of any tissue characteristic should be made with some level of caution. The standard acquisition methods presented here represent only a starting point for defining a full imaging protocol. Meeting both scan time and precision requirements requires further consideration and, in practice, is often challenging.

The current material has been presented without citing original literature. However, the information provided, and much more, can be found in the following suggested readings, sorted by topic area:

Modeling relaxometry in brain:
- Whittall, K. P., Mackay, A. L., Graeb, D. A., Nugent, R. A., Li, D. K. B., and Paty, D. W. In vivo measurement of T2 distributions and water contents in normal human brain. Magnet Reson Med 37, 34–43 (1997)
- Laule, C., Vavasour, I. M., Kolind, S. H., Li, D. K. B., Traboulsee, T. L., Moore, G. R. W., and MacKay, A. L. Magnetic resonance imaging of myelin. Neurotherapeutics 4, 460–484 (2007)
- Cohen-Adad, J. What can we learn from T2* maps of the cortex? Neuroimage 93, 189–200 (2014)
- Barta, R., Kalantari, S., Laule, C., Vavasour, I. M., MacKay, A. L., and Michal, C. A. Modeling T1 and T2 relaxation in bovine white matter. J Magn Reson 259, 56–67 (2015)
- Does, M. D. Inferring brain tissue composition and microstructure via MR relaxometry. Neuroimage 182, 136–148 (2018)

432 **Chapter 27** Quantitative relaxometry mapping

- Möller, H. E., Bossoni, L., Connor, J. R., Crichton, R. R., Does, M. D., Ward, R. J., Zecca, L., Zucca, F. A., and Ronen, I. Iron, Myelin, and the Brain: Neuroimaging Meets Neurobiology. Trends Neurosci 42, 384–401 (2019)

Compartmental modeling and exchange:

- Woessner, D. E. Brownian motion and its effects in NMR chemical exchange and relaxation in liquids. Concept Magnetic Res 8, 397–421 (1996)
- Dortch, R. D., Horch, R. A., and Does, M. D. Development, simulation, and validation of NMR relaxation-based exchange measurements. J Chem Phys 131, 164502 (2009)

Magnetization transfer effects on relaxometry:

- Edzes, H. T. and Samulski, E. T. The measurement of cross-relaxation effects in the proton NMR spin-lattice relaxation of water in biological systems: Hydrated collagen and muscle. J Magn Reson 31, 207–229 (1978)
- Gochberg, D. F. and Gore, J. C. Quantitative magnetization transfer imaging via selective inversion recovery with short repetition times. Magn Reson Med 57, 437–441 (2007)
- Malik, S. J., Teixeira, R. P. A. G., and Hajnal, J. V. Extended phase graph formalism for systems with magnetization transfer and exchange. Magnet Reson Med 80, 767–779 (2018)

Mono-exponential models of iron and more:

- Hardy, P. A., Gash, D., Yokel, R., Andersen, A., Ai, Y., and Zhang, Z. Correlation of R2 with total iron concentration in the brains of rhesus monkeys. J Magn Reson Imaging 21, 118–127 (2005)
- Rooney, W. D., Johnson, G., Li, X., Cohen, E. R., Kim, S., Ugurbil, K., and Springer, C. S. Magnetic field and tissue dependencies of human brain longitudinal 1H2O relaxation in vivo. Magn Reson Med 57, 308–318 (2007)
- Langkammer, C., Krebs, N., Goessler, W., Scheurer, E., Ebner, F., Yen, K., Fazekas, F., and Ropele, S. Quantitative MR Imaging of brain iron: A postmortem validation study. Radiology 257, 455–462 (2010)
- Stüber, C., Morawski, M., Schäfer, A., Labadie, C., Wähnert, M., Leuze, C., Streicher, M., Barapatre, N., Reimann, K., Geyer, S., Spemann, D., and Turner, R. Myelin and iron concentration in the human brain: A quantitative study of MRI contrast. Neuroimage 93, 95–106 (2014)
- Berkowitz, B. A. Oxidative stress measured in vivo without an exogenous contrast agent using QUEST MRI. J Magn Reson 291, 94–100 (2018)

MRI methods of relaxometry:

- Prasloski, T., Mädler, B., Xiang, Q., MacKay, A., and Jones, C. Applications of stimulated echo correction to multicomponent T2 analysis. Magnet Reson Med 67, 1803–1814 (2012).
- Alonso-Ortiz, E., Levesque, I. R., and Pike, G. B. MRI-based myelin water imaging: A technical review. Magnet Reson Med 73, 70–81 (2014)
- Lutti, A., Dick, F., Sereno, M. I., and Weiskopf, N. Using high-resolution quantitative mapping of R1 as an index of cortical myelination. Neuroimage 93, 176–188 (2014)
- Lee, J., Hyun, J., Lee, J., Choi, E., Shin, H., Min, K., Nam, Y., Kim, H. J., and Oh, S. So you want to image myelin using MRI: An overview and practical guide for myelin water imaging. J Magn Reson Imaging 53, 360–373 (2021)

27.4 Conclusion and suggested readings

Propagation of error:

- Lankford, C. L. and Does, M. D. On the inherent precision of mcDESPOT. Magnet Reson Med 69, 127–136 (2013)
- Bouhrara, M. and Spencer, R. G. Fisher information and Cramér-Rao lower bound for experimental design in parallel imaging. Magnet Reson Med 79, 3249–3255 (2018)
- Lankford, C. L. and Does, M. D. Propagation of error from parameter constraints in quantitative MRI: Example application of multiple spin echo T2 mapping. Magnet Reson Med 79, 673–682 (2018)

CHAPTER

MR fingerprinting: concepts, implementation and applications

28

Dan Ma

Case Western Reserve University, Cleveland, OH, United States

28.1 Introduction

MR fingerprinting (MRF) is a novel quantitative MR technique that allows simultaneous quantification of multiple tissue properties in a short scan time. Since it was first published in *Nature* in 2013, the technology has demonstrated high scan efficiency for volumetric multi-parametric imaging in times on the order of five to ten minutes, high robustness in scanning different parts of the body including brain, prostate, musculoskeletal system, abdomen and heart, and high accuracy and reproducibility in both phantom and human validations. MRF thus has the potential to enable widespread clinical use and standardization of quantitative MR.

The basic concept of MRF is analogous to the "fingerprinting" technique, where a unique fingerprint, a comprehensive database, and a matching algorithm are required to identify all information in regard to a person. Similarly, the goal of MR fingerprinting is to obtain all physiological or physical properties, such as relaxation, diffusion, perfusion, and so on, of a tissue from its MR signal. The process is to use an imaging sequence to generate different signal signatures (or fingerprints) that depend on many tissue properties simultaneously. Next, a dictionary that contains simulated signals from all foreseeable combinations of tissue properties is generated. Finally, a pattern recognition algorithm is applied to identify signal features, extract underlying tissue properties and convert them into quantitative maps. Based on this general concept, the initial implementation of MRF (Ma et al., 2013) was able to provide four maps (T_1, T_2, off-resonance, and proton density) in 12 seconds per slice of scan time and showed the highest scan efficiency as compared to other fast quantitative methods. The high error tolerance was additionally demonstrated when only 2% of the data were sampled in an accelerated scan, and when the last 20% of a healthy volunteer's scan was motion corrupted.

As compared to conventional quantitative methods, the key innovation of MRF is a fundamental rethinking of the entire acquisition, processing, visualization, and usage of MR images. First, there is no requirement of the signal shape in data acquisition. The signal features can come from signal magnitudes, phases, temporal evolutions, and number of tissue dimensions. To this end, instead of using repeated or serial acquisitions to create exponential curves from all tissues, variable excitation patterns and/or timings are typically applied to create signals with random shapes and to produce a simultaneous sensitivity to multiple tissue properties. Second, the concept of building a dictionary in MRF is also innovative and powerful. A dictionary contains simulated signals based on either analytical models or numerical models. There is a large flexibility of simulating signal evolutions, for example from different time scales, ranging from micro-seconds to the whole acquisition time, and different resolutions,

Advances in Magnetic Resonance Technology and Applications, Volume 4, ISSN 2666-9099. https://doi.org/10.1016/B978-0-12-822479-3.00044-0
Copyright © 2021 Elsevier Inc. All rights reserved.

436 Chapter 28 MR fingerprinting: concepts, implementation and applications

ranging from micrometer scale of a microvasculature network to millimeter scale of an MR voxel. It is also convenient to account for confounding factors in the signal simulation, including commonly faced B_0, B_1 inhomogeneity, and RF imperfections. The comprehensive simulation allows separation of physiological or pathological features from external environmental variations, which enables more accurate and reproducible quantitative estimation. Finally, the model-based pattern recognition permits high error tolerance, which is crucial for clinical translation. Similar to conventional fingerprinting techniques, which often contend with smudges and partial fingerprint information, MR scans also face measurement errors, such as thermal noise, system and gradient imperfections, subject motion, and artifacts from accelerated scans. Some of these errors can be accounted for in the signal simulation, and some can be tolerated directly through pattern recognition. Such acquisition errors may globally reduce the probability of a match, but as long as the errors do not cause another fingerprint to become the most likely match, the correct quantitative identification will still be made. As will be shown in the following sections, the high error tolerance allows highly efficient and robust scans with large acceleration factors. This chapter covers a general overview of MRF technology, current clinical applications, and potential future directions.

28.2 Basic framework of MRF

A flowchart of the basic framework of MRF is illustrated in Fig. 28.1. There are three main compartments of the MRF framework: data acquisition, dictionary generation, and pattern recognition. The data acquisition involves design of sequence parameters (Fig. 28.1A), sampling trajectories (Fig. 28.1B), and reconstruction methods to generate an image series (Fig. 28.1C) or spatial-temporally varying signals (Fig. 28.1F). In parallel, a dictionary is generated through simulation (Fig. 28.1D), based on the prior knowledge of signal models, the sequence parameters, and system conditions. Finally, a matching algorithm is applied to match the acquired signals to the dictionary (Fig. 28.1E). Once the match is identified, the underlying tissue properties can be extracted and translated into quantitative maps (Fig. 28.1G). This flowchart represents a generalized framework, with a large flexibility in the design of each compartment. In the following sections, we will discuss each compartment in more detail.

28.3 Data acquisition

The main goal of the MRF sequence design is to generate incoherent signals that are sensitive to multiple tissue properties of interest and are separable in processing. As described in the introduction, there is no constraint on the signal shapes, so nearly any sequence design can be used as an MRF acquisition, and multiple sequence modules can be combined in a single acquisition. A basic sequence is composed of parameters, including RF pulses (flip angle, phase, frequency, RF profile, power), timing (repetition time TR, echo time TE, inversion time TI), gradients (spatial encoding, spoiling, diffusion/velocity encoding), and number of repetitions or time points. These parameters can be varied selectively or simultaneously during an MRF scan to create temporally and spatially incoherent signals.

Although any design is possible, the majority of the current MRF implementations are based on steady-state sequences, because of their high scan efficiency. This type of sequence consists of a train of excitation, encoding gradients, and readout blocks in one repetition and acquires one or multiple

28.3 Data acquisition

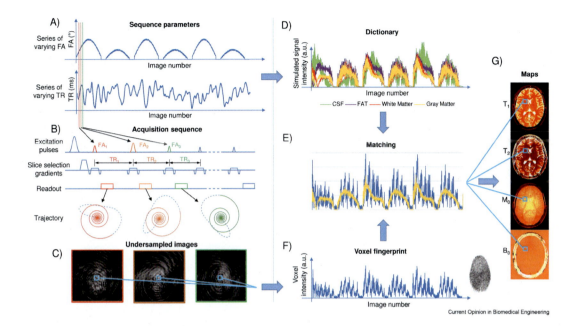

FIGURE 28.1

Overview of the MRF framework. Figure taken from Panda et al. (2017).

echoes in each block (or TR, TR $\leq T_2$). Because there is no time for the spins to fully relax, the acquired signals thus have a mixture of contrasts from T_1, T_2, and other factors such as B_0 and B_1. Opposite from conventional steady-state imaging, where a steady-state signal is desirable and achieved by repeatedly applying the same acquisition blocks, MRF varies parameters in each acquisition block, meaning that the signals are always in a *transient* state. In this way, a larger fraction of the available signal evolution can be used to obtain unique information.

The initial implementation of the MRF scan by (Ma et al., 2013) was based on an inversion-recovery steady-state free-precession sequence (MRF-bSSFP or MRF-TrueFISP), as shown in Fig. 28.1. The choice was based on the extensive existing knowledge about the IR-TrueFISP signal and its sensitivity to T_1, T_2, and off-resonance frequency (Ehses et al., 2013). Fig. 28.1D shows the simulated signal evolutions that would be expected from four commonly encountered tissues of the brain (fat, white matter, gray matter, and cerebrospinal fluid) using Bloch simulation. Each tissue type has characteristic T_1 and T_2 values, and thus each signal evolution has a different shape. Note also that all signals are in transient states, meaning that new signal changes can be expected by acquiring for a longer time.

Although the MRF-TrueFISP sequence provides signals with high SNR and multi-parametric sensitivity, one drawback is the well-known banding artifacts at the locations where the dephasing of the spins exceeds multiples of π (Scheffler and Lehnhardt, 2003). To move such artifacts outside of the anatomy-of-interest, high levels of magnetic field homogeneity or short TR times are required. However, this is challenging in scans performed at high field strengths, or for scans with a large tissue coverage. To overcome these artifacts, MRF scans based on partially spoiled or fully spoiled steady-state sequences were proposed, for example MRF-FISP (Jiang et al., 2015). These sequences introduced unbalanced gradients, which partially or fully spoiled signal coherence, and thus reduced the signal sensitivity to off-resonance. The outputs of these sequences thus only include T_1, T_2, and proton density maps. With the cost of reduced SNR from gradient spoiling, these approaches eliminated banding artifacts, and thus greatly improved the robustness of MRF. Examples of MRF-FISP results from different clinical areas are shown in Fig. 28.2.

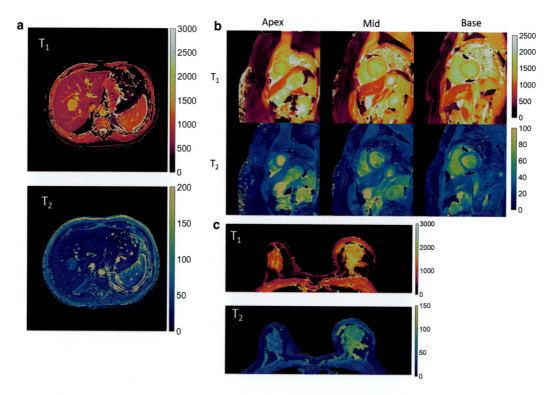

FIGURE 28.2

Examples of MRF maps from (a) an abdominal scan of a patient with lung adenocarcinoma metastatic to the liver, (b) multi-slice cardiac scans of a healthy subject, (c) a breast scan of a patient with invasive ductal carcinoma in left breast. Figure taken from McGivney et al. (2020).

Other sequence variations have been proposed to improve the tissue coverage by using simultaneous multi-slice (SMS, see Chapter 3) (Ye et al., 2016) or 3D imaging (Ma et al., 2018), and to quantify other tissue properties, such as T_2^* (Wang et al., 2019), perfusion (Su et al., 2016), chemical exchange (Heo et al., 2019), and system properties, such as B_0 and B_1 field inhomogeneities (Cloos et al., 2016). Fig. 28.3 shows an example of 3D MRF results of a brain scan, with 1 mm isotropic image resolution from (Ma et al., 2019). As the MRF scans evolved from neural to body imaging, special sequence designs and motion compensation algorithms were proposed to compensate for periodic (cardiac MRF (Hamilton et al., 2017)) or spontaneous motions (MORF (Mehta et al., 2018)). By fully taking advantage of the flexibility in sequence design, work has also been directed to reduce RF energy deposition and to improve patient comfort by directly converting loud scan noise to music (Ma et al., 2015). A detailed summary of these sequences can be found in the review paper by Poorman et al. (2020).

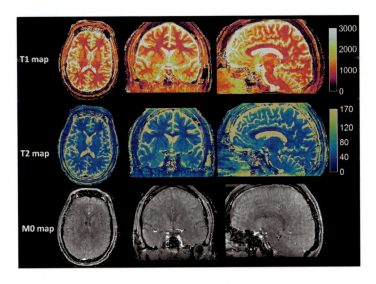

FIGURE 28.3

3D T_1, T_2 and M_0 maps generated from an MRF scan of a healthy subject. Figure taken from Ma et al. (2019).

28.4 Scan acceleration

Because MRF is based on pattern recognition, where the form of all predicted signal evolutions is known, MRF is less sensitive to errors during the measurement than conventional quantitative methods. This feature offers new opportunities to accelerate the MRF scan through rejection of spatial undersampling errors (aliasing). Similar to the sequence design that aims to maximize incoherence in the temporal domain, the key prerequisite of rejection aliasing artifacts through pattern recognition is to make the artifacts incoherent to the true signal.

In the initial implementation (Ma et al., 2013), high scan acceleration was achieved by using a single-shot variable density spiral trajectory in each readout block (Fig. 28.1B). This spiral trajectory only sampled $\sim 1/48^{th}$ of the normally required data for each image, corresponding to a factor of 48 faster scan time. The variable density spiral trajectory was used, because it has higher sampling efficiency and generates incoherent artifacts as compared to Cartesian undersampling. The spiral trajectory was also rotated from one timepoint to the next during the scan, making aliasing artifacts temporally incoherent. The interaction of the temporal and spatial incoherence in MRF facilitated the separation of artifacts and real signals without causing bias in the pattern recognition step. As a result, although the acquired images (Fig. 28.1C) were severely corrupted by aliasing artifacts and the signal evolution

440   Chapter 28 MR fingerprinting: concepts, implementation and applications

from a pixel in Fig. 28.1F was buried in highly oscillating noise, these artifacts were incoherent with the expected MRF signals, so they were largely filtered by the following pattern recognition step in Fig. 28.1E. Fig. 28.1G shows high quality estimates of the tissue property maps without any artifacts present in reconstructed images. Applying such a high undersampling rate substantially reduced the scan time from ~15 minutes of acquiring 1000 fully sampled images to only 12 seconds, making a multi-parametric scan clinically feasible. Higher acceleration factors have been reported by using radial or arbitrary trajectories (Ma et al., 2015; Cloos et al., 2016), simultaneous multi-slice (Ye et al., 2016) and three-dimensional acquisitions (Ma et al., 2018). These acquisition strategies have made MRF scans fast enough for 2D body and cardiac scans within a single breath hold, and 3D whole-brain scans with 1 mm isotropic resolution in less than 6 minutes.

The ability of rejecting artifacts and extracting multiple tissue properties eventually depends on the amount of information acquired from both temporal and spatial domains. To compensate for the low SNR in each image, a high number of images, ranging from hundreds to thousands, or more, temporal samples are typically required, which prolongs the scan time. One approach to reduce the scan time is to apply advanced reconstruction algorithms to improve the quality of the image series before feeding them to the pattern recognition step. To this end, any reconstruction algorithms that explore spatial and temporal redundancy and enforce data consistency, such as parallel imaging, compressed sensing, and low-rank subspace, can be applied. A discussion of reconstruction algorithms that have been applied to MRF can be found in various review papers, e.g., (McGivney et al., 2020). An important aspect of MRF reconstruction is that the image series (Fig. 28.1C) are an intermediate output of the entire framework. It is thus not intuitive to determine how "good" the necessary image quality is in the reconstruction step to obtain noise-free quantitative maps, as demonstrated by the difference in image quality between Figs. 28.1C and 28.1G. For this reason, studies have started to focus on evaluating the quality of the maps, instead of each reconstructed image, by optimizing the whole framework, which will be discussed later in this chapter.

28.5 Dictionary generation

In MRF, a dictionary is constructed that contains signal evolution from all foreseeable combinations of tissue- and system-related properties. All signal evolutions are simulated on a computer using analytical or numerical models to predict spin behaviors. The inputs of the simulation are acquisition parameters, such as flip angles, RF phases, dephasing from gradients, TRs and TEs, tissue properties of interest, such as T_1, T_2, diffusion, perfusion, and system properties, such as RF slice profile, B_0 and B_1 inhomogeneities. The output of the simulation is typically a 2D matrix, with a temporal dimension containing signals at each TE, and the property dimension containing all possible combinations of tissue and system properties.

There are various ways of creating a dictionary. The classic Bloch equations were used in the initial implementation to simulate signal evolutions from an MRF-TrueFISP scan that are dependent on T_1, T_2, and off-resonance. Extended phase graph (EPG) (Weigel, 2015), which was used in MRF-FISP and other FISP-based implementations, is a more efficient way of simulating echo signals from sequences with spoiling gradients. In MR vascular fingerprinting (MRvF) (Christen et al., 2014), a micro-vasculature network was constructed, which contained 96 randomly distributed vessels, to simulate vascular fingerprints from a gradient echo sampling of the FID and SE (GESFIDE) sequence. The signals from MRvF depended on three tissue properties, vessel radius R, cerebral blood volume (CBV), and the oxygenation saturation level (SO$_2$). Other tissue properties, such as T_2^*, intra-voxel phase distribution, flow, diffusion, and so on, have been incorporated into dictionary simulation in other studies as well. Several studies used multi-compartmental models to account for partial volumes or tissue interactions, such as tissue and pass-through artery models for MRF-ASL, water-fat models for water-fat separation, and two-compartment magnetization transfer and chemical exchange models. Apart from tissue properties, Ma and colleagues demonstrated that simulating slice profile and B$_1$ effects in the MRF-TrueFISP dictionary improved the accuracy and robustness of the results (Ma et al., 2017). This correction method applies to other sequences as well, because slice profile and B$_1$ are two main confounding factors that deviate actual flip angles from the ideal inputs. In most MRF applications, the dictionary only needs to be generated once prior to imaging, and can be used for multiple subjects. One example of an exception is cardiac MRF (Hamilton et al., 2017), in which ECG triggering was applied during the scan so that each readout was planned in the diastole of the heartbeat. In this case, a subject-specific dictionary had to be generated after each scan.

The size of the dictionary depends on the complexity of the signal models, the number of properties-of-interest, as well as the range and step size of each property. Ideally, a dictionary should contain samples of multi-dimensional property space with a wide range and infinitely fine resolution. In practice, there is a balance between resolution and size of the dictionary. The practical choice of range and resolution of the simulation may depend on anatomy and prior-knowledge of the target properties. For example, an MRF-TrueFISP dictionary for neuro imaging may have possible T_1 values between 100 ms to 5000 ms (in increments of 20 ms below 2000 ms and in an increment of 300 ms above), T_2 values between 20 and 3000 ms (in increments of 5 ms below 100 ms, and an increment of 10 ms above), and off-resonance values between -400 to +400 Hz (an increment of 1 Hz between $\pm$ 40 Hz, and larger increment above). As the model becomes more complex and the number of inputs increases, the simulation time and size of the dictionary can become a challenge for MRF implementation. For example, the dictionary for MRF-FISP has 18,838 columns, representing all possible T_1 and T_2 combinations. The dictionary for MRF-TrueFISP has an additional off-resonance dimension, which increases the dictionary size to 563,784 columns. In the case where the sequence is also sensitized to quantify T_1, T_2, off-resonance and T_2^*, the number of columns was reported to be over 30 million in (Wang et al., 2019).

To mitigate the size of the dictionary, various methods have been proposed to compress either the time or/and property dimensions of the dictionary. Singular value decomposition (SVD) was used to reduce the time dimension, enabling a compression of 80–99% by projecting the dictionary onto a subspace spanned by the first few singular vectors (McGivney et al., 2014). Computing the SVD of a large matrix can be memory-intensive, and in the case where the full dictionary may be too large to store and process, a randomized SVD approach has been applied to approximate the singular vectors of the dictionary, without needing to store the full dictionary in memory (Yang et al., 2018). The number of elements in the tissue property will grow exponentially as the number of inputs increases, which is more problematic. Papers both by Yang (Yang et al., 2018) and Hamilton (Hamilton et al., 2015) proposed two-step mapping methods. In the first step, initial estimate of the tissue properties, such as T_1, T_2, and chemical exchange, were derived by matching the acquired signal to a coarse dictionary, where the step size of each tissue property is large. The second step is to refine the estimation by using either polynomial interpolation or gradient descent to determine more accurate results. Deep learning methods may be a natural fit to address the challenge in dictionary size, because all elements in the dictionary are from simulation, and thus can provide infinite numbers of training data. Once trained,

442 **Chapter 28** MR fingerprinting: concepts, implementation and applications

the network can generate signal evolutions using feedforward calculation that's more than 100 times faster. Yang et al. used generative adversarial networks (GAN) to efficiently generate MR fingerprints, reducing the simulation time of a MRF-FISP dictionary from 2 hours to 7 seconds (Yang et al., 2020). Fast dictionary simulation through deep-learning is also beneficial when the dictionary needs to be updated for each scan, such as for cardiac MRF (cMRF). Hamilton and Seiberlich (2020) proposed a fully connected network to generate a cMRF dictionary in less than 1 s when given ECG timing information as input, which removed a major bottleneck in cMRF data processing.

28.6 Pattern recognition

After the acquisition and dictionary generation, the final step is to generate multiple quantitative maps through pattern recognition. This step selects a signal vector or a weighted set of signal vectors from the dictionary that best corresponds to the observed signal evolution. All the tissue or system properties that were used to build this signal vector in the dictionary can then be retrieved simultaneously. Currently, the most commonly used method calculates the inner product between the acquired signal in each pixel and all signal vectors from the dictionary. The signal vector in the dictionary with the highest inner product values is considered as the "match". The implementation of this method is straightforward, and the dot-product result is not affected by scaling or constant offset between the two signals. This is an exhaustive search method that guarantees the global maximum within the range of the simulation, and has been shown to be accurate and robust to the high degree of aliasing artifacts in several of the initial MRF studies.

One can immediately recognize that the computational time of this exhaustive searching method depends linearly on the size of the dictionary, which can be prohibitively long in some cases. Calculating the inner product in the low-rank subspace after SVD compression proposed by McGivney and colleagues is 3–5 times faster (McGivney et al., 2014). Gauley and colleagues proposed a fast group matching method that first divided the full dictionary into groups based on the inherent correlation of the signals in the dictionary and filtered out all groups with poor matching possibilities. The dot-product was then only performed in a few groups with high correlation to the acquired signals. It was reported that the computational time was nearly two orders of magnitude faster than direct matching (Cauley et al., 2015). Since 2018, several machine learning approaches have been proposed to accelerate the pattern matching step, or to bypass the dictionary generation and exhaustive search steps to directly generate maps from the acquired images. In the latter case, a neural network was trained to learn a nonlinear mapping, which took measured signals as inputs and directly outputs tissue property maps (Chen et al., 2020). This approach has lower memory requirement since only the network weights and biases need to be saved. The processing time is also substantially shorter, because only a rapid feedforward calculation is needed. The details of machine learning methods are reviewed by Hamilton and Seiberlich (2020).

28.7 New promise for clinical translation

Quantitative MR is one major step closer to establishing imaging biomarkers for disease diagnosis and treatment. It may become a paradigm shift for converting the current standard-of-care of visual and

28.7 New promise for clinical translation

qualitative MR diagnosis to a quantitative acquisition and analysis framework. These tissue property maps would provide reproducible numbers that are associated with the underlying microstructure and microenvironment of tissues, which may enable earlier disease detection, more accurate diagnosis, and better treatment monitoring. In summary, the key benefits of MRF for clinical applications include high scan efficiency and robustness, multi-dimensional sensitivity and specificity, and high repeatability.

First, MRF is a technology that allows simultaneously multi-parametric imaging in a clinically feasible time. All the quantitative maps are from the same scan, so they are perfectly co-registered. In addition, MRF signal-based partial volume analysis allows tissue-segmentation from the same data and from the same pattern recognition step, providing additional segmented maps (such as gray matter, white matter, CSF) without using other post-processing tools. Fig. 28.4 shows the 3D tissue fraction maps generated from the MRF scan of the same volunteer as from Fig. 28.3. All image positions are the same as Fig. 28.3. Currently, MRF scans for various anatomies have been developed. For example, high-resolution brain imaging for both adult and pediatric patients have been achieved with a total scan time of 19 seconds for a single slice and 6 minutes to cover the whole brain (Chen et al., 2019); sub-millimeter (0.6x0.6 mm^2) hip articular cartilage imaging with a scan time of only 1.2 minutes (Cloos et al., 2019); 2D kidney imaging in 15 seconds within a single breath hold, and 3D breast imaging in 6 minutes; and cardiac cine imaging for combined ejection fraction, T_1 and T_2 in 10 seconds. MRF scans have also been robustly applied on 1.5T, 3T, and 7T scanners. These maps can be used to synthesize

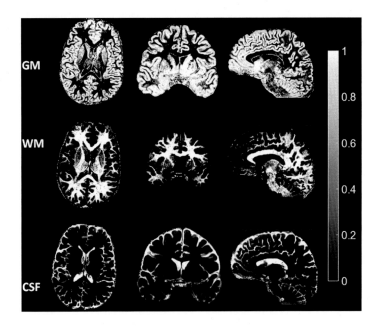

FIGURE 28.4

3D brain tissue fraction maps, including gray matter, white matter and CSF, generated from an MRF scan of a healthy subject. Figure taken from Ma et al. (2019).

infinite numbers of weighted images, including T_1-weighted, T_2-weighed, and FLAIR images that are commonly seen in clinical MR, without additional scan. An overview of clinical areas where the MRF scans were applied can be found in the review paper by Poorman et al. (2020).

Second, apart from improved scan efficiency, the concept of simultaneous encoding and quantification of multiple tissue properties is actually essential to gain multi-dimensional tissue sensitivity and specificity. In fact, signals acquired from any MR scan are inevitably affected by multiple physiological and physical properties. If these properties are quantified separately, by assuming that other effects are negligible, the unique joint sensitivity is no longer retained. This multi-dimensional quantification has become a main approach to resolve complicated, but real tissue environments. In this sense, multi-parametric analysis would allow a more comprehensive characterization of pathological processes and therapeutic responses.

Finally, MRF has shown high repeatability and reproducibility in both phantom and *in vivo* studies. Jiang et al. initially performed a repeatability study using the ISMRM/NIST relaxation phantom. The phantom was scanned over 34 consecutive days, and the variance was within 5–8% (Jiang et al., 2017a). Körzdörfer et al. conducted 2D MRF scans on healthy volunteers on 10 scanners from a single manufacturer, including different models at four different sites. The intra-scanner repeatability was in the range of 2%–3.1% for T_1 and 3.1%–7.9% for T_2 (Körzdörfer et al., 2019a). Table 28.1 lists the T_1 and T_2 values measured from various brain regions from this study. Accounting for actual scan conditions and tissue complexity has made the MRF scan more robust and the resulting maps more reproducible.

Table 28.1 Measured T_1 and T_2 values in Segmented Tissue Compartments of the brain.

Tissue Compartment	$\overline{T_1}$ (msec)	$^\sigma\overline{T_1}$ (msec)	$^\sigma T_1$ (msec)	$\overline{T_2}$ (msec)	$^\sigma\overline{T_2}$	$^\sigma T_2$ (msec)
Gray matter	1372	12.5	144.6	52.7	0.7	9.0
Frontal gray matter	1385	22.1	146.5	55.6	1.2	8.5
Temporal gray matter	1397	13.2	147.8	53.2	0.9	8.5
Parietal gray matter	1360	26.9	148.2	51.1	0.7	9.2
Occipital gray matter	1368	17.3	161.3	53.6	0.8	12.0
Insula gray matter	1398	37.2	133.7	52.6	0.9	9.3
Thalamus	1286	26.3	77.7	45	2.4	3.6
Caudate nucleus	1359	31.1	63.7	50.1	2.8	3.3
Putamen	1266	35.8	61.7	45	2.7	4.1
White matter	954	15.4	64.4	38.7	0.9	3.1
Frontal white matter	933	16.5	63.4	37.7	1.2	2.9
Temporal white matter	954	16.7	65.5	38.7	1.1	2.6
Parietal white matter	946	16	58.1	39.4	0.9	2.9
Occipital white matter	980	18.5	66.8	39.9	0.7	2.9
Pallidum	1008	43.6	49.1	29.1	2.2	1.9
Corpus callosum	871	21.2	44.0	33.9	0.9	3.0
Cerebrospinal fluid	2330	69.5	604.7	213.9	22.9	165.9

Note.—The mean value ($\overline{T_1}$ and $\overline{T_2}$), the standard deviation of the mean value over volunteers ($^\sigma\overline{T_1}$ and $^\sigma\overline{T_2}$), and the average standard deviation in a region of interest ($^\sigma T_1$ and $^\sigma T_2$) are displayed.

28.8 Clinical applications

In general, the clinical applications of MRF seek to address two questions: whether multi-parametric maps are sensitive to detect subtle changes of tissues that are typically overlooked by clinical MR protocols, and whether these maps are able to improve specificity of disease diagnosis and treatment management. The purpose is to provide image-based guidance for election of appropriate diagnostic and management options, as well as accurate prognostic information in the early course of management. In this chapter, we will focus on neural imaging applications.

It is known that normal tissues possess various amount of water content, macromolecular, and iron concentrations, which manifests as different contrasts in MR images. In one of the first human studies of MRF, Badve and colleagues used T_1 and T_2 from MRF to measure the brain parenchymal changes related to normal aging and demonstrated gender-based differences in normal aging (Badve et al., 2015). Chen et al. used 2D MRF to track T_1, T_2, and myelin fraction changes of normal developing children in the first five years of life. A marked decrease of T_1 and T_2 values until the age of 20 months was observed, followed by a slower decrease for all white matter region (Chen et al., 2019).

Tissue and disease characterization is one of the main applications of quantitative MRI, by comparing tissue properties between normal and diseased tissues, or among pathological tissues with various types. Badve and colleagues used T_1 and T_2 maps acquired from 31 patients to successfully differentiate low-grade gliomas from metastases and from peritumoral regions of glioblastomas (Badve et al., 2017). A multi-modality multi-parametric study analyzed 18F-FET PET-MRI and MRF images from 42 patients with suspected primary brain tumors, and showed that the combined analysis enabled high-quality image-based tumor decoding and phenotyping for differentiation of low-grade vs high-grade gliomas, and for prediction of the mutational status of ATRX, IDH1, and 1p19q (Haubold et al., 2019).

Multi-parametric image analysis has also shown promising results in characterizing other neurological diseases. Ma et al. demonstrated that MRF maps were able to distinguish epileptic lesions from non-epileptic lesions. Fig. 28.5 shows MR images from a patient with right temporal-parietal epilepsy (Ma et al., 2019). The official radiology report indicated bilateral periventricular nodular heterotopias (PVN) with uniform signal intensity (Fig. 28.5a). Review of the MRF maps revealed a significant T_1 increase in the nodules at the right occipital horn from the T_1 map (Fig. 28.5b). This distinct signal abnormality was not appreciable on the conventional MRI. The patient underwent sterostatic-EEG, targeting multiple brain regions, including the nodules as shown in Fig. 28.5c. The nodules with abnormal signals shown by MRF were consistent with the interictal SEEG signal and ictal onset of a typical seizure. In addition to the findings of heterotopia, elevated T_1 values were also seen in the normal-appearing WM adjacent to the active epilepsy lesion (Fig. 28.5e,f), which was also not identified by conventional MRI images. A separate study (Liao et al., 2018) used MRF to identify subtle T_1 and T_2 changes in hippocampus between patients with mesial temporal lobe epilepsy (MTLE) and healthy controls. Quantitative comparison among both sides of the hippocampus in patients and healthy controls reduced incorrect diagnosis of bilateral hippocampal sclerosis (HS) as unilateral, and thus improved the diagnosis rate of MTLE from 69.7% to 96.9% (Liao et al., 2018). Other than T_1 and T_2, the MRF-ASL scan developed by Su and colleagues was applied to Moyamoya patients. Diminished CBF and lengthened bolus arrival time were identified from three patients that could not be detected with regular ASL (Su et al., 2016).

446 **Chapter 28** MR fingerprinting: concepts, implementation and applications

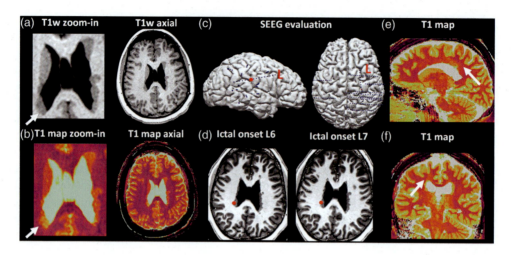

FIGURE 28.5

MRF results from an epilepsy patient with right temporo-parietal epilepsy. Figure taken from Ma et al. (2019).

28.9 New techniques and directions

The promising results of MRF are fostering further development of this technology for larger scale clinical studies for various diseases. One direction of the new techniques focuses on optimizing the throughput of the entire imaging and post-processing pipeline in clinical settings. This involves optimizations targeting a minimal scan time, high accuracy and precision, or high sensitivity to various tissue properties.

Though flexibility in sequence design is a main advantage of the MRF framework, it can lead to a prohibitively large optimization problem. In addition, MRF is a framework with multiple steps, including acquisition design, image reconstruction, dictionary generation, and pattern matching. The quantitative results are thus dependent on the performance of all steps. For example, as demonstrated in Fig. 28.1, the pattern matching step has a high error tolerance for measurement errors, even though the SNR of the reconstructed image series is substantially lower than the criteria for typical image reconstruction methods. This nonlinearity is one example of the challenges to define a proper cost function within a computationally feasible range for MRF: the optimization of each individual step does not necessarily lead to an overall better performance, and metrics of analysis for each step in the process must be implemented. The complexity of the cost function will affect both the optimization landscape of the problem and the computational techniques that are able to provide a reliable solution. Although current studies typically optimize MRF acquisition and reconstruction separately, optimization of multiple steps of MRF may be incorporated in a comprehensive framework (Jordan et al., 2021), and this would be a significant step in optimizing the full MRF framework.

Comprehensive computational modeling and resolving complex tissue environments is another direction. Many studies have proposed models with more tissue or system properties, or with multicompartmental microstructure networks to explain MR signals. Similar to other model-based analysis, many discussions have arisen about which model is more valid (as "all models are wrong") and how to interpret the results (one tissue property is not accurate if not accounting for dozens of other tissue properties). Especially in MRF, as all acquisition parameters can be flexibly varied across time, many effects become time-varying and can no longer be considered as simple scaling factors. One related issue is that the advantage of dictionary-based matching may decrease as more complicated models (>4 tissue properties) are considered. Many studies have proposed to use conventional optimization methods, or hybrid pattern matching and local minimization methods to address this issue.

In recent years, machine learning and deep learning techniques have emerged in MRF development and clinical studies with two main directions. The first direction is to use deep learning to improve MRF technology, for example efficiently building large size dictionaries or directly predicting tissue properties by using end-to-end deep learning models. These methods have shown promising results for solving nonlinear, non-convex, and high dimensional problems. The second direction is to use deep learning to integrate MRF with other clinical information, such as from clinical examinations, laboratory tests, and other image modalities, to assist clinical diagnosis and treatment planning. Because all MRF scans are prospective scans, limited amounts of human data, especially patients' data, currently posit one of the main challenges for the development of new MRF technology and clinical applications. However, MRF development over recent years has made this quantitative imaging technology readily available for clinical adoption, with short scan time, simple implementation, and high reproducibility. As more clinical evidence become available in the near future, MRF may eventually become a critical step of promoting data-driven and evidence-based precision medicine.

References

Badve, C., et al., 2015. Simultaneous T 1 and T 2 brain relaxometry in asymptomatic volunteers using magnetic resonance fingerprinting. Tomography 1 (2). https://doi.org/10.18383/j.tom.2015.00166.

Badve, C., et al., 2017. MR fingerprinting of adult brain tumors: initial experience. American Journal of Neuroradiology 38 (3), 492–499. https://doi.org/10.3174/ajnr.A5035.

Cauley, S.F., et al., 2015. Fast group matching for MR fingerprinting reconstruction. Magnetic Resonance in Medicine 74 (2), 523–528. https://doi.org/10.1002/mrm.25439.

Chen, Y., et al., 2020. High-resolution 3D MR fingerprinting using parallel imaging and deep learning. NeuroImage 206, 116329. https://doi.org/10.1016/j.neuroimage.2019.116329.

Christen, T., et al., 2014. MR vascular fingerprinting a new approach to compute cerebral blood volume, mean vessel radius, and oxygenation maps in the human brain. NeuroImage 89, 262–270. https://doi.org/10.1016/j.neuroimage.2013.11.052.MR.

Cloos, M.A., et al., 2016. Multiparametric imaging with heterogeneous radiofrequency field. Nature Communications 7, 12445. https://doi.org/10.1017/CBO9781107415324.004.

Hamilton, J.I., Griswold, M.A., Seiberlich, N., 2015. MR fingerprinting with chemical exchange (MRF-X) to quantify subvoxel T1 and extracellular volume fraction. Journal of Cardiovascular Magnetic Resonance 17 (Suppl 1), W35. https://doi.org/10.1186/1532-429X-17-S1-W35.

Hamilton, J.I., et al., 2017. MR fingerprinting for rapid quantification of myocardial T1, T2, and proton spin density. Magnetic Resonance in Medicine 77 (4), 1446–1458. https://doi.org/10.1002/mrm.26216.

Haubold, J., et al., 2019. Non-invasive tumor decoding and phenotyping of cerebral gliomas utilizing multiparametric 18F-FET PET-MRI and MR fingerprinting. European Journal of Nuclear Medicine and Molecular Imaging 47, 1435–1445. https://doi.org/10.1007/s00259-019-04602-2.

Jiang, Y., et al., 2015. MR fingerprinting using fast imaging with steady state precession (FISP) with spiral readout. Magnetic Resonance in Medicine 74 (6), 1621–1631. https://doi.org/10.1002/mrm.25559.

448 Chapter 28 MR fingerprinting: concepts, implementation and applications

Jiang, Y., et al., 2017a. Repeatability of magnetic resonance fingerprinting T1 and T2 estimates assessed using the ISMRM/NIST MRI system phantom. Magnetic Resonance in Medicine 78 (4), 1452–1457. https://doi.org/10.1002/mrm.26509.

Jordan, S.P., Hu, S., Rozada, I., et al., 2021. Automated design of pulse sequences for magnetic resonance fingerprinting using physics-inspired optimization. Proceedings of the National Academy of Sciences of the United States of America 118 (40), e2020516118. https://doi.org/10.1073/pnas.2020516118.

Körzdörfer, G., Kirsch, R., et al., 2019a. Reproducibility and repeatability of MR fingerprinting relaxometry in the human brain. Radiology 292 (2), 429–437. https://doi.org/10.1148/radiol.2019182360.

Ma, D., et al., 2013. Magnetic resonance fingerprinting. Nature 495 (7440), 187–192. https://doi.org/10.1038/nature11971.

Ma, D., Coppo, S., et al., 2017. Slice profile and B1 corrections in 2D magnetic resonance fingerprinting. Magnetic Resonance in Medicine 78 (5), 1781–1789. https://doi.org/10.1002/mrm.26580.

Ma, D., Jiang, Y., et al., 2018. Fast 3D magnetic resonance fingerprinting for a whole-brain coverage. Magnetic Resonance in Medicine 79 (4), 2190–2197. https://doi.org/10.1002/mrm.26886.

Ma, D., et al., 2019. Development of high-resolution 3D MR fingerprinting for detection and characterization of epileptic lesions. Journal of Magnetic Resonance Imaging 49 (5), 1333–1346. https://doi.org/10.1002/jmri.26319.

McGivney, D., et al., 2014. SVD compression for magnetic resonance fingerprinting in the time domain. IEEE Transactions on Medical Imaging 33 (12), 2311–2322. https://doi.org/10.1109/TMI.2014.2337321.

Scheffler, K., Lehnhardt, S., 2003. Principles and applications of balanced SSFP techniques. European Radiology 13 (11), 2409–2418. https://doi.org/10.1007/s00330-003-1957-x.

Su, P., et al., 2016. Multiparametric estimation of brain hemodynamics with MR fingerprinting ASL. Magnetic Resonance in Medicine. https://doi.org/10.1002/mrm.26587.

Wang, C.Y., et al., 2019. Magnetic resonance fingerprinting with quadratic RF phase for measurement of T 2* simultaneously with δ f, T 1, and T 2. Magnetic Resonance in Medicine 81 (3), 1849–1862. https://doi.org/10.1002/mrm.27543.

Yang, M., et al., 2018. Low rank approximation methods for MR fingerprinting with large scale dictionaries. Magnetic Resonance in Medicine 79 (4), 2392–2400. https://doi.org/10.1002/mrm.26867.

Further reading

Chen, Y., et al., 2018. Three-dimensional MR fingerprinting for quantitative breast imaging. Radiology 290 (1), 33–40. https://doi.org/10.1148/radiol.2018180836.

Chen, Y., et al., 2019. MR fingerprinting enables quantitative measures of brain tissue relaxation times and myelin water fraction in early brain development. NeuroImage 186, 782–793. https://doi.org/10.1016/J.NEUROIMAGE.2018.11.038.

Cloos, M.A., et al., 2019. Rapid radial T1 and T2 mapping of the hip articular cartilage with magnetic resonance fingerprinting. Journal of Magnetic Resonance Imaging 50 (3), 810–815. https://doi.org/10.1002/jmri.26615.

Ehses, P., et al., 2013. IR TrueFISP with a golden-ratio-based radial readout: fast quantification of T1, T2, and proton density. Magnetic Resonance in Medicine 69 (1), 71–81. https://doi.org/10.1002/mrm.24225.

Hamilton, J.I., Seiberlich, N., 2020. Machine learning for rapid magnetic resonance fingerprinting tissue property quantification. Proceedings of the IEEE 108 (1), 69–85. https://doi.org/10.1109/JPROC.2019.2936998.

Heo, H.Y., et al., 2019. Quantifying amide proton exchange rate and concentration in chemical exchange saturation transfer imaging of the human brain. NeuroImage 189, 202–213. https://doi.org/10.1016/j.neuroimage.2019.01.034.

Jiang, Y., et al., 2017b. MR fingerprinting using the quick echo splitting NMR imaging technique. Magnetic Resonance in Medicine 77 (3), 979–988. https://doi.org/10.1002/mrm.26173.

Körzdörfer, G., Jiang, Y., et al., 2019b. Magnetic resonance field fingerprinting. Magnetic Resonance in Medicine 81 (4), 2347–2359. https://doi.org/10.1002/mrm.27558.

Liao, C., et al., 2018. Detection of lesions in mesial temporal lobe epilepsy by using MR fingerprinting. Radiology 288 (3), 804–812. https://doi.org/10.1148/radiol.2018172131.

Ma, D., et al., 2015. Music-based magnetic resonance fingerprinting to improve patient comfort during MRI examinations. Magnetic Resonance in Medicine. https://doi.org/10.1002/mrm.25818.

McGivney, D.F., et al., 2020. Magnetic resonance fingerprinting review part 2: technique and directions. Journal of Magnetic Resonance Imaging 51 (4), 993–1007. https://doi.org/10.1002/jmri.26877.

Mehta, B.B., et al., 2018. Image reconstruction algorithm for motion insensitive MR fingerprinting (MRF): MORF. Magnetic Resonance in Medicine 80 (6), 2485–2500. https://doi.org/10.1002/mrm.27227.

Mehta, B.B., et al., 2019. Magnetic resonance fingerprinting: a technical review. Magnetic Resonance in Medicine 81 (1), 25–46. https://doi.org/10.1002/mrm.27403.

Panda, A., et al., 2017. Magnetic resonance fingerprinting – an overview. Current Opinion in Biomedical Engineering 3, 56–66. https://doi.org/10.1016/j.cobme.2017.11.001.

Poorman, M.E., et al., 2020. Magnetic resonance fingerprinting part 1: potential uses, current challenges, and recommendations. Journal of Magnetic Resonance Imaging 51 (3), 675–692. https://doi.org/10.1002/jmri.26836.

Weigel, M., 2015. Extended phase graphs: dephasing, RF pulses, and echoes - pure and simple. Journal of Magnetic Resonance Imaging 41 (2), 266–295. https://doi.org/10.1002/jmri.24619.

Yang, M., et al., 2020. Game of learning Bloch equation simulations for MR fingerprinting. available at: http://arxiv.org/abs/2004.02270.

Ye, H., et al., 2016. Accelerating magnetic resonance fingerprinting (MRF) using t-blipped simultaneous multislice (SMS) acquisition. Magnetic Resonance in Medicine 75 (5), 2078–2085. https://doi.org/10.1002/mrm.25799.

CHAPTER

Quantitative multi-parametric MRI measurements

29

Gunther Helms

Department of Clinical Sciences Lund (IKVL), Lund University, Lund, Sweden

29.1 Introduction

Quantitative MRI (qMRI) goes beyond the rationale of conventional clinical MRI to highlight anatomical structure or functional properties by optimizing local contrast. Through systematic variation of sequence parameters, MR images of different contrast are created. Then, "maps" of local MR or physiological parameters of the living organism are estimated from the observed intensities. These spatially resolved metrics can be evaluated in clinical imaging research for cross-sectional and longitudinal studies, or can serve as biomarkers of pathology, or can be used as observables for biophysical models of tissue microstructure.

Taking the step beyond qualitative interpretation of MR contrast, the development and validation of biophysical models is undergoing active development. In brain, it is traditionally focused on the established relationship between "structural" MRI contrast and myelin, ferritin or other forms of iron, and bulk water including cerebrospinal-fluid (CSF) and vasogenic edema. Multi-parametric quantification approaches will thus help in the differentiation of biophysical signal origin and allow for more sophisticated biophysical modeling.

In MRI, measurement of water signal is exploited as an intrinsic probe of tissue microstructure and interaction with hydrated biomolecules. The molecular dynamics and thermal motions of water molecules determine the particular lengths and time scales of their interaction with tissue. The evolution of magnetization during an MRI pulse sequence is described by the MR parameters of the equations of Bloch, Torrey, and McConnell, giving a classical framework of the stochastic properties of water at the Larmor frequency, that is, the Zeeman splitting at the local static field B_0 in terms of the relaxation times. Note that the B_0 range of commercial human MR systems (currently 0.1T to 9.4T) still allows for a consistent interpretation of image contrast and MR parameters, despite their varying physical values.

MR parameters are derived from models of the MR experiment, and thus share the limited resolution of MRI. Since they represent a sub-volume-weighted voxel average, their specificity may be limited by their "aggregate" nature. For example, the T_2^*-decay of a gradient-echo signal is influenced by a residual macroscopic B_0 gradient and microscopic inhomogeneity as well as different local T_2 and magnetic susceptibilities at the mesoscopic scale. The main rationale behind quantitative multi-parametric measurements is to gain complementary information on the behavior of magnetization in the voxel. From this, partial volumes and/or microscopic properties of tissue can be derived via biophysical models. Increasingly, validation experiments are performed *ex vivo* to relate macroscopic maps to underlying microscopic tissue properties.

452 Chapter 29 Quantitative multi-parametric MRI measurements

This chapter will present a mainly sequence-centered approach to multi-parametric measurements. These usually employ a particular pulse sequence to render the MR parameters that govern its signal equation. The combination of these parameters may then be exploited to formulate biophysical models of underlying tissue properties on a sub-voxel scale. State-of-the-art methods and evaluation software will be presented for spin-echo and gradient-echo MRI. The specific issues of estimating the water content (or proton density, PD) will be explained.

Major applications that make use of different quantitative techniques to address specific microscopic properties will be outlined. Prime examples are g-ratio mapping (see Section 29.3.3.3) or to access the directional influence on relaxation (see Section 29.3.3.4). Due to the scope and complexity of ongoing research on biomarkers and biophysical models, the reader is referred to the relevant literature for details.

29.2 MRI sequences for multi-parametric brain mapping

The conceptually simplest approach to measure an MR parameter is based on the signal equation of an MR experiment, which can be fitted to the image intensities obtained according to the values of predefined sequence parameters, such as echo times (TE) for T_2 or T_2^*, or inversion times (TI) for T_1. Hence, multi-parametric quantitative MRI requires protocols of repeated scans that are adapted to fitting the range of relaxation times in the brain while controlling for error progression, thus compromising on their immediate diagnostic value. Usually, sources of systematic errors need to be accounted for, such as technical imperfections, including slice profile effects or flip angle inhomogeneity. Using the same pulse sequence usually reduces the amount of raw data needed, and thus increases time efficiency, since each acquisition provides information on multiple MR parameters. This renders parameter maps at the same spatial resolution and with identical exposure to B_0 and B_1 imperfections (see Section 29.2.5). When combining techniques based on different sequences, co-registration, interpolation, and sequence-specific bias can become an issue.

29.2.1 Spin-echo sequences

The earliest multi-parametric measurements utilized multi-slice spin-echo (SE) imaging to estimate mono-exponential T_1, T_2, and PD of tissue via fitting of the Bloch equations. The foremost target of spin-echo mapping has been the classification of voxels in terms of tissue classes.

29.2.1.1 Multi-parameter SE mapping

Modern multi-parametric techniques require just a few images representing different TEs and TIs to provide maps of T_1, T_2, and PD. Measurement times are kept within 5 minutes by use of anisotropic voxels and regularization to restrict the parameter space fitting to low degrees of freedom (Warntjes et al., 2016). Since the slice profiles for inversion, excitation, and refocusing have to be taken into account, this requires dedicated protocols supplied by the manufacturers, which are matched with commercial evaluation software.

Exemplifying a biophysical model that goes beyond tissue classification, the combination of T_1, T_2, and PD are then modeled by contributions from four fractional contributions to water content with their properties empirically chosen to represent the micro-environments of myelin, cellular matrix, free-

29.2 MRI sequences for multi-parametric brain mapping

water-like CSF, and "excess water" representing expanded extracellular space/edema (Warntjes et al., 2016) undergoing exchange. Assuming a specific PD value, these components are converted into sub-volumes (adding up to 1) to characterize healthy and diseased brain tissue (Fig. 29.1). The biophysical

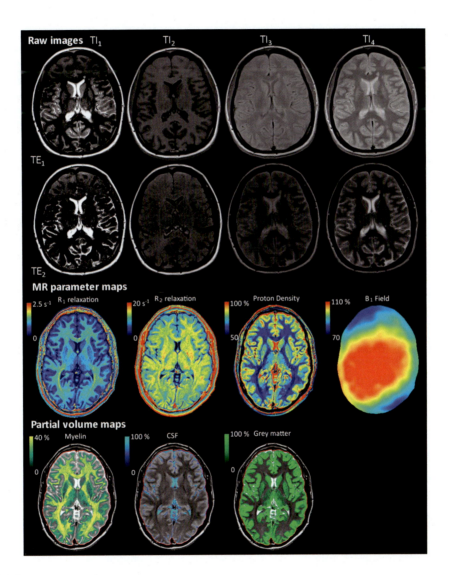

FIGURE 29.1

Multi-parametric measurements using spin-echoes: 2D turbo-spin-echo measurement using SyMRI (Warntjes et al., 2016). Top rows: MR images obtained at two different TEs and four different TIs at 3T. Third row: Color-coded maps of $R_1 = 1/T_1$, $R_2 = 1/T_2$, PD, and relative B_1^+. Bottom row: Partial volumes of myelin, CSF, and GM as derived from a heavily constrained biophysical model. (Images courtesy of M. Warntjes, SyMRI).

454 **Chapter 29** Quantitative multi-parametric MRI measurements

model behind the commercial software yields partial volumes of myelin in addition to those of standard white and gray matter (WM/GM) and CSF tissue types.

29.2.1.2 Multiple T_2 from spin-echoes

Careful multi-SE measurements at short TE-spacings show that T_2 relaxation in brain is multi-compartmental. The presence of a short observable component of T_2 between 10 and 20 ms being assigned to water trapped inside myelin is now firmly established (for a review see MacKay and Laule, 2016). Single-slice acquisition using Carr–Purcell–Meiboom–Gill (CPMG) sequences have now been replaced by 3D-encoded multi-gradient-and-spin-echo (GRASE) measurements (Prasloski et al., 2012). Data are evaluated by regularized inversion on a logarithmic T_2 grid, correcting for B_1^+ inhomogeneities by modeling the decay using the extended phase graph (EPG) algorithm. When properly representing the receive sensitivity (see Section 29.2.5), distributions of PD and T_2 can be obtained (Whittall et al., 1997). Assumptions on T_2 and PD of myelin water allows one to extract the volume fraction of myelin from T_2 measurements (Warntjes et al., 2016).

29.2.2 Gradient-recalled echo sequences

Gradient-recalled echoes (GRE) are the basis of fast steady-state MRI techniques, and thus are suited for 3D mapping at higher resolution than spin-echo MRI. After simple non-linear transforms, the parameters PD, T_1, T_2/T_1, and T_2^* can be obtained by linear regression, that is, by direct calculation of the inverse.

29.2.2.1 Multiple gradient-echoes

Gradient-echo imaging is in essence multi-parametric, because the signal magnitude is dephased by the dispersion of B_0 across the voxel, whereas the phase evolves with the mean B_0 in the voxel. Multiple gradient-echo measurements thus provide both the effective transverse relaxation T_2^* and the Larmor frequency $\Delta\omega_0$.

From maps of $\Delta\omega_0$, the distribution of the magnetic susceptibility $\chi(\mathbf{x})$ is obtained via field-to-source inversion (see Chapter 22). $\chi(\mathbf{x})$ is represented by a single dipole source per voxel, estimated by division of the z-component of the dipole field in k-space, notwithstanding the equation's ill-posed nature along the "magic angles" 54.7° and 125.3° with respect to $\mathbf{B_0}$, due to division by zero. The fast-paced development of these so-called quantitative susceptibility mapping (QSM) methods has resulted in a number of different software packages, featuring different solutions for the removal of slowly varying background inhomogeneity and regularized inversion. Both $1/T_2^*$ and χ correlate with non-heme iron content and their measurement benefits from higher field strengths (Fig. 29.2).

29.2.2.2 Spoiled gradient-echoes

Spoiled gradient-echo sequences (with common acronyms SPGR, FLASH, or T_1-FFE) allow one to access additional parameters from the dynamic steady-state of longitudinal magnetization M_z. With increasing flip angle α, $S(\alpha)/\sin\alpha$ changes from representing the equilibrium M_0, or PD-weighting, to a heavily T_1-weighted state. Hence, maps of T_1 and the fully relaxed signal amplitude can be easily obtained by varying the flip angle (VFA). Because the local flip angle shows considerable spatial variation across the brain, naïve fitting to the nominal flip angle will result in biased maps of T_1 and signal amplitude S_0. Such VFA experiments therefore need to be complemented by flip angle mapping for

29.2 MRI sequences for multi-parametric brain mapping

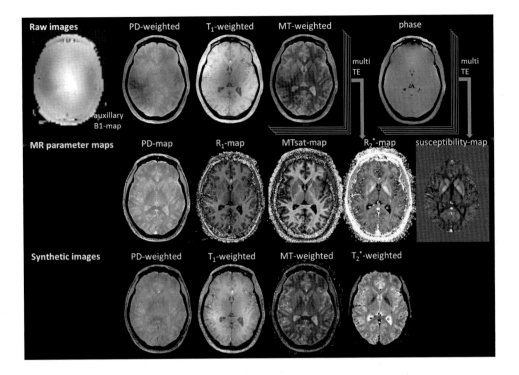

FIGURE 29.2

Multi-parametric measurements using gradient-echoes: 3D spoiled gradient-echo measurement. Top row: MR images of predominant PD-, T_1-, and MT-weighting at 7T obtained at eight different TEs and an independently acquired B_1-map. Only the first echo is shown. Middle row: Maps of PD, $R_1 = 1/T_1$, MT saturation, and $R_2^* = 1/T_2^*$ calculated using the hMRI toolbox (Tabelow et al., 2019). The map of magnetic susceptibility was obtained from multi-echo phase images using MEDI. Grayscale bars are omitted for the sake of space. Bottom row: Synthetic images calculated from the bias-corrected, calibrated MR parameters. The T_2^*-weighted image was calculated at TE = 19.7 ms exceeding TR = 18 ms.

bias correction. The VFA method has been popular, owing to the simplicity of the signal equation and protocol optimization, and the fact that the pulse sequence is readily available.

Spoiled gradient-echo imaging is also used for quantification of the binary spin bath model of magnetization transfer (MT). Additional RF pulses are implemented before the readout, which predominantly saturate the "MRI invisible" pool of motionally restricted or "bound" protons associated with macromolecules. Since spoiling precludes exchange effects on transverse magnetization, the ensuing MT effect is relatively easy to model. By varying the offset frequency and power of the "MT pulse", this sequence has been utilized to fit the two-pool model (or binary spin bath) for quantitative magnetization transfer (qMT) with an auxiliary VFA to determine the observed T_1. In this time-consuming procedure, a frequency-selective MT pre-pulse is applied at different frequency offsets and pulse powers (Sled, 2018).

456 Chapter 29 Quantitative multi-parametric MRI measurements

Reduction of the acquisition to a minimum of two flip angles and a single MT-experiment still allows estimation of PD, T_1, and the MT saturation (MTsat) by inversion of an empirical signal equation (Helms et al., 2008). This semi-quantitative measure for MT refers to the additional percent saturation of water M_z per TR created by the MT pulse (Helms et al., 2008). In the context of spoiled GRE imaging, "multi-parameter mapping" refers to combination with a multi-echo readout (see Section 29.2.2.1). Because signal equations can be simplified to a good approximation, parameter maps of T_1, T_2^*, MT, and PD can be calculated analytically (Fig. 29.2). A toolbox for SPGR-based multi-parameter mapping is available within the SPM framework (https://www.fil.ion.ucl.ac.uk/spm/) that can handle flexible protocols (hMRI, Tabelow et al., 2019). Since high spatial resolution can be achieved, this has been applied to cortical mapping (see Section 29.3.1) and post-mortem studies (see Section 29.3.4).

29.2.2.3 Balanced steady-state free precession

The balanced steady-state free precession (bSSFP) sequence with echo formation in the center of the TR and with refocusing gradient moments, shows an increasing degree of T_2/T_1 weighting at higher flip angles. Thus, 3D maps of T_2/T_1 can be obtained from bSSFP images in a similar fashion to the T_1 maps that can be obtained from spoiled GRE images. MT effects can be imposed by varying the duration, and hence power, of the RF pulses, but the presence of residual transverse magnetization complicates a closed form signal equation.

At 1.5T, an inversion pulse can be combined with a bSSFP readout to yield T_1 maps by inversion recovery and thus T_2 maps too (Schmitt et al., 2004). At 3T and higher field strengths, however, bSSFP acquisition is limited by higher specific absorption rates (SAR) and banding artifacts, where the B_0 offset creates destructive interference in the precessing transverse component.

29.2.2.4 Combination of spoiled and balanced acquisition (DESPOT)

The combination of spoiled and gradient-recalled VFA experiments to yield 3D maps of T_1, T_2, and S_0 at high isotropic resolutions in a relatively short time has been dubbed DESPOT1/2 (driven equilibrium single pulse observation of T_1 and T_2) (Deoni et al., 2003). For dual flip angles (DFA), T_1, and T_1/T_2 can be obtained directly by inverting the signal equations. As mentioned above, these maps are strongly susceptible to bias caused by inhomogeneous B_1^+ and B_0. DESPOT1 needs to be complemented with an inversion-recovery-prepared train of rapid acquisitions of gradient-echoes (MP-RAGE) to correct for B_1 inhomogeneity. The B_0 bands of DESPOT2 can be shifted and eliminated by phase cycling (Deoni, 2009).

A signal model of the first-order exchange between myelin water and cellular water has been implemented into DESPOT theory (Deoni et al., 2008). Fitting multi-component mcDESPOT comprises removal of B_1^+ bias and B_0-related banding artifacts and relies on a genetic algorithm to yield the myelin water fraction in brain tissue (Fig. 29.3). It has been used to study myelination in children and demyelinating disease.

29.2.2.5 Multi-parameter MP2RAGE

T_1 can also be estimated from the regularized division of a T_1-weighted and a PD-weighted image acquired by two consecutive RAGE trains after inversion (MP2RAGE). This technique is especially popular at high and ultra-high B_0, because the influence of B_1^+ inhomogeneities on T_1 estimation can be reduced. Similarly as for steady-state imaging, implementation of a multi-echo readout may be used for T_2^* and susceptibility mapping at ultra-high field, where TE can be shortened (Caan et al., 2018).

29.2 MRI sequences for multi-parametric brain mapping   **457**

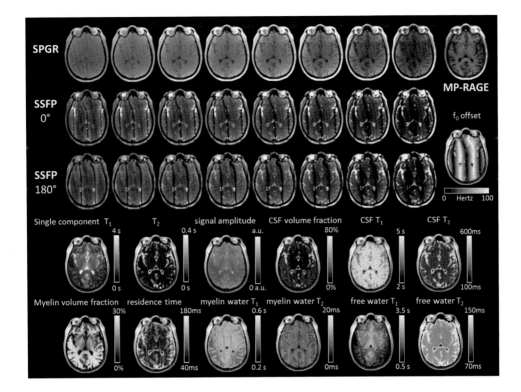

FIGURE 29.3

Combining spoiled and refocused steady-state images to fit multiple-components using mcDESPOT: Rows 1–3 show raw images of three VFA series of the steady-state signals from spoiled (SPGR) and refocused (SSFP) gradient-echo sequences. The banding artifacts of SSFP are controlled by a linear shim field and shifted by RF phase alternation (180°). The f$_0$ offset map appears modulo 100 Hz, corresponding to TR = 5 ms. B_1^+ inhomogeneity is determined by a low-resolution MP-RAGE. Rows 4 and 5 show parameter maps overlaid on an MP-RAGE image. A single-component model yields maps of T_1, T_2, and signal amplitude. The mcDESPOT model estimates a non-exchanging signal component of CSF and exchanging components of myelin water and free water. With their T_1 and T_2 estimates, these components contribute in varying proportions to the observed signal. The residence time of myelin water is calculated from the exchange kinetics. Data acquired at 3T and 1.7 mm resolution courtesy of the core facility "MR-Research in the Neurosciences", Göttingen University Medical Center.

29.2.3 Echo-planar imaging

By virtue of its capability to encode a 2D image in a single shot, echo-planar imaging (EPI) provides versatility and speed for encoding any MR parameter. Firstly, T_2^* or T_2 can be estimated by varying the TE of a GRE- or SE-EPI readout, respectively, e.g., in combination with diffusion MRI. For mapping T_1, magnetization-prepared schemes have evolved from the 2D Look-Locker sequence into measurements with full 3D coverage by slice-shifted multi-slice inversion recovery EPI (Polders et al., 2012) at sub-millimeter resolution. Usually, multi-slice acquisition allows for a long TR to achieve full relaxation. Higher spatial resolution and reduced distortions can be achieved by using segmented EPI. EPI-encoding of a few k-space lines can also be used to accelerate turbo gradient-echo-and-spin-echo (GRASE) acquisition. Recently, an acquisition time of 3 minutes has been achieved for T_1, T_2, and T_2^* mapping by combining inversion recovery with a GRASE-like readout using highly accelerated 3D EPI (Wang et al., 2019).

29.2.4 MR fingerprinting

Fingerprinting (see also Chapter 28) is an approach for extracting qMRI maps using non-repetitive MRI pulse sequences for data acquisition and dictionary fitting approaches for parameter estimation. The Bloch simulations can easily accommodate any type of pulse sequence, including non-repetitive sequences (e.g., with pseudo-random changes in flip angles and TR). This higher flexibility can be used for speeding up the acquisition and/or improving the conditioning of the inverse problem by an informed choice of acquisition parameters. The improved conditioning promises higher precision and efficiency compared to conventional approaches. However, fingerprinting also requires more precise modeling of the MRI signal, since although it can enhance the sensitivity to the MR parameters of interest, it can also lead to artifacts and biases due to inadequate forward models (Mehta et al., 2019). By its design, MR fingerprinting is a highly time-efficient multi-parametric method, and the heavily undersampled images are just an intermediate step in the processing.

29.2.5 Bias correction, calibration, and PD

Image intensities are influenced by the spatial dependence of B_0 and B_1 fields, as well as the combination and relative position of receive coils. To obtain accurate parameter maps such sources of bias need to be accounted for in the quantification model. This applies particularly to PD, which always appears together with the receive sensitivities in the signal amplitude that can be removed from the equation by dividing two images. Such ratios provide "semi-quantitative" metrics that retain a residual dependence on other parameters imposed by sequence and scanner hardware. They are thus locally reproducible, but not accurate or physically specific. To obtain accurate maps, sources of bias are either hard-coded in the model, such as specific slice profile shapes or inversion factors, or "calibrated" via additionally acquired information, such as B_0 and B_1^+ maps, or scans of opposite gradient polarity to correct for distortions and eddy currents.

The maximum signal amplitude is obtained by accounting for decay of transversal magnetization in spin-echoes or gradient-echoes. The intensity value in arbitrary units is proportional to PD, the gain and combinations of sensitivity of the receive coils. These have to be kept constant to be eliminated by division with a reference image. The spatial sensitivity of receive elements is routinely acquired to reconstruct parallel partial acquisitions, but referenced to the main volume transmit coil when operated in receive mode. By applying such empirical corrections of intensity bias, PD may be estimated reasonably well from the expected signal at zero TE and full T_1 relaxation. Note that this pragmatic approach ignores the fact that the receive field cannot be accurately determined by experiments conducted outside the near-field regime, where the pseudo-static simplification of the principle of reciprocity applies. PD is commonly given as "water content" in percent units [p.u.] relative to the number of protons in pure water at 37°C, as calibrated in an external phantom or tissue of well-known PD, such as CSF or adult WM.

29.3 **Applications**

Since conventional MRI strives to optimize local contrast specific to the diagnostic problem of interest, it accepts variation between scans in terms of signal scaling in arbitrary units [a.u.] and bias fields. The pertinent problems for follow-up studies (reproducibility) and tissue characterization are addressed by qMRI. As envisioned at the outset of MRI, multi-parametric qMRI provides characterization of brain tissue as the water protons probe their microscopic environments. Thus, multi-parametric techniques will increase the specificity, since MR parameters are susceptible by varying degrees to the main drivers of MR contrast in the brain, chiefly myelinated axons and iron in blood or stored in the form of ferritin. Thus brain development in childhood and normal ageing have emerged as major applications of qMRI.

29.3.1 **Synthetic MRI**

A complete set of multiple parameters (comprising at least PD, T_1, and T_2 or T_2^*) can be used to calculate a "synthetic image" of an underlying pulse sequence for arbitrary acquisition parameters, i.e., other than those used to generate the primary images, from which the maps were obtained (Fig. 29.2). Thus a set of high-contrast images can be created for diagnostic purposes. The parameter range may even be extended to a range that may be technically unfeasible (Callaghan et al., 2016), e.g., zero TE or TE > TR in fast GRE imaging. Like the parametric maps they are based on, these synthetic images will show much reduced influence of bias, e.g., spatial variation of flip angles. Despite its diagnostic potential, however, clinical use of synthetic MRI is still at the stage of being purely a research tool.

29.3.2 **Tissue classification**

One of the first applications of multi-parametric mapping was the classification of pixels for segmentation of brain in terms of WM, GM, and CSF, before the availability of bias field correction in segmentation software. The search for non-invasive biomarkers of pathological changes follows the same rationale. Note that underlying morphological changes need to be accounted for when applying qMRI to parametric mapping of change, dubbed voxel-based quantification (VBQ, Draganski et al., 2011). For example, multi-parametric measurements provide insight into structural and morphological changes of the brain with age (Lorio et al., 2014). Recent advances comprise segmentation of the thalamus and the mid-brain and brain stem. The underlying concept of class-specific MR properties can be used to represent a voxel in terms of its partial volume constituents as derived from multiple parameter maps (Fig. 29.1).

Owing to the advances in high-resolution multi-parametric mapping, however, this coarse categorization is increasingly being replaced by characterizing specific anatomical structures, as indicated by the specific appearance of, e.g., the pyramidal tract and optic radiation, and the iron-rich deep brain nuclei on conventional MRI. Regional WM is addressed by a tract-specific approach, and GM by mapping of cortical profiles and areas (Dick et al., 2012).

29.3.3 **Biophysical models of microstructure**

Multi-parameter measurements can reveal systematic relationships between the MR parameters that lead to biophysical models of tissue of ever increasing complexity. One example is cross-relaxation

460 **Chapter 29** Quantitative multi-parametric MRI measurements

between MRI-invisible macromolecules and free water (Edzes and Samulski, 1977). Since cross-relaxation and exchange processes are fast on the timescale of T_1 (about 1 s), a single-exponential T_1 is observed. Note that in the context of modeling applications, the use of "relaxation rates"—i.e., the inverse of the relaxation times, which for T_1 is given by $R_1 = 1/T_1$—is preferred, because rates can be represented as a sum or the weighted average of local processes. The macromolecular contributions to T_1 relaxation (hydration fraction and exchanging protons) lead to a linear relationship of R_1 with the inverse water content (WC) (Fullerton et al., 1982): $R_1 = R_{10} + r_w/WC$.

A short T_1 (or high R_1) used as a surrogate measure for low water content has been well established, and T_1-dominated MR contrast is often referred to as "structural MRI". The mono-exponential T_1, T_2, and T_2^* relaxation times used in the Bloch equation should be considered as parsimonious, largely due to operational restrictions on timing, SNR, stability, etc.

29.3.3.1 Compartments

Observation of multiple relaxation components indicates compartmentalization. Due to the very low T_2 of immobile protons, T_2 is shortened more by macromolecular content than T_1, and is thus more sensitive to compartmentalization, either by low permeability (myelin water) or spatial separation at distances greater than the diffusional displacement ("partial volume effect").

Exchange is modeled by (pseudo-)first-order kinetics, where the rate constants reflect the equilibrium magnetization of the compartments. The slow exchange of myelin water with the bulk of tissue water in WM was first assessed by combining MT and multi-component T_2 measurements (Stanisz et al., 1999). Two McConnell equations coupled by exchanging water have become the standard concept for relaxation in WM.

Measurements of compartmental exchange—if not based on diffusion measurements, where spatial and temporal scales can be controlled by experiment—usually require a combination of parameters to be measured. Each of these provides information on different temporal and spatial scales as defined by relaxation and exchange processes. These range from static phenomena, such as susceptibility at a scale beyond one voxel, to the ultrastructural scale of fast processes, such as MT or T_2 of myelin water. Without properly accounting for relaxation, the exchange cannot be accurately estimated and *vice versa*.

A typical example for estimating compartment sizes is mcDESPOT (see Section 29.2.2.5), which models the effect of exchange with myelin water on the steady-state signals observed by DESPOT (Fig. 29.3).

29.3.3.2 Modeling relaxation by empirical relaxivities

The understanding of relaxation processes at the microscopic or mesoscopic scale are complex and notoriously difficult to transfer to the aggregate observations at the level of an imaging voxel. Multi-parametric information allows for an empirical multivariate approach. An MR parameter may even be used as a "surrogate" metric to represent the concentration of its main driver. The contribution of macromolecules to T_1 and T_2 relaxation can be explored using MT-based metrics as a surrogate concentration. Macromolecular content is the main driver of R_1, but contributes to R_2^* to a lower degree. R_2^* is mainly driven by iron content (Fig. 29.4). Modeling R_1 by MT saturation and R_2^* as a surrogate for iron has a high predictive value in normal brain (Callaghan et al., 2014).

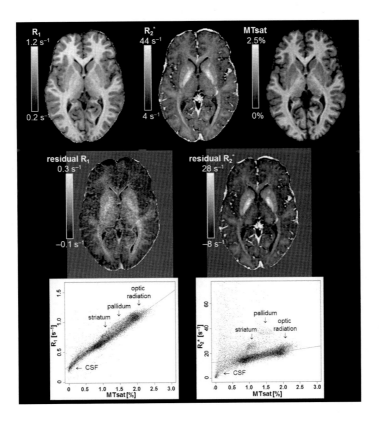

FIGURE 29.4

Revealing contributions to T_1 and T_2^* relaxation: Top row: Maps of R_1, R_2^*, and MT saturation (MTsat) from multi-parametric gradient-echo qMRI (Tabelow et al., 2019). Under the assumption that macromolecular content is represented by MTsat and contributes linearly to R_1 and R_2^*, local contributions to R_1 and R_2^* that are driven by macromolecules can be removed by subtraction. Bottom row: Scatter-plots of R_1 and R_2^* over MTsat in brain from the depicted axial slice demonstrate the contributions of macromolecules. Some clusters of the main linear correlation can be assigned to specific anatomical regions. The regression lines were obtained by excluding pixels of $R_2^* > 25$ s^{-1}, $R_2^* < 10$ s^{-1}, and MTsat $< 0.5\%$. Middle row: Maps of residual R_1 and R_2^* show little contrast at the subcortical boundary, but highlight iron-rich GM and anisotropic WM tracts instead. Values in CSF are negative due to negligible macromolecular content.

29.3.3.3 g-Ratio estimation

Emerging approaches to map the axonal g-ratio, i.e., the ratio between the lumen and the outer diameter of myelinated axons, combine diffusion and relaxation measurements. The axonal sub-volume is derived from diffusion measurements, whereas the myelin sub-volume can be calibrated from various surrogate parameters, such as PD, MT, or the myelin water fraction as reviewed in (Mohammadi and Callaghan, 2021). Expanding on Section 29.2.5, it should be mentioned that the conversion from

462 **Chapter 29** Quantitative multi-parametric MRI measurements

MRI signal components to sub-volumes requires assumptions about the specific proton densities. For microscopic compartments, these cannot be derived experimentally.

29.3.3.4 Directional dependence

Via the microscopic B_0 distribution created by subspaces of different magnetic susceptibility (e.g., venules and myelinated axons), structural anisotropy imposes a dependence on the relative orientation to the B_0 field (Fig. 29.4). Static effects have been observed on χ and T_2^* (Wharton and Bowtell, 2012) and described by a hollow cylinder model. Via diffusion, T_2 and T_1 are also varied to a minor degree (Knight et al., 2018). Small directional variations in MT correlate with simulations, where the semi-solid absorption lineshape accounts for anisotropic distribution of lipid bilayers (Pampel et al., 2015). The parameters of predominant direction and degree of anisotropy are derived from diffusion tensor imaging.

29.3.4 Post-mortem MRI

Post-mortem MRI allows higher resolution through longer measurement times and may serve as a link between *in vivo* MRI and histological examinations. In the context of searching for biomarkers and assessing biophysical models, post-mortem samples can be scanned prior to validation by destructive techniques.

Multi-parametric measurements are increasingly applied to study the effects of temperature, changes of hemoglobin, autolysis, and fixation of tissue. Except for PD, the contrast of MR images changes post mortem as relaxation and diffusion are governed by the stochastic motion of water. Despite changing values, the contrast of parameter maps may allow for visual comparison of *in vivo* and post-mortem scans and fixed tissue (Fig. 29.5).

29.4 Discussion

The field of multi-parametric mapping has considerably expanded during the past two decades. Development has been driven by progress in scanner technology, yielding higher resolution or faster measurements, stabilization improvements (such as motion correction), and ever more sophisticated modeling of the MR sequence and scanner behavior.

Until recently, mainly single MR parameters have been correlated with biological properties of brain tissue and their changes in ageing and disease. This has laid the foundation for the interpretation of MR images. For example, a shorter T_1 is taken to represent higher myelin content in cortex, a long T_2 represents free bulk water in WM lesions, and a short T_2^* in the basal ganglia indicates the accumulation of iron. Multi-parametric MRI measurements thus provide simply more information on healthy tissue or pathology. Although this time-honored approach of using MR parameters as "biomarkers" has been proven useful, MR parameters should be regarded as aggregate at the voxel level, and as surrogate markers of tissue properties as biophysical modeling becomes more widespread.

The endeavor of modeling tissue microstructure at a scale beyond voxel size to include partial volumes, compartments, and exchange (see Section 29.3.3) is a rapidly developing field. It has been the drive to develop specifically multi-parametric quantitative MR methods that has provided the input

29.4 Discussion   463

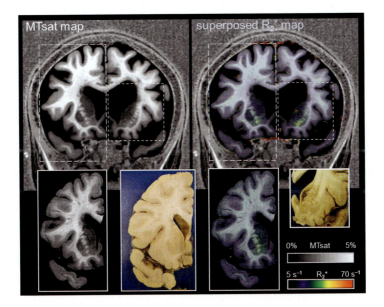

FIGURE 29.5

Post-mortem MRI using MT and R_2^* as surrogate metrics for structural content and iron: Post-mortem MRI using multi-parameter mapping of MT saturation and R_2^* at ambient temperature. Values of MT saturation (grayscale) are inherently corrected for changes in T_1 and used as a surrogate marker for macromolecular content; transparent color-coded overlays of R_2^* for local iron. Large images show an *in situ* MR acquisition of a woman aged 85 years; the inserts show co-registered parameter maps and surface views of formalin-fixed hemispheres. The maps reveal bilateral loss of substance in the striatum and focal iron in the right caudate (collaboration with W.J. Schulz-Schaeffer, Neuropathology, Göttingen University Medical Center).

to such models. However, adequate quality assurance (QA) has to be performed to control systematic error (bias), especially when comparing results obtained on scanners of different makes and models.

The quantification routines that are provided with the software included on clinical MR scanners mostly refer to a single parameter and often lack rigorous bias correction and calibration. To address this, an increasing amount of dedicated processing software for multi-parameter mapping has been made available on an open or commercial basis. Unlike the hMRI toolbox (Tabelow et al., 2019), these routines are mostly adapted to specific protocols or scanners, especially when the processing involves sophisticated modeling and bias correction. Measurement protocols, biophysical models, and processing software are usually optimized in conjunction. The concept behind the SyMRI software (Warntjes et al., 2016) is an educative example of these three levels: MR protocol, deriving aggregate MR parameters from signal modeling, and deriving sub-volume information from a highly constrained tissue model that includes exchange.

Deriving these MR parameters can be considered as solving an inverse problem with the image intensities as input. This may involve regularization and/or constraints that trade off bias and residues to yield a meaningful solution. The available algorithms for QSM present different solutions for dipole field inversion and background phase correction. Grossly deviating inputs may render the problem ill-posed or introduce systematic errors, as in the mcDESPOT protocol, where an intricate combination of scans provides the necessary information for the joint estimation of compartment sizes from exchange and B_1 and B_0 bias fields.

Forward modeling the magnetization dynamic is becoming increasingly popular as the models easily become too complex to cast the signal in a closed-form signal equation, such as in MP2RAGE or when using the extended phase graph algorithm to calculate the T_2 decay for imperfect SE refocusing. This also allows incorporation of sources of systematic errors, e.g., by creating bias field-dependent look-up tables. Fortuitously, increasing computer hardware performance enables more flexible computational solutions to the inversion problem, supporting more complex models and data acquisition schemes. This is highlighted by the rapid expansion of MR fingerprinting to encompass biophysical exchange models (Mehta et al., 2019).

Repeatability and reproducibility of multiple parameters demand a high stability of scanner performance, which is currently under investigation by multi-site multi-platform comparisons. After accounting for the specific model and make of the scanner and individual pre-scan adjustments, biases remain the main barrier to achieving full comparability of quantitative MRI. These obstacles can be addressed by standardized protocols and by adaption to platform-specific settings.

References

Caan, M., Bazin, P.-L., Marques, J., de Hollander, G., Dumoulin, S., van der Zwaag, W., 2018. MP2RAGEME: T1, T2*, and QSM mapping in one sequence at 7 Tesla. Hum. Brain Mapp. 40, 1786–1798.

Callaghan, M.F., Helms, G., Lutti, A., Mohammadi, S., Weiskopf, N., 2014. A general linear relaxometry model of R1 using imaging data. Magn. Reson. Med. 73, 1309–1314.

Callaghan, M.F., Mohammadi, S., Weiskopf, N., 2016. Synthetic quantitative MRI through relaxometry modelling. NMR Biomed. 29, 1729–1738.

Deoni, S.C., 2009. Transverse relaxation time (T2) mapping in the brain with off-resonance correction using phase-cycled steady-state free precession imaging. J. Magn. Reson. Imaging 30, 411–417.

Deoni, S.C., Rutt, B.K., Arun, T., Pierpaoli, C., Jones, D.K., 2008. Gleaning multi-component T1 and T2 information from steady-state imaging data. Magn. Reson. Med. 60, 1372–1387.

Deoni, S.C., Rutt, B.K., Peters, T.M., 2003. Rapid combined T1 and T2 mapping using gradient recalled acquisition in the steady state. Magn. Reson. Med. 49, 515–526.

Dick, F., Tierney, A.T., Lutti, A., Josephs, O., Sereno, M.I., Weiskopf, N., 2012. In vivo functional and myeloarchitectonic mapping of human primary auditory areas. J. Neurosci. 32, 16095–16105.

Draganski, B., Ashburner, J., Hutton, C., Kherif, F., Frackowiak, R.S.J., Helms, G., Weiskopf, N., 2011. Regional specificity of MR contrast parameters in normal ageing revealed by voxel-based quantification (VBQ). NeuroImage 55, 1423–1434.

Edzes, H., Samulski, E., 1977. The measurement of cross-relaxation effects in the proton NMR spin-lattice relaxation of water in biological systems: hydrated collagen and muscle. J. Magn. Res. 31, 207–229.

Fullerton, G., Potter, J., Dornbluth, N., 1982. NMR relaxation of protons in tissues and other macromolecular water solutions. Magn. Reson. Imaging 1, 209–228.

Helms, G., Dathe, H., Kallenberg, K., Dechent, P., 2008. High-resolution maps of magnetization transfer with inherent correction for RF inhomogeneity and T1 relaxation obtained from 3D FLASH MRI. Magn. Reson. Med. 60, 1396–1407.

Knight, M.J., Damion, R.A., Kauppinen, R.A., 2018. Observation of angular dependence of T1 in the human white matter at 3T. Biomed. Spectrosc. Imaging 7, 125–133.

Lorio, S., Lutti, A., Kherif, F., Ruef, A., Dukart, J., Chowdhury, R., Frackowiak, R.S., Ashburner, J., Helms, G., Weiskopf, N., Draganski, B., 2014. Disentangling in vivo the effects of iron content and atrophy on the ageing human brain. NeuroImage 103, 280–289.

MacKay, A.L., Laule, C., 2016. Magnetic resonance of myelin water: an in vivo marker for myelin. Brain Plast. 2, 71–79.

Mehta, B.B., Coppo, S., Mcgivney, D.F., Hamilton, J.I., Chen, Y., Jiang, Y., Ma, D., Seiberlich, N., Gulani, V., Griswold, M.A., 2019. Magnetic resonance fingerprinting: a technical review. Magn. Reson. Med. 81, 25–46.

Mohammadi, S., Callaghan, M.F., 2021. Towards in vivo g-ratio mapping using MRI: unifying myelin and diffusion imaging. J. Neurosci. Methods 358, 108990.

Pampel, A., Müller, D., Anwander, A., Marschner, H., Möller, H., 2015. Orientation dependence of magnetization transfer parameters in human white matter. NeuroImage 114, 136–146.

Polders, D.L., Leemans, A., Luijten, P.R., Hoogduin, H., 2012. Uncertainty estimations for quantitative in vivo MRI T1 mapping. J. Magn. Res. 244, 53–60.

Prasloski, T., Rauscher, A., Mackay, A.L., Hodgson, M., Vavasour, I.M., Laule, C., Mädler, B., 2012. Rapid whole cerebrum myelin water imaging using a 3D GRASE sequence. NeuroImage 63, 533–539.

Schmitt, P., Griswold, M.A., Jakob, P.M., Kotas, M., Gulani, V., Flentje, M., Haase, A., 2004. Inversion recovery TrueFISP: quantification of T_1, T_2, and spin density. Magn. Reson. Med. 51, 661–667.

Sled, J.G., 2018. Modelling and interpretation of magnetization transfer in the brain. NeuroImage 182, 128–135.

Stanisz, G.J., Kecojevic, A., Bronskill, M.J., Henkelman, R.M., 1999. Characterizing white matter with magnetization transfer and T2. Magn. Reson. Med. 42, 1128–1136.

Tabelow, K., Balteau, E., Ashburner, J., Callaghan, M.F., Draganski, B., Helms, G., Kherif, F., Leutritz, T., Lutti, A., Phillips, C., Reimer, E., Ruthotto, L., Seif, M., Weiskopf, N., Ziegler, G., Mohammadi, S., 2019. hMRI – a toolbox for quantitative MRI in neuroscience and clinical research. NeuroImage 194, 191–210.

Wang, F., Dong, Z., Reese, T.G., Bilgic, B., Manhard, M.K., Chen, J., Polimeni, J.R., Wald, L.L., Setsompop, K., 2019. Echo planar time-resolved imaging (EPTI). Magn. Reson. Med. 81, 3599–3615.

Warntjes, M., Engström, M., Tisell, A., Lundberg, P., 2016. Modeling the presence of myelin and edema in the brain based on multi-parametric quantitative MRI. Front. Neurol. 7, 1–15.

Wharton, S., Bowtell, R., 2012. Fiber orientation-dependent white matter contrast in gradient echo MRI. Proc. Natl. Acad. Sci. USA 109, 18559–18564.

Whittall, K., Mackay, A., Graeb, D., Nugent, R., Li, D., Paty, D., 1997. In vivo measurement of T2 distributions and water contents in normal human brain. Magn. Reson. Med. 37, 34–43.

PART 10

Neurovascular imaging

CHAPTER 30

Neurovascular magnetic resonance angiography

Kevin M. Johnson

Departments of Medical Physics and Radiology, University of Wisconsin – Madison, Madison, WI, United States

30.1 Introduction

The brain's vascular system is crucial to its function, with a network composed of arteries supplying oxygenated blood from the heart, a network of active small vessels and capillaries, which provide flow regulation and nutrient exchange, and the venous system for waste removal and the recirculation of deoxygenated blood. Magnetic resonance angiography (MRA) and the related technique of magnetic resonance venography (MRV) are used to visualize disease in arteries and veins, both of which are susceptible to gross pathologic changes and subclinical remodeling. Native vascular diseases include wall thickening and luminal narrowing with atherosclerosis, arteriovenous malformations, which shunt blood from the arterial to the venous system, and aneurysms, locally enlarged arteries. These native vascular diseases can be considered abnormal remodeling of the vascular wall and the general risk is hemorrhage or impaired blood delivery. Since geometry is highly coupled to remodeling and resulting blood flow, most current diagnostic imaging has focused on measuring the blood-filled lumen of the vasculature. The size and shape of the lesions is often sufficient to guide treatments (e.g., a large aneurysm would indicate that treatment is needed). This chapter provides a brief introduction to the vascular system, an overview of MRI techniques used to visualize vessels, and a comparison of MRA methods.

30.2 Macrovasculature of the brain

30.2.1 Anatomy

Fig. 30.1 shows MRA images of the brain highlighting its unique vascular system. Oxygenated arterial blood to the brain is supplied by multiple major arteries, namely the left and right internal carotid artery (ICA) and the basilar artery (BA), the latter of which is formed from the confluence of the left and right vertebral arteries. The arterial supplies are connected at the base of the brain in the circle of Willis (CoW), which allows for a level of collateral filling, mixing the blood from multiple supply arteries. From the CoW, there are multiple branches, including the middle cerebral arteries (MCAs), which provide blood to the left and right hemispheres of the brain. These major arteries feed into a vast array of branching arteries and extremely small perforating vessels, which are not well visualized with standard MRA sequences. Venous drainage occurs along a paired network, draining from the inside out to the superior sagittal sinus (SSS) and straight sinus (SS), among other veins.

Advances in Magnetic Resonance Technology and Applications, Volume 4, ISSN 2666-9099. https://doi.org/10.1016/B978-0-12-822479-3.00047-6
Copyright © 2021 Elsevier Inc. All rights reserved.

470 Chapter 30 Neurovascular magnetic resonance angiography

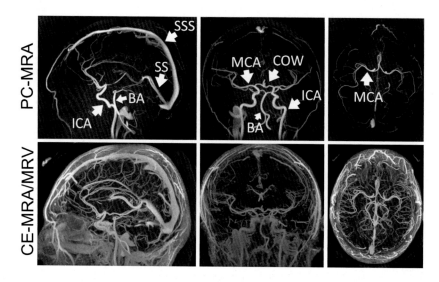

FIGURE 30.1

Sagittal, coronal, and axial limited maximum intensity projections (over 40 mm) acquired with two MRA techniques, one using motion-based phase contrast (PC-MRA) and the other (CE-MRA/MRV) using an exogenous, intravascular contrast agent (Ferumoxytol). The PC-MRA shows the major feeding and draining vessels of the brain, whereas the CE-MRA shows the more dense macrovascular spaces regardless of flow rate. Major feeding arteries are labeled (MCA=middle cerebral artery, BA=basilar artery, ICA=internal carotid artery, CoW=circle of Willis) and draining veins (SS=straight sinus, SS=the superior sagittal sinus).

30.2.2 Blood flow

Roughly 500 mL/min of blood is delivered to the brain with a peak arterial velocity of ∼100 cm/s. Blood flow is generally fastest in the major feeding arteries and slower in distal arteries and in the venous system; however, flow can be much higher or lower depending on disease. The flow is pulsatile from cardiac contraction and expansion, but this pulsatility is dampened by the compliance of the vasculature. This leads to a high level of pulsatility in the major feeding arteries and limited pulsatility in deep cerebral veins. However, as the venous system is largely depressurized, the flow and geometry of large draining veins is variable, due to changes in intrathoracic pressure from respiration, and is altered with changes to hydration status and posture. Such flow variations can lead to ghosting artifacts in MRA and other sequences if not accounted for.

30.3 Contrast methods

Most MRA methods are bright blood in nature, providing bright vessels with dark background tissue. Unfortunately, the native T_1 and T_2 of blood is not sufficiently different from gray and white matter to provide the required contrast in itself. Thus, neurovascular MRA techniques focus on three primary alternative contrast mechanisms based on the localized motion of blood, the inflow and bulk transport

30.3 Contrast methods

of blood, and the use of exogenous contrast media. Each of these techniques has its own advantages and disadvantages with the selection of technique guided by the clinical question to be answered.

30.3.1 Effect of motion on imaging

The velocity of blood is relatively high and must be considered for all MRA techniques. In the case of inflow and contrast-agent-based techniques, the sequence needs to be minimally sensitive to blood motion; however, purposeful sensitization can also be used to image the vasculature. This is certainly the case for black blood imaging, which provides negative contrast and allows for visualization of the vessel wall. For further reading on black blood imaging, see Chapter 31 and also (Henningsson et al., 2020).

To enable bright blood neurovascular MRA, while avoiding off-resonance artifacts, spoiled gradient echo (GRE) sequences are commonly utilized with a single echo collected after excitation. We can characterize the flow sensitivity of these sequences using a Bloch simulation from excitation to readout, which models motion. For example, magnetization moving at a velocity (v) will have the position:

$$x(t) = x_0 + v \cdot t, \tag{30.1}$$

where x_0 is the initial position and t is the time at the start of simulation. During a single TR, gradients are played out resulting in a precessional frequency that changes over time:

$$\omega(t) = \gamma G_x(t) x(t), \tag{30.2}$$

where ω is the frequency and G_x is the gradient strength; here in one direction. We can separate this based on the position in Eq. (30.1):

$$\omega(t) = \gamma G_x(t) x_0 + \gamma G_x(t) v \cdot t \tag{30.3}$$

and integrate the frequency to determine the phase over time:

$$\phi(t) = \gamma \int_0^t G_x(t) x_0 dt + \gamma \int_0^t G_x(t) v \cdot t dt, \tag{30.4}$$

which represents the k-space and the velocity dependent phase, usually written as:

$$\phi(t) = k_x(t) x_0 + \gamma M_1(t) v. \tag{30.5}$$

Here, k_x is the k-space position and M_1 is the 1st moment of the gradients, both of which change over time. The 1st moment is similar to the b-value in diffusion imaging, but is modeled after coherent flow rather than Brownian motion. Nevertheless, the first moment describes how sensitive a given sequence is to motion, with the 1st moment plotted for several frequency encoding options in Fig. 30.2. There is an interaction between the 1st moment and spatial encoding, which leads to motion–dependent spatial shifts (for more details please see (Nishimura et al., 1991)). Aside from these shifts, the observed signal can be described using a voxel model with parameters evaluated at the echo time (TE):

$$I(x_0, t) = \int \rho(v) e^{i \gamma M_1(\text{TE}) v} dv, \tag{30.6}$$

where I is the complex image after a Fourier transform from k-space to image space, and $\rho(v)$ is the spin density as a function of velocity within a given voxel. For simplicity and characterization of sequences, we can assume that the velocity distribution is uniform with a mean value v_{mean} and a range v_{range}. In this case, the signal will be

$$I(M_1(\text{TE})) = I_0 \operatorname{sinc}\left(\frac{\gamma M_1(\text{TE}) v_{\text{range}}}{2\pi}\right) e^{i\gamma M_1(\text{TE}) v_{\text{mean}}}; \tag{30.7}$$

here I_0 is signal when disregarding flow. From this, we can see that the 1st moment influences both the image magnitude and also the phase, with these being related to v_{range} and v_{mean}, respectively.

Controlling the 1st moment is important for imaging vascular structures, and artifacts can arise if this is not minimized. For example, full-echo sequences sampling from $-k_{\text{max}}$ to k_{max} along the frequency encode direction are rarely used for angiography. Instead, partial (minimum-) echo readouts are usually employed, with or without flow compensation. Flow compensation provides reduced sensitivity to motion-induced artifacts, including signal loss due to intravoxel dephasing, but also ghosting artifacts arising due to phase variations from flow pulsatility. This comes at the cost of longer echo times and minimum TRs and is often only applied along the frequency encoding direction.

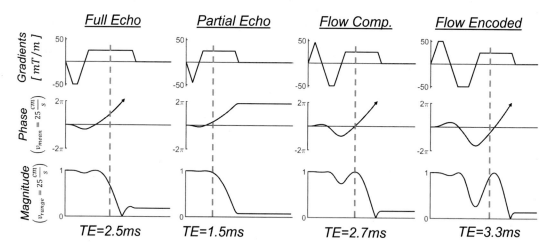

FIGURE 30.2

Comparison of frequency-encoding readout strategies for a GRE sequence showing the gradient waveform, signal phase for $v_{\text{mean}} = 25$ cm/s, and signal magnitude with range of velocities of $v_{\text{range}} = 25$ cm/s. Full-echo sampling symmetrically in k-space leads to a substantial 1st moment at the echo time and to velocity-dependent phase and signal loss. This can be compensated for by using a partial echo, which samples k-space asymmetrically and reduces the minimum echo time and the 1st moment. Alternatively, a bipolar readout can be introduced to provide flow compensation, which nulls the 1st moment at the echo time, or flow encoding, which is used for phase-contrast MRA.

30.3.2 Phase contrast MRA

Motion encoding is also the basis for phase contrast (PC) velocity imaging, which aims to directly measure velocity fields. PC-MRI exists in multiple forms, including 2D or 3D, one- or three-directional velocity encoding, and cardiac-cycle-resolved or time averaged. With recent advances in acquisition acceleration, it has become possible to acquire 3D images with temporal resolution over the cardiac cycle, known as 4D-Flow MRI; however, 3D imaging without cardiac gating is most commonly used for angiography. In all cases, PC-MRI is performed using velocity-encoding bipolar gradients, as shown in Fig. 30.2, which offsets the 1st moment at the echo time. This allows the sampling of Eq. (30.7) at multiple 1st moment values, but with a fixed TE that can be used to solve for velocity for each voxel. Fig. 30.3 shows example images from such a sequence. For PC-MRI, the phase evolution caused by the velocity of the moving blood must also be separated from phase arising from the coils, from chemical shift, and from magnetic susceptibility. The bulk of this phase is independent of the 1st moment and is assumed to be constant for a given echo time, giving the image phase:

$$\phi(x) = \phi_B + \gamma \vec{M}_1 (TE) \cdot \vec{v}(x),$$ (30.8)

where ϕ_B is the background phase, $\vec{M}_1$ is the 1st moment vector, and $\vec{v}$ is the mean velocity vector. We can acquire multiple images using two or more 1st moment values, which will allow us to solve for the velocity. For example, to encode in a single direction, we can acquire one image with flow compensation ($\vec{M}_1 (TE) = 0$), and then a second acquisition with a non-zero first moment in a desired dimension. This will result in a phase difference between the two acquisitions of

$$\Delta\phi(x) = \gamma \Delta\vec{M}_1 (TE) \cdot \vec{v}(x),$$ (30.9)

where Δ signifies the difference between the two acquisitions. This provides one direction of velocity encoding, along the direction of $\vec{M}_1$. For 2D flow imaging, $\vec{M}_1$ is typically along the slice encoding direction, but for 3D applications three interleaved acquisitions are performed with $\vec{M}_1$ played out sequentially in each of the three orthogonal directions. Velocity can then be determined using a solution to Eq. (30.9):

$$v(x) = \frac{\Delta\phi(x)}{\gamma \Delta M_1 (TE)} = V_{enc} \frac{\Delta\phi(x)}{\pi},$$ (30.10)

where V_{enc} is defined as the velocity magnitude that creates a phase of π at the echo time. The V_{enc} also corresponds to the range of velocities which can be measured without artifact, as the angle of a complex signal is only detectable from $-\pi$ to π. Velocities greater than the V_{enc} will phase wrap and erroneously appear to be a velocity within $-V_{enc}$ to V_{enc}. For three-directional encoding, at least four images with differing velocity encoding gradients are required, corresponding to the unknown background phase and three velocity directions. This requirement for multiple images ultimately limits the achievable spatial resolution with PC-MRI compared to other techniques.

Velocity images can be used to create a phase contrast angiogram (PC-MRA). For pure angiographic applications, it is common to calculate an angiogram using the raw complex data:

$$PC\text{-}MRA_{cd} = \sqrt{\sum_{i=1}^{N} |I_i - I_0|^2},$$ (30.11)

474 **Chapter 30** Neurovascular magnetic resonance angiography

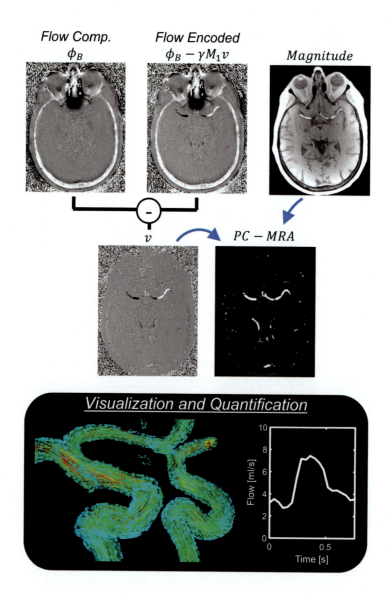

FIGURE 30.3

Source phase images from a PC-MRI experiment, in which one acquisition is collected with flow compensation and a second is collected with flow encoding. These images are then subtracted and scaled to remove the common background phase and converted to velocity. This velocity information can be combined with magnitude information to produce a PC-MRA image. Such data can also be processed to yield flow visualization and quantification, such as the streamlines and flow shown in the ICA.

where I_0 is a flow-compensated image that is complex-subtracted from all images before they are combined using root sum-of-squares. This approach can produce bright contrast from both the velocity-induced phase (v_{mean}) and magnitude signal loss (v_{range}). Alternatively, the PC-MRA field can be calculated from the velocity field and signal magnitude, using a pseudo complex difference:

$$\text{PC-MRA} = I_{avg} \sin\left(\frac{\pi |\vec{v}|}{2V_{enc}}\right), \tag{30.12}$$

where I_{avg} is the average signal magnitude. This function is heuristic in nature, and there is not a universal method for calculating the PC-MRA. This second method of calculating a PC-MRA can produce images with reduced background tissue signal, due to phase corrections applied in post processing and is compatible with more complex multi-point flow encoding schemes. For both methods, the V_{enc} can be set during acquisition to highlight different vascular structures. A V_{enc} of $\sim$100 cm/s is appropriate for the large arteries. Lower V_{enc} values can be used to highlight smaller arteries, veins, and provide robustness to slow flow; however, this will come at the cost of longer echo times, a higher level of signal loss from intravoxel dephasing, and errors where the velocity is higher than the V_{enc}.

A major advantage of PC-MRI is its ability to quantify velocity fields, which can be used to visualize flow and derive hemodynamic information. This requires a segmentation of the vasculature, often directly from the PC-MRA and also post-processing corrections to the velocity data. Though numerous inaccuracies exist in the PC velocity data, residual background phase is the main correctable factor. This background phase arises from imperfect gradient waveforms due to eddy currents, and is typically removed using second- or third-order polynomial fitting to background tissue. After this correction, various measures can be extracted from the flow field, especially from 4D-flow acquisitions. These include those based on flow (mean flow, flow pulsatility) and also processed variables, such as wall shear stress (WSS). The main limiting factor in using PC-MRI quantitatively in the brain is the high required spatial resolution to capture the flow fields in the smaller vascular anatomy. Given the typically 1 mm spatial resolution achievable PC-MRI, such quantification is limited to large vessels.

30.3.3 Inflow-based MRA

The very purpose of the neurovascular system is to transport blood into and away from brain tissue, and this bulk transport also leads to the transport of magnetization into and out of the brain volume. This specifically leads to a different RF pulse history for blood and tissue. For example, inflowing blood often will have a dramatically higher signal than stationary tissue signal. Such inflow affects almost all imaging techniques and should therefore be considered as a potential confounding source of contrast and mitigated if undesirable. This is especially true at higher field strengths, where the RF field is more heterogeneous and the T_1 of blood is longer. In the case of inflow-based MRA, angiographic images are formed using RF pulses, which maximize the inflow signal while minimizing static tissue signal.

Inflow is the basis for time-of-flight (TOF) angiography, which is widely used for non-contrast neurovascular angiography due to its ability to provide high spatial resolution. TOF exists in 2D and 3D variants, with 2D used in cases of slow flow or motion and 3D used to provide high spatial resolution and signal-to-noise ratio (SNR). Both 2D and 3D TOF are based on relatively simple gradient-recalled echo (GRE) sequences, for which inflow is relatively straightforward to model. Consider a simple 3D imaging experiment in which a slab is imaged with a 3D GRE sequence, as shown in Fig. 30.4. With

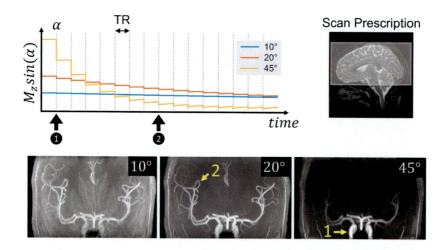

FIGURE 30.4

The maximal signal for a gradient-echo sequence (longitudinal magnetization normalized by flip angle) as a function of time spent in the imaging volume. The signal will initially be much higher, and then, depending on the TR and flip angle, will decay to a lower steady state value. With the prescription shown using an axial slab orthogonal to blood flow into the brain, vessels will be enhanced relative to background signals from gray and white matter. Choosing the flip angle and TR is a balance between enhancing rapidly-filling (Point 1) and slow-to-fill (Point 2) vessels. Limited coronal maximum intensity projections of a single-slab 3D TOF acquisition (bottom row) demonstrate this tradeoff, and a moderate TR and flip angle is often chosen, such as here with a TR=30 ms and a flip angle of 20°.

an axial imaging slab, blood entering the volume from the inferior edge will not have experienced any excitation; thus it will enter the imaging volume with its maximal magnetization. Ignoring T_2^* decay, the signal for the first excitation after entering the volume will be

$$S_0 = M_z^- \sin(\alpha) = M_0 \sin(\alpha(x_i)), \qquad (30.13)$$

where S_i is the signal for the ith excitation, M_z^- is the longitudinal magnetization just before excitation, and $\alpha(x_i)$ is the flip angle for the position of the magnetization at the ith excitation. Between this excitation and the next, the magnetization will recover:

$$M_z^- = M_0 + (M_z^+ - M_0)e^{-TR/T_1}, \qquad (30.14)$$

where M_z^+ is the magnetization after the previous excitation and equal to

$$M_z^+ = M_z^- \cos(\alpha(x_i)). \qquad (30.15)$$

Applying this procedure iteratively, the longitudinal magnetization can be derived as a function of position and time spent in the volume. The magnetization, and resulting signal level, will eventually reach a steady-state value that is much lower than the initial inflow-enhanced value. Assuming the T_1

of blood to be 1600 ms at 3 tesla and TR=30 ms, the initial signal will be $\sim16\times$ higher for a flip angle of 45° and $\sim4\times$ for a flip angle of 20°. As shown in Fig. 30.4, the choice of flip angle and TR determine how fast magnetization is driven to its steady-state value, with higher flip angles and shorter TRs driving the signal faster to a steady-state value.

For the intracranial vasculature, 3D TOF is the preferred method, and whereas 2D TOF uses similar principles, a full discussion is excluded for brevity. Modern TOF acquisitions are essentially inflow-optimized GRE acquisitions. First, these sequences are flow compensated along at least the frequency-encoding direction and often use highly selective asymmetric RF excitation pulses. Second, the RF pulse flip angle and TR are tuned to provide sufficient contrast, usually resulting in an acquisition with a moderate TR (10–40 ms) and flip angle (10–40°), based on desired flow sensitivity and the T_1 of blood at the imaging field strength. As both T_1 and SNR increase with field strength, 3D TOF performs significantly better at high field. Third, it is common to geometrically alter the excitation to maximize inflow contrast, as shown in Fig. 30.5. Specifically, multiple overlapping thin slab acquisitions (MOTSA, see Blatter et al., 1991) are used to reduce the time spins spend in the image volume. Furthermore, the excitation profile of each slab is often designed to be variable, with lower flip angles used at the inflowing edge and higher values used at the outflow. Together, these aid in creating higher and more uniform contrast across the slab, although the assumptions remain that flow is unidirectional, and reduced contrast will occur in tortuous vessels or vessels with slow flow, and in veins flowing in the opposite direction. Contrast can be partially restored by applying off-resonant magnetization transfer (MT) pulses between imaging excitation to further reduce the background signal (Edelman et al., 1992; Pike et al., 1992). This is based on the premise that blood does not exhibit a strong MT effect, due to the lack of a bound macromolecule pool, whereas tissue, especially white matter, does. Thus MT pulses can be applied which reduce the signal from gray and white matter with limited effect on blood. This results in higher contrast at the cost of increased RF energy deposition, which can be limiting at high field strengths.

While 3D TOF is an effective technique for imaging the brain vasculature and is widely used clinically and in research settings, it remains challenging in cases of slow flow. Typically, contrast is lost between the vasculature and background tissue after blood is within the excited volume for more than ~500 ms. To greatly enhance slow flow visualization, inflow-based angiography can alternatively be achieved using arterial spin labeling (ASL). As described in Chapter 12, ASL can be used to label blood prior to entering the imaging volume. With images taken with a label present and a separately acquired control reference, a complex subtraction of the images will result in only the labeled blood itself. Unlike perfusion ASL, angiographic ASL is performed without an extended post-label delay, is generally not coupled with background suppression pulses, and uses a flow-robust imaging readout (e.g., GRE). This decoupling of imaging and inflow sensitization allows background-free intracranial MRA to be achieved, and thus contrast exists regardless of inflow time. Due to signal decay of the label, exponentially with the T_1 of blood, the practical limit is closer to ~5 s. With this substantial reduction in slow-flow limitation, single-slab intracranial inflow MRA images are feasible with improved depiction of anatomy even in cases of complex or tortuous flow. Furthermore, small modifications to the pulse sequence allow vessel-selective tagging and visualization of inflow dynamics, although this comes at the cost of lower SNR and longer acquisition times for equivalent resolution.

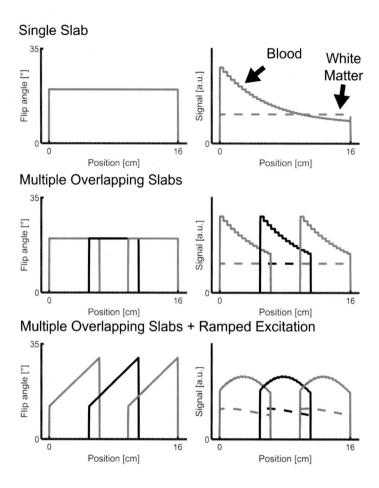

FIGURE 30.5

Comparison of signal assuming left-to-right blood motion at 15 cm/s for three excitation paradigms. As in Fig. 30.4, imaging with a single slab results in blood signal that is enhanced upon initially entering the slab, but which decays to a level below that of white matter as more RF pulses are applied. Acquiring data with three overlapping slabs reduces the inflow saturation, resulting in higher blood-to-tissue contrast across the slab. These three slabs are combined across the overlapping regions, but there remains a sharp flow enhancement transition. The use of multiple slabs excited with a ramped flip angle reduces the initial enhancement (which drives decay to equilibrium), allowing for a more uniform signal enhancement. These plots will depend on the flow velocity in the slab selection direction.

30.3.4 Contrast-enhanced MRA

Contrast-enhanced MRA (CE-MRA), utilizing exogenous T_1-shortening contrast agents, can be more robust to slow flow, thus providing brain filling patterns, and be acquired in less time than MRA based on inflow or motion enhancement. When CE-MRA was introduced in the late 1990s it made

30.3 Contrast methods

incredible inroads to almost every vascular territory and is by far the most dominant method for MR angiography outside the head. In the neurovascular system, CE-MRA has been less pervasive and is challenged by the small caliber of intracranial vessels and the rapid transit of blood across the brain's capillary network. CE-MRA has two basic forms, single frame or time resolved, both of which are acquired during the dynamic passage of an intravenously delivered bolus injection of a gadolinium-based contrast agent (e.g. gadoterate meglumine). In each case, the passage of contrast agent requires care to capture an arterial image in which the vasculature is not obscured by enhancing tissues and veins.

To achieve high quality CE-MRA, strategies must be used to provide acceleration, mitigate timing errors, and remove background signal. CE-MRA utilizes heavily T_1-weighted 3D GRE, typically using partial-echo sampling without flow compensation and high imaging bandwidth to provide the shortest possible TR. Prior to contrast injection, a pre-contrast mask will usually be collected and subtracted in k-space to remove signal from non-enhancing tissue. Subsequently, contrast is injected during which image(s) are acquired. A temporal resolution of 1 s with 0.5 mm spatial resolution would be sufficient to detect most abnormal intracranial filling patterns and prevent most significant errors from venous and perfusion overlap. However, this leads to an estimated required acceleration >100× for full brain coverage. This is far greater than what is achievable with parallel imaging acceleration. Thus for the past several decades, CE-MRA techniques have been developed to share information across a larger temporal footprint, while still reconstructing images that represent the desired temporal frame.

For example, single-frame MRA can be performed by (1) timing the acquisition to start as soon as the arterial vasculature is filled with contrast, and (2) collecting a single 3D image with k-space data collection, starting at the center and progressing to the edge. Correct timing can be achieved by monitoring the upstream arterial signal in real time with a rapid dynamic acquisition or using a test bolus at a lower dose with the same injected volume and protocol. Although a single phase is collected, k-space will still be modulated by the contrast dynamics and CE-MRA images can have substantial artifacts at vessel edges, including ringing and edge enhancement (Maki et al., 1996). To compensate for these artifacts, the injection protocol can be tailored to match the temporal footprint of the acquisition time. Alternatively, images can be collected in the steady state, providing a combined MRA and MRV.

As an alternative to single-frame imaging, dynamic CE-MRA can be performed by simply collecting multiple frames during the acquisition, an example of which is shown in Fig. 30.6. To achieve this, it is most common to use "view sharing" strategies, which share sections of k-space across frames. Keyhole imaging is perhaps the most basic view sharing acquisition and updates a central region of k-space each frame, with the resolution-providing edges of k-space being shared across all frames. More complex strategies exist (e.g., TRICKS, TWIST, 4D-TRAK), which update the peripheral regions of k-space more frequently to reduce artifacts from mismatch between the center and edge of k-space (Korosec et al., 1996). Recent developments in reconstruction algorithm techniques, including compressed sensing, low rank approximation, and deep learning, provide opportunities for substantially higher accelerations. All of these techniques exploit known information about the underlying structure (e.g., few vessels, similar temporal dynamics, etc.). With these techniques the required acceleration factors of 100× may be possible, as is shown in Fig. 30.6. However, similar to the adoption of view sharing schemes, the impact of new artifacts on clinical interpretation must be considered.

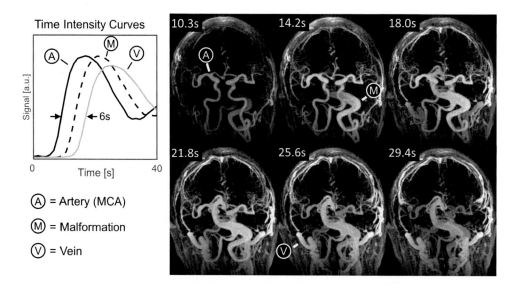

FIGURE 30.6

Dynamic contrast-enhanced MRA images showing the temporal evolution of contrast in a subject with a vascular malformation, dilatation of the vertebral and basilar arteries. Mask-subtracted CE-MRA is shown collected with 1.26 s temporal resolution using a constrained reconstruction approach (Extreme MRI) and 3D radial sampling. As shown in the time-intensity curves, there is a brief time window in which the arterial system is enhanced, while the veins are not. This is location-dependent and can be modified with pathology. In this case, the arterial malformation has substantially slowed flow and enhances later than the arteries fed by the internal carotids. Nevertheless, temporal dynamics aid in visualizing and characterizing vascular structures.

30.4 Comparisons of techniques

Inflow, motion, and contrast-enhanced MRA techniques are all used clinically with the specific technique chosen based on the expected disease. Non-contrast techniques perform extremely well with normal vasculature, but can be subject to artifacts with disease, particularly slow flow. Despite this, they often achieve higher spatial resolution using extended acquisition times, and hence improved depiction of small vascular structures. In particular, 3D-TOF can often provide superior depiction of arterial stenosis (vessel lumen narrowing from atherosclerosis) and small aneurysms (bulged/ballooned blood vessels). CE-MRA and some of the emerging non-contrast techniques (e.g., ASL-MRA) provide more robustness when vessels are tortuous or when flow is slow. This includes in recirculating flow regions distal to arterial stenosis. Fig. 30.7 shows an example comparison in a subject with a slow-flow vascular malformation that is challenging to visualize, the same subject shown in Fig. 30.6. As shown in the images, non-contrast 3D-TOF and PC-MRA poorly visualize the structure, whereas appropriately timed CE-MRA provides excellent depiction. Interestingly, negative contrast black-blood imaging with T_1-weighted 3D fast spin echo imaging (e.g., CUBE/SPACE) provides perhaps the best depiction. Fig. 30.8 shows another comparison example; in this case, comparing dynamic ASL-MRA with PC-MRA and a post-contrast CE-MRA in a subject with an arteriovenous malformation (AVM).

In AVMs, there are high-flow feeding arteries, which feed a nested vascular shunt (nisus) direct to draining veins. These can be challenging to assess with CE-MRA, due to extremely rapid transit from the feeding arteries to draining veins. Here, inflow-based ASL-MRA is able to provide the extremely high temporal resolution (500 ms) needed to depict the feeding arteries and draining veins. These are also visible in PC-MRA and CE-MRA, but require careful inspection to trace the arteries.

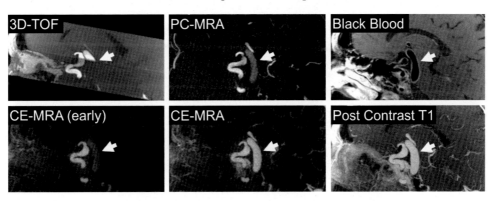

FIGURE 30.7
Sagittal images from the same subject as in Fig. 30.6, demonstrating challenges with slow flow in the vascular malformation (arrow). Bright-blood images are shown as 8 mm limited maximum intensity projections. Non-contrast 3D-TOF and PC-MRA techniques poorly visualize the vessel lumen, due to a long inflow time and slow blood velocity, respectively. CE-MRA techniques provide the opportunity to visualize the vascular structures; however, acquisitions must be timed to provide adequate filling of the vascular structures-of-interest. As an alternative to bright-blood MRA, black-blood images can be collected with T_1-weighted 3D spin-echo sequences. Such sequences can provide depiction of extremely slow flow, especially when combined with high resolution post-contrast T_1-weighted images.

30.5 Summary and outlook

For intracranial applications, common MRA techniques are based on inflow, motion, and exogenous contrast agents. Each of these techniques can be used to image the intracranial vasculature, with the selection of the technique dependent on the features of the expected vascular disease. These techniques can depict both the arterial and venous system and complement structural imaging. This includes identifying abnormal vascular anatomy that may affect perfusion, characterizing upstream vascular lesions, leading to tissue damage including stroke, and providing segmentations to avoid the inclusion of vessels in quantitative measures. MR angiography is largely limited by the relatively slow acquisition speed of MRI, and will improve with advances in accelerated acquisition and reconstruction. Higher acceleration will improve the achievable spatial and temporal resolution of established techniques, and will also enable emerging techniques, such as 4D-Flow and ASL-MRA. Long term, it is likely that "lumenographic" techniques may become insufficient to grade vascular lesions. Here, MRI holds potential to become a dominant and comprehensive technique, providing proxy measures of vessel wall health and the status of the downstream tissue.

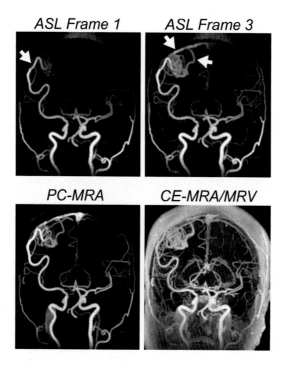

FIGURE 30.8

Comparison of multi-delay ASL-MRA, PC-MRA, and CE-MRA/MRV for the identification of feeding and draining veins of an arteriovenous malformation (AVM). In the first frame of this pCASL-based ASL sequence, the feeding artery is identified. In the third ASL frame, 1 s later, two draining veins can be visualized. The same vessels are present in the PC-MRA, especially visible due to their high flow rate; however, velocity data may be challenging to interrogate in the dense nidus of the AVM. CE-MRA, here without time resolution, shows the higher spatial fidelity, but can be challenging to acquire with sufficient temporal resolution for such fast flowing structures.

References

Blatter, D.D., Parker, D.L., Robison, R.O., 1991. Cerebral MR angiography with multiple overlapping thin slab acquisition. Part I. Quantitative analysis of vessel visibility. Radiology 179, 805–811. https://doi.org/10.1148/radiology.179.3.2027996.

Edelman, R.R., Ahn, S.S., Chien, D., Li, W., Goldmann, A., Mantello, M., Kramer, J., Kleefield, J., 1992. Improved time-of-flight MR angiography of the brain with magnetization transfer contrast. Radiology 184, 395–399. https://doi.org/10.1148/radiology.184.2.1620835.

Henningsson, M., Malik, S., Botnar, R., Castellanos, D., Hussain, T., Leiner, T., 2020. Black-blood contrast in cardiovascular MRI. J. Magn. Reson. Imaging, e27399. https://doi.org/10.1002/jmri.27399.

Korosec, F.R., Frayne, R., Grist, T.M., Mistretta, C.A., 1996. Time-resolved contrast-enhanced 3D MR angiography. Magn. Reson. Med. 36, 345–351. https://doi.org/10.1002/mrm.1910360304.

Maki, J.H., Prince, M.R., Londy, F.J., Chenevert, T.L., 1996. The effects of time varying intravascular signal intensity and k-space acquisition order on three-dimensional MR angiography image quality. J. Magn. Reson. Imaging 6, 642–651. https://doi.org/10.1002/jmri.1880060413.

Nishimura, D.G., Jackson, J.I., Pauly, J.M., 1991. On the nature and reduction of the displacement artifact in flow images. Magn. Reson. Med. 22, 481–492. https://doi.org/10.1002/mrm.1910220255.

Pike, G.B., Hu, B.S., Glover, G.H., Enzmann, D.R., 1992. Magnetization transfer time-of-flight magnetic resonance angiography. Magn. Reson. Med. 25, 372–379. https://doi.org/10.1002/mrm.1910250217.

Further reading

Edelman, R.R., Koktzoglou, I., 2019. Noncontrast MR angiography: an update. J. Magn. Reson. Imaging 49, 355–373. https://doi.org/10.1002/jmri.26288. An overview detailing emerging noncontrast MRA techniques and their applications.

Henningsson, M. Malik, S. Botnar, R. Castellanos, D. Hussain, T. Leiner, T., n.d. Black-blood contrast in cardiovascular MRI, J. Magn. Reson. Imaging n/a, e27399. https://doi.org/10.1002/jmri.27399. An overview of black blood imaging methods and applications to provide depiction of the vessel wall rather than lumen.

Markl, M., Frydrychowicz, A., Kozerke, S., Hope, M., Wieben, O., 2012. 4D flow MRI. J. Magn. Reson. Imaging 36, 1015–1036. https://doi.org/10.1002/jmri.23632. White paper focussed on principles of 4D-Flow.

Youn, S.W., Lee, J., n.d. From 2D to 4D phase-contrast MRI in the neurovascular system: will it be a quantum jump or a fancy decoration? J. Magn. Reson. Imaging n/a. https://doi.org/10.1002/jmri.27430. A detailed review paper detailing the use cases of 4D-Flow for intracranial applications.

Turski, P., Scarano, A., Hartman, E., Clark, Z., Schubert, T., Rivera, L., Wu, Y., Wieben, O., Johnson, K., 2016. Neurovascular 4DFlow MRI (phase contrast MRA): emerging clinical applications. Neurovascular Imaging 2, 8. https://doi.org/10.1186/s40809-016-0019-0. An overview of emerging applications of 4D-Flow for Neurovascular Applications.

Carr, J.C., Carroll, T.J. (Eds.), 2012. Book Providing a More Detailed Overview of Non-contrast and Contrast Enhanced MRA Techniques. Magnetic Resonance Angiography: Principles and Applications. Springer-Verlag, New York.

CHAPTER

Neurovascular vessel wall imaging: new techniques and clinical applications

31

Chun Yuan[a], Mahmud Mossa-Basha[a], Zachary Miller[a], and Zechen Zhou[b]

[a]*Department of Radiology, University of Washington, Seattle, WA, United States*
[b]*Philips Research North America, Cambridge, MA, United States*

31.1 Introduction

Neurovascular imaging, considering its importance in assessing the blood supply to the brain, plays a key role in both clinical and research applications. Biomarkers for blood supply rely on assessing the vessel luminal integrity (angiographic imaging, see Chapter 30), the vessel wall (the main focus of this chapter), and blood flow and tissue perfusion (see Chapters 12–14). Magnetic resonance imaging (MRI) has played an important role in all these areas due to its high spatial resolution, lack of ionizing radiation, and newly developed techniques targeting various areas of the vessel wall. This chapter focuses on vessel wall imaging (VWI) in the carotid and intracranial arteries. VWI, by definition, aims to visualize normal and diseased blood vessels, enable quantitative measurement of vessel wall thickness, and other morphological features, and characterize wall tissue composition, especially diseased arteries, such as atherosclerosis. The first section of this chapter discusses the technical background and newly developed techniques for vessel wall imaging, and the second discusses current applications of VWI techniques in the carotid and intracranial arteries.

31.2 Imaging technology

VWI usually requires multi-contrast, high-resolution, large-coverage, black-blood, and rapid imaging features in the MRI sequence and acquisition design to meet the clinical needs for atherosclerotic plaque diagnosis (Yuan et al., 2020). Characterization of different plaque components for vulnerability stratification relies on their distinct physical properties that can be decoded by multi-contrast MR scans (Fig. 31.1). High-resolution imaging is also clinically necessary to evaluate vessel wall condition and disease progression stages accurately, particularly for intracranial vessels. In addition, the large-coverage scan strategy (Yuan et al., 2020) provides a single-scan solution for screening the entire vascular bed, which helps to improve the acquisition efficiency of diagnostic information. Furthermore, black-blood imaging techniques ensure good image contrast between lumen and vessel wall that enable more accurate plaque morphological measurements. However, these imaging requirements may result in long scan times or may need compensation for image quality loss. Therefore rapid imaging

Advances in Magnetic Resonance Technology and Applications, Volume 4, ISSN 2666-9099. https://doi.org/10.1016/B978-0-12-822479-3.00048-8
Copyright © 2021 Elsevier Inc. All rights reserved.

techniques to accelerate clinical workflow, while preserving image quality, are important in VWI techniques.

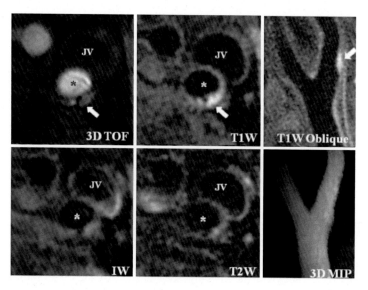

FIGURE 31.1

An atherosclerotic plaque with intraplaque hemorrhage (white arrows) can be found in the left internal carotid artery (*). This lesion has low plaque burden (percent wall volume=36%) and normal MRA (3-dimensional TOF, maximum intensity projection). JV: jugular vein; TOF: time of flight; MIP: maximum intensity projection. Reproduced with permission from Zhao et al., 2011.

VWI analysis is another critical aspect to extraction of diagnostic information from the acquired images and for assisting in clinical interpretation of plaque morphologies and components. Vessel wall analysis can be applied for many purposes from screening to full comprehensive vascular analysis, including artery tracing, plaque segmentation, and characterization, for diagnosing different vascular pathologies, such as vasculitis, atherosclerosis, and arteriosclerosis. Development of automatic analysis tools will be beneficial for standardized and efficient clinical diagnosis procedures.

In this section, we will introduce the currently available imaging and analysis techniques for VWI, and briefly discuss some examples of emerging approaches to improve VWI in terms of acquisition, reconstruction, and analysis.

31.2.1 Vessel wall imaging sequences

The most widely used vessel wall imaging sequences can generally be divided into two major categories, depending on the flow suppression techniques. The first category of VWI sequence relies on a flow suppression preparation pulse, which can be easily integrated with any fast acquisition module (e.g., spoiled gradient echo, balanced steady-state free precession). The design of flow suppression preparation pulses has also evolved from the basic thin-slab flow suppression methods (e.g., saturation bands, double inversion-recovery, quadruple inversion-recovery) to the most recent large-coverage flow suppression methods (e.g., inversion recovery, T_2-prepared inversion recovery, motion sensitized driven equilibrium MSDE (Wang et al., 2010), delay alternating with nutation for tailored excitation DANTE (Li et al., 2012)). In particular, flow-sensitive gradient-based techniques (i.e., MSDE, DANTE) are currently used in many 3D VWI exams across different anatomies, and supported by multiple vendors. The other category of VWI sequence does not rely on extra preparation modules, but on the intrinsic flow suppression effects within the acquisition module (e.g., fast/turbo spin-echo, PSIF), where the flowing spins fail to establish coherent echo pathways. Specifically, 3D turbo spin-echo (TSE) with a variable flip angle (VFA) refocusing pulse train is the most common 3D VWI solution for whole-body vessel wall exams and is well supported by almost all major vendors (e.g., 3D CUBE/SPACE/VISTA on GE/Siemens/Philips, respectively), considering its robustness to field inhomogeneity, high signal-to-noise ratio (SNR) property, and flexible compatibility with multiple imaging contrasts. For intracranial VWI (IVWI), T_1-weighted 3D TSE VFA scans are often performed with an anti-drive or tip-down module at the end of the echo train to suppress the cerebrospinal fluid (CSF) and improve T_1 contrast (Kerwin et al., 2007). For other contrast weightings of 3D TSE VFA scans, CSF and blood can be jointly suppressed by additional DANTE preparation. Different VWI sequences can be combined to produce multi-contrast and black-blood images, but the optimal sequence and scan parameter selection typically depends on the vascular beds and applications. Beyond the imaging contrasts provided by different MR properties, exogenous contrast agents (e.g. gadolinium chelates) can also enhance the delineation of outer wall and highlight atherosclerotic plaque composition and vessel wall activity (Yuan et al., 2020). With increasing application of contrast media deposition, low-dose contrast-enhanced VWI or VWI without contrast administration may be a potential future development trend.

Recently, a few technical advances have been made with respect to IVWI sequence design. A new concept in general sequence design and optimization has demonstrated its feasibility by leveraging reinforcement learning techniques, but its evaluation is still in the early stages. Further development of such approaches may also facilitate more robust, time-efficient, and non-intuitive pulse sequences for IVWI application. On the other hand, recent studies have shown the potential to improve overall SNR and image sharpness of whole-brain 3D TSE IVWI by changing the strategy of VFA design, since deep learning-based techniques can be used to enhance the point spread function along the phase-encoding and slice-encoding planes (Fig. 31.2). This framework offers an additional tool to optimize pulse sequences by leveraging improved image formation theory and processes.

31.2.2 Vessel wall imaging acceleration

Multi-contrast, high-resolution, large-coverage VWI scans may have long image acquisition times, which prevents VWI from clinical accessibility, because long exam times may cause image quality degradation due to patient motion, and thus reduce clinical workflow efficiency. Rapid imaging techniques are therefore valuable in improving clinical translation of VWI to more hospitals and imaging centers. Parallel imaging and partial Fourier acquisition are the most applicable techniques for whole-brain IVWI acceleration on most clinical scanners. By leveraging data redundancy and prior information (e.g., multi-channel receiver information, image content close to being real-valued), they can provide 2- to 4-fold overall scan time reduction, whilst maintaining acceptable image quality for diagnosis. Compressed sensing, as one of the latest MR innovations, enables additional acceleration capability by using the prior knowledge that images can be sparsely represented in a transformed domain, which allows 5- to 6-fold scan time reduction, while preserving similar quality to parallel imaging

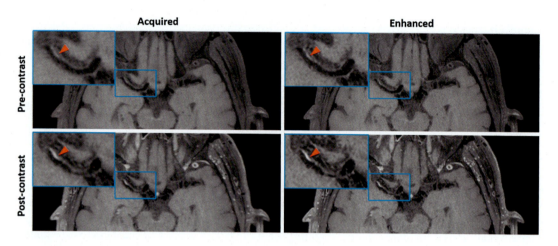

FIGURE 31.2

Example of convolutional neural network-based (CNN-based) image enhancement from a patient acquired with optimized 3D T_1-weighted TSE sequence for intracranial vessel wall imaging. For both pre- and post-contrast images, CNN-enhanced results can provide clearer definition of the intracranial vessel wall and atherosclerotic plaque (as shown by red arrows) in the right middle cerebral artery. From Yuan et al., 2020.

reconstruction at a lower acceleration factor. With these acceleration techniques, a whole-brain T_1-weighted 3D TSE based IVWI with isotropic resolution of 0.5 mm–0.6 mm isotropic can be acquired in around 5–6 mins, which has already shown promising results for frontline clinical routine use.

There are some emerging advancements in different technical development areas. 3D IVWI is typically acquired with Cartesian encoding in clinical settings. For parallel imaging and compressed sensing, the aliasing caused by sub-sampling can only propagate within the phase and slice-encoding planes. By using non-Cartesian encoding, such aliasing can be distributed across the entire 3D space so that the full power of coil sensitivity spatial encoding can be used for unfolding/parallel imaging reconstruction to reduce noise amplification effects. Wave encoding, as one special non-Cartesian encoding strategy (see Chapter 1), has shown some benefits in IVWI application. In compressed sensing, the current method of sparsifying images on most of MR scanners is by use of a wavelet transform, which is a fixed and universal transform and may not be optimal for certain applications.

Deep learning offers a data-driven framework to train a tailored deep neural network that can represent the image in a more appropriate transformed sparse domain for a targeted application, resulting in a more accurately restored image than the universal or learned sparse transform with shallow architectures. With a deep neural network as the prior knowledge for compressed sensing, accelerated 3D IVWI may better preserve the pathologies in reconstructed MR images. Deep learning-based approaches can also enhance the image quality of accelerated IVWI in the downstream image formation process, including denoising to suppress the residual noise, and super-resolution to improve structure delineation. Besides the separate acceleration of multi-contrast scans, proper translation of shareable knowledge from acquired images to guide subsequent serial imaging and reconstruction would enable even higher acceleration of multi-contrast IVWI.

It is also worth mentioning that the approach of temporal-spatial low-rank modeling allows highly accelerated dynamic volumetric imaging to be achieved in a clinically acceptable time, which can resolve motion issues during scanning, and offers potential for quantitative parametric mapping. Compared to well-established sequence designs, more advances are expected in the realm of imaging acceleration, particularly with the aid of deep learning techniques.

31.2.3 Vessel wall imaging analysis

VWI provides a rich but complex set of images, where multiple contrast weightings of the same anatomy are produced. Information from different weighted images needs to be combined for interpretation of vessel wall composition. Though such interpretation is common in radiology, the major challenges of VWI analysis are the small size and variable plaque composition within a small region of plaque. Manual review is workable for plaque component identification (Kerwin et al., 2007). However, quantification requires segmentation from multiple image slices and leads to longer review times and increased inter- and intra-reader variability. Automatic segmentation methods can provide reproducible measurements, whereas human observers can check for accuracy of component identification and further train the models for improved performance. An additional challenge in VWI is caused by the fact that VWI interpretation is not yet routine in clinical practice. Therefore vessel wall analysis requires intensive training at specialist centers. These factors also reduce the opportunity for a wide-ranging use of this technology. Once trained and validated, the deep learning systems may provide an opportunity for more medical centers to bring the benefits of plaque imaging to their patients.

Some software packages have already been developed and widely used for automated or semi-automated vessel wall assessment in different VWI studies. Fig. 31.3 illustrates an example of plaque information that can be generated using the CASCADE software tool (University of Washington, Seattle, USA, Kerwin et al., 2007). Both identification and quantification of plaque components have been shown to predict clinical outcomes. Multiple plaque components, such as lipid-rich necrotic core (LRNC), calcification, intraplaque hemorrhage (IPH), loose matrix, fibrous cap, and fibrous tissue, can be identified using vessel wall MRI. The presence of IPH in the carotid arteries is associated with stroke or transient ischemic attack in the ipsilateral side. Plaques with large LRNC, IPH, and a disrupted fibrous cap are deemed to be higher risk for events. Moreover, plaque composition is also known to affect the progression of disease. For example, the presence of IPH is known to stimulate plaque progression in the same artery. Quantitative measurements of the vessel wall were instrumental in describing such clinical associations. A combination of qualitative and quantitative information from plaque analysis form the basis of risk scores.

Automatic plaque component identification and quantification requires several processing steps. The essential step for quantification is plaque segmentation, where each image pixel is classified into a plaque component label. Several semi-automated methods for plaque analysis using machine learning-based methods have been demonstrated (Chen et al., 2018). While these methods have shown promise in fast segmentation of plaque components, there are additional improvements in accuracy that may be possible to obtain using deep convolutional neural network-based (CNN-based) methods(Shi et al., 2019; see also Fig. 31.3).

Relatively straight arteries, such as the carotid bifurcation segment or short peripheral artery segments, may be more amenable to direct CNN-based segmentation. More complicated vessel geometries, such as the coronary arteries or intracranial arteries, will require pre-processing to extract the artery centerline as the first step. Identification of the artery centerline can be done manually, either by drawing

490 Chapter 31 Neurovascular vessel wall imaging

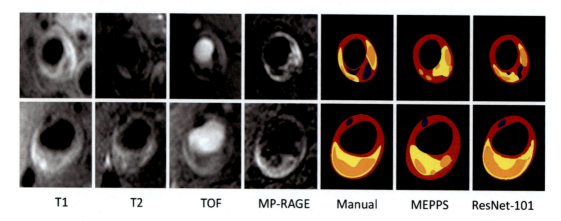

FIGURE 31.3

Deep learning-based segmentation for vessel wall and plaque components using a deep neural network (ResNet-101) compared to conventional machine learning method (MEPPS) shows better correspondence to the reference standard manual reader's contours. Contours shown are LRNC (yellow), IPH (orange), calcification (dark blue), and fibrous tissue (red). MEPPS is a built-in plaque component segmentation method in the CASCADE software package. MEPPS: morphology-enhanced probabilistic plaque segmentation; CASCADE: computer-aided system for cardiovascular disease evaluation. Reproduced with permission from Dong et al., 2017.

lumen/wall contours or by identifying an image ROI to process. However, fully automated end-to-end analysis of scans requires automated methods to locate the artery. Studies have demonstrated the feasibility of CNN-based artery location methods in carotid black-blood VWI applications. Locating long and tortuous arteries, such as intracranial arteries, requires a different approach, because it is difficult to obtain an image slice perpendicular to the axis of the artery.

For IVWI, the intracranial arteries can be traced using deep learning-based segmentation on non-contrast MRA (Chen et al., 2018). Fig. 31.4 shows results of intracranial arteries identified on TOF MRA, indicating that even distal arteries can be detected well, which can be used to quantify the variations of intracranial vessels. Following such artery tracing, slices axial to the artery at each point can be calculated automatically, and these axial slice coordinates can propagate to other image weightings of IVWI for in-plane plaque segmentation with the registration transform matrix.

Beyond the process of artery tracing, plaque segmentation, and quantification, an additional step is required to compile these elements into a clinically interpretable form that is predictive of patient outcome. A wealth of informative studies exist linking VWI features to clinical outcomes. Using traditional multivariate analysis, carotid IPH has been demonstrated to be predictive of recurrent cerebrovascular events in patients with symptomatic high-grade carotid stenosis. Similarly, IPH has been shown to be predictive of fibrous cap rupture. Currently, a few studies attempt to associate VWI features with clinical outcomes using more advanced models. However, the predictive ability of conventional models can potentially be improved by using deep neural networks, which may also identify new risk predictors that were not identified by classical methods.

With the advent of new deep learning-based techniques, VWI has entered a new age for rapid image formation and quantitative analysis that may improve the current clinical workflow and diagnostic con-

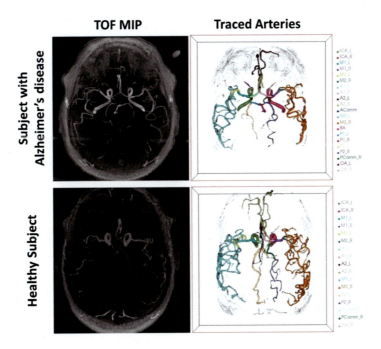

FIGURE 31.4

Arterial centerlines shown in different colors were extracted from 3D TOF images, and labeled with anatomical segments. This quantification tool (iCafe) can better represent the variations of intracranial blood supply during cognitive decline. Distal artery length measurement by iCafe is reduced in subjects with mild cognitive impairment or dementia compared to cognitively normal subjects. iCafe: intracranial artery feature extraction.

fidence. New VWI-based risk predictors may demonstrate its unique value for different neurovascular applications.

31.3 Current applications

The *American Journal of Neuroradiology* recently published two white papers (Mandell et al., 2017; Saba et al., 2018) authored by experts from the American Society of Neuroradiology (ASNR) vessel wall imaging study group on carotid and intracranial vessel wall imaging. There is extensive discussion of current and future clinical applications for both vascular territories. In this section, we focus our attention on recent developments related to clinical applications for these vessels.

31.3.1 The carotid artery

In the carotid artery, many recent studies have focused on the role of vessel wall imaging in embolic stroke of undetermined source (ESUS, sometimes referred to as cryptogenic stroke) case evaluation.

ESUS has been reported in up to 40% of ischemic stroke patients. One of the hypotheses for ESUS is that some of these patients may have carotid atherosclerosis that causes less than 50% stenosis, but is at high risk of rupture due to the status of the vessel wall and underlying atherosclerotic plaque. Imaging carotid atherosclerosis with MRI enables us to visualize telltale features of culprit lesions, which can help to find or exclude large artery atherosclerosis as the underlying etiology, and optimize secondary prevention accordingly for individual patients.

In one of the earlier studies by Freilinger et al., the authors applied carotid VWI to 32 consecutive patients with cryptogenic stroke and non-stenosing (<50%) carotid atherosclerosis (Freilinger et al., 2012). A multi-contrast MRI protocol detected complicated lesions, including fibrous cap rupture, intraplaque hemorrhage, and mural thrombus, in 12 (37.5%) of the plaques ipsilateral to the stroke, whereas none were found on the contralateral side, which showed signals consistent with fibroatheroma and pathological intimal thickening as the predominant lesion type. This pilot study concluded that arterio-arterial embolism from complicated, non-stenosing carotid atherosclerotic plaques may play a role in a subgroup of patients previously diagnosed with cryptogenic stroke. This study led to a prospectively designed, multi-center study: the carotid plaque imaging in acute stroke (CAPIAS) study (Bayer-Karpinska et al., 2013), which aims to determine the frequency, characteristics, clinical, and radiological long-term consequences of ipsilateral complicated American Heart Association lesion Type VI carotid artery plaque in patients with cryptogenic stroke.

There is a series of recent studies based on MRI, CT, and ultrasound that all point to a similar observation that, among ESUS subjects, there were carotid lesions with intraplaque high-intensity signal, intraplaque hemorrhage (IPH), above a certain thickness, and non-stenotic plaque ipsilateral to the side of infarction. Furthermore, there are two recent reporting-based studies involving over 1000 subjects that provided quantitative reports supporting the argument of VWI of carotid in ESUS subjects.

Zhao et al. performed a multi-center prospective study to determine the prevalence of high-risk carotid plaques among patients with cerebral ischemic symptoms in the anterior circulation and with evidence of carotid plaque determined by ultrasound (Zhao et al., 2017). Based on 1047 recruited subjects and VWI MRI of the carotid artery, the investigators found that approximately two thirds of high-risk plaques (HRP) were in arteries with <50% stenosis and that maximum wall thickness was found to be a stronger discriminator than stenosis for HRP detection. Detailed analysis of plaque burdens of carotid lesions (Fig. 31.5) in these carotid arteries found that among subjects with <50% stenosis, 12.6% had HRP ipsilateral to the side of stroke and the rest did not (Watase et al., 2019). Besides HRP features, wall thickness was a major factor of difference.

In a recent report by Kamel et al. (2020), the investigators examined the causes of stroke that may be reclassified after accounting for non-stenosing carotid plaques with high-risk features. They included 1721 acute ischemic stroke patients and used carotid MR angiography to identify the presence of IPH as evidence of HRP, and found almost 21% of ESUS subjects might be reclassified to be stroke caused by large artery atherosclerosis and, interestingly, 23% of subjects with cardioembolic source stroke might be stroke from multiple sources.

These findings highlight the issues of under-appreciated carotid plaques and their significant impact in the determination of the source of stroke. VWI MRI, with its ability to identify HRP and measure plaque burden and vessel wall morphology, will play an ever more important role for clinical applications in this area.

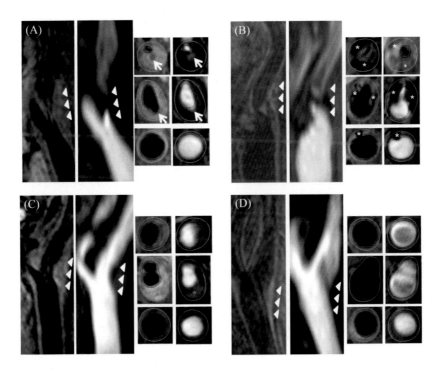

FIGURE 31.5

Example magnetic resonance images of the four groups. (A) SS(+)/HRP(+): significant stenosis with ulceration (white arrow); (B) SS(+)/HRP(−): significant stenosis with calcified plaque (white asterisk); (C) SS(−)/HRP(+): no significant stenosis with IPH (orange asterisk); (D) SS(−)/HRP (−): no significant stenosis with small plaque. Red outline, lumen; light blue outline, outer vessel wall; white arrowheads, outer vessel wall. (SS = significant stenosis, HRP = high-risk plague, IPH = intraplaque hemorrhage). From Watase et al., 2019.

31.4 Intracranial arteries

IVWI is a reliable and reproducible technique, specifically for intracranial atherosclerotic plaque detection and characterization and aneurysm evaluation (Mossa-Basha et al., 2015). This technique has also shown value in disease characterization (Hartman et al., 2019). The clinical applications of IVWI also continue to expand, as the body of literature grows, providing additional predictive value of IVWI with vascular disease states, as well as new insights into vascular pathophysiology. We will discuss the value of IVWI in specific arterial disease states.

31.4.1 Intracranial atherosclerosis

Intracranial atherosclerosis disease (ICAD) is a leading cause of ischemic stroke worldwide, and is seen more frequently in certain ethnicities, including East Asian, Black, and Hispanic populations. ICAD, similar to atherosclerosis elsewhere in the vascular tree, has a number of ways in which it can result in ischemic stroke, including perforator ostial occlusion, hypo-perfusion, and plaque rupture with *in-situ* thrombosis or artery-to-artery embolus (López-Cancio et al., 2014).

The reference standards for evaluation of ICAD are luminal imaging techniques, such as CT angiography, MRA, and digital subtraction angiography (DSA). However, stenosis assessment frequently underestimates the presence and burden of ICAD. This is because ICAD frequently outwardly remodels, and can reach significant burden before resulting in appreciable luminal stenosis (Fig. 31.6). In the evaluation of 339 autopsy cases with ischemic stroke, 40% of ICAD lesions that were found showed minimal to no stenosis (Mazighi et al., 2008). IVWI can be more sensitive for the detection of ICAD. In the performance of IVWI in 1765 subjects aged 67–90 years, the prevalence of ICAD was 31%, with 9% showing $\geq 50\%$ stenosis (Suri et al., 2016). The prevalence of ICAD with $\geq 50\%$ stenosis was 8% in whites and 12% in blacks. A recent meta-analysis (Wang et al., 2019), which included 21 studies with 463 patients without luminal stenosis on MRA and 651 patients with stenosis<50%, showed that the prevalence of non-stenotic plaque in patients with acute/subacute infarct is 50.6%, whereas the prevalence of plaques with <50% was 51.2%.

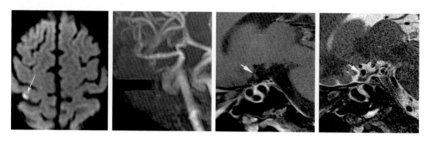

FIGURE 31.6

Axial DWI (left image) shows punctate infarcts in the right MCA territory (arrow), likely representing embolic infarcts. The right MCA and ICA show normal luminal caliber on TOF MRA (left middle image). Sagittal T_1 post-contrast vessel wall MRI image (right middle image) shows outwardly remodeling lesion (short arrow), which on sagittal T_2-weighted image (right image) shows heterogeneous T_2 signal with a juxtaluminal T_2 hyperintense band (short arrow) representing an irregular fibrous cap.

The first paper on IVWI evaluated the intracranial vertebral arteries of 30 patients and the internal carotid arteries of 62 patients with post-contrast T_1-weighted turbo spin-echo sequences (Aoki et al., 1995). The group found that the degree of wall enhancement correlated with patient age (p<0.05), and was thought to relate to ingrowth of vasa vasorum. Though ICAD primarily shows eccentric wall involvement on IVWI, some studies have indicated that approximately 10% of ICAD lesions can show concentric wall thickening and enhancement (Mossa-Basha et al., 2015). T_2-weighted IVWI can help identify juxtaluminal T_2 hyperintensity in ICAD, representing the fibrous cap.

IVWI may be able to help identify characteristics that are associated with culprit lesions. Atherosclerosis frequently shows outward remodeling, and symptomatic ICAD lesions with outward remodeling are significantly associated with increased micro-embolic events on transcranial Doppler, as compared to symptomatic ICAD lesions without outward remodeling. Symptomatic plaques are also more likely to show outward remodeling, whereas asymptomatic plaque more commonly have inward remodeling. In the evaluation of 137 plaques in 42 patients (Qiao et al., 2016), there was an association between outward remodeling and downstream ischemic stroke when controlling for plaque burden (odds ratio

1.34). In addition, posterior circulation plaques more frequently showed outward remodeling (54% vs 29.9%, p=.011) and larger plaque burden (77.7 vs 69, p=.008). Whereas both symptomatic and asymptomatic plaques can show enhancement, non-enhancing lesions are typically non-culprit (Qiao et al., 2014). In addition, there is an association between plaque enhancement and vulnerability (odds ratio 34.6, 95% confidence interval 4.5–266.5) when adjusted for plaque thickness. Culprit plaques showed a higher degree of quantitative enhancement when compared to non-culprit lesions (25.9%±13.4 vs 13.6%±12.3, P=0.003). Intraplaque hemorrhage is known to have a significant association with plaque vulnerability in carotid atherosclerotic disease. Similarly, associations between intracranial intraplaque hemorrhage and vulnerability have been found. In 109 stenotic middle cerebral artery ICAD lesions (46 symptomatic and 63 asymptomatic), there was a significant difference in the presence of lesion T_1 hyperintensity (Xu et al., 2012), corresponding to intraplaque hemorrhage (19.6% of symptomatic vs 3.2% of asymptomatic lesions, p=0.01).

The location of ICAD lesions can also confer stroke risk and a pattern of ischemic events. Plaque location can be determined by middle cerebral artery anatomy, as related to flow dynamics. In the evaluation of plaque location in 130 subjects (57 with acute deep brain infarct, 28 with white matter lesions, and 45 controls), ICAD lesions were found along the superior middle cerebral wall on the side ipsilateral, rather than contralateral to the acute infarcts in the basal ganglia (69.2% vs 37.5%, P = 0.025)(26). With symptomatic middle cerebral artery stenosis, ICAD is more likely to involve the superior wall and, similarly, patients with perforator infarcts are more likely to have superior wall ICAD involvement than those without perforator infarcts.

31.4.2 Cerebral aneurysms and post-aneurysm rupture

Cerebral aneurysms represent an arterial malformation, in which the sidewall of intracranial arteries protrude, typically to form an outpouching. Aneurysms typically occur at arterial branching points due to altered flow dynamics, most commonly involving the anterior communicating artery, origin of the posterior communicating arteries, and branch points of the middle cerebral arteries. The major concern for aneurysms is the potential that they may rupture, and result in catastrophic subarachnoid hemorrhage. Aneurysmal subarachnoid hemorrhage carries a high risk of significant morbidity or mortality.

Traditionally, intracranial aneurysms are evaluated using luminal imaging techniques, including DSA, CT angiography, and MR angiography. These techniques are valuable in aneurysm detection as well as anatomic visualization for treatment decision-making and planning. Risk classification schemes for aneurysm rupture risk generally rely heavily on angiographic imaging characteristics, specifically aneurysm size and location. This includes the recently developed PHASES score, which incorporates size and location, as well as clinical factors, specifically hypertension, age, ethnicity, and history of previous aneurysm rupture (Greving et al., 2014). Though aneurysm size is considered a significant risk for aneurysm rupture, with progressive increase in rupture risk with increasing aneurysm size, considering the overall prevalence of small aneurysms, and despite their lower rupture rate, subarachnoid hemorrhage most frequently results from small anterior circulation aneurysms. In the assessment of 10,272 aneurysms, 47% of unruptured aneurysms measured <5 mm, as did the largest proportion of ruptured aneurysms at 26% (Greving et al., 2014). This highlights the limitations of current algorithms used for aneurysm risk stratification, which heavily rely on aneurysm luminal imaging characteristics.

IVWI has the potential to more directly assess aneurysm vulnerability through visualization of wall changes that may confer increased risk of rupture (Fig. 31.7). Hartman et al. (2019) evaluated 65 unruptured intracranial aneurysms in 45 patients with IVWI, and found that aneurysms with PHASES>3 as

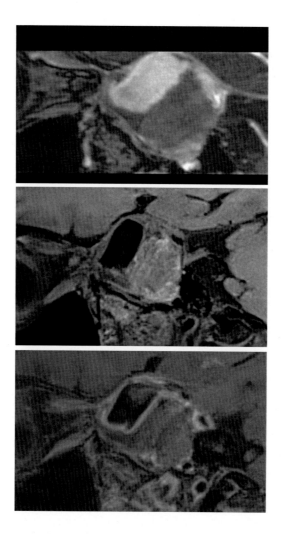

FIGURE 31.7

43-year-old with left 6th nerve palsy. Sagittal reconstruction of post-contrast 3D TOF MRA (top image) shows partially thrombosed left cavernous ICA aneurysm, with luminal flow-related enhancement. Sagittal T_1 pre- (middle image) and post- (bottom image) contrast vessel wall images also show the partially thrombosed aneurysm with dark patent lumen and isointense thrombus. There is enhancement of the aneurysm walls on the post-contrast T_1 vessel wall image.

compared to those with PHASES≤3 were significantly more likely to show wall enhancement (42.1% vs 14.8%, p=0.022), greater extent of enhancement (mean: 2.9 vs 2.2 quadrants, p = 0.063), and wall thinning (9.2% vs 0%, p = 0.044). Gariel et al. (2020) evaluated 145 small unruptured intracranial aneurysms (mean size 4.1 mm) in 129 patients, with baseline IVWI and subsequent longitudinal luminal imaging. Twelve aneurysms showed growth (considered a surrogate for rupture) at 2 years, 8 of which showed wall enhancement before or concurrently with aneurysm growth. Multivariate analysis showed that increased wall enhancement, and not size, was associated with aneurysm growth (relative risk, 26.1 (95% CI, 7.4–91.7), P<0.001). Sensitivity, specificity, positive predictive value, and negative predictive value for aneurysm growth of aneurysm wall enhancement was 67%, 100%, 96%, and 100%, respectively. These findings support the value of enhancement in potentially differentiating aneurysm stability. Although multiple studies have shown overlap with the presence of enhancement in stable aneurysms, aneurysms with non-enhancing walls are consistently stable, which can help contribute to aneurysm stability evaluation.

With conventional imaging modalities, there are marked limitations in predicting patients who will have poor outcomes after aneurysmal subarachnoid hemorrhage. IVWI may better predict post-aneurysm rupture outcomes than current clinical and imaging algorithms (Mossa-Basha et al., 2018), including the development of angiographic vasospasm and delayed cerebral ischemia. In 31 consecutive patients who underwent aneurysm coiling (9 unruptured and 22 ruptured), enhancing arterial segments were more frequently seen in ruptured aneurysm cases as compared to unruptured cases (29.9% vs 6.2%; odds ratio 6.5 (2.5–16.7)). Per-segment analysis showed significant association between arterial segment enhancement and development of vasospasm when controlling for modified Fisher score of hemorrhage (odds ratio 3.9, (1.7–9.5)). With aneurysmal subarachnoid hemorrhage, arterial wall enhancement has also been shown to be significantly associated with development of delayed cerebral ischemia (p<0.04).

31.4.3 Intracranial vasculopathy differentiation

One of the major applications for IVWI is differentiation of intracranial vasculopathies (Mandell et al., 2017). Although DSA is considered the gold standard for differentiation of intracranial vasculopathies, including vasculitis, reversible cerebral vasoconstriction syndrome (RCVS), intracranial atherosclerosis (ICAD), Moyamoya disease (MMD) and dissections, its accuracy for disease differentiation ranges from 31–43% (Mossa-Basha et al., 2016, 2017). IVWI has shown the ability to differentiate vasculopathies, due to its ability to directly visualize pathology of the arterial wall rather than the effects on blood flow, as is seen with luminal imaging techniques. In the evaluation of 29 patients (21 with ICAD, 4 with vasculitis, 4 with RCVS), with 118 lesions (81 ICAD, 22 RCVS, 15 vasculitis) who underwent multicontrast IVWI, it was found that the inclusion of T_2-weighted sequences in addition to T_1-weighted pre- and post-contrast IVWI helped improve sensitivity of differentiating ICAD from other vasculopathies from 90.1% to 96.3% (Mossa-Basha et al., 2015). ICAD lesions were significantly more likely to have eccentric wall involvement (90.1%) than reversible cerebral vasoconstriction syndrome (8.2%; P<0.001) and vasculitic lesions (6.7%; P<0.001), and were also more likely to have T_2 hyperintensity than the other two vasculopathies (79% versus 0%; P<0.001). There were also significant differences in the presence, intensity, and pattern of enhancement between the various vasculopathies, with RCVS showing minimal to no enhancement, vasculitis with intense homogeneous enhancement, and ICAD having heterogeneous enhancement of varying degrees (Mossa-Basha et al., 2015).

IVWI can improve diagnostic accuracy for vasculopathy differentiation, when compared to luminal imaging alone. In 54 patients with 201 arterial lesions (Mossa-Basha et al., 2017), the inclusion of IVWI assessment, as compared to luminal imaging assessment alone, significantly improved diagnostic accuracy (per-lesion analysis 88.8% vs 36.1%, p<0.001; per-patient analysis 96.3% vs 43.5%, p<0.001).

Chapter 31 Neurovascular vessel wall imaging

This significant improvement in accuracy applied to each vascular disease (vasculitis, ICAD, RCVS) individually as well. The classic diagnostic imaging differentiator of vasculopathy type is proximal or distal branch involvement. However, there was no significant correlation between the arterial segment of lesion involvement and diagnosis. In addition, eccentric pattern of disease on IVWI was much more strongly associated with ICAD diagnosis as compared to eccentric pattern on luminal imaging (κ 0.69 vs 0.18, p<0.001). Inter-reader agreement was stronger for IVWI as compared to luminal imaging for lesion diagnosis (κ 0.72 vs κ 0.04) and pattern of involvement (κ 0.87 vs κ 0.02).

In the evaluation of 21 Moyamoya vasculopathy patients (8 MMD, 10 ICAD Moyamoya syndrome, 3 vasculitis) who underwent IVWI (Mossa-Basha et al., 2016), the inclusion of IVWI over luminal imaging alone resulted in significant improvement in diagnostic accuracy (86.8% vs 31.6%, p<0.001). Multiple studies have shown idiopathic MMD to most frequently show no or minimal wall enhancement with no wall thickening, and normal T_2-weighted wall signal characteristics, whereas ICAD Moyamoya pattern shows eccentric enhancement, juxtaluminal T_2 wall hyperintensity, and outward remodeling with pronounced wall thickening (Mossa-Basha et al., 2016), and vasculitis shows intense, homogeneous wall enhancement with isointense T_2 wall signal relative to gray matter (Mossa-Basha et al., 2016, 2017). Occasionally MMD can show circumferential wall enhancement. However, there should be no wall thickening and there should be negative remodeling, which is in contrast to ICAD Moyamoya syndrome, which shows wall thickening and positive remodeling.

References

Aoki, S., Shirouzu, I., Sasaki, Y., Okubo, T., Hayashi, N., Machida, T., Hoshi, E., Suzuki, K., Funada, N., Araki, T., et al., 1995. Enhancement of the intracranial arterial wall at MR imaging: relationship to cerebral atherosclerosis. Radiology 194 (2), 477–481. https://doi.org/10.1148/radiology.194.2.7824729. Epub 1995/02/01.

Bayer-Karpinska, A., Schwarz, F., Wollenweber, F.A., Poppert, H., Boeckh-Behrens, T., Becker, A., Clevert, D.A., Nikolaou, K., Opherk, C., Dichgans, M., Saam, T., 2013. The carotid plaque imaging in acute stroke (CAPIAS) study: protocol and initial baseline data. BMC Neurol. 13, 201. https://doi.org/10.1186/1471-2377-13-201. Epub 2013/12/13.

Chen, L., Mossa-Basha, M., Balu, N., Canton, G., Sun, J., Pimentel, K., Hatsukami, T.S., Hwang, J.N., Yuan, C., 2018. Development of a quantitative intracranial vascular features extraction tool on 3D MRA using semiautomated open-curve active contour vessel tracing. Magn. Reson. Med. 79 (6), 3229–3238. https://doi.org/10.1002/mrm.26961. Epub 2017/10/17.

Dong, Y., Pan, Y., Zhao, X., Li, R., Yuan, C., Xu, W., 2017. Identifying carotid plaque composition in MRI with convolutional neural networks. In: IEEE International Conference on Smart Computing (SMARTCOMP).

Freilinger, T.M., Schindler, A., Schmidt, C., Grimm, J., Cyran, C., Schwarz, F., Bamberg, F., Linn, J., Reiser, M., Yuan, C., Nikolaou, K., Dichgans, M., Saam, T., 2012. Prevalence of nonstenosing, complicated atherosclerotic plaques in cryptogenic stroke. JACC Cardiovasc. Imaging 5 (4), 397–405. https://doi.org/10.1016/j.jcmg.2012.01.012.

Gariel, F., Ben Hassen, W., Boulouis, G., Bourcier, R., Trystram, D., Legrand, L., Rodriguez-Regent, C., Saloner, D., Oppenheim, C., Naggara, O., Edjlali, M., 2020. Increased wall enhancement during follow-up as a predictor of subsequent aneurysmal growth. Stroke 51 (6), 1868–1872. https://doi.org/10.1161/strokeaha.119.028431. Epub 2020/05/14.

Greving, J.P., Wermer, M.J., Brown, R.D. Jr., Morita, A., Juvela, S., Yonekura, M., Ishibashi, T., Torner, J.C., Nakayama, T., Rinkel, G.J., Algra, A., 2014. Development of the PHASES score for prediction of risk of rupture of intracranial aneurysms: a pooled analysis of six prospective cohort studies. Lancet Neurol. 13 (1), 59–66. https://doi.org/10.1016/s1474-4422(13)70263-1. Epub 2013/12/03.

Hartman, J.B., Watase, H., Sun, J., Hippe, D.S., Kim, L., Levitt, M., Sekhar, L., Balu, N., Hatsukami, T., Yuan, C., Mossa-Basha, M., 2019. Intracranial aneurysms at higher clinical risk for rupture demonstrate increased wall enhancement and thinning on multicontrast 3D vessel wall MRI. Br. J. Radiol. 92 (1096), 20180950. https://doi.org/10.1259/bjr.20180950. Epub 2019/01/18.

Kamel, H., Pearce, L.A., Ntaios, G., Gladstone, D.J., Perera, K., Roine, R.O., Meseguer, E., Shoamanesh, A., Berkowitz, S.D., Mundl, H., Sharma, M., Connolly, S.J., Hart, R.G., Healey, J.S., 2020. Atrial cardiopathy and nonstenosing large artery plaque in patients with embolic stroke of undetermined source. Stroke 51 (3), 938–943. Epub 2020/01/02.

Kerwin, W., Xu, D., Liu, F., Saam, T., Underhill, H., Takaya, N., Chu, B., Hatsukami, T., Yuan, C., 2007. Magnetic resonance imaging of carotid atherosclerosis: plaque analysis. Top. Magn. Reson. Imaging 18 (5), 371–378.

Li, L., Miller, K.L., Jezzard, P., 2012. DANTE-prepared pulse trains: a novel approach to motion-sensitized and motion-suppressed quantitative magnetic resonance imaging. Magn. Reson. Med. 68 (5), 1423–1438. https://doi.org/10.1002/mrm.24142. Epub 2012/01/13.

López-Cancio, E., Matheus, M.G., Romano, J.G., Liebeskind, D.S., Prabhakaran, S., Turan, T.N., Cotsonis, G.A., Lynn, M.J., Rumboldt, Z., Chimowitz, M.I., 2014. Infarct patterns, collaterals and likely causative mechanisms of stroke in symptomatic intracranial atherosclerosis. Cerebrovasc. Dis. 37 (6), 417–422. https://doi.org/10.1159/000362922. Epub 2014/07/12.

Mandell, D.M., Mossa-Basha, M., Qiao, Y., Hess, C.P., Hui, F., Matouk, C., Johnson, M.H., Daemen, M.J., Vossough, A., Edjlali, M., Saloner, D., Ansari, S.A., Wasserman, B.A., Mikulis, D.J., 2017. Neuroradiology VWISGotASo. Intracranial vessel wall MRI: principles and expert consensus recommendations of the American society of neuroradiology. Am. J. Neuroradiol. 38 (2), 218–229. https://doi.org/10.3174/ajnr.A4893. Epub 2016/07/28.

Mazighi, M., Labreuche, J., Gongora-Rivera, F., Duyckaerts, C., Hauw, J.J., Amarenco, P., 2008. Autopsy prevalence of intracranial atherosclerosis in patients with fatal stroke. Stroke 39 (4), 1142–1147. https://doi.org/10.1161/strokeaha.107.496513. Epub 2008/03/01.

Mossa-Basha, M., Hwang, W.D., De Havenon, A., Hippe, D., Balu, N., Becker, K.J., Tirschwell, D.T., Hatsukami, T., Anzai, Y., Yuan, C., 2015. Multicontrast high-resolution vessel wall magnetic resonance imaging and its value in differentiating intracranial vasculopathic processes. Stroke 46 (6), 1567–1573. https://doi.org/10.1161/strokeaha.115.009037. Epub 2015/05/09.

Mossa-Basha, M., de Havenon, A., Becker, K.J., Hallam, D.K., Levitt, M.R., Cohen, W.A., Hippe, D.S., Alexander, M.D., Tirschwell, D.L., Hatsukami, T., Amlie-Lefond, C., Added, Yuan C., 2016. Value of vessel wall magnetic resonance imaging in the differentiation of moyamoya vasculopathies in a non-Asian cohort. Stroke 47 (7), 1782–1788. https://doi.org/10.1161/strokeaha.116.013320. Epub 2016/06/09.

Mossa-Basha, M., Shibata, D.K., Hallam, D.K., de Havenon, A., Hippe, D.S., Becker, K.J., Tirschwell, D.L., Hatsukami, T., Balu, N., Yuan, C., 2017. Added value of vessel wall magnetic resonance imaging for differentiation of nonocclusive intracranial vasculopathies. Stroke 48 (11), 3026–3033. https://doi.org/10.1161/strokeaha.117.018227. Epub 2017/10/17.

Mossa-Basha, M., Huynh, T.J., Hippe, D.S., Fata, P., Morton, R.P., Levitt, M.R., 2018. Vessel wall MRI characteristics of endovascularly treated aneurysms: association with angiographic vasospasm. J. Neurosurg. 131 (3), 859–867. https://doi.org/10.3171/2018.4.Jns172829. Epub 2018/09/22.

Qiao, Y., Zeiler, S.R., Mirbagheri, S., Leigh, R., Urrutia, V., Wityk, R., Wasserman, B.A., 2014. Intracranial plaque enhancement in patients with cerebrovascular events on high-spatial-resolution MR images. Radiology 271 (2), 534–542. https://doi.org/10.1148/radiol.13122812. Epub 2014/01/31.

Qiao, Y., Anwar, Z., Intrapiromkul, J., Liu, L., Zeiler, S.R., Leigh, R., Zhang, Y., Guallar, E., Wasserman, B.A., 2016. Patterns and implications of intracranial arterial remodeling in stroke patients. Stroke 47 (2), 434–440. https://doi.org/10.1161/strokeaha.115.009955. Epub 2016/01/09.

Saba, L., Yuan, C., Hatsukami, T.S., Balu, N., Qiao, Y., DeMarco, J.K., Saam, T., Moody, A.R., Li, D., Matouk, C.C., Johnson, M.H., Jäger, H.R., Mossa-Basha, M., Kooi, M.E., Fan, Z., Saloner, D., Wintermark, M., Mikulis, D.J., Wasserman, B.A., 2018. Neuroradiology VWISGotASo. Carotid artery wall imaging: perspective and guidelines from the ASNR vessel wall imaging study group and expert consensus recommendations of the American Society of Neuroradiology. Am. J. Neuroradiol. 39 (2), E9–E31. https://doi.org/10.3174/ajnr.A5488. Epub 2018/01/11.

Shi, F., Yang, Q., Guo, X., Qureshi, T.A., Tian, Z., Miao, H., Dey, D., Li, D., Fan, Z., 2019. Intracranial vessel wall segmentation using convolutional neural networks. IEEE Trans. Biomed. Eng. 66 (10), 2840–2847. https://doi.org/10.1109/TBME.2019.2896972. Epub 2019/02/01.

Suri, M.F., Qiao, Y., Ma, X., Guallar, E., Zhou, J., Zhang, Y., Liu, L., Chu, H., Qureshi, A.I., Alonso, A., Folsom, A.R., Wasserman, B.A., 2016. Prevalence of intracranial atherosclerotic stenosis using high-resolution magnetic resonance angiography in the general population: the atherosclerosis risk in communities study. Stroke 47 (5), 1187–1193. https://doi.org/10.1161/strokeaha.115.011292. Epub 2016/04/09.

Wang, J., Yarnykh, V.L., Yuan, C., 2010. Enhanced image quality in black-blood MRI using the improved motion-sensitized driven-equilibrium (iMSDE) sequence. J. Magn. Reson. Imaging 31 (5), 1256–1263. https://doi.org/10.1002/jmri.22149.

Wang, Y., Liu, X., Wu, X., Degnan, A.J., Malhotra, A., Zhu, C., 2019. Culprit intracranial plaque without substantial stenosis in acute ischemic stroke on vessel wall MRI: a systematic review. Atherosclerosis 287, 112–121. https://doi.org/10.1016/j.atherosclerosis.2019.06.907. Epub 2019/06/30.

Watase, H., Canton, G., Sun, J., Zhao, X., Hatsukami, T.S., Four, Yuan C., 2019. Different carotid atherosclerotic behaviors based on luminal stenosis and plaque characteristics in symptomatic patients: an in vivo study. Diagnostics (Basel) 9 (4). https://doi.org/10.3390/diagnostics9040137. Epub 2019/10/02.

Xu, W.H., Li, M.L., Gao, S., Ni, J., Yao, M., Zhou, L.X., Peng, B., Feng, F., Jin, Z.Y., Cui, L.Y., 2012. Middle cerebral artery intraplaque hemorrhage: prevalence and clinical relevance. Ann. Neurol. 71 (2), 195–198. https://doi.org/10.1002/ana.22626. Epub 2012/03/01.

Yuan, C., Hatsukami, T., Mossa-Basha, M. (Eds.), 2020. Vessel Based Imaging Techniques - Diagnosis, Treatment, and Prevention. Springer Nature, Switzerland.

Zhao, X., Underhill, H.R., Zhao, Q., Cai, J., Li, F., Oikawa, M., Dong, L., Ota, H., Hatsukami, T.S., Chu, B., Yuan, C., 2011. Discriminating carotid atherosclerotic lesion severity by luminal stenosis and plaque burden: a comparison utilizing high-resolution magnetic resonance imaging at 3.0 Tesla. Stroke 42 (2), 347–353. https://doi.org/10.1161/STROKEAHA.110.597328.

Zhao, X., Hippe, D.S., Li, R., Canton, G.M., Sui, B., Song, Y., Li, F., Xue, Y., Sun, J., Yamada, K., Hatsukami, T.S., Xu, D., Wang, M., Yuan, C., Collaborators CIS, 2017. Prevalence and characteristics of carotid artery high-risk atherosclerotic plaques in Chinese patients with cerebrovascular symptoms: a Chinese atherosclerosis risk evaluation II study. J. Am. Heart Assoc. 6 (8). https://doi.org/10.1161/JAHA.117.005831. Epub 2017/08/14.

PART 11

Advanced magnetic resonance spectroscopy

CHAPTER

Single voxel magnetic resonance spectroscopy: principles and applications

32

Ivan Tkáč and Gülin Öz

Center for Magnetic Resonance Research, Department of Radiology, University of Minnesota, Minneapolis, MN, United States

32.1 Introduction

Magnetic resonance spectroscopy (MRS) is an MR modality that provides unique biochemical information from a selected volume of tissue non-invasively. Only nuclei with non-zero nuclear spins (e.g., ^{1}H, ^{13}C, ^{31}P) can be detected by MRS. In this chapter, we will focus exclusively on proton (^{1}H) MRS, which is the most widely used application due to its sensitivity (high gyromagnetic ratio and natural abundance) and its feasibility on all MRI scanners, without requirements for additional hardware. The capability of ^{1}H MRS to discriminate between different chemical compounds is based on the phenomenon called chemical shift. The chemical shift represents a small change in the resonance frequency of the observed nucleus, resulting from a change in the electron density surrounding it. These effects are caused by the structure of the particular chemical compound, which directly links resonance frequencies to chemical properties. However, the chemical shift is not a property of the whole molecule, but is a unique property of each magnetically equivalent group of nuclei within the molecule. In other words, the ^{1}H MR spectrum of a chemical compound has as many resonances (signals) with different chemical shifts as the number of magnetically non-equivalent hydrogen nuclei (protons) in the molecule. Since the chemical shift is proportional to the strength of the static magnetic field (B_0), it became much more practical to express it in field-independent, dimensionless units (parts per million, ppm) as the ratio of the frequency difference from a chosen reference (in Hz scale) divided by the resonance frequency (in MHz scale). In addition, chemical bonds mediate the interaction between protons bound in the same molecule (scalar spin-spin coupling called J-coupling), which results in fine splitting of resonances. Differences in chemical shifts of magnetically non-equivalent protons combined with their J-coupling pattern (through 2 or 3 bonds) make the ^{1}H MR spectrum uniquely specific for a particular chemical compound (brain metabolite), rather like a fingerprint. This feature of ^{1}H MRS, in principle, enables us to detect and quantify individual chemical compounds in their complex mixtures. However, there are a number of technical obstacles and limitations to achieve this goal of quantifying a wide range of metabolites in selected human brain regions *in vivo*. First, concentrations of the most abundant brain metabolites are about four-orders of magnitude lower than that of water protons, which are utilized for most MRI techniques. Second, spectra of brain metabolites strongly overlap, which makes their unambiguous assignment and quantification challenging. Ultra-high magnetic fields are particularly beneficial for MRS, because both sensitivity and chemical shift dispersion progressively improve

Advances in Magnetic Resonance Technology and Applications, Volume 4, ISSN 2666-9099. https://doi.org/10.1016/B978-0-12-822479-3.00050-6
Copyright © 2021 Elsevier Inc. All rights reserved.

503

504 **Chapter 32** Single voxel magnetic resonance spectroscopy

with B_0 field strength. However, the B_0 field strength is not enough to maximize the neurochemical information that is potentially available. Reliable quantification of a wide range of brain metabolites (neurochemical profiling) requires high-quality ^1H MR spectra and appropriate processing tools. This chapter is dedicated to single-voxel MRS methods. The description of advanced MR spectroscopic imaging (MRSI) techniques, which provide spatial distribution of brain metabolites, is the topic of Chapters 33 and 34. The following sections will describe advanced ^1H MRS acquisition techniques, data processing steps, and currently available metabolite quantification methods. Finally, examples of advanced ^1H MRS applications will be highlighted to demonstrate the power of *in vivo* neurochemical profiling.

32.2 Acquisition techniques and calibration procedures

Neurochemical profiling requires high quality ^1H MR spectra. The quality of the final spectrum depends on multiple factors, including the localization performance of the pulse sequence, water suppression (WS) efficiency, B_0 field homogeneity, appropriate power calibration, physiological motion, and the B_0 drift of the MR scanner. In addition, benefits of high fields (sensitivity and chemical shift dispersion) could be offset by increased spatial B_0 and transmit B_1^+ field inhomogeneities, increased chemical shift displacement error (CSDE), increased spectral linewidth, and increased specific adsorption rate (SAR). ^1H MRS can benefit from high B_0 fields only if the effects of these factors that lower spectral quality are minimized as much as possible.

32.2.1 Advanced localization techniques

32.2.1.1 Ultra-short echo-time STEAM

The primary goal of the localization pulse sequence is to maximize the signal from the selected volume-of-interest (VOI) and eliminate all signals originating from outside of the VOI (such as subcutaneous lipid contamination and spurious echoes). In addition, it is extremely important that CSDE of the localization sequence (displacement of the VOI for off-resonance signals) is reasonably small. Last, but not least, it is desirable that the minimum achievable echo-time (TE) of the pulse sequence is short to minimize signal intensity loss due to T_2 relaxation effects and J-evolution of coupled spin systems. Standard pulse sequences (stimulated-echo acquisition mode (STEAM), point-resolved spectroscopy (PRESS)), originally developed for 1.5T MR scanners, did not meet the requirements for ultra-high magnetic fields. The ultra-short-TE STEAM sequence that incorporates VAPOR (variable pulse power and optimized relaxation delays) water suppression interleaved with outer volume suppression (OVS) was developed for the first 7T MR scanner installed at the University of Minnesota (Tkac et al., 2001). This sequence had excellent localization performance, highly efficient WS, and acceptably small CSDE (7% per ppm in each localization direction). In addition, the minimum TE was as short as 6 ms, which minimized signal loss caused by T_2 relaxation. Furthermore, this sequence allowed metabolite quantification with negligible T_1 and T_2 relaxation effects when a long repetition time (TR = 5 s) was used. This sequence was optimized for a peak transmit B_1^+ field as high as 40 μT, which required B_1 shimming (explained later) for whole-brain coverage at 7T. However, the main limitation of this sequence was the fact that the stimulated-echo-based STEAM sequence provided only 50% of the signal available from the VOI. The total acquisition time could be shortened by 75% if a high-performance, full-intensity sequence was available.

32.2.1.2 Short-echo, full intensity technique: semi-LASER

The problem was successfully resolved by a new pulse sequence VAPOR-sLASER (Oz and Tkac, 2011; Scheenen et al., 2008), shown in Fig. 32.1. The semi-LASER (sLASER; localization by adiabatic selective refocusing) sequence appears to be the best available compromise based on MR scanner hardware performance (available peak B_1^+), localization performance, and minimum TE of 25–30 ms, and therefore was recommended by community consensus for use at high and ultra-high fields (Wilson et al., 2019). In sLASER, two pairs of broadband 180° adiabatic pulses reduce the CSDE in two slice-selection directions down to 3% at 7T. The CSDE in the third direction (selected by a 90° pulse) remained the same as for STEAM (7%). Transmit-receive head RF coils commonly used at 7T can generate a transmit B_1^+ field of at least 25 μT, which is sufficient for RF pulses used in the sLASER sequence with TE ≤ 30 ms (Oz et al., 2021). However, 3T MR scanners in a standard hardware configuration always use a body transmit RF coil, which limits the available peak B_1^+ on some platforms of MR scanners. A solution was introduced by replacing the frequency-modulated rephasing 180° pulses by gradient-modulated pulses (e.g., frequency offset corrected inversion (FOCI) and gradient offset independent adiabaticity (GOIA)), which are capable of selecting slices using substantially lower peak B_1^+ (15 μT) without compromising the CSDE. The sLASER localization sequence offers additional advantages. The series of four consecutive refocusing RF pulses keeps some properties of the CPMG (Carr–Purcell–Meiboom–Gill) pulse train that slows down the J-evolution and T_2 relaxation, which helps to minimize signal loss for echo-times as long as 30 ms. The sLASER sequence is combined with additional OVS pulses to improve its localization performance, particularly in the direction parallel to slice excitation (Fig. 32.1). These OVS pulses help to suppress unwanted coherences originating from outside of the VOI (subcutaneous lipids, spurious echoes of water from distant regions) (Oz and Tkac, 2011).

32.2.1.3 Spectral editing techniques

Reliable quantification of some weakly represented metabolites, such as γ-aminobutyric acid (GABA) and glutathione (GSH), is challenging, because their spectra overlap with resonances of other metabolites that have much higher concentrations. Quantification of GABA and GSH is feasible from short TE spectra acquired at 7T, but becomes less reliable at 3T. An alternative for quantification of these two important brain metabolites is the J-difference editing technique. Editing pulse sequences use frequency-selective editing RF pulses in alternating scans on a selected resonance of the metabolite-of-interest, which affects the evolution of the resonance coupled by a scalar spin-spin interaction. Subtraction of alternating scans eliminates all resonances unaffected by the editing pulse, which considerably simplifies the quantification of GABA or GSH. The MEGA-sLASER technique appears to be the optimum editing pulse sequence for 3T currently available. The robustness of the editing sequences is improved by interleaved navigator pulses for real-time frequency updates, because spectral editing is very sensitive to the B_0 drift of the magnet (typically after high gradient duty-cycle MRI sessions).

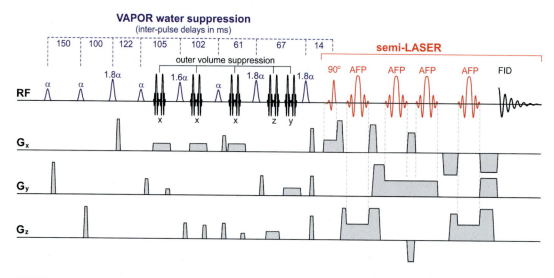

FIGURE 32.1

The scheme of the sLASER sequence with VAPOR water suppression. Outer volume suppression pulses are used to improve the localization performance, especially in the direction parallel to the slice-selective excitation pulse. Relative flip angles of frequency-selective water suppression RF pulses and inter-pulse delays of the VAPOR pulse train optimized for 7T are highlighted (in blue).

32.2.2 Water suppression techniques
32.2.2.1 VAPOR water suppression

The neurochemical information provided by ^{1}H MRS can be severely compromised if the strong signal originating from brain water is not properly suppressed. The VAPOR water suppression was recently recommended for single-voxel ^{1}H MRS (Tkac et al., 2021; Wilson et al., 2019). The most important advantage of this WS technique is its low sensitivity to variations in transmit B_1^+ field and T_1 relaxation of water protons. The residual water signal is nearly independent of the nominal flip angle of VAPOR pulses (the flat region between 60–100 deg in Fig. 32.2A), which makes the WS robust and insensitive to spatial inhomogeneity in B_1^+ typical for ultra-high magnetic fields. This property of VAPOR simplifies the adjustment of the VAPOR RF power. In addition, minimized sensitivity to T_1 is essential for efficient WS, because T_1 values of water from white matter (WM), cortical gray matter (GM), and cerebrospinal fluid (CSF) are very different, both at 3T (WM 840 ms, GM 1500 ms, CSF 4000 ms) and 7T (WM 1200 ms, GM 2100 ms, CSF 4400 ms; Fig. 32.2A). The frequency selectivity of VAPOR (at 50% of the residual M_z magnetization) is typically set to ±0.3 ppm from the water resonance frequency at 4.7 ppm, which is narrow enough not to suppress resonances of *myo*-inositol (4.05 ppm), lactate (4.10 ppm), and the H1-α signal of glucose (5.23 ppm). On the other hand, this frequency selectivity also guarantees decent WS outside of the VOI, where the water resonance frequency can be shifted due to B_0 inhomogeneity. The VAPOR timing scheme allows interleaved OVS, which improves the localization performance of the pulse sequence. The disadvantage of VAPOR is its overall duration (~720 ms), which prohibits short TRs (<1 s). Moreover, VAPOR suppresses signals of downfield exchangeable protons (e.g., –NH–) and may affect quantification of some metabolites (creatine, glutamate) by a water-mediated magnetization-transfer mechanism.

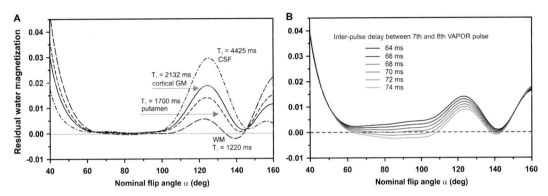

FIGURE 32.2

(A) Simulated dependence of the residual water signal on nominal flip angle at 7T for tissues with different T_1 relaxation times of water. (B) Simulated dependence of the residual water signal on nominal flip angle for an average tissue T_1 of 1500 ms at 7T for different inter-pulse delay between 7th and 8th water suppression pulses.

32.2.2.2 ^{1}H MRS without water suppression

These disadvantages of VAPOR WS can be resolved by the metabolite-cycling (MC) technique, which utilizes frequency-selective adiabatic RF pulses to invert the metabolite signals in the upfield or downfield part of the spectrum relative to water in alternating acquisitions, while leaving the water resonance unaffected. Addition and subtraction of these alternating scans allow the separation of the metabolite signals from the water signal and its sidebands (Tkac et al., 2021). This technique (MC-STEAM, MC-sLASER) was successfully utilized to acquire ^{1}H MR spectra from the human brain at 9.4T (Giapitzakis et al., 2018). This approach allows acquisition of signals from exchangeable protons that resonate downfield from the water signal. In addition, the metabolite-cycling technique is preferable when acquiring MRS data from small VOIs, when the signal-to-noise (SNR) of single scans is not sufficiently high for performing frequency and phase correction (more in the next section). Similarly, advantages of the metabolite-cycling technique have been demonstrated in diffusion-weighted ^{1}H MRS, where large fluctuations in phase are common.

32.2.3 Adjustment procedures and acquisition protocols
32.2.3.1 Adjustment of B_0 homogeneity

The resonance frequency is directly proportional to the magnetic field B_0. Therefore, acquiring MRS data from the VOI with a spatially inhomogeneous B_0 field leads to variations in resonance frequency, which consequently result in broadening of acquired signals. In general, the MRS data quality is much more sensitive to B_0 inhomogeneity than MRI. Since the natural linewidth of brain metabolites at 7T is around 10 Hz (due to T_2 relaxation and microscopic B_0 inhomogeneity) and resonances of different metabolites are often separated by less than 10 Hz, the B_0 inhomogeneity within the VOI should be

508 **Chapter 32** Single voxel magnetic resonance spectroscopy

less than 0.01 ppm (i.e., $\Delta B_0 < 0.0000007$ mT at 7T). The B_0 field is always distorted across the body of the subject, due to differences between magnetic susceptibility of air and tissue. The experimental minimization of B_0 variation is performed in a process called B_0 shimming. Magnet shim coils are designed to generate B_0 field shapes that resemble lower-order spherical harmonic functions (usually up to the 2nd-order) (Juchem et al., 2020). The B_0 shimming procedures map the field and set the appropriate currents in the shim coils to counteract the B_0 inhomogeneities within the region-of-interest. There are two B_0 mapping strategies, mapping along projections or using full three-dimensional B_0 maps. Methods based on projections (such as fast automatic shimming technique by mapping along projections (FASTMAP)) typically outperform 3D methods in very fine B_0 adjustments necessary for single-voxel ^{1}H MRS. Sparse B_0 sampling (6 projections for adjusting all 1st and 2nd-order shim terms) results in very short acquisition times, which allow performing 2 to 3 iterations for very fine B_0 shimming without a serious time penalty. In addition, methods such as FASTMAP can be used in a regime independent of eddy-current bias on the B_0 mapping procedure.

32.2.3.2 Calibration of transmit B_1^+ field

Adjustment of the transmit RF power is one of the routine steps in the beginning of any MRI scan. This step is necessary, because properties of the RF coil depend on the coil loading by the examined subject. The standard RF power adjustment (typically performed on a slice) does not necessarily provide an accurate value for the VOI selected for MRS, due to spatial B_1^+ inhomogeneity, which is typical for ultra-high B_0 fields. Since the performance of the ^{1}H MRS sequence is highly sensitive to RF misadjustment, VOI-based RF power adjustment is highly recommended (Oz et al., 2021). If the MRI scanner is equipped with a parallel transmit system and array coils, phases and/or amplitudes of each element of the array have to be optimized to eliminate destructive interferences of B_1^+ fields inside of the VOI. This procedure (called B_1 shimming) must be performed before the VOI-based power adjustment.

32.2.3.3 Adjustment of VAPOR power and timing

Precise calibration of the RF power is not only important for the localization sequence, but can also be used to automatically set the RF power for the VAPOR water suppression. The automatic setting of the VAPOR RF power must be properly calibrated to guarantee that the calculated power (i.e., VAPOR desired preset flip angle) agrees with the requested power (nominal flip angle) in the center of the flat region (around 85 deg) of the residual water signal dependence curve, shown in Fig. 32.2A. If necessary, fine minimization of the residual water signal can be performed using the delay between the 7th and 8th VAPOR RF pulses (Figs. 32.1 and 32.2B) (Tkac et al., 2021).

32.2.3.4 ^{1}H MRS data acquisition

Since ^{1}H MRS has inherently low sensitivity, signal averaging must be used to increase the SNR. During this data averaging period (5–10 min), processes such as physiological motion, small head motion, and magnet B_0 drift lead to variations in frequency and phase of acquired signal. If these effects are uncorrected, the final averaged spectrum quality is deteriorated. Therefore each individual scan has to be stored separately to enable correction of these effects in post-acquisition data processing. When metabolite data are acquired using VAPOR WS, acquisition of few scans ($\sim$4) without WS is necessary, as the unsuppressed water signal is used in data processing for eddy-current removal and as a metabolite quantification reference.

32.2.4 Prospective motion correction

Small variations in signal frequency and phase resulting from physiological motion (respiratory and cardiac) can be easily eliminated by frequency and phase correction in the data processing pipeline (i.e., retrospective motion correction) when single-scans are saved separately. However, this procedure does not solve the problem of changing VOI position associated with subject movement. Methods have been developed to track the head motion by external optical devices or by navigator MRI scans interleaved with the MRS sequence. Motion tracking information then allows updating the real-time position of the VOI inside the head (prospective motion correction). These procedures help, but are not sufficient to prevent spectral quality degradation due to B_0 field changes induced by head motion. The most advanced pulse sequences combine motion tracking with interleaved B_0 shimming (FASTMAP-based, linear terms only) as recently demonstrated (Andronesi et al., 2021; Deelchand et al., 2019). This powerful feature of combining the motion correction with the B_0 shimming is shown in Fig. 32.3. This approach is very promising for ^{1}H MRS in children and patients with movement disorders, where suppressing subject motion can be rather challenging.

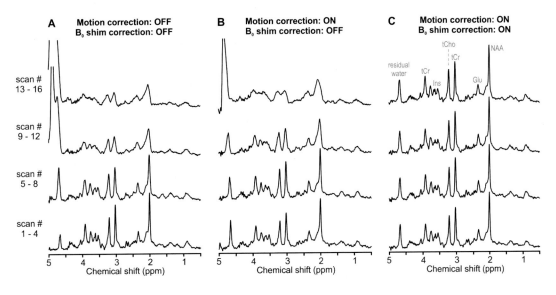

FIGURE 32.3

Performance of prospective motion and B_0 shim correction during translation along the Z-axis. ^{1}H MR spectra (sLASER, TE = 26 ms, TR = 10 s, 4 averages per spectrum) acquired from the prefrontal cortex of a single subject at 7T under the 3 different conditions: (**A**) no correction, (**B**) motion correction only, (**C**) B_0 shim and motion corrections. At baseline, the spectra between all conditions were comparable. Scan # 1 – 4: baseline (no subject motion); scan # 5 – 8: head motion 0 – 4 mm; scan # 9 – 12: head motion 4 – 12 mm; scan # 13 – 16: head displaced by ~12 mm relative to the baseline.

32.2.5 Across-vendor standardization of sLASER

The previous sections described the benefits of the sLASER localization pulse sequence, but this technique is not available for ^{1}H MRS users in their standard software on clinical 3T MR scanners yet. A multi-institutional consortium was formed to resolve this pulse sequence availability problem (Deelchand et al., 2021). Across-vendor (Siemens, Philips, GE) standardization of sLASER was challenging, due to differences in peak B_1^+ available on different vendor platforms. This problem was resolved by using gradient-modulated refocusing RF pulses (GOIA-WURST). In addition, the sLASER sequence was combined with VAPOR WS and OVS, as shown in Fig. 32.1). The initial results of implementing this sequence with identical acquisition parameters on three different vendor platforms (highlighted in Fig. 32.4) were very encouraging and resulted in consistently high quality spectra from multiple brain regions relevant for neurological disorders.

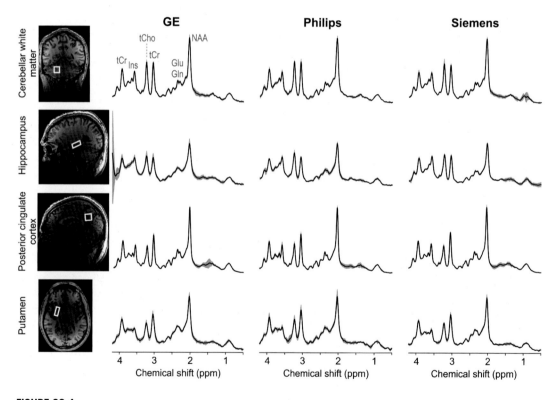

FIGURE 32.4

Mean (black) and standard deviation (gray) of the sLASER ^{1}H MR spectra (TE = 30 ms, TR = 5 s, 64 averages) acquired from five brain regions on GE, Philips and Siemens 3T scanners across all 5 different subjects on each scanner. Voxel locations are shown on the T_1-weighted images. All spectra were normalized to the tNAA peak. The large variation in hippocampus spectra on the GE platform was related to inefficient water suppression in one subject.

32.3 Data processing and metabolite quantification

32.3.1 MRS data preprocessing

Raw ^{1}H MRS data require a number of processing (sometimes called preprocessing) steps. First, signals from multiple coil channels of the receive RF coil array are combined. Data from each receive channel are corrected for phase differences between channels, and then combined using weighting factors based on individual coil sensitivities. Second, the effects of residual eddy currents are eliminated using the unsuppressed water signal. Third, frequency and phase variations between individual transients (scans) are removed. Fourth, individual transients are examined to see if they meet the basic quality requirements (SNR, linewidth), and corrupted outliers are eliminated. Finally, all transients are summed, and the resulting spectrum is used for metabolite quantification.

32.3.2 Spectral fitting and metabolite quantification

Short TE spectra of metabolites are strongly overlapped, even at high and ultra-high B_0 fields, despite increased chemical shift dispersion. All currently available spectral fitting programs (e.g., linear combination of model spectra (LCModel); versatile simulation, pulses, and analysis (VeSPA); totally automatic robust quantitation in NMR (TARQUIN); Java-based magnetic resonance user interface (jM-RUI)) are based on a linear-combination approach. The experimental spectrum is decomposed into metabolite spectra from the basis set (Fig. 32.5). The basis set contains spectra of MRS-detectable brain metabolites (concentration above ~0.5 µmol/g). These metabolite spectra (typically 20–25) should be simulated specifically for each pulse sequence and its parameters. An important part of the fitting procedure is the handling of the broad signals underlying metabolite spectra. These broad signals originate from fast-relaxing mobile macromolecules (cytosol proteins). The macromolecule spectrum (experimentally measured or parameterized) is typically included in the basis set. The uncertainty of the model fit parameter estimates is provided by Cramér–Rao lower bounds. The unsuppressed water signal is most commonly used as an internal reference for metabolite quantification. Metabolite concentrations have to be corrected for relaxation effects, unless MRS data were acquired using ultra-short-TE localization methods. However, this correction requires a number of simplifying assumptions, because accurate values of water and metabolite T_2 relaxation times are not necessarily available, due to their dependence on B_0 field strength, tissue type (GM, WM, CSF), brain region, and, partially, also on subject age. In addition, relaxation properties of protons bound in different groups within the same molecule may be different.

32.4 Applications of advanced ^{1}H MRS techniques

Here we highlight select applications of advanced ^{1}H MRS in the brain. The highlighted studies were chosen for their ability to demonstrate the benefits of the advanced techniques vs conventional MRS approaches. The theme in many of the selected studies is that changes with disease or physiology are detectable in *individual* subjects, rather than in the cohort setting. Such an ability clearly requires high quality, artifact-free spectra with high sensitivity and resolution, and is essential for the utility of any technology in the clinical decision-making setting.

512 Chapter 32 Single voxel magnetic resonance spectroscopy

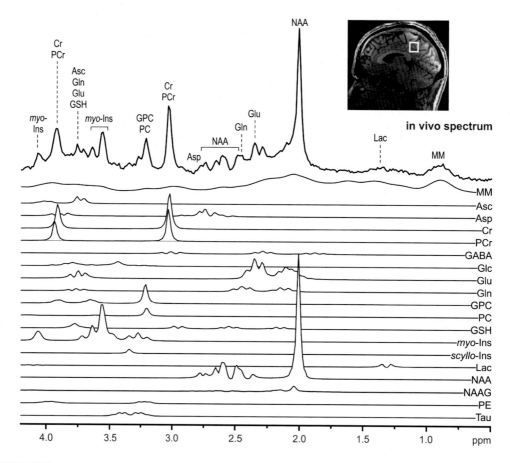

FIGURE 32.5

The LCModel analysis of an *in vivo* ^{1}H MR spectrum acquired from a human brain at 3T (sLASER, TE = 28 ms, TR = 5 s, 160 averages, VOI = 8 mL, posterior cingulate cortex). Macromolecules (MM), ascorbate (Asc), aspartate (Asp), creatine (Cr), phosphocreatine (PCr), γ-aminobutyric acid (GABA), glucose (Glc), glutamate (Glu), glutamine (Gln), glycerophosphocholine (GPC), phosphocholine (PC), glutathione (GSH), *myo*-inositol (*myo*-Ins), *scyllo*-inositol (*scyllo*-Ins), lactate (Lac), N-acetylaspartate (NAA), N-acetylaspartylglutamate (NAAG), phosphoethanolamine (PE), taurine (Tau).

32.4.1 Brain cancers

Tumors are the largest clinical indication for ^{1}H MRS. In the past decade, most clinical reports on MRS in brain tumors utilized conventional ^{1}H MRS technology ($B_0 \leq 3T$) and vendor-provided MRS packages. Successful application of MRS was possible mainly due to the large spectral changes in cancers (e.g. reduction in total N-acetylaspartate (tNAA) and elevation in total choline). Advanced single voxel techniques are now used for brain tumor applications to detect more subtle changes, e.g. to detect novel neurochemicals.

An ability to detect the oncometabolite 2-hydroxyglutarate (2HG) with ^{1}H MRS was demonstrated in glial tumors with isocitrate dehydrogenase 1 (IDH1) and 2 (IDH2) mutations. The association of IDH1 and 2 mutations with improved survival of patients with gliomas makes 2HG an important prognostic biomarker. Therefore, improved detection of 2HG has been investigated using an sLASER sequence optimized for 2HG detection (Emir et al., 2016). sLASER was chosen in this work due to its minimal CSDE and insensitivity to transmit field (B_1^+) inhomogeneities at 7T. This study successfully distinguished tumors with cytosolic IDH1 mutations from those with mitochondrial IDH2 mutations for the first time based on ~3-fold higher levels of 2HG in IDH2 mutant tumors (Emir et al., 2016).

More recently, another novel oncometabolite, cystathionine, was detected in gliomas with codeletion of chromosome arms 1p and 19q, which is a favorable prognostic marker, using edited MRS at 3T (Branzoli et al., 2019). The *in vivo* detection and quantification of these oncometabolites by MRS now allows *noninvasive* identification of glioma subtypes.

32.4.2 Neurological and psychiatric diseases

Neurochemical abnormalities in neurological and psychiatric diseases are typically subtler than cancers, making robust and highly reproducible MRS acquisition protocols more important for clinical utility. Hence, advanced ^{1}H MRS protocols have been successfully used in studies of Alzheimer disease, Parkinson's disease (PD) (Holmay et al., 2013), amyotrophic lateral sclerosis (ALS) (Cheong et al., 2019), Huntington's disease (Adanyeguh et al., 2018), spinocerebellar ataxias (Joers et al., 2018), multiple sclerosis, migraine, depression (Godlewska et al., 2018) and schizophrenia among others. These studies demonstrated that advanced MRS methods enhance understanding of disease pathology (Adanyeguh et al., 2018), allow monitoring of pathology at different disease stages, including the earliest, premanifest period (Joers et al., 2018), and help monitor treatment response (Holmay et al., 2013). The majority of these studies were done at high and ultra-high field, where the standard PRESS implementation suffers from large CSDE, providing additional motivation to use advanced ^{1}H MRS sequences. Here we highlight some of these studies that took advantage of an sLASER protocol at 7T for optimal sensitivity to detect subtle neurochemical abnormalities in the brain.

A clear added value of ^{1}H MRS over conventional structural MRI is an ability to predict progressive changes in the brain, e.g. in neurodegenerative diseases, based on neurochemical changes that precede cell loss and tissue atrophy. A study that reported the neurochemical correlates of functional decline in ALS showed that ^{1}H MRS was a better predictor of study withdrawal due to disease progression than the standard clinical scale (Cheong et al., 2019). Namely, the motor cortex tNAA-to-*myo*-inositol ratio distinguished patients who withdrew from the study from those who completed all visits with almost no overlap, while there was substantial overlap in the clinical scores of these patient groups. Along the same lines, neurochemical abnormalities were detected at the premanifest stage in carriers of hereditary ataxia mutations with an estimated disease onset within 10 years (Fig. 32.6) (Joers et al., 2018).

Finally, neurotransmitter imbalances have been an intensely investigated topic in psychiatric diseases. A recent study of non-medicated patients with major depression revealed elevated glutamine levels in the striatum without a group difference in glutamate levels in any of the regions investigated using advanced ^{1}H MRS methods (Godlewska et al., 2018). Such studies where glutamate and glutamine signals are reliably separated are poised to shed light on altered glutamatergic activity in such psychiatric disorders.

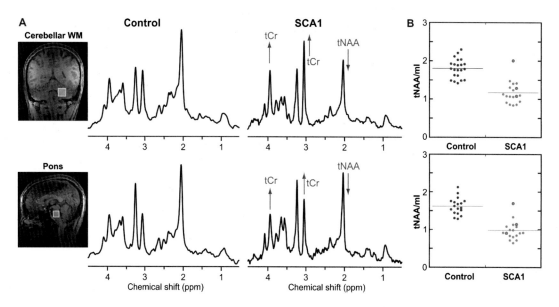

FIGURE 32.6

Detection of neurochemical abnormalities before ataxia onset in spinocerebellar ataxia 1 (SCA1). (A) ^{1}H MR spectra (sLASER, 7T, TE = 26 ms, TR = 5 s, 64 transients) obtained from a patient with SCA1 at premanifest stage are shown in comparison to a matched control. VOI locations in the cerebellar white matter and pons are shown on T_1-weighted images (left). Neurochemical abnormalities that are visually apparent in SCA1 vs control spectra (lower tNAA and higher tCr) are marked. (B) Total N-acetylaspartate-to-*myo*-inositol ratios (tNAA/mI) separate patients from controls with almost no overlap (right). Data from 3 premanifest patients with SCA1 are denoted as points encircled with black. Two premanifest subjects with estimated ataxia onset within 10 years display tNAA/mI values in the same range as manifest patients, whereas one premanifest subject with estimated ataxia onset more than 10 years previously has tNAA/mI levels in the control range.

32.4.3 Metabolic diseases

^{1}H MRS provides an ideal imaging modality to study metabolic disorders *in vivo*. While conventional ^{1}H MRS methods have been highly successful in investigations of inherited metabolic diseases that demonstrate large spectral changes, ^{1}H MRS techniques with robust localization and minimal CSDE at high field have been important for optimal SNR in studies focusing on real time metabolic measurements. Specifically, advanced single-voxel MRS methods have been utilized in studies where different glycemia levels are maintained in healthy volunteers and in patients with diabetes for dynamic measurements of energy metabolites, such as lactate (Wiegers et al., 2016) and glucose (Seaquist et al., 2017). Because small changes in metabolite concentrations are followed in these studies to gain insights into real time metabolic (Wiegers et al., 2016) or transport (Seaquist et al., 2017) activity, the voxel selection needs to be the same for all resonances-of-interest and the SNR needs to be high enough to enable sufficient time resolution. Thus, advanced MRS methods have been chosen in these studies. Importantly, advanced MRS methods have opened the door to studies of previously inaccessible VOIs, such as the hypothalamus, a region central to whole-body glucose regulation (Fig. 32.7) (Seaquist et al., 2017).

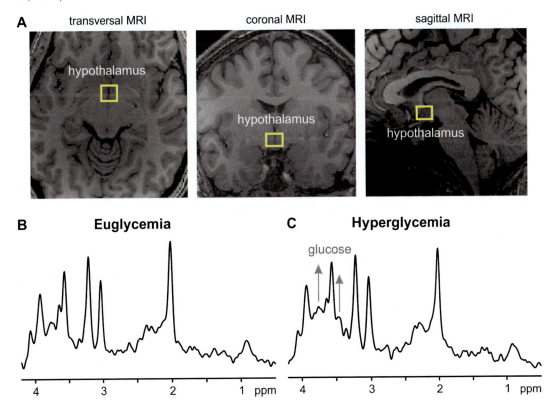

FIGURE 32.7

Measurement of glucose concentration increase in the hypothalamus during hyperglycemia. MR spectra (sLASER, 3T, TE = 28 ms, TR = 5 s, 128 transients) obtained from a healthy participant during euglycemia (blood glucose 5 mM) and hyperglycemia (blood glucose 23.4 mM). (**A**) The VOI location is shown on T_1-weighted images. (**B**) ^{1}H MR spectrum acquired during euglycemia and (**C**) hyperglycemia. Elevation of glucose in the brain tissue is marked in the hyperglycemia spectrum. Monitoring brain glucose levels as a function of blood glucose allows estimation of glucose transport kinetics in the hypothalamus.

32.4.4 Functional MRS

Advanced ^{1}H MRS techniques (ultra-short-TE STEAM, sLASER) opened a new avenue to investigate dynamic changes in concentrations of metabolites induced by brain stimulation. Functional MRS (fMRS) has been successfully applied at ultra-high B_0 fields to assess neurochemical changes during stimulation in the human visual or motor cortices. Concentration changes in glutamate, lactate, aspartate and glucose as small as 0.2 μmol/g were detected in the visual cortex using a block-designed paradigm of visual stimulation (Fig. 32.8) (Bednarik et al., 2015). The observed functional changes of metabolite concentrations were in agreement with an overall increase in oxidative energy metabolism during neuronal activation. These fMRS studies likely represent the current limits of sensitivity to detect metabolite concentration changes with advanced MRS techniques.

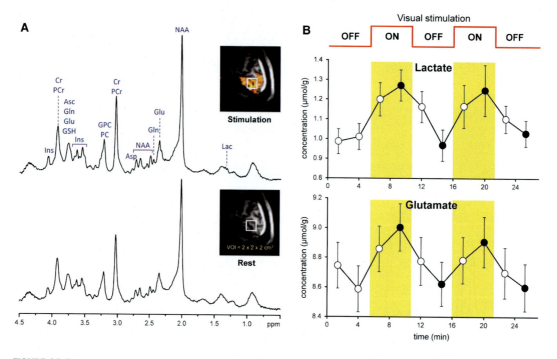

FIGURE 32.8

(A) ^{1}H MR spectra acquired from the occipital cortex during visual stimulation and rest periods (sLASER, TE = 26 ms, TR = 5 seconds, 32 averages, data acquired during the second halves of stimulation and rest periods. Inset: functional MRI - VOI selected in the activated brain region (visual cortex). (B) Time courses of lactate and glutamate concentrations during the visual stimulation paradigm (32 averages, 2.7 min resolution) in individual subjects (N = 12). Statistically significant changes in lactate (p < 0.002) and glutamate (p < 0.0005) were observed between stimulation and rest periods (second-half, black points).

32.5 Conclusions

The advanced ^{1}H MRS applications highlighted above demonstrate the power of this technique. Reliable *in vivo* neurochemical profiling in the human brain is feasible, but requires advanced pulse sequences and appropriate calibration (B_0 and B_1^+) and processing procedures. The pulse sequence is the key element determining the localization performance (maximum signal from the VOI, minimum signal contamination from outside of the VOI, minimum CSDE, and efficient WS). The VAPOR-sLASER technique described in this chapter appears to be the optimal pulse sequence currently available to meet these criteria. We hope that major MRI vendors will speed up the process of implementing this pulse sequence into their standard MRS packages and make it available on clinical 3T MRI scanners as soon as possible.

Acknowledgments

The preparation of this manuscript was in part supported by the National Institute of Neurological Disorders and Stroke (NINDS) grant R01 NS080816. The Center for Magnetic Resonance Research is supported by the National Institute of Biomedical Imaging and Bioengineering (NIBIB) grant P41 EB015894 and the NINDS Institutional Center Cores for Advanced Neuroimaging award P30 NS076408. We would like to thank Drs Dinesh K. Deelchand and James M. Joers for their assistance with figure preparation.

References

Adanyeguh, I.M., Monin, M.L., Rinaldi, D., Freeman, L., Durr, A., Lehericy, S., Henry, P.G., Mochel, F., 2018. Expanded neurochemical profile in the early stage of Huntington disease using proton magnetic resonance spectroscopy. NMR Biomed. 31.

Andronesi, O.C., Bhattacharyya, P.K., Bogner, W., Choi, I.Y., Hess, A.T., Lee, P., Meintjes, E.M., Tisdall, M.D., Zaitzev, M., Van Der Kouwe, A., 2021. Motion correction methods for MRS: experts' consensus recommendations. NMR Biomed. 34, e4364.

Bednarik, P., Tkac, I., Giove, F., Dinuzzo, M., Deelchand, D.K., Emir, U.E., Eberly, L.E., Mangia, S., 2015. Neurochemical and BOLD responses during neuronal activation measured in the human visual cortex at 7 Tesla. J. Cereb. Blood Flow Metab. 35, 601–610.

Branzoli, F., Pontoizeau, C., Tchara, L., Di Stefano, A.L., Kamoun, A., Deelchand, D.K., Valabregue, R., Lehericy, S., Sanson, M., Ottolenghi, C., Marjanska, M., 2019. Cystathionine as a marker for 1p/19q codeleted gliomas by in vivo magnetic resonance spectroscopy. Neuro-Oncol. 21, 765–774.

Cheong, I., Deelchand, D.K., Eberly, L.E., Marjanska, M., Manousakis, G., Guliani, G., Walk, D., Oz, G., 2019. Neurochemical correlates of functional decline in amyotrophic lateral sclerosis. J. Neurol. Neurosurg. Psychiatry 90, 294–301.

Deelchand, D.K., Berrington, A., Noeske, R., Joers, J.M., Arani, A., Gillen, J., Schar, M., Nielsen, J.F., Peltier, S., Seraji-Bozorgzad, N., Landheer, K., Juchem, C., Soher, B.J., Noll, D.C., Kantarci, K., Ratai, E.M., Mareci, T.H., Barker, P.B., Oz, G., 2021. Across-vendor standardization of semi-LASER for single-voxel MRS at 3T. NMR Biomed. 34, e4218.

Deelchand, D.K., Joers, J.M., Auerbach, E.J., Henry, P.G., 2019. Prospective motion and B0 shim correction for MR spectroscopy in human brain at 7T. Magn. Reson. Med. 82, 1984–1992.

Emir, U.E., Larkin, S.J., De Pennington, N., Voets, N., Plaha, P., Stacey, R., Al-Qahtani, K., Mccullagh, J., Schofield, C.J., Clare, S., Jezzard, P., Cadoux-Hudson, T., Ansorge, O., 2016. Noninvasive quantification of 2-hydroxyglutarate in human gliomas with IDH1 and IDH2 mutations. Cancer Res. 76, 43–49.

Giapitzakis, I.A., Shao, T., Avdievich, N., Mekle, R., Kreis, R., Henning, A., 2018. Metabolite-cycled STEAM and semi-LASER localization for MR spectroscopy of the human brain at 9.4T. Magn. Reson. Med. 79, 1841–1850.

Godlewska, B.R., Masaki, C., Sharpley, A.L., Cowen, P.J., Emir, U.E., 2018. Brain glutamate in medication-free depressed patients: a proton MRS study at 7 Tesla. Psychol. Med. 48, 1731–1737.

Holmay, M.J., Terpstra, M., Coles, L.D., Mishra, U., Ahlskog, M., Oz, G., Cloyd, J.C., Tuite, P.J., 2013. N-acetylcysteine boosts brain and blood glutathione in gaucher and Parkinson diseases. Clin. Neuropharmacol. 36, 103–106.

Joers, J.M., Deelchand, D.K., Lyu, T., Emir, U.E., Hutter, D., Gomez, C.M., Bushara, K.O., Eberly, L.E., Oz, G., 2018. Neurochemical abnormalities in premanifest and early spinocerebellar ataxias. Ann. Neurol. 83, 816–829.

Juchem, C., Cudalbu, C., De Graaf, R.A., Gruetter, R., Henning, A., Hetherington, H.P., Boer, V.O., 2020. B0 shimming for in vivo magnetic resonance spectroscopy: experts' consensus recommendations. NMR Biomed., e4350.

Oz, G., Deelchand, D.K., Wijnen, J.P., Mlynarik, V., Xin, L., Mekle, R., Noeske, R., Scheenen, T.W.J., Tkac, I., Experts' Working Group on Advanced Single Voxel 1H MRS, 2021. Advanced single voxel (1) H magnetic resonance spectroscopy techniques in humans: experts' consensus recommendations. NMR Biomed. 34, e4236.

Oz, G., Tkac, I., 2011. Short-echo, single-shot, full-intensity proton magnetic resonance spectroscopy for neurochemical profiling at 4 T: validation in the cerebellum and brainstem. Magn. Reson. Med. 65, 901–910.

Scheenen, T.W., Klomp, D.W., Wijnen, J.P., Heerschap, A., 2008. Short echo time 1H-MRSI of the human brain at 3T with minimal chemical shift displacement errors using adiabatic refocusing pulses. Magn. Reson. Med. 59, 1–6.

Seaquist, E.R., Moheet, A., Kumar, A., Deelchand, D.K., Terpstra, M., Kubisiak, K., Eberly, L.E., Henry, P.G., Joers, J.M., Oz, G., 2017. Hypothalamic glucose transport in humans during experimentally induced hypoglycemia-associated autonomic failure. J. Clin. Endocrinol. Metab. 102, 3571–3580.

Tkac, I., Andersen, P., Adriany, G., Merkle, H., Ugurbil, K., Gruetter, R., 2001. In vivo 1H NMR spectroscopy of the human brain at 7 T. Magn. Reson. Med. 46, 451–456.

Tkac, I., Deelchand, D., Dreher, W., Hetherington, H., Kreis, R., Kumaragamage, C., Povazan, M., Spielman, D.M., Strasser, B., De Graaf, R.A., 2021. Water and lipid suppression techniques for advanced (1) H MRS and MRSI of the human brain: experts' consensus recommendations. NMR Biomed. 34, e4459.

Wiegers, E.C., Rooijackers, H.M., Tack, C.J., Heerschap, A., De Galan, B.E., Van Der Graaf, M., 2016. Brain lactate concentration falls in response to hypoglycemia in patients with type 1 diabetes and impaired awareness of hypoglycemia. Diabetes 65, 1601–1605.

Wilson, M., Andronesi, O., Barker, P.B., Bartha, R., Bizzi, A., Bolan, P.J., Brindle, K.M., Choi, I.Y., Cudalbu, C., Dydak, U., Emir, U.E., Gonzalez, R.G., Gruber, S., Gruetter, R., Gupta, R.K., Heerschap, A., Henning, A., Hetherington, H.P., Huppi, P.S., Hurd, R.E., Kantarci, K., Kauppinen, R.A., Klomp, D.W.J., Kreis, R., Kruiskamp, M.J., Leach, M.O., Lin, A.P., Luijten, P.R., Marjanska, M., Maudsley, A.A., Meyerhoff, D.J., Mountford, C.E., Mullins, P.G., Murdoch, J.B., Nelson, S.J., Noeske, R., Oz, G., Pan, J.W., Peet, A.C., Poptani, H., Posse, S., Ratai, E.M., Salibi, N., Scheenen, T.W.J., Smith, I.C.P., Soher, B.J., Tkac, I., Vigneron, D.B., Howe, F.A., 2019. Methodological consensus on clinical proton MRS of the brain: review and recommendations. Magn. Reson. Med. 82, 527–550.

CHAPTER

Magnetic resonance spectroscopic imaging: principles and applications

33

Wolfgang Bogner, Bernhard Strasser, Petr Bednarik, Eva Heckova, Lukas Hingerl, and Gilbert Hangel

High-field MR Center, Department of Biomedical Imaging and Image-guided Therapy, Medical University of Vienna, Vienna, Austria

33.1 Introduction

MR spectroscopic imaging (MRSI) is a powerful extension of single-voxel MRS. Rather than probing the neurochemical profile within only one voxel, state-of-the-art MRSI provides three-dimensional maps of multiple neurochemical compounds, in some cases over the whole brain. This is enabled by mapping three spatial dimensions and the chemically specific spectral dimension simultaneously. Since 1982, when MRSI was originally proposed, it has become an important research tool for neuroscience, but, like many other MRI techniques, it has had difficulties translating into a widely used tool for routine clinical practice (Öz et al., 2014) due to its lack of simplicity and robustness. A susceptibility to artifacts (e.g., instabilities, field inhomogeneities, and nuisance signals), in particular, and a lack of automation and quality assurance of the increasingly large data sets, were considerable limitations, which had to be gradually overcome. Excessive data size led to prohibitively lengthy reconstruction and quantification times (Maudsley et al., 2020).

In parallel, there has been an ongoing trend toward human MRI at ultra-high-field (UHF) with the result that 7T whole-body MR scanners have become available for routine clinical use recently with a resultant gain in sensitivity and spectral resolution (i.e., chemical specificity) (Henning, 2018). Yet, 3T scanners are still more common, and thus alternative means by which to improve chemical specificity, such as spectral editing, have evolved. Spectral editing has thus far been mostly single-voxel MRS-dominated, but an increasing number of MRSI implementations are emerging (Maudsley et al., 2020). Complementary information can be obtained by less common multi-nuclear (e.g., ^{31}P, ^{13}C, ^{2}H)-MRSI techniques, a main driving factor of which is the rapid rise of hyperpolarization technology, with its translation from animal to human applications. All this has led to an increasing demand for fast and efficient MRSI-encoding and processing techniques.

Thus, MRSI provides valuable intrinsically multi-parametric and quantitative images of multiple neurochemical compounds that are complementary to the structural and functional information provided by other MRI techniques.

Advances in Magnetic Resonance Technology and Applications, Volume 4, ISSN 2666-9099. https://doi.org/10.1016/B978-0-12-822479-3.00051-8
Copyright © 2021 Elsevier Inc. All rights reserved.

519

520 Chapter 33 Magnetic resonance spectroscopic imaging

33.2 Principles & advanced techniques
33.2.1 Acquisition & reconstruction
33.2.1.1 Spatial localization

In contrast to MRI, MRSI frequently uses prelocalization (e.g., cuboid volumes) to remove unwanted nuisance signals (e.g., extracranial lipids). Common prelocalization schemes are stimulated-echo- or spin-echo-based, and employ conventional radiofrequency (RF) pulses. Motivated by single-voxel MRS at ≥ 3 tesla, the use of adiabatic RF pulses, which provide more accurate spatial selection, has become increasingly common. Unfortunately, prelocalization prevents an investigation of cortical brain regions, and, combined with adiabatic RF pulses, leads to high specific absorption rates (SAR) and signal loss associated with long echo times (TE). Recent UHF-MRSI approaches are therefore more similar to MRI. They employ single-slice or slab-selective localization without preselection to enable whole-brain investigations using either single-refocusing or echo-less free induction decay (FID)-MRSI acquisition (Maudsley et al., 2020; Henning, 2018). In parallel, significant progress has been achieved in making MRSI acquisition more robust via the development of hardware- and software-based retrospective/prospective motion and instability correction techniques (Andronesi et al., 2021).

33.2.1.2 MRSI encoding & decoding

To encode the chemically-specific frequency dimension (ω) simultaneously with up to three spatial imaging dimensions (x, y, z), MRSI must sample the so-called k-space (k_x, k_y, k_z) not just once, such as in MRI, but repeatedly within very small time intervals (i.e., < ms) along a temporal dimension, k_t. These time intervals are inversely proportional to the spectral bandwidth (SBW), which must be broad enough to cover the entire spectrum without aliasing. For the encoding of the image space, any MRI encoding technique can be used, such as phase- or frequency-encoding. However, with increasing SBW and spatial resolution demands, non-Cartesian k-space sampling trajectories are becoming more popular (Fig. 33.1) (Bogner et al., 2020).

Phase encoding is the slowest among all the spatial encoding techniques. Only a single k-space point is acquired per repetition time (TR). Yet, due to its simplicity, it is the only option implemented on commercial whole-body MR systems. In contrast, spatial-spectral encoding (SSE) is up to two magnitudes faster with usually negligible SNR loss, but increases the stress on gradient hardware and is more prone to hardware imperfections. The first proposed SSE technique was echo planar spectroscopic imaging (EPSI). In MRI terms, EPSI is a multi-echo gradient-echo pulse sequence with several hundred echoes. For each echo, frequency encoding along k-space lines is repeated after very short time intervals to reach a sufficiently high SBW. Currently, not only k-space lines, as in EPSI, but several other trajectories for navigating through k-space are available, including spirals, concentric rings, or rosettes.

Parallel imaging exploits the intrinsic spatial localization of multi-channel receive coils to accelerate MRI/MRSI acquisitions. Each coil element "sees" only a fraction of the investigated object. Hence, some spatial information is inherently encoded into the detected signal and some of the "traditional" encoding steps can be omitted. Omitting these encoding steps (i.e., undersampling) causes image aliasing, but the full spatial information can be recovered by solving an overdetermined system of linear equations or an optimization problem. MRSI accelerations by one order of magnitude have been shown when exploiting coil sensitivity information in all three spatial dimensions, but the biggest challenge is residual aliasing, which can cause strong lipid artifacts.

33.2 Principles & advanced techniques

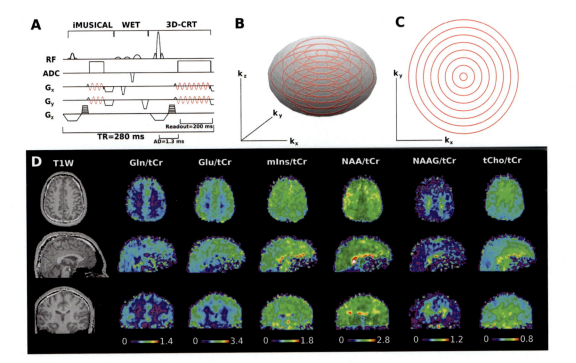

FIGURE 33.1

(A) FID-MRSI pulse sequence diagram with 3D-CRT (concentric ring trajectory) encoding via sine- and cosine-modulated gradients in k_x and k_y and a trapezoidal partition-encoding gradient in k_z. Pulse sequence parameters were TR=280 ms, AD=1.3 ms, readout duration 200 ms, 64x64x39 matrix, 9:21 min acquisition time. In 3D k-space, this corresponds to an ellipsoidal volume (B) covered by stacked 2D-CRT (C), with their maximal distance given by the Nyquist criterion for all three directions. (D) Metabolic ratio maps of a healthy volunteer in the transverse, sagittal, and coronal plane for voxels with CRLBs<40. Adapted from Hingerl et al. (2019) with permission from *Investigative Radiology*.

Compressed sensing is another reconstruction technique that relies on undersampling. Whereas parallel imaging omits regular spatial encoding patterns and requires multi-channel receive coils, the omitted spatial encodings for compressed sensing must be pseudo-random, which results in incoherent aliasing and random undersampling that can even extend to the frequency domain. No special hardware is necessary, but the detected signal must be compressible (i.e., a "sparsifying" transform to a signal containing mainly zeros must exist). If that is the case, prior knowledge is used to retrieve the full spatial/spectral information. The main problems are slow, usually iterative, decoding and the risk of enforcing the prior knowledge too strongly (over-regularization).

When combined with shortening of the TR, SSE can achieve remarkable accelerations, even at UHF with a reported 300-fold faster scanning than clinical ^{1}H-MRSI. Spatial resolutions <3 mm isotropic over the whole brain have been shown in clinically attractive scans times of ~10–15 min. There are, however, cases (e.g., hyperpolarized ^{13}C-MRSI or dynamic ^{1}H-MRSI) where further acceleration is

522 Chapter 33 Magnetic resonance spectroscopic imaging

necessary. In such cases, SSE can be combined with undersampling in image- and frequency-encoded domains (Bogner et al., 2020; Hingerl et al., 2019).

For even faster scanning, the goal of MRSI reconstruction can be reformulated to incorporate additional spatial (e.g., anatomical imaging) or spatial/spectral prior information. Rather than reconstructing the chemical composition at each spatial point, it is only reconstructed within a few anatomical compartments. Instead of deriving hundreds of unknowns (voxels), only a few unknowns need to be calculated, thus requiring fewer "traditional" encoding steps. This results in the highest acceleration factors (Ma et al., 2015).

33.2.2 MRSI processing & quantification

MRSI processing pipelines include several reconstruction and spectral preprocessing steps before the quantification of spectra can be performed to obtain metabolic maps. As the spatial dimensions increase, the data storage requirements, complexity, and computation time are typically four to five orders of magnitude higher than for single-voxel MRS. Thus, processing times of several hours are not uncommon for volumetric MRSI with (tens of) thousands of voxels even on powerful computers. Promising attempts to reduce processing times, not only by increasing computer power, but also via improved algorithms and advanced machine-learning exist, but have not yet been established (Maudsley et al., 2020).

State-of-the-art MRSI reconstruction is largely consistent with that in MRI, including coil combination and spatial Fourier transform, or for non-Cartesian MRSI gridding on Cartesian coordinates and correction of k-space trajectory imperfections. Beyond this, some steps are MRS-specific to account for the spectral dimension, including removal of ghosting artifacts in the frequency dimension, spatial propagation of unsuppressed nuisance signals (e.g., lipids), and inherently low SNR/spatial resolution of MRSI. Recent developments rely on acquisition techniques that maximize sensitivity, reduce sampling noise, and enable high-resolution strategies that incorporate *a priori* spatial/spectral information for constrained spatial reconstruction (Bogner et al., 2020).

After the image reconstruction, the preprocessing of MRSI includes, at a minimum, the typical steps used in single-voxel MRS, such as removal of residual water and lipid nuisance signals, frequency/line-shape/phase correction, and spectral Fourier transformation. However, MRSI voxels are much smaller, and the large water signal is suppressed, leaving only the metabolite signals with low signal-to-noise ratios (SNR) to perform these preprocessing steps. This is more challenging. Therefore recent MRSI preprocessing employs extrinsic, non-water suppressed MRI data, interleaved MRI navigators, or MRSI without water suppression (e.g., metabolite-cycling) (Bogner et al., 2020).

Given the large number of spectra in MRSI, fully automated spectral analysis for spectral quantification is essential. Iterative parametric modeling and incorporation of *a priori* spectral information are widely used, but they are slow and have difficulties dealing with a broad range of spectral qualities. This is impractical for MRSI. Newer algorithms using machine-learning will play an increasing role to overcome this limitation (Maudsley et al., 2020; Gurbani et al., 2019).

Integrating advanced MRSI into the clinical workflow therefore calls for efficient processing of large data sets and combination with other imaging modalities to support further analysis steps. Processing multi-channel, high-resolution, volumetric MRSI has large memory requirements, which are frequently not met on MR scanners, and lengthy processing interferes with subsequent MRI protocols. Efforts to integrate state-of-the-art, whole-brain MRSI on commercial MR scanners have therefore been launched recently (Maudsley et al., 2020).

An important step toward clinical acceptance is quality control, which is essential to reduce false-positive and false-negative results. Traditional quality assessment metrics (e.g., Cramér–Rao lower bounds (CRLB), linewidth, SNR) must be interpreted with caution, especially in pathologies. Though the spectral quality has gradually improved over time, there is still a large variability in the spectral qualities obtained in MRSI, and the sheer number of spectra per data set do not permit visual inspection. Subject and scanner instabilities and outer volume contamination can cause additional MRSI-typical artifacts that can be difficult to recognize. Automated assessment tools have therefore been investigated (e.g., based on machine-learning) (Fig. 33.2) (Maudsley et al., 2020).

For the comparative analyses of metabolic maps between subjects or across multiple studies, signal normalization is required. Though estimation of metabolite concentrations via internal referencing to other compounds with "known" concentrations has become the standard in single-voxel MRS, this includes several assumptions and estimated correction factors, which are more complicated to assess in MRSI (e.g., water concentration, relaxation times, and mixed tissue contributions) so that using metabolite ratios is still common in MRSI.

The combined spatial and multi-parametric information of MRSI presents opportunities for novel quantitative analyses, such as automated atlas-based registration, which benefit from whole-brain coverage. This naturally supports the use of voxel-based analysis methods, which allows comparisons between data sets from different subjects or subject groups after registering multiple images to a standard frame of reference. Thereby, single-subject metabolite maps can be compared to mean values from a control group to account for normal regional variations of brain metabolite levels (Maudsley et al., 2009).

The multi-parametric nature of MRSI allows for multiple metabolite maps to be analyzed together, using techniques for pattern recognition analysis and using also other MRI contrasts. Early results indicate considerable potential for these analysis approaches. However, these methods have not been widely implemented and require consistent imaging protocols that have not yet been established.

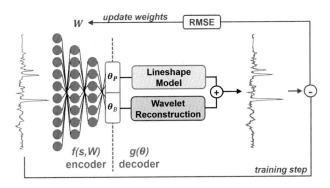

FIGURE 33.2

Schematic of the convolutional encoder–model decoder (CEMD) architecture, which uses a convolutional neural network (CNN) to learn a low-rank representation of input spectra and uses known models for the baseline and peak components of spectra to train the CNN. Adapted from Gurbani et al. (2019) with the permission of *Magnetic Resonance in Medicine*.

33.2.3 Advanced scanner hardware and ultra-high magnetic fields

MR scanner hardware has a critical influence on the quality of obtained MRSI data. Fortunately, there have been significant advances in that respect, including more sensitive multi-channel RF coils, faster-switching gradients for SSE, better B_0-shim hardware, motion/field-monitoring devices, and, most important of all, UHF magnets that improve both sensitivity and spectral resolution (Maudsley et al., 2020; Henning, 2018; Juchem et al., 2020).

Among the multitude of MR applications, MRSI of ^{1}H and multi-nuclei (e.g., ^{31}P, ^{23}Na, ^{13}C, ^{2}H) are some of the largest beneficiaries from UHF. At higher field strength, the SNR increases substantially (for some nuclei even super-linearly), enabling better tradeoffs between higher spatial resolution and shorter measurement times. High spatial resolutions are important to reduce lipid contamination and improve intra-voxel field homogeneities. The resulting higher spectral separation at ≥ 7 tesla allows more accurate metabolite quantification (e.g., better separation of glutamate vs glutamine, myo-inositol vs glycine, and N-acetyl aspartate vs N-acetylaspartylglutamate in ^{1}H-MRSI, or, for ^{31}P-MRSI, improved splitting of PE/PC, GPE/GPC, or α-ATP/NADH resonances). Other metabolites, such as the major inhibitory neurotransmitter γ-aminobutyric acid (GABA), rely on spectral editing methods to overcome the spectral overlap of resonances with more abundant metabolites, even at 7T. Only at 9.4T and above may a direct mapping of GABA be feasible without editing, if intra-voxel B_0 inhomogeneities can be kept sufficiently low, using advanced B_0-shimming and a high spatial resolution (Juchem et al., 2020; Motyka et al., 2019). Possible solutions to improve B_0-homogeneity include dynamic shimming, additional shim inserts, or integrating shim elements into RF coils (Juchem et al., 2020) (Fig. 33.3). Another prominent source of UHF artifacts is the increased chemical shift displacement error (CSDE), which causes mis-mapping of metabolites proportional to their chemical shift difference in the slice-selection direction. High-bandwidth pulses are needed to counteract this effect (Kreis et al., 2020). In addition, in ^{1}H-MRSI, transmitted B_1 fields become increasingly inhomogeneous due to wave-propagation and skin depth effects, thereby rendering the efficiency of applied RF pulses position-dependent and causing specific-absorption-rate (SAR) hotspots. Adiabatic pulses provide a possible solution. They are insensitive to transmit B_1 errors and overcome CSDE-related problems. Yet, adiabatic pulses have other limitations, the most important being the increased SAR, which leads to long TRs and associated SNR loss. Parallel transmit technology is another way to overcome transmit B_1 inhomogeneities, but requires expensive hardware and challenging redesign of RF pulses, and has therefore been rarely used in MRSI. A general problem at UHF is the faster T_2/T_2^* relaxation, which favors MRSI acquisition techniques with a short-TE or FID sampling. FID-MRSI is therefore becoming increasingly common, not only for ^{2}H- and ^{31}P-MRSI, but also for ^{1}H-MRSI at UHF, due to a variety of advantages, including the absence of T_2- and J-evolution-related signal loss, low SAR, negligible CSDE, and insensitivity to transmit B_1 errors. This enables a jump in spatial resolution toward that of clinical diffusion MRI. Critical components to reach these high spatial resolutions in clinically acceptable scan times are fast-switching gradients, which are fundamental for rapid high-resolution SSE, highly-sensitive multi-channel receive coils to enable efficient parallel imaging, and advanced B_0-shimming to avoid losses in SNR and chemical specificity.

33.2.4 Multi-nuclear MRSI

The increasing availability of UHF-MRI and hyperpolarization technology have been the main driving factors behind multi-nuclei-sensitive MRSI. Most common are ^{31}P-MRSI and hyperpolarized ^{13}C-

33.2 Principles & advanced techniques

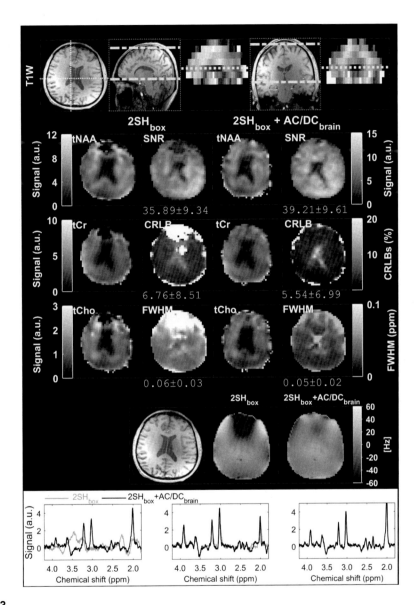

FIGURE 33.3

Comparison of MRSI data obtained with the standard second-order spherical harmonics shim, 2SH$_{box}$, to the AC/DC shim superimposed on the 2SH$_{box}$ shim, 2SH$_{box}$+AC/DC$_{brain}$, in a healthy volunteer. tNAA, tCr, tCho, SNR, CRLB of tCr, full width at half maximum (FWHM), and B$_0$ maps, as well as sample spectra, are compared between the two shim conditions and anatomical images are shown at the top. The sample spectra are taken from a left anterior, left central, and right posterior position. The 2SH$_{box}$ and 2SH$_{box}$+AC/DC$_{brain}$ spectra are shown in gray and black, respectively. The values under the maps indicate the mean and standard deviation calculated over the whole-brain slab. A clear improvement in all maps and the frontal and central spectra can be seen when using 2SH$_{box}$+AC/DC$_{brain}$ instead of 2SH$_{box}$. Adapted from Esmaeili et al., *Scientific Reports 2020* under CC BY license.

526 Chapter 33 Magnetic resonance spectroscopic imaging

MRSI. Though well-established preclinically and outside the brain, multi-nuclear MRSI is less common in brain imaging. While typically the lower sensitivity of multi-nuclear MRSI is a limiting factor compared to ^{1}H-MRSI, the lack of residual water/lipid contamination make multi-nuclear MRSI generally more robust.

[31]P nuclei have an approximately 15 times lower sensitivity, but a 100% natural abundance and much larger spectral dispersion than ^{1}H nuclei (de Graaf). Moreover, ^{31}P-MRSI provides complementary information by detecting major constituents of cell energy metabolism, including concentrations of phosphocreatine, inorganic phosphate, and ATP, as well as intracellular pH. For decades, ^{31}P-MRSI was confined to phase-encoded FID-MRSI, but in recent years, new methods to push the limitations on scan time, SNR, and resolution have been proposed. This includes introducing spatial-spectral encoding and undersampled ^{31}P-MRSI, which were shown for 3T and up to 9.4T. Whereas combinations of these acceleration techniques have been shown (Henning, 2018; Bogner et al., 2020), they will probably remain a niche technique due to the inherently low SNR available for ^{31}P-MRSI unless combined with the application of spatial-spectral prior knowledge (e.g., SPectroscopic Imaging by exploiting spatiospectral CorrElation (SPICE), allowing ^{31}P-MRSI with $6.9 \times 6.9 \times 10 \, mm^3$ nominal resolutions in the brain to be acquired even at 3T within ~15 minutes) (Ma et al., 2015). Next to improved acquisition sequences, improved double-tuned multi-channel-receive ^{31}P/[1]H-coils have brought significant SNR increases from 3T to 9.4T. Unfortunately, established MRS methods to improve sensitivity and spectral resolution become more challenging at UHF, such as [1]H-decoupling and nuclear Overhauser effect (NOE) enhancement within safe SAR limits.

Muscle metabolism is the most common application for ^{31}P-MRS(I), but there were few applications for this technique in the brain. Of these, whole-brain measurements of intra- and extracellular pH in brain tumors is one application with which to investigate tumor metabolism, as elevated pH appears to precede tumor progression. Significant changes in metabolism associated with neurodegenerative (e.g., increased phosophocreatine and pH in the hippocampus in Alzheimers' disease) and psychiatric disorders (e.g., phosphocholine and phosphoethanolamine increases in depression) have been found (Rijpma et al., 2018).

MRSI of hyperpolarized ^{13}C-compounds that mark metabolic pathways is a highly promising technique. Although hyperpolarized ^{13}C-MRSI is already further developed in other human organs, such as the prostate, it is only now starting to translate from animal studies to initial clinical studies for the human brain (Wang et al., 2019). In 2018, MRSI of deuterated glucose and potentially other deuterated substances was introduced in humans *in vivo* (De Feyter et al., 2018). It was successfully demonstrated in volunteers and glioma patients and could become a powerful alternative to FDG-PET, not only for imaging of the Warburg effect, but also to quantify metabolic fluxes non-invasively (Fig. 33.4).

33.2.5 Spectrally-edited MRSI

Spectral editing techniques utilize the scalar (J)-coupling between spins to separate spectrally overlapping resonances and are most commonly applied as J-difference editing (Bogner et al., 2017). In J-difference editing, two averages are subtracted, with one of these having a target resonance inverted by an editing pulse, causing it to remain after subtraction. Edited-MRSI requires higher motion/scanner stability and robustness to B_1/B_0-inhomogeneities than single-voxel MRS (Andronesi et al., 2021). A commonly targeted metabolite is GABA, which is hard to quantify otherwise, due to its low concentration and spectral overlaps. Though MEGA-PRESS pulse sequences remain the workhorse for

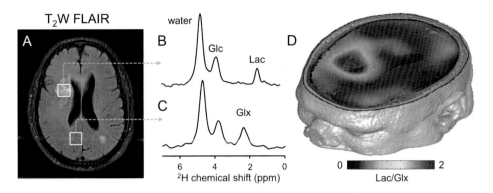

FIGURE 33.4

Deuterium metabolic imaging (DMI) of human brain glucose metabolism *in vivo*. (A) Clinical T_2-weighted, fluid-attenuated inversion recovery (FLAIR) MR images of a patient with a recurring glioblastoma multiforme (GBM) brain tumor. (B, C) Deuterium (2H) MR spectra extracted from a 3D DMI data set, originating from the regions indicated in (A), acquired approximately 60 minutes following oral administration of [6,6'-2H2]-glucose. Apart from the naturally abundant water signal, the 2H MR spectrum from normal-appearing brain tissue (C) contains peaks from the substrate, [6,6'-2H2]-glucose (Glc), and a downstream product, [4-2H]-glutamate+glutamine (Glx), formed following metabolism in the glycolytic pathway and the tricarboxylic acid cycle. The 2H MR spectrum from the tumor region (B) shows increased lactate (Lac), characteristic of the Warburg effect. (D) A Lac/Glx ratio map demonstrates a high contrast-to-noise measure of anaerobic over aerobic metabolism, thereby providing unique metabolic information not available from standard clinical MR images. Adapted from De Feyter et al. (2018) with permission from *Science Advances*.

GABA-editing, recent research applications have evolved to use adiabatic spatial-selection pulses (e.g., MEGA-LASER/sLASER especially using low-power/high-bandwidth, gradient-modulated adiabatic pulses) instead to overcome CSDE and transmit B_1 errors, at UHF and MRSI, in particular (Choi et al., 2021). Combining spectral editing with MRSI is becoming increasingly popular and has been implemented in combination with rapid spatial-spectral readout strategies (e.g., EPSI, spirals and concentric rings). Using a B_1/B_0-insensitive editing pulse sequence allows the acquisition of relatively high-resolution maps over entire brain slices without volume selection and without macromolecular contamination of the GABA signal when combined with efficient lipid-suppression strategies (Fig. 33.5) (Moser et al., 2019). Another important innovation has been the possibility to simultaneously edit multiple target metabolites (e.g., glutathione and GABA) using a spectral Hadamard encoding approach (Chan et al., 2019). In particular, the ability to correct motion and scanner instabilities (e.g., using volumetric navigators in real-time or retrospectively) has resulted in a jump in reproducibility for spectrally-edited MRSI (Bogner et al., 2013).

33.2.6 Emerging MRSI techniques

Two emerging MRS methods that have brought entirely new insights into brain metabolism and cellular integrity are functional and diffusion-weighted MRS. Thus far, studies have been mostly restricted to single-voxel MRS, but initial promising MRSI pilot data have been shown recently, which illustrate the potential of functional MRSI (fMRSI) and diffusion-weighted MRSI (dwMRSI) to access

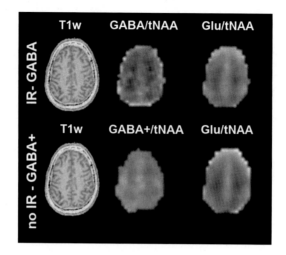

FIGURE 33.5

A comparison of GABA/GABA+ and Glu to NAA ratios acquired with edited MRSI at 7T (Moser et al., 2019). Using inversion-recovery, the macromolecular background can be suppressed, visibly enhancing the apparent GABA contrast between the WM and the GM.

new biomarkers for clinical studies and neuroscience. fMRSI is a tool with which to image dynamic changes in brain metabolism as a result of neuronal activation, whereas dwMRSI can be used to map the cell-type-specific dimensions of brain cells via the diffusion properties of metabolites within these cells. In both cases, the scan time per dynamic timepoint or per diffusion-weighted scan, respectively, must be short to allow multiple similar MRSI scans to be performed in succession, requiring very fast spatial-spectral encoding strategies. At the same time, an outstanding temporal stability is paramount to accurately quantify the small signal intensity changes that allow assessment of functional and microstructural information. See Fig. 33.6.

33.3 Applications
33.3.1 Clinical applications

Though MRSI has a wide array of potential clinical applications, as illustrated by studies on migraine, ADHD, stroke/ischemia, leukodystrophies, or HIV-associated dementia, clinical studies that are focused on brain tumors, epilepsy, demyelinating, and neurodegenerative, or psychiatric disorders are by far the most common (Maudsley et al., 2020; Wilson et al., 2019).

33.3.1.1 Brain tumors

Imaging of brain tumors is the main clinical application of ^{1}H-MRSI today, but clinical protocols are mostly limited to single-voxel MRS or single low-resolution slices, and the quantification of tCho/tNAA ratios as a marker for tumor infiltration. The application of ^{1}H-MRSI was mostly focused on preop-

33.3 Applications   529

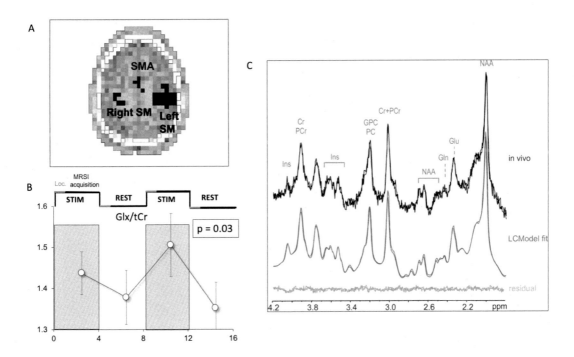

FIGURE 33.6

Functional MRSI (pilot study). A. Masks (in black) were created by thresholding of parametric maps resulting from a functional BOLD-fMRI experiment activating supplementary motor area (SMA) and bilateral primary sensorimotor cortex (SM). Masks were down-sampled to the resolution of MRSI data (5x5x4.8 mm^3) acquired with a 3D FID-MRSI (Hingerl et al., 2019). B. Mean time-course (N =12) of Glx/tCr obtained in the left primary sensorimotor cortex during the stimulation paradigm of single-finger opposition. Data were compared with the standard paired t-test (STIM vs REST). Loc. - autoalign localizer. C. Sample spectra from two REST blocks acquired in the left sensorimotor cortex and their quantification in LCmodel.

erative grading, radiation planning, and tumor delineation. In contrast, recent clinical studies using state-of-the-art ^{1}H-MRSI show a wealth of complementary metabolic information that can be visualized in brain tumors. Today's ^{1}H-MRSI techniques map not only tCho, tCr, and tNAA, but also, beyond that, 2HG, *myo*-Ins, Gln, Glu, Gly, and GSH, which are potent markers for mutation-status, astrocytosis, tumor metabolism, tumor grade, and oxidative stress. In addition, the improvements in brain coverage and spatial resolution could make ^{1}H-MRSI highly attractive, as it allows the heterogeneous metabolism of brain tumors to be studied in previously unseen detail (Fig. 33.7) (Hangel et al., 2019).

A key metabolite of interest in MRS of brain tumors is 2-hydroxyglutarate (2HG), a product of mutated isocitrate-dehydrogenase (IDH), which has recently come to prominence in cancer research as a treatment target and highly potent prognostic marker (Choi et al., 2012). Consequently, a whole array of MRS methods at 3T and 7T, mostly based on spectra-editing and optimized J-evolution, has emerged. Several of these techniques have also been translated into MRSI versions to enable imaging of elevated 2HG concentrations in IDH-mutant gliomas in clinical studies.

530 Chapter 33 Magnetic resonance spectroscopic imaging

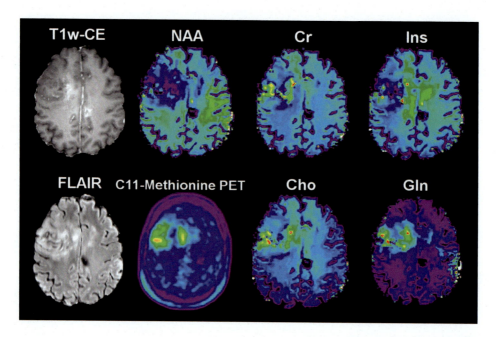

FIGURE 33.7

High-resolution metabolite maps of a recurrent low-grade glioma based on 7T FID-MRSI, with additional super-resolution compared to routine 3T imaging and PET. With sufficient resolution, metabolic heterogeneities within the tumor can be resolved. Gln, in particular, shows promise as a new biomarker next to the established tCho (Hangel et al., 2019).

Multiple approaches for segmentation, based on or augmented by MRSI, have been proposed, using metabolic information to better define tumor margins and to differentiate tissue types, with different computational/deep-learning algorithms. High-performing acquisition strategies, such as EPSI, were applied in several studies that evaluated the impact of radio- and chemotherapy on tumor metabolism by identifying remaining infiltration, thus visualizing changes in NAA, tCho, lactate, and lipids during treatment, which correlate with treatment outcome. MRSI was found to increase the treatment volumes in radiation therapy and to indicate larger tumor volumes than PET.

Using 7T systems, MRSI of gliomas can more easily separate Gln from Glu, and Gly from *myo*-Ins (Hingerl et al., 2019), which are potent target metabolites of modern cancer research.

33.3.1.2 Epilepsy

Epilepsy is a disruption of regular brain activity caused by different pathologies. MRSI is an obvious candidate with which to map changes in neurotransmitters and metabolites in (suspected) epileptic foci, but early available MRSI methods were hampered by long measurement times, low resolution, a lack of coverage and motion, and only changes in NAA, tCr, and tCho could be detected, with findings limited to a decrease in NAA ratios to tCr/tCho. Whole-brain MRSI at 3T has improved resolution and coverage and enabled finding decreased NAA/tCr in neocortical epileptogenic foci. Other 3T research found a positive correlation between seizure frequency and Glu/tCr in epileptic children. Using 7T MRSI, a correlation between decreased NAA/tCr and patient outcome in resected tissue was found, and 7T 3D-MRSI identified even increases of Glu and GABA in epilepsy patients. Also defining interregional correlations between NAA, Glu, and GABA as neurotransmitter networks, which is a promising new concept that may expand our understanding of epilepsy (van Veenendaal et al., 2018).

33.3.1.3 Demyelinating & neurodegenerative diseases

Due to its ability to map NAA, *myo*-Ins, and Cho, ^{1}H-MRSI is a powerful imaging tool with which to visualize neuronal integrity, gliosis, and de/re-myelination among other metabolites in demyelinating and neurodegenerative disorders.

MRSI studies in multiple sclerosis (MS) have investigated the role of widespread axonal damage (reduced NAA, NAA/tCr, NAA/tCho) even in the earliest clinical stages and supplied evidence of gray matter pathological involvement. MRSI has confirmed the greater degree of inflammation and myelin damage in relapsing-remitting MS over progressive MS by measuring tCho, elucidated the relevance of reactive gliosis (increased *myo*-Ins, *myo*-Ins/tNAA) to the accumulation of neurological disability, characterized the pathological development of lesions, and enabled the measurement of pathology-driven oxidative stress (reduced GSH). Recent high-spatial-resolution FID-MRSI has improved the neurometabolic assessment of small, focal T_2-hyperintense lesions (Fig. 33.8). MRSI may also facilitate the distinction of MS from neuromyelitis optica, the latter of which is characterized by the lack of diffuse axonal injury (Swanberg et al., 2019).

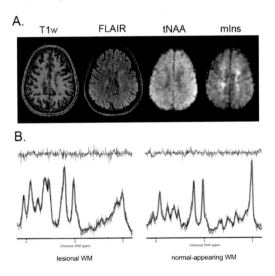

FIGURE 33.8

N-acetylaspartate and myo-inositol metabolic images and corresponding MRI of a multiple sclerosis patient acquired at 7T (A) and representative spectra from lesional and normal-appearing white matter (B).

In adult adrenoleukodystrophy, MRSI at 7T revealed early white-matter degeneration and demyelination, as yet unseen on clinical MRI. It also showed potential in the establishment of early diagnosis in acute disseminated encephalomyelitis.

532 **Chapter 33** Magnetic resonance spectroscopic imaging

MRSI permitted the detection of axonal degeneration in the motor cortex and other regions implicated in the pathophysiology of amyotrophic lateral sclerosis (ALS). The NAA decrease indicated a correlation with disability and improved the diagnostic accuracy of multi-parametric MRI in ALS. NAA/tCr ratios proved to be a surrogate marker of therapeutic efficacy.

In addition to the abundant ^{1}H-MRSI findings of reduced NAA, NAA/tCr, and increased *myo*-Ins, *myo*-Ins/tNAA, or *myo*-Ins/tCr levels, which imply widespread neurodegeneration and reactive gliosis in Alzheimer's disease (AD), an altered energy metabolism (increased PCr and Pi) was observed by ^{31}P-MRSI in brain regions with early degeneration. Neurometabolic changes in mild cognitive impairment (MCI) were found to be significantly larger than those observed for normal aging, and elevated hippocampal *myo*-Ins/tNAA may help to predict MCI conversion to dementia. Finally, MRSI was found to be useful in discriminating different forms of dementia.

Metabolic alterations in the substantia nigra, including reduced NAA and GSH concentrations, were also detected using MRSI in Parkinson's disease. Longitudinal studies showed abnormal tNAA/tCr decline of the substantia nigra in Parkinson's disease. Finally, MRSI measures of NAA in the basal ganglia were able to differentiate Parkinsonian variants from idiopathic Parkinson's disease.

33.3.1.4 Psychiatric disorders

Brain studies congruently point to distinct metabolic alterations in psychiatric disorders (Maddock and Buonocore, 2011), although the exact extent and localization of these changes remain uncertain, offering important prospects for MRSI. In agreement with neurobiological and single-voxel MRS studies, MRSI showed NAA, Cho, or Cr deficits in most psychiatric disorders and provided evidence of their response to therapy. Though quantification of these three abundant metabolites remains relatively straightforward, even with less advanced methods at lower fields, their quantification benefits from improved stability and quantification accuracy at higher fields. UHF-MRSI with short TE offers an opportunity to accurately separate and quantify glutamate and glutamine. Most MRSI studies have reported their sum, as reliable separation is not possible at low fields. Glutamate, the main excitatory neurotransmitter, is the most promising MRSI target in schizophrenia and other psychiatric conditions. Glutamate deficiencies were also detected in bipolar and major depressive disorders. Altered glutamate levels are accompanied by GABA abnormalities due to an excitatory/inhibitory imbalance in schizophrenia and autism spectrum disorder, but GABA cannot be reliably quantified with MRSI at lower fields, and even single-voxel MRS requires advanced spectral editing. Spatially heterogeneous glutamate/GABA disturbances pose an opportunity for novel 3D-MRSI approaches (Moser et al., 2019), which could be utilized in clinical settings (Spurny et al., 2020). Glutamate, together with lactate, is related to glucose combustion and ATP production. Facilitated lactate and attenuated glutamate production is caused by anaerobic glycolysis in the cytosol, due to compromised glucose oxidation in the mitochondria. Lactate and glutamate dissociation point to mitochondrial metabolic deficits, and to the shift from oxidative to anaerobic glucose metabolic pathways (De Feyter et al., 2018), which are considered critical in schizophrenia and bipolar disorder pathophysiology, and thus need to be reliably quantified using advanced MRSI. ^{1}H-MRSI, indeed, found resting lactate disturbances in unmedicated patients with bipolar disorders. According to 7T-MRSI, there is an association between regional disturbances in tCho/tCr, NAA/tCr, Glu/tCr, *myo*-Ins/tCr, GABA/tCr, and GSH/tCr in patients with major depressive disorders and mindfulness-based cognitive therapy and a reduction in depression severity. This indicates potential implications for MRSI in measurements of treatment response and postulation of individualized pharmacotherapy.

33.3.2 Advanced MRSI in neuroscience

MRSI methods have contributed to an understanding of the fundamental properties of neural circuits. The availability of accurate measures of glutamate and GABA, which are critically involved in the balance between excitation and inhibition in local neuronal circuits and in the regulation of neuronal output, provided breakthroughs in understanding brain physiology (Stanley and Raz, 2018). Glutamate and GABA are involved in memory formation and neural plasticity. The relationship between GABA levels and learning performance was demonstrated in the hippocampus using edited 3D-MRSI (Spurny et al., 2020). Glutamate was also linked to normal and impaired cognition and reflected task-evoked responses to physiological stimulations and cognitive tasks. The detection of subtle functional glutamate responses requires unprecedented temporal stability, and only preliminary studies have been performed with FID-based, single-slice ^{1}H-MRSI in mice, and 3D-MRSI in humans in the barrel and sensorimotor cortex, respectively. Assessing the spectral linewidth of water allows the simultaneous acquisition of neurochemical and BOLD responses similar to interleaved BOLD-fMRI/MRS experiments. An understanding of metabolic variations throughout the normal brain caused by body mass index or sex, as well as metabolic measures during brain development and aging, are essential for accurate appreciation of regional metabolic alterations in various diseases. Metabolic alterations, indeed, crucially affect cognitive outcomes. To date, studies have not provided normative values for the extended spectrum of metabolites that are becoming available with advanced MRSI approaches. Novel MRSI methods applied at UHF promise to increase our understanding of various contributors to discrepancies in brain metabolism in health and disease.

33.4 Conclusions & outlook

Ultimately, we need accurate concentration maps of as many metabolites as possible and metabolic concentration maps that we can trust without looking back at the spectra. This is the ultimate goal of MRSI development, so as to reach users with a broad range of experience levels.

We have not fully arrived at all the advanced MRSI techniques, but some methods are already being used commonly in neuroscience and have reached routine clinical use (e.g., brain tumor imaging), while an array of even more powerful, emerging MRSI techniques are waiting right at the gate (Maudsley et al., 2020; Bogner et al., 2020). To make these techniques broadly accessible, several obstacles in the acquisition, reconstruction, quantification, and analysis of data still remain.

1) Mitigation of artifacts that occur during the acquisition and that originate from different sources, including subject-specific motion-related artifacts (Andronesi et al., 2021) and scanner-inherent imperfections (Juchem et al., 2020), is a rapidly evolving field of research, which will soon turn these new MRSI techniques into robust neuroimaging tools.

2) High-resolution, whole-brain MRSI raw data can reach $\sim$100 Gbyte in size. A significant challenge to overcome is their rapid online reconstruction to eliminate the need for lengthy (often custommade) offline reconstruction pipelines (Maudsley et al., 2020).

3) Fully automated quality assurance and quantification of several 100,000 spectra requires rapid MRSI-optimized quantification software that is not established yet, but promising attempts via GPU-optimization and based on deep-learning are emerging and awaiting validation (Bogner et al., 2020).

4) Ultimately, the increasing number of simultaneously acquired neurochemical compounds poses a challenge to their analysis and meaningful interpretation, also in combination with other multi-

534   Chapter 33 Magnetic resonance spectroscopic imaging

parametric MRI techniques. Similar challenges are being faced by other quantitative MRI and imaging sciences, in general, and thus, advanced machine-learning algorithms to tackle this major challenge are under intense investigation (Maudsley et al., 2020; Gurbani et al., 2019).

As all the previously introduced techniques and ideas to overcome these remaining challenges have arisen from academic research, they remain out of reach of potential clinical MRS users. MRI manufacturers have been hesitant to adapt the new MRS technologies of the last two decades, but only their contribution to MRS implementation can lead to a widespread adoption of these new methods.

Clearly, all this is less of an issue for single-voxel MRS, which already provides more accurate and reproducible results within tolerably short analysis times today, but changes in metabolite levels without knowledge of their spatial distribution are frequently not pathology-specific, in the same way as most other MRI parameters (e.g., T_1 or T_2 relaxation) would be unspecific. This makes the ability of MRSI to map spatial distributions so valuable and the development of accurate and robust MRSI techniques worthwhile.

References

Andronesi, O.C., Bhattacharyya, P.K., Bogner, W., et al., 2021. Motion correction methods for MRS: experts' consensus recommendations. NMR Biomed. 34 (5), e4364. https://doi.org/10.1002/nbm.4364.

Bogner, W., Hess, A.T., Gagoski, B., et al., 2013. Real-time motion- and B0-correction for LASER-localized spiral-accelerated 3D-MRSI of the brain at 3T. NeuroImage 88C, 22–31. http://www.ncbi.nlm.nih.gov/pubmed/24201013. (Accessed 27 March 2015).

Bogner, W., Hangel, G., Esmaeili, M., Andronesi, O.C., 2017. 1D-spectral editing and 2D multispectral in vivo ^{1}H-MRS and ^{1}H-MRSI - methods and applications. Anal. Biochem., 529.

Bogner, W., Otazo, R., Accelerated, Henning A., 2020. MR spectroscopic imaging—a review of current and emerging techniques. NMR Biomed. https://onlinelibrary.wiley.com/doi/abs/10.1002/nbm.4314.

Chan, K.L., Oeltzschner, G., Saleh, M.G., Edden, R.A.E., Barker, P.B., 2019. Simultaneous editing of GABA and GSH with Hadamard-encoded MR spectroscopic imaging. Magn. Reson. Med. 82 (1), 21–32. https://onlinelibrary.wiley.com/doi/abs/10.1002/mrm.27702.

Choi, C., Ganji, S.K., DeBerardinis, R.J., et al., 2012. 2-hydroxyglutarate detection by magnetic resonance spectroscopy in IDH-mutated patients with gliomas. Nat. Med. 18 (4), 624–629. https://doi.org/10.1038/nm.2682. https://www.ncbi.nlm.nih.gov/pmc/articles/PMC3615719/?tool=pmcentrez&r+endertype=abstract%5Cn.

Choi, I-Y., Andronesi, O.C., Barker, P., et al., 2021. Spectral editing in 1H magnetic resonance spectroscopy: experts' consensus recommendations. NMR Biomed. 34 (5), e4411. https://doi.org/10.1002/nbm.4411.

De Feyter, H.M., Behar, K.L., Corbin, Z.A., et al., 2018. Deuterium metabolic imaging (DMI) for MRI-based 3D mapping of metabolism in vivo. Sci. Adv. 4 (8), eaat7314.

de Graaf, R.A. In Vivo NMR Spectroscopy. John Wiley & Sons, Ltd, Chichester, UK. http://doi.wiley.com/10.1002/9781119382461.

Gurbani, S.S., Sheriff, S., Maudsley, A.A., Shim, H., Cooper, L.AD., 2019. Incorporation of a spectral model in a convolutional neural network for accelerated spectral fitting. Magn. Reson. Med. 81 (5), 3346–3357. http://doi.wiley.com/10.1002/mrm.27641.

Hangel, G., Jain, S., Springer, E., et al., 2019. High-resolution metabolic mapping of gliomas via patch-based super-resolution magnetic resonance spectroscopic imaging at 7T. NeuroImage 191, 587–595. http://www.ncbi.nlm.nih.gov/pubmed/30772399. (Accessed 30 October 2019).

Henning, A., 2018. Proton and multinuclear magnetic resonance spectroscopy in the human brain at ultra-high field strength: a review. NeuroImage 168, 181–198. http://www.ncbi.nlm.nih.gov/pubmed/28712992.

Hingerl, L., Strasser, B., Moser, P., et al., 2019. Clinical high-resolution 3D-MR spectroscopic imaging of the human brain at 7 T. Invest. Radiol., 1. http://journals.lww.com/10.1097/RLI.0000000000000626.

Juchem, C., Cudalbu, C., Graaf, R.A., et al., 2020. B 0 shimming for in vivo magnetic resonance spectroscopy: experts' consensus recommendations. NMR Biomed. https://onlinelibrary.wiley.com/doi/abs/10.1002/nbm.4350.

Kreis, R., Boer, V., Choi, I-Y., et al., 2020. Terminology and concepts for the characterization of in vivo MR spectroscopy methods and MR spectra: background and experts' consensus recommendations. NMR Biomed. https://onlinelibrary.wiley.com/doi/10.1002/nbm.4347.

Ma, C., Lam, F., Liang, Z-P., 2015. Encoding and Decoding with Prior Knowledge: From SLIM to SPICE. eMagRes. John Wiley & Sons, Ltd, Chichester, UK, pp. 535–542. http://doi.wiley.com/10.1002/9780470034590.emrstm1441.

Maddock, R.J., Buonocore, M.H., 2011. MR Spectroscopic Studies of the Brain in Psychiatric Disorders, pp. 199–251. http://link.springer.com/10.1007/7854_2011_197.

Maudsley, A.A., Domenig, C., Govind, V., et al., 2009. Mapping of brain metabolite distributions by volumetric proton MR spectroscopic imaging (MRSI). Magn. Reson. Med. 61 (3), 548–559. http://doi.wiley.com/10.1002/mrm.21875.

Maudsley, A.A., Andronesi, O.C., Barker, P.B., et al., 2020. Advanced magnetic resonance spectroscopic neuroimaging: experts' consensus recommendations. NMR Biomed. https://onlinelibrary.wiley.com/doi/abs/10.1002/nbm.4309.

Moser, P., Hingerl, L., Strasser, B., et al., 2019. Whole-slice mapping of GABA and GABA+ at 7T via adiabatic MEGA-editing, real-time instability correction, and concentric circle readout. NeuroImage 184, 475–489. https://linkinghub.elsevier.com/retrieve/pii/S1053811918308243.

Motyka, S., Moser, P., Hingerl, L., et al., 2019. The influence of spatial resolution on the spectral quality and quantification accuracy of whole-brain MRSI at 1.5T, 3T, 7T, and 9.4T. Magn. Reson. Med. 82 (2), 551–565. https://onlinelibrary.wiley.com/doi/abs/10.1002/mrm.27746.

Öz, G., Alger, J.R., Barker, P.B., et al., 2014. Clinical proton MR spectroscopy in central nervous system disorders. Radiology 270 (3), 658–679. http://pubs.rsna.org/doi/10.1148/radiol.13130531.

Rijpma, A., van der Graaf, M., Meulenbroek, O., Olde Rikkert, M.G.M., Heerschap, A., 2018. Altered brain high-energy phosphate metabolism in mild Alzheimer's disease: a 3-dimensional 31 P MR spectroscopic imaging study. NeuroImage Clin. 18, 254–261. https://linkinghub.elsevier.com/retrieve/pii/S2213158218300317.

Spurny, B., Seiger, R., Moser, P., et al., 2020. Hippocampal GABA levels correlate with retrieval performance in an associative learning paradigm. NeuroImage 204, 116244. https://linkinghub.elsevier.com/retrieve/pii/S1053811919308353.

Stanley, J.A., Raz, N., 2018. Functional magnetic resonance spectroscopy: the "new" MRS for cognitive neuroscience and psychiatry research. Front. Psychiatry, 9. http://journal.frontiersin.org/article/10.3389/fpsyt.2018.00076/full.

Swanberg, K.M., Landheer, K., Pitt, D., Juchem, C., 2019. Quantifying the metabolic signature of multiple sclerosis by in vivo proton magnetic resonance spectroscopy: current challenges and future outlook in the translation from proton signal to diagnostic biomarker. Front. Neurol., 10. https://www.frontiersin.org/article/10.3389/fneur.2019.01173/full.

van Veenendaal, T.M., Backes, W.H., Tse, D.H.Y., et al., 2018. High field imaging of large-scale neurotransmitter networks: proof of concept and initial application to epilepsy. NeuroImage Clin. 19, 47–55. https://linkinghub.elsevier.com/retrieve/pii/S2213158218301128.

Wang, Z.J., Ohliger, M.A., Larson, P.E.Z., et al., 2019. Hyperpolarized 13 C MRI: state of the art and future directions. Radiology 219 (2), 273–284. http://pubs.rsna.org/doi/10.1148/radiol.2019182391.

Wilson, M., Andronesi, O., Barker, P.B., et al., 2019. Methodological consensus on clinical proton MRS of the brain: review and recommendations. Magn. Reson. Med. 82 (2), 527–550. https://onlinelibrary.wiley.com/doi/abs/10.1002/mrm.27742.

CHAPTER

Non-Fourier-based magnetic resonance spectroscopy

34

Peter Adany[a], In-Young Choi[a,b], and Phil Lee[a,c]

[a]*Hoglund Biomedical Imaging Center, University of Kansas Medical Center, Kansas City, KS, United States*
[b]*Department of Neurology, University of Kansas Medical Center, Kansas City, KS, United States*
[c]*Department of Radiology, University of Kansas Medical Center, Kansas City, KS, United States*

34.1 Introduction

Magnetic resonance spectroscopic imaging (MRSI) provides a powerful means to measure and quantify MR-detectable chemicals involved in metabolism and other processes in humans and animals from spatially localized tissue volumes. MRSI has become indispensable in the diagnosis, prognosis, and treatment of diseases, including cancers and metabolic disorders, and studies of exogenous influences on brain metabolic function in health and disease. Intrinsic limitations of MRSI with low spatial resolution have prompted the development of non-Fourier MRSI reconstruction methods beyond standard Fourier reconstruction, which promise improved spatial resolution, SNR, and scan time through the incorporation of *a priori* information. This chapter will summarize the background and state-of-the-art of non-Fourier reconstruction techniques in MRSI.

The concepts of standard MRSI reconstruction include the Fourier transform, Shannon–Nyquist sampling theory, and linear algebra, and background on these topics can be found in a variety of references (De Graaf, 2007; Strang, 2006; Shannon, 1949). MRSI reconstruction is grounded in the mathematical concept of a *transformation*, with input data sampled in an instrument space (e.g., frequency), and output data represented in a physical space (e.g., spatial coordinates). Often, this is expressed using the matrix formalism of linear algebra. For example, the one-dimensional discrete Fourier transform of size N can be expressed as an $N \times N$ matrix, F. The model relationship between spatial data vector p and a k-space data vector s is a matrix multiplication,

$$s = F\,p. \tag{34.1}$$

The matrix inverse, F^{-1}, reconstructs spatial data, $\hat{p}$, from s:

$$\hat{p} = F^{-1}s. \tag{34.2}$$

The columns of F^{-1} are a *basis* for p if they are linearly independent and span the space of p. In the case of the discrete Fourier transform, F is unitary, where its inverse is the complex conjugate transpose, $F^{-1} = F'$. In other cases, the matrix may be $N \times M$, and the matrix pseudoinverse, denoted †, may be used. For example, in spectral localization by imaging (SLIM), the model is expressed in terms of a compartmental geometry matrix as

$$s = G\,c \tag{34.3}$$

and solved as

$$\hat{c} = G^\dagger\,s. \tag{34.4}$$

The coefficients c represent contributions from anatomical shapes. Therefore every SLIM reconstruction has a different $G^\dagger$ and requires the additional knowledge of the underlying anatomical structures, which is obtained from higher resolution MRI in the same scan session. This is an example of a non-Fourier reconstruction, and it minimizes the mean squared error. Finally, general constrained optimization finds some solution $\hat{c}$ that minimizes a more general cost function.

Localization in MRSI refers to the ill-posed problem of reconstructing the arbitrary spatial function from a limited number of k-space observations. Traditionally, the low spatial resolution of MRSI required visual interpretation of voxels, graphically superimposed or compared statistically with high-resolution MRI. This process was formalized and improved upon by SLIM, which incorporates high-resolution anatomical shape information directly into the reconstruction. Localization concepts for MRSI have been reviewed (Lee et al., 2017; Liang et al., 1992), emphasizing the use of *a priori* information to improve resolution and overcome common artifacts caused by B_0 and B_1 inhomogeneities.

The major strength of non-Fourier techniques for MRSI resides in their ability to incorporate *a priori* information to improve spatial resolution or specificity, reduce noise, nuisance signals, and scan time. Examples of non-Fourier techniques include the following: accelerated MRSI using coil sensitivity mapping (e.g., generalized autocalibrating partial parallel acquisition (GRAPPA)); denoising and super-resolution using constrained reconstruction (e.g., total variation denoising); MRSI localization using a *geometry* matrix derived from anatomic compartment shapes (i.e., SLIM); and partially-separable and low-rank representation of signals with spatial and spectral priors (e.g., spatiospectral correlation (SPICE)). Historically, it is worth noting some conceptual advances that aimed to overcome the limitations of the Fourier transform in spectral analysis. These include the short time Fourier transform (Gábor, 1946), linear prediction methods, including the autoregressive model (Akaike, 1969), and multi-resolution analysis using wavelets (Mallat, 1989).

34.2 MRSI reconstruction using Fourier and non-Fourier approaches

34.2.1 Basic concepts of MRSI reconstruction

Classically, MRSI is an extension of single voxel spectroscopy (SVS) in which the FID is fully sampled, and the acquisition is repeated with varying phase encodings applied before each FID. The signal in MRSI, simplified to ignore B_0 and B_1 field inhomogeneities and a scaling factor, can be expressed as

$$s(\boldsymbol{k}, t) = \int_{\text{FOV}} \rho(\boldsymbol{r}, t)\, e^{-j2\pi \boldsymbol{k}\cdot\boldsymbol{r}}\, d\boldsymbol{r}, \tag{34.5}$$

where ρ is the apparent MR spin density, $\boldsymbol{k}$ is the phase encoding vector, t is time, and $\boldsymbol{r}$ is the spatial coordinate vector. Vectors are denoted in bold type throughout. Eq. (34.5) reflects that the linear gradient in MRI is a physical counterpart of harmonic analysis, as devised by Mansfield (Garroway et al.,

34.2 MRSI reconstruction using Fourier and non-Fourier approaches   **539**

1974). Recovery of the spatial function $p(\boldsymbol{r},t)$ from the spatial frequency-time domain signal $s(\boldsymbol{k},t)$ is given by the inverse Fourier transform,

$$p(\boldsymbol{r},t) = \iiint_{-\infty}^{\infty} s(\boldsymbol{k},t)e^{j2\pi kx}\,d\boldsymbol{k}. \tag{34.6}$$

In general, Eq. (34.6) requires $s(\boldsymbol{k},t)$ to be known for all $\boldsymbol{k} \in \mathbb{R}^3$. However, when $p(\boldsymbol{r},t)$ is non-zero only over a finite interval (e.g. finite object size), $p(\boldsymbol{r},t)$ can be represented unambiguously by discrete samples. The k-space step size is related to the field of view as $\Delta k_x = 1/\text{FOV}_x$.

Though it is necessary to acquire an infinite number of discrete k-space samples to recover $p(\boldsymbol{r},t)$ perfectly, in practice k-space samples are significantly undersampled or truncated due to experimental constraints, e.g., scan time and SNR. The results of truncated k-space are reduced spatial resolution and ringing artifacts, which often degrade MRSI data quality via nuisance signal artifacts of residual water and lipid signals originating from the scalp in proton MRSI. The basic problems and capabilities of Fourier and non-Fourier reconstructions are illustrated below.

Fig. 34.1 shows the MRSI processing results of a simplified simulated object, where the image is the first time point of a two-dimensional plane within the MRSI slab, with a uniform phase over the image. A "brain" structure-of-interest is made by the parallelogram shape with signal amplitude set as one ($1\times$). A second structure, consisting of a thin curved section, represents a nuisance scalp lipid source, with a $12\times$ signal amplitude. For the following examples, MRSI has k-space dimensions of 50×128 with phase encoding in the horizontal direction only (1D MRSI) to illustrate the effect of truncation of k-space.

When the k-space is adequately sampled, the discrete Fourier transform (DFT) provides a straightforward and artifact-free reconstruction with correct values of signal intensity in each compartment (Fig. 34.1A, right).

However, when only a limited k-space is sampled as in typical MRSI acquisitions, the reconstructed image exhibits the well-known ringing artifact, due to the large oscillating point spread function (PSF) sidelobes (Fig. 34.1B). The width of the central lobe of the PSF indicates the resolution of the system, defined as the minimum separation distance by which two point-objects can be individually identified. The ringing effect can be understood through the convolution property of the Fourier transform, i.e., multiplication in the spatial frequency domain is equivalent to convolution in the spatial domain. In the truncated discrete case, the PSF is

$$h(x) = \Delta k \sum_{n=-\frac{N}{2}}^{\frac{N}{2}-1} e^{j2\pi n \Delta kx} = \Delta k \frac{\sin(\pi \Delta kx N)}{\sin(\pi \Delta kx)} e^{-j\pi \Delta kx}. \tag{34.7}$$

The limiting case of this function is a sinc function as Δk approaches 0. The reconstruction obtained by extending the dimensions beyond the acquired k-space is known as *zero padding* of k-space, and the result is an interpolated higher resolution image with the ringing convolution profile of Eq. (34.7). To reduce the magnitude of rining sidelobes, a typical approach is *apodizing* the k-space, e.g., with a Hamming filter (Fig. 34.1C). Apodization is simply the multiplication of k-space with a lowpass filter. Although apodization is effective at reducing the ringing artifact, it broadens the width of the PSF, reducing the effective resolution.

Alternatively, the missing k-space could be filled back in, aided by additional information about the underlying structure of the data. The Papoulis-Gerchberg (PG) algorithm is a rather successful iterative

540 Chapter 34 Non-Fourier-based magnetic resonance spectroscopy

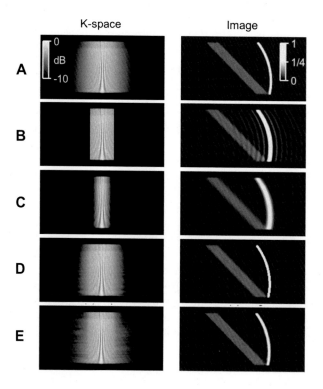

FIGURE 34.1

Example Fourier and non-Fourier reconstructions, with the object k-space (left) and image (right). Simulation used 256×128 image and 50×128 MRSI k-space dimensions with one-dimensional phase encoding in the horizontal axis. The original (true) data are shown in the top row. The left column displays k-space data (logarithmic scale). The right column shows the spatial reconstruction (linear grayscale with clipping). The reconstructions shown are (A–E): full k-space (true), zero padded, zero padded with Hamming filter, finite-support extrapolation of k-space using Papoulis-Gerchberg (PG) algorithm, and autoregressive model k-space extrapolation. The PG algorithm extrapolated only the thin structure (scalp lipid), as in a typical application in MRSI to selectively remove scalp lipid signals.

k-space extrapolation method that has been widely used in MRSI of the brain to remove interfering lipid signals originating from the scalp (Papoulis, 1975). PG algorithm utilizes spatial boundary information obtained from high-resolution MRI. The boundary of the lipid source can be obtained with good accuracy from MRI obtained in the same scan session as the MRSI data. Using a mask of the lipid region as a spatial constraint, the PG algorithm could effectively remove the ringing artifact from the high-intensity compartment (Fig. 34.1D). Note that the PG algorithm was used to extend the k-space data only from the nuisance signal source, e.g., the scalp, though it does not significantly modify signals coming from other sources.

Linear prediction, such as the autoregressive and moving average (ARMA) models, offers another class of extrapolation method; however, they have been infrequently used in MRSI due to their sensitivity to the noise and variability of k-space data. The autoregressive (AR) model is a simple one, which

34.2 MRSI reconstruction using Fourier and non-Fourier approaches **541**

can be fitted to the central k-space data to predict outer k-space based on the assumption of the continuation of the k-space patterns. Determining the optimal order for an AR model is difficult, especially for heterogeneous input data (e.g., MRSI data). In the simulation example (Fig. 34.1), no choice of AR order worked perfectly; an AR model order of 5, i.e., AR(5), worked best. Since the AR model primarily captured the periodic components, apodization was required to model the decaying components of the k-space profile. AR modeling poses difficulty in determining the model order, but when successful it was able to extrapolate the k-space with surprising quality (Fig. 34.1E).

34.2.2 Reconstruction of MRSI using SLIM and SLOOP

Spectral localization by imaging (SLIM) (Hu et al., 1988) is a reconstruction technique for MRSI that outputs the spectra of distinct anatomic structures rather than imaging voxels. Major structures, e.g., white matter (WM) and gray matter (GM) in the brain, can be delineated from high-resolution MRI. These become *compartments* in SLIM, often with further division of larger shapes, such as global GM and WM into smaller shapes. For SLIM, a compartment is presumed to be a spatially homogeneous signal source. Solving the linear system (as in Eq. (34.4)) obtains the contributions of the individual structures that best explain the data in the least squared sense. The output of a SLIM reconstruction is a set of M compartment spectra, rather than voxels (requiring a sufficient number of k-space acquisitions, $N \geq M$). A SLIM reconstructed image can be composed by scaling the binary compartment maps by their respective SLIM coefficients and summing. SLIM has favorable convergence properties: in the limit of large N, SLIM recovers the compartmental average value, even in the presence of inhomogeneities (Hu and Wu, 1993).

SLIM reconstruction can be characterized by evaluating the spatial response function (SRF). Similar to the concept of the pointspread function, the SRF describes the characteristic response of a compartment at all spatial points, defined as (von Kienlin and Mejia, 1991)

$$\text{SRF}_m\,(\boldsymbol{r}) = \sum_{n=0}^{N-1} g_{mn} e^{-j2\pi \boldsymbol{k}\cdot\boldsymbol{r}}, \tag{34.8}$$

where g_{mn} are elements of the pseudoinverse matrix $G^{\dagger}$. The average of SRF_m over compartment m is equal to 1 in any non-pathological case. The average of SRF_m outside compartment m provides a measure of the degree of immunity to signal leakage from other areas. Signal leakage in SLIM occurs due to compartmental signal inhomogeneities and can be assessed as the spatial average of SRF.

In Fig. 34.2, SLIM reconstruction is shown with identical k-space data and spatial encoding setup as the previous examples. Phase encoding is one dimensional in the horizontal direction. The SLIM reconstruction is highly oversampled in this case, and the spectral response functions (SRFs) indicate robust localization, with strong rejection (low amplitudes) in opposite compartments and dense phase variations that provide needed cancellations of signals.

When the MRSI acquisition is reduced to a more stringent 8×8 phase encoding size (Fig. 34.3A), extreme loss of details is seen in the MRSI Fourier reconstruction (shown with 256×128 points using zero padding). A zoomed-in view of the k-space shows the drastically reduced coverage. The SLIM reconstruction with this scheme is still exact; however, the SRF has broader sidelobes than the previous larger k-space example, which suggests greater susceptibility to signal leakage from other compartments.

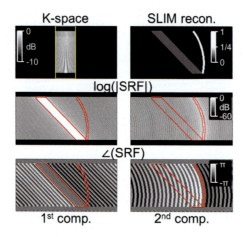

FIGURE 34.2

SLIM reconstruction using the same setup as Fig. 34.1. The input k-space data are bounded within a vertical outline, as shown (top, left). The SLIM reconstructed image is made by scaling the input compartment images by the SLIM coefficients (top, right). Spatial response functions (SRFs) are shown separately for each compartment with magnitude and phase images. Solid outlines indicate the input compartments over the SRF images. At large MRSI dimensions, the SLIM matrix is highly overdetermined. The SRF shows strong spatial dropoff and dense phase variations in the opposite compartments, indicating robust localization performance.

SLIM allows flexibility in the choice of k-space encodings compared with Fourier reconstruction. An extension of SLIM, called spectral localization with optimal pointspread function (SLOOP) (von Kienlin and Mejia, 1991), uses optimization of the k-space sampling pattern to improve SNR and/or localization accuracy in a given scan duration. SLOOP may use the same number of phase encoding steps with a different k-space sampling pattern that has been tailored to better match the expected k-space energy, e.g., within a 16×16 window (Fig. 34.3B). The SRF of SLOOP exhibits some random and coherent patterns, but it retains similar spatial profiles as the basic SLIM scheme. The improvement of SLOOP is measured in terms of the SRF value within opposite compartments. In this example, SLOOP reduced the potential cross-contamination from the lipid compartment into the brain compartment by 33%. SLOOP has been mainly used in *in vivo* ^{31}P MRSI studies (von Kienlin et al., 2001).

34.2.3 GSLIM solution for inhomogeneous compartments

As the previous examples illustrated, SLIM reconstruction is highly advantageous in terms of achievable SNR and anatomical specificity with few k-space encodings. However, SLIM uses some assumptions that limit its applicability. Firstly, SLIM assumes spatial homogeneity of the compartments. Structures such as the GM and WM tissues are not globally homogeneous. Inhomogeneity leads to compartmental signal leakage, unless it can be removed by preprocessing, or properly accounted for in the signal model.

Generalized series spectral localization by imaging (GSLIM) aims to discover signal variations within compartments using the SLIM framework (Liang and Lauterbur, 1991). In GSLIM, the ordinary

34.2 MRSI reconstruction using Fourier and non-Fourier approaches

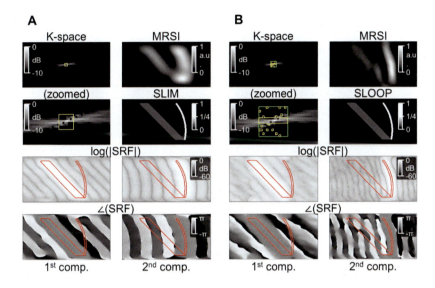

FIGURE 34.3

SLIM reconstruction with 8×8 k-space, reconstructed at image dimensions of 256×128. The traditional Fourier reconstruction is shown (top row). The SLIM reconstruction is shown in (A). The k-space view has been zoomed in to show the reduced coverage (N=64 k-space points). SLIM using optimized and sparsely sampled k-space with the SLOOP approach is shown in (B). The k-space sampling pattern was broadened to a 16×16 region with the same number of k-space points as (A). Solid outlines indicate the input compartments over the SRF images. The SRFs exhibit greater sidelobe amplitudes and broader phase cancellation patterns than the previous example. In comparison with SLIM, the SLOOP SRFs exhibit better response using the same number of k-space points, with excellent magnitude dropoff outside compartments, and dense phase cancellation in the opposite compartments.

SLIM system is evaluated first. Then, residual spatial variation is recovered as the convolution of an arbitrary function and the SLIM k-space. This holds the compartment shapes as fixed inputs and recovers spatial variation as an additional multiplicative factor.

Different brain compartment inhomogeneities were simulated as shown in Fig. 34.4 (TRUE: right column). The SLIM reconstruction from these data reflected the averaging capability of SLIM (left column). The GSLIM reconstruction was able to accurately capture both the compartmental average and the residual inhomogeneity, as shown (middle column). The strength of GSLIM is adding to SLIM the ability to recover the hidden compartmental signal variations and to reduce inter-compartmental signal leakage caused by compartmental inhomogeneities to the extent that Fourier reconstruction permits. One weakness of GSLIM is its inability to incorporate measured maps of extrinsic signal inhomogeneities, especially B_0 and B_1 inhomogeneities, which significantly affect the model (G).

In MRSI, B_0 and B_1 inhomogeneities greatly impact reconstruction quality and quantitative accuracy. A non-uniform B_1 adds spatial modulation as do intrinsic tissue heterogeneities, but unlike intrinsic tissue variations, the B_1 field can be measured to good accuracy using quick imaging scans. Similarly, non-uniform B_0 results in problematic line broadening and compartmental leakage, especially with larger compartments. Uneven B_0 causes modulations and dispersal of the k-space over the

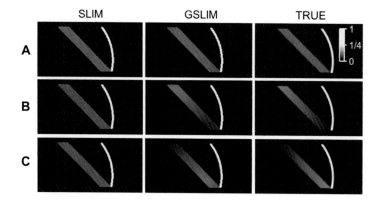

FIGURE 34.4

Comparison of SLIM and GSLIM with reconstructions in presence of compartmental inhomogeneity. Reconstructions used 16×16 input k-space (N=256). Input images were generated without (A) and with linear signal intensity variations (B, C). GSLIM effectively recovered the inhomogeneities, whereas SLIM yielded only the compartmental averages (B, C). These show how GSLIM could be used to explore intrinsic heterogeneity of defined tissue structures in SLIM-type reconstructions.

time course of the FID. Therefore a major goal in MRSI reconstruction has been to incorporate and properly compensate for B₀ and B₁ field inhomogeneities during MRSI reconstruction. Several modifications of SLIM have been proposed, which incorporate corrections for B₀ and/or B₁ inhomogeneities, including BSLIM (Khalidov et al., 2007), *star*SLIM (Passeri et al., 2014), NL-CSI (Bashir and Yablonskiy, 2006), BASE-SLIM (Adany et al., 2016), SLAM (Zhang et al., 2013), and SPLASH (An and Shen, 2015). Effectively, each of these non-Fourier reconstructions improves the basis through some use of prior information. Alternatively, preprocessing may be required to correct for B₁ and B₀ using other techniques. These corrections are less straightforward in the low-resolution regime of MRSI, e.g., see SPICE (Peng et al., 2010), SPREAD (Dong and Peterson, 2009), and "overdiscrete" sensitivity encoding (SENSE) reconstruction (Kirchner et al., 2016).

34.2.4 BASE-SLIM for B₀ and B₁ corrections

An imperfect B₀ and receive coil sensitivity (B₁) introduces spatial and spatio-temporal modulations, which are difficult to correct, especially at the lower resolutions of MRSI. In SLIM, these effects violate assumptions and lead to compartmental leakage. Uneven B₀ also leads to spectral line broadening. The B₀-adjusted sensitivity encoded SLIM (BASE-SLIM) technique considers B₀ and B₁ inhomogeneities as additions in the signal model of SLIM. BASE-SLIM defines the geometry matrix elements as

$$h_{n_c,m}(t) = \sum_r B_{1(c)}(r) \, p_m(r,t) \, e^{-j2\pi k_{n_c} \cdot r + j\gamma \Delta B_0(r) t}, \tag{34.9}$$

where $h_{n_c,m}$ are the entries of the $N \times M$ BASE-SLIM geometry matrix; $N = N_p N_c$, where N_p is the number of phase encodings and N_c the number of receiver coils, $B_{1(c)}(r)$ is the spatial receiver coil sensitivity profile, γ is the proton gyromagnetic ratio, and $\Delta B_0(r)$ is the spatial B₀ frequency deviation.

34.2 MRSI reconstruction using Fourier and non-Fourier approaches

The BASE-SLIM geometry matrix is evaluated over the time course of the FID. Therefore, the spatial response function changes over time, reflecting the influence of measured B_0 and B_1 perturbations in the reconstruction. The SRF of a BASE-SLIM reconstruction is shown in Fig. 34.5 at several timepoints.

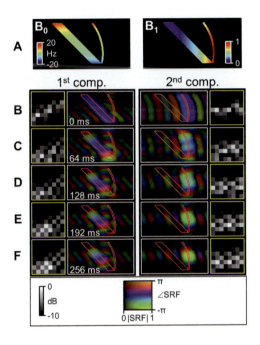

FIGURE 34.5

BASE-SLIM-simulated spatial response functions (SRF) showing the inclusion of B_0 and B_1 field maps as prior information in the MRSI reconstruction. The B_0 field inhomogeneity leads to a time-dependent SRF, shown at different timepoints of the free induction decay (from 0 to 256 ms, B–F) for the 1st and 2nd compartments. In the pseudo-colored SRF, phase is indicated by the color (hue), and magnitude is indicated by intensity (value). The B_1 heterogeneity results in amplitude variations of the SRF. The B_0 and B_1 field maps are shown in (A), bounded by the input compartments. The k-space of each SRF is shown next to its spatial view. Red outlines show the input compartments overlaid with the SRFs.

Fig. 34.6 demonstrates the efficacy of the BASE-SLIM technique using simulations and *in vivo* data (Adany et al., 2016). In simulated data in Fig. 34.6A, simple input spectra were assigned at 2.01 ppm and 1.3 ppm as the mock signals of N-Acetylaspartate (brain) and scalp lipid, respectively. The B_0 and B_1 field maps were simulated, as shown in Fig. 34.5. In the presence of B_0 and B_1 inhomogeneities, ordinary SLIM reconstruction, as well as BASE-SLIM with only partial corrections for B_0 and B_1, resulted in inaccurate signal amplitudes and compartmental leakage (Fig. 34.6A, bottom three). When both B_0 and B_1 were corrected, the reconstruction was effectively exact (Fig. 34.6A, top). BASE-SLIM could successfully reconstruct spectra from GM and WM with good spectral quality and characteristic spectral patterns of GM and WM after incorporating B_0 and B_1 information (Fig. 34.6B).

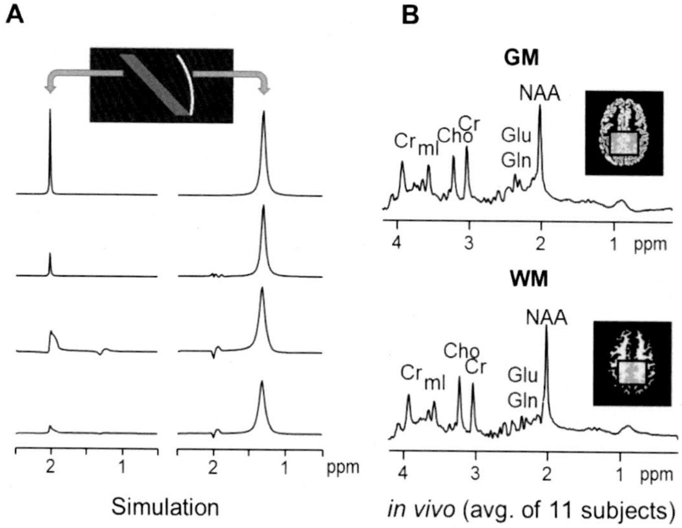

546 Chapter 34 Non-Fourier-based magnetic resonance spectroscopy

FIGURE 34.6

BASE-SLIM reconstruction. Simulated data (A) and averaged spectra from 11 subjects (B). Simulated input signals were generated based on compartments and simulated B_0 and B_1 maps (Fig. 34.5). The first compartment was assigned a singlet at 2.01 ppm (representing N-Acetylaspartate) with a T_2 value of 280 ms. The second compartment was assigned a singlet at 1.3 ppm (representing a lipid) and T_2 of 38 ms. The inputs were scaled to have equal peak spectral amplitudes. BASE-SLIM reconstructions were carried out with all combinations of B_0 and B_1 correction (four spectra pairs). Results are shown with un-corrected (SLIM) results (A, bottom), B_1 correction only (A, second row from bottom), B_0 correction only (A, third row from bottom), and B_0 and B_1 corrected (BASE-SLIM) spectra (A, top). On the right, example group-averaged BASE-SLIM reconstructed *in vivo* GM and WM spectra of 11 subjects, which were acquired using a semi-LASER sequence with TE/TR = 35/1600 ms, FOV = 20×20 cm^2, matrix = 16×16, slice thickness = 2 cm.

34.2.5 Constrained and parameterized reconstruction concepts

In SLIM, the compartments are considered fixed prior information, and the problem can be stated as

$$\operatorname*{argmin}_{c} \|Gc - s\|^2. \tag{34.10}$$

Alternatively, the problem can be stated from the perspective of subsampled data consistency (Manjón et al., 2010). In this view, there is a *high-resolution* MRSI, x, that is consistent with acquired *low resolution* MRSI, s (where their k-spaces intersect) and additional constraints from high-resolution MRI. Then, the problem may take a form such as (Jain et al., 2017)

$$\operatorname*{argmin}_{x} \|H(x) - s\|^2 + \lambda R(x), \tag{34.11}$$

where H implements the k-space sampling and transformation of image data x, and $R(x)$ is a regularization term balanced against the least squares term by the regularization parameter λ. The constraint

34.2 MRSI reconstruction using Fourier and non-Fourier approaches   **547**

$R(x)$ measures agreement between some features of x and some prior rule or information derived from other data (MRI). This approach is featured in recent works, such as patch-based super-resolution of MRSI in multiple sclerosis (Hangel et al., 2019) and others.

34.2.6 Spatiospectral correlation (SPICE)

Another novel approach to high-resolution non-Fourier MRSI reconstruction is the method of spectroscopic imaging by exploiting spatiospectral correlation (SPICE). SPICE utilizes concepts of a *union of subspaces* and *partially separable functions*. A multivariate function, $g(x,t)$, is separable if it can be expressed as $g(x,t) = u(x)v(t)$, and it is considered partially separable if the following holds (Haldar and Liang, 2007):

$$g(x,t) = \sum_{\ell=1}^{L} u_\ell(x) v_\ell(t),$$
(34.12)

where L is the separability order. For example, a two-dimensional Gaussian function is separable, i.e., $e^{-(x^2+y^2)} = e^{-x^2} e^{-y^2}$, whereas a super-Gaussian, such as $e^{-(x^2+y^2)^2} = e^{-x^4} e^{-2x^2 y^2} e^{-y^4}$, is not.

It is worth noting that the singular value decomposition (SVD) finds the partially separable representation of a matrix, of the order of the matrix rank. An interesting example of this is when the matrix simply contains an image $I(x, y)$, letting x, y be the columns and rows, respectively. The SVD yields the u_ℓ and v_ℓ of Eq. (34.12) as the left- and right-singular vectors. These vectors can be multiplied and scaled by their singular values, and then summed to reconstruct the image. In SPICE, separability is applied to the spatial and temporal variables, presumed separable to a small order (i.e., $L \sim 5$) (Haldar and Liang, 2007). Additionally, SPICE uses the concept of a union of subspaces that composes the signals of water (w), lipid (l), and metabolites (m) as follows:

$$p(x,t) = \sum_{w=1}^{L_w} p_w(x,t) + \sum_{l=1}^{L_l} p_l(x,t) + \sum_{m=1}^{L_m} p_m(x,t).$$
(34.13)

With this model and sufficient measurement of the separable basis, the metabolite spectral coefficients can be recovered using an optimization algorithm. Applications of SPICE have taken advantage of hybrid sampling approaches and incorporation of spectral prior information to achieve fast high-resolution MRSI (Lam et al., 2016).

Most recently, deep learning was incorporated as a learned basis (Lam et al., 2020). Recent advances in machine learning promise new and undiscovered possibilities for MRSI, including improved reconstruction and easier and faster interpretation of spectra and diagnosis using established convolutional neural networks (CNN) and other emerging techniques that tackle non-image data. As these concepts mature, the well-developed concepts of non-Fourier localization may strengthen and yield exciting new capabilities in MRSI.

548 Chapter 34 Non-Fourier-based magnetic resonance spectroscopy

34.3 Conclusions

Non-Fourier reconstruction of MRSI offers solutions to overcome major limitations of traditional Fourier reconstruction in MRSI, such as its low spatial resolution and detection sensitivity, by incorporating valuable prior information into the reconstruction. The advantages of non-Fourier reconstruction are increased SNR, reduced scan time, and improved spatial specificity and quantification accuracy. An important aspect to consider for robust non-Fourier reconstruction of MRSI is fidelity of prior information, including spatial alignment between MRSI and high-resolution MRI, and accuracies of B_0 and B_1 maps. Non-Fourier-based MRSI techniques are still an emerging area of research and further work is needed to realize their full potential, e.g., by developing optimized algorithms to balance the spectral information content vs spatial resolution/specificity.

References

Adany, P., Choi, I.-Y., Lee, P., 2016. B0-adjusted and sensitivity-encoded spectral localization by imaging (BASE-SLIM) in the human brain in vivo. NeuroImage 134, 355–364.

Akaike, H., 1969. Fitting autoregressive models for prediction. Annals of the Institute of Statistical Mathematics 21, 243–247.

An, L., Shen, J., 2015. Image-guided spatial localization of heterogeneous compartments for magnetic resonance. Medical Physics 42, 5278–5286.

Bashir, A., Yablonskiy, D.A., 2006. Natural linewidth chemical shift imaging (NL-CSI). Magnetic Resonance in Medicine 56, 7–18.

De Graaf, R.A., 2007. In: In Vivo NMR Spectroscopy: Principles and Techniques. John Wiley & Sons, Chichester, West Sussex, England; Hoboken, NJ.

Dong, Z., Peterson, B.S., 2009. Spectral resolution amelioration by deconvolution (SPREAD) in MR spectroscopic imaging. Journal of Magnetic Resonance Imaging 29, 1395–1405.

Gábor, D., 1946. Theory of communication. Journal of the Institution of Electrical Engineers 93, 429–457.

Garroway, A.N., Grannell, P.K., Mansfield, P., 1974. Image-formation in NMR by a selective irradiative process. Journal of Physics C: Solid State Physics 7, L457–L462.

Haldar, J.P., Liang, Z.P., 2007. Spatiotemporal imaging with partially separable functions. In: 4th IEEE International Symposium on Biomedical Imaging: from Nano to Macro, 2007. 12–15 April 2007, pp. 988–991. ISBI 2007.

Hangel, G., Jain, S., Springer, E., Heckova, E., Strasser, B., Povazan, M., Gruber, S., Widhalm, G., Kiesel, B., Furtner, J., Preusser, M., Roetzer, T., Trattnig, S., Sima, D.M., Smeets, D., Bogner, W., 2019. High-resolution metabolic mapping of gliomas via patch-based super-resolution magnetic resonance spectroscopic imaging at 7T. NeuroImage 191, 587–595.

Hu, X., Levin, D.N., Lauterbur, P.C., Spraggins, T., 1988. SLIM: spectral localization by imaging. Magnetic Resonance in Medicine 8, 314–322.

Hu, X., Wu, Z., 1993. SLIM revisited. IEEE Transactions on Medical Imaging 12, 583–587.

Jain, S., Sima, D.M., Sanaei Nezhad, F., Hangel, G., Bogner, W., Williams, S., Van Huffel, S., Maes, F., Smeets, D., 2017. Patch-based super-resolution of MR spectroscopic images: application to multiple sclerosis. Frontiers in Neuroscience 11, 13.

Khalidov, I., Van De Ville, D., Jacob, M., Lazeyras, F., Unser, M., 2007. BSLIM: spectral localization by imaging with explicit B0 field inhomogeneity compensation. IEEE Transactions on Medical Imaging 26, 990–1000.

Kirchner, T., Fillmer, A., Henning, A., 2016. Mechanisms of SNR and line shape improvement by B0 correction in overdiscrete MRSI reconstruction. Magnetic Resonance in Medicine.

Lam, F., Li, Y.D., Guo, R., Clifford, B., Liang, Z.P., 2020. Ultrafast magnetic resonance spectroscopic imaging using SPICE with learned subspaces. Magnetic Resonance in Medicine 83, 377–390.

Lam, F., Ma, C., Clifford, B., Johnson, C.L., Liang, Z.P., 2016. High-resolution (1) H-MRSI of the brain using SPICE: data acquisition and image reconstruction. Magnetic Resonance in Medicine 76, 1059–1070.

Lee, P., Adany, P., Choi, I.Y., 2017. Imaging based magnetic resonance spectroscopy (MRS) localization for quantitative neurochemical analysis and cerebral metabolism studies. Analytical Biochemistry 529, 40–47.

Liang, Z.P., Boda, F.E., Constable, R.T., Haacke, E.M., Lauterbur, P.C., Smith, M.R., 1992. Constrained reconstruction methods in MR imaging. Reviews of Magnetic Resonance in Medicine 4, 67–185.

Liang, Z.P., Lauterbur, P.C., 1991. A generalized series approach to MR spectroscopic imaging. IEEE Transactions on Medical Imaging 10, 132–137.

Mallat, S., 1989. A theory for multiresolution signal decomposition: the wavelet representation. IEEE Transactions on Pattern Analysis and Machine Intelligence II, 674–693.

Manjón, J.V., Coupé, P., Buades, A., Collins, D.L., Robles, M., 2010. MRI superresolution using self-similarity and image priors. International Journal of Biomedical Imaging 2010, 425891.

Papoulis, A., 1975. New algorithm in spectral analysis and band-limited extrapolation. IEEE Transactions on Circuits and Systems 22, 735–742.

Passeri, A., Mauca, S., Bene, V.D., 2014. Radiofrequency field inhomogeneity compensation in high spatial resolution magnetic resonance spectroscopic imaging. Physics in Medicine and Biology 59, 2913–2934.

Peng, X., Nguyen, H., Haldar, J., Hernando, D., Wang, X.P., Liang, Z.P., 2010. Correction of field inhomogeneity effects on limited k-space MRSI data using anatomical constraints. Annual International Conference of the IEEE Engineering in Medicine and Biology Society 2010, 883–886.

Shannon, C.E., 1949. Communication in the presence of noise. Proceedings of the Institute of Radio Engineers 37, 10–21.

Strang, G., 2006. Linear Algebra and Its Applications. Thomson, Brooks/Cole, Belmont, CA.

von Kienlin, M., Beer, M., Greiser, A., Hahn, D., Harre, K., Kostler, H., Landschutz, W., Pabst, T., Sandstede, J., Neubauer, S., 2001. Advances in human cardiac P-31-MR spectroscopy: SLOOP and clinical applications. Journal of Magnetic Resonance Imaging 13, 521–527.

von Kienlin, M., Mejia, R., 1991. Spectral localization with optimal pointspread function. Journal of Magnetic Resonance 94, 268–287.

Zhang, Y., Gabr, R.E., Zhou, J., Weiss, R.G., Bottomley, P.A., 2013. Highly-accelerated quantitative 2D and 3D localized spectroscopy with linear algebraic modeling (SLAM) and sensitivity encoding. Journal of Magnetic Resonance 237, 125–138.

PART 12

Ultra-high field neuro MR techniques

CHAPTER

Benefits, challenges, and applications of ultra-high field magnetic resonance

35

Karin Markenroth Bloch[a] and Benedikt A. Poser[b]
[a]Lund University, Lund, Sweden
[b]Maastricht University, Maastricht, The Netherlands

35.1 Introduction

The technical development that has characterized the field of MR since the early 1980s continues at breathtaking speed. For many years, one primary focus was to increase the main magnet field strength (B_0), to address the limited sensitivity which is a general drawback of MR. At the time of writing, over 40,000 MRI machines are installed worldwide. The vast majority have field strengths of 1.5T or 3T, but it was always recognized that higher B_0 would bring advantages to both SNR and image contrast, improving differentiation of tissue types. Clinical whole-body 4T magnets were introduced in the late 1990s, but did not make it into widespread use as the gain was quite incremental relative to the required engineering effort. The main early driver for development of higher field strength systems came with the discovery of the blood oxygenation level-dependent (BOLD) effect that allows for non-invasive measurement of brain activation, as the BOLD sensitivity and specificity increase more than linearly with field strength. In the 1990s, the first 7T (300 MHz) whole-body magnets were installed in institutions with a primary interest in neurosciences and the study of brain function. Early investigations into clinical use took advantage of the markedly increased T_2^* contrast at ultra-high field (UHF) to depict iron-rich deep brain structures at unprecedented resolutions. The number of human 7T MRI scanners has rapidly increased to a total of about 90 systems at the time of writing. The availability of the first FDA approved commercial system in 2018, and a second vendor's in 2020, has further accelerated this trend, so that 7T systems are now increasingly found in hospitals and institutions without a main focus on MR methods development.

The exploration of even higher magnetic fields continues, with a few whole-body 9.4T and one 10.5T systems now in use, two 11.7T magnets being commissioned, and efforts ongoing to build 14T human MRI scanners. While the by-far dominant use of UHF is in neuro and musculoskeletal applications, much current research focuses on applications in the torso, including cardiac, kidney, and prostate imaging. However, the technical challenges that need to be overcome for body imaging are much greater than encountered in the head.

This chapter aims to give an overview of UHF MR in a neuroimaging context by first providing an overview of the basic physical motivations for going to higher fields. It will then describe the challenges and limitations of working at higher field strengths, and outline some of the currently available

554   **Chapter 35** UHF benefits, challenges & applications

solutions. This chapter also provides a discussion of the potentials of UHF by highlighting some of the neuro applications that benefit from UHF. For a complete review of UHF MR, the reader is referred to (Ladd et al., 2018).

35.2 Advantages and opportunities at ultra-high field

The efforts to develop technology and applications for ultra-high field MR scanners are motivated by the substantial gains brought by the higher field strength. This section describes the main advantages, which are also summarized in Table 35.1.

Table 35.1 Overview of the main consequences, and their respective advantages and disadvantages when increasing the magnetic field strength.

	Change with B_0	Advantages	Disadvantages
SNR	↑	Increased sensitivity	
Chemical shift	↑	Increased spectral resolution (MRS, CEST, fat suppression)	Larger RF pulse bandwidths required
T_1	↑	Background suppression, label persistence (MRA, ASL)	Long TR and TI required
T_2	↘	T_2w BOLD	Short TE needed (diffusion), broader linewidths (MRS)
T_2^*	↓	T_2^*w BOLD fMRI, phase imaging, QSM	B_0 inhomogeneities, geometrical distortions
Susceptibility effects	↑		
B_1 effects	↑	Parallel transmission, parallel reception	Increased SAR and B_1 inhomogeneities
Physiology effects	↑		Increased nausea, dizziness and other effects

35.2.1 Signal-to-noise ratio (SNR)

The most well-known advantage of UHF is the increased SNR, and this has been the major argument to justify the expense and research effort into MR at stronger fields; despite considerable technical advances in hardware, sequences, and reconstruction algorithms over the years, the low sensitivity of MR remains a significant limitation.

It is commonly stated that the MR signal-to-noise ratio (SNR) increases about linearly with B_0, since the equilibrium polarization scales linearly with the polarizing magnetic field. This is confirmed experimentally at lower fields, where it generally holds true that the noise is dominated by the sample for all *in vivo* applications. At higher fields, with hence higher Larmor frequencies, this approximation no longer holds, and the variation of SNR with field strength has a complex dependence on object size, object shape, and object composition. Going beyond 3T, this leads to an overall greater-than-linear SNR

35.2 Advantages and opportunities at ultra-high field

benefit with increasing B_0. In one study comparing SNR in the brain at 3T, 7T, and 9.4T, it was found that SNR goes up with B_0 to the power of 1.65 (Pohmann et al., 2016). For the case of going from 3T to 7T, this corresponds to an SNR increase by a factor of 4.0, instead of just 2.3, which would be the case for a linear increase.

Another very useful property is the increased performance of parallel imaging at UHF, owing to reduced noise penalties in accelerated/undersampled acquisitions incurred by the coil array's geometry factor (Wiesinger et al., 2004). Since, effectively, all proton MRI applications at UHF target higher spatial resolutions and rely on parallel imaging to stay within reasonable acquisition times, this is a fortunate property. The most commonly used commercial head receive coil currently at 7T has 32 channels, but promising results have been shown with custom-built coil arrays of 64 channels and higher.

Any MR application will benefit from higher SNR. An obvious choice is to trade the gain for a higher spatial resolution in structural and functional acquisitions than is attainable at lower fields. Alternatively, the increase in SNR can be spent on more highly undersampled scans, which enable shorter acquisition time or better temporal resolution of dynamic processes, such as fMRI or perfusion measurements. Shorter acquisitions are less prone to motion corruption as the time the subject has to lie still is shortened. These considerations become increasingly relevant as UHF moves towards clinical applications.

There are also applications that *in vivo* become feasible only at UHF, as they are too SNR-starved at lower fields and would therefore be impracticable due to the need for long averaging. Examples include the imaging of nuclei other than water protons (such as ^{23}Na, ^{13}C, ^{31}P, ^{39}K) (Niesporek et al., 2019), certain spectroscopic imaging applications (Henning, 2018), or techniques based on chemical exchange saturation transfer (CEST) (van Zijl and Yadav, 2011; van Zijl et al., 2018).

35.2.2 Spectral resolution

With increasing Larmor frequency, the spectral separation of the resonances in the frequency spectrum also increases. This leads to an improved ability to quantify metabolites reliably via peaks that would be indistinguishable due to overlap at lower fields, or that would require spectral editing to tease them apart.

35.2.2.1 MR spectroscopy and spectroscopic imaging

Adding to the increased SNR, the higher spectral resolution makes MR spectroscopy (MRS) and spectroscopic imaging (MRSI) of water and other nuclei some of the largest beneficiaries of stronger fields. Examples of the results that can be obtained at 7T and 9.4T are given in Fig. 35.1. The immediate advantage of increased SNR is a greater freedom in trading between measurement time and spatial resolution. Higher spatial resolution might be desired by a particular application for better metabolite localization, but the use of smaller voxels is in itself an important aspect in managing intra-voxel field inhomogeneities and reducing lipid contamination. Careful B_0 shimming to minimize field inhomogeneity in the region of interest is thus also crucial to retain the advantages of UHF (Juchem et al., 2020). B_0 inhomogeneity and shimming techniques will be discussed later in this chapter.

The key benefit of the increased spectral separation at UHF is more accurate metabolite quantification (Henning, 2018). For proton MRS, for example, there is better separation of the important metabolites glutamate vs glutamine, myo-inositol vs glycine, and N-acetylaspartate vs N-acetylaspartylglutamate. However, even at 7T other metabolites, including the major inhibitory neuro-transmitter γ-aminobutyric acid (GABA), rely on spectral editing or model fitting methods to overcome the spectral overlap of resonances with more abundant metabolites. Direct quantification of GABA and other low-concentration metabolites becomes possible at 9.4T, provided that a good B_0 shim can be achieved. The faster T_2 and T_2^* relaxation at UHF poses a challenge for MRSI, in that it requires an acquisition readout with short TE. To address this, even direct (non-echo) sampling of the FID has become more common at UHF (see Chapters 32 and 33).

35.2.2.2 Chemical exchange saturation transfer (CEST)

The additional spectral separation at UHF also benefits CEST (van Zijl and Yadav, 2011), a rapidly developing technique for oncological diagnostics, tumor staging, and post-operative follow-up (see Chapter 25). CEST enables the detection of signals from low-concentration macromolecules, such as proteins and peptides, whose protons resonate at a frequency that is somewhat offset from the free water protons. Signals from these protons can be measured indirectly by observing their saturated proton magnetization being transferred into the free water pool. In a CEST sequence, high-energy saturation is applied at the offset frequency of interest, followed by, for instance, a fast turbo-flash or echo-planar image readout. In addition to the higher SNR, the advantage of UHF results in large part from the increased spectral dispersion of resonances. As the bandwidth of RF pulses is largely B_0 independent, this improves the selective saturation of the narrow bandwidth of interest. Further sensitivity advantage arguably results from the longer T_1 at UHF (see below), which allows for more saturation build-up during the extended saturation trains.

35.2.3 Changes in relaxation times and contrast

MR relaxation times are field strength-dependent, and thus change at UHF. For common tissues, T_1 relaxation times increase, whereas T_2 shortens somewhat, and T_2^* shortens considerably with field strength. Depending on the application, this creates opportunities or challenges, and the complex inter-play of different individual changes often means that a 3T application cannot simply be copied to 7T when seeking the maximum benefit of UHF.

35.2.3.1 T_1-weighted imaging

Longitudinal (or spin-lattice) relaxation time T_1 increases with B_0. T_1 relaxation is caused by spin-lattice energy exchanges, and this exchange is most efficient when the molecular tumbling rate matches the Larmor frequency. Hence, for protons in molecules with lower mobility, the exchange rate will decrease and T_1 will increase. Water has a broad range of tumbling frequencies, and consequently its T_1 is least affected by B_0 changes. In practice, T_1 values of tissues in the brain increase, but also differ proportionately less between different tissue types.

T_1-weighted MPRAGE and MP2RAGE are staple sequences to study brain structure at a resolution and contrast that is not feasible at lower fields (Fig. 35.2). The lengthening of T_1 is not *per se* beneficial in FLASH and turbo-flash type readouts, since the lower Ernst angle and reduced attainable steady-state signal partially offsets the SNR gain from higher B_0. Despite this, at 7T, whole-brain acquisitions at 0.6 mm isotropic resolution in less than 10 minutes are in routine practice, and advanced acquisition strategies, such as wave-CAIPI sampling provide further speed-up. *In vivo* 7T T_1-weighted images have been shown at voxel sizes as small as 250 μm in combination with prospective motion correction

35.2 Advantages and opportunities at ultra-high field   557

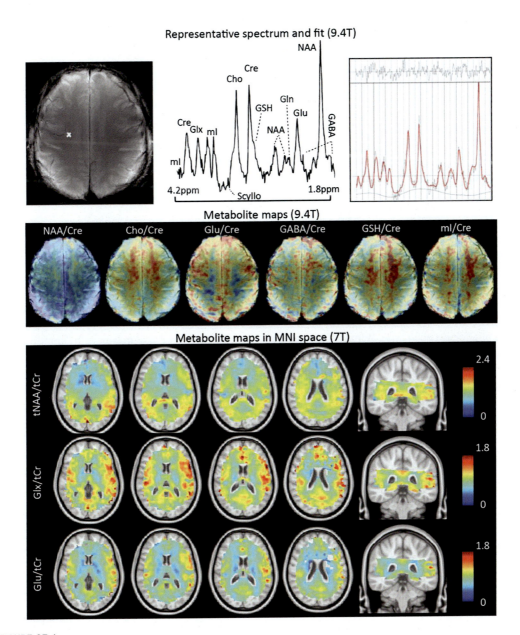

FIGURE 35.1

Top panel: Ultra-high resolution (128×128 matrix) data acquired at 9.4T using a single-slice FID MRSI sequence at the voxel location shown to the left. To the right, the LC-Model spectrum fit. **Middle panel**: Corresponding metabolite ratio maps in ultra-high resolution (128×128) for different metabolites. **Bottom panel**: Partial volume corrected and MNI-averaged metabolite maps derived from 23 subjects. Data acquired at 7T using a FID MRSI sequence and a lipid crusher coil. *Figures were kindly provided by Sahar Nassirpour, MPI Tübingen (9.4T data) and Alex Bhogal, UMC Utrecht (7T data).*

(Fig. 35.2, middle row). UHF has been highly enabling for identification of clinically relevant tissue anomalies, including tissue segmentation and volumetry in research and clinical applications.

For other applications, the longer T_1 is advantageous. In perfusion imaging with arterial spin labeling the magnetic label lasts longer, allowing for a longer acquisition window, and hence larger volume coverage. In sequences with extended saturation trains, such as CEST, a more efficient saturation is achieved, due to less T_1 decay occurring during the saturation period. A clinically relevant example that benefits greatly from the longer T_1 is time-of-flight angiography (TOF), thanks to both enhanced inflow effects and better background suppression (von Morze et al., 2007). This permits neurovascular imaging without exogenous contrast enhancement at resolutions up to 150 µm, however requiring prohibitively long scan times for routine use (Fig. 35.2, bottom left).

35.2.3.2 T_2-weighted imaging

Although having a weak field dependence at lower field strengths, the transverse (or spin-spin) relaxation time T_2 begins to be more strongly affected by field strengths at 7T and higher, where the contribution of molecular diffusion and chemical exchange to the T_2 signal attenuation become more pronounced. The T_2 of different tissues and fluids are affected differently by the field strength increase, but generally become shorter.

The T_2 changes lead to changes in T_2 contrast, and hence different image appearance than at lower field strengths. In the commonly used turbo-spin-echo (TSE) sequences, the contrast can be tuned by the choice of effective echo time. With the increased SNR at UHF, T_2-weighted images with submillimeter resolutions and high contrast reveal fine anatomical structures. One example is high-resolution imaging of the hippocampus and subsequent segmentation of its subfields, as shown in Fig. 35.3. The drastic shortening of blood T_2 also has positive implications for the spatial specificity of the fMRI BOLD signal, especially in predominantly T_2-weighted BOLD. Other methods, such as diffusion-weighted EPI are disadvantaged by the faster T_2 decay: use of shorter TE to compensate is prohibited by the EPI readout duration, whereas the desire for typically higher spatial resolution at UHF adds further challenge. This makes diffusion EPI at UHF an uphill battle. In addition, it requires strong gradients or not yet commonly available advanced acquisition schemes, such as segmentation or spiral imaging, for it to be competitive with clinical high-end MR scanners.

T_2-weighted imaging and different contrast preparations with FLAIR and double inversion recovery (DIR) are important in clinical applications. Two general challenges when transferring those to UHF are the RF power deposition, which results from the use of high flip angles and long refocusing trains, and the contrast variation and even signal loss due to B_1 inhomogeneity, as will be discussed below.

35.2.3.3 T_2^*-weighted and phase imaging

Transverse relaxation time T_2^* is the combined effect of T_2 relaxation and dephasing caused by local microscopic field inhomogeneities: $1/T_2^* = 1/T_2 + \gamma \Delta B_0$. ΔB_0 denotes the difference in local fields, the (static) effect which leads to a rapid free induction decay, but is reversible in a spin-echo experiment. T_2^* shortens considerably at UHF, an effect driven by iron and myelin content of the tissue.

Strongly T_2^*-weighted magnitude images to provide a qualitative measure of iron and myelin concentration can be obtained with gradient-echo imaging at relatively short TE. Quantitative values for T_2^* are readily obtained by exponential fitting to multi-echo GRE images. One great benefit of short T_2^* is the easily achievable phase contrast, and phase itself contains supplementary information in addition to the magnitude images. It is not surprising that high-resolution gradient-echo phase images were

35.2 Advantages and opportunities at ultra-high field

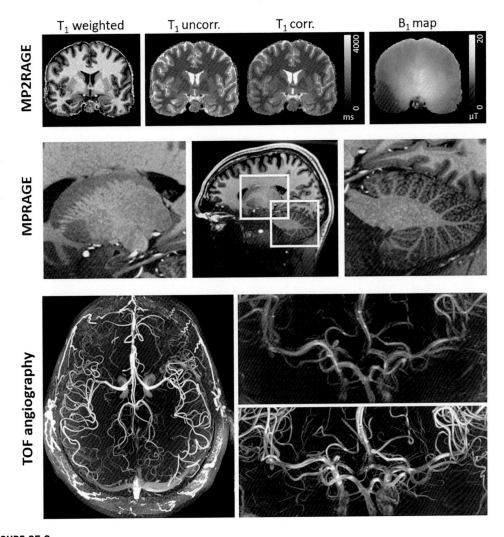

FIGURE 35.2

Applications of T_1-weighted structural imaging at 7T. **Top row**: Images from an MP2RAGE acquisition at 0.6 mm isotropic resolution. Images from the two MP2RAGE inversion images (not shown) can be combined to yield a T_1-weighted image optimized for GM/WM/CSF contrast (left), and to obtain T_1 maps (middle). Errors in the T_1 maps of about 100–500 ms due to B_1 inhomogeneity are corrected using an SA2RAGE B_1 map acquisition (right). **Middle row**: 250 μm isotropic MPRAGE data, acquired with prospective motion correction and averaged over eight sessions. The two outer panels show zoomed views to highlight the exquisite anatomical detail revealed at this resolution. **Bottom row**: Examples of time-of-flight angiography, at isotropic resolution of 0.3 mm (left). MRA at 250 μm (top right) is readily achievable with partial brain coverage, but the long acquisition time makes it subject motion blurring. The use of prospective motion correction enables MRA with a resolution of even 150 μm (bottom right). *Images were kindly provided by Sriranga Kashyap, Maastricht University (MP2RAGE), Falk Lüsebrink, Otto-von-Guericke University (MPRAGE), Jon Polimeni, Martinos Center / MGH (TOF MRA, left) and Hendrik Mattern, Otto-von-Guericke University (TOF MRA, right).*

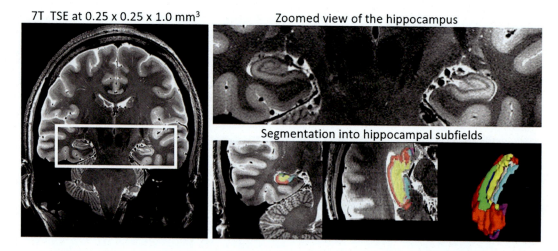

FIGURE 35.3

High-resolution imaging of the hippocampus using T_2-weighted turbo-spin-echo (TSE) imaging at 7T. **Left**: Coronal slice at 250 μm in-plane resolution. **Top right**: Zoomed view of the same image revealing the fine hippocampal structure. **Bottom right**: Example of segmentation into hippocampal subfields. *Images courtesy of Sriranga Kashyap, Maastricht University (personal communication).*

amongst the first celebrated results at 7T. The signal phase $\Delta\Phi = \gamma \Delta\chi \, TE \cdot B_0$ is directly proportional to echo time TE, B_0, and tissue susceptibility (χ). Stronger phase contrast than at 3T can thus be achieved at 7T at just half the TE, leading to time-efficient acquisition while benefiting from the higher SNR at UHF. Moreover, opportunities are created by phase being a quantitative measure, unlike the arbitrarily scaled magnitude images.

Two commonly used techniques that take advantage of phase contrast are susceptibility-weighted imaging (SWI) and quantitative susceptibility mapping (QSM) (Liu et al., 2015). In SWI, magnitude contrast is multiplied by a mask obtained from filtered phase images (see Chapter 22). Fine structures of locally differing susceptibility lead to signal suppression, irrespective of whether they are paramagnetic or diamagnetic, and the result is a contrast enhancement of these structures. For example, SWI images provide an enhanced but arbitrary contrast around deoxyhemoglobin-containing veins, iron-rich structures, such as the deep brain nuclei or microbleeds. QSM, on the other hand, gives a contrast based on the quantification of susceptibility, thereby also distinguishing between diamagnetic and paramagnetic tissues. QSM processing only uses the filtered phase data, and deconvolution with a dipole kernel yields the tissue susceptibility from the field perturbations that are captured by the phase images. Examples of T_2^*-weighted and phase imaging are shown in Fig. 35.4.

Another important application that relies on (predominantly) T_2^* contrast is blood oxygenation level-dependent (BOLD) fMRI (Ugurbil, 2016). Neuronal activation is accompanied by local changes in oxygen extraction, blood flow and blood volume, which result in a net reduction in local deoxyhemoglobin concentration and susceptibility. This manifests in magnitude signal changes in time series measurements that allows the concerned brain regions to be identified by means of correlation analysis against an externally applied stimulus.

35.2 Advantages and opportunities at ultra-high field

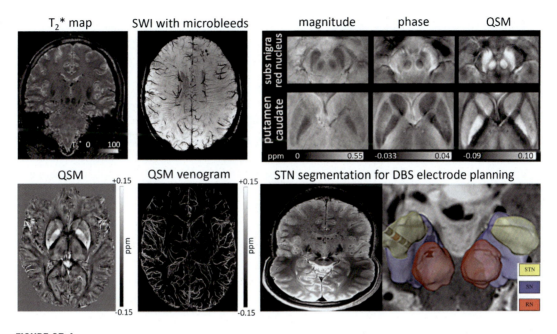

FIGURE 35.4

Applications of T_2^*-weighted imaging and phase imaging at 7T. **Top left**: T_2^* map at 0.25×0.25×1.0 mm³ resolution, obtained by log-linear fit to four gradient echoes. **Top center**: Susceptibility weighted reconstruction (0.4×0.4×1.0 mm³) reveals fine venous vessels and microbleeds, as seen in the frontal brain. **Bottom left and center**: Axial slice of a QSM data set and derived venogram reconstruction (0.33×0.33×1.25 mm³) as an alternative to SWI. **Top right**: High-resolution magnitude, phase and QSM images (0.5 mm iso.) of the substantia nigra and putamen illustrating the complementarity of the different contrasts that can be obtained from a single GRE acquisition (here, a 15-fold undersampled whole-brain wave-CAIPI GRE at three head orientations). **Bottom right**: Segmentation of the subthalamic nucleus from high-contrast T_2^* and T_2 images to aid the planning of deep brain stimulation electrode placement. *Images kindly provided by Sriranga Kashyap, Maastricht University (top left), Jens Theysohn, University Hospital Essen (top center), Berkin Bilgic, Martinos Center / MGH (top right), Hendrik Mattern, Otto-von-Guericke University (bottom left and center), Noam Harel, University of Minnesota / CMRR (bottom right).*

The activation-induced BOLD signal change increases stronger than linearly with field strength, while being increasingly weighted towards the microvasculature around the site of neuronal activation (Uludag et al., 2009). This favorable behavior results from the relative contribution of four MRI contrast mechanisms that make up the BOLD signal: two intravascular components that effectively vanish as blood T_2 shortens, a positive bias towards extravascular static dephasing (effectively a T_2^* effect, which increases linearly with B_0), and extravascular dynamic dephasing (signal attenuation from stochastic motion around the capillaries), which has a quadratic dependence on B_0. Although the T_2^* BOLD sensitivity gain at UHF enables fMRI at laminar resolutions, the specificity is compromised by veins at the pial surface. Cerebral blood volume (CBV) contrast using the vascular space occupancy technique is an attractive alternative for sub-millimeter fMRI at superior sensitivity. For a full discussion of fMRI at UHF, the reader is referred to Chapter 36.

562   Chapter 35 UHF benefits, challenges & applications

Depending on application, the short T_2^* at UHF may not be an advantage. Although providing the desired contrast at a microscopic level, the faster spin dephasing also results in artifacts, particularly in gradient-echo and EPI images.

35.3 Challenges encountered at ultra-high field

Higher field strengths bring their own challenges, which for a long time precluded widespread use of UHF. Two decades of technological advances, paired with new methods that are less susceptible to these issues, have brought 7T to a level where it is now seen as mature enough for clinical neuro applications. Further inventive developments continue unabated and promise new solutions and methods. This section discusses these challenges and the current state of available solutions, and an overview is given in Table 35.1.

35.3.1 B_0 inhomogeneity

B_0 inhomogeneity refers to spatial variation in the static magnetic field, mostly caused by the presence of the subject in the magnet (Ladd et al., 2018). The absolute offset in local B_0, equivalently resonance frequency, scales linearly with field strength. The resulting local field gradients are most pronounced in regions containing different magnetic susceptibility, such as tissue-air and tissue-bone interfaces, and most extreme around metal implants. The frequency offsets manifest themselves differently depending on the sequence. In sequences with low effective acquisition bandwidth, such as echo-planar imaging (EPI), this causes geometric distortions and intensity variations (Fig. 35.5, top row). In EPI, this can be partially reduced by using parallel imaging to shorten the echo-planar readouts. Further corrections are typically made in image processing using separately acquired field maps or distortion maps. In gradient-echo sequences, through-slice spin dephasing causes signal voids that increase in severity with longer echo time and for thicker slices. Spectrally selective pulses designed to excite or saturate specific frequency bands may result in poor water excitation or lipid suppression in regions of strong field offset. In spectroscopy, B_0 variation within the target voxel causes the spectral peaks to broaden and reduce in amplitude (hence reduce SNR, see Fig. 35.5, middle row). This potentially leads to overlap between neighboring metabolite peaks, partially counteracting the major benefit of UHF for spectroscopy, namely the linearly increasing separation between peaks on the frequency axis (also see Chapters 32–34). Careful B_0 shimming on the target region is therefore imperative at UHF to reduce the undesired effects of B_0 inhomogeneity (Juchem et al., 2020). Many UHF systems are equipped with shim coils up to third order. Promising developments based on high-density shim arrays have also been shown, with many small local shim coils used to achieve correction of local field offsets to even higher orders. This concept has been extended by letting the elements of receive arrays to double as B_0 shim coils. The advantage is not only the large number of shim coils, but also the proximity to the head (Fig. 35.5, bottom row).

Frequency fluctuations induced by breathing also scale linearly with B_0, at UHF manifesting strongly as image blurring or artifacts in segmented acquisitions. The respiratory motion of the air- and blood-filled chest alters the frequency at the location of the head by up to tens of Hertz at 7T, especially in the case of obese subjects. Head motion also disturbs the local B_0, adding to the image artifacts caused by the motion itself. Frequency stabilization with phase navigator echoes is routinely used in

35.3 Challenges encountered at ultra-high field

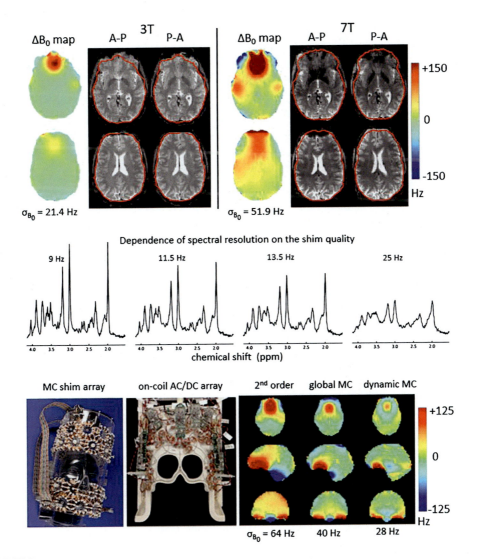

FIGURE 35.5

Effects of B₀ inhomogeneity at UHF and promising solutions. **Top row**: B₀ field maps and EPI acquisitions at 3T and 7T after typical whole-brain second-order shimming, showing the linear increase of inhomogeneity with B₀. The effect of inhomogeneities on EPI is highlighted by the differing geometric distortions when reversing the phase encoding. **Middle row**: Proton spectra obtained at different shims, which result in linewidths between 9 Hz (very good shim) and 25 Hz width (poor shim), showing how an inadequate shim leads to severe peak amplitude reduction and broadening. **Bottom row**: Advanced shim coils for local shimming to higher orders. **Left**: Multi-coil shim insert with local coils in cylindrical arrangement. **Middle**: RF coil array, in which the receive elements double as shim coils (AC/DC array), allowing for placement very close to the head. **Right**: Head shims obtained with second-order shim, global MC shim and slice-by-slice shim with the AC/DC array. *Figures kindly provided by Jason Stockmann, Martinos Center / MGH (top row and bottom row center/right) and Christoph Juchem, Columbia University (middle row, and bottom left).*

564 **Chapter 35** UHF benefits, challenges & applications

some sequence types, including EPI and GRE, with a correction to zeroth order being applied during image reconstruction. Some recent scanners also use feedback for real-time adjustment of the RF transmit frequency. More sophisticated is the use of real-time B_0 shimming with fast-switchable shims to allow for higher-order correction, but this technology is not yet widely available. Another niche approach is to continuously monitor the spatial distribution of the field fluctuations with magnetic field probes, and use the information either for real-time shim adjustment or for higher-order compensations during the reconstruction process.

35.3.2 RF power and B_1 inhomogeneity

35.3.2.1 Challenges posed by SAR and heating

The RF power required to achieve a given flip angle increases nearly quadratically with B_0, which in practice can be limiting at UHF since the regulatory limits for global and local RF power deposition are the same regardless of field strength (Fagan et al., 2021). The restrictions by global SAR are largely removed by the use of local transmit coils that limit RF exposure to the body part of interest, unlike whole-body RF transmission that is used at lower field strengths. Local hotspots of tissue heating result from the spatial variation in the RF field and specifically its electric field component. These hotspots, in terms of local (10 g) tissue-averaged SAR, set the upper limit for the permissible energy deposition, and are approximated from electromagnetic field simulations of the RF coils with human head tissue models. The inclusion of safety margins to account for variations in head anatomy and size and placement within the coil results in local SAR limits that are commonly more restrictive than the global SAR. This further adds to the practical limitations set by the already strongly increased RF power requirement at UHF. Most affected are high flip angle sequences with multiple inversion pulses (e.g., FLAIR), slice-selective 2D turbo-spin-echo, and those requiring long saturation pulses (e.g., CEST). To avoid being forced to prolong TR or reduce the number of slices to comply with the power limitations, 3D volume-selective TSE sequences commonly replace the more power-demanding 2D slice-selective scans.

35.3.2.2 Causes and challenges of B_1 inhomogeneity

Inhomogeneity in the radiofrequency (RF) transmission field remains the most obdurate challenge at UHF. With increasing B_0, and hence Larmor frequency, the required RF wavelength becomes shorter. As the wavelength approaches the typical dimensions of the human body, this leads to interactions between the object and the RF field, causing spatial variations in both B_1 amplitude and phase (Vaughan et al., 2006). The consequence is spatially varying flip angles across the object, even when using a volume transmit coil, in turn leading to variations in signal and image contrast. In the human head, the effect begins to be seen at 3T, where it is generally not detrimental. At UHF, regions of partial or even full signal or contrast loss are commonly observed. With typical head coil arrays, the brain regions most affected by incorrect low flip angles are the temporal lobes and cerebellum, whereas the central part of the brain generally gets flip angles that are too high. Although short-TR gradient-echo sequences with low excitation flip angles are relatively forgiving to B_1 inhomogeneity, any acquisitions that rely on high flip angles can be severely affected. This includes single and multiply refocused spin-echo sequences and sequences with one or more inversion pulses.

Spatially varying image contrast makes automatic image processing more challenging. Tissue segmentation algorithms developed for lower field strength images typically do not perform sufficiently

35.3 Challenges encountered at ultra-high field

well when applied to UHF data, requiring manual intervention or careful region-specific adjustment. AI-augmented algorithms have shown potential for improving both segmentation robustness and speed.

Diagnostic image interpretation of UHF images requires radiological training and experience to confidently distinguish possible lesions from artifacts and regional contrast and signal variations, as was the case during the transition from 1.5T to 3T.

35.3.2.3 Dealing with B_1 inhomogeneity

Parallel transmission (pTx) is the much talked-about solution to B_1 inhomogeneity, but in practice most UHF neuroimaging still relies on adaptation of more established techniques.

In all MR imaging, the transmitter power has to be calibrated to the desired flip angles. Due to the B_1 distribution patterns at UHF, a global calibration will only yield the correct flip angle in a limited region (Hoult, 2000), whereas in other parts of the brain the flip angles are too high or too low (see Fig. 35.6, bottom row). In 2D acquisitions it is possible to perform the adjustment in a slice-wise manner, even automatically by using machine learning techniques to predict the relative slice B_1. This somewhat improves local B_1 homogeneity and reduces total SAR, but at the time of writing is not available for many sequences or across scanner platforms.

Non-pTx RF pulses

Adiabatic pulses provide one effective way of addressing transmit inhomogeneity. They are largely insensitive to variations in B_1 amplitude and frequency, as long as they are applied at sufficient power to pass the adiabatic threshold. Such pulses are most commonly used as inversion pulses. A disadvantage of adiabatic pulses is their long duration and their high power/SAR requirement, which can be restrictive at UHF. While relatively straightforward waveforms based on hyperbolic secants are used at 3T, UHF MRI has driven the tailoring of more SAR-efficient adiabatic inversion pulses, such as WURST or TR-FOCI (Hurley et al., 2010). Nevertheless, their performance under SAR constraints is often compromised in regions of poor B_1, such as the temporal lobes or cerebellum.

Dielectric pads

A highly pragmatic and frequently employed means to reduce B_1 inhomogeneity is the use of dielectric pads (Teeuwisse et al., 2012). These are thin pouches (e.g., in square shape of 10–15 cm size, a few millimeters thick) filled with a high-permittivity material, such as calcium-titanate. Their placement allows for a coarse steering of the effective B_1 field by impedance-matching the head to the incoming B_1 field, creating a closer-to-spherical head shape, and by acting as a secondary local source of RF field. The pads are especially useful for increasing B_1 in the temporal lobes. Significant signal improvements are thus achieved for scans with spin-echoes or inversions, in addition to better performance of adiabatic pulses.

Parallel RF transmission (pTx)

Parallel RF transmission provides a flexible control of B_1 (Padormo et al., 2016). pTx head coils typically consist of eight separate transmit elements with unique spatial profiles, which can be independently driven in RF amplitude, phase, and waveform. Since the overall B_1 is determined by the superposition of these individual transmit fields, pTx allows for spatiotemporal control of B_1. A schematic view is given in Fig. 35.6, top row.

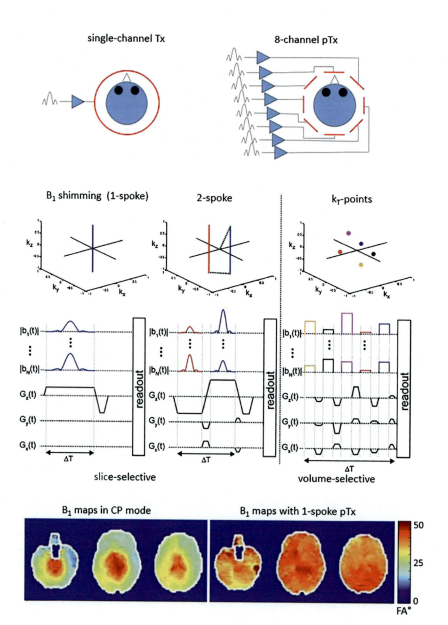

FIGURE 35.6

Top row: Schematic illustrations of single-channel RF transmission with a circularly polarized (CP) volume coil, and eight-channel parallel transmission with a pTx array, where the complex pulse waveform can be individually controlled on each channel. **Middle row**: Illustration of static and dynamic spokes and k_T-points pTx. **Bottom row**: Exemplary B_1 maps at 7T in standard CP mode (left) and 8-channel pTx with 1-spoke multi-band excitation (right). Whereas CP mode excitation suffers from the characteristic "central brightening", the use of pTx allows for a much greater flip angle homogeneity at all slice locations. *Figures kindly provided by Sebastian Schmitter, PTB Berlin (pulse diagrams) and Xiaoping Wu, University of Minnesota / CMRR (B_1 maps).*

Although the same type of pTx head coil (8-channel transmit/32-channel receive) is available at most 7T sites, routine use is hindered by cumbersome workflow and sequence implementations that require scarce expertise. SAR safety implementations are either prohibitively restrictive or left as the responsibility of each individual research site. B_1 mapping, pulse calculations, and SAR estimates can add 10–15 minutes to the examination time. Routine use of pTx is expected to increase with the new generation of 7T systems that offer better integrated pTx, efforts towards FDA approval, and significant advances in calibration-free pTx (see below), all helping to make it accessible to non-expert operators.

In the following, we describe the two ways in which pTx is used, namely static and dynamic pTx, how they are simplified into calibration-free pTx, and finally show some imaging examples at different contrasts. For a complete review of pTx techniques, the reader is referred to (Padormo et al., 2016).

Static pTx - B_1 shimming

In static pTx (commonly called B_1 shimming or RF shimming), the same RF pulse shape is applied on each channel and merely adjusted per channel in phase, and optionally amplitude (Vaughan et al., 2006). The goal is to optimize the complex superposition of the B_1 fields from the individual channels in the target region by finding the set of phase (and amplitude) settings that satisfy a given optimization criterion. Typical choices are root mean square error (RMSE), coefficient of variation, or transmit efficiency. Knowledge of the relative transmit sensitivities of each coil is sufficient, and those can be measured in a few seconds. B_1 shimming is most suitable for homogenizing the B_1 field in a defined target region-of-interest, while offering only limited ability to mitigate inhomogeneity over a larger volume or the whole brain. A measurement sequence can also use different B_1 shims for different sequence elements: an example is arterial spin labeling (ASL, see Chapter 12), where different B_1 shims can be used for the labeling pulse versus the imaging readout. The toggling between different RF shims within a pulse sequence is usually referred to as dynamic B_1 shimming.

Dynamic pTx

In dynamic pTx (full pTx), each channel transmits different and independently modulated RF pulse shapes. The flip angle is given by the Bloch equations and depends on the pulse's temporospatial B_1 evolution and concurrently applied gradient trajectory, as well as the B_0 distribution that affects the spins' phase along the typically long pTx pulse duration. pTx pulse design is complicated by the non-linearity of the Bloch equations. For small flip angles, a linear approximation can be used, but computationally demanding optimization algorithms are required when that condition is not met. For dynamic pTx pulse calculation, absolute B_1 maps for each channel must be measured in a prescan procedure, which typically takes several minutes. k_T-points pulses (Cloos et al., 2012) are the typical choice for non-selective excitations, such as used in 3D whole-brain MPRAGE and GRE imaging (Fig. 35.6, middle right). This approach consists of a train of a few (5–8) very short rectangular subpulses, interspersed with small gradient blips that map out a 3D trajectory of points at which the RF energy is deposited along the pulse. Being non-selective and typically low flip angle, k_T-points excitation pulses can be very short (1–2 ms), which leaves them suitable for fast echo-train readouts. A similar technique is the technique of SPINS pulses, which uses a continuous RF pulse under a continuous 3D spiral gradient. The benefit of k_T-points pTx over regular circularly polarized or quadrature mode pulses has been shown for a wide range of imaging sequences, including MP(2)RAGE, GRE, SPACE, and FLAIR.

The 2D counterpart to k_T-points is the technique of 2D spokes pulses (Setsompop et al., 2008), the common choice for slice-selective pTx pulses (Fig. 35.6, middle left). This method consists of a short train of typically 2–3 conventional slice-selective pulses, separated by x-y gradient blips, which distribute the excitation energy in the slice plane. Various successful implementations for the head have been shown, but the method's practical utility for high flip angles does not match that of k_T-points. The total duration of 2D spokes pulses is several milliseconds, making them more sensitive to B_0 off-resonance and eddy current effects than regular non-pTx or k_T-points pulses. Moreover, different spokes pulses are needed for different slice locations (at least 10–15 separately designed pulses to cover the whole brain), adding to the computational complexity.

Calibration-free pTx

Recognizing the similarity in B_1 and B_0 distributions across different human heads has led to the concept of universal pulses as a calibration-free solution to pTx (Gras et al., 2017). Universal pulses are generated by optimizing across a larger input set of subject-specific B_1 and B_0 maps. The resulting pTx pulse can be applied on any typical subject or patient, and will yield a near-optimal result in flip angle homogeneity compared to the dynamic pTx with full in-scan calibration (Fig. 35.7). Calibration-free pTx has been demonstrated at 7T for non-selective (k_T-points), slice-selective (2D spokes), and multi-band pulses, and used for excitation, refocusing, and inversion. The concept has also been adapted for static pTx.

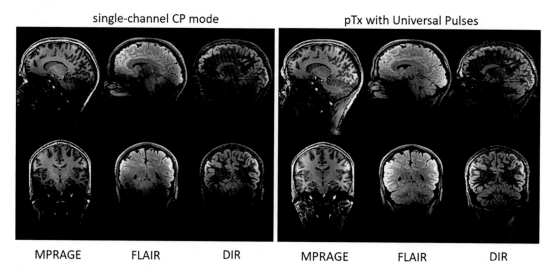

FIGURE 35.7

Effect of B_1 inhomogeneity on 7T structural imaging with T_1w-MPRAGE, T_2-prepared FLAIR and double inversion recovery (DIR), and mitigation by the use of pTx. **Left**: Acquisition with single-channel transmission shows loss of signal and contrast in all images, especially in the temporal lobes and cerebellum. **Right**: Homogeneous signal and contrast is obtained with a calibration-free form of pTx, universal pulses. Image resolution and acquisition times: MPRAGE: $0.8 \times 0.8 \times 0.8$ mm³, TA 6' 35"; FLAIR: $1.0 \times 1.0 \times 1.0$ mm³, TA 9' 48"; DIR: $1.0 \times 1.0 \times 1.0$ mm³, TA 11' 54". *Images courtesy of Nicolas Boulant, CEA Neurospin.*

35.3.3 Physiological effects

Being scanned at UHF can be accompanied by enhanced physiological sensations compared to those experienced at lower field strength (Hansson et al., 2020; Ladd et al., 2018). There are three aspects of MRI that are responsible for physiological effects: the main static magnetic field, the time-varying gradient field, and the radiofrequency field. UHF-specific effects of the RF field are discussed at length in previous sections.

Most frequently observed at UHF are transient effects attributed to the motion through the main magnetic field when moving a participant into and out of the scanner. These include temporary nausea, dizziness, metallic taste, or visual sensations in the form of light flashes (magnetophosphenes). While subjects report these effects more often at UHF, they are long known also from lower field strengths, and owing to their transient nature have not been regarded as being of any concern. The perception of transient effects is highly dependent on the individual, and the most effective way to reduce these sensations is to move the patient bed slowly. Initial fears that unpleasant sensations related to UHF may discourage volunteers to participate in UHF studies have not proven true. Predominant complaints are independent of field strength, including acoustic noise or discomfort from lying still. Some studies have reported a temporarily reduced cognitive performance after a 7T scan, which is believed to be related to vestibular effects.

The time varying magnetic fields from the fast gradient switching may cause a physiological response by peripheral nerve stimulation (PNS), an effect that has been well studied at lower fields. Since it is caused by the gradient switching for image encoding, it is not *per se* field strength dependent. However, greater experience of PNS has been reported at 7T, which is plausible given the typically higher spatial resolution at UHF, and hence use of higher gradient amplitude and slew rate.

Finally, tissue heating due to RF power exposure must be considered and be kept within regulations, as discussed above. The physical sensation of getting warm, however, is less common at UHF.

35.4 Summary

Curiosity about the function and morphology of the human brain has been the major driver for field strengths of 7T and above. The successes in primarily the neurosciences have been accompanied by rapid development of both hardware and methods to overcome the challenges posed by B_0 and B_1 inhomogeneities and SAR limitations. Those efforts have now brought us close to fully exploiting the key opportunities at UHF: SNR gain, contrast changes, functional sensitivity, and spectral resolution. With that, 7T neuroimaging has entered a realm of fast emerging new applications beyond research and development, demonstrating clinical benefit in an increasing number of areas (see following chapters on fMRI and clinical applications). This development is boosted by the availability of commercial 7T systems with regulatory approval for clinical use, and the continued efforts to improve technical solutions and integrate them into an efficient workflow. Examples are calibration-free parallel transmission and AI-based SAR assessments, both methods which will allow for the use of pTx without time penalty and overly conservative power limits.

In parallel, the frontiers of even more extreme field strengths continue to be explored, yielding further technological breakthroughs which will benefit UHF in general. Without doubt, the future holds promise of further advances in methodology and applications, promoting research and clinical goals.

References

Cloos, M.A., Boulant, N., Luong, M., Ferrand, G., Giacomini, E., Le Bihan, D., et al., 2012. kT-points: short three-dimensional tailored RF pulses for flip-angle homogenization over an extended volume. Magnetic Resonance in Medicine 67 (1), 72–80.

Fagan, A.J., Bitz, A.K., Bjorkman-Burtscher, I.M., Collins, C.M., Kimbrell, V., Raaijmakers, A.J.E., et al., 2021. 7T MR safety. Journal of Magnetic Resonance Imaging 53 (2), 333–346.

Gras, V., Boland, M., Vignaud, A., Ferrand, G., Amadon, A., Mauconduit, F., et al., 2017. Homogeneous non-selective and slice-selective parallel-transmit excitations at 7 Tesla with universal pulses: a validation study on two commercial RF coils. PLoS ONE 12 (8), e0183562.

Hansson, B., Markenroth Bloch, K., Owman, T., Nilsson, M., Latt, J., Olsrud, J., et al., 2020. Subjectively reported effects experienced in an actively shielded 7T MRI: a large-scale study. Journal of Magnetic Resonance Imaging 52 (4), 1265–1276.

Henning, A., 2018. Proton and multinuclear magnetic resonance spectroscopy in the human brain at ultra-high field strength: a review. NeuroImage 168, 181–198.

Hoult, D.I., 2000. Sensitivity and power deposition in a high-field imaging experiment. Journal of Magnetic Resonance Imaging 12 (1), 46–67.

Hurley, A.C., Al-Radaideh, A., Bai, L., Aickelin, U., Coxon, R., Glover, P., et al., 2010. Tailored RF pulse for magnetization inversion at ultrahigh field. Magnetic Resonance in Medicine 63 (1), 51–58.

Juchem, C., Cudalbu, C., De Graaf, R.A., Gruetter, R., Henning, A., Hetherington, H.P., et al., 2020. B(0) shimming for in vivo magnetic resonance spectroscopy: experts' consensus recommendations. NMR in Biomedicine, e4350.

Ladd, M.E., Bachert, P., Meyerspeer, M., Moser, E., Nagel, A.M., Norris, D.G., et al., 2018. Pros and cons of ultra-high-field MRI/MRS for human application. Progress in Nuclear Magnetic Resonance Spectroscopy 109, 1–50.

Liu, C., Li, W., Tong, K.A., Yeom, K.W., Kuzminski, S., 2015. Susceptibility-weighted imaging and quantitative susceptibility mapping in the brain. Journal of Magnetic Resonance Imaging 42 (1), 23–41.

Niesporek, S.C., Nagel, A.M., Platt, T., 2019. Multinuclear MRI at ultrahigh fields. Topics in Magnetic Resonance Imaging 28 (3), 173–188.

Padormo, F., Beqiri, A., Hajnal, J.V., Malik, S.J., 2016. Parallel transmission for ultrahigh-field imaging. NMR in Biomedicine 29 (9), 1145–1161.

Pohmann, R., Speck, O., Scheffler, K., 2016. Signal-to-noise ratio and MR tissue parameters in human brain imaging at 3, 7, and 9. 4 tesla using current receive coil arrays. Magnetic Resonance in Medicine 75 (2), 801–809.

Setsompop, K., Alagappan, V., Gagoski, B., Witzel, T., Polimeni, J., Potthast, A., et al., 2008. Slice-selective RF pulses for in vivo B1+ inhomogeneity mitigation at 7 tesla using parallel RF excitation with a 16-element coil. Magnetic Resonance in Medicine 60 (6), 1422–1432.

Teeuwisse, W.M., Brink, W.M., Haines, K.N., Webb, A.G., 2012. Simulations of high permittivity materials for 7 T neuroimaging and evaluation of a new barium titanate-based dielectric. Magnetic Resonance in Medicine 67 (4), 912–918.

Ugurbil, K., 2016. What is feasible with imaging human brain function and connectivity using functional magnetic resonance imaging. Philosophical Transactions of the Royal Society of London. Series B, Biological Sciences 371 (1705).

Uludag, K., Muller-Bierl, B., Ugurbil, K., 2009. An integrative model for neuronal activity-induced signal changes for gradient and spin echo functional imaging. NeuroImage 48 (1), 150–165.

van Zijl, P.C., Yadav, N.N., 2011. Chemical exchange saturation transfer (CEST): what is in a name and what isn't? Magnetic Resonance in Medicine 65 (4), 927–948.

van Zijl, P.C.M., Lam, W.W., Xu, J., Knutsson, L., Stanisz, G.J., 2018. Magnetization transfer contrast and chemical exchange saturation transfer MRI. Features and analysis of the field-dependent saturation spectrum. NeuroImage 168, 222–241.

Vaughan, T., Delabarre, L., Snyder, C., Tian, J., Akgun, C., Shrivastava, D., et al., 2006. 9.4T human MRI: preliminary results. Magnetic Resonance in Medicine 56 (6), 1274–1282.

von Morze, C., Xu, D., Purcell, D.D., Hess, C.P., Mukherjee, P., Saloner, D., et al., 2007. Intracranial time-of-flight MR angiography at 7T with comparison to 3T. Journal of Magnetic Resonance Imaging 26 (4), 900–904.

Wiesinger, F., Van De Moortele, P.F., Adriany, G., De Zanche, N., Ugurbil, K., Pruessmann, K.P., 2004. Parallel imaging performance as a function of field strength–an experimental investigation using electrodynamic scaling. Magnetic Resonance in Medicine 52 (5), 953–964.

CHAPTER

Neuroscience applications of ultra-high-field magnetic resonance imaging: mesoscale functional imaging of the human brain

36

Jonathan R. Polimeni[a,b,c]

[a]Athinoula A. Martinos Center for Biomedical Imaging, Massachusetts General Hospital, Charlestown, MA, United States
[b]Department of Radiology, Harvard Medical School, Boston, MA, United States
[c]Division of Health Sciences and Technology, Massachusetts Institute of Technology, Cambridge, MA, United States

36.1 Introduction

Today, functional magnetic resonance imaging (fMRI) is the most widespread tool for noninvasively measuring activity across the entire brain and has produced much of our recent knowledge of its functional organization in humans. For this reason, fMRI has become indispensable for human neuroscience. One of the most promising new directions for human fMRI has been ultra-high field (UHF) fMRI, typically defined as operating at magnetic field strengths of 7 tesla and above. Although this technology has been available for nearly two decades (Uğurbil, 2018), the technology is now mature and widespread enough for routine neuroscience studies. The advantage of UHF MRI stems from the increasing imaging sensitivity afforded by the higher field strength, but also from the enhancement of several forms of contrast with higher field strengths, such as the blood oxygenation level-dependent or BOLD contrast: the most common fMRI signal used today. These increases in imaging sensitivity and functional contrast together provide a supra-linear increase in BOLD fMRI detection power with increasing magnetic field. This makes fMRI one of the most compelling applications of UHF, and indeed many of the early successes of UHF MRI that drove its continued development were in the domain of human fMRI. The boost in fMRI sensitivity with higher fields is a currency that can be "spent" in various ways, and it is most commonly spent on increased imaging resolution. Therefore, the main application of UHF fMRI today is the study of fine-scale structures of functional organization that can only be resolved with the smaller voxel sizes afforded by the increased field strength. Because UHF MRI can provide imaging sensitivity and resolution that cannot be achieved at conventional field strengths, it has enabled new classes of neuroscientific studies that can be performed with human fMRI.

This chapter will provide a brief overview of current trends in neuroscience applications of UHF MRI, focused mainly on human neuroimaging in healthy volunteers. Because of the explosive growth in the use of UHF MRI over the past 10 years, the applications of the technology have become more

Advances in Magnetic Resonance Technology and Applications, Volume 4, ISSN 2666-9099. https://doi.org/10.1016/B978-0-12-822479-3.00055-5
Copyright © 2021 Elsevier Inc. All rights reserved.

574 Chapter 36 Neuroscience applications of UHF fMRI

diverse, although here we will showcase the benefits for a handful of exemplary applications. Additional examples can be found in the literature provided in the ***Further Readings*** listed at the end of the chapter.

36.2 Considerations for fMRI studies at UHF: imaging resolution and quality

There are several factors to consider when moving to higher field strengths. One is physiological noise (structured noise fluctuations in the BOLD fMRI signal driven by physiological dynamics, such as respiratory or cardiac cycles), which also increases in amplitude with field strength. These increased noise levels partly counteract and diminish the functional sensitivity gains. However, smaller fMRI voxels contain proportionately reduced levels of physiological noise such that the noise in these voxels is instead dominated by thermal-noise sources. Therefore, high-resolution BOLD fMRI acquisitions enjoy the expected sensitivity boost at higher field. This means that studies conducted at large voxel sizes of approximately 1.5 mm or larger (depending on the hardware configuration) may actually *not* benefit from moving to UHF from conventional field strengths, because of the large physiological noise contributions, and for this reason most UHF fMRI studies are performed at high resolution. What this means is that high-resolution BOLD fMRI acquisitions are not just a *benefit* of moving to UHF MRI, they are also in some sense a *requirement*. Fortunately, even for studies that do not require high resolution *per se*, including studies examining large-scale brain organization, fMRI with small voxels combined with anatomically-informed smoothing can still provide higher overall sensitivity and tissue specificity than conventional large-sized voxels. This is because the small voxels contain more signal from the tissue-of-interest (e.g., cortical gray matter) and less noise contamination from surrounding tissue (e.g., cerebrospinal fluid). Therefore, acquiring fMRI data with voxels small enough to adequately sample the cortex is advantageous even for studies investigating large-scale brain organization, and so a wide range of studies can benefit from moving to UHF MRI.

Although the increased sensitivity with higher field strength can enable these smaller voxels, there are several constraints on the achievable imaging resolution. Even though UHF MRI provides increased sensitivity that can itself be used to compensate for signal-to-noise ratio losses associated with increased imaging resolution, it is not always possible to achieve a specific desired imaging resolution in practice, i.e., one cannot simply "crank up" the resolution on a given MRI system. There are many reasons for this. One is that image encoding is constrained by hardware, such as the gradient coil, which cannot always switch quickly enough (due to engineering constraints), to achieve the desired small voxels. However, more often, the imaging performance is not limited by the hardware itself, but rather by safety limits imposed by the human body (Polimeni and Wald, 2018). Because of this, on some UHF systems, the imaging is limited by encoding, i.e., there is ample sensitivity that could enable small voxels, but the MRI scanner cannot provide the desired voxel sizes. Often these encoding limits can be circumvented by advanced acquisition strategies such as parallel imaging acceleration, which themselves sacrifice sensitivity, leaving the acquisition starved for sensitivity. A recent example of a technique that aims to overcome the encoding limits on current-generation scanners is shown in Fig. 36.1, where standard single-shot fMRI acquisitions are replaced with a multi-shot approach to achieve more encoding needed to acquire a 600 micron isotropic fMRI voxel size, albeit at some loss in image sensitivity. This trade-off between sensitivity and encoding represents a fundamental trade-off in high-resolution image acquisition. Often, cutting-edge high-resolution UHF fMRI acquisitions push the MRI scanner

36.2 Considerations for fMRI studies at UHF: imaging resolution and quality

to its encoding limits to achieve peak performance, then compensate for sensitivity losses through data averaging.

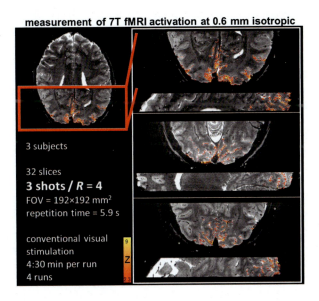

FIGURE 36.1

Accelerated-segmented VFA-FLEET acquisition for high-resolution 7T fMRI. Activation of the visual cortex measured in three subjects at 0.6 mm iso. Statistical activation maps (Z score) are overlaid on the cropped mean EPI images from a single run in axial and sagittal views for each subject. (Adapted from Berman et al., Magn. Reson. Med. 85, 120–139, 2021, with permission.) (*Figure courtesy: A. Berman, Martinos Center, MGH.*)

Today there are several UHF MRI technologies that can contribute to the encoding needed to achieve small voxels and high image quality, which are covered in detail in other chapters in this book. However, it is worth noting that, at the advent of UHF MRI, there were concerns that image artifacts—specifically susceptibility-induced geometric distortion in the echo-planar imaging (EPI) method used universally for fMRI—would be too severe at these field strengths to be practically useable. This was before accelerated parallel imaging became commonplace. Acceleration can reduce EPI distortion, and any remaining distortion can be further eliminated with postprocessing. Today, perhaps the highest-quality EPI can be achieved at UHF (Setsompop et al., 2016), and because of this, high-quality EPI is increasingly used for fast anatomical imaging as well.

Thus, the imaging performance achieved by UHF fMRI today is sufficient to provide resolutions well below the 1-mm scale. Though non-standard fMRI data analysis strategies must be employed to maintain these high imaging resolutions during data analysis (Polimeni et al., 2018), these strategies are becoming more routinely available. The pressing questions then are: What are the advantages of such high resolution? And the more basic question: Given that the fMRI signals only track hemodynamic changes related to neural activity, do these imaging resolutions go beyond what is really needed for human fMRI?

576 **Chapter 36** Neuroscience applications of UHF fMRI

36.3 Relating functional MRI to neural activity: what is currently known?

The fundamental limitation of fMRI in its application to neuroscience is that the fMRI signals are all indirect measures of neural activity (Logothetis, 2008). All currently used fMRI methods track changes in blood flow, volume, or oxygenation, or a combination thereof, that occur *alongside* neural activity. Although fMRI has produced much of our recent knowledge of the large-scale functional organization in the human brain, the ability of fMRI to yield insights into human brain function is ultimately limited by how closely the fMRI signals reflect neural activity.

Because one of the main uses of fMRI is localizing brain activity, the *neural specificity* of fMRI is often viewed in terms of the *spatial specificity*, that is, the ability to infer the precise location of the underlying neural activity from the observed fMRI response. This spatial specificity is often characterized by a point-spread function, as a simplification, and classic early fMRI studies using the technologies available at the time estimated that fMRI exhibited a point-spread of about 2 mm or more. However, converging evidence, mainly from optical microscopy in small animal models, has overturned this belief and suggests that changes in blood flow in response to neuronal activity are far more precisely coordinated than previous estimates. Indeed, it seems that as new technologies for quantifying specificity emerge, the estimates of specificity improve, suggesting that the closer we look, the finer blood flow regulation appears to be (Goense et al., 2016). Supporting these observations, new mechanisms of fine-scale blood flow regulation and coordination within the microvasculature have been identified that can produce localized changes in the hemodynamics underlying the fMRI signals, provided that responses within the large vessels of the macrovascular can be removed or otherwise avoided. The relevant question then is whether the "biological resolution" of fMRI—by which we mean *the precision of blood flow regulation in response to neural activity*—is better than the imaging resolution achievable with modern UHF MRI technology (Polimeni and Wald, 2018). The ultimate biological resolution of fMRI is still unknown (Drew, 2019), although naturally, it is likely not a fixed quantity and will vary across the brain, and yet it appears that it may be sufficient to infer neural activity within the basic modules of functional architecture in the human cerebral cortex: namely cortical columns and layers.

This updated view regarding the biological resolution of fMRI may seem difficult to accept, given that the hemodynamic response is widely viewed as coarsely related to neural activity. It is perhaps mainly for this reason that traditional systems neuroscience has not fully embraced fMRI. However, it is worth noting that there is ample concrete, empirical evidence that hemodynamics-based techniques are capable of resolving fine-scale structures in the brain. Conventional optical imaging of intrinsic signals is used to map out neural activity based on light absorption changes in oxy- and deoxyhemoglobin, and indeed has been used to discover two-dimensional patterns of functional architecture. A more recent example of this technique is shown in Fig. 36.2, where the patterns of light absorption (in this case driven by changes in oxyhemoglobin) can be used to clearly resolve cortical columns selective for preferred visual stimulus orientation or the preferred eye. This is perhaps the most clear and convincing demonstration of the spatial specificity achievable by hemodynamics-based measures of neural activity. Note that direct comparisons of the activation patterns detected in these optical data and fMRI data are complicated by several factors: the blood absorption signals measured with optical imaging are purely intravascular, whereas the signals measured with fMRI are generally a complex mixture of intravascular and extravascular effects, and some degree of spatial blurring is present in both modalities, either due to the optical properties of the tissue or due to blurring occurring during the MR image formation. Nevertheless, these optical imaging data indicate that blood flow and oxygenation regulation in the brain are sufficient to robustly resolve these fine-scale features of functional architecture.

36.3 Relating functional MRI to neural activity: what is currently known?

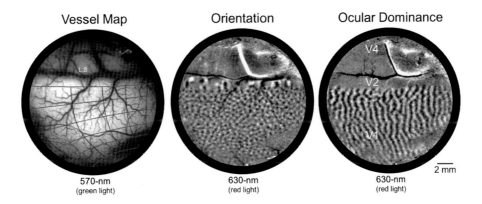

FIGURE 36.2

Optical imaging of cerebral cortical columns based on hemodynamics. Images of exposed macaque visual cortex using different wavelengths of light. Whereas the green-light illumination (570-nm wavelength) produces a vessel map, the red-light illumination (630-nm wavelength) is absorbed by oxyhemoglobin. Activation maps resulting from presenting oriented visual stimuli reveals the cortical columnar systems for orientation preference, and presenting visual stimuli to one eye reveals the cortical columnar system for ocular dominance. Both columnar systems end at the border between visual areas V1 and V2, with some evidence of orientation tuning within V2. Scale bar = 2 mm. (Adapted from Lu et al., Neuroimage 148, 160–168, 2017, with permission.)

Beyond spatial specificity, there are other aspects of the hemodynamic response that must be considered when assessing neural specificity of fMRI. The *temporal specificity* of fMRI has received less attention, although classic reviews considered this question in detail (Bandettini, 1999; Menon and Kim, 1999). Though there is a long-held belief that the hemodynamic response is "sluggish", mounting evidence points to a rapid response in the capillary bed that can be detected with sufficiently high spatial and temporal imaging resolution. A new class of "fast fMRI" studies have demonstrated that indeed the fMRI signal can track neural activity to unexpectedly high temporal frequencies up to 0.75 Hz at 7T, and perhaps with the extra sensitivity provided by 9.4T up to 1.0 Hz; an experiment demonstrating these fast fMRI responses measured in the visual cortex is summarized in Fig. 36.3. This is significant, as this will allow fMRI techniques to investigate dynamics of high-level cognition that evolve on these time scales such as attention, sleep, awareness, and language, and enable experiments with more naturalistic designs. Because these fast fMRI techniques sacrifice sensitivity for temporal resolution, and because of the low amplitudes typical of these rapid fluctuations in the fMRI signal, UHF fMRI can compensate for these losses to allow for the detection and tracking of these dynamic cognitive processes.

Beyond spatial and temporal localization, there are many questions regarding how to relate the amplitude of the fMRI response to the amplitude of the underlying neural response. Several studies have demonstrated ambiguities in the interpretation of BOLD signal increases, indicating that an increase in neural activity cannot be clearly inferred from increases in the BOLD response. Decreases of the BOLD signal during activation, generally termed "negative BOLD responses", also can be challenging to interpret, and may, in some cases, reflect neural inhibition, whereas in other cases may reflect vascular effects. Still, there are many relevant aspects of neural activity that seem at least now to be beyond the

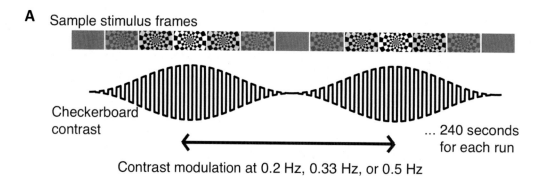

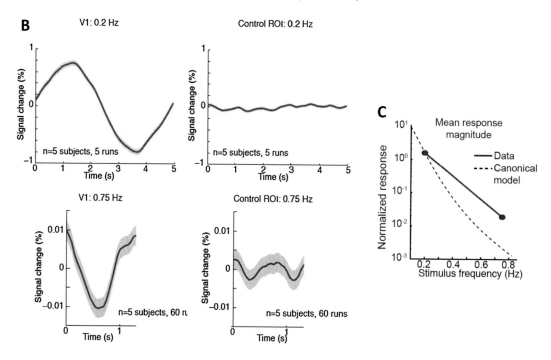

FIGURE 36.3

Fast fMRI can track stimulus-driven neural oscillations up to 0.75 Hz. (A) Design of visual oscillatory visual stimulus used to probe fast fMRI responses in human visual cortex. Stimulus consisted of a standard radial checkboard flashing at 12 Hz, and the luminance contrast was modulated at several frequencies of interest. (B) Stimulus-triggered mean BOLD response to 0.2 Hz and 0.75 Hz stimuli averaged across primary visual area V1. A non-visually activated gray matter control ROI does not show oscillatory responses, suggesting that the detected oscillation is caused by neural activity, rather than by motion or physiological noise. (C) Mean BOLD response amplitude measured in visual cortex (solid line). The dashed line depicts the predicted amplitude of the BOLD response to this stimulus as a function of stimulus modulation frequency. The BOLD responses to the 0.75 Hz stimulus modulation were approximately 10× larger than those predicted from the canonical hemodynamic response model, suggesting that the hemodynamic response to these rapidly oscillating stimuli is faster than expected. (Adapted from Lewis et al., Proc. Natl. Acad. Sci. USA 113, E6679–E6685, 2016, with permission.)

36.4 Prospects for "mesoscale fMRI" of cortical maps, columns, and layers   **579**

reach of fMRI, such as distinguishing between excitatory and inhibitory neural activity, subthreshold postsynaptic activity versus spiking, or the influences of neuromodulators on local activity.

Several approaches have been suggested to extract information from the fMRI signal that can be more directly related to neural activity and exploit the intrinsically high spatial and temporal resolution of the hemodynamic response. Several alternative pulse sequence approaches have matured extensively in recent years and appear to provide increased neural specificity for fMRI (Huber et al., 2019). FMRI signals, such as spin-echo-based BOLD and non-BOLD fMRI based on tracking changes cerebral blood volume or CBV, are especially well suited to UHF MRI, and methods for measuring changes in cerebral blood flow or CBF are challenging at UHF, but promising. Each of these alternative fMRI signals is sensitive to different aspects of the hemodynamic response, yet they each reflect changes predominantly from the microvasculature. Still, there are several complexities in the origins of many of these alternative fMRI signals, and more work will be needed to properly interpret data acquired with these methods. In comparison to standard gradient-echo BOLD—which exhibits the highest functional sensitivity of all fMRI signals, yet poor neural specificity, due to the dominance of large vein contributions—these alternative fMRI methods provide improved specificity at the expense of sensitivity. Again, this is where UHF MRI can help by providing increased imaging sensitivity to partially compensate for the relatively low sensitivity of these alternative fMRI techniques.

Other ongoing modeling efforts have been proposed to retain the high sensitivity of gradient-echo BOLD, while achieving high specificity through inferring the microvascular component of the measured response, in effect an attempt to "put the genie back in the bottle" and undo the draining vein effects. Although the proposed modeling makes assumptions about the vascular anatomy and coupling of the various components of the hemodynamic response through the vascular network, this approach to interpreting fMRI data is promising; future studies may integrate measurements from multiple fMRI contrasts together with similar models to better relate these measurements to the underlying neural activity, akin to the approach taken in the calibrated BOLD framework.

Overall, it appears that fMRI intrinsically has the potential to provide a faithful representation of neural activity if large vessel contamination can be avoided and if the remaining fMRI signal can be properly interpreted. Although the ultimate biological resolution is still unknown, recent human UHF fMRI studies suggest that the achievable resolution today is sufficient to investigate brain function at the spatial scale of basic modules of functional architecture: cortical columns and layers.

36.4 Prospects for "mesoscale fMRI" of cortical maps, columns, and layers

The achievable spatial specificity of human fMRI has substantially advanced in recent years, and now enables imaging of mesoscale features of functional architecture, such as the fine-scale details of topographic maps, cortical columns, cortical layers, and small subcortical nuclei. In addition to the earliest high-resolution studies providing evidence that some component of the BOLD response could reflect the underlying columnar organization, and because ground truth was available for the columnar patterns, this provided the initial glimpses of what high-resolution fMRI could achieve, which was further established with more complete maps of columnar patterns. A more recent example exploited the ground truth of visuotopic mapping in human primary visual cortex (V1) to impose a resolution test pattern, as summarized in Fig. 36.4, which similarly helped demonstrate the high resolution achievable with human fMRI.

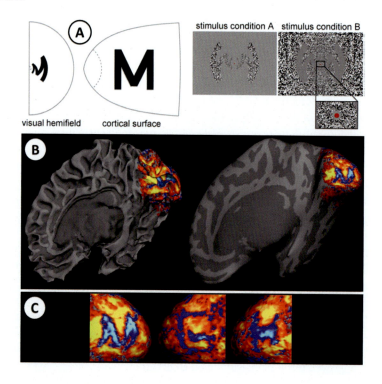

FIGURE 36.4

High-resolution 7T fMRI imposing a spatial activation pattern on human V1. (A) Because of the warping of the visual field onto V1, to impose neuronal activity in the shape of the letter "M", the visual stimulus has to be pre-warped based on the known topographic mapping. (B) Activation in response to this stimulus is difficult to discern in the original folded representation of the cortex, but once the surface model is inflated, it is easier to appreciate the pattern of activation. (C) This paradigm can be used to generate several "test patterns" to evaluate the spatial specificity of human 7T fMRI. (Adapted from Polimeni et al., Neuroimage 52, 1334–46, 2010, with permission.)

Although the early studies of cortical columns aimed to detect these columnar systems, a new direction has been to first map out, and then more closely evaluate the feature selectivity of distinct columnar systems within individual cortical areas. An example is shown in Fig. 36.5, where two interdigitated columnar systems of the secondary visual cortex (V2) were first identified, then their spatial frequency tuning shown to be consistent with the known columnar segregation of magnocellular and parvocellular streams in visual cortex.

Perhaps the most exciting recent development in human fMRI has been the emerging field of "laminar fMRI", which attempts to localize fMRI activation to within distinct cerebral cortical layers (Norris

36.4 Prospects for "mesoscale fMRI" of cortical maps, columns, and layers

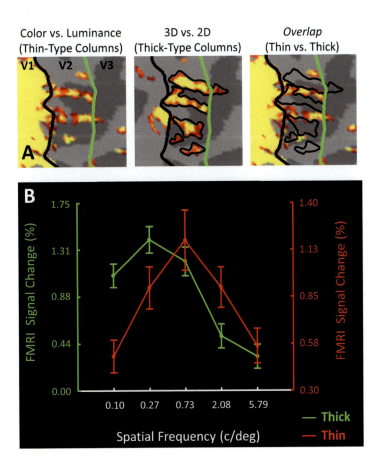

FIGURE 36.5

Investigating functional properties of interdigitated columnar systems within human extrastriate visual cortex. (A) Interdigitated color- and disparity-selective columns within cortical area V2. Thin-type stripes exhibit selectivity for color, whereas thick-type stripes exhibit selectivity for disparity, and the two columnar systems exhibit minimal overlap as expected from classical histology studies. (Adapted from Nasr et al., 2016, with permission.) (B) Responses within area V2 to achromatic stimuli at a range of spatial frequencies, demonstrating a preference for low spatial frequency in thick-type stripes and high spatial frequency in thin-type stripes, consistent with the known columnar segregation of magnocellular and parvocellular streams in visual cortex. BOLD responses in thin- and thick-type stripes are indicated in red and green, respectively. (Adapted from Tootell and Nasr, J. Neurosci. 37, 8014–8032, 2017, with permission.)

and Polimeni, 2019a). Because several cortical layers are the well-known inputs and outputs along canonical feedforward and feedback pathways of brain communication, the localization of brain activation to specific layers could provide information regarding which pathway is engaged, potentially enabling fMRI to decipher brain networks and discern the directionality of information flow in the communications between cortical areas. This topic is surveyed in detail in Parts 5 and 6 of this book.

The most successful acquisition methods for laminar fMRI to date are those that provide purely microvascular weighting, including the 3D-GRASE method for BOLD fMRI and the SS-SI VASO method for cerebral blood volume or CBV fMRI, although many studies have used small-voxel gradient-echo BOLD fMRI, combined with careful analyses to avoid macrovascular effects.

One of the key challenges in laminar fMRI is the interpretation of the activation maps, which is complicated by the close resemblance between the vascular architecture and the neuronal architecture in the cerebral cortex: at the microscopic scale there are multiple vascular "layers" of capillary beds that run parallel to the neuronal layers, and at the mesoscopic scale there are mid-sized intracortical vessels, such as diving arterioles and ascending venules, that run perpendicular across the layers and couple the hemodynamics across the neural layers. This means that even techniques that remove the largest vessels at the macroscopic scale may still be vulnerable to biases towards seeing stronger activations in locations with higher capillary density and a coupling/mixing of activations across layers.

Laminar fMRI thus faces several challenges. The first is to account for these vascular biases. Because the vascular anatomy in some ways reflects the functional anatomy of the cortex, it can often be difficult to separate out vascular biases and the underlying patterns of neural activity. Furthermore, it is well known that the microvasculature varies dramatically across brain regions, suggesting that these biases may vary regionally. In fact, it has been proposed that cortical areas may be defined on the basis of their "angioarchitecture" (Pfeifer, 1940), again suggesting a tight structure-function relationship between the patterns of vascular anatomy and neural activity.

The second challenge is that our knowledge of the patterns of laminar connectivity across cortical areas is incomplete, therefore even if vascular biases have been removed it can be difficult to interpret the underlying pattern of neural activity. Prior theories of a canonical microcircuit that is common to several cortical areas have given way to more nuanced theories, in which the patterns of input and output pathways are far more complex and vary across cortical areas.

Finally, knowledge of the functional roles of cortical layers and what stimuli or tasks engage specific pathways, and in what layer would neural activity be localized when those pathways are engaged, is still incomplete. Indeed, there have been some disagreements over what might be the expected pattern of neural activation to specific stimuli, even in well-studied cortical areas (Self et al., 2017). The tight intercommunication between layers in intracortical circuits and the rapid spread of neural activity between layers with a cortical column make it difficult to predict what the spatial pattern of neuronal activity should be, even if the inputs and outputs of a given cortical area are known. In other words, if input from a specific pathway were to arrive in a given cortical area in the known input layer, it is not a given over the time scales of an fMRI measurement that the strongest neural activation would persist within this input layer, therefore it may not be possible to infer which layer is receiving input on the basis of where the strongest fMRI activity is observed. If the sequence of neural events could be discerned with fMRI techniques, the input layer to a cortical area could potentially be identified based on where neural activity occurred first in time.

Nevertheless, even with these questions on how to generate hypotheses regarding the expected patterns of neural responses across layers, laminar fMRI may be well-suited to exploratory studies seeking to discover patterns of connections between neural populations. With clever experimental designs and careful control experiments, it should be possible to employ this technique to better understand functional circuitry in the human brain.

36.5 Individual-focused neuroscience and single-subject fMRI at high fields

Typically, high-resolution fMRI is applied in studies examining fine-scale organization of the brain, such as cerebral cortical columns and layers, and for this reason these studies perform all analyses at the single-subject level. Not only does spatial normalization used in group-level studies result in loss of spatial resolution, but fine-scale features, such as cortical columns, are known to exhibit distinct patterns across subjects, therefore averaging columnar activation patterns across individuals would not be valid. Nevertheless, high-resolution fMRI data often have limited sensitivity, and the effect sizes of interest are small, therefore to achieve both high sensitivity and high spatial specificity many runs of fMRI data—often well over an hour of total fMRI data acquisition—are required.

It may be true that fMRI studies at conventional resolutions are also sensitivity limited, and can also see more with the increased sensitivity that comes with more averages. For example, recent studies using conventional whole-brain 3T fMRI acquisitions examined whole-brain activation in response to a simple visual stimulus after averaging 100 runs across 10 sessions (Gonzalez-Castillo et al., 2015). It was found that, after averaging, this massive number of data activations was detected over nearly the entire brain. One of the main findings was the response in regions outside of the visual cortex, whose time-courses did not resemble the stimulus timing, suggesting that typical fMRI analyses performed on typical data may only detect responses that match the modeled activation time-course, and therefore meaningful, repeatable responses that do not match the model go undetected. This led the authors to suggest that false negatives may be pervasive in standard studies, which could be attributed either to low measurement sensitivity or to inappropriate response models or both.

Along these same lines, a recent set of studies acquired resting-state fMRI data in individual subjects over 24 experimental sessions at 3T and investigated subject-specific functional connectivity maps from these data (Braga and Buckner, 2017). They identified a fractionation of the default network into two spatially distinct, adjacent, interdigitated subnetworks from the resting-state data, and these subnetworks also exhibited distinct responses to several tasks of high-level cognitive function. They similarly found a fractionation of the fronto-parietal control network and the dorsal attention network within association cortex, and demonstrated that these networks also have complex and fine-scale inter-digitated relationships, although the subnetworks exhibit the same general progression across subjects. These fine-scale patterns could be identified at 3T using best-practice analysis methods designed to preserve the spatial resolution in the data. Remarkably, these subnetworks could also be seen in individual subjects from single experimental sessions at 7T, suggesting that 7T fMRI may, in some cases, provide sufficient sensitivity for single-subject fMRI. A demonstration of this fractionation observed in multi-session 3T data and again in single-session 7T data is shown in Fig. 36.6. Further studies from this group replicated these findings and identified that several individual sub-networks identified in the resting-state data exhibited strong overlap with activation patterns evoked by tasks of high-level cognitive function, such as social function and memory and also language processing. This demonstration of striking fine-scale differences in these maps of cognitive functions at the individual level, and the ability to generate sufficient imaging sensitivity to detect these at the single-subject level without relying on group averaging, is of key importance both to cognitive neuroscience and to the maturing field of psychiatric neuroimaging. Therefore, the extra sensitivity available with UHF fMRI can make major contributions to this field as well.

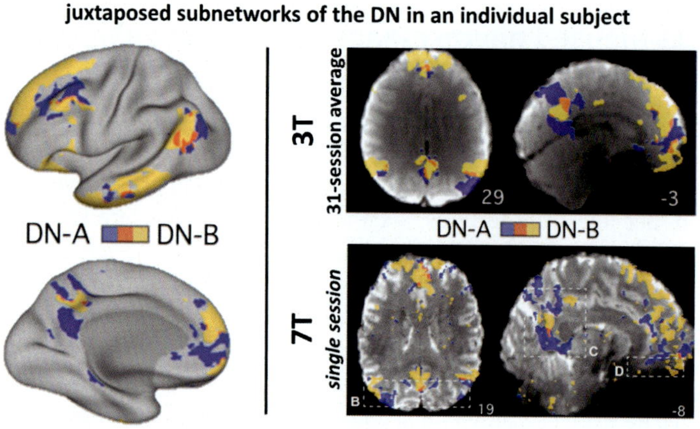

FIGURE 36.6

Examples of highly-powered single-subject 7T fMRI data. (A) Braga et al. reveal how the default network (DN) fractionates into two spatially separated sub-networks, DN-A and DN-B, within an individual subject after pooling data across 31 sessions of resting-state BOLD-fMRI at 3T. (Adapted from Braga and Buckner, 2017, with permission.) (B) The study was later repeated at 7T, where the fractionation of the DN into two subnetworks can be seen within the individual from a single experimental session consisting of 24 minutes of resting-state BOLD-fMRI data. (Adapted from Braga et al., J. Neurophysiol. 121, 1513–1534, 2019, with permission.) (*Figure courtesy: O. Viessmann, Martinos Center, MGH.*)

36.6 What role should UHF fMRI play in modern neuroscience?

Considering the potential neuroscience applications summarized above, the question arises of how can and should UHF fMRI play a role in modern neuroscience. Although it is clear that UHF fMRI enables investigation of functional organization at fine spatial scales, it may be argued that these modules of functional architecture would be more completely and definitively understood using invasive recording in animal models, where their precise spatial arrangement and tuning properties of the neurons could be better discerned. Still, it is valuable to image these features in humans, as it is not guaranteed that all aspects of fine-scale organization are present in the same way in both humans and animal models. Investigations into cognition and human behavior are more straightforward to conduct in humans, and recent high-resolution fMRI studies have demonstrated that these advanced techniques are applicable not only to low-level sensory or motor regions, but also to brain areas subserving these high-level functions (Finn et al., 2020).

Despite this progress, most fMRI studies, including high-resolution studies, engage primarily in brain mapping or *localizing* fMRI responses (i.e., the "where" question), and draw conclusions about brain function based on where the activity is found, given the anatomical context. This paradigm even extends to new domains, such as laminar fMRI, where conclusions are drawn based on which layer or layers appear to be activated and the *a priori* known functional roles of those layers. What is less common and more challenging is to apply fMRI to understanding brain computation and the underlying neural mechanisms of these computations. Although mapping out the "data structures" of the brain,

36.6 What role should UHF fMRI play in modern neuroscience?   585

including topographic maps, columnar systems, and laminar patterns of connectivity, can shed insight into the associated "algorithms" of brain computation, identifying the algorithms themselves requires adapting techniques of computational neuroscience to fMRI. Recent work has attempted to identify representations encoded within fMRI data, however understanding brain computation with fMRI will likely require, e.g., explicit circuit models that also account for the transformation of neural activity to observed hemodynamics. As the resolution and neuronal specificity of UHF fMRI continues to increase, it may become possible to further isolate activation along feedforward and feedback pathways and to investigate the recurrent interactions between multiple brain areas to map out these functional circuits.

A major advantage of fMRI is its ability to measure activation across the entire brain, which is a necessity to characterize functional circuity and the interactions between cortical and subcortical regions. Though the spatial coverage accessible to invasive optical imaging techniques has grown dramatically in recent years, techniques such as EEG/MEG have been adapted to detect activation in subcortical structures, and PET imaging has been extended to produce dynamic images of brain function. Meanwhile, fMRI is still perhaps the most versatile technique for dynamic imaging across the entire human brain. This advantage can be further exploited by extending current high-resolution fMRI techniques beyond the cerebral cortex to include important subcortical and cerebellar sites as well. Although several fMRI acquisition technologies currently in use achieve high spatial resolution through restricting coverage to a small field of view, new techniques are becoming available that can provide high resolution with whole-brain coverage.

As stated above, a major question faced by fMRI is what is the ultimate *specificity*, both in space and time, of fMRI *in humans*, and how does it vary across the brain? Not only does vascular architecture vary dramatically between brain regions, but it is likely that neurovascular coupling varies as well, further complicating the interpretation. This is especially relevant for studies investigating functional interactions and circuity across distant brain regions. Because much of the fundamental research into neurovascular coupling is performed in small animal models using optical microscopy, another pressing question is to what extent can invasive animal studies estimate specificity in humans? Given the major differences in vascular anatomy and topology across species, and observed differences in hemodynamics, as well as the strong effects of anesthesia and sedation on neural activity, neurovascular coupling, and vascular activity, it is unclear to what extent the question of the ultimate specificity of the fMRI signals can be fully answered in animal models.

As we gain more insight into the relationship between neural activity and hemodynamics, questions regarding the specificity, both in space and time, of the fMRI signals will be further clarified. Though the ultimate specificity of fMRI is still unknown (and it likely varies across brain regions), there is reason to believe that the biological resolution is still higher than our currently achievable imaging resolution. Hopefully this will continue to inspire technological advances aimed at increasing our imaging capabilities to better match the biological resolution, to harness the potential of fMRI to more faithfully reflect neuronal activity than it does today. What then are the current limits to spatiotemporal *imaging* resolution, and how do we move past them (Polimeni and Wald, 2018)? Will this require smarter, more efficient pulse sequences? Faster gradient coils? Denser RF coil arrays? Bigger magnets? Or perhaps *all four*? Ongoing efforts into creating special-purpose UHF MRI scanners designed for specific imaging modalities, such as fMRI, combined with advanced (and relatively inexpensive) field sensing and field control technologies, will soon provide the enhanced sensitivity and encoding needed to further improve spatiotemporal resolution. It is important to remember, however, that the spatial and temporal specificity of brain hemodynamics, while unknown, are not limitless, and there likely will be some fine-scale features of functional organization that can never be resolved with any hemodynamics-based measure. Nevertheless, it may be many years before imaging resolution catches up to even our current best estimates of the biological resolution of fMRI.

Finally, to date most high-resolution fMRI studies have sought to observe fine-scale patterns of functional architecture that were already known to exist in the brain from classical neuroscience studies, including those based on invasive neural recordings or *post-mortem* histology. These fMRI studies have been helpful in answering important questions regarding the specificity of fMRI and its ability to detect known features, but scientifically these studies have largely been confirmatory in nature. It is not always safe to assume that all features of functional architecture observed in animal models will be recapitulated in humans, as noted above, thus confirmation of these features in humans is helpful. Still, the neuroscientific insights from these confirmatory studies are limited. *When, then, can high-resolution fMRI move past confirmatory human studies, and become a "discovery science"?* What will it take for high-resolution fMRI to be properly validated so that we can use it to uncover new aspects of fine-scale functional organization? Accounting for and removing vascular effects to improve our interpretation of the fMRI activation pattern would help achieve this goal, although it is unclear how to evaluate when this would have been accomplished well enough. Moving towards acquisitions with less pronounced vascular biases will certainly help. Perhaps for now high-resolution UHF fMRI will still require multimodal validation, and the scientific tools of replication and reproducibility, plus careful experimental design, will help us build confidence in our findings.

36.7 Summary/conclusions

The increased sensitivity and neural specificity afforded by UHF MRI has clearly expanded the reach of human fMRI, making it possible to investigate the human brain at the scale of the basic modules of functional architecture. Though it is still unclear what are the fundamental limits of human fMRI in reporting neural activity—in terms of both localizing neural signals in space and time, or understanding the various aspects of neural activity through fMRI—evidence suggests that we have not yet reached the limit. These new capabilities afforded by UHF fMRI enable investigations into fine-scale functional organization of the brain in individual subjects, including whole-brain functional circuitry, and are poised to provide insights into brain computation.

Acknowledgments

The author gratefully acknowledges useful discussions with Drs Avery Berman, Jingyuan Chen, Laura Lewis, Shahin Nasr, Ville Renvall, Olivia Viessmann, and Larry Wald. Special thanks also to Dr Anna Roe for providing the images presented in Fig. 36.2, to Drs Berman and Viessmann for providing Figs. 36.1 and 36.6, respectively, and to Drs Rodrigo Braga, Shahin Nasr, Roger Tootell, and Laura Lewis for kind permission to reproduce figures from their work. This work was supported in part by the NIH NIBIB (grants P41-EB030006 and R01-EB019437), the NIH NIMH (grant R01-MH124004), by the *BRAIN Initiative* (NIH NIMH grants R01-MH111419 and U01-EB025162), and by the MGH/HST Athinoula A. Martinos Center for Biomedical Imaging.

References

Bandettini, P.A., 1999. The temporal resolution of functional MRI. In: Moonen, C.T.W., Bandettini, P.A. (Eds.), Functional MRI. Springer-Verlag, Berlin, pp. 205–220.

Berman, A.J.L., Grissom, W.A., Witzel, T., Nasr, S., Park, D.J., Setsompop, K., Polimeni, J.R., 2021. Ultra-high spatial resolution BOLD fMRI in humans using combined segmented-accelerated VFA-FLEET with a recursive RF pulse design. Magn. Reson. Med. 85, 120–139. https://doi.org/10.1002/mrm.28415.

Braga, R.M., Buckner, R.L., 2017. Parallel interdigitated distributed networks within the individual estimated by intrinsic functional connectivity. Neuron 95, 457–471.e5. https://doi.org/10.1016/j.neuron.2017.06.038.

Braga, R.M., Van Dijk, K.R.A., Polimeni, J.R., Eldaief, M.C., Buckner, R.L., 2019. Parallel distributed networks resolved at high resolution reveal close juxtaposition of distinct regions. J. Neurophysiol. 121, 1513–1534. https://doi.org/10.1152/jn.00808.2018.

Drew, P.J., 2019. Vascular and neural basis of the BOLD signal. Curr. Opin. Neurobiol. 58, 61–69. https://doi.org/10.1016/j.conb.2019.06.004.

Finn, E.S., Huber, L., Bandettini, P.A., 2020. Higher and deeper: bringing layer fMRI to association cortex. Prog. Neurobiol. https://doi.org/10.1016/j.pneurobio.2020.101930.

Goense, J., Bohraus, Y., Logothetis, N.K., 2016. fMRI at high spatial resolution: implications for BOLD-models. Front. Comput. Neurosci. 10, 66. https://doi.org/10.3389/fncom.2016.00066.

Gonzalez-Castillo, J., Hoy, C.W., Handwerker, D.A., Roopchansingh, V., Inati, S.J., Saad, Z.S., Cox, R.W., Bandettini, P.A., 2015. Task dependence, tissue specificity, and spatial distribution of widespread activations in large single-subject functional MRI datasets at 7T. Cereb. Cortex 25, 4667–4677. https://doi.org/10.1093/cercor/bhu148.

Huber, L., Uludağ, K., Möller, H.E., 2019. Non-BOLD contrast for laminar fMRI in humans: CBF, CBV, and CMRO2. NeuroImage 197, 742–760. https://doi.org/10.1016/j.neuroimage.2017.07.041.

Lewis, L.D., Setsompop, K., Rosen, B.R., Polimeni, J.R., 2016. Fast fMRI can detect oscillatory neural activity in humans. Proc. Natl. Acad. Sci. USA 113, E6679–E6685. https://doi.org/10.1073/pnas.1608117113.

Logothetis, N.K., 2008. What we can do and what we cannot do with fMRI. Nature 453, 869–878. https://doi.org/10.1038/nature06976.

Lu, H.D., Chen, G., Cai, J., Roe, A.W., 2017. Intrinsic signal optical imaging of visual brain activity: tracking of fast cortical dynamics. NeuroImage 148, 160–168. https://doi.org/10.1016/j.neuroimage.2017.01.006.

Menon, R.S., Kim, S.G., 1999. Spatial and temporal limits in cognitive neuroimaging with fMRI. Trends Cogn. Sci. https://doi.org/10.1016/S1364-6613(99)01329-7.

Nasr, S., Polimeni, J.R., Tootell, R.B.H., 2016. Interdigitated color- and disparity-selective columns within human visual cortical areas V2 and V3. J. Neurosci. 36, 1841–1857. https://doi.org/10.1523/JNEUROSCI.3518-15.2016.

Norris, D.G., Polimeni, J.R., 2019a. Laminar (f)MRI: a short history and future prospects. NeuroImage 197, 643–649. https://doi.org/10.1016/j.neuroimage.2019.04.082.

Pfeifer, R.A., 1940. Die angioarchitektonische areale Gliederung der Grosshirnrinde, auf Grund vollkommener Gefässinjektionspräparate vom Gehirn des Macacus Rhesus. G. Thieme, Leipzig.

Polimeni, J.R., Fischl, B., Greve, D.N., Wald, L.L., 2010. Laminar analysis of 7T BOLD using an imposed spatial activation pattern in human V1. NeuroImage 52, 1334–1346. https://doi.org/10.1016/j.neuroimage.2010.05.005.

Polimeni, J.R., Renvall, V., Zaretskaya, N., Fischl, B., 2018. Analysis strategies for high-resolution UHF-fMRI data. NeuroImage 168, 296–320. https://doi.org/10.1016/j.neuroimage.2017.04.053.

Polimeni, J.R., Wald, L.L., 2018. Magnetic resonance imaging technology — bridging the gap between noninvasive human imaging and optical microscopy. Curr. Opin. Neurobiol. 50, 250–260. https://doi.org/10.1016/j.conb.2018.04.026.

Self, M.W., van Kerkoerle, T., Goebel, R., Roelfsema, P.R., 2017. Benchmarking laminar fMRI: neuronal spiking and synaptic activity during top-down and bottom-up processing in the different layers of cortex. NeuroImage. https://doi.org/10.1016/j.neuroimage.2017.06.045.

Setsompop, K., Feinberg, D.A., Polimeni, J.R., 2016. Rapid brain MRI acquisition techniques at ultra-high fields. NMR Biomed. 29, 1198–1221. https://doi.org/10.1002/nbm.3478.

Tootell, R.B.H., Nasr, S., 2017. Columnar segregation of magnocellular and parvocellular streams in human extrastriate cortex. J. Neurosci. 37, 8014–8032. https://doi.org/10.1523/JNEUROSCI.0690-17.2017.

Uğurbil, K., 2018. Imaging at ultrahigh magnetic fields: history, challenges, and solutions. NeuroImage 168, 7–32. https://doi.org/10.1016/j.neuroimage.2017.07.007.

Further reading

Recent review articles on the topic of neuroscience applications of UHF MRI

De Martino, F., Yacoub, E., Kemper, V., Moerel, M., Uludağ, K., De Weerd, P., Uğurbil, K., Goebel, R., Formisano, E., 2018. The impact of ultra-high field MRI on cognitive and computational neuroimaging. NeuroImage 168, 366–382. https://doi.org/10.1016/j.neuroimage.2017.03.060.

Dumoulin, S.O., Fracasso, A., van der Zwaag, W., Siero, J.C.W., Petridou, N., 2018. Ultra-high field MRI: advancing systems neuroscience towards mesoscopic human brain function. NeuroImage 168, 345–357. https://doi.org/10.1016/j.neuroimage.2017.01.028.

Huber, L., Finn, E.S., Chai, Y., Goebel, R., Stirnberg, R., Stöcker, T., Marrett, S., Uludag, K., Kim, S.G., Han, S.H., Bandettini, P.A., Poser, B.A., 2020. Layer-dependent functional connectivity methods. Prog. Neurobiol. https://doi.org/10.1016/j.pneurobio.2020.101835.

Lawrence, S.J.D., Formisano, E., Muckli, L., de Lange, F.P., 2019. Laminar fMRI: applications for cognitive neuroscience. NeuroImage 197, 785–791. https://doi.org/10.1016/j.neuroimage.2017.07.004.

Schluppeck, D., Sanchez-Panchuelo, R.M., Francis, S.T., 2018. Exploring structure and function of sensory cortex with 7 T MRI. NeuroImage 164, 10–17. https://doi.org/10.1016/j.neuroimage.2017.01.081.

van der Zwaag, W., Schäfer, A., Marques, J.P., Turner, R., Trampel, R., 2016. Recent applications of UHF-MRI in the study of human brain function and structure: a review. NMR Biomed. https://doi.org/10.1002/nbm.3275.

Recent Special Issues on related topics

Yacoub, E.S., Wald, L.L. (Eds.), 2018. Special Issue: "Pushing the spatio-temporal limits of MRI and fMRI". NeuroImage.

Polimeni, J.R., Uludağ, K. (Eds.), 2018. Special Issue: "Neuroimaging with ultra-high field MRI: present and future". NeuroImage.

Norris, D.G., Polimeni, J.R. (Eds.), 2019b. Special Issue: "MRI of cortical layers". NeuroImage.

Lewis, L.D., Vizioli, L., Yacoub, E.S. (Eds.), forthcoming. Special Issue: "How pushing the spatiotemporal limits of fMRI can advance human neuroscience". Prog. Neurobiol.

CHAPTER

Clinical applications of high field magnetic resonance

37

Louise Ebersberger[a], Mark E. Ladd[b], and Daniel Paech[a]

[a]*German Cancer Research Center (DKFZ), Division of Radiology, Heidelberg, Baden-Württemberg, Germany*
[b]*German Cancer Research Center (DKFZ), Division of Medical Physics in Radiology, Heidelberg, Baden-Württemberg, Germany*

37.1 Proton MRI/MRS at UHF

37.1.1 High-resolution proton imaging at ultra-high field strength ($\geq$ 7 tesla)

Magnetic resonance imaging (MRI) at ultra-high magnetic field (UHF) strengths ($B_0 \geq 7$ tesla (T)) provides an increase in resolution and image contrast in comparison to conventional MRI at lower field strengths. This makes UHF MRI a powerful technique to non-invasively assess normal and abnormal brain tissue with high spatial resolution. There is a fast-growing body of evidence that UHF MRI has the potential to improve depiction of anatomical substructures, and therefore diagnostic confidence. However, as discussed in previous chapters the acquisition of high-quality whole-brain MRI at high field is hampered by increased inhomogeneity in the B_0 and B_1 fields, particularly at the skull base, where distortions become greater with increasing B_0. Such limitations need to be overcome before UHF MRI can be fully integrated into clinical diagnostic work-up and decision making.

37.1.1.1 Clinical applications

Conventional high-resolution proton imaging is still the mainstay of clinical imaging at 7T. The following section summarizes the most important *in vivo* and clinical applications of UHF MRI.

37.1.1.2 Brain anatomy

Techniques based on magnetic susceptibility imaging benefit particularly from UHF, enabling visualization of brain structures that have been difficult to depict with scanners at lower field strengths. Early investigations of anatomical brain structures with high resolution using UHF MRI showed that post-processed phase images sensitive to magnetic susceptibility enhance the inherent brain gray/white matter contrast in gradient-echo images, which can be used to study internal anatomical brain structures. Consequently, MR venograms, using deoxyhemoglobin as an intrinsic contrast agent, can also be obtained with high quality at UHF. Susceptibility-weighted imaging (see Chapter 22) can not only be used to depict cerebral cavernous malformations, but also non-vascular lesions, for instance to discriminate between multiple sclerosis (MS) white matter lesions and benign white matter hyperintensities.

MR angiography (MRA), using 3D arterial time-of-flight (TOF) at UHF, has enabled the visualization of small intracranial vessel lumina and the characterization of vessel walls, far beyond the circle of Willis. Therefore 7T TOF MRA can help to better identify small vessel occlusion or atherosclerotic stenosis. See Fig. 37.1.

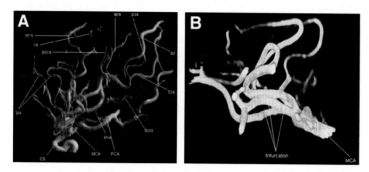

FIGURE 37.1

(A) Data from a healthy volunteer acquired with TOF MRA at 7T, showing the left middle cerebral artery (MCA) and its branches with great detail. (B) The magnified view depicts an anatomic variation, a trifurcation of the MCA. Figure from Heverhagen et al. Invest Radiol, 43, 568–73, 2008.

Dysfunction of dopaminergic neurotransmission of the substantia nigra and ventral tegmental area is associated with neurological and neuropsychological diseases, including Parkinson's disease (PD) and schizophrenia. Unfortunately, these midbrain structures are difficult to assess with conventional clinical MR imaging. Eapen et al. showed that gradient- and spin-echo (GE and SE,) as well as fast-field echo (FFE) sequences at 7T, provide sufficient contrast-to-noise ratio (CNR) to evaluate the anatomy of the midbrain. The FFE sequence, in particular, reveals vascular details and substructure information within the midbrain regions that could be useful for examining structural changes in midbrain pathologies (Eapen et al., 2011).

Deistung et al. explored the potential for UHF MRI to depict the intricate anatomy of the human brainstem *in vivo* by acquiring T_2-weighted images, quantitative maps of longitudinal relaxation rate (R_1 maps), and effective transverse relaxation rate (R_2^* maps), magnetic susceptibility maps, and direction-encoded track-density images (Deistung et al., 2013). Small anatomical substructures (e.g., the substantia nigra and red nuclei) were visible in all contrasts. Similar results have been obtained by others, who demonstrated that magnetization-prepared rapid-acquisition gradient-echo (MPRAGE) and MP2RAGE sequences provide clear depiction of the cranial nerves at 7T. Such detailed anatomical information could be helpful for the diagnosis of cranial nerve disorders, such as trigeminal neuralgia related to an affection (e.g., inflammation or compression) of the nerve root.

37.1.1.3 Brain cancer

Currently, MRI at clinical field strengths of up to 3T is a cornerstone in the diagnosis and treatment planning of brain cancer. Gliomas are the most frequent primary brain tumors in adults. Patients with high-grade glioma (HGG, WHO Grade III-IV) still face poor prognosis, despite gross total resection followed by radio-chemotherapy as the therapy of choice. One of the major problems is the aggressive and diffuse infiltration of tumor cells, preferably along white matter tracts, which often remains invisible on conventional imaging. Due to increased signal-to-noise-ratio (SNR) and higher spatial resolution at 7T, UHF MRI could also enhance visualization of tumor infiltration into neighboring tissues, thus refining current target volume definition in neurosurgery or radiotherapy. Recently, integration of 7T MR imaging into radiotherapy treatment planning for brain tumors was shown to be technically feasible. Moreover, intermediate- and long-term imaging manifestations of radiotherapy-related changes in normal-appearing brain tissue can be assessed using 7T susceptibility-weighted imaging (SWI).

7T TOF MRA enables characterization and quantification of the internal vascular morphology of brain tumors, making this method potentially useful in future studies for the evaluation of therapy response, particularly anti-angiogenic therapies. Regarding tumor enhancement following injection of an intravenous contrast agent, comparisons between 7T MRI and lower field strengths have shown no differences in the presence and size of the enhancing region. However, Noebauer-Huhmann et al. reported better visibility and lesion delineation at 7T following full-dose contrast agent administration (Noebauer-Huhmann et al., 2015). Half the routine contrast agent dose at 7T yielded higher lesion enhancement than the full dose at 3T, which indicates the possibility of dose reduction at 7T.

These results demonstrate that UHF MRI can be utilized for a more detailed imaging of brain tumors, enabling a more accurate diagnosis and therapy response evaluation.

37.1.1.4 Vascular imaging

Stroke caused by vascular occlusion or bleeding and other cerebrovascular diseases are major causes of death and disability worldwide. MRI is the most sensitive imaging technique to detect acute brain infarctions and to characterize incidental cerebrovascular lesions, such as white matter hyperintensities, lacunes, and microbleeds.

In a study performed by Novak and colleagues, seventeen subjects with minor ischemic infarcts were examined using T_2-weighted gradient-echo and rapid acquisition with relaxation enhancement (RARE) images at 8T, with in-plane resolution up to 200 µm. 8T MRI revealed infarcts and microvasculature pathologies with high resolution that were not apparent on routine MRI at 1.5T (Novak et al., 2005).

Another major clinical advancement of UHF MRI is its ability to detect cortical microinfarcts, which is only possible to a limited extent at 3T. Cortical microinfarcts are associated with atherosclerosis and are believed to be of microembolic origin.

UHF MRI has also proven useful in the depiction of cerebral aneurysms and arteriovenous malformations (AVMs). Wrede et al. demonstrated highly sensitive delineation of unruptured intracranial aneurysms using 7T MRA within a clinical setting comparable to the gold standard, digital subtraction angiography (DSA) (Wrede et al., 2017). 7T TOF MRA has been shown to enable the detection of microaneurysms with diameters $\leq$ 1 mm. Furthermore, non-enhanced 7T MPRAGE, together with 7T arterial TOF MRA, have been found superior to 1.5T arterial TOF MRA in the characterization of AVMs regarding the identification of draining veins, the nidus, and feeder(s), which is relevant for both neurosurgical and endovascular neuroradiological treatment. Future investigations need to additionally acquire dynamic information about the blood flow patterns within the AVM, e.g., provided by phase-contrast 4D flow imaging with higher SNR at 7T compared to 3T.

37.1.1.5 Neurodegenerative diseases

Another important application of vascular imaging at 7T is in the field of neurodegenerative diseases. The increased sensitivity of SWI at 7T leads to improved detection of deoxyhemoglobin (as seen in microbleeds or cavernomas) or calcifications with UHF MRI. Because microbleeds and white matter lesions are associated with vascular dementia, 7T and higher field strength provide improved sensitivity

592 **Chapter 37** Clinical applications of high field magnetic resonance

for an early diagnosis. In addition, cortical microinfarcts are detectable at UHF (see previous section), a common finding in neuropathological studies of aging and dementia or Alzheimer's disease (AD).

Generally, a close relationship between vascular and degenerative pathology in the human hippocampus is suggested. In this context, it has recently been shown that human hippocampal vascularization can be assessed *in vivo* using 7T angiography, which may aid linking vascular anatomical phenotypes to neurodegenerative and vascular pathology.

Besides vascular imaging, more precise volumetric assessments of the hippocampal subfields and entorhinal cortex (ERC) can be performed at 7T, showing volume reductions in patients with AD in all hippocampal subfields and ERC compared with healthy controls and patients with mild cognitive impairment.

For the detection and treatment of PD, T_2^*-weighted images and susceptibility-weighted images obtained at UHF have been shown to better visualize the substantia nigra and its inner organization, which allows better identification of potential targets for deep brain stimulation (DBS) compared to 3T MRI.

37.1.1.6 Epilepsy

Epilepsy is a complex neurological disorder associated with epileptic seizures caused by a sudden neuronal dysfunction. This dysfunction can be caused by structural abnormalities, such as dysplastic tissue or calcifications. MRI is a highly sensitive modality for identifying these potentially epileptogenic regions and selecting patients for surgical treatment.

Given the gain in CNR and SNR at 7T, it is not surprising that UHF MRI has been found to be superior in detecting possible epileptogenic zones compared to MR scans at 3T or 1.5T. UHF MRI was able to reveal structural abnormalities not previously detected at 3T in patients with focal cortical dysplasia (FCD), and the lesions appeared more distinct compared to 3T scans. Similar results have been found for patients with focal epilepsy and drug-resistant epilepsy. Furthermore, a greater soft-tissue contrast of the hippocampal architecture could be achieved in patients suffering from mesial temporal sclerosis (MTS) by employing 7T MRI. Likewise, Zhang et al. found that UHF MRI may improve visualization of the internal hippocampal structure. However, the gain in image resolution at 7T did not add predictive value concerning the surgical outcome (Zhang et al., 2019). See Fig. 37.2.

In addition to better detection of structural lesions, UHF MRI might also enable the identification of new MR biomarkers associated with epilepsy. Multi-echo gradient-echo MRI at 7T has been applied to investigate the cortical microstructure in patients with FCD, and higher frequency shifts have been associated with regions of dysplastic tissue. Feldman et al. found asymmetric distribution of perivascular spaces in patients with epilepsy by using a T_2-weighted SE sequence at 7T (Feldman et al., 2018). Thus the quantification of perivascular spaces could be a potential novel MR biomarker for studying epilepsy and might help identify or confirm suspected seizure onset zones. Moreover, the investigation of hippocampal and temporal lobe volumes and fluctuation amplitudes measured at 7T revealed lateralization effects in patients with temporal lobe epilepsy, whereas healthy controls demonstrated a symmetric distribution, thus providing a potential method to detect local abnormalities.

The image quality provided by ultra-high field strengths has already been shown to be helpful for detecting structural lesions and epileptogenic zones. At the same time, UHF MRI facilitates the search for new MR biomarkers for studying the effects of epilepsy on the human brain. This might lead to more precise diagnosis of epilepsy subtypes in the future and contribute to presurgical decision-making.

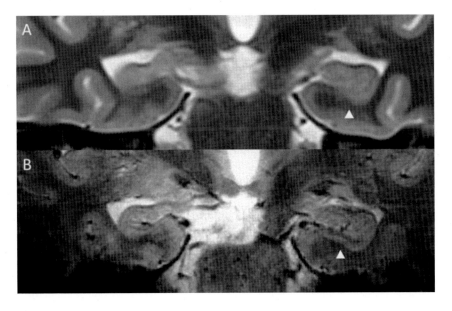

FIGURE 37.2

Patient with mesial temporal sclerosis in the right hippocampal formation (arrow head) with (A) T_2-weighted coronal slice acquired at 3T and (B) a T_2^*-weighted gradient-echo (GE) image acquired at 7T, with greater structural detail. Figure from Obusez *et al. Neuroimage*, 168, 459–476, 2018.

37.1.2 Proton MRS

Magnetic resonance spectroscopy (MRS) is an effective tool for investigating metabolites and neurotransmitters and their turn-over rates. This non-invasive and non-ionizing imaging technique offers the capability to measure over 20 metabolites and compounds in the human brain, thus playing an important role in neuroimaging. Proton MRS, either as a single-voxel or multivoxel method, is primarily applied in clinical practice, because protons have the highest MR sensitivity. In this context, UHF MRI provides increased spectral resolution and sensitivity that markedly improve the obtained spectra (see Chapters 32 and 33). MRS has to be considered as part of a combined diagnostic approach, including morphologic and functional MRI, whereby complementary methods, such as dynamic contrast-enhanced MRI, can be employed to detect areas of increased vascularization.

37.1.2.1 Feasibility studies

In 2001, Tkáč and colleagues demonstrated the feasibility of 7T ^{1}H MRS in 18 healthy subjects (Hingerl et al., 2020). Characteristic spectral patterns of metabolites, e.g., myo-inositol and taurine, were discernible in the *in vivo* spectra, and overlapping multiplets of J-coupled spin systems, such as glutamine and glutamate, could be resolved. At 9.4T, Nassirpour and colleagues recently demonstrated that high-resolution (97 μL nominal voxel size) metabolite maps can be acquired in 3.75 minutes by combining an improved sensitivity encoding (SENSE) reconstruction with a B_0 correction of spatially

594   Chapter 37 Clinical applications of high field magnetic resonance

over-discretized magnetic resonance spectroscopic imaging (MRSI) data (Nassirpour et al., 2018). The acquired data included spectra of 18 brain metabolites.

37.1.2.2 Brain tumors

In patients with glioma, metabolite maps obtained at 7T enable the assessment of an extended neurochemical profile compared to 3T approaches, and the identification of metabolic activities beyond morphologically visible deviations. Hingerl et al. used a free induction decay MRSI sequence with rapid concentric ring trajectory at 7T for metabolic mapping (8 metabolites) of the whole cerebrum (Hingerl et al., 2020). In one patient with glioma, 200% higher choline, up to 100% increased glutamine, and increased glycine were found in tumor tissue. Since increased choline (Cho) levels are also observed in benign disorders, e.g., in inflammation, the specificity of MRS may significantly increase through the acquisition and evaluation of multiple metabolites, as now available at UHF. Therefore such insights into metabolic features could further our understanding of the altered pathophysiological metabolism in tumors with impact on therapy planning and prognostication.

37.1.2.3 Other applications

Investigations in patients with MS demonstrated the potential of MRS at 7T to quantify biomarkers, such as glutathione (GSH), γ-aminobutyric acid (GABA), glutamate, and other metabolites relevant in MS. Furthermore, 7T MRS has been applied in patients with amyotrophic lateral sclerosis (ALS). In a study performed by Atassi et al., 13 ALS participants and 12 age-matched healthy controls (HC) underwent 7T MRI and MRS. N-acetylaspartate (NAA) was decreased by 17% and glutamate (Glu) was decreased by 15% in people with ALS compared to controls, indicating neuronal injury and/or loss in the precentral gyrus (Atassi et al., 2017). Therefore 7T ^{1}H MRS may enable non-invasive assessment of molecular changes related to neuronal injury and/or loss in patients with MS and neurodegenerative, or neuroinflammatory diseases.

37.1.3 Quantitative exchange-label turnover (qELT) for measuring metabolic fluxes

qELT is a quantitative magnetic resonance spectroscopy (qMRS) technique that permits the measurement of metabolic fluxes. The method is based on proton (^{1}H) magnetic resonance spectroscopy for quantifying the exchange between deuterium (^{2}H) and protons (Rich et al., 2020). qELT was inspired by recent studies highlighting the ability of deuterium MRS (DMRS) to measure metabolic kinetics after the administration of deuterated substances. However, deuterium exhibits low sensitivity in comparison to protons. With qELT, Rich et al. unified the advantages of the high sensitivity provided by ^{1}H spectroscopy with the ability of DMRS to furnish information about metabolic kinetics.

This method is especially useful for quantification of compounds involved in energy metabolism, such as glucose (Glc) and lactate. The requirements of deuterium-labeled glucose and standard MR scanners with proton spectroscopy are easy to fulfill and make this method easily applicable. The measurement is performed 60 minutes after administration of [6,6'-^{2}H$_2$] Glc, allowing the deuterium-labeled substrate to be metabolized to detect its various downstream metabolites, including deuterated lactate, deuterated GABA, and glycine. Some of the most important findings of Rich et al. include the feasibility of detecting lactate and other glycolytic metabolites in glioblastoma through single-voxel acquisition, showing similar results compared to previous studies employing DMRS. Furthermore, qELT permits *in vivo* mapping of cerebral metabolism by providing insights into cerebral energy consumption and neurotransmitter levels. qELT broadens the applicability of MR spectroscopy immensely by enabling the effective measurement of metabolic fluxes.

37.1.4 Functional MRI at ultra-high field strengths

At 3T, a spatial resolution of about $2 \times 2 \times 2$ mm^3 is attainable for fMRI images based on the blood-oxygenation-level-dependent (BOLD) signal. The resolution at 7T profits from higher SNR together with reduced partial volume effects, which renders an improved resolution of about $1 \times 1 \times 1$ mm^3. This resolution, in conjunction with a higher CNR at UHF strengths, enables improved visualization of the anatomical organization of the cortex, the cerebellum, and subcortical structures, permitting more detailed investigation of neuronal organization (see Chapters 17 and 36) and leading to a better understanding of brain connectivity. The application of fMRI at UHF has emerged as a powerful technique in neuroimaging and an unparalleled tool for investigating neuronal activity. See Fig. 37.3.

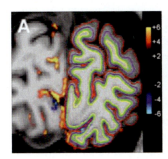
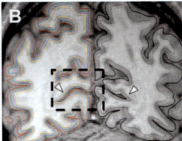
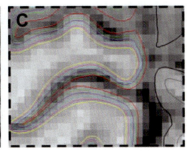

FIGURE 37.3

UHF MRI renders laminar analysis of fMRI activation possible. (A) The activation patterns are projected onto the high-resolution anatomical data. (B) Single axial slice of multi-echo MPRAGE data with cortical surface reconstruction overlaid; (C) magnified view of right calcarine sulcus. Figure from Polimeni et al. *Neuroimage*, 52, 1334–46, 2010.

37.1.5 Chemical exchange saturation transfer (CEST)

Chemical exchange saturation transfer (CEST) MRI is a state-of-the-art technique that permits large signal amplification of low-concentration molecules *in vivo* (see Chapter 25). CEST MRI approaches are based on the chemical exchange between solute-bound protons and protons of free bulk water. Solute-bound protons are labeled by selective radiofrequency (RF) saturation. The subsequent proton exchange leads to a magnetization transfer to free bulk water that to a large extent depends on the concentration of cellular proteins. Therefore CEST MRI may add valuable information in diagnostic oncology prior to invasive procedures and in the follow-up setting for therapy monitoring.

The majority of CEST studies published have aimed at quantifying the amide proton transfer (APT) effect that resonates at approximately +3.5 parts per million (ppm) relative to the water proton signal. The APT signal is most commonly assessed using the magnetization transfer ratio asymmetry (MTR$_{asym}$) approach proposed by Zhou et al. (2003), usually referred to as APT-weighted (APT-w) MRI in the literature.

596 **Chapter 37** Clinical applications of high field magnetic resonance

UHF scanners and newly proposed metrics have enabled more sophisticated quantifications that allow correction of confounding effects. These include, for example, conventional broad magnetization transfer (MT), direct water saturation (spillover), and interfering metabolite resonances, by using multi-pool Lorentzian fit analysis on data with high spectral resolution (Zaiss et al., 2015). Beyond that, such approaches make the simultaneous quantification of multiple CEST pools possible (e.g., relayed nuclear Overhauser effects (rNOE) and amine resonances). Consequently, CEST MRI extends the available repertoire of MR biomarkers in diagnostic oncology and is currently being investigated in numerous clinical studies.

37.1.5.1 Clinical applications

Early response assessment and prognostication are major challenges in daily clinical decision making for patients with glioma. Investigations of APT-w MRI during the follow-up (or ongoing therapy) in patients with glioma consistently reported increased APT signals in progressive tumors compared to tumors classified as stable disease or treatment-related changes. Additionally, the APT signal was found to be inversely correlated with survival and progression-free survival (PFS) in patients with glioma. rNOE imaging during ongoing radiotherapy also enabled treatment responders to be distinguished from non-responders in patients with glioma. In patients with newly diagnosed glioma, APT and rNOE CEST signals were shown to be associated with a response to first-line chemo-radiation therapy prior to treatment.

Regarding histopathologic features, APT(-w) CEST MRI has been shown to correlate with WHO tumor grade. APT-mediated CEST signals were also shown to be associated with the IDH mutation status in newly diagnosed gliomas. Mutations in enzymes encoded by the IDH gene cause widespread downregulation of protein expression, resulting in decreased APT signals in IDH-mutant gliomas. For rNOE effects, associations with tumor grade and cellularity have also been found. rNOE signals were found to be decreased in both high-grade and low-grade glioma. See Fig. 37.4.

The vast majority of CEST studies at UHF have been applied in neuro-oncological diseases. Few non-oncologic applications of CEST MRI have so far been reported at UHF, whereas various studies covering a broad disease spectrum have been published on CEST MRI at 3T, particularly in stroke. At 7T, a multi-pool CEST MRI approach, including APT and rNOE imaging, has recently been demonstrated by Msayib and colleagues in patients with acute ischemic stroke (Msayib et al., 2019).

Another promising CEST technique established at 7T has been reported by Davis et al. for the detection of glutamate in the human brain, named GluCEST MRI (Davis et al., 2015). GluCEST has been shown to correctly lateralize temporal lobe seizure in patients with previously determined non-lesional temporal lobe epilepsy. Furthermore, peritumoral GluCEST signals were found to be associated with recent seizures and drug-refractory epilepsy in patients with glioma. Generally, CEST MRI may extend the repertoire of available MR biomarkers that could assist in the non-invasive diagnosis and follow-up of patients with various diseases.

37.1.6 Dynamic glucose-enhanced (DGE) MRI

Direct detection of glucose using MRI or MRS is constrained by limited spatial resolution even at UHF, because of the very low *in vivo* glucose concentration. The spontaneous exchange between the five hydroxyl groups of d-glucose and the protons of free bulk water is the common physical principle of existing glucose-enhanced MRI approaches. The indirect detection via the water proton signal

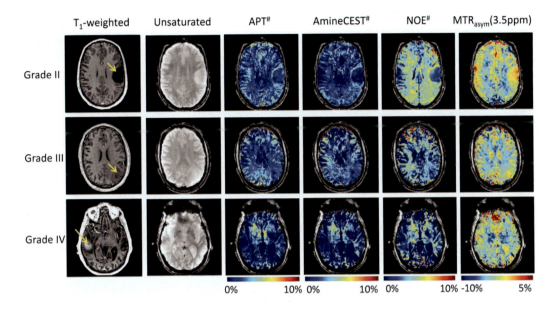

FIGURE 37.4

Comparison of MR signals (from left to right: T_1-weighted, unsaturated, and APT#, AmineCEST#, NOE#, and MTR$_{asym}$ (3.5 ppm) maps superimposed on corresponding unsaturated image) from three different patients with WHO Grade II, III, and IV tumor, respectively. Figure from Heo *et al. J Magn Reson Imaging*, 44, 41-50, 2016.

yields strong (negative) signal amplification proportional to the local glucose concentration. DGE MRI contrasts are calculated as (relative) signal intensity differences between a timepoint *t* and a reference signal obtained from baseline acquisitions prior to intravenous glucose administration. Consequently, DGE MRI contrasts are prone to motion-induced artifacts and require sophisticated motion correction approaches to reduce these artifacts.

In contrast to clinically used gadolinium-based MR contrast agents, glucose is not confined to the intravascular space and the extracellular extravascular space. Glucose signal changes can therefore theoretically be attributed to concentration changes in the intravascular space, the extravascular and extracellular space, and the intracellular space. Future studies are needed to continue the evaluation of the origin of the measured glucose signal and the potential benefit for clinical routine.

37.1.6.1 Clinical applications

First applications in patients with glioma were performed by Xu et al. employing CEST MRI (Xu et al., 2015) and by Schuenke et al. and Paech et al. using an adiabatically prepared CESL approach (Schuenke et al., 2017; Paech et al., 2017). Increased glucose concentrations were found in areas of disrupted blood-brain barrier (BBB), partially overlapping with gadolinium-enhanced T_1-weighted images and relative cerebral blood volume (rCBV) maps. Increased glucose concentrations were also reported in areas outside the disrupted BBB. Future studies may correlate such findings with the results of histopathological analysis following surgical treatment.

598 **Chapter 37** Clinical applications of high field magnetic resonance

In addition to major signal contributions from BBB leakage and tissue perfusion, CEST and CESL signals may also be altered by pH, because an acidic tumor microenvironment can enhance DGE signals through proton exchange rate modulation. Recently, the feasibility of DGE MRI has been demonstrated at 3T field strength (Herz et al., 2019). However, small effect sizes currently limit robust signal quantification at field strengths less than 7T. For this reason, DGE MRI may gain further attention for clinical applications in the near future as the number of UHF scanners in clinical imaging continuously increases.

37.2 X-nuclei imaging in metabolic and functional imaging

The trend toward higher field strengths not only offers higher resolution for proton (^{1}H) imaging, but also increases the applicability of X-nuclei imaging and spectroscopy. The term X-nuclei unites all non-proton nuclei with a non-vanishing spin, such as sodium (^{23}Na), phosphorous (^{31}P), potassium (^{39}K), chlorine (^{35}Cl and ^{37}Cl), fluorine (^{19}F), and the oxygen-17 isotope (^{17}O). These nuclei are directly involved in many biological processes. Hence, X-nuclei imaging is able to provide metabolic and functional information that cannot be obtained via conventional proton MRI. However, low sensitivity and concentration, short relaxation times, and complex MR interactions pose challenges. Nonetheless, these imaging markers have received attention, as they provide access to cerebral metabolism, ionic fluxes, and cell homeostasis in a non-invasive manner.

A prerequisite for MRI is a non-vanishing spin resulting in a magnetic moment, brought about by an odd number of protons and/or neutrons. The most important nuclei for MR imaging and their magnetic properties are listed in Table 37.1.

Table 37.1 Overview of the nuclei most commonly used for MRI and their physical properties. The spin is designated with I, whereas γ corresponds to the gyromagnetic ratio, α to the natural abundance, and Z to the abundance in the human body. The relative SNR of the X-nuclei compared to conventional proton SNR is specified at the same concentration. Table modified from Ladd, 2018 (*in:* Schlegel W., Karger C.P., Jäkel O. (eds.) *Medizinische Physik*. Berlin, Heidelberg: Springer Spektrum) and Ladd et al. *Prog Nucl Magn Reson Spectrosc*, 109, 1–5, 2018.

Nucleus	I [$\hbar$]	γ [MHz/T]	α [%]	Relative sensitivity [%]	SNR relative to ^{1}H [%]	Typical *in vivo* concentration c [mol/L] of the isotope
^{1}H	1/2	42.6	99.99	100	100	79
^{17}O	5/2	-5.8	0.04	0.0011	0.00815	0.015
^{19}F	1/2	40.1	100	83.3	88.5	≈ 0.001
^{23}Na	3/2	11.3	100	9.25	35.0	0.041
^{31}P	1/2	17.2	100	6.63	16.4	0.003*
^{35}Cl	3/2	4.2	75.78	0.356	3.64	0.027
^{39}K	3/2	2.0	93.26	0.0473	1.02	0.108

* *For ^{31}P, the in vivo concentration is given for PCr in brain tissue.*

37.2.1 Sodium-23 (^{23}Na) MRI

In X-nuclei MRI, sodium ^{23}Na imaging is one of the most established MR techniques, due to its high natural abundance in the human body and its relatively high gyromagnetic ratio compared to other X-nuclei.

Sodium plays a vital role in many physiologic processes. The flux of sodium ions in organisms drives the transmission of action potentials, maintenance of cell homeostasis, and regulation of physical properties, such as pH, blood volume, and blood pressure. In brain tissue, 80% of the total sodium is distributed within the cells, though at a much lower concentration ($[Na^+]_i$ = 8-15 mM) than in the extracellular compartment ($[Na^+]_e$ = 145 mM). This gradient is sustained by the ubiquitous Na^+/K^+-ATP pump, illustrated in Fig. 37.5. On this basis, it is evident that sodium MRI offers a wide variety of possible applications for the investigation of physiologic and pathophysiologic processes in the human body, and has proven useful for investigating neurodegeneration and neuroinflammation, brain tumors, energetic imbalances, and excitability disturbances.

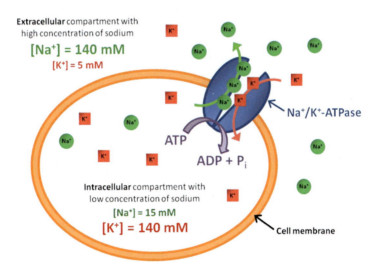

FIGURE 37.5

The Na^+/K^+-ATP pump transports two potassium ions inside the cell in exchange for three sodium ions, creating a chemical and electrogenic gradient. Figure from Madelin and Regatte, *J Magn Reson Imaging*, 38, 511–29, 2013.

37.2.1.1 Multiple sclerosis

MS is a potentially disabling neuroinflammatory disease of the central nervous system most commonly diagnosed in young adults. The first study to investigate MS using ^{23}Na MRI was conducted in 2013 by Inglese et al. at a field strength of 3T; they found that patients with MS showed increased tissue sodium concentration levels in acute and chronic lesions and in normal-appearing white matter compared to healthy controls (Inglese et al., 2010). Since then, brain sodium accumulation has been positively cor-

600 **Chapter 37** Clinical applications of high field magnetic resonance

related with disability, disease progression, lesion evolution, and cognitive impairment. Furthermore, sodium is highly sensitive to disruption of the BBB and vasogenic tissue edema in contrast-enhancing lesions, and was found to be a promising marker for monitoring patients with progressive MS. According to Fleysher et al., technical advances, such as triple quantum filtered ^{23}Na MRI (Fleysher et al., 2010), provide information about the intracellular sodium concentration and the intracellular volume fraction in MS. The increase in the total sodium concentration (TSC) was found to be caused mainly by neuronal mitochondrial dysfunction. A recent study showed that intralesional heterogeneity could be observed when employing high-resolution ^{23}Na MRI, potentially making contrast-enhancing media unnecessary if the lesion is of sufficient size.

37.2.1.2 Brain cancer

Apart from MS, ^{23}Na MRI has also been used to characterize cerebral tumors non-invasively. As early as the late 1990s, focal brain tumor growth could be monitored employing sodium imaging. The TSC is increased in brain tumor tissue compared to normal-appearing areas, thus ^{23}Na MRI has been used for characterizing tumor proliferation and evaluation of therapy response (Laymon et al., 2012). Sodium MRI for brain tumor imaging has been compared to other imaging techniques, such as ^{1}H spectroscopy, ^{18}F-fluoroethyltyrosine (FET) positron emission tomography (PET), ^{18}F-fluorodeoxyglucose (FDG) PET, and ^{18}F-fluorothymidine (FLT) PET, as seen in Fig. 37.6. Though ^{23}Na MRI showed some advantages over these modalities, more patient data are needed to investigate the potential of sodium imaging for diagnostics and therapy assessment.

37.2.1.3 Other applications in neuroimaging

A variety of other cerebral diseases have been explored with ^{23}Na MRI. Abnormal sodium concentrations in tissue have proved to be a potential marker for pathophysiologic processes in neurodegenerative diseases, such as amyotrophic lateral sclerosis, Huntington's disease, and AD. Shimizu et al. conducted a study examining changes on ^{23}Na MRI after cerebral infarction (Shimizu et al., 1993). The use of a double-tuned ^{1}H/^{23}Na head coil and an optimized protocol have shortened the examination time of clinical sodium imaging, even enabling the investigation of acute stroke within 22 minutes of acquisition time (Neumaier-Probst et al., 2015). Furthermore, Grover et al. found that ionic dysfunction in symptomatic patients with mild traumatic brain injury can be visualized through ^{23}Na MRI (Grover et al., 2018). Sodium measurements of patients with migraine revealed increased sodium concentration in the cerebral spinal fluid compared to healthy controls, indicating a possible therapeutic approach. The first non-invasive evidence of altered sodium concentrations in epilepsy has recently been demonstrated by Ridley et al. The results showed a decrease in sodium concentration in the epileptogenic region directly after seizure, whereas the sodium levels were chronically elevated during interictal phases (Ridley et al., 2017). Overall, ^{23}Na MRI is emerging as a promising tool in the field of neuroimaging with broad applicability.

37.2.2 Dynamic oxygen-17 (^{17}O) MRI

The 17-oxygen isotope (^{17}O) is non-toxic and the only stable oxygen isotope that can be detected via MRI. The natural abundance of ^{17}O is very low (0.038%); therefore the concentration of the isotope is usually enhanced through inhalation of enriched ^{17}O$_2$ gas during the measurement. The oxygen

37.2 X-nuclei imaging in metabolic and functional imaging

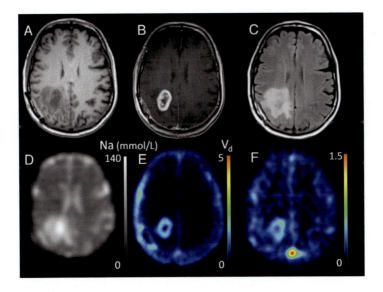

FIGURE 37.6

Patient with right-sided posterior frontoparietal glioblastoma. The images include a (A) MPRAGE structural MRI, (B) contrast-enhanced T_1 MRI, (C) fluid-attenuated inversion recovery (FLAIR), (D) sodium MRI, (E) F-18 FLT PET tracer distribution volume, and (F) a normalized F-18 FLT PET image (0 to 2 minutes post tracer injection) showing early tracer wash-in. The MR images were acquired at 3T. Figure from Laymon et al. *Magn Reson Imaging*, 30, 1268–78, 2012.

isotope is only detectable by MRI when bound in water ($H_2^{17}O$), which is produced through oxidative phosphorylation in mitochondria. The signal of this metabolized tissue water can then be measured using ^{17}O MRI. The cerebral metabolic rate of oxygen consumption (CMRO$_2$) can be determined by fitting a metabolic model to the dynamic $H_2^{17}O$ signal. Hence, ^{17}O MRI is a promising imaging technique for investigating cerebral oxygen metabolism in a direct manner.

37.2.2.1 Clinical applications

The unfavorable MR properties of ^{17}O make the application of this method quite challenging. These properties, in conjunction with the extreme cost of $^{17}O_2$ gas (approximately $2000 per liter), have resulted in only a limited number of clinical studies with ^{17}O MRI. In the clinical context, this method has been primarily used for brain tumor imaging. Hoffmann et al. were the first to demonstrate the feasibility of clinical ^{17}O MRI by examining a patient with glioblastoma. They found decreased CMRO$_2$ values within the tumor tissue and highlighted the importance of partial-volume correction (PVC) for ^{17}O data to improve the accuracy of quantitative CMRO$_2$ values (Hoffmann et al., 2014). Recently, Paech and colleagues conducted a study employing dynamic ^{17}O MRI to compare patients with brain tumors to healthy controls (Paech et al., 2020). See Fig. 37.7. They found that both high-grade and low-grade gliomas exhibited a decrease in CMRO$_2$ in the tumor volume in accordance with the Warburg effect.

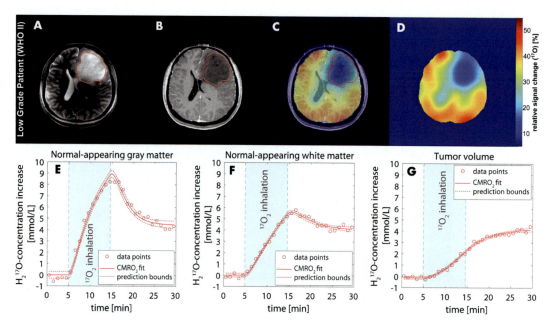

FIGURE 37.7

Dynamic and anatomical information from a patient with low-grade brain tumor. Images include: (A) structural T_2 MRI, (B) contrast-enhanced MPRAGE MRI and relative ^{17}O signal change, (C) with MPRAGE overlay and (D) without. The corresponding signal evolution with metabolic fits are provided for (E) normal-appearing gray matter, (F) normal-appearing white matter, and (G) tumor volume. Figure from Paech et al. Radiology, 295, 181–189, 2020.

Beyond brain tumors, ^{17}O MRI offers great potential for investigating oxygen metabolism in patients with stroke. In contrast to the BOLD effect, CMRO$_2$ and oxygen extraction fraction (OEF) can be directly quantified, and the method is logistically more accessible for acute ischemic stroke than 15-oxygen PET, since the latter requires a cyclotron on site. Other possible applications of this modality are neurodegenerative diseases, such as AD or PD.

37.2.3 Phosphorus-31 (^{31}P) MR spectroscopy

Though ^{1}H MRS is the most prevalent method in the field of spectroscopy, phosphorous (^{31}P) spectroscopy provides complementary information about cellular energy expenditure and membrane metabolism. ^{31}P spectroscopy permits the detection of energy substrates, such as adenosine-triphosphate (ATP), adenosine-diphosphate (ADP), phosphocreatine (PCr), and free phosphate (Pi). The intracellular pH level can be deduced indirectly from the shift difference between the PCr and Pi resonances. The detection of the phosphomonoesters phosphorylethanolamine (PE) and phosphorylcholine (PC), as well as the phosphodiesters glycerophosphorylethanolamine (GPE) and glycerophosphorylcholine (GPC), yields structural and functional information about the cellular and mitochondrial membranes.

37.2.3.1 Clinical applications

^{31}P spectroscopy has been used to investigate numerous neurological diseases. Over the years, PD has in particular been a focus of ^{31}P spectroscopy research. With this method, mitochondrial dysfunction and alterations in membrane phospholipid metabolism have been identified as pathologic changes in patients with PD. Furthermore, hypometabolism in affected brain areas could be a possible predictor for cognitive impairment. In addition, ^{31}P spectroscopy is a suitable tool for differentiating metabolic patterns due to PINK1 gene mutation or based on differences in sex. However, no metabolic abnormalities were identified in early-stage PD. Barbiaroli et al. were able to detect abnormal phosphate metabolite and ion concentrations in multisystemic atrophy (MSA), hypothesizing that ^{31}P spectroscopy might be a non-invasive diagnostic tool for differentiating MSA from PD (Barbiroli et al., 1999). In patients with AD, one study reported that high-energy phosphate and membrane metabolism play a subordinate role in the pathophysiology of AD, whereas, more recently, another study showed increased PCr and pH levels in regions of early degeneration. Alterations in mitochondrial function detected via ^{31}P spectroscopy have also been reported for epilepsy and in patients suffering from acute traumatic brain injury.

At high magnetic fields, ^{31}P spectroscopy profits from increased SNR, and thus better resolution, enabling the measurement of the creatine kinase rate and ATP synthesis rate in the human brain at 7T. Moreover, the nicotinamide adenine nucleotide (abbreviated as NAD^+, in the oxidized and NADH in the reduced state) content and the NAD^+/NADH redox state can be detected by employing ^{31}P spectroscopy. A method called proton observed phosphorous editing (POPE) results in improved detection of ^{1}H–^{31}P coupled metabolites *in vivo*. Finally, Mirkes and colleagues demonstrated the feasibility of high-resolution pH mapping in the human brain and patients with brain tumors at 9.4T (see Fig. 37.8). Overall, ^{31}P spectroscopy is a versatile method for investigating energy and membrane metabolism in the human brain, giving insights into the pathophysiology of cerebral diseases.

37.2.4 Other X-nuclei

37.2.4.1 Exploring cellular homeostasis employing ^{35}Cl and ^{39}K MRI

Together with sodium and calcium, chlorine and potassium are among the most common ions in the human body. These ions play an important role in cellular excitability and signal transmission. In comparison with sodium, the sensitivity, and therefore the SNR, of ^{35}Cl and ^{39}K MRI is very low, which is why obtaining clinical images with these modalities in justifiable scan time is challenging. However, the value of ^{35}Cl and ^{39}K MRI in neuroimaging has been demonstrated in rats for a glioma and stroke model, bringing attention to these imaging techniques.

The feasibility of potassium ^{39}K MRI in humans has been shown in the last decade. Whereas this method is used solely in non-clinical neuroimaging studies, the focus of human ^{39}K MRI lies in cardiac and muscle imaging, because of the higher potassium concentration in these tissues. Nagel et al. conducted the first feasibility study for ^{35}Cl MRI in humans, examining muscle and brain tissue in healthy controls and patients with glioblastoma (Nagel et al., 2014). The results showed an increase in chlorine within the tumor tissue, yielding insight into pathologic changes in cancer.

37.2.4.2 ^{19}F MRI for excellent specificity

Fluorine-19 exhibits almost the same sensitivity as proton MRI, but its abundance in the human body is almost zero. In light of this fact, fluorinated compounds can be applied as exogenous MR-detectable

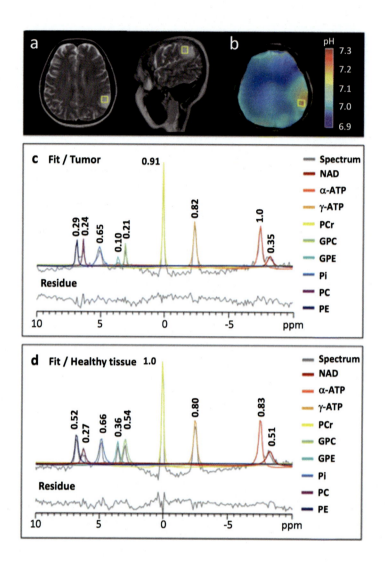

FIGURE 37.8

Anatomical images and data obtained with ^{31}P MRS from a patient with suspected high-grade glioma with adjacent low-grade glioma anteriorly, hardly visible. (A) turbo-spin-echo (TSE) images, (B) pH maps with slightly alkaline pH visible in both tumor areas, (C) fitted ^{31}P spectrum from highlighted voxel in TSE image within the brain lesion, (D) ^{31}P spectrum of the contralateral healthy hemisphere. Figure from Mirkes *et al*. MAGMA, 29, 579–89, 2016.

tracers, offering high specificity and enabling the observation of various biological processes without background signal. At the present time, ^{19}F MRI is used primarily in preclinical research focusing on macrophage response in inflammatory processes, such as myocarditis or after cerebral infarction. Recently, this modality has also been established for lung imaging and used in healthy volunteers and patients with various lung diseases.

37.2.4.3 Perspectives for X-nuclei imaging

In conclusion, X-nuclei imaging provides a non-invasive measure for investigating cerebral metabolism, cellular homeostasis, and numerous neurological diseases, thus proving to be an effective neuroimaging tool. To date, X-nuclei imaging modalities are predominantly used in preclinical research. In the future, with increasing magnetic field strengths and in the light of new technical developments, X-nuclei imaging could play an important role in clinical routine.

37.3 Impact of UHF in clinical neuroimaging

The introduction of UHF scanners has had a major influence on the possibilities in neuroimaging. All MRI techniques, including susceptibility-weighted, structural, and angiographic, profit considerably from the boost in SNR and CNR, which permits high-resolution imaging. This enables the precise visualization of anatomical sub-structures or cerebral blood flow, greatly benefiting clinical decision-making in the field of vascular and neurological diseases. Furthermore, UHF proton imaging permits the identification of novel MR biomarkers that provide information about diseases, such as brain cancer or epilepsy. In addition to this gain in morphological information, UHF imaging enhances the specificity of functional imaging techniques, or even renders their application possible for the first time in a clinical setting. For fMRI, advances in field strength permit sub-millimeter detection of the BOLD signal, providing insights into brain connectivity. The advent of UHF scanners has sparked significant progress in preclinical techniques, such as qELT, CEST imaging, DGE MRI or X-nuclei imaging, techniques that furnish metabolic information about physiological and pathophysiological processes.

UHF MRI already plays a key role in neuroscience and preclinical neuro research, and its role in clinical diagnostics is sure to expand as more systems with clinical approval as medical devices are installed. In the future, further increases in field strength will advance our capabilities in clinical research and surely lead to significant advances in these imaging techniques.

References

Atassi, N., Xu, M., Triantafyllou, C., Keil, B., Lawson, R., Cernasov, P., Ratti, E., Long, C.J., Paganoni, S., Murphy, A., Salibi, N., Seethamraju, R., Rosen, B., Ratai, E.-M., 2017. Ultra high-field (7tesla) magnetic resonance spectroscopy in amyotrophic lateral sclerosis. PLoS ONE 12, e0177680.

Barbiroli, B., Martinelli, P., Patuelli, A., Lodi, R., Iotti, S., Cortelli, P., Montagna, P., 1999. Phosphorus magnetic resonance spectroscopy in multiple system atrophy and Parkinson's disease. Mov. Disord. 14, 430–435.

Davis, K.A., Nanga, R.P., Das, S., Chen, S.H., Hadar, P.N., Pollard, J.R., Lucas, T.H., Shinohara, R.T., Litt, B., Hariharan, H., Elliott, M.A., Detre, J.A., Reddy, R., 2015. Glutamate imaging (GluCEST) lateralizes epileptic foci in nonlesional temporal lobe epilepsy. Sci. Transl. Med. 7, 309ra161.

Deistung, A., SchÄFer, A., Schweser, F., Biedermann, U., GÜLlmar, D., Trampel, R., Turner, R., Reichenbach, J., 2013. High-resolution MR imaging of the human brainstem in vivo at 7 Tesla. Front. Human Neurosci. 7.

Eapen, M., Zald, D.H., Gatenby, J.C., Ding, Z., Gore, J.C., 2011. Using high-resolution MR imaging at 7T to evaluate the anatomy of the midbrain dopaminergic system. Am. J. Neuroradiol. 32, 688–694.

Feldman, R.E., Rutland, J.W., Fields, M.C., Marcuse, L.V., Pawha, P.S., Delman, B.N., Balchandani, P., 2018. Quantification of perivascular spaces at 7T: a potential MRI biomarker for epilepsy. Seizure 54, 11–18.

606 Chapter 37 Clinical applications of high field magnetic resonance

Fleysher, L., Oesingmann, N., Inglese, M., 2010. B(0) inhomogeneity-insensitive triple-quantum-filtered sodium imaging using a 12-step phase-cycling scheme. NMR Biomed. 23, 1191–1198.

Grover, H., Qian, Y., Boada, F.E., Lakshmanan, K., Flanagan, S., Lui, Y.W., 2018. MRI evidence of altered callosal sodium in mild traumatic brain injury. Am. J. Neuroradiol. 39, 2200–2204.

Herz, K., Lindig, T., Deshmane, A., Schittenhelm, J., Skardelly, M., Bender, B., Ernemann, U., Scheffler, K., Zaiss, M., 2019. T1ρ-based dynamic glucose-enhanced (DGEρ) MRI at 3 T: method development and early clinical experience in the human brain. Magn. Reson. Med. 82, 1832–1847.

Hingerl, L., Strasser, B., Moser, P., Hangel, G., Motyka, S., Heckova, E., Gruber, S., Trattnig, S., Bogner, W., 2020. Clinical high-resolution 3D-MR spectroscopic imaging of the human brain at 7 T. Invest. Radiol. 55, 239–248.

Hoffmann, S.H., Radbruch, A., Bock, M., Semmler, W., Nagel, A.M., 2014. Direct (17)O MRI with partial volume correction: first experiences in a glioblastoma patient. MAGMA 27, 579–587.

Inglese, M., Madelin, G., Oesingmann, N., Babb, J.S., Wu, W., Stoeckel, B., Herbert, J., Johnson, G., 2010. Brain tissue sodium concentration in multiple sclerosis: a sodium imaging study at 3 tesla. Brain 133, 847–857.

Laymon, C.M., Oborski, M.J., Lee, V.K., Davis, D.K., Wiener, E.C., Lieberman, F.S., Boada, F.E., Mountz, J.M., 2012. Combined imaging biomarkers for therapy evaluation in glioblastoma multiforme: correlating sodium MRI and F-18 FLT PET on a voxel-wise basis. Magn. Reson. Imaging 30, 1268–1278.

Msayib, Y., Harston, G.W.J., Tee, Y.K., Sheerin, F., Blockley, N.P., Okell, T.W., Jezzard, P., Kennedy, J., Chappell, M.A., 2019. Quantitative CEST imaging of amide proton transfer in acute ischaemic stroke. NeuroImage Clin. 23, 101833.

Nagel, A.M., Lehmann-Horn, F., Weber, M.A., Jurkat-Rott, K., Wolf, M.B., Radbruch, A., Umathum, R., Semmler, W., 2014. In vivo 35Cl MR imaging in humans: a feasibility study. Radiology 271, 585–595.

Nassirpour, S., Chang, P., Kirchner, T., Henning, A., 2018. Over-discretized SENSE reconstruction and B0 correction for accelerated non-lipid-suppressed 1H FID MRSI of the human brain at 9.4 T. NMR Biomed. 31, e4014.

Neumaier-Probst, E., Konstandin, S., Ssozi, J., Groden, C., Hennerici, M., Schad, L.R., Fatar, M., 2015. A double-tuned (1) H/(23) Na resonator allows (1) H-guided (23) Na-MRI in ischemic stroke patients in one session. Int. J. Stroke 10 (Suppl A100), 56–61.

Noebauer-Huhmann, I.-M., Szomolanyi, P., Kronnerwetter, C., Widhalm, G., Weber, M., Nemec, S., Juras, V., Ladd, M.E., Prayer, D., Trattnig, S., 2015. Brain tumours at 7T MRI compared to 3T—contrast effect after half and full standard contrast agent dose: initial results. Eur. Radiol. 25, 106–112.

Novak, V., Abduljalil, A., Novak, P., Robitaille, P., 2005. High-resolution ultrahigh-field MRI of stroke. Magn. Reson. Imaging 23, 539–548.

Paech, D., Nagel, A.M., Schultheiss, M.N., Umathum, R., Regnery, S., Scherer, M., Wick, A., Platt, T., Wick, W., Bendszus, M., Unterberg, A., Schlemmer, H.P., Ladd, M.E., Niesporek, S.C., 2020. Quantitative dynamic oxygen 17 MRI at 7.0 T for the cerebral oxygen metabolism in glioma. Radiology 295, 181–189.

Paech, D., Schuenke, P., Koehler, C., Windschuh, J., Mundiyanapurath, S., Bickelhaupt, S., Bonekamp, D., Bäumer, P., Bachert, P., Ladd, M.E., Bendszus, M., Wick, W., Unterberg, A., Schlemmer, H.-P., Zaiss, M., Radbruch, A., 2017. T1ρ-weighted dynamic glucose-enhanced MR imaging in the human brain. Radiology 285, 914–922.

Rich, L.J., Bagga, P., Wilson, N.E., Schnall, M.D., Detre, J.A., Haris, M., Reddy, R., 2020. (1)H magnetic resonance spectroscopy of (2)H-to-(1)H exchange quantifies the dynamics of cellular metabolism in vivo. Nat. Biomed. Eng. 4, 335–342.

Ridley, B., Marchi, A., Wirsich, J., Soulier, E., Confort-Gouny, S., Schad, L., Bartolomei, F., Ranjeva, J.P., Guye, M., Zaaraoui, W., 2017. Brain sodium MRI in human epilepsy: disturbances of ionic homeostasis reflect the organization of pathological regions. NeuroImage 157, 173–183.

Schuenke, P., Koehler, C., Korzowski, A., Windschuh, J., Bachert, P., Ladd, M.E., Mundiyanapurath, S., Paech, D., Bickelhaupt, S., Bonekamp, D., Schlemmer, H.-P., Radbruch, A., Zaiss, M., 2017. Adiabatically prepared spin-lock approach for T1ρ-based dynamic glucose enhanced MRI at ultrahigh fields. Magn. Reson. Med. 78, 215–225.

Shimizu, T., Naritomi, H., Sawada, T., 1993. Sequential changes on 23Na MRI after cerebral infarction. Neuroradiology 35, 416–419.

Wrede, K.H., Matsushige, T., Goericke, S.L., Chen, B., Umutlu, L., Quick, H.H., Ladd, M.E., Johst, S., Forsting, M., Sure, U., 2017. Non-enhanced magnetic resonance imaging of unruptured intracranial aneurysms at 7 Tesla: comparison with digital subtraction angiography. Eur. Radiol. 27, 354–364.

Xu, X., Yadav, N.N., Knutsson, L., Hua, J., Kalyani, R., Hall, E., Laterra, J., Blakeley, J., Strowd, R., Pomper, M., 2015. Dynamic glucose-enhanced (DGE) MRI: translation to human scanning and first results in glioma patients. Tomography 1, 105.

Zaiss, M., Windschuh, J., Paech, D., Meissner, J.-E., Burth, S., Schmitt, B., Kickingereder, P., Wiestler, B., Wick, W., Bendszus, M., Schlemmer, H.-P., Ladd, M.E., Bachert, P., Radbruch, A., 2015. Relaxation-compensated CEST-MRI of the human brain at 7 T: unbiased insight into NOE and amide signal changes in human glioblastoma. NeuroImage 112, 180–188.

Zhang, Y., Lv, Y., You, H., Dou, W., Hou, B., Shi, L., Zuo, Z., Mao, W., Feng, F., 2019. Study of the hippocampal internal architecture in temporal lobe epilepsy using 7T and 3T MRI. Seizure 71, 116–123.

Zhou, J., Payen, J.-F., Wilson, D.A., Traystman, R.J., Van Zijl, P.C.M., 2003. Using the amide proton signals of intracellular proteins and peptides to detect pH effects in MRI. Nat. Med. 9, 1085–1090.

Index

0–9
3D diffusion imaging, 118
3D TOF, 477

A
Acceleration
  in-plane, 124
  scan, 439
  vessel wall imaging, 487
Acceleration-selective ASL, 183
Acquisition, 520
  balanced, 456
  Cartesian, 6, 7, 18
  DCE, 204
  DSC, 204
  DSI, 13
  DWI, 13, 109
  efficient, 187
  EPI, 14, 57, 116
  fMRI, 15, 47, 249, 585
  gradient-echo, 17
  GRE, 204
  HARDI, 13
  methods, 426, 427, 431
  MR, 24, 34
  MRF, 436
  MRI, 18, 19, 24
  MRSI, 520, 539, 541
  MSE, 427
  MT, 17
  partial Fourier, 23
  PROPELLER, 120, 121
  protocols, 5, 128, 195, 272, 507, 513
  scheme, 13, 47, 49, 63, 231, 234, 241, 243
  simultaneous multi-slice, 37
  snapshot, 13
  snapshot-CEST, 18
  spoiled, 456
  strategies, 10, 203, 440
  techniques, 109, 504, 522
  TOF, 477
Acute ischemic stroke, 211, 362, 367, 596, 602

Acute stroke, 211, 214, 362
Advanced acquisition methods, 205
Advanced localization techniques, 504
Advanced MRSI, 522, 532, 533
Advanced scanner hardware, 524
AIF
  global, 202
  local, 202
Along-the-tract analysis, 153
Alzheimer's disease neuroimaging initiative (ADNI), 8
Amide CEST MRI, 393
Amide proton transfer (APT), 595
Amine CEST signal, 394
Amyotrophic lateral sclerosis (ALS), 366, 513, 532, 594
Analysis
  along-the-tract, 153
  connectome-based, 153
  data-driven, 252
  fiber-tracking, 165
  fixel-based, 154
  group-level, 253
  multivariate, 252
  single-subject, 288
  statistical, 252, 315
  subject-level, 253
  tract geometry, 154
  tract-based, 151
  univariate, 252
  vessel wall imaging, 489
  voxel-wise, 150
  whole-brain, 253
Apparent diffusion coefficient (ADC), 158, 212
Arterial input function (AIF), 199
Arterial spin labeling (ASL), 15, 47, 179, 188, 211, 214, 231, 477, 567
Arterial transit time (ATT), 16, 184
Artifacts
  cause, 165
  EPI, 240
  from accelerated scans, 436
  ghosting, 46, 470, 472, 522

610 Index

streaking, 353
Artificial intelligence (AI), 12, 205
Atlas-based segmentation, 98
Auto-calibration signal (ACS), 11
Automated segmentation, 97
AxCaliber, 167
Axonal diameter distribution (ADD), 170

B

b-vecs, 138
B_0
  homogeneity, 507
  inhomogeneity, 242, 506–508, 555, 562
  shimming, 508, 509, 555, 562, 564
B_1
  inhomogeneities, 564, 565
  shimming, 504, 508, 567
B_1^+
  inhomogeneities, 454, 456, 508
Background fields, 344
Background suppression (BS), 184
Balanced acquisition, 456
Balanced steady-state free precession, 456
BASE-SLIM, 544
Bias, 74
  correction, 458
Biomarker, 319, 462
Biophysical modeling, 189
Biophysical models, 459
Biophysical tissue properties, 16
Blip-up-blip-down fieldmaps, 132
Block designs, 267
Blood
  flow, 16, 199, 206, 469, 470, 560
    velocity, 184
  magnetization, 49, 185
    water, 179, 180, 182, 183, 187
  signal, 179, 184, 375
Blood oxygenation level-dependent (BOLD), 560
Blood-brain-barrier (BBB), 16
Blood-oxygenation-level-dependent (BOLD), 232, 309, 595
BOLD
  fMRI, 279, 310, 573, 582
  signal, 14, 78, 247, 249–251, 253, 280, 310, 313, 319, 561, 577
Brain
  activation, 247, 258, 553, 581

activity, 14, 247, 255, 265, 277, 288, 309, 310, 314, 316, 324, 530, 576
aging, 328, 329
anatomical coordinate system, 53
anatomy, 11, 86, 147, 258, 589
cancer, 197, 198, 204, 279, 512, 590, 600
connectivity, 295, 323, 324, 329
connectome, 295, 328
function, 261, 277, 288, 323, 329, 553, 579, 584, 585
perfusion, 15, 16, 178, 196, 197
segmentation, 11, 96, 100
stem involvement, 361
surgery, 332
tumors, 153, 223, 279, 528, 529, 594
bSSFP acquisition, 456

C

Camera-based motion tracking systems, 58
Carotid artery, 491
Carr–Purcell–Meiboom–Gill (CPMG), 120, 454, 505
Cartesian acquisitions, 6, 7, 18
Cavernomas, 218, 280, 281, 361, 591
CBV fMRI, 582
Central vein sign, 363
Cerebral amyloid angiopathy (CAA), 360
Cerebral aneurysms, 495
Cerebral blood flow (CBF), 16, 177, 198, 212, 231, 367
Cerebral blood volume (CBV), 198, 212, 441, 561
Cerebral microbleeds, 346
Cerebral venous sinus thrombosis, 361
Cerebrovascular diseases, 211, 367
Cerebrovascular reserve, 215
Cerebrovascular response, 232
Chemical exchange saturation transfer (CEST), 17, 373, 388, 394, 398, 399, 555, 556, 558, 595, 598
  data, 392
  dynamic, 388
  effects, 389, 390, 392, 394, 396, 398, 399
  fingerprinting, 394
  MRI, 595, 596
  pool, 389, 391, 396, 596
  preparation, 392, 396, 398
  pulsed, 391
  sequence, 396, 556
    scheme, 392
Chemical shift displacement error (CSDE), 504, 524

Chronic hypoperfusion, 213, 215
Clinical
  applications, 528
  fMRI, 283, 285
  impact, 54
  neuroimaging, 605
  scales, 331
  translation, 31, 320, 333, 415, 436, 442
Clinico-radiological paradox, 330
Cloverleaf navigator, 63
Clustering segmentation methods, 99
Cognitive
  abilities, 324
  states, 326, 327
  subtraction, 263
Coil inhomogeneity, 130
Coil sensitivity, 23, 37, 44, 63, 64, 113, 119, 544
  calibration, 46
Coil-space navigator, 64
Collapsed fat navigator, 63
Collinearity, 75
Compartments, 460
Complex fiber architecture, 165
Compressed sensing (CS), 13, 30
Computed tomography (CT), 195, 213
Connectivity strength, 304
Connectome, 152, 153, 171, 295, 300, 302, 309, 324, 328, 330, 334
  approaches, 336
  brain, 295, 328
  features, 324, 326
  flexibility, 326
  functional, 309, 310, 318, 324, 326, 327, 334
    static, 325, 327
  structural, 297, 325, 327
Connectome-based analysis, 153
Connectomics, 329–332
Constrained spherical deconvolution (CSD), 154, 299
Continuous ASL (CASL), 181
Contrast
  agent, 49, 195–197, 342, 346, 363, 367, 388, 396, 479, 589, 591
    bolus, 196, 367
  enhancing lesions, 408
  estimates, 76
  FLAIR, 12
  methods, 470
  neuro MRI, 11

  phase, 473, 558
Contrast-based perfusion MRI, 195
Contrast-enhanced MRA (CE-MRA), 478
Convolutional neural networks (CNN), 547
Coronal slice orientation, 38, 50
Corpus callosum (CC), 151
Creatine, 394

D
Data acquisition, 21–23, 27, 238, 436, 458, 464
Data quality, 56
Data-driven analysis, 252
DCE acquisitions, 204
Deep brain stimulation (DBS), 332, 366, 592
Deep learning, 81, 92, 100, 488, 547
Degrees of freedom (DoF), 89
Dementia, 223, 224, 532
  vascular, 223, 224
Demyelinating, 406, 531
  disease, 404, 405, 456
Demyelination, 366, 377, 404, 405
DESPOT, 456
Developmental venous anomalies (DVA), 216, 218
DGE signal, 396
Dictionary generation, 440
Diffuse axonal injury (DAI), 361
Diffusion
  coefficient, 158
  restricted, 161
  time, 157
Diffusion spectrum imaging (DSI), 13, 14
Diffusion tensor (DT), 147
Diffusion tensor imaging (DTI), 13, 221, 297
Diffusion-weighted imaging (DWI), 13, 110, 115, 131, 323
  acquisitions, 13, 109
  MS-EPI, 112
  multi-shot EPI, 110
Diffusion-weighted MRSI (dwMRSI), 527
Digital subtraction angiography (DSA), 494, 591
Discrete cosine transform (DCT), 30
Discrete Fourier transform (DFT), 539
Disease
  biomarkers, 324
  characterization, 412, 493
  metabolic, 514
  neurodegenerative, 366, 531, 591
  neurological, 407, 513
  pathways, 330

612 Index

psychiatric, 513
vascular, 481, 493, 498
Disease-related brain changes, 319
Distortion, 123, 126, 131
   correction, 250
dMRI, 38, 46–48, 51, 147, 158–160, 172, 296
   acquisition times, 49
   signal, 48, 157, 160, 161, 165, 167, 297, 300
Double inversion recovery (DIR), 558
Drug development, 282
Drug-resistant epilepsy, 592
DSC acquisitions, 204
DSI acquisitions, 13
Dual echo-time fieldmaps, 132
Dual flip angles (DFA), 456
Dynamic causal modeling (DCM), 255
Dynamic contrast-enhanced (DCE), 195
Dynamic glucose-enhanced (DGE) MRI, 596
Dynamic susceptibility contrast (DSC), 195, 212

E

Echo planar imaging (EPI), 6, 238, 249, 457
   acquisitions, 14, 57, 116
   artifacts, 240
   readout, 42, 46, 238, 241
Echo planar spectroscopic imaging (EPSI), 520
Eddy current-induced distortions, 124
Eddy current-induced field, 134
Effect of motion on imaging, 471
Efficient acquisition, 187
Elliptical sampling (ES), 6
Encoding gradients, 109, 110, 126, 436, 473
Endovascular reperfusion therapy, 211
Epilepsy, 224, 278, 530, 592, 600, 603
   drug-resistant, 592
   focal, 592
   lesional, 280
   non-lesional, 278
Equilibrium magnetization, 379, 383, 460
Ernst angle, 14
Event-related designs, 268
Extended phase graph (EPG), 428, 440, 454
External motion trackers, 58
Extravascular extracellular space (EES), 198

F

Fast spin echo (FSE), 120
Fat suppression (FS), 15

Fiber density (FD), 154
Fiber orientation distributions (FOD), 154, 297
Fiber orientations, 297, 300
Fiber tractography, 151, 154
Fiber-bundle cross-section (FC), 154
Fiber-tracking analysis, 165
FID navigators, 64, 66
Field cameras, 60
Fixel-based analysis, 154
FLAIR, 12, 335, 361, 363, 403, 444, 558, 564
   contrast, 12
   example, 12
   images, 12, 363
Flip angle, 237, 343, 454, 565, 567
Fluid attenuated inversion recovery (FLAIR), 403
fMRI, 14, 38, 47, 51, 231, 243, 247, 261, 262, 267,
      271, 274, 277, 278, 285, 288, 315, 323, 573
   acquisition, 15, 47, 249, 585
   BOLD, 279, 310, 573, 582
   clinical, 283, 285
   data, 252, 253, 283, 288, 320, 576, 585
   experiments, 263, 266, 278
   functional connectivity, 309
   human, 573, 575, 580, 586
   laminar, 580
   mesoscale, 579
   response, 283, 576, 577
   resting-state, 255, 268
   results, 257, 258, 282, 288, 290
   sensitivity, 281, 573
   signals, 71, 234, 262, 283, 290, 576, 579
   single-subject, 583
   studies, 78, 251–253, 258, 285, 319, 574, 576, 583,
      584, 586
   task, 253, 263
   temporal specificity, 577
   ultra-high field (UHF), 271, 274, 573–575, 577, 583,
      584, 586
   validating, 290
   voxels, 267, 574
fMRSI, 528
Focal
   brain damage, 282
   epilepsy, 592
   lesions, 153, 415
Focal cortical dysplasia (FCD), 592
FOCI-pulse, 181
Fourier approaches, 538
Fractional anisotropy (FA), 13, 71, 150

Free induction decay (FID), 520
Frequency encoding (FE), 111
Frequency offset corrected inversion (FOCI), 505
Function
    arterial input, 199
    brain, 261, 277, 288, 323, 329, 553, 579, 584, 585
    orientation
        density, 165
        distribution, 13
    point spread, 109, 539
    response
        hemodynamic, 238, 253
        spatial, 541
        spectral, 541
Functional
    connectivity (FC), 247, 255, 257, 258, 271, 309–313, 315, 318, 323, 326, 328, 334
    connectome, 309, 310, 318, 324, 326, 327, 334
    correlations, 318
    imaging, 166
    localization, 263
    MRI, 14, 38, 84, 171, 231, 247, 257, 261–263, 309, 320, 323, 336, 576, 593, 595
    MRS, 515
Fusiform face area (FFA), 263

G

g-ratio estimation, 461
GABA, 533
GBCAs, 197
Generative adversarial networks (GAN), 58, 442
Ghosting artifacts, 46, 470, 472, 522
Global AIF, 202
Global signal regression, 313
GluCEST, 596
Glutamate, 394, 532, 533
    deficiencies, 532
Gradient offset independent adiabaticity (GOIA), 505
Gradient-echoes
    multiple, 454
    spoiled, 454
Gradient-recalled echo sequences, 454
Gradients, 59, 131, 436
    encoding, 109, 110, 126, 436, 473
    extra-vascular field, 234
    linear, 62, 125, 134
    non-linearities, 131
    readout, 6, 241

    z-shim, 240
GRAPPA, 26, 27, 48, 110, 112, 538
    kernels, 44, 46
        convolution, 28
    reconstruction, 29, 46
    weights, 44
Gray matter (GM), 5, 96, 297, 423, 506, 541
GRE acquisition, 204
Group-level analysis, 253
GSLIM solution, 542

H

HARDI acquisition, 13
Hemodynamic response function (HRF), 238, 253
High angular resolution diffusion imaging (HARDI), 300
High-resolution proton imaging, 589
Hippocampal sclerosis (HS), 445
Histogram analysis, 149
Homodyne high-pass filter, 344
Human
    fMRI, 573, 575, 580, 586
    tissues, 342
Human connectome project (HCP), 8, 128, 319
Hydroxyl CEST signals, 394
Hypoperfusion
    ASL, 224
    chronic, 213, 215

I

iEPI acquisition method, 112
Image
    acquisition, 185
    FLAIR, 12, 363
    formation, 237
    reconstruction, 112
    registration algorithms, 86, 88
Imaging
    3D diffusion, 118
    altered relaxation properties, 235
    large-scale population, 8
    MT, 407, 414
    parallel, 6, 7, 37
    perfusion, 47, 49, 196, 198, 211–213, 215, 217, 221, 222, 226, 335, 367, 558
    phase, 558, 560
    spectroscopic, 555
    susceptibility-weighted, 359
    vascular, 591

614 Index

vessel wall, 485–487, 489
X-nuclei, 598, 605
In-plane acceleration, 124
Independent component analysis (ICA), 251, 257, 269, 310, 313, 333
Individual-focused neuroscience, 583
Inertial measurement units (IMU), 59
Inference, 76
Inflow-based MRA, 475
Inhomogeneous compartments, 542
Internal carotid artery (ICA), 469
Intracranial arteries, 493
Intracranial atherosclerosis (ICAD), 493
Intracranial vasculopathy differentiation, 497
Intrinsic connectivity networks (ICN), 323
Inversion recovery signal, 382
Iron mapping, 365
Iron rims, 363
Ischemic stroke, 158, 159, 215, 281, 363, 493, 494
acute, 211, 362, 367, 596, 602

K

K-space, 62, 520
navigators, 62

L

Label fusion, 98
Laminar fMRI, 580, 582, 584
Large-scale population imaging, 8
Laterality, 290
Learning, 327
Lesional epilepsy, 280
Lesional pathologies, 278
Lesions
focal, 153, 415
vascular, 481
white matter, 97, 330, 591
Linear gradients, 62, 125, 134
Linear model, 71, 74
Lipid signal, 394, 539
Local AIF, 202
Local tractography methods, 300
Localizing fMRI responses, 584
Localizing seizure activity, 281
Longitudinal relaxation, 424
Longitudinal segmentation, 101

M

Machine learning approaches, 58

Macromolecular protons, 373, 404–406, 411, 412, 415, 422
Macrovasculature, 469
Magnetic resonance angiography (MRA), 469
Magnetic resonance spectroscopic imaging (MRSI), 537, 594
Magnetic resonance spectroscopy (MRS), 221, 503, 593
Magnetic resonance venography (MRV), 469
Magnetic susceptibility, 124, 232, 341, 589
Magnetization, 185, 232
blood, 49, 185
dynamic, 464
equilibrium, 379, 383, 460
exchange, 424, 425
transfer effects, 180–183
Magnetization transfer (MT), 373, 387, 403, 455, 477, 596
Magnetization transfer ratio (MTR), 377, 403
Magnetization transfer-based MRI, 403
Marker-based systems, 59
MB RF pulse, 38, 39, 50, 51
Mean absolute error (MAE), 76
Mean diffusivity (MD), 13, 150
Mean squared error (MSE), 32
Mean transit time (MTT), 198, 199, 212
Measuring metabolic fluxes, 594
Mesial temporal lobe epilepsy (MTLE), 445
Mesial temporal sclerosis (MTS), 592
Mesoscale fMRI, 579
Metabolic diseases, 514
Metabolite quantification, 504, 508, 511, 524
Metastases, 223
Methods
acquisition, 426, 427, 431
clustering segmentation, 99
contrast, 470
edge-based, 99
feature-based, 100
local tractography, 300
motion tracking, 54
MRSI, 533
non-contrast perfusion, 192
retrospective correction, 57
slice shifting, 38
thresholding, 97
MICRO SWI, 348
Microbleeds (MBs), 342, 347, 359, 560, 591

cerebral, 346
Microstructure, 459
  tissue, 13
Microvascular blood volume, 198
Middle cerebral arteries (MCA), 469
Mild cognitive impairment (MCI), 532
Mitigating motion, 55
Mixture models, 99
Modeling, 421, 422
  biophysical, 189
  relaxation, 460
Models
  animal, 405
  biophysical, 459
  linear, 71, 74
  mixture, 99
  prediction, 81
  signal, 64, 426, 436, 456, 542
Molecular markers, 220
Motion
  encoding, 473
  metrics, 56
  tracking methods, 54
Movement, 130
  gross, 128
  subject, 128, 138
  within a volume, 128, 140
Movement-induced signal loss, 129, 140
MR
  acquisitions, 24, 34
  fingerprinting, 458
  properties, 232
  scanner, 125, 373, 463
  signal, 4, 5, 15, 22, 61, 154, 177, 195, 196, 266, 435, 446
    derivation, 197
    generation, 196
  spectroscopy, 555
MRA
  contrast-enhanced, 478
  inflow-based, 475
  phase contrast, 473
MRF, 436
  acquisition, 436
  scans, 437, 438, 440, 443, 444, 447
MRS
  data preprocessing, 511
  functional, 515

proton, 593
MRSI, 504, 519, 520, 522, 523, 526, 530–532, 537–539, 541, 555
  acquisition, 520, 539, 541
  advanced, 522, 532, 533
  decoding, 520
  encoding, 520
  Fourier reconstruction, 541
  localization, 538
  methods, 533
  multi-nuclear, 524
  processing, 522, 539
  quantification, 522
  reconstruction, 522, 537, 538, 544
  spectrally-edited, 526
  studies, 531, 532
  techniques, 527, 533, 534
  volumetric, 522
  voxels, 522
MS-EPI DWI, 112
MSE acquisition, 427
MT
  acquisition, 17
  effect, 374, 376–378, 382, 384, 385, 404, 413, 477
  experiment, 375
  imaging, 407, 414
  imaging-derived metrics, 404
  pulsed, 379, 384
  saturation, 375–377, 379, 380, 384, 391, 456, 460
    flip angles, 380
    pulse, 380, 384
MTR, 377, 405
Multi-band acquisitions, 115
Multi-modal approaches, 101
Multi-nuclear MRSI, 524
Multi-parameter MP2RAGE, 456
Multi-parameter SE mapping, 452
Multi-parametric brain mapping, 452
Multi-shot EPI DWI, 110
Multiple comparisons, 77
Multiple gradient-echoes, 454
Multiple sclerosis (MS), 330, 349, 365, 377, 378, 407, 412, 531, 589, 599
Multiple spin echo (MSE), 427
Multivariate analysis, 252
Multivoxel pattern analysis (MVPA), 255
Mutual information (MI), 91
Myelin, 161, 365, 376, 377, 380, 403, 404, 406, 422–425, 451, 452, 454

616 Index

water, 385, 423–426, 429, 454, 456, 460
  fraction, 424, 456, 461
  signal, 427
Myelination, 377, 456

N

Navigator, 60–63, 112, 241
  cloverleaf, 63
  coil-space, 64
  collapsed fat, 63
  FID, 64, 66
  k-space, 62
  object-space, 63
  orbital, 62
  signal, 63
  spherical, 63
  volumetric, 63
Neoplasms, 219
Network connectivity changes, 328
Neural
  activity, 232, 235, 238, 576
  adaption, 266
  signal, 309, 313
  specificity, 576
Neurite density, 13
Neurodegenerative diseases, 366, 531, 591
Neuroimaging, 600
  clinical, 605
Neurological disease, 407, 513
Neuroscience, 262, 533
  individual-focused, 583
Non-contrast perfusion methods, 192
Non-contrast SWI, 348
Non-EPI diffusion imaging, 120
Non-Fourier approaches, 538
Non-lesional epilepsy, 278
Non-neurosurgical applications, 281
Normal brain development, 412
Nuclear Overhauser effect (NOE), 526

O

Open science, 258
Orientation density function (ODF), 165
Orientation dispersion (OD), 13
Orientation distribution function (ODF), 13
Outer volume suppression (OVS), 504
Oxygen extraction fraction (OEF), 367, 602
Oxygen saturation, 367

P

Parallel imaging (PI), 6, 7, 37
Parametric designs, 265
Parkinson's disease (PD), 413, 458, 513, 590
Partial Fourier (PF), 6
  acquisitions, 23
Partial volume effects (PVE), 202
Pathological
  brain aging, 328
  brain processes, 329
  specificity, 403, 408, 414
Pathology segmentation, 97
Penumbra, 211
Perfusion, 49, 177, 179, 195, 197, 198
  abnormalities, 211, 218
  ASL, 477
  brain, 15, 16, 178, 196, 197
  imaging, 47, 49, 196, 198, 211–213, 215, 217, 221,
    222, 226, 335, 367, 558
  MRI, 216, 218, 223–225
  parameters, 190, 198, 201, 204, 212, 214, 221
  quantification, 184, 189, 198, 201
Permeability parameters, 198
pH-weighted MRI, 394
Phase
  aliasing, 344, 346
  contrast, 473, 558
    MRA, 473
  encoding, 6, 109, 520, 541
  imaging, 558, 560
  information, 343
  mask, 341, 342, 345, 346
  modulation function, 38
  signal, 344, 353, 560
Physiological
  confounds, 250
  effects, 569
  noise regression, 313
Plasticity, 166
Point spread function (PSF), 109, 539
Pool size ratio (PSR), 380
Positron emission tomography (PET), 147, 195, 215,
    261, 600
Post-aneurysm rupture, 495
Post-labeling delay (PLD), 16
Post-mortem MRI, 462
Postmortem human studies, 405, 406
Preprocessing, 248

Primary CNS lymphoma, 223
Principal component analysis (PCA), 251, 273, 314
Principal diffusion direction (PDD), 297
Projection on convex sets (POCS), 23
Prominent hypointense vessel sign (PHVS), 362
PROPELLER, 61
   acquisitions, 120, 121
Prospective correction, 65
Prospective motion correction, 56, 509, 556
Protein conformation, 394
Proton density (PD), 458
Proton MRI/MRS, 589
Proton MRS, 593
Proton MRSI, 539
Proton observed phosphorous editing (POPE), 603
Pseudo-continuous ASL (pCASL), 16, 181
Pseudoprogression, 221
Pseudoresponse, 222
PSF-EPI, 116
PSR, 405
Psychiatric disorders, 513, 532
Pulsed ASL (PASL), 180
Pulsed CEST, 391
Pulsed MT, 379, 384
Pulsed qMT, 380

Q

qMT
   pulsed, 380
Quality assurance (QA), 463
Quality control (QC), 252
Quantification, 46, 97, 377, 378, 505, 507, 592, 594
   perfusion, 184, 189, 198, 201
     results, 394
     routines, 463
Quantitative exchange-label turnover (qELT), 594
Quantitative magnetization transfer (qMT), 374, 455
Quantitative MT (qMT), 378
Quantitative perfusion parameters, 198
Quantitative permeability parameters, 202
Quantitative susceptibility mapping (QSM), 349, 351, 359, 364, 454, 560

R

Radial kurtosis (RK), 13
Radiation necrosis, 222
Radiation therapy (RT), 149, 221
Reacquisition, 65

Readout, 398
   EPI, 42, 46, 238, 241
   gradient, 6, 241
Reconstruction, 520, 546
Region of interest (ROI), 5
   analysis, 149
Region-based methods, 100
Regional analysis, 253
Registration, 54, 61–63, 92, 251, 290
   marks, 86, 88, 90
Regularization, 80
Relative spatial shifts, 42
Relayed nuclear Overhauser effects (rNOE), 394
Remyelination, 377, 406
Renovation quality (RQ), 81
Reperfusion therapy, 212, 213
Representational similarity analysis (RSA), 255
Response prediction, 332
Resting state, 310
   fMRI, 255, 268
   networks, 318
Restricted diffusion, 161
Retrospective correction methods, 57
Reversible cerebral vasoconstriction syndrome (RCVS), 497
RF
   phase modulation, 37
   power, 564
   pulses, 5, 38, 40, 51, 118, 119, 180, 181, 183, 436, 455, 456, 475, 505, 507, 520, 524, 556, 567
   shimming, 567
Root mean square error (RMSE), 567
rsfMRI, 247, 248, 250–253, 255, 268–270

S

SAR, 564
Scan acceleration, 439
Scanner
   MR, 125, 373, 463
Segmentation, 186
   evaluation, 102
   structure, 97
Selective inversion recovery (SIR), 376, 379, 382–384, 404
Self-navigation, 61
Semi-LASER (sLASER), 505
Sensitivity, 157, 165, 283
   fMRI, 281, 573
   signal, 438

618 Index

Signal
  amine CEST, 394
  amplitude, 236, 429, 454, 458, 539, 545
  ASL, 179
  baseline, 235
  blood, 179, 184, 375
  BOLD, 14, 78, 232, 247, 249–251, 253, 280, 309, 310, 313, 319, 561, 577
  decay, 109, 118, 158, 162, 163, 170, 234, 235, 422, 427, 477
  derivation, 195
  DGE, 396
  dMRI, 48, 157, 160, 161, 165, 167, 297, 300
  fMRI, 71, 234, 262, 283, 290, 576, 579
  hydroxyl CEST, 394
  intensity, 29, 376, 445, 504, 539
  inversion recovery, 382
  lipid, 394, 539
  magnitude, 428, 475
  model, 64, 426, 436, 456, 542
  MR, 4, 5, 15, 22, 61, 154, 177, 195, 196, 266, 435, 446
    derivation, 197
  MRI, 21, 231, 232, 235, 238, 458, 462
  navigator, 63
  net, 232, 234, 422
  neural, 309, 313
  phase, 344, 353, 560
  sampling, 238
  sensitivity, 438
  targeting, 181
  variation, 137, 424, 565
  vector, 442
  water, 376, 379, 451, 507
    myelin, 427
Signal-to-noise ratio (SNR), 3, 554
Similarity measure, 90
Simultaneous multi-slice (SMS), 37
Simultaneous slice excitation, 38
Single voxel spectroscopy (SVS), 53, 538
Single-band (SB), 38
Single-subject analyses, 288
Single-subject fMRI, 583
Singular value decomposition (SVD), 201, 441, 547
SIR qMT, 384
sLASER, 510
Slice shifting method, 38
Slice timing correction, 249

SLIM, 541
SLOOP, 541
SMS, 38, 47
  image reconstruction, 43
Spatial
  encoding strategies, 5
  filtering, 312
  localization, 520
  response function (SRF), 541
  smoothing, 250
  specificity, 576
  transformer network (STN), 93
Spatiospectral correlation (SPICE), 547
Specific absorption rate (SAR), 14, 38, 456, 520
Specificity, 157, 165, 285, 423, 585
  pathological, 403, 408, 414
Spectral editing techniques, 505
Spectral fitting, 511
Spectral localization by imaging (SLIM), 541
Spectral resolution, 555
Spectral response function (SRF), 541
Spectrally-edited MRSI, 526
Spectroscopic imaging, 555
Spherical deconvolution (SD), 297
Spherical navigator, 63
Spin-echo (SE), 204, 454
  sequences, 452
Spoiled acquisition, 456
Spoiled gradient-echoes, 454
Spontaneous activity, 318
Spontaneous remyelination, 405
SS-EPI DWI, 109
Static functional connectome, 325, 327
Static structural connectome, 309
Statistical analysis, 252, 315
Streaking artifacts, 353
Stroke
  acute, 211, 214, 362
  ischemic, 158, 159, 215, 281, 363, 493, 494
  outcome prediction, 281
Structural connectome, 297, 325, 327
Structure segmentation, 97
Subject movement, 128, 138
Subject-level analysis, 253
Subtractive logic, 263
Superior longitudinal fasciculus (SLF), 151
Superior sagittal sinus (SSS), 469
Surgical planning, 277
Susceptibility-by-movement interaction, 133

Susceptibility-induced distortions, 124
Susceptibility-induced field, 130, 132
Susceptibility-weighted imaging (SWI), 350, 359
  high field, 350
  images, 345, 346, 349, 359–361, 364, 560
  non-contrast, 348
  pitfalls, 349
  processing, 345
  pulse sequence, 342
Synthetic MRI, 459

T

Target mismatch, 213
Task design, 283
Task fMRI (tfMRI), 247, 249, 253, 263, 268, 270
Temporal filtering, 250, 312
Temporal lobe epilepsy (TLE), 278, 592
Temporal signal-to-noise ratio (tSNR), 236, 398
Temporal specificity, 577
Thresholding methods, 97
Time-varying dynamics, 326, 327
Tissue, 96, 459
  human, 342
  microstructure, 13
  segmentation, 96
TOF acquisitions, 477
Total generalized variation (TGV), 31
Total intracranial volume (TIV), 96
Total sodium concentration (TSC), 600
Tract geometry analysis, 154
Tract-based analysis, 151
Tractograms, 151
Tractography, 97, 138, 151, 165, 300
  algorithms, 296, 300, 302, 304
  analysis, 165
  approaches, 297
  streamlines, 303
Transformation space, 88
Transverse relaxation, 423
Transverse relaxometry, 427
Traumatic brain injury (TBI), 198, 361
Treatment planning, 332
Treatment response assessment, 221
Tumor, 363
  grading, 219
Turbo spin-echo (TSE), 42, 403

U

Ultra-high field (UHF), 554, 562, 573, 574, 589, 605
  fMRI, 271, 274, 573–575, 577, 583, 584, 586

  magnetic, 524
  MRI, 565, 573–575, 579, 586, 589–593, 605
  strength, 589, 595
Ultra-short echo-time STEAM, 504
Univariate analysis, 252

V

Validating fMRI, 290
VAPOR power, 508
VAPOR water suppression, 506, 508
Variable density magnetization transfer (vdMT), 384
Variable flip angle (VFA), 487
Variance inflation factor (VIF), 79
Variational network (VN), 33
Vascular
  dementia, 223, 224
  disease, 481, 493, 498
  imaging, 591
  lesions, 481
  malformations, 216
Vessel wall imaging (VWI), 485
  acceleration, 487
  analysis, 489
  sequence, 486
Virtual dissection, 300
Volumetric
  MRSI, 522
  navigators, 63
Voxel-wise analysis, 150

W

Wall shear stress (WSS), 475
Water
  myelin, 385, 423–426, 429, 454, 456, 460
  relaxation, 376, 389
  saturation, 375, 379, 388, 389, 391, 398
  signal, 374–376, 379, 451, 507
Water content (WC), 460
Water suppression (WS), 504, 506
Water-selective excitation (WE), 15
White matter (WM), 96, 297, 506, 541
  lesions, 97, 330, 591
Whole-brain analysis, 253

X

X-nuclei, 603
  imaging, 598, 605

Z

Z-shim gradients, 240

Printed in the United States
by Baker & Taylor Publisher Services